TOO MUCH BLOOD

TOO MUCH BLOOD

Bill Talbitzer

VANTAGE PRESS
New York Washington Atlanta Hollywood

FIRST EDITION

Published by Vantage Press, Inc.
516 West 34th Street, New York, New York 10001

Manufactured in the United States of America
Standard Book Number 533-03801-4

Library of Congress Catalog Card Number 78-57825

PREFACE

Several books have been written about the Juan Corona murder case. There were numerous magazine articles, newspaper stories, and television documentaries presented concerning this most bizarre and unusual case. Reporters and writers from all over the world came to Sutter County, California, to write their stories and to report their observations. Many reporters and writers genuinely attempted to write and report a truthful account of the daily chain of events which, from my perspective, appeared to never end. The efforts of some produced headlines that were purely fictional, without foundation or factual information. I personally considered most reporters a complete nuisance—an appendix, unwanted and unnecessary. At first the majority of news accounts were very complimentary, and news people were very friendly in their attempt to gather the news and facts about this case. Later, when information became a scarcity due to court-imposed gag rules, reporters turned to the defense attorney and the suspect, who provided them with wild stories and antics which most in their journalistic careers had never before anticipated nor experienced. They met each afternoon after the court had recessed for the day in a bar near the courthouse where the defense attorney, after several drinks, would talk to anyone and everyone—these stories usually appeared in the next issue of the newspaper. A defense attorney who promised to expose to the world the real killer—a Perry Mason approach which eventually backfired and never came to pass.

Herein lies the most accurate accounting of the case written by the only author who possessed all of the factual data available concerning the Corona murders. Bill Talbitzer was provided complete access to all crime reports, correspondence, crime scene photographs, personal and confidential files and memorandums, all of which are contained in the files of the Sutter County Sheriff's Office. Mr. Talbitzer personally toured and viewed the total crime scene area where all the graves were located.

As the Sheriff-Coroner of Sutter County, California, I was in charge of and took total responsibility for the investigation and subsequent arrest of Juan Corona. My office had the obligation of locating and exhuming the bodies, identifying the victims, protecting, searching for, and collecting all the evidence, locating and interviewing each and every witness, conducting follow-up investigation of all subsequent leads, arranging for expert and scientific analysis of the evidence collected, and presenting the ultimate case results to the district attorney for prosecution.

After a lengthy, tedious, and tiring trial, several court motions, demonstrations by reactionary groups, relentless badgering by reporters, harassing phone calls, and correspondence from every weirdo in the nation, this case finally came to an end.

The defendant Juan Corona was found guilty of twenty-five consecutive counts of first-degree murder. Some reporters and writers were shocked. They had been beguiled and bamboozled by the defense attorney. They wrote the stories as he wanted them to, with the promise of a later journalistic reward which never materialized.

Bill Talbitzer was the exception. He explored for himself the factual information concerning this case. I personally attest to the authenticity and truthfulness of his effort—this book.

Roy D. Whiteaker
Sheriff-Coroner
County of Sutter

FOREWORD

The material used in writing this book was obtained from the official, the unofficial, and the confidential files of the Sutter County Sheriff's Department, as well as from the official transcript of the trial.

The files contained much information that was never released to the public until now because it never became a part of the public record. However, it would be impossible to properly outline the entire Corona case without including it in the story.

The real story of the murders and the circumstances that surrounded them will never be told. Only the murderer and the victims were present when the crimes were committed. Certainly, the dead do not speak and, if Corona actually was the criminal, no one, so far as is known, ever obtained a statement from him.

Nor was the story ever adequately covered by the press. Not that the press wasn't willing. It was handicapped.

The rule of silence that was imposed by Sheriff Roy Whiteaker and District Attorney G. Dave Teja in the very beginning, together with the "gag" orders issued by the courts, effectively sealed off the facts of the case from the public. The reporters, intense and aggressive as they were, had no access to the information that was being gathered by the investigators, and they were prevented by law from talking to any potential witness.

At the same time, the demands of editors who constantly cried for fresh news for each edition placed the reporters in the field in the position of having to supply stories which they had no way of checking for truth and reliability.

Their only source of information became the defense attorney, who was ever willing to talk but who obviously would speak only of those things which might enhance the position of his client.

The same situation continued throughout the four months of trial and, although the press was privy to everything that went on in the courtroom, some of the evidence and the testimony that influenced the jury escaped the attention of the reporters. Again, that was probably because the defense attorney was the only trial principal who would talk. His daily press conferences provided the reporters with the last words they heard at the end of each session, including the testimony that was recorded during the off-the-record sessions in the judge's chambers.

The author believes that this story, obtained from records heretofore unavailable, is the most complete account of the Corona case yet written. Whether Corona was given an effective defense is yet to be decided by the courts. Whether he was guilty, as the jury decided, or innocent, as many people still declare, cannot be determined here. The purpose of this book is to display the facts as they were developed by the investigators and let the reader decide.

The delinquencies and the inadequacies of the courtroom antagonists at times seemed to overshadow the murders themselves. It was a credit to the jurors that they were able to survive the periods of confusion and extraneous oratory and still retain the ability to concentrate on the testimony which they considered in reaching their decision.

No doubt there will be arguments for many years about the trial and the verdict. A final decision will never be reached, and no attempt is being made to reach one here.

This is only the story of twenty-five murders which occurred in a quiet, peaceful northern California farm community, the investigation that followed, and the trial that was supposed to end it all but didn't.

TOO MUCH BLOOD

Chapter 1

Like the quality of mercy, the gentle rain was falling from the heavens over Fairfield, California, as the crowd began to gather in front of the Solano County Courthouse.

It was just before noon on January 18, 1973, and two hours earlier the news that the jury in the case of the *People* v. *Juan Vallejo Corona* had reached a verdict had been reported. The principals in the trial had been notified and had begun to assemble.

Inside the building the Corona family had already filed through the security checkpoint and into the recently renovated courtroom: The wife, Gloria, a small, pretty woman with a look of lingering sadness that had shadowed her clear, even features for the past eighteen months; the four small daughters in their neat, starched, little-girl dresses and shiny patent leather slippers; Candida Corona, the defendant's grim-faced mother now past seventy years of age and showing the deep lines that a life of hard work had etched into her face; and Pedro, the scowling younger brother ever resentful and always convinced that his brother was a victim of the inequities of law enforcement. Other family members and their friends soon filled more than a quarter of the available seats.

In the jammed hallway, spectators and press alike lined up to be searched by the beefed-up security force of sheriff's deputies, while outside, where other deputies had taken up stations around the building, television crews were setting up their microphones in the hope of interviews after the verdict had been read. The rain continued to fall softly but steadily without the wind that sometimes accompanied such winter squalls. Those who waited outside the building sought shelter beneath the short overhanging roof that covered the entrance. From a side room a bailiff led the defendant to his seat at the defense counsel's table. Corona, dressed in his dark blue suit and with his hair neatly groomed showed no more emotion than he had during any of his many court appearances since he was first charged with hacking and stabbing to death twenty-five transient farm workers during the early months of 1971. Their bodies had been found buried in graves that were concealed in peach orchards and in the heavy underbrush which lined the banks of the Feather River north of Yuba City.

The thirty-eight-year-old farm labor contractor had been accused of luring the transients from Marysville's skid row by offering them work on the Jack Sullivan ranch where all but one of the bodies were found. It had been the most sensational crime in the history of California and probably in the nation. It made news in every corner of the world.

By 12:15 P.M. the court had been convened and the jury of ten men and two women filed slowly, almost reluctantly, into the courtroom. They showed the strain of their eight days of deliberation and the four months of trial that preceded them. They were tired, and they had every right to be.

Since the previous September 11 they had listened to more than 3 million words of testimony during a thirteen-week parade of witnesses to the stand. They had examined more than 900 items of evidence and they had been subjected to a mind-boggling pressure that grew in intensity as the trial ground on.

Those who filled the seventy-seven-seat courtroom tried to second-guess the verdict by studying the somber faces of the jury while Corona sat stolidly staring straight ahead. There was no need for the bailiff to rap for silence as the judge entered through a door behind the bench. The stillness of the grave was in the room.

It had been an intense, often unruly and constantly acrimonious trial marked by frequent clashes between the opposing attorneys and sometimes between the judge and the attorneys. The judge was Richard E. Patton, one of the most astute and respected jurists in the state. Since being appointed to the case on February 24, 1972, he had functioned under almost constant tension in presiding over one of the most sensational murder trials in the nation's history. Yet he never relaxed the complete control of the case which he assumed when he was first introduced to it. During the preceding four months he had assessed fourteen fines and fourteen jail sentences against Richard Elwyn Hawk, the defense attorney, and he had also fined and sentenced to jail on two occasions both G. Dave Teja, the Sutter County district attorney and Bartley C. Williams, Teja's special prosecutor. Even Corona had been fined twice, a total of $550 for failing to obey court orders on the advice of his attorney. For Corona the fines meant nothing. He was flat broke and he had already spent 602 days in jail.

Now the verdict was in. It was handed to the court clerk who passed it on to the judge. "In the case of the People of the State of California against Juan Vallejo Corona, as to count one of the information, guilty as charged." Twenty-four more times the same monotonous, stilted language of the law was repeated, and Corona stood convicted of twenty-five counts of first-degree murder.

It took just twenty-eight minutes to read the entire verdict.

The Corona family gasped and several of them burst into tears. Their friends and followers were visibly angry. The members of the press, most of whom had been willing to bet on an acquittal, rushed for the telephones to let the world know of the verdict. Hawk was speechless with anger and disappointment, while the prosecution team sighed with surprised satisfaction. They really hadn't expected to win.

Outside where the radio and television crews were waiting in anticipation of interviewing a freed Corona, and where the photographers were readying their equipment, a crowd began to gather.

In an on-the-spot interview Hawk bitterly accused the

sheriff, the prosecution and even the judge of conspiring to assure a conviction. The Corona family and their vociferous adherents from the several "Corona Defense" groups that emerged after his arrest not only cried "Foul" but also shouted their contempt for the court.

Many members of the newspaper, radio, and television contingents, who had been beguiled by Hawk's loquacity and his air of supreme self-confidence, hinted at legal shenanigans.

The Corona controversy, which had begun to build shortly after his arrest, was accelerated by the verdict. Instead of settling the issue, the decision of the jury only clouded it further. When one member of the panel, Mrs. Naomi Underwood, publicly charged that she had been coerced into voting for the verdict against her better judgment, the arguments flared again.

No one, it seemed other than the sheriff and his officers and eleven members of the jury, believed that Corona was guilty. But those eleven had no doubts in their minds. Their lives had been dominated for four months by a trial that would create legal and public arguments for many years in the future. They had lived in a pressure cooker of their own doubts and responsibilities for more than a week while they wrestled with a duty which suddenly none of them wanted.

On at least one occasion they had been forced to walk through a gauntlet of the Corona family, men, women, and children all waiting outside the courthouse and gazing at them pleadingly, hopefully, accusingly as they filed from the building toward the bus that would take them to their lodgings after a day of deliberations.

They had taken fifteen ballots during the eight days and had boiled the case down to sixteen points upon which they based their final decision. They had come to the conclusion that there was only one answer to what had been described throughout the world as "The crime of the century." Of the sixteen vital points that their deliberations involved, there were several that presented what they considered to be absolute evidence of guilt. They had decided that:

There was just too much human blood of too many different

types on too many of Juan Corona's possessions.

There was too much evidence that Juan Corona had been seen driving away from Marysville's skid row with too many men whose bodies had been found later in isolated graves.

There were too many witnesses who had seen Corona at too many times and in too many places where he had no business being and where several of the bodies had been found later.

There was no logical reason for Corona to keep a ledger containing the names of men who had been found viciously murdered and buried in the remote graves. Too, the dates written beside the names in the book seemed to coincide too closely with what was learned later to be the last times they had been seen alive.

However, the jury had heard only the prosecution's case during the trial. Despite Hawk's assertions during his opening argument that he would put Corona on the stand and that he would establish an indisputable alibi for him, he rested his case without presenting a defense. He had even promised the jury, and the world at large through the press, that he would reveal the name of the *real* killer during the course of the trial, but that he failed to do.

It was enough to make one wonder if Corona had received an effective or even an adequate defense. The Richard Hawk who so positively informed the jury at the very start of the trial that he would walk Corona out of the courtroom a free man was not the same Richard Hawk who so quietly threw in the sponge at the end. It was as though he had something else on his mind.

As it turned out, he had.

As the foreman of the jury, Ernest Phillips, later said, the lack of a defense case and the failure of Corona to testify "bothered them." However, he added that the jury had not decided the issue on any one feature of the trial "but on the continuity or the string." That string, apparently, had been the one that tied the sixteen points together.

Now the verdict was in and the long, complex trial was finished. For Corona, it meant the end of a way of life that he had carefully laid out for his family when he first obtained a labor contractor's license more than ten years before.

For Judge Patton, it was the end of what was probably the most climactic episode in his career.

For Sheriff Roy Whiteaker and his staff it meant the end of more than eighteen months of hope, despair, frustration, harassment, and then, finally, the satisfaction that comes with vindication.

Surprisingly, for Gloria Corona, the wife who had stood staunchly by her husband all through that long period, it meant the end of "fourteen years in hell," as she told a close friend after the trial was over and before she filed for divorce. The Corona marriage, the investigation revealed, had not been the happy one that had been so widely publicized.

There were many facets to the Corona case that were not aired during the trial, and there were many others that were never fully displayed to the public. Thus, there was much, much more to the case than was ever revealed. In fact, there is every indication that there were more victims than the twenty-five that were found. Those who investigated the bloody chapter in Ameican criminal history are convinced that there are at least eight bodies still buried in some remote spots in Sutter County's farm areas.

Had it not been for the sheer savagery of the killings and the magnitude of the crime itself, the situation that developed might have provided the plot for a comic opera. There have been few criminal cases anywhere that became as screwed up as the Corona case, mainly because of the Pollyannaish preparation for the trial by the prosecution. Add to that the flea-on-a-hot griddle coverage of the crime itself and the trial that followed, the bombastic audacity of the defense counsel, and the vocal but disorganized attempt to influence the outcome by partisan activists, and the result was a raucous chapter in the history of California jurisprudence that will be remembered for years.

And sitting squarely in the middle of the mess was the Sutter County Sheriff's Department, subjected to attacks by the press and the Corona adherents and forbidden by court order and departmental policy to speak out in its own defense. While the prosecution was busy trying Corona for the crimes he was charged with and getting absolutely no help from the defense, Hawk was vigorously trying the sheriff's department and was getting lots of help from the prosecution.

Chapter 2

It had been a long, hard row for the youngest sheriff in the state to hoe since May 20, 1971, when it all began.

That was the day when Goro Kagehiro, a Japanese peach farmer whose acreage lay north of Yuba City, appeared at the Live Oak City Police Department a few miles further north of his ranch. Kagehiro reported that he had seen an open hole in his orchard at about noon the day before while he was inspecting the trees. When he returned to the same spot in the orchard at 6:30 that evening, the hole had been filled.

The rancher was a little upset. Although it was not unusual for county or state agricultural officials to dig an occasional hole for a soil sample, this particular excavation had been too big for that. The more Kagehiro thought about it, the more curious he became. He could only conclude that somebody had buried something in his orchard—maybe some stolen property that could be retrieved later.

The police at Live Oak pointed out that the ranch lay outside the city limits and was in the jurisdiction of the Sutter County Sheriff's Department. They would, they said, notify the sheriff and a deputy would be sent to investigate.

By the time Kagehiro returned to his orchard, at 8:10 A.M., Deputy Steve Sizelove was waiting for him in the driveway. The rancher told his story to the deputy and offered to go with the officer to search for whatever might be buried. Taking a couple of shovels the men drove to a remote section of the orchard which was hidden from any nearby roads or dwellings.

Kagehiro apologized for the trouble he was causing, but Sizelove shrugged it off. "We might as well dig it out and find out if there is anything there," he said, and he and the rancher set to work with the shovels. It was 8:20 A.M. when they began to dig.

The husky Sizelove, twenty-six years old and a deputy for only three years, was popular with his fellow officers and he was also the butt of many practical jokes. He was a native of the county and had gone into police work with the intent of making it a career.

As he dug into the loose dirt about two feet from the surface, he struck a denim pants leg and, reaching down, felt solid flesh under the cloth. Here was another one, he thought, and said to himself, "Those dirty bastards have buried a dead fish in a pair of jeans and now they've framed me into digging it up."

A little bit deeper, he uncovered a shoe, and when he reached to pick it out of the hole, it came loose and a human foot was revealed. At that point, he began to do everything right. He carefully noted the time in his notebook as 8:40 A.M. and then told Kagehiro to walk back to the patrol car with him where he radioed the office to report his find. He was ordered to hold everything until Detective Sergeant John Purcess and Detective Harold Cochran, who were in a patrol car enroute to Marysville, arrived. Purcell was the department's chief deputy coroner and chief criminal deputy.

Sizelove walked back to search near the grave and observed a tire track about eight feet away. He carefully placed his briefcase at the near end to protect it and then waited for the other officers.

At 9:00 A.M. Purcell and Cochran arrived, and right after them came Whiteaker, Undersheriff Frank Cartoscelli, and Deputy Roger Mason, the department's photographer and identification officer. Purcell was put in charge of the investigation and he ordered the area carefully checked for possible evidence before digging was resumed. Cochran was ordered to make a plaster of paris impression of the tire track, and a kit was sent from the Yuba City office for that purpose. When it arrived, Cochran carefully prepared the mixture and just as carefully poured the plaster of paris over the tracks. Then, as it began to harden, Cochran, following prescribed police procedure which he had learned in academy criminology classes, wrote into the plaster the date, the time, the place, the reason, and then he signed it.

That tire impression was to become a skeleton in the investigative closet and a source of embarrassment to the prosecution.

Then, as Mason began to take pictures of each step of the operation, the grave was fully uncovered and the victim was removed. The body was that of a white male who had been horribly murdered. A cursory inspection at the scene showed that the man had been viciously chopped on the back of the head several times with some type of heavy knife or axe, and he had also been stabbed in the left chest. There were severe wounds on his right hand, indicating that he had attempted to fend off at least two of the blows before he was killed.

With the body laid out on the ground, Sizelove leaned close to the face and exclaimed, "I know this guy! His name is Whitacre!"

The sheriff, in no mood to take a joke at that time, replied, "How would you like to start walking a beat in the rice fields, Sizelove?"

"No, no sheriff. That's really his name. I stopped him on the Colusa Highway four days ago and talked to him. I've got a field identification card on him in the office."

Cochran, who had finished taking the tire impression, also looked at the corpse and told the sheriff that, he, too, had seen him in the area on the same day Sizelove saw him.

The body was taken to the morgue in Yuba City where it was quickly identified as that of Kenneth Edward Whitacre, forty-one years old, whose last known residence was Alameda, California. Since quitting his job as a truck driver for the telephone company twelve years before, he had become one of the faceless wanderers who follow the crops in California year after year, stopping for a time, working just long enough to buy a bottle or two of wine, and then moving on to another skid row in another town. His police "rap sheet" showed arrests, mostly for drunkenness, dating from 1959. On one occasion he had been arrested for robbery in

Oakland in 1966 and had been sent to the California State Prison's medical facility at Vacaville for a ninety-day psychiatric observation. He had been discharged on January 31, 1967.

His only outstanding features were two ugly, bucktooth snags in the front of his mouth and the long, army-type overcoat he wore even in hot weather. He had never married, and the possessions found on his body were few. Some homosexual literature and a couple of Bibles were found, and that was all. Positive identification was made from his fingerprints, and he was eventually cremated at Marysville at the request of his brother and other family members.

Purcell's official report contained the information that the grave was seven feet, ten inches in length and three feet, six inches deep. Samples of dirt were taken from it and tested for bloodstains, but none were found. An immediate autopsy at the morgue revealed that the victim had died of a stab wound in the left chest inflicted by a knife with at least a seven-inch blade. It also noted the deep lacerations on the back of the head, one on the left cheek, and the wounds on the right hand. At least two separate weapons were used, the autopsy surgeon said, because the head wounds were made by a heavier blade than the chest wound.

Purcell ordered that Whitacre's clothing, together with his meager possessions and the tire impression, be locked up as evidence.

The sheriff assigned several deputies to try to trace Whitacre's movements, and they immediately got positive results. He had been in the area for the past several days. Both Cochran and Sizelove had seen him on Monday morning, May 17, and other residents had observed him plodding along the roads west of Yuba City on Tuesday. Later that afternoon he asked a young bicyclist for directions to a highway that would take him to Oakland, and the next morning between 8:30 and 9:00 A.M. he was seen on the Colusa Highway by both Carol Jean Bordsen and William Forderhase. The last time he was seen alive was between noon and 1:00 P.M. that same day by thirteen-year-old Gina Chapman, who was confined to her home on Larkin Road, north of the Colusa Highway, because of illness. The girl said she recognized Whitacre by the long overcoat and by the prominent front teeth when he looked toward her house and smiled. The home was located less than a mile from where the body was later found.

At that time Whitacre had less than six hours to live.

The body was found early enough in the day to allow the Marysville *Appeal-Democrat* to have a story in the evening edition, and the result was several telephone calls to the sheriff's office by persons who believed they had seen the victim within recent days. There was one call, however, that was even more interesting. The owners of a ranch located near Kagehiro's orchard called to say that they had observed a hole on their property.

Purcell went immediately to the ranch and was shown a spot in the peach orchard where a hole had been covered. The rancher explained that the hole had been seen a month before and he had watched it for a week before deciding to fill it in. The rancher was taken the next day to the spot where Whitacre's body had been found and said the hole in his orchard was identical to Whitacre's grave. Deputies later excavated the hole that the rancher had filled in and confirmed the statement.

The day following the finding of the body was a busy one for the sheriff's staff, and it also brought some new developments.

Kagehiro, who was interviewed by Detective Jerry Gregory, explained that he had been in the orchard to inspect the work of a crew that was thinning peaches. He said the crew had been recruited by Juan Corona and had finished work at noon. The men had been paid off by the labor contractor at the Jack Sullivan ranch where Corona had the use of the labor camp. Corona, Kagehiro said, had worked for him for several seasons as well as for Sullivan, whose much larger ranch was adjacent to his.

Gregory, having obtained a picture of the victim which was taken by Mason in the morgue, went next to the Sullivan Ranch where he showed it to Raymond Duron, the foreman. Duron had never seen Whitacre before and neither had any of the workers who were nearby and to whom he showed the photograph.

Gregory asked if Duron knew where Corona could be found and he replied that the contractor was working at the labor camp that day. Corona was called from the camp and Duron showed him the picture, asking in Spanish if Whitacre had ever been a member of one of the crews. Duron explained that the picture was that of a murder victim, and Corona replied that he had never seen the man before, handing the picture back. Then the labor contractor asked to see it again and said, "This fellow looks like he is already dead." Duron replied, "Yes, he is dead."

Back at the office there was another call waiting for Gregory. This one was from Sergeant Ollie Coleman of the Marysville Police Department who told of an incident that had occurred about a year ago in the Guadalajara Café in Marysville.

The cafe, Coleman said, was owned by Natividad Corona, half-brother to Juan. It was located in the skid-row section of the town and was a popular gathering spot for Mexican farm workers. Coleman reported that a farm worker had been badly cut in the cafe and that both Natividad and Juan had been suspects in the case. He also said an informant had told him that Juan was known to have fits of temper so extreme that members of his family had had to take ropes at times and tie him up until he calmed down.

Gregory got the name of Coleman's informant and interviewed the man, also a Mexican farm worker. After promising that he would not use the man's name, Gregory was told that Coleman's information was correct and also said that Corona was seen in the cafe on the night of the cutting and was carrying a short-handled hoe, such as those used for weeding beans.

The informant then volunteered that Natividad was "queer" and that if anyone talked about it to Juan or even brought up the subject of homosexuality in his presence, Juan would go into one of his fits of temper.

That night, as he reviewed the information collected thus far in the case, Sheriff Whiteaker noted the interesting coincidence that Corona had been working on the Kagehiro ranch on the day Whitacre was murdered and that he had also been a suspect in the Guadalajara Cafe cutting. Interesting enough, the sheriff thought, to warrant a background check on the labor contractor; as soon as one of the detectives could find some free time, the check would be made.

Purcell and Cartoscelli also remembered the Corona name. As Purcell told the sheriff, it had happened in May, 1969, when Deputy Bill Heise while on patrol observed a youth running through an orchard near the Sullivan Ranch. Heise radioed for assistance in stopping the youth and both Cartoscelli and Purcell responded. When he was finally stopped, the runner turned out to be a badly frightened teenager who could not understand English.

By coincidence, Jesse Escovedo, an off-duty Marysville police officer at the time, drove past and was hailed by the Sutter County officers. Acting as an interpreter, Escovedo learned that the boy had recently been smuggled in from Mexico to work in the harvest and he owed Juan Corona $170 for his passage. That day, he said, Corona had demanded payment, and when the youth could not come up with the money, Corona grabbed a machete from his pickup truck and started after him.

Cartoscelli called the U. S. Border Patrol, and an agent came and picked the youth up. He said his department was in the process of conducting an undercover operation in the Marysville–Yuba City area and requested that no report of the incident of that day be made by the Sutter County officers.

The murder investigation continued sporadically for the next three days, hampered somewhat by numerous other duties that called for attention by Whiteaker's department, which numbered only thirty-seven people, including clerks, jailers, bailiffs, and other office personnel.

Then, on the twenty-fifth, everything went to hell.

Chapter 3

At 7:45 that Tuesday morning, Duron called the sheriff's office to report what appeared to be a grave in one of Sullivan's peach orchards. By 8:20 Purcell and Gregory were at the ranch and

Duron led them to the spot, which was several hundred yards from where Whitacre's body had been found five days before. Ernesto Garcia, one of his workers, Duron said, had spotted a depression in the orchard and, remembering the grave that had yielded Whitacre's body, had reported immediately to Duron. The foreman told his employer and was advised to notify the sheriff.

Cartoscelli arrived at 8:50, and within ten minutes the officers had uncovered a body. At that point everything stopped until the sheriff and Mason arrived, along with the police chiefs of both Live Oak and Yuba City, as well as Sullivan, the ranch owner. Whiteaker ordered a backhoe and Tom Jernigan arrived at 9:50 A.M. to help with the excavation. Within minutes the badly decomposed body of a white male was lifted from the grave and taken to the morgue.

While the digging was going on, Purcell had observed a pick-up truck drive slowly along the nearby road. Within minutes the same vehicle drove back the other way. The driver who was so interested in the activity was Juan Corona.

Whiteaker, remembering the empty hole on the nearby ranch and still concerned with the Whitacre investigation, decided on a sweeping search of the orchards in the vicinity. Calling in his off-duty deputies and as many reserves as he could muster, he ordered a foot-by-foot canvass of the several thousand acres radiating from the site of the grave.

As the search began, Purcell went to the funeral home in Yuba City where the body had been taken. There, Dr. Charles Clement, a pathologist, had been called in and was examining the corpse. The man was five feet, ten inches tall, had black hair and had apparently been wearing his entire wardrobe when he was killed: two pairs of dark pants, a blue suit coat, a gray coat sweater, a red, white, and blue plaid shirt, an undershirt, and a pair of red and white boxer shorts. There was only one shoe, a black oxford.

His worldly possessions made a very small collection on a nearby table. A can of snuff, a bar of Ivory soap, another bar of soap, unwrapped; a five-inch pink comb, a package of Safeway matches, and two sales slips from the same Marysville store, one for twenty-nine cents, the other for twenty-three cents, and both dated May 8, 1971; a safety razor and a small amount of Beech Nut chewing tobacco.

The autopsy revealed that he had been chopped several times on the back and both sides of the head and then had been stabbed in the left chest. Unlike Whitacre, there were no defensive-type wounds on his hands.

Because of the condition of the body it was impossible to take fingerprints by the normal, rolling method, therefore, Dr. Clement amputated the tips of the fingers and thumbs and Purcell sent them to Sacramento in the custody of Deputy Seth Reynolds. There they could be tested in the C.I.I.'s sophisticated laboratory which had equipment designed to obtain fingerprints from partially decomposed fingers. It would be several days before positive identification could be established.

The search continued through the ranch property north of town with the crew now augmented by officers and reserves from the Yuba City Police Department. Throughout the warm spring afternoon the searchers walked the rows of peach trees laden with fruit that would ripen within the next three months while clouds formed over the distant Northern Sierra Mountains bringing rain toward the valley, just what nobody needed right then.

Detective Denver Duncan, a former peach farmer himself and a long-time resident of the area—his ranch was within two miles of the search area—suggested that maybe there was a more appropriate site to be looked into. As he told Cartoscelli, Sizelove, and Deputy Bill Rodemaker, "If I was a nut and was going to kill a guy and bury him, I'd take him over close to the river where the soil is sandy and easier to dig in."

The four officers crawled into Deputy Wilbur Terry's jeep and headed east. A short time before, the state had built a section of new freeway that extended north from Yuba City almost to Live Oak, bypassing a section of former Highway 99-East which bisected the Sullivan holdings. With Cartoscelli driving, the jeep rolled across the new freeway, crossed the old 99-E, and drove into the Sullivan ranch yard where the labor camp was located.

There, Juan Corona for the past seven years had housed the members of the crews he recruited during the cultivating and harvest seasons.

The buildings consisted of a messhall in which Corona maintained his office, a long, low bunkhouse, and a utility shed.

A road extended east toward the river, still a half-mile away, and was separated by a high levee from the section of the ranch where the labor camp was located. That levee protected the ranch from the Feather River, which, until the Oroville Dam was completed thirty-five miles upstream in 1968, rampaged over the lower sections of the ranch almost every winter. The land closest to the river was mostly sand and silt, covered with blackberry bushes, buck brush, wild vines and oak and cottonwood trees. Except for a few narrow paths carved out by fishermen, the area is practically impenetrable and the river is concealed.

Cartoscelli drove the jeep past the labor camp, along the curving dirt road and up over the levee. There the road turned south and wound and twisted its way along the river, turning eventually in a southwesterly direction.

Rodemaker suddenly whooped, "Hold it! We'd better check this out!" As the vehicle slowed, Rodemaker jumped off the rear seat and strode back up the road where he leaned over to inspect the ground next to the roadway. The others found him peering at a series of small mounds of fresh dirt that seemed to lead off into the underbrush. Carefully Rodemaker brushed at the first mound of dirt and revealed a red stain. There were similar stains on each of the other mounds and the trail led to what appeared to be a fresh grave.

The third body had been found, the body that was to cause so much confusion and argument in the months to come.

The sheriff was called to the scene, and while Cartoscelli and Sizelove began digging out the grave, the others began looking through the thick underbrush. More officers were summoned to the area and two more graves were quickly located. The victim found in the grave that Rodemaker had spotted, had apparently been buried within the last couple of days. The body was that of a white man with the small finger of the left hand missing, evidently the result of an old injury. The remains were placed in a plastic body bag and numbered. Counting Whitacre, five days before, it was the third body found.

At the same time, about 140 yards north, or closer to the Sullivan labor camp, another body was being retrieved. That one, also white and male, was placed in a body bag and given the number four. Squares of paper with the numbers on them were placed in the bags. Both bodies were laid alongside the road where they could easily be picked up and placed in a hearse for delivery to the funeral parlor. The possessions of each victim and the evidence found in the graves were noted in writing by Gregory, who had become the recording officer, and sealed in plastic bags. Numbers corresponding to those placed in the body bags were put on tags and fastened to the plastic evidence bags.

Meanwhile, four more gravesites had been located, and crews were engaged in excavating them. Mason was trying to keep up with the diggers and was photographing each excavation. Cartoscelli, as undersheriff, was in charge of the digging crews, and Purcell was keeping track of the sequence in which the bodies were retrieved. Gregory was listing descriptions and listing the personal possessions and the evidence.

It was just after dark when the hearse arrived to pick up the first two bodies that were lying alongside the road. The first body was placed in the hearse on the right side and the second was placed on the left. When the hearse arrived at the mortuary, the bodies were taken from the vehicle in the order in which they were picked up and, because the body tags had not been properly sealed, the numbered tags fell out onto the floor. The driver and his helper saw the tags lying there, picked them up, and placed them on the bodies in the order in which they were picked up beside the road. Unknowingly, they had placed tag number three on body number four, and vice versa.

It was a simple mistake, but it was to have repercussions that created an eighteen-month-long headache for the investigators, particularly Cartoscelli.

The autopsy revealed that the third victim found had been dead less than three days and possibly had been killed as late as the day before he was found. The fourth body, however, had been dead for at least two weeks and possibly longer.

The importance of the numbering became apparent when the plastic bags containing the evidence found in the graves were eventually examined; for when number three was exhumed it was Sizelove, helping with the digging, who called Cartoscelli's attention to two pieces of paper lying on the body.

They were two meat receipts issued by a Marysville market to Juan Corona on May 21.

That meant two important things. One, the victim had been killed after Whitacre's body was found five days before. And two, Juan Corona, who had been only a fringe suspect before, was now the prime suspect in the case!

There was no time to straighten out the mistake right then; in fact, there was no time even to discover it. The crews along the riverbank were digging up bodies in wholesale lots, and the morticians were urgently needed to haul them back to town. Thus, nobody at that time noticed the switch in numbers and it was to be weeks before it came to be known.

The digging continued after darkness fell with the aid of floodlights furnished by the Live Oak Fire Department. By this time, Whiteaker had contacted Teja, who came to the scene to get a firsthand view of the action. A quick conference with the sheriff, after learning of the meat receipts, convinced Teja a strategy session was in order. The two officials realized that it would be late before all of the bodies could be retrieved from graves already found. Maybe now was the time to go over the file that Whiteaker had been compiling.

The sheriff and the district attorney had not been idle. Teja had been notified earlier in the day when the second body had been found, and Whiteaker had relayed his growing suspicion of Corona. The Marysville Police Department's reports of the Guadalajara Cafe cutting had been studied, and the labor contractor had been definitely tied to that case. There was also an indication that Corona had once been confined to a mental institution, and a check of the records in the courthouse confirmed that fact. Duron who had known Corona for many years—in fact, he had attended Corona's wedding—had told Purcell earlier that day that "Corona is crazy."

The Marysville police also had a missing person's report on a Sigurd Emil Beierman, who, according to the man who reported him missing, had last been seen driving away from Marysville with Corona in the latter's tan-colored van almost two months before.

At 9:00 P.M. Whiteaker contacted two deputies and ordered that Corona be placed under observation. When Corona and his wife left their home shortly after that hour, police "tailed" them to a market where they stayed for forty-five minutes. The couple then drove to the Sullivan ranch, where Corona parked near the mess hall for another fifteen minutes before driving home. Inside the house the lights were turned out five minutes later and the trailing officers remained on watch until they were relieved by other deputies.

Out in the river bottoms, deputies exhumed bodies five, six, seven, eight, and nine; and what Whiteaker considered to be the clincher came when the last one was examined. The left thumb and index finger were missing as the result of an old injury, and the description tallied with that listed in the missing person report on Beierman.

Whiteaker and Teja decided to act at once.

As the bodies were being recovered, the news began to filter out of Marysville by radio and news wires that more than just an ordinary murder case was developing. Reporters began to converge on the sheriff's office asking questions that the harassed desk sergeants had been forbidden to answer. As the evening wore on, the number of news media representatives increased and the demands for news became more insistent. A hasty security perimeter was established at the site where the bodies were being found to keep spectators and press alike at bay. Manning the defense perimeter was to become a twenty-four-hour-a-day task for the next several weeks.

As the word of the grisly discoveries filtered through the community, the number of telephone calls to the sheriff's office increased sharply. The harried deputies, many of them called from their homes after having completed their regular day's work, responded to all calls of prowlers, suspected gravesites in fields and yards, and demands for neighborhood protection.

An atmosphere of near-terror permeated Yuba City, almost equivalent to that of sixteen years before when the Feather River burst through the levee at Shanghai Bend, south of town, during the terrible Christmas-week flood, December 23, 1955. Most of the city was flooded, most of the population was evacuated and forty people lost their lives during that horror-filled night.

Yuba City had overcome that disaster, had rebuilt, and had again become the dignified, even austere, city that sat like a somewhat haughty dowager on the right bank of the scenic Feather River, looking with lofty disdain toward raucous, bawdy Marysville to the east. The city had been founded in 1849 by Sam Brannan, the man who had first shouted the news of the discovery of gold in California as he raced through the streets of San Francisco holding high a small bottle of the precious metal that had been found in the American River at Coloma. Brannan was an early-day entrepreneur who had gotten his start in California when Brigham Young had sent him from Salt Lake City with instructions to found a Mormon colony on the coast. Instead, Brannan used the money Young had supplied him with to lay the foundations of a business empire that soon dominated the entire state.

His main enterprise was supplying the eager argonauts who poured into California to frantically chase the Golden Fleece. With the discovery of gold on the Feather by John Bidwell, and the opening of the Northern Mines in the mountains to the east, Brannan decided that a trading post at a point near the confluence of the Yuba and the Feather would pay off.

He was not, however, the first pioneer to see the opportunity that the wide, sweeping valley offered. Some years before, John Augustus Sutter, California's first empire builder, had established a farm less than three miles downstream. Called the "Hock" or "Upper" Farm, it became a final refuge for Sutter after the gold-crazed invaders had driven him from his vast lands.

Yuba City never did amount to much of a supply point for

the mines. New Mecklenburg, which later became Marysville, grabbed off that plum, but Yuba City's future lay just ahead. The rich soil lent itself well to the growing of fruits, rice, grains, and vegetables, and by shortly after the turn of the century, Yuba City was proudly proclaiming itself as "The Peach Bowl of the World." With the establishment of agriculture came also a solid, sedate way of life that continued generation after generation. There was never a skid row in Yuba City. The city fathers were historically adamant about that!

Now, the calm demeanor of the community began to crack. There was a monster at large somewhere in the tangled undergrowth of the river bottoms, and no one knew when it would carry the attack to the more affluent sections of the city. Hunting rifles and shotguns were brought from closets and placed close at hand, and neighbors hurriedly made plans to protect their neighborhoods. It was another source of worry for the sheriff, who feared that some innocent wayfarer seeking information or directions might be shot as he approached a house.

Whiteaker was mighty anxious to achieve some sort of action that would calm the community. At the rate bodies were being found, there was no telling what might happen if the population were to panic.

The time had come to move in on Juan Corona.

Whiteaker and Teja were busy in the district attorney's office drafting the language of a search warrant that would be served on the suspect. That job began at 10:45 P.M. and continued until after 2:00 A.M.

In his request for a warrant the sheriff listed the circumstantial evidence that he had already compiled as well as conjectures of his own. The missing person report, and the finding of Beierman's body, the Guadalajara cutting, the two meat receipts found in the grave of the nine-fingered man, and the previous mental commitment were all detailed.

The sheriff then added his own opinion that the nature of the wounds on the victims, the savagery of the attacks, the disposition of the bodies, as well as the sheer number of the victims "indicates that the slayer is at least seriously mentally ill and is probably a homicidal maniac." The sheriff added that autopsy reports indicated the wounds were made by at least two separate weapons.

He requested that the court permit him to search the Corona home, the labor camp, and the Corona vehicles for "knives, axes, machetes, and anything else in the way of weapons," as well as for employment records, bloodstained clothing or weapons, bloodstained vehicles, and even one black oxford shoe believed to belong to victim number two who had only one shoe when his body was found.

John Houk, presiding judge of the Sutter County Superior Court, had been called at his home and told that the request for the warrant was being prepared. He agreed to come to the courthouse and to issue the warrant if the requirements of the law were met.

At the same time, Cartoscelli, who had closed the digging site for the night, was organizing two search parties at the request of Whiteaker and Teja. One, under the direction of Captain John B. Littlejohn and Purcell, would search the Corona home and vehicles, and the other, with himself in charge, would search the buildings at the labor camp. Cartoscelli briefed the officers on what was to be searched for and explained how the evidence was to be handled. Mason was to do the photography at both scenes while other officers were assigned to record all of the items that were expected to be found.

The only problem remaining was to devise a way to elude the press which congregated in a clamoring group outside the small sheriff's office. For that, Whiteaker devised a special strategy.

Judge Houk signed the search warrant at 2:30 A.M. and the sheriff and Teja returned to Whiteaker's office. There they huddled briefly in a back room and then, as if having received an urgent call, strode quickly and silently from the building giving the appearance of two men on their way to an emergency situation. They jumped into the sheriff's car and sped out of the driveway with the press in full pursuit.

While Teja and Whiteaker were driving an erratic course

around the Yuba City area with the dogged "newsies" hanging close behind them, the special search crews left the sheriff's office by another exit. At the Corona home, located in a neat, orderly, middle-class neighborhood, and at the Sullivan Ranch, roadblocks were quickly established to seal off both points.

Chapter 4

It was just after 3:00 A.M. when Littlejohn knocked on the door of the Corona home with the search warrant in his hand. Corona himself opened the door and, when he saw Littlejohn, in full uniform, he attempted to push it closed, but the burly captain pushed his way into the house. He told Corona the reason he and the others were there.

Corona was wearing a pair of dark trousers, and Littlejohn's first move was to make a pat search of his person. He removed a pocket knife from Corona's pocket, then he began to read the search warrant. When Corona indicated that he did not understand what was being read to him, Littlejohn sent for an interpreter.

Jesse Escovedo was an interpreter with much experience in police work and had gone with Cartoscelli's crew to the labor camp to aid in the questioning of any workers who might be there. As it turned out, he wasn't needed because, as the officers drove into the yard in police cars, the occupants of the bunkhouse—there were about a half dozen, Cartoscelli estimated—fled into the darkness and did not return.

Escovedo was therefore immediately available and, at Littlejohn's radioed request, was driven to the Corona home. There Littlejohn instructed him to read the entire search warrant, word for word. It was unusual, but the cautious Littlejohn didn't intend to leave any loopholes which a sharp defense attorney could wiggle his client through later on. After the reading was finished, Corona was asked if he understood, and he replied that he did. Littlejohn then asked Escovedo to read the "Miranda warning," a recitation of a suspect's constitutional rights as prescribed by the United States Supreme Court in a famous decision of 1966. Corona replied that he understood that also.

While the formalities were being taken care of in the living room, the other officers were conducting a thorough search of the rest of the house and the garage. Mrs. Corona, who was very upset, was trying to quiet her four small, crying daughters, while the maid, eighteen-year-old Graciella Carlos, huddled silently in a corner.

Littlejohn and Purcell remained with the suspect while the search continued and the evidence was being accumulated. Duncan entered the master bedroom and took from an upright filing cabinet, two ledgers, a bundle of check stubs, and other business papers. As he glanced through the ledgers, Duncan saw that one was not a regular farm record. It contained only a jumble of names and dates, but it lacked the social security numbers, dates of beginning and end of employment, and wages paid as would normally be found in such a book.

The ledger was to become one of the most controversial, and at the same time damning, pieces of evidence that would be used against Corona.

In the garage, Cochran and Deputy Seth Reynolds began their search, which also turned up evidence that would later become important. Beneath the front seat of the Corona van, Cochran found a zipper bag containing two pairs of bloodstained men's shorts, a bolo machete, and several nine-millimeter pistol cartridges. In the rafters of the garage he found a denim jacket with what appeared to be bloodstains, and leaning against a wall he found a posthole digger with what looked to him like bloodstains and human hairs on the blade.

Reynolds, at the same time, examined the back of the van and saw what he took to be blood spatters on the walls and on the spare tire. Crawling under the vehicle, he saw stains on the gas tank and on the inside of the rear bumper. They looked as if they had been formed by a heavier substance being washed from the vehicle with water.

In the trunk of the Corona family car, an Impala coupe, Reynolds found a headband with what looked like bloodstains as well as a floor mat with spatters. Both vehicles, as well as a pick-up truck with Corona's name printed on the side, were confiscated.

At the labor camp Caroscelli's crew was also collecting what they considered to be evidence. The mess-hall building, where Corona had his office, was locked from the inside so Sizelove was boosted through a window and then let the others in.

Rodemaker found a knife with a long, thin blade, called a "Tennessee Toothpick" in one drawer of the desk, along with a nine-millimeter Browning automatic pistol in a holster and a partial box of cartridges. When he examined the pistol closely, he saw that it was cocked and there was a shell in the firing chamber. Cartoscelli asked Mason to put down his camera long enough to unload the weapon. Further inspection revealed dark stains on both the pistol and the knife.

The desk also yielded a pen that was unusual and, as it later turned out, very important. It was a ballpoint pen that contained six ink cartridges, each a different color. The pen was gathered up with the other items and carefully placed in an evidence bag.

In the sink a religious candle was burning in a holder, and it was snuffed out. The holder was also taken as evidence, as were several kitchen knives.

Back at the Corona home, the search was concluded at 4:45 A.M., and Littlejohn and Purcell formally placed Corona under arrest for nine counts of murder. Escovedo explained the arrest to the suspect in Spanish and added a suggestion that Corona might need an attorney. Corona said practically nothing during the entire episode until just before he was taken from the house. He asked his wife to notify his brother Pedro and also to arrange for the feeding of breakfast to his small crew at the Sullivan ranch later in the morning. He was then led from his home to a waiting police car, a blanket covering his head.

When the car containing Corona, Littlejohn, and Purcell arrived at the sheriff's office, a large contingent of the news media was waiting. Corona was led inside with the blanket covering the upper part of his body. There he was booked, fingerprinted, photographed, and placed in a cell in the women's section of the jail. That section was isolated from the other prisoners and was not used because Sutter County's women prisoners were confined in the more modern Yuba County jail in Marysville.

At the Twin Cities Mortuary, Doctors Clement and Thomas P. Connolly worked throughout the night examining the bodies that were found the day before.

Although they were not pathologists, the two surgeons had, in the past, performed autopsies on hundreds of victims of violent deaths in the area.

The body of the first man found—actually, the second victim in the case—was later determined to be that of Charles Cleveland Fleming. He had been savagely chopped on the back of the head and had been stabbed in the left chest. He and Whitacre were the only victims found on the west side of the freeway and, in a somewhat complicated numbering system devised by the sheriff's officers, was number W-2. Whitacre was listed as W-1.

Body number three, or the second one found the previous day, bore the number E-1 on the sheriff's list but was number four on the records of the mortician. It was dug from the grave in which the damning meat receipts were found and was mis-numbered when the tags of bodies three and four were mixed up at the mortuary. The body, dead less than forty-eight hours, according to the surgeons, was that of Melford Everette Sample, who had also been chopped on the back of the head and stabbed in the left chest.

The real body number four remained unidentified by name but became notorious because of the numbering mistake. The victim had been dead for at least two weeks and possibly longer, according to the doctors. He was the only victim who was wearing a full beard. There were no personal possessions found.

The body in grave number five had also been buried for several weeks. Through a bank passbook in his pocket the officers tentatively identified him as Donald Dale Smith.

A Social Security card found on victim number six bore the name of John Joseph Haluka. His possessions consisted of $7.09 in cash and a small package of cigarette tobacco. Repetitiously, the doctors noted the chop wounds, but unlike the others, he had not been stabbed in the left chest.

There was no way of identifying number seven because nothing had been found on his person. The body had been dead for several weeks and was badly decomposed

The identification of victim number eight became pretty easy when doctors removed his false teeth and found a Social Security number carved in one of the plates. Warren Jerome Kelley also had tattoos on the fingers of both hands along with initials and scrolls inscribed on both arms. He had also been chopped on the back of the head and had been stabbed not once, but twice, in the left chest.

Beierman's body had been the eighth found on May 25 and the ninth found to date in the case.

Doctors Clement and Connolly had informed Whiteaker and Teja that it would be impossible for the bodies to be kept in Yuba City because of the lack of facilities. The sheriff and the district attorney, therefore, had called on Sacramento County that day for help and were told that the bodies could be moved to the coroner's morgue in that city. In addition, Sacramento County Coroner George Neilsen said he would send Joseph Masters and Pierce Rooney, both forensic pathologists of extensive experience, to Yuba City that very day to help with the autopsies.

The Yuba City doctors had also notified the sheriff that most of the bodies were so badly decomposed that it would be impossible to roll the fingers for identifying prints. It was decided by Whiteaker and Teja that the tips of the victims be amputated and sent to Sacramento for examination in the laboratory there.

Accordingly, the finger tips of six of the cadavers were excised and each digit placed in a plastic tube. The tubes for each victim were then sealed in separate plastic bags, ten to the bag except for the nine-fingered man from grave number three, and Seth Reynolds was called to make the trip to Sacramento with them.

Reynolds delivered the bags and obtained a receipt for them. As he approached Yuba City on his way home, he radioed his position to the office and was ordered to proceed directly to the

Sullivan ranch. There he was told by Purcell that members of the huge press corps were trying by every possible means to infiltrate the digging scene. Purcell said the eager newsies were renting helicopters, motorboats, motorbikes, and were even trying to work their way up the thickly overgrown riverbanks to get into the restricted area.

Purcell ordered Reynolds to set up a security ring and to keep everybody out regardless, unless they had authorization from the sheriff to enter.

Reynolds informed Purcell that he had delivered the fingers and had obtained a receipt for them. He was told to set up his guards first and then to turn in the receipt later.

Several hours later Reynolds delivered the receipt to Purcell, who immediately made copies of it and forwarded it to the office of the district attorney.

Unfortunately, Reynolds, in all of the turmoil that followed, neglected to make out a report of his trip to Sacramento.

The mass of evidence that was collected at the house and the labor camp was listed by Littlejohn and Gregory before being stowed away. There was a lot of it, and it all had to be tagged by the officers. Everything that could possibly be used to cut or kill a person was picked up, including short-handled hoes, hatchets, butcher knives, cleavers, and even a wooden club that looked as though it might have bloodstains on it. The file cabinet was taken, together with additional receipts for supplies purchased by Corona, including one from the same meat company that issued those found in grave number three, checkbooks, a cigarette lighter, a ring, articles of clothing that appeared to be stained, and even two burlap bags full of blankets that were found in the garage, and a pair of rubber boots and a shovel, both with dark stains, found in the back of the van.

By that time, the officers who had been digging the night before were reporting for more of the same. At that time, also, Roy Van den Heuval, the county's public defender, arrived at the office. He had been called by Teja, who wanted to make certain that Corona had legal counsel as the law required. Van den Heuval had not yet been appointed, but he was ready to provide whatever legal advice Corona might need.

The latter was a confused and badly frightened man. Escovedo had told him in Spanish that "they are digging up bodies by the river" and that he was suspected of killing the victims. He had not been questioned because he had indicated that he did not want to talk to the police, nor did he want to talk to Van den Heuval. When he was asked if he had an attorney, he replied:

"My family is getting one for me."

Van den Heuval talked to Teja before he left the building and was told that a complaint charging Corona with nine counts of murder was even then being drawn up. Teja said he expected to arraign the labor contractor that same day and Van den Heuval said he would attend the session.

While that was going on, Cartoscelli was organizing a detail of six deputies to go back to the riverbottoms where three more possible gravesites had been reported found by deputies. By 11:00 A.M. three more bodies had been recovered, all of them had been chopped on the back of the head and all of them stabbed in the left chest.

There were other similarities, too.

As in the case of the eight bodies that had been found the day before, all of the victims' shirts had been pulled up over their heads, and their arms were raised and crossed over their faces, yet not touching the skin itself. Too, the trousers were either pulled down or missing altogether, and the sexual organs of several were exposed. The details were listed in the reports that were written by the officers who found the bodies. As had been done the day before, the remains were placed in body bags and numbered before being removed to the Chapel of the Pines in Yuba City.

An autopsy later revealed a dissimilarity in the body of victim number eleven. The man had also been shot in the back of the head, but the bullet wound was not readily seen because of the severe chop wounds. The victim was tentatively identified as William Henry Kamp, sixty-three, by a Colorado driver's license and a Social Security card found in his wallet, which also contained a five-dollar bill and three one-dollar bills, and a five-cent piece. A coin purse contained a quarter, four dimes, four nickels, and six pennies. In his pockets officers found an aspirin bottle, a gold religious coin, a cheap pocket watch, a money order receipt, a plastic comb, and some personal papers.

Body number ten was that of a Negro who was missing two upper front teeth. All that was found on the body was a package of Safeway matches.

Number twelve was a white man, six feet tall and very thin. There was nothing at all on the body to identify him.

With the twelfth body in the morgue, Cartoscelli, who had been on duty for twenty-four hours without letup, called it a day.

Back at the sheriff's office, the members of the media now numbered over a hundred. Whiteaker, looking out the window at the mob on the courthouse lawn, turned to the woman at the desk and wistfully said, "Now I know how Custer felt when he saw all those Indians coming."

While Cartoscelli went home for some much-needed rest, the other officers concentrated on searching for leads that might help to identify the victims. They were also interested in discovering any facts, or even rumors, that would tie Corona more tightly into the case.

The C.I.I. (California Bureau of Investigation and Identification) had sent Don E. Stattlemyer a criminalist, from Sacramento, to assist in the case at Whiteaker's request and to examine the evidence that had been found *to date*.

Stottlemyer received the items that had been taken from the Corona home and the labor camp and then was taken to the garage where the Corona vehicles had been impounded to examine them. From the interior of the van he scraped bloodstains from the spare tire and the walls and also from the inside of the rear bumper. In the trunk of the Impala he found a red hair and also scraped some stains from the rear latch.

All of the evidence which was found had been spread out on tables at the sheriff's pistol range south of town for inspection by the experts.

However, there was one notable exception. The evidence from the Whitacre grave, including the tire impression, was not included.

All of the items that were considered to be important to the case were taken to the laboratories in Sacramento where they could be examined more thoroughly by Stottlemyer and other experts.

Purcell took advantage of the break in the body search to talk to Roy DeLong, who had reported Beierman missing. DeLong, fifty-two, was a resident of a skid-row hotel and a familiar figure in the section of town where the farm workers congregated. DeLong had talked to Officer Ronald Huff of the Marysville Police Department earlier in the month to report that his friend, "Pete" Beierman, was missing. Beierman had been a resident of Marysville for over twenty years and, after his wife died three years before, had taken to hanging around a mission that Chris Bergtholdt operated for the transient farm workers. The mission had been financed by Ghagat Singh Thiara and was called the "Men's Day Center."

Beierman had his Social Security checks sent there, and DeLong reported him missing on May 6 after he had failed to pick up one that was delivered on April 4 and another which was delivered on May 5. DeLong told Huff that he had last seen his friend six weeks before. He said they were standing on the corner of Third and D streets when a man walked up and asked Beierman if he wanted to work. The last DeLong saw of Pete was when he climbed into a tan-colored panel truck and drove away with his employer. DeLong said he did not know who the man was but said he believed he was a Mexican. He also said Beierman was missing parts of two fingers on one hand.

By the midmorning the number of reporters, cameramen, and photographers had swelled, and they were still coming from all parts of the nation. The Yuba City story was developing into the greatest news drama in many years. Twelve murder victims found and the Lord only knew how many more there would be. The clamorous newsmen were getting louder in their demands for information. Finally, Whiteaker decided to talk to them.

Having ordered his staff to say nothing to anybody about the case for fear of fouling up a later trial, the sheriff had made up his mind to give only the barest facts about the crime.

Chapter 5

Although at thirty-one he was the youngest sheriff in California, and despite the fact he had been sheriff for less than five months, Roy Whiteaker was no johnny-come-lately to the law business. The newsies were about to find out that they were dealing with a very shrewd dude.

A native of Arkansas, his family had moved to Los Angeles when he was four years old. He attended elementary and high schools there and then had enlisted in the army in 1958. He served three years as a military policeman, mostly in the Panama Canal Zone where he met and married his wife. He was discharged in 1961 and moved to Northern California where, in 1962, he joined the Yuba City Police Department.

Police work turned out to be Whiteaker's cup of tea, and he rose to the position of detective in 1965. An ambitious man with a growing family, he was determined to succeed in his profession.

He attended a narcotics school sponsored by the Federal Bureau of Narcotics and also attended Yuba Community College near Marysville and graduated with a degree in police science.

Sacramento State University was located fifty-three miles away, and he made that round trip each night to complete courses there. He received a lifetime teaching credential from the California State Department of Education at the end of two years.

In 1970 he decided to challenge H. P. "Shug" Ollar, the incumbent sheriff of Sutter County, and won rather easily. He took office on January 4, 1971, and was still in the process of reorganizing the department and establishing his own policy when he suddenly became front-page copy all over the world.

Whiteaker met the press on the front lawn of Yuba City's Victorian era courthouse. Speaking in a quiet, controlled voice, the trim, neatly dressed six-footer gave the essential details of the case. He announced that twelve bodies had been found and, yes, he expected that more would be discovered. No, he could not guess at a final figure, but as new victims were found the press would be informed.

The suspect, he said, was Juan Vallejo Corona. He was thirty-six years old and was a farm labor contractor. Not much else was known about him at the present time because the investigation was still continuing.

Singling out one question from a dozen shouted at him, the sheriff said, "We are certain that we have the right man. We are convinced he committed the murders." He explained that some of the bodies had apparently been buried for as long as six weeks or more and suggested that a large, heavy knife, perhaps a machete, had been used to kill the men. However, he added, at least two of the graves had been dug within forty-eight hours of the time the bodies were discovered.

After assuring the reporters that he would meet with them again the following day and that they would be kept informed if more victims were discovered, Whiteaker broke off the conference and retreated to his office.

There he began to make arrangements for Corona's arraignment, which was scheduled to begin within minutes. It had been decided to arraign the suspect in the sheriff's office rather than take him to the justice court, which was located in another part of the building. That would eliminate the necessity of having to walk Corona through the mass of photographers who were waiting with cameras at the ready in hope of getting a shot of the man who was making headlines throughout the world.

Whiteaker appointed Littlejohn to take charge of security and to protect the prisoner every time he was moved from his cell. It was an apt selection.

Littlejohn joined the Sutter County department in 1959 after getting an honorable discharge from the Air Force, where he had been a staff sergeant.

During the next eight years he was promoted to sergeant, then lieutenant, and finally to captain in 1967. Educationally, he also advanced. He obtained a degree in police science from Yuba College and an advanced certificate from the State Peace Officers Standards and Training Commission. He also earned a lifetime teaching credential in police science.

Littlejohn was not only experienced and smart; he was also

tough. "There is not going to be a Jack Ruby case around here," he asserted when he took over the job of providing security for Corona. Members of the press and spectators soon learned to keep their distance when the prisoner had to appear in public. Littlejohn prescribed a minimum distance between his charge and the public and strictly enforced it.

Shortly after noon Corona, with a blanket covering his head and shoulders, was led from his cell to the sheriff's office and faced Judge J. J. Hankins of the Yuba County Justice Court. Hankins was asked to preside because he was an attorney, while the justice court judge in Yuba City was not. There had been some discussion among the legal fraternity recently as to the propriety of nonlawyers sitting as judges in cases involving felonies.

Hankins went over the charges briefly and then asked Corona, "Do you have an attorney?"

Corona replied that he did not, and when asked if he had talked to a lawyer he pointed to Van den Heuval and said, "well, this man, he come and see me."

Hankins then asked if the defendant had money to hire an attorney and suggested that a defense might cost as much as $20,000. Corona didn't have that kind of money, and Hankins appointed Van den Heuval as the defense attorney of record until such time as Corona might want to make other arrangements. Van den Heuval immediately asked for a week's continuance. It was granted, and the brief session was all but over.

The only other matter was to act on a motion by Teja, who asked that all parties be restrained from talking in public about the case. Teja pointed out that large numbers of media people were constantly pressing the sheriff for information, interviews with the defendant, and pictures of Corona. Such pretrial publicity, he said, could be prejudicial to the defense. Judge Hankins then issued an order forbidding the district attorney, the sheriff or his deputies, and the court attachés from discussing the case and from giving "any information other than that information which is public record and in the records of the court." Hankins himself went into the hallway where the horde of newsmen were gathered and told them of the gag order.

Corona was led back to his cell where he was visited by his wife, Gloria, and his brother, Pedro. A tearful meeting, apparently. Gloria was crying and Pedro was grim as they left the jail.

The telephones were still ringing as the hundreds of calls kept coming into the office. Newspapers, television and radio stations from all over the nation and a few from Europe—all were asking for the latest developments. Calls from ordinary people inquired whether long-missing sons, brothers or uncles were among the victims.

Because of the sheriff's announcement that Corona had been arrested and charged with the murders, the calls from frightened residents among Yuba City's 14,000 population had dropped sharply, but the total number of calls not only failed to decrease but actually increased because the cranks were now calling in.

One woman called in to say that she was clairvoyant and had had a dream in which there had been revealed to her a map showing the location of numerous graves. The call was dutifully checked out by a deputy sheriff who visited the woman. She had sketched a map of her dream-produced gravesites, which turned out to be located several miles from the Yuba City area.

Another woman called in to tell the sheriff, "Juan Corona could not possibly have killed those men because my brother did it. I know it was my brother because he was so mean to me as a child."

There were many similar calls and then there was one from a woman who insisted on talking only to the sheriff. Two detectives finally agreed to talk to the woman, who gave her name as Ruby Lillard and who said she had information about Corona that was known only by her. She was asked to come to the office.

Nobody ever did figure out whether Ruby Lillard was crazy on the day she talked to the two detectives—and later when she testified before the grand jury—or whether she went wacky later on. Regardless, it was a strange and involved story that she told the detectives and then later repeated to Whiteaker.

Ruby was well known among the denizens of the skid-row hotels where she had occasionally shared a bed with them either for a small fee or even gratis if the recipient of her favors could supply a small potion of cheap whiskey or fortified wine. She was also officially listed as "legally blind" by the state welfare department and was therefore eligible for special assistance. In her case, the assistance was in the form of a concession to operate a snack bar in the State Division of Highways building in Marysville.

At the time she talked to the detectives Ruby was about fifty-two years old, had been through a couple of nondescript marriages, and had the look of one who had made several trips "around the turf," as the saying went in the end of town she liked to frequent.

She had met Juan Corona in 1957, she said, when he was only a boy. He told her that his brother, Natividad, had sent him to her but she couldn't understand what else he was saying until he said he was sick. He said. "Call doctor. Call police," Mrs. Lillard said. She said she did not call the police or a doctor because Corona added that he was "sick in the head" and that his heart "turn over." She said she saw Corona again in 1958, and at that time he said, "I think bad things." She asked him what kind of bad things and said he drew pictures of men, then made several slash marks across the heads with the pencil. Then he said, "He dead. I kill him," she told the sheriff.

Strangely, she said, the pictures of the men had no eyes. Whiteaker was to be reminded of that remark some weeks later.

Mrs. Lillard told of meeting Corona in a small park in Marysville's skid row, and again he said he was sick and asked her to call the police. She said she talked to a police officer who told her that Corona didn't want to work but wanted welfare instead. He couldn't be arrested unless he committed a crime, the officer told her.

She said Juan told her, "Maybe if I kill someone they get me a doctor. I kill everybody."

Mrs. Lillard said she laughed at him and asked, "Juan, what would you do with the bodies?" She said Juan asked her how bodies were disposed of and she told him they were buried in a hole. He asked her how big the hole should be and she described the size of a grave.

Mrs. Lillard said she ran into Corona again two years later in a bar she had purchased in Marysville, but she didn't recognize him. He told her that he had been working hard and had gotten a home and a wife, but his wife had left him. He said he was still sick and wanted help and asked how it was done in the United States. She told him to go to the welfare department. "They help?" he asked. When told they would he said, "I go."

During the next two or three years she had seen Corona on other occasions, and each time he said he was still sick. Once, in 1963, she said, Natividad asked her to join a celebration the family was having in the Guadalajara Cafe, which he had purchased in partnership with Raymond Duron, a family friend and Jack Sullivan's foreman. Duron was to remain a silent partner until he sold his share to Natividad.

On the party occasion, she said, Juan was present but was slumped in a chair. The family said he was "sick," she said. Juan got up from the chair, she related, and stood with his head back, sniffing. She said he appeared to recover somewhat and then said, "Nothing no one can do," and walked out the door.

Mrs. Lillard also said Gloria Corona came to her in 1965 after the couple had married, and told her "Juan's sick."

She said she went out to the street and found Corona slumped over the fender of an automobile. She said two police officers came up at that point and both began to beat him, thinking he was drunk. She cried for them to stop, saying, "He is not drunk! He doesn't drink!"

She said the officers then talked to Corona a few minutes, then took him away, but she never found out where. There was no police report of the incident.

Then, there was one other time the two met, a time she remembered vividly.

It was on a night a couple of years before when she met Corona in Marysville and he had asked her to go with him to bury some garbage. As the fascinated Whiteaker listened, she told of riding with Corona through Yuba City, then north and onto the levee either on or near the Sullivan Ranch. They had parked near some trees close to the river and Corona got out of the truck. She said she asked him what kind of garbage he was going to bury and he replied, "Wino garbage."

There wasn't a sound, she said. It was "death quiet." Then she heard a slight movement and then, "Only a minute later I heard a terrible blow, a thud, hit the bottom of the van."

She said it was inside the van but that she couldn't see because she was still sitting in the front seat where Corona had told her to stay. She was frightened, she said, because the blow was like a "sort of concussion, knocked me off my equilibrium." She said the springs of the truck went down but she couldn't feel them come up. She could not see outside the van but she heard a sniffing sound, "Like an animal, and it was in the van. It was outside and it came near the driver's side. I locked the door."

The she said "the thing" went around the back of the vehicle and came around to the other side. She locked that door too, she said, then lay down and held both doors. She thought there was an animal sniffing around the truck.

She said she looked out and saw a shadow as it went into the trees. "Then I heard nothing for quite awhile. In fact, it was breaking day before he came back to the truck."

She said Corona got into the vehicle, asked her where she lived, and drove her home. Then, she said, he didn't want to let her out of the van.

He said, "I no let you go. You tell my brothers."

She finally got out of the van, she said, and didn't see Corona again except casually on occasion in the skid-row area.

Whiteaker relayed the details of his conversation with Mrs. Lillard to Teja, but the district attorney didn't get a chance to follow it up.

There wasn't much time to do anything for the next few days. A late afternoon telephone call from Ray Duron saw to that.

Another possible gravesite had been found on the Sullivan ranch, Duron said. His workers, he added, were looking for more sites at his instructions.

Chapter 6

The clouds had been gathering over the valley, and there was every indication that it was going to rain again. Maybe, the sheriff thought, it might be better to wait until morning to probe the newest site. After all, if there was a body there it wasn't going to go anywhere and the security force would keep the place closed off to the public and the press.

The next morning, Cartoscelli and his digging crew went to the ranch while Purcell, Gregory, and Harrison were assigned to begin an intensive investigation into Corona's background and to seek any further information they could find that might affect the case.

At the ranch, Cartoscelli learned that other possible sites had been found, and Duron sketched a rude map showing approximate locations. Later, a newsman got a hint of that map and then surmised that it might have been found at the Corona home during the search. The thought was no sooner formed than it turned into a glaring headline—"Death Map!"

It had rained on and off during the night and the ground was turning soggy. The heavy cloud cover remained as Cartoscelli's crew began digging at 9 A.M., and by 9:40 the body of the thirteenth victim had been uncovered. A half-empty wine bottle and an empty dog food bag were lifted from the grave, and then the body with the now familiar chop wounds in the back of the head and the knife thust in the left chest, was laid out on the ground.

The index, middle, ring, and little fingers of the left hand were missing as the result of an old injury, and a black leather glove for the hand was found in the grave. The victim, later identified as Clarence Hocking, had the usual sparse personal possessions on his person. A plastic comb, a small amount of adhesive tape, nail clippers, a toothbrush, a small bottle of Lucky Tiger hair oil, and a package of cigarette papers were all placed in a bag and numbered. A similar number was written on a tag which was placed in the body bag.

Newsmen had been allowed by the sheriff to watch the digging but were kept at a distance of forty yards. Whiteaker had gone to the ranch to watch his deputies at work. Now he held another press conference. It was brief and to the point. The sheriff said his men would continue to search "until we quit finding bodies," and he refused to speculate on how many more might turn up. However, he said, he was sure more would be found. He also promised, and delivered, "mug shots" of the suspect.

Just before noon it began to rain again, a rain that turned into a gully washer that drove the men to shelter. Deputies and reporters alike, antagonists of a sort just minutes before, now huddled in the sparse shelter of the labor camp buildings bound together in misery but still held apart by the gag order that prohibited the officers from talking to the press about the case.

The rain slackened early in the afternoon and Duron led the deputies back over the levee and then south to a fork in the dirt road where three of his men had reported seeing Corona four days before. There had been no reason for the labor contractor to be in that area. The men, brothers Moses and Jose Ramirez and Jesus Machuca, had reported the incident to Duron after the three bodies had been found the day before.

At 1:30 P.M. the fourteenth body was found in a grave somewhat more shallow than the others. It took less than forty-five minutes to exhume the body, and officers tentatively identified it as that of James S. Howard. The victim had two pill bottles in his pockets with his name on them and a bus ticket made out for a trip to Sacramento on May 1, 1971.

The fifteenth body was found a few minutes later and was quickly brought out of its grave. The victim, male and white, was fully clothed but the trousers were unzippered. Again, a tentative identification was made by means of four food-stamp books, a food-stamp application form, and a set of dentures, all of which had the name Jonah Smallwood on them.

The bodies, numbered and bagged, were sent along to the Twin Cities Mortuary and from there to the more capacious Sacramento County Morgue.

Duron then led the searchers to another section of the orchard, about a mile to the north where other workers had reported seeing Corona. It took more than three hours of combing the brush before the telltale indentations were found. This time there were five of them.

Whiteaker was there and so was Teja as the digging began. The deputies were beginning to feel the effects of exhuming putrid, decaying bodies that had been buried in the soft soil. The stench was so heavy in the damp air that the officers were smoking cigars at a furious rate in an effort to make the tobacco smoke conceal the nauseous fumes that arose from the graves.

The digging proceeded rapidly with the aid of Jim Kilmer's backhoe and it was taking no longer than thirty to forty minutes to retrieve each body.

However, the deputies lost a lot of time when they ran into what could be considered false holes. In some sections the soft earth covered a layer of heavy hardpan less than two feet from the surface. On five different occasions the searchers began to dig in telltale indentations in the ground only to find that the original digging had stopped when the hardpan was struck.

If, indeed, as the theory was now being advanced, the murderer had had his victims dig their own graves, he had shown them a macabre consideration by making certain that the digging was easy for them.

Number sixteen was only three feet below the surface with the legs bent at the knees and pressed against the chest. A Social Security card bore the name of Elbert T. J. Riley. Besides the card, the victim had only two cents in his pockets.

Number seventeen, found nearby just a few minutes later, was also in a shallow grave. Papers in a wallet found in the grave indicated the man might be Paul B. Allen. His attack had been even more vicious than those suffered by the others. Half of his face had been hacked away and his brain was exposed through a gaping hole in the skull. He had just two dollars in his pockets along with a black eye patch and a Bull Durham bag containing a safety razor and the remnants of a bar of soap.

It was getting darker by this time, and floodlights were called in. By their light grave number eighteen was opened and the body of Edward Martin Cupp, identified by personal papers found on the body, was exposed. Deputies also found change totaling $1.81 and a tobacco tin on the body.

There was a slight delay before the next two bodies were exhumed. Rodemaker had found some tire tracks between the two graves and had sent for a plaster of paris kit.

When the kit arrived, Rodemaker followed the same procedure as had Cochran on the day Whitacre's body was found seven days before. Seven days! *God!* thought the sheriff, *had it only been a week since this whole crazy thing started?*

As Rodemaker carefully mixed the plaster of paris and then poured the solution into the tracks while a deputy held a flashlight to help him see what he was doing, an interested spectator was Teja, who watched as Rodemaker, before the plaster of paris was fully hardened, wrote the date, time, place, the reason for the impression, and then signed his name in the material. The impression was then lifted from the ground and placed in a department vehicle. Later, a report of the incident was written and copies were sent to Teja's office.

After the delay caused by copying the tire tracks, the work of retrieving bodies number nineteen and twenty went on. Near grave number nineteen the deputies found a red hardhat which had been cast into some bushes. The victim had suffered the usual chop wounds on the back of the head and the familiar stab wound in the left chest. He also had been chopped on the right and left arms, indicating that he had attempted a futile defense against his killer.

The hardhat, the sheriff learned before the night was over, was the proudest possession of Albert Hayes, well known as "Scratch" in the lower end of Marysville.

The twentieth victim was difficult to identify mainly because it was not immediately possible to determine whether he was black, Mexican, or white. As it turned out, he was none of those. When identification was finally established, it was learned that he was Raymond Reand Muchache, a Maidu Indian.

The magnitude of the story that was developing into the

"crime of the century" awed even the most cynical reporters who had flocked to the small town on the Feather River.

Twenty bodies! All of them viciously murdered apparently by the same person! As District Attorney Teja said, "It is a totally unreal case!" No one among the 150 members of the news media who had been assigned to Yuba City had ever covered anything to match this one!

The press was frustrated at every turn. The sheriff wouldn't talk, and neither would his deputies. All Van den Heuvel would say was, "They've got the wrong man!" The big questions were still unanswered:

Who was this fellow Juan Corona?

Why, out of 45,000 residents of Sutter County, was he the one arrested?

What was the motive for the murders?

The reporters, continually pounded by the hard-nosed editors who were demanding fresh angles to the story, were reduced to interviewing each other. The result was some stories that made lurid headlines but which, for the most part, had little basis in fact.

The sheriff, too, was asking the same questions. Despite the fact that Corona had lived in Yuba City for the past fifteen years and had been a labor contractor for twelve of them, he was pretty much unknown ouside the farming and Mexican communities.

He had no past criminal record except for that affair in the Guadalajara Cafe the year before and which Whiteaker was now determined to reinvestigate.

He had a comfortable, modern home in a quiet, orderly neighborhood. He apparently paid his bills and he was well thought of by the ranchers for whom he supplied crews of farm laborers. Both Kagehiro and Sullivan, for whom he had worked for several years, had already described him as a hardworking, conscientious contractor who would go out of his way and make an extra effort to make sure a job was well done.

There was, of course, the commitment to the mental hospital sixteen years before, but that was only for three months. There were a lot of people in the area who had been confined in similar institutions in the past and had recovered to become solid, substantial citizens.

If Corona had indeed killed these men, Whiteaker asked himself, why?

The pattern had already developed. There was no doubt that the killings had been done by a homicidal maniac. Too, because most of the victims were missing their trousers or at least had them open in front, and because the penises of several were exposed, there didn't seem to be any doubt that there was a homosexual angle. There was probably also a clue in the fact that the victims had all been winos, the type who hung out in Marysville's skid row, homeless and adrift, and who traditionally only worked sporadically, just enough to buy a bottle of cheap wine and rent a flop in a skid-row flophouse once in awhile.

Take the positions of most of the bodies when the graves were uncovered. Why were the arms crossed above the face? Why were the shirts pulled up over the heads?

Were these ritual-type killings, as some of the news reports had suggested? It was ridiculous to consider that the men had been killed in order that their Social Security cards could be stolen and then sold south of the border to wetbacks. A couple of newspapers had carried that story but Social Security credentials had been found on some of the victims, so that theory was out.

Certainly, robbery wasn't the motive. Men such as the victims rarely carried any money around with them because they spent what little they earned as fast as they earned it. Also, while it didn't amount to much, money had been found on some of the men.

It was a real puzzler, and the county's new sheriff was expected to find the answers. There was only one way to do it—lots of leg work, a great deal of patience, and the checking of every report, every rumor, every whisper, no matter how silly they seemed on the surface.

The first thing, it seemed, would be to go into Juan Corona's background, and Whiteaker turned that problem over to his investigators.

Chapter 7

Purcell received the reports of the telephone calls that were coming into the office and assigned these which were worth following up to investigators. Anything which had to do with Corona's background was to be placed in a separate file for the sheriff to study. Copies of all reports were to go to the district attorney.

The investigators quickly learned that the Mexican farm workers were reluctant to talk about any member of the Corona family. Juan and his brothers were known to be bound together by strong family ties, and any affront to one would call for fast retaliation from the others. However, by promising some informants to keep their names confidential, and by promising others that they would not have to testify, the officers began to learn a lot about the suspect.

Corona had first come to California in 1950 when he slipped across the border from his native Autlan illegally. He worked in the fields of the Imperial Valley for awhile then drifted into the Sacramento Valley, where he worked in the crops around Stockton and picked grapes in Lodi. His older half-brother, Natividad, had come to the States several years before and was comfortably settled in Marysville, where Juan visited him on occasion.

Corona left the farm work and went into construction for awhile, making his home in Sacramento. At nineteen he met a girl in Sacramento and, because her family forced it, he married her in Reno in 1953. The marriage lasted only a few months and Corona went back to the crops. He eventually went to Marysville where Natividad was a labor contractor and found plenty of work. Juan lived with his half-brother working in his crews and slowly learning the labor contracting business by serving as a crew foreman at times.

In December, 1955, the terrible flood which took forty lives occurred, and it had a strange effect on Juan. It was Natividad who filed a petition in the Yuba County Superior Court on January 11, 1956, asking that his half-brother be committed to a mental hospital. Natividad said that Juan believed that he was living in a land of ghosts because he thought everybody had been killed in the flood. The people he saw on the streets he believed were all dead. He spent most of his time reading the Bible, Natividad testified.

Juan was confined in the security ward of the county hospital where two doctors, J. J. Salopek and Benjamin Miller, neither of them psychiatrists, examined him. Their report described him as "divorced, Catholic, confused, disoriented, delirious and suffering from hallucinations extending over the past month." His physical condition was good, the report said, but his mental condition was confused and he was suffering from delusions.

The condition was diagnosed as schizophrenia and it was recommended that he be transferred to a state hospital for treatment. He was twenty-two years old at the time.

Corona was transported in handcuffs to DeWitt State Hospital in Auburn, on January 17, where he was admitted. The first report described him as being "combative" upon admission and added that he was suffering from "schizophrenic reaction, paranoid type."

He began to undergo shock treatments every other day and, by the end of the first week, wanted to go home. He went to the hospital office and demanded to be released, threatening to kick the door down if he was not. It was 8 P.M. and the attendant on duty called for assistance as Corona began kicking the door. He was placed in seclusion for twenty-four hours and, upon being released, apparently caused no more trouble.

Coincidentally, one of the witnessing signatures on a consent form to allow Corona to receive medical and dental treatment at the hospital was that of Ray Duron. The other signature was Natividad's.

After three months the doctors decided that Corona was well enough to be released. Because they had been informed when he first entered the hospital that he was an illegal alien, hospital officials notified the Border Patrol and Corona was sent back to Mexico.

Late in 1956, he received a "green card" permitting him to

work in the United States, and returned to Marysville. He resumed working for his brother and followed the crops through the valley, usually finishing the year by picking olives in Corning. He continued to live with Natividad for the next two years until the latter decided to give up his labor contracting business and open the Guadalajara Cafe in partnership with Duron. Natividad allowed Juan to use his state contracting license, for which Juan would pay a percentage of the profits.

By this time he was a muscular twenty-six-year-old, five feet, 11 inches tall, and weighing a full 180 pounds. He liked to dress well, with his thick, black hair neatly combed and his shoes always shined. His deep, brown eyes were nearly concealed by heavy, black brows and he rarely smiled

In 1960 he met Gloria Moreno Cuesas, twenty-four, who had also been born in Autlan. Gloria was helping her mother cook for a crew of farm workers in a labor camp near Yuba City. She had been in Yuba City for several years and was very popular among the younger crowd. At the time she met Juan she was engaged to a young Yuba City man of Mexican descent.

The pretty, shapely Gloria often attended the dances that were held in Yuba City, and it was at one of those events that she met Juan. Nobody could ever understand what attracted her to him but, shortly after the meeting the couple were married in Reno, Nevada. It was to be the beginning of Gloria's self-described "fourteen years of hell."

For Corona it was a marriage of convenience. He needed a cook for his farm laborers and, in Gloria, he found a woman who could and would work long hours and could also satisfy his fierce sex drive.

As a family man, Corona was a good provider. He purchased a home in Live Oak, twelve miles up the road from Yuba City, and later bought the more modern and newer home on Richland Road. During the next seven years they had four daughters to whom Juan was a stern, yet kind, father.

While the press went to a great length to describe Corona as a loving, devoted husband, there were some contradictions. If Gloria was living with a man who was kind and loving, then she was certainly accident-prone. Medical records indicated such injuries as a broken nose, a lacerated tongue, cuts and bruises on the head and shoulders, and crushed veins in the legs during the course of her marriage. There were other incidents, too, that never came to the attention of doctors.

However, in the manner of her people, Gloria never complained except to one or two close friends. Outwardly, she gave the appearance of a loyal wife who was satisfied with her lot.

Corona was a grim, introverted man who made few friends, if any. He joined the Charros, a Mexican society devoted to horsemanship, and often attended the meetings though seldom took part in the discussions. However, he was always willing to contribute financially when the organization needed money.

He also became active in the Catholic Church, where he was a generous contributor. He organized and attended retreats and other church activities and was described by his parish priest as a "good man."

In his work he was successful, and the growers liked him. He was able to get contracts when other contractors could not, but even so he had some problems. An olive grower in Oroville said he kept "the dirtiest kitchen I ever saw," and he was ordered off a ranch near Yuba City for failing to keep his camp clean. Another grower said he fired him because he failed to feed his workers properly.

However, none of the growers who hired him had any complaints about the quality of his work. Even those who disputed his habits were more than willing to have him harvest their crops.

His crews were almost always made up of Mexicans. He would not work women and children, except in emergencies, and he despised the Anglo wino. Only when there was absolutely no other labor available would he consider working a wino. They were no good, he said. They would work only long enough to earn the price of a bottle of wine and then would want to go to town and get drunk.

The members of the news media who began to circulate in the community asking questions about Corona got answers that contradicted those the deputies received. It was widely reported in the media that Corona was an even-tempered man who had no bad habits and was easy to get along with.

There were indications that such was not always the case.

Duron, the old family friend who had helped Corona get the contract at the Sullivan ranch in 1966, knew something of Corona's temper. Back in 1968, he told Gregory, Duron had lined up two crews to start the peach harvest. The regular ranch crew was to start one day and Corona was told to start his crew the day after.

Instead, Corona showed up on the ranch with a crew on the first day and Duron told him that he could not begin work until the morrow.

He said Corona became agitated, leaped in his bus, spun it around the parking lot with screeching tires a couple of times and then parked it behind the mess hall.

A short time later, Duron said, he was walking across the yard with two men whom he had just supplied with picking bags when he heard a motor behind him. He looked around and saw the vehicle heading directly toward him, and the trio had to leap frantically to one side to keep from getting run over.

Corona was a good worker he said, but he didn't have much sense. In fact, Duron said, Corona was "crazy."

Leroy Parent, manager of a credit firm that had mortgages on the Corona equipment, said he had sent Riley Smith, one of his employees, to Corona's home in the summer of 1969 to inspect the vehicles. Smith came back to the office to report that Corona had become angry at some of the questions and had "roughed him up." Parent said he then went to see Corona and related that Corona lunged through the door at him.

He asked Corona the necessary questions and the latter was "obnoxious and loud" at some of them but calm at the others.

In March, 1971, Corona had appealed to the county welfare department for assistance because there was no farm work. His appeal was denied on the grounds that it was fraudulent and, the case worker reported, Corona "went to pieces" and became abusive in the offices. His anger was so obvious that those in the offices were afraid of him.

A Mexican woman living in Gridley told officers that she would not talk if her name was to be used. When assured that it would not be, she said all of the Mexican people were afraid of Corona and his brothers. She said she was told that Juan had cut a man in the Guadalajara Cafe but would talk no further about it because, she said, "I've heard some of the deals the Coronas have done, and they don't do it themselves or do it with someone who knows you or knows them. They just pay a complete stranger to do it."

She also said she heard that Juan, as well as Natividad, was homosexual and that everyone was scared of him.

The owner of the tavern where the Mexican farm workers gathered had two Mexicans working for him. He had said both of them told him Juan Corona was a man to stay away from. They would have nothing to do with him, they said.

Anna Marie Ford, a grocery clerk, was also interviewed by Gregory after she had called the sheriff's office to say she had some information.

It had happened way back in 1961, she said, when she was clerking in a store. Two men became engaged in a loud and angry argument which ended when one left. The other, whom she knew as a truck driver, apologized to her for the disturbance and said the other man, whom she identified as Juan Corona, had made an indecent proposal to him.

Another interview took Gregory to the California Prison for Women at Frontera where he talked to Lorraine Hattie Saling. She was in prison after a felony conviction and told a prison matron that she knew something about Corona.

The woman told Gregory that she had gone to a Marysville motel with Corona on several occasions and said that he wanted her to perform unnatural sex acts with him. She refused to say whether she did or did not; however, she told Gregory that she had heard Corona had cut a man in the cafe but she was never afraid of him and he had never harmed her.

A farm worker at the Sullivan ranch, who would not allow his name to be used, told Gregory that the Mexican people talked about Juan being "queer." They said he was crazy and that he liked sex too much and liked to kill while doing it. He himself had worked for Corona, he said, and had heard the remarks often.

Larry John Tanner also had an interesting meeting with Corona.

Tanner, a transient, was temporarily staying at a mission in Oroville in October, 1970, when he and two other men decided to try to get work picking olives at the Berkeley Olive Groves outside of town.

Corona had the contract to supply the picking crews, and Tanner said they talked to him about work. He said Corona lectured them for fifteen minutes or more about the drinking habits of winos and said he would not stand for any drinking by his crews. As he talked, Tanner said, he became more and more agitated and angry and repeated himself several times. Finally, he told the three to get into his pickup, which was parked in the labor camp, and wait while he obtained picking buckets for them.

Tanner said while he was sitting in the pickup he felt with his foot an object under the seat. He said he reached down and found a cleaver and a butcher knife which he pulled out to look at.

Tanner said he turned to the other two and said, "This guy ain't kidding. You'd better pick olives real good "

He put the cleaver and knife back under the seat and Corona came out of a mess hall with three buckets. Tanner said he and his companions were the only three Americans on the job. He said Corona continued to make derogatory remarks about Anglo winos as they drove to the grove. Corona told them he didn't like to hire Americans because they drank too much and kept the other workers awake at night. Tanner and his friends stayed on the job only long enough to earn enough money so they could move on from Oroville.

All of the information obtained was turned over to the sheriff and the district attorney for study, and Whiteaker turned his attention to the Guadalajara incident. However, the discovery of still more bodies in the orchards and along the river caused another delay in those plans.

The telephone calls were still coming in at a fantastic rate, and there was also a report from the Tehama County Sheriff's Department at Red Bluff, eighty miles to the north, about a body that had been found in the Sacramento River near Corning, almost eighteen months before. The Tehama sheriff thought it might be of interest to Whiteaker because the body had been that of a man who was murdered in the same fashion as those who were being found in Sutter County.

It was going to be necessary to check that one out, too; but first, there were some more suspected gravesites to be probed.

On May 29 the deputies were back in the river bottoms with their shovels. They quickly found the grave of John Henry Jackson, sixty-four years old and black, and dead of chops to the back of the head. There was no stab wound in the chest, however. His possessions were as sparse as those of the other victims; a package of paper matches, a small roll of friction tape, one nine-volt battery, and two metal buttons.

Lloyd Wallace Wentzel's body was found in a grave at the edge of an orchard, dead of the usual wounds and more easily identified than some of the others. He had a social welfare identification card along with a harmonica, four filter-tip cigarette butts, some food-stamp coupons; his cash assets consisted of one five-cent piece.

The last body found on that day was that of Mark Beverly Shields, whose identity was first established by his name on a pill bottle found in his pocket. There was nothing else found in the way of possessions. Shields had been stabbed twice, slashed on the back of the head several times, and had probably tried to defend himself because his left forearm was slashed and broken.

That brought the total to twenty-three bodies and called for more screaming headlines around the world. It was the last body to be found for almost a week; however, the search of the orchards and riverbank continued.

Then, on June 3, another gravesite was found and from it was lifted the body of Sam Bonafide, fifty-five, who also was known as Joe Carriveau. Of all of the victims, he was the only one who had ever worked for Corona. Social Security records obtained later showed that he had earned a total of forty dollars while employed by Corona during the last quarter of 1970. He was identified by a bank passbook found in his pocket. He also had thirty-five cents in change, a pocket knife, two pocket watches, a key ring with five keys, a nail clipper, and an empty money bag from a Marysville bank.

The following day the last recorded victim was found. He was Joseph J. Maczak, fifty-five, whose body was found under a layer of trash that had also been buried with him. On his person were identification papers, a safety razor, a pocket watch, a pocket knife, cigarette tobacco papers, a comb, and two apples, both rotten.

There were, in addition, some other items found that proved to be of interest to the investigators. A shattered glass holder for a religious candle similar to the one found when deputies searched the mess hall the morning of the twenty-sixth, a child's stocking, some grass cuttings and other household rubbish.

And among that household rubbish nestled two slips of paper that were to have a devastating effect on the outcome of the trial. They were two bank deposit slips imprinted with Juan Corona's name.

Chapter 8

Teja became directly involved in the investigation as soon as the magnitude of the crime became apparent. He was more of a cop at heart than he was an attorney, and he had often in the past gone to the scenes of major crimes to give advice on the collecting of evidence and the interrogation of suspects.

He was a native of the county, and his father was still farming the family orchards which he had purchased many years before. Bachan Teja had been an East Indian immigrant when he first arrived in Yuba City area. Eventually, he became active in political affairs and was active in the local Democratic Party affairs.

His son, Dave, had been elected district attorney in 1962 when he was twenty-eight years old. He had already served his apprenticeship as a prosecutor by serving as deputy district attorney for John Hauck, who had headed the office before being appointed to the Superior Court bench.

Teja, already becoming bald at thirty-seven years of age, was a stocky five feet, ten inches tall and going slightly to fat. He was a longtime friend of Whiteaker and had supported the new sheriff in his bid for election. He was popular in the county, having been elected to office three times. His only opposition had come in the last election, and he had brushed that aside. His record as a prosecutor was good, although he had never been faced with the possibility that he would have to try a case with the dimensions of the one facing him now.

For that reason, he was anxious to be in on all of the phases of the investigation to make sure that no vital evidence was overlooked.

He became convinced that Corona was guilty when those meat receipts were found in grave number three with the nine-fingered man. He was damn well going to prove it in court if the case ever got there!

Teja had two investigators on his staff, and he assigned then to work with the sheriff's department full-time. That gave Purcell, as chief investigator, a crew of twelve men with which to pursue the investigation. Additionally, Whiteaker got help from the Yuba City and Marysville police departments and was also provided with the services of investigators from the Yolo County Sheriff's Department and the Sacramento County Sheriff's Office. The latter department furnished the services of Sergeant Dave Perales, a Mexican-American who would probe for information that was not available to the Anglo officers in the Mexican community.

The press now had more information than it had been intended to give them. Judge Hankins provided it when he released the contents of the search warrant thet had been served on Corona at his home. By law, such documents must be returned to the court after they have been executed, and generally they are public records. In this case, Teja and Whiteaker expected that the information contained in the document would be covered by Hankins' gag order which was issued on the twenty-sixth. However, when the search warrant was returned on the twenty-eighth, newsmen who had learned in advance that it would be done were waiting outside Hankins' small courtroom. When Harrison appeared and gave the document to the judge, the reporters asked to see it and Hankins obligingly complied. He even had copies made for distribution, thus making sure that everybody who was covering the story got a look at it.

Thus, the world now knew the reasons for Corona's arrest; they knew of the meat receipts found in the third grave, the missing person report of Beierman, the commitement to the state mental hospital, Duron's remark that Corona was crazy, the Marysville police report on the Guadalajara Cafe cutting, and the list of possible weapons seized at the Corona home and labor camp.

The material was not only good for a new rash of headlines, but it also led to even more speculation on the part of the press. Teja was determined that such disclosures would not occur again.

Thereafter he directed all potential witnesses who gave statements to investigators would be served with court orders restraining them from discussing their statements with anyone other than those who were officially connected with the case. It was bewildering to many of the informants, who had given their statements in Spanish with the aid of interpreters, to be handed a legal paper written in English which only a few of them could make any sense of, and which forbade them to talk about their experience even to their own families.

The reporters had learned that most of the victims had come from the lower end of Marysville. They headed in that direction in search of stories which would augment the scanty information they were able to get from the few official releases that were coming from the sheriff and the district attorney.

It might be a good idea, they thought, to interview some of the winos and derelicts who hung out in the fleabag hotels and the sleazy taverns that made up the upper Sacramento Valley's most widely known skid row.

It turned out to be a field day for the interviewees. The newsies moved in with their cameramen, their photographers, and their expense money, and the winos were suddenly drinking on some of the nation's most prestigious publications.

The skid-row residents, who had been living by their wits for most of their lives, knew exactly what to say in order to keep their visitors interested. Some fine human interest stories came out of the shabby section of the old Gold Rush town that had been founded on the Feather and Yuba Rivers as a trading post nearly 130 years before.

In a way, John Augustus Sutter had also had a hand in the establishment of the outpost that was to become Marysville. In 1842, having extended his holdings into what later became Yuba County, Sutter leased a substantial portion of the land to Theodore Cordua, who immediately established a stock ranch and a trading post. He named the place New Mecklenburg and it sat there in lonely contemplation of its future until 1848 when gold was discovered at a spot on the Yuba called Rose's Bar, about eight miles upstream.

The Argonauts flocked into the region, and New Mecklenburg was soon bursting at the seams. M. C. Nye purchased the place and called it Nye's Rancho, but many of the miners moved a few miles east and set up a camp which they called Yubaville, after the river that flows east from the Sierra before meeting the Feather south of Yuba City.

The place grew so fast that it was impossible for the building program to keep up with the influx, and it wasn't long until it became the jumping-off place for the prospectors who were heading for the northern mines. As Yubaville grew, so did its civic pride. By 1849 it had become the head of navigation on the Feather and the most important supply point in the north. It also had the dubious reputation of being one of the bawdiest, most unbridled camps in the West.

The core of solid citizens, more interested in commerce than mining and rapidly getting rich by supplying the gold-hungry hordes who were racing toward the distant mountains in ever-increasing numbers, decided that the place should have a new name.

Charles Covillaud, a young lawyer who had landed in the camp earlier that year had brought with him his bride, the beautiful Mary Murphy Covillaud, one of the survivors of the tragic Donner party.

During the town meeting that had been called to discuss the name change, the suggestion that the town be named in honor of the beautiful Mary was accepted, and it was Marysville from that time forward. By 1855 it was the third largest city in the entire state.

If by changing the name of the town, the citizens thought they might also change its lecherous reputation and rakish character, they were mistaken. As the years rolled on, the character of the town changed very little, if at all. The veneer of respectability even today barely conceals the ribald, salty posture that made it the liveliest Gold Rush town of them all 120 years before.

Through the erosion of time the section of the city that had once been the center of commerce for all of the northern mines degenerated into a seedy, disreputable district, frequented by those individuals, men and women alike, who found both their livelihood and their pleasures in that nether world peopled by the perpetually poor and the social misfits.

The shoddiness extended not only through the former commercial district but also through the nearby neighborhood where the once ostentatious mansions of the Gold Rush era moguls were now decaying, crumbling wrecks.

Such was the source of the victims who were found in the graves along the Feather in the not-so-merry month of May.

Chapter 9

Purcell and other investigators were sifting through the hundreds of telephone calls that were coming into the office and trying to separate those which came from people who claimed to have seen Corona in the vicinity of the graves. There were several of them.

David Schmidl, a twenty-five-year-old Live Oak farmer, had taken his girlfriend—later his wife—Sharon Reeves, twenty-three, to the river for some night catfishing on May 19. He told Harrison that it was between 9 P.M. and 10 P.M. and the location was directly east of the Sullivan ranch.

Schmidl did not see Corona, he said, but he saw the latter's pickup truck, which he recognized because the vehicle had Corona's name painted on the side.

The next day Harrison interviewed Miss Reeves, who corroborated Schmidl's statement with a couple of embellishments. While her fiancé walked down to the river's edge, she said, she waited for him in Schmidl's pickup truck. She said she saw Corona come out of a brushy area carrying a shotgun. She said he put the weapon in his pickup, then got into the driver's seat and drove away in a hurry. He left so fast, she said, that he didn't wait for his two dogs, which were running along the road behind the vehicle when she last saw them. She described Corona's red and white pickup as having his name printed on its side.

Miss Reeves was certain that it was a gun Corona was carrying, and continued to insist that it was a gun during questioning later before the grand jury and even during the trial many months later.

Jacob C. Compton, thirty-eight, a surveyor for the California Department of Water Resources, was in the river bottoms during the last week in April, 1971, examining the banks for high water damage. On the day in question Compton was on the Sullivan ranch property during the morning when he saw a brown van come from one of the orchards. Compton said he stopped about 1,000 feet from the vehicle when it stopped and the driver got out, looked around, and then drove toward the ranch.

On the afternoon of that same day, Compton told Harrison, he was working on the Yuba County side of the river at about 3 P.M. when he saw the same van drive into the same area it had visited in the morning. It stayed only a few minutes, he said.

His co-worker, Steve Makis, told Harrison that he did not see the van in the morning but that afternoon he had seen it from the Yuba County side. Both men said they had seen other vehicles in the vicinity during the several days they worked along the river-banks and had also seen tracks left by other cars or trucks at various times.

Ernesto Garcia, a Sullivan worker, told a fellow worker, Joe Vesita, that he had seen Corona in the orchard near the river late at night the previous January. Vesita relayed the information to Duron, who reported it to the sheriff's department and Garcia was interviewed.

He had been spraying at about 10 P.M. and he saw Corona come out of the orchard. Later, when Garcia went to the ranch for more spraying materials, he saw Corona near the messhall and asked him why he had been in the orchard. Corona told him he had been looking for his dog.

Garcia said he told Corona, "Well, your dog has been tied up here in the ranch yard all the time."

Duron told Vesita to check out the area where Corona had been seen by Garcia, and a grave containing one of the victims was found there on May 29.

James Cummings, the ranch carpenter, was hanging a new door on the barn about the middle of May when he saw Corona back a blue van up next to the levee. He said he saw Corona go into the orchard, stay there about 45 minutes, and then leave. Cummings thought it was odd that Corona should be there because there was no one working in the orchard at the time.

When he finally reported the incident to Duron, on May 29, the foreman and three other workers inspected the spot and found another grave.

Juan Sanchez told his foreman that he too had seen Corona drive the blue panel truck to the northeast corner of the river bottom orchard on a day several weeks before. Sanchez said Corona was there for a long time—maybe two hours, although nobody was working in the vicinity. Later, three bodies were found in that general area.

John Reed Gaither, twenty-five, of Sacramento, attended a family picnic on the Prindiville ranch, next door to Sullivan's, the previous April 11. He told officers that he decided to walk along the river, north toward the Sullivan ranch, for some target shooting. He told Harrison that while he was firing his pistol at some tin cans, he saw a van which he described as white. There was nobody around it, he said, but when he showed the spot to officers, it was in the vicinity of some of the gravesites.

Sullivan was contacted again and said that Corona had furnished crews for the ranch for the past five years but only during the pruning and harvesting seasons. Therefore, there was no reason for Corona to haul men to the ranch after the previous March 15. In fact, Sullivan said, there was no reason for Corona to even be on the ranch property, outside the camp area, after that date.

On the twenty-ninth, Corona, with the blanket covering his head, was moved across the river to the more modern Yuba County jail at Marysville. Whiteaker wanted more security and more seclusion than the old and decrepit Sutter County jail could offer. In Marysville, Corona was placed in a cell in an isolated section, there to await his next appearance in court.

Van den Heuval had obtained from Teja what information the district attorney was willing to surrender and, after several hours of study and research, had just about decided to defend Corona on the grounds of mental incompetency. After looking over the 1956 commitment to DeWitt and studying the comments of Duron and other witnesses who had described Corona's erratic temperament, the public defender felt the court would agree to a commitment to a mental institution. That could prevent the case from getting into court, where a jury could go over the evidence. Van den Heuval had apparently made up his mind already that Corona was guilty.

On June 2 Corona was moved from the Yuba County jail to the Sutter County Justice Court for arraignment on nine counts of first-degree murder. Reporters and photographers were on hand to try for pictures of the suspect as he was put into a patrol car, but they were disappointed. When Corona came out of the jail he had his coat draped over his head and shoulders. The grim, burly Littlejohn was there to insist that the spectators be kept at a distance.

Van den Heuval entered a plea of innocent to all nine counts during the hearing, which was closed to press and spectators. He entered a motion that Teja be forced to turn over to him all of the information that his and the sheriff's investigators had collected on the Corona case. Under the law, a defendant is entitled to such information because it is often an unhappy fact that the prosecution has more resources with which to gather such material than the defense—particularly a defendant such as Juan Corona, a man too poor to employ the counsel and professional help needed for an adequate defense.

Teja resisted the motion, but Judge Hankins ruled in favor of the defense. He ordered that the information be given to Van den Heuval within forty-eight hours.

The hearing lasted less than ten minutes, and it turned out to be Van den Heuval's last appearance for the defense, although he did not know it at the time. While he continued to plan for Corona's defense, the latter's brother, Pedro, was making some plans of his own.

Pedro had been told by a friend that there was an attorney in Concord who was an expert at representing minority defendants who were charged with serious crimes. The younger Corona was already disenchanted with Van den Heuval, who had suggested that Juan might not be right in the head. That was an insult to the whole Corona family, and such a man could not be allowed to defend Juan. He told his friend that he would like to talk to this lawyer.

Richard E. Hawk was indeed a successful attorney, and it was true that he had often successfully defended poor people who could not have otherwise expected to receive representation. When he was contacted by Pedro's friend, he quickly agreed to come to Yuba City and talk to the defendant. He arrived on Sunday, June 11, and visited Juan in the Yuba County jail.

That afternoon it was agreed by members of the Corona family and by Juan that Hawk would take over the defense. Hawk met with Van den Heuval that same evening and made all the arrangements to substitute as the attorney of record. Van den Heuval typed up the letters and notified Hankins by phone that

Hawk would file them the very next morning.

Just about everybody connected with the prosecution and all of the members of the press—at least those who were still on the scene—were caught by surprise. The news contingent had been drastically reduced since the finding of the twenty-fifth body. The weight of the story remained the same, but the sensationalism that was generated by the discovery of corpse upon corpse was no longer present to justify continuing headlines. For the most part the Corona story had become inside page news. Hawk was about to change that.

Chapter 10

Richard Hawk had been born in Walla Walla, Washington, the son of a one-time policeman who had operated a tavern for several years and then had purchased a beer distributorship. He had attended Stanford University at Palo Alto, California, and had graduated in 1954 with a bachelor of science degree. He had married a classmate and had returned to Walla Walla, where he went to work for his father. The following year he gained admission to Stanford Law School and got his degree from there in 1957.

His first job as a lawyer had been with a Burlingame law firm where he was handed the dull, bookworm tasks which traditionally fell to the new kid in the office. He had little opportunity to actually practice law and, although he now had a family of two children and a wife to support, he decided to quit. He hooked on with an attorney in Pittsburg, California, who handed him all of the "losers" that came into the office. It was a frustrating experience for a young, ambitious, and extremely sharp young lawyer.

His income decreased drastically and his wife, not used to the austerity of poverty, left him and returned to her parents with the son and daughter. It was the low point of his life, and he thought often of bunching the whole thing and finding a new line of work.

However, despite the losses in court and the personal adversities, Hawk was learning. He himself didn't realize how good a trial lawyer he was becoming until he was appointed by the court to represent a man who was accused of murdering his girlfriend. Using the defense that his client had blacked out and didn't remember what had happened, Hawk got a hung jury on the first trial and then got his man acquitted. Everyone agreed that his work had been brilliant and his courtroom footwork had been masterful. He got a lot of publicity and was on his way.

By the time he got that fateful phone call from Pedro's friend on May 8, Hawk was chopping in high cotton. His kids had come back to live with him. He had a beautiful home in Concord, an airplane, cars, money, and a substantial income. He had all of the criminal cases he cared to handle and he also got a good chunk of the civil work, which was where the money lay. His new wife, Geneva, a slim girl of Mexican extraction, was good-looking, smart, and sharp as a tack.

Hawk had also developed an ability to cross-examine hostile witnesses that made him the envy of the Contra Costa Bar. He was incisive, quick-witted, and could be discouragingly blunt when necessary. He did his homework in every case, no matter how small, and when he walked into a courtroom, he was, "Ready!"

As for his fee for defending Corona, Hawk wasn't too worried. Juan owned two homes and three vehicles, all of which could be sold. His brothers might be able to chip in a little more, although Juan was practically broke.

There was, however, an ace in the hole that could be expected to produce some money. There was a good chance that the Mexican-American residents of the state, if they could be convinced that one of their own was being "jobbed" by the police, might be willing to pungle up some defense money. The man who might get the ball rolling was already in Yuba City.

Richard Lopez had arrived from his home in Stockton on May 31. A cement finisher by trade, Lopez had been very active in the Chicano movement in Northern California for several years. He wore an impressive, sweeping black mustache, and when he dressed in khakis with a peaked army hat of the General John J. Pershing era, he looked surprisingly like the late, legendary Pancho Villa.

Lopez was a member of such organizations as La Raza Unida (The United People), MAPA (The Mexican-American Political Association) and several ultraliberal Anglo groups.

He also had connections with the Brown Berets, a militant Chicano youth organization. Its members were fond of parading about in paramilitary uniforms topped by a brown beret. Hawk was going to find a way to make colorful, if not effective use of that later on.

Lopez was a militant but nonviolent spokesman for his people, and he quickly became convinced that the Corona case offered a "cause" that could further publicize the plight of the Chicano. His contribution was to found the "La Raza Unida Defense Fund for Juan Corona." Fred Montez, owner of a grocery store and a friend of the Corona family, became the treasurer.

Hawk had it figured that the defense fund would produce thousands of dollars to aid Corona. The blacks had done it for Angela Davis, he reasoned, why not the Mexicans? Whether he was right or not, nobody ever knew. It was never learned exactly how much money was raised. There was never an audit, and Hawk claimed that the amount was so small that he went broke furnishing his own funds to finance the defense in the end.

Hawk had one more fund-raising idea but he was going to wait awhile to put that one into effect. Eventually, it was going to embarrass him.

Now that he was officially defending Corona, Hawk's first move was to ask for a continuance to July 13. Then he met the press outside the courthouse.

Gag order or no gag order, nobody was going to stop Richard Hawk from talking to his friends in the press corps. He told the press, just as Van den Heuval had a couple of weeks before, "They've got the wrong guy." Juan was innocent, he said. His client was very upset. "He should be. The State of California is trying to put him in the gas chamber!"

In answer to a question, Hawk replied, "There is no reason to plead not guilty by reason of insanity." He was to vigorously refuse to discuss the subject many times in the future when reporters suggested that a dual plea was indicated

The dual plea was one of "not guilty" and "not guilty by reason of insanity." It was rare in California for murder defendants, particularly in sensational cases such as this, not to enter such a plea. It was a way of coppering the bet. A conviction of murder might be mitigated by a finding that the defendant was mentally unsound at the time the crime was committed.

Corona went back to jail and the investigation accelerated. With Hawk on the scene, it was a lead-pipe cinch that there was not going to be any plea bargaining or any other easy out for the prosecution. This guy was going to fight!

Chapter 11

While one group of investigators continued to follow leads provided by telephone calls, another group began to look into the Guadalajara Cafe affair which had occurred some seventeen months before.

It was February 25, 1970, when Jose Romero Raya, a twenty-three-year-old farm worker was found in the men's room of the cafe, lying in a pool of his own blood and with part of his brain oozing from a gaping head wound. He had been slashed and chopped on the head and face. He was rushed to a Marysville hospital and from there to an intensive care center in Chico, fifty miles to the north. Doctors worked for nine hours in surgery and succeeded in saving his life, but he emerged from the hospital weeks later scarred for life and a very bitter young man.

The Marysville police were called and began an investigation which, for some unknown reason, was allowed to wither away just when it seemed that it was going to bear fruit.

It was Natividad who called police to report the cutting early on the morning of the twenty-fifth. Raya had been in the cafe for several hours along with several other farm workers, and just before 1 A.M. had excused himself from his drinking partner to go to the rest room. Natividad, when questioned by Marysville officers, said a man who was unknown to him, had come from the rest room at 1:15 A.M. and told him "There is a dead man back there." Natividad investigated and then made his telephone call.

The cafe owner had never before seen the man who told him about the injured man and wouldn't be able to recognize him if he saw him again, he told the officers. About the only fact the police learned that night was that everybody in the cafe was lying when they were questioned.

However, suspicion had fallen on Natividad and there was no doubt that it bothered him. Several days later he appeared at the Marysville police station to talk to Captain John Gust. He now remembered the man who had told him about the man lying in the restroom, he said.

It was his half-brother, Juan Corona, and he added the information that Juan had been committed to a mental hospital in 1956.

Juan was called and asked to come to the police station where officers asked him what he knew about the cafe cutting. Nothing, he said, he hadn't even been around at the time. He had been in Mexico to visit his mother.

He was told that the officers knew he had returned from Mexico several weeks before but he still maintained that he was not present in the cafe. When the officers reminded him that they could put him in the place that night, he suddenly changed his story and admitted he had been there but had left at 10:30 P.M., almost three hours before Raya had been found. When he was told that other witnesses placed him in the cafe much later than that, he insisted he was telling the truth.

He was asked if he would take a lie detector test and he readily agreed. However, when the Marysville police called the C.I.I. to ask for a polygraph expert to make the test, they were told that there was only one on the staff and he was on leave. The expert would not be back on duty for another two weeks, they were told. At that point the police ended their investigation, despite the conflicting statements they had received.

In the light of the investigation that was pursued by the Sutter County Sheriff's Department, a big question remains today.

If Juan Corona had been found to have been the man who cut Raya, and had the case been properly tried in a criminal court, would there have been twenty-five bodies found in the peach orchards across the river fifteen months later?

For when the Sutter County investigators completed their file on the case, and in the light of Raya's own statements later on, it became apparent that Juan Corona was a logical, if not the *most logical* suspect in the incident.

When Raya returned from the hospital he told officers that he did not know who had cut him. Later, he obtained the services of an attorney and filed a suit against Natividad and Juan. Raya had a friend, Chavella Vasquez, who also served as his interpreter and therefore, presumably, knew more about the incident than any person other than the victim.

While the Raya lawsuit was pending, Natividad sold his properties in Yuba and Sutter counties, and returned to Mexico where he settled in Jalisco, Guadalajara. He was worth about $400,000, according to the best estimates.

Included in the property that Natividad hurriedly disposed of was a blue panel truck. He sold that vehicle to Pedro, who took immediate possession.

The blue panel truck was eventually to figure in the Fairfield verdict almost three years later.

Raya eventually won a judgment for $250,000 by default but never collected a dime.

When Whiteaker's officers began their investigation, Raya continued to insist that it was Natividad who had attacked him, but others who were in the cafe that night told a different story.

Trinidad Sepeda was working as a waitress that night because the regular waitress, Katherine Meza, also called Catalina by many of the patrons, was unable to perform. Catalina had been imbibing some of the establishment's merchandise and was in no condition to carry food as well. She therefore spent much of the evening drinking with Raya. She did not stray from the bar that night because she could not dance. It wasn't that she had had too much to drink. She had two broken ribs suffered when she involved herself in a fight between two patrons in another bar a couple of nights before.

Trinidad was involved in an off and on marriage with Fidel Juarez Lopez at the time and Lopez was also in the cafe having just returned from a meeting of Charros which was also attended by Juan. With Lopez were his two brothers and a cousin, all in the United States illegally and all looking for farm work.

Trinidad related that Natividad was suffering from a bad cold thus she was not only taking his place as the bartender but was also trying to wait on tables and cook the food as well.

It was only a few minutes before the cutting was discovered that she saw Juan come into the cafe. Raya had been having an animated conversation with Natividad about getting a check cashed but, she said, there was no anger involved.

She lost track of things about that time, she said, because she finally was able to convince Natividad that he should eat, and when he agreed, she went into the kitchen to warm over some ribs and tortillas.

She was returning from the kitchen with the food when she saw Natividad hurry from the direction of the men's room and go to the phone. She asked Catalina what was wrong and was told that there was a dead man in the rest room. Lopez and his brothers and cousin were just leaving the place in a rush.

Lopez came to her home the next morning, she said, and told her that Juan had done the cutting. Trinidad also told the officers another interesting tidbit.

She said that about an hour after Raya was carried from the cafe, Juan called on the telephone. He asked for "Corona" as he always did when he called, and she got the impression that Juan had been involved in "some kind of trouble or something." She said she told Natividad about the call and was told to tell Juan to call back. Juan did not call back, she told the officers.

Catalina agreed that she had been in the cafe when Raya was cut, and she was very upset about it. She and the young man were very close. Raya called her "mother" and she called him "son."

She said she noticed that Natividad was tending bar that night and also that Juan was sitting at the bar talking to Lopez. It was Lopez, she said, who came from the rest room and told Natividad about the cutting. She said Natividad went back "real fast" and then came back repeating aloud the telephone number of the Marysville Police Department.

About that time, she said, Juan left the cafe and so did Lopez and his relatives.

She said that Natividad called on her a few days later because he had the idea that she knew who cut Raya. She said he told her, "I didn't do it, and if you know, I wish you would please talk."

"Well," she replied, "I don't know."

After Raya got out of the hospital, she said he told her first that three men had assaulted him. Later, after he filed his lawsuit, he told her it was Natividad.

Neither of the women was trying to protect Natividad because of a romantic attachment to the handsome cafe owner. They knew, as did all of the habitués of the Guadalajara, that Natividad only had eyes for men. He was an avowed and admitted homosexual and made no effort to hide it.

Lopez denied that he had been the man who found Raya lying in the men's room, but the rest of his story coincided with that told by the women. He had attended the meeting of the Charros, he said, and about 11 P.M. he walked down the street to the Guadalajara. Juan Corona was sitting outside in his pickup truck, and he walked over to ask the labor contractor if he could provide work for his relatives. They had recently arrived from Mexico, he said, and had no papers.

He said Corona told him that he would meet him at 5 A.M. the next day and would take his relatives to Pedro's labor camp. Lopez went inside the cafe to talk to his brothers and cousin who were waiting for him. He was telling them the good news when Juan walked in.

Juan offered to buy him a drink, he said, and he agreed to

have a bottle of pop. It was after midnight by this time, and he and Juan talked for a bit. Juan ordered a cup of coffee and drank about half of it during their conversation.

Then Corona walked back toward the rest rooms, was there a short time, and came back, walking fast and looking neither to the right or left. He walked past Lopez without a word, left the building, and Lopez said he saw him get into his pickup and leave. Within another few minutes Lopez saw Natividad come back from the rear of the building and he told him that a man was hurt. Lopez gathered up his relatives and rushed them out of the cafe before the police arrived.

Raya, interviewed by Gregory more than fifteen months after he was cut, continued to insist that it was Natividad who cut him. However, Gregory got some additional information that assumed real importance.

On the night of February 24, 1970, Raya met Corona earlier in the evening. He told Gregory that he was with Nick Ramirez in front of a theater in Marysville at about 10 P.M., he said, and Corona walked up and asked the two of them if they wanted to go to work. When Raya said they would, Corona told them to get in his pickup and he would drive them to the Sullivan ranch where the job was. Raya said he and Ramirez refused to leave at that time but offered to meet Corona the following morning at 6 A.M. in front of the Tower Theater. Corona insisted that they go with him to the ranch that night, but Raya continued to refuse.

They left it like that, and Raya went on to the Guadalajara and a lengthy—and painful—leave of absence from all farm labor.

The sheriff had a lot of information and certainly enough circumstantial evidence to figure that Juan Corona had a more than accidental involvement in the Guadalajara incident, but he had no weapon nor did he have a motive. There were rumors, of course, and there was a theory, but neither would stand up in court.

There was a report, voiced by two of the bar patrons, that Corona was carrying a short-handled hoe in a paper sack when he went into the cafe. If that was so, he must have taken it out with him, because no weapon of any kind was found either in the building or anywhere around it.

As for the theory, police officers who studied the reports surmised that Juan, seeing his half-brother and Raya in animated conversation when Raya wanted to cash the check, might have guessed that his brother was suggesting a homosexual relationship and become insanely angry.

It was only rumor and theory, and neither was ever to be tried out in court. The Guadalajara incident was effectively excluded from the Corona trial by Hawk although part of what Raya said did have a bearing on the ultimate outcome.

Chapter 12

The other officers were making some progress in finding potential witnesses who could tie Corona to the disappearance of the victims from their Marysville haunts.

To get that information the investigators were forced to rely on the foggy, often wine-befuddled memories of men who had no stature whatever in any community to which their wandering mode of life took them. It was certainly not like taking a calm, logical statement from a bank official or a merchant, for instance. These were guys who, on one hand, saw in the police only a ticket to ten days in the bucket, and on the other knew the cops were not in the habit of believing anything a wino told them.

Yet there had to be some information in skid row. That's where the cadavers originally came from, wasn't it? Somewhere in the cheap wine joints and the crummy flophouses, there were some people with information.

The orders of the sheriff were plain. Find them and find out what they know!

Charles Miller was chief of the Linda Fire Department, which served an unincorporated area south of Marysville. A friend of his, John Matoon of Marysville, said he had a wino living with him, but the man had disappeared for several days.

Detective Fred Smith drew that one, and he called on Matoon. The wino's name was "Smokey," Matoon said, but that's all he knew about him.

Smith's next stop was at Chris Bergtholdt's mission where he learned that Smokey was really Nick Brboro, and not too hard to find. He was a swamper at the Guadalajara Cafe.

Nick told the officers he had been hanging around skid row for a few days and just forgot to go home. When he was asked if he knew Juan Corona, he said he didn't, but he did say that along about the middle of May he was approached by a Mexican who asked him if he wanted to dig some holes to bury garbage in. "I didn't want to dig no holes," Nick said. Who was the guy who asked him? He didn't know him, but he knew that he was the brother of the guy who owned the Guadalajara. He went to the station and identified Corona's mug shot, and then added something else.

A friend of his by the name of "Scratchy" hadn't been seen around for quite awhile. He was a little guy who always wore a hardhat that was painted red.

It was the same hardhat that was found near the grave that held the body of Albert Hayes, victim number nineteen. Smokey didn't have to worry anymore about his pal's whereabouts.

Cochran and Duncan, making the rounds of the bars, picked up a rumor that Byron Shannon, a black labor recruiter for a rival labor contractor, had been bragging that he knew plenty about Corona.

Finding Shannon was not very difficult, and he was willing, even anxious, to talk.

He was pretty well acquainted with Elbert Riley because he loaned him money last May 10 after Riley had been picked up by the California Highway Patrol and charged with drunk driving. After Riley was released from jail Shannon loaned him twenty-seven dollars to pay the impound fees on his car, and then loaned him and a companion, Jonah Smallwood, fifteen dollars to get a room and a meal. They promised him that they would go to work for Shannon's employer, J. B. Johnson, the following week and pay off the debt.

Shannon said Riley and Smallwood went on a drunk, and the next time he saw them was in "Wino Park," a favorite hangout next to the Yuba River levee.

The little patch of greenery, almost hidden from above by the freeway overpass, was a haven for the bums and the out-of-work loafers who lacked the money to justify their presence in one of the nearby taverns. It was meticulously maintained by the city park department, and its green grass and shade trees could cool and shelter a man who was just coming off of, or going into, a prolonged bout with the grape. The police rarely rousted anyone from the park so long as his activities did not breach the peace to an unbearable extent.

Shannon was a frequent visitor to the park during those seasons when the demand for casual farm workers was high. Thus it was, with the thinning season reaching a peak, that he went to the park on May 12 in search of Riley and Smallwood, his debtors.

He told the police that he was in the company of Willis Lasby, who ran a shoeshine stand outside a nearby tavern. Willie's trade in that particular end of town was not so brisk as to prevent him from taking time off at his pleasure, and he customarily spent much of his day in the park.

On this day, Shannon said, he, Willie, Riley, Smallwood, and a man with only one eye were sitting in the park when Juan Corona drove up with another man in the pickup. Corona asked if they wanted work and Riley, Smallwood, and the one-eyed man answered that they did. Lasby also offered to go to work but, Shannon said, Corona told him, "I don't want no colored."

The last he saw of the other three men, said Shannon, was when they drove away from the park with Corona and the other man, whom he said was also a Mexican. It was his understanding, he said, that the men were going to work on the Sullivan ranch.

Shannon also had had some connection with John Henry Jackson, the twenty-first victim found. He said he had met Jackson at the mission early in January when the latter asked him for a job. There was no work available at the time, and the two didn't talk again until the first week in May. At that time, Shannon said, the two were talking on a street corner, a block from Wino Park, when Corona drove up and stopped at the intersection. Jackson shouted to Corona, asking for work. While Corona sat in the pickup, Jackson walked to the window on the driver's side and talked to the contractor. Then, said Shannon, he turned around and hollered, "Well, I ain't going with you. I'm going with this fellow." He said Jackson threw his bedroll into the back of the pickup and left with Corona. He had never seen Jackson again, he said.

It was now time to talk to Lasby. His name was Willis, and he was also called "Cleanhead" at times. He was not too much help to the investigators because, he said, he was drunk on the day he was with Shannon at the park. He couldn't remember the men who got into the pickup truck, although he was sure there were three of them but he thought they were Mexicans or Indians. There were other men already in the truck, he said, and all of them appeared to be Mexicans. He could not recognize Corona as the driver although he said he had seen Corona pick up workers before at the mission.

About the only comment of value he could offer was a statement that he had asked Shannon who the contractor was who was driving the pickup, and Shannon replied, "That's Juan Corona."

James Garfield Pervis was another name that was bandied about in skid row. He had had an experience with Corona, it was said, but was not too anxious to talk about it.

Duncan found him on a downtown Marysville street late at night, and Pervis talked. He told Duncan that he had been working on his car the previous April 10 when he had to go to town for some parts. Pervis lived in Yuba City and was walking across the bridge into Marysville when Corona drove up in his pickup.

It was about four o'clock in the afternoon, he said, and Corona asked him if he'd like to work a couple of hours around the labor camp. Pervis said he refused because he wanted to get the work on his car completed. Corona urged him to take the job, he said, but again he refused.

Pervis had known Corona by sight for several years and was certain of his identification. He said the pickup was "a two-tone green job."

Ishmael Kenneth Walton was another man with something to say that the investigators wanted to hear.

He and Donald Dale Smith were sitting around the Day Center sometime around the first of May when a Mexican asked if one of them wanted to work. He needed someone to dig a hole for garbage, he said.

Walton said he refused the job and also advised Smith not to take it. Smith also refused, but the Mexican picked up another man, about fifty years old, and drove away. Walton said the pick-up truck was "kind of yellow." He knew the driver was Corona, he said, because other men at the Day Center told him so.

Walton said he refused the job and told Smith not to go because "there was something funny about it. You know, a man isn't going to hire somebody to dig holes for garbage. There's too many garbage dumps around."

Walton also said Corona often picked up workers around the Day Center. He always picked up one at a time, he said, and they were always white men.

Roy Lee English had a lot to say to the investigators, but he never got a chance to say it in court. His story was made all the more interesting because he was about one brick shy of a load when Purcell talked to him.

He had worked for Corona a few times during the busy seasons, he said, and he also was acquainted with Beierman, Smallwood, Muchache, and others. He often saw the men around the Day Center and in Wino Park.

"About all I can tell you," he said, "is these guys kept disappearing. I thought they was on a drunk. I didn't know he was killing them. They didn't come back, then I got suspicious. I suspected something, but I couldn't visualize just what was going on and you know, it wasn't none of my business."

He had worked for Corona at the Sullivan camp before, he said, and one night, about ten o'clock, Corona woke him up.

"Well, he asked me to dig a hole and I said, 'Hell no,' I wanted no kind—I'm no damn garbage pit. I said, 'I'm too drunk. I'm going to town to do something with my pay'. He said, 'No, I want you to dig me a hole' and I said 'No, I don't want to dig no Goddamn holes'."

Shannon said Corona would "go in and out of the bunkhouse late at night. Yah, that's something else I don't like—to be woke up when I'm working in the night."

He was asked if he had been awakened at night and he said, "Yah, time and time again late at night he asked me to do something. Hell, I couldn't even get out of bed. You know how I am when I'm drinking. When I lay down, I'm ———."

Asked again if Corona came in late at night to try to get him to do something, English replied, "Yah. I said, 'Hell no, I'm sleeping, get somebody else.' "

"It gives you a funny feeling when you know you have worked for a damn fool like that and wind up still alive."

After going over his statement, the investigators agreed that English was just not the kind of witness who would impress a jury. He was not only an ex-felon, thus being open to impeachment by the defense, but he was also an erratic rumpot who could turn a jury off in no time.

There was also the distinct possibility that English was calling upon his imagination to furnish some of the details he was relating. Nowhere were officers ever to find any evidence that English had worked for Corona in the past, much less having stayed overnight in the labor camp.

Roy had apparently been reading the papers and following the story on television.

Aquinalbo Baclaan was not much help to the prosecution either when Duncan caught up to him in response to another skid-row rumor.

Baclaan said he had worked for Corona for one day about May when he was approached by the contractor at the Brunswick Club in Marysville. It was about 7 A.M. and Corona drove him to the Sullivan ranch for a thinning job.

They drove to the ranch in the van and Corona said not one word on the way. Neither did he make any overt gestures or attempt to take any backroad shortcuts.

When they arrived at the ranch, Corona told him that if he wished to eat lunch he would be fed in the mess hall, but Aquinalbo preferred to work straight through.

He worked until 5 P.M., he said, when Corona picked him up and returned him to Marysville, dropping him off across the street from the Guadalajara. Corona asked him to check with the bartender and find if anyone in the cafe wanted to work the next day. He did, and informed Corona that nobody in the bar wanted a job. Corona paid him ten dollars in cash, he said.

Aquinalbo said he saw Corona again the next morning, but he had already agreed to work for another man that day.

Chan Singh Khera, owner of an orchard just south of the site where Fleming was found on May 25, also contacted the sheriff during the time when bodies were still being found.

Khera said he had known Corona since 1962 and had hired him many times. He was a good contractor and his work was always satisfactory. In fact, he had made arrangements for Corona to do some thinning for him in June.

It was about two or three days before Fleming's body was discovered that Khera ran into Corona on a road about 200 yards southeast of the spot where Whitacre had been buried. He told Corona that he would be able to use him in about a month and Corona drove on in his van. Corona was alone at the time.

It was slow, tedious police work, and for every smidgin of worthwhile information that was gathered, there were dozens of leads that turned out to be duds. Like the interview with English. That was a complete waste of time.

Then, there were the two boys who told their parents they saw blood dripping from the trunk of an automobile on Rio Oso Road, south of Marysville. The press made a big thing out of that one, speculating that maybe the real killer was still on the loose because Corona was already in jail.

It took several days to trace that report, which was finally cleared up when the deputies learned the blood had come from a freshly butchered beef that had been hauled from one ranch to another after it had been slaughtered.

There was also the report from the Stockton Police Department. They had received a call from a department store where a Mexican farm worker, badly beaten, had purchased some new clothes. He told the clerk that he had been beaten by Juan

Corona but had managed to escape and fled Yuba City.

That one also came to a dead end, but not before Gregory spent two valuable days running it down in Stockton.

It occurred right while the Corona case was attracting the maximum publicity. Domingo Torres Riso appeared in a Stockton clothing store on May 30 to replace the bloody clothing he was wearing. He had been badly beaten about the face and head and, when he presented a check to pay for the articles, the clerk noticed he was from Yuba City. The clerk said jokingly, "You look like you might have met up with Juan Corona."

For some ungodly reason, Riso told the clerk that he had been working for Corona in an orchard and was suddenly attacked by the labor contractor. The story got away from him and just kept getting bigger. If this Anglo wanted a sensational yarn, Riso was the man to give it to him.

Corona was trying to kill him, he said, because he thought he was a white wino. When he cried out in Spanish, Corona stopped beating him and he ran.

As soon as Riso left the store, the excited clerk called the police, but they were unable to locate the bloodstained customer immediately. They notified Purcell and promised to try to find the man and hold him for questioning.

Gregory left for Stockton, and the next day Riso was located by the local police. A little bit shaken by the uproar he had caused, Riso told Gregory the true story. He had gotten into a fight in a Marysville tavern on the twenty-ninth and quickly learned that he was over-matched. After absorbing a thorough shellacking, he left town and wound up in Stockton the next morning.

When the clerk suggested that he might have been whipped by Corona, Riso went along with the gag and told his colorful story. It was just a harmless joke on the clerk, he said, but Gregory couldn't find any humor in it.

The real story was checked out in Marysville, and a disgusted Gregory filed a report that increased the size of the file but added nothing of value to the investigation.

There was no doubt that every police agency in the state was aware of the Yuba City situation and anxious to help if possible.

Take the case of the perambulating poet. That call came in from Eureka, a good 300 miles from Yuba City on the north coast of California. The police there had picked up Anthony Doocy, a transient farmer laborer, on a drunk charge. When they booked him they found in his pocket a poem entitled "Tramp." It had to do with orchard graves and farm laborers working in Yuba City. On the off chance that Doocy might know something important the Sutter County sheriff was notified.

Gregory took off for Eureka and what turned out to be another fruitless interrogation.

Doocy, who was not the brightest fellow who ever picked a peach and who butchered iambic pentameter, hadn't been in Yuba City for two years. During his ramblings through the state he had read a newspaper here and there, and from that information had written a poem. He often wrote poems for himself, mostly when he was partially full of the "creature."

He didn't know anything about the Yuba City affair, and he didn't know any of the victims, except possibly Beierman. When shown Pete's picture he thought he remembered having seen him around the Day Center a couple of years before.

Another dead end, but maybe one of those wild, far-out reports might pay off with some valuable information eventually.

Chapter 13

Now, however, it was time to take stock of the current status of the investigation. Among the dozens of reports that had already been written there was sufficient circumstantial evidence to connect Corona with the murders, but no jury would ever convict on the basis of that material alone.

There was some physical evidence that might, upon expert examination, provide some important clues, but the real value of that wouldn't be determined until the specialists did their work.

And, of course, there were twenty-five victims, indisputable proof that murder—brutal, ruthless, barbarous—had been committed.

Only the number made the crime significant. Individually, the murders had no traumatic impact on the public. In a community such as Yuba City, so small that the obituaries in the local newspaper were generally those of family friends, the death of a stranger—or even of two strangers—was rarely noticed. The violent deaths of twenty-five strangers was news, and the incident had hurled the rural community into the national spotlight; however, the attitude of the natives was still pretty impersonal.

They had not been missed in life when they made their periodic pilgrimages along the fruit trails, and neither were they missed in death. Their comings and goings in the narrow, disreputable world in which they lived had been of no interest to anyone, even to their contemporaries.

The main topics of conversation along the streets and at cocktail parties were:

Who is going to bury these people? and

How much is this thing going to cost the taxpayers by the time the trial is over?

The boys at the C.I.I. had done their jobs pretty well as far as identifying the murdered men was concerned. Whiteaker had a list of twenty-one names that had been confirmed, and they were still working on the other four—although they never were identified.

The sheriff was aided in his attempts to identify the victims by the Salvation Army and the records of local blood banks throughout the state.

It was a little-known fact that the "Sallies" kept pretty good records on transients who stayed with them for any length of time in their various mission centers, Data such as Social Security numbers, scars, tattoos, physical descriptions, birthplaces, and even notations of personality traits were all listed by the S.A. and then filed away. It became available to Whiteaker at his request.

The blood banks were exceptionally valuable in supplying

names and other identifying intelligence of those men who made a practice of selling their blood for a few dollars when they were "in the shorts." Even more important were the records of blood types that were turned over to the investigators.

When all of the information, the rap sheets, and the mug shots had been obtained, it made a pitiful collection. Looking at the worn, ravaged features staring out of the police photographs, it was hard to believe that once they might have been cuddled close to a loving mother's breast.

It was almost impossible to see them being dandled on a proud grandfather's knee, or being led, scrubbed and sparkling, to their first day of school.

Had they ever felt, in the first flush of young manhood, that the world was something to be overcome by their youthful strength and ambition?

There was a time, many years ago, that Charles Cleveland Fleming felt the pride of fatherhood and the love of his children. The native of Louisiana, born July 15, 1903, had been raised in a solid, God-fearing home. The trace of his background turned up two daughters and two sisters, still living in Louisiana. His police record began with an arrest for drunkenness in Shreveport in 1949 and continued with arrests for vagrancy in California, Washington, and back to California. The final entry on the rap sheet said simply: "5/26/71, Yuba City, Dead." There was no longer a place for Fleming in Louisiana. Just four days after his sixty-eighth birthday, on July 19, 1971, he was cremated at Sierra View in Marysville.

Melford Everette Sample was a Nebraska boy, born in Greeley on April 6, 1912. He was twenty-nine years old when he marched away to World War II. After the war he married and moved to California, where his family broke up in 1951. His wife, Virginia, returned to Greeley and told police that she had not heard from or of him for twenty years. His sister, Bernice, wrote him faithfully, forwarding her letters to the addresses that he sent her from time to time. Her last letter, written on May 1, 1971, said she was worried about him and wished he could settle down. She hoped he was getting his teeth fixed, and she relayed the news that his niece had just had a new baby. Would he, she asked, send her an address where she should send his next veteran's pension check?

On July 26, 1971, Sample found his permanent address. He, too, was cremated at Sierra View, almost 2,000 miles from the small Nebraska farming community he had left thirty years before.

Donald Dale Smith was no stranger to Yuba City. He had worked in and out of the area for many years, laboring in the orchards that clung to the base of the Sutter Buttes, a volcanic upthrust that doninated the flat Sacramento Valley. The "smallest mountain range in the world," the Buttes were called, and they had served as a landmark for Captain Luis Arguello, the Spanish explorer who had, in 1820, named the nearby river "El Rio de Las Plumas," the River of the Feathers.

Born in Kansas on June 23, 1910, Smith had been a wanderer for many years. He had spent some time in most of the jails in the valley, including Marysville's, but never for anything more serious than being drunk in public. Smith never hurt anyone in his whole life—except himself—since he was a boy in the tree-shaded plains town of Frankfort, Kansas.

His sister in Frankfort and his brother in Atlanta, Georgia, remembered him with dim but fond memories. On August 3, 1971, he was cremated at Sierra View in the valley that he had often told police he liked better than any place he had ever been.

The $255.22 that he had accumulated in a savings account in the Bank of America in Roseville was turned over to the public administrator to help pay the funeral expenses.

John Haluka was a long way from his native Perth Amboy, New Jersey, when he wandered into the valley looking for work. He had been running away from something almost all of his life. He was born on October 9, 1918, in a home that was comfortable if not affluent, but had it been a mansion, it would still not have been strong enough to hold him. He was a "mover" by instinct, and he was long gone from New Jersey before he was twenty years old.

Haluka headed for the Golden State of California and worked

in the fields and the avocado groves when the urge was on him. When the Selective Service Law went into effect in 1940, he registered for the draft but, when he was called to the colors early in 1942, he ignored the summons. That brought a federal complaint, and he was picked up by the San Diego police. He managed to escape from jail and was able to remain at liberty throughout the war. When he was picked up on several occasions for vagrancy and drunkenness after the war, the subject of the federal complaint never came up.

In the spring of 1971, he wandered into Marysville, broke but, in the manner of his kind, unworried. Whiteaker notified his sister, Anna, who was still living in New Jersey, that her brother had been murdered. It would be up to Sutter County to bury him, she said; there was just no money available.

On December 13, 1971, he was buried in Sutter Cemetery, where the Buttes everlastingly looked down upon the everlasting dead.

Warren Jerome Kelley was truly a homeless man, Born in Texas in 1909, he started out in the right direction and then lost his way in a maze of bottles, according to his police record. His family, including a wife, Ruby, a son, a daughter, and a brother, had no use for him whatsoever. His was a way of life that they could not accept.

His wanderings took him all over the country, and along the way he developed a liking for tattoos. Letters on the fingers of his right hand spelled out "true," and on the left hand, "love." Scrolls, flowered designs, and initials covered his arms. In the end they helped to identify his remains.

Kelley was buried in the Sutter Cemetery on October 14, 1971.

Bhagat Singh Thiara, who farmed a large peach orchard near Yuba City, had been worried about William Emery Kamp. Kamp had worked for him for two seasons and had left the ranch on January 23, leaving his possessions in the modest cabin Thiara provided for him.

The employer and employee had struck up a friendship that was founded on a mutual devotion to religion.

For many years after he left St. Paul, Minnesota, where he was born on December 17, 1907, Kamp was a heller. He discovered a liking for the bottle that led him to drift with the tide of footloose transients who worked the farms and the orchards of the nation. During his odyssey, he used a number of aliases and he was jailed many times for being drunk in public. He took his last drink in 1961 when a prolonged bout with the bottle ended in the drunk tank of the Oakland, California, City Jail.

Kamp met Thiara at the Day Center which the rancher had established and continued to support. That was early in 1970, and Kamp moved onto the Thiara ranch.

No longer attracted by the skid-row fleshpots, Kamp spent his off-hours reading his Bible, sometimes pausing to write down an interesting passage in a notebook he kept with him at all times. Whenever the opportunity was offered, he preached to the derelicts who frequented Wino Park and the Day Center.

Thiara thought of calling the sheriff to report Kamp's disappearance after he had been gone from the ranch for several weeks, but then decided not to. It wouldn't have done any good; by the time the thought crossed the rancher's mind his friend and employee was already dead.

When he was buried in Sutter Cemetery on October 22, 1971, the religious medal that was found on his body went into the grave with him.

Clarence Hocking never liked to stay in one place, but neither did he like to stray too far from the Sacramento Valley. His police record indicated that he had been a visitor in most of the towns and a tenant in many of the jails for almost ten years.

A native of Illinois where he was born January 11, 1918, Hocking made hardly a ripple as he drifted through life. Never married, there were no family ties to hold him except for a sister who lived in Linden, California, just outside of Stockton.

His only recognition as a member of the human race came first when his body was exhumed from an orchard grave on May 26 and last, when he was buried in Sutter Cemetery on October 1, 1971.

James Wylie Howard couldn't wait to get out of New Mexico

where he was born in the hamlet of Elida on May 25, 1907. It was just sixty-four years and one day before he was found in a grave along the banks of the Feather River.

Before he was twenty-five years old he had shaken the New Mexico dust from his heels and was trying to settle in Oklahoma. The drought and the dust storms drove thousands of people from that state during the Depression years, Howard among them.

He joined the exodus to California and became one of the legion of "fruit tramps." While thousands of the once-scorned "Okies" were clawing their way upward to positions of substance—and in some cases even wealth—in their communities, Howard slipped further down the social ladder and became a wino. He never married.

Members of his family, upon learning of his murder, had the body shipped to Sacramento where he was buried in Mt. Vernon Memorial Park on July 6, 1971.

When World War II came along, Jonah Raggio Smallwood was working in Gainesboro, Tennessee, the town where he was born on October 5, 1914. He left his job and joined the navy, serving until he was honorably discharged in 1952. He had done an extra hitch because he once thought of making it a career.

He had married while he was in the service and became the father of seven children. It proved to be too much of a load for him to cope with. One day he just walked out and hit the road. Life was tough for a guy with only a third-grade education, and jobs were hard to come by. For Smallwood, the future held just one bottle after another, a short stay with the Salvation Army once in awhile, and a police record that covered six full pages.

Somewhere along the line, his wife obtained a divorce, but it didn't mean anything to Jonah. He never saw her or any of the kids after he left.

Normally a quiet, even introverted, man, Smallwood was mean and quarrelsome when he was drinking. Therefore, he had few friends.

His family claimed the body and took him back home to Gainesboro where he was buried in Pherris Cemetery on September 30, 1971.

Elbert T. J. Riley was only sixteen years old when World War II broke out, but he was in it before it ended. He was born in Arkansas on January 14, 1925, and, after he was discharged from the army in 1947, he became a journeyman carpenter.

He moved to California, got married in the little town of Exeter in the San Joaquin Valley and set out to be a regular family man. Daughter Shirley came along in 1949, and the Riley family was about the happiest one in town.

The only fly in the milk of marital happiness was Elbert's liking for the cup. Because of that, things went from bad to worse until his wife, Linda, had enough. They separated and Riley hit the skids for keeps.

For a time he tried to send support money to his wife, but all of a sudden there was no job left. In 1966 he was arrested on a warrant charging him with failure to provide for his child, but he escaped from the jail in Tulare. He was arrested for escape and served his time, then went back to following the crops.

His family lost track of him completely until they got the word that he was one of the Yuba City dead. His father and his daughter claimed the body and he was buried on August 24, 1971, in the Exeter District Cemetery.

Paul Buell Allen had two handicaps that prevented him from leading a normal life. He was a complete and dedicated alcoholic and he was also missing his right eye, lost somewhere along the foggy, uncertain trail that he had been following for the past twenty years.

Had he been a working citizen of the community with his lust for strong drink, Allen would have been considered a sick man with a serious social problem. His position in the social strata, however, gave him only the status of a wino, a condition for which the "good" people had found no cure.

Born in Arkansas on December 19, 1911, he served in the army during the war, even though he was married at the time. After the war he found it difficult to settle down, and that led to a divorce. From there it was all downhill until he arrived in Marysville in the late spring of 1971 and probably took his last job.

Paul Allen was buried in the Fort Smith National Cemetery in his native Arkansas on July 25, 1971.

Edward Martin Cupp was the victim of leniency.

He was arrested in Sacramento early in May, and on May 8, was given a sentence of forty days in the county jail and a year's probation. Then the jail sentence was suspended also and Cupp was free to go to Marysville, where he expected to find work in the orchards. Had he served only half of that jail sentence he certainly wouldn't have been found in that soggy grave next to the Feather on May 29.

Cupp brightened the Christmas of 1927 for his mother and father when he was born on December 23. He was too young for World War II, but the army took him in 1948. A quickie marriage lasted less than three months. The restrictions of service life were not for him, and he went AWOL early in 1949, only to be arrested on February 8 of that year and confined to the stockade in Jackson, Mississippi.

After he got his undesirable discharge, he set out to steal his way across the country. He got as far as Willow Springs, Missouri, where he was arrested for stealing an automobile, and was sent to a prison farm at Jefferson City.

He escaped within a matter of three months and took off for the Far West. That felony conviction and the escape that followed handicapped him in his search for work. He had to take jobs that did not require such documents as Social Security card and references; a precarious and uncertain existence at best. He kept his nose clean until that Sacramento drunk that resulted in his arrest. Evidently the statute of limitations had run out in Missouri because his fingerprints cleared the F.B.I. files.

So the court was lenient and, as a result, Cupp was dead. He was buried in the Sutter Cemetery on October 1, 1971.

"Scratchy" Hayes hit the road long before he was twenty-one years old. Things had been tough back in Pennsylvania where he was born on April 5, 1913. Too young to reap the benefits of the plush times during the Roaring Twenties, Albert Leon Hayes arrived at young manhood just in time to experience the bitter, hard times that came with the Crash of '29. By that time he was seventeen and on his own and he wasn't even twenty-one when he was arrested in Salt Lake City for being drunk and trespassing in March, 1934, tough charges in a town that was still steeped in the teetotaler philosophy of Brigham Young.

He directed his rambling feet toward the West Coast and arrived in California in time to take in the fruit harvest of that year. As far as Scratchy was concerned, it was a good way of life. A fellow could work whenever he wanted to earn enough for a bottle or two of cheap wine, travel as free as the breeze simply by grabbing a handful of boxcars and, when the work was slack, there were missions in just about every town. A guy could always get a meal with no more effort than it took to sit through a thirty-minute sermon by a sky pilot.

Somewhere along the line, Scratchy picked up a hardhat which he painted red and wore like a name plate. It was his identification among the bums and the cops of dozens of towns from Los Angeles to the Oregon-Washington border.

Scratchy didn't make many mistakes as he wandered up and down the coast—never argued with the cops, did his short hitches in jail quietly and smoothly, and got along well with his skid-row acquaintances. Nobody ever got mad at Scratchy.

Nobody that is, except whoever dumped his hacked and battered body into that grave along the Feather River in the spring of 1971.

Scratchy was another one who was buried by the county in the Sutter Cemetery on September 16, 1971.

For a man who could rightfully lay claim to a substantial portion of Northern California through birthright, Raymond Reand Muchache couldn't find a place to settle down.

Born September 19, 1923, in Fall River, Muchache was a Maidu Indian, entitled to a piece of the multimillion dollar settlement the federal government was offering his people for their tribal lands, which had been taken from them more than 100 years before.

But Muchache just couldn't get along with the other Maidus because of an abrasive temperament which was easily inflamed by the wine that was so easy to come by. He was "rousted" from McCloud, Alturas, Susanville—all of the towns that he knew while he was growing up.

His residence in the Sacramento Valley below his native hills was marked by a series of short, farm labor jobs and a series of jail sentences handed out after arrests for being drunk in public.

When Muchache became the twentieth body to be exhumed from the orchard graveyard, there was no difficulty in finding relatives to notify. His cousins, uncles, and aunts appeared to claim the body and a benevolent Bureau of Indian Affairs provided the funds for his burial in the Fall River Mills Cemetery.

The only thing that made John Henry Jackson stand out among the congregation of the Bergthodt's Mission was his color. John Henry, named after the legendary "steel drivin' man" was black. A quiet man who worked hard and drank his wine in solitude, Jackson disappeared one day as quietly as he had so many times before during his annual visits to Marysville.

There were no relatives. Only a friend, Anna Lishinsky of Monticello, New York, where Jackson had been born on April 4, 1907. He, too, was buried in the Sutter Cemetery on October 14, 1971.

Lloyd Wallace Wentzel was happy to get probation after he was sentenced to the Sacramento County jail on April 23, 1971. The sentence was for fifty days because Wentzel had appeared once too often in front of a judge who was weary of seeing his name time after time on the drunk calendar.

Even after being released, Wentzel continued to hang around Sacramento's lower end of town. There was really no place else for him to go right then. He had been a wanderer for much of his life since he was born in South Dakota on June 11, 1910.

When May arrived, however, Wentzel knew it was time to move on if he was to get in on some of the work around Marysville. On May 14 he purchased a bus ticket and arrived in the Hub City on the same day.

It was just fifteen days later that his body was found in the orchard in grave number twenty-two. Better he should have had to serve that fifty days the judge had given him five weeks before.

Wentzel had one relative, a sister living in Arizona. He was also buried in Sutter Cemetery on October 14, 1971.

The story of Mark Beverly Shields was the story of hundreds of men like him, the faceless, nondescript, ragged wanderers who harvested the crops year after year and staggered up and down the dirty streets of a hundred skid rows every winter.

A native of California, Shields was born on July 15, 1914, in Santa Rosa, a sedate, comfortable city lying north of San Francisco. He grew up in normal, middle-class surroundings and, with his normal, middle-class schoolmates, went off to join the army when World War II erupted. After that there was no more normalcy.

Shields followed an ever-developing thirst into the fields and the orchards of California, foregoing the comforts of married life for the bliss that he found in the thousands of empty wine bottles that he scattered in his wake.

His grave was not as lonely as those of the others. He was buried within a hundred yards of the mess hall and bunkhouse on the Sullivan ranch. In searching for relatives, the deputies ran across the names of his mother and his brother, both still living in California. Listed on his latest booking slip as the person to be notified in case of death was the name of Hattie Lorraine Saling, the woman who claimed to have had those rendezvous with Juan Corona in a Marysville motel.

His family and his veteran's status enabled him to be buried in Sierra View Memorial Park in Marysville.

The man who was found in the twenty-fourth grave was a strange one. He had two names and two birthdates as well as a bank account. Sam Bonafide was also known as Joe Carriveau. Sam was listed as having been born in the State of Washington on February 10, 1916, while Joe was born in Puerto Rico on November 29, 1919. Sam served in the army in World War II while Joe's only army connection was with the Salvation Army, where he was allowed to stay for a few days while sobering up in 1957. That was the last prolonged drunk for either Sam or Joe.

Sam liked to work in the harvests, and he worked his way along the West Coast from top to bottom year after year. In Dunsmuir he stopped long enough to establish a bank account that contained $310.40 by the time he was found in grave number twenty-four.

A sister and a stepbrother were notified, but they did not claim the body. Sam—or Joe—was buried in Sutter Cemetery on October 22, 1971.

Joseph J. Maczak had lived among the debris of the world of the farm worker for most of his life, and in the end he was buried in debris.

When he was found in grave number twenty-five on June 4, an accumulation of rubbish was covering part of his body. Polish Joe Maczak was born on St. Patrick's Day, March 17, 1916, in Illinois. He headed west as soon as he was grown sufficiently to leave the nest and found just the kind of work he liked, following the fruit. In his youth he acquired horseshoe tattoos on his left forearm which helped to identify him in the end.

He never acquired any more possessions than he could comfortably wear or carry in his pockets. He didn't want to. He had learned long ago that living was for today and memories are for tomorrow.

The sheriff located a sister in Los Angeles, but there was nobody to claim the body. Joe Maczak, born on St. Patrick's Day, was buried on Columbus Day, October 12, 1971, in Sutter Cemetery.

There was no great outpouring of public sympathy for the deceased despite the efforts of visiting newsmen to probe the conscience of the communities of Yuba City and Marysville. There was general agreement that a terrible tragedy had occurred and almost—but not all—of the residents thought it was a shame that the men had been killed. However, it was an impersonal sympathy, about like that displayed when a stray dog is struck by an automobile.

After all, these men were complete strangers, especially in Yuba City, where winos were not allowed to linger even long enough to spend the money they earned in the orchards. Their acquaintances at the Day Center and in Wino Park didn't even know their right names.

It was too bad it had to happen in Yuba City, because it made the town look bad. The worst thing about the whole deal was the snickering from that bunch of donkeys across the river in Marysville. They always were jealous of Yuba City's reputation for decency, nice kids, clean streets and, particularly, no cathouses. About the only excuse Yuba City could offer was to point out, "They came from Marysville, didn't they?"

There were some, however, who felt that the departure of the victims should be marked with some solemnity. Father Joseph Bishop set the tone when he held a memorial Mass at St. Isadore's Church for the murdered men and the Corona family. There were 250 parishioners present for the service, and the television crews were on hand to record the proceedings.

Father Bishop asked for the repose of the souls of the dead and the mercy and sympathy of the living on behalf of the family of the suspect.

The Marysville and Yuba City Ministerial Fellowship decided to allow the residents of both counties to join them in a massive memorial service which they scheduled for June 8. They decided to hold it on the Yuba City High School football field because of the huge crowd they expected to attend.

A bare 200 people, many of them representing the news media, attended the service in which six ministers took part.

The politicians got into the act quickly with pompous statements to the effect that laws should be devised to protect farm workers from such tragic situations. None were able to say just exactly what the laws should delineate in the way of regulation, but at least they got their names in the papers.

Mrs. Judy Freeman, a Marysville housewife, started a fund to provide headstones for the graves of those men who would be buried in the potter's field plot in the Sutter Cemetery. It was expected that the cost would be $5,000. Mrs. Freeman's dedicated and untiring efforts resulted in $732 being raised. A Chicago firm, whose president read of the proposed fund, agreed to provide the required numder of markers at no charge.

What little public interest there had been in the dead men died quickly. Within a week after the memorial service, it was impossible to find more than a handful of people in both counties who could recall the name of even one of the deceased.

Chapter 14

The American people can get a laugh out of just about any situation, and they proved it now. The rash of Corona gags began to circulate around the state and around the nation, one or two of them even showing up on big-time television shows.

One of the most widely circulated was a business card, purported to be Corona's, with the words "Sorry I missed you!" written diagonally across it.

Further up-country, a small town wag placed an ad in his local weekly paper announcing, "Security plan for farm workers. Built in layaway program. Call or write, Juan V. Corona, Yuba City, Calif."

The riddle was also a knee slapper. It went like this:

"What's the fastest thing on wheels in the world?"

"A farm worker going through Yuba City on a bicycle."

There were more of them, so many more that they became boring after a time. As is always the case, within a short time there was something else for people to talk about and, had it not been for Richard Hawk, the Corona case would have faded to indifferent and intermittent copy.

Hawk kept the interest up by making bombastic statements to the press whenever there was a member of the media available. He couldn't understand, he said, how Whiteaker could justify breaking into a man's home in the wee hours of the morning and arresting him on the flimsy, ridiculous evidence they had found.

They had arrested the wrong man, he asserted, and they knew it, but Dave Teja was determined to get the State of California to kill Juan Corona anyway.

Hawk was making good copy, and he was keeping the case alive in the media but Whiteaker had no time to listen. He had other things on his mind such as the ledger which was found in Corona's home.

The original had been turned over to the handwriting experts at the C.I.I., but the sheriff had kept copies for study by himself and his investigators.

Duncan, the detective who found the ledger in Corona's home, pointed out that no farmer or labor contractor who was responsible for keeping track of his employees, their working hours, and their wages as required by law would keep such a ledger. Whereas the regular farm records would consist of a series of names and orderly columns of figures, this particular book had only a series of poorly written names, dates, Spanish phrases, and initials.

A quick perusal of pages 50, 51, and 52, revealed eight names of men whose bodies had been discovered in the graves, and dates which the investigation revealed coincided closely with the dates when they dropped out of sight in Marysville.

There was, for instance, the name of Mark Beverly Shields and the date April 28, 1971. Sam Bonafide was listed along with the date of May 6, 1971. The name Smith was written with no first name but with the notation Camino Rio Oso—Bear River Road—and the date of May 9, 1971. Duncan and Whiteaker figured that would be Donald Ray Smith.

Warren Kelley's middle name was spelled Gerome rather than with a "J." The date was March 30, 1971, with the initials S.R. following. Could the S.R. mean Sullivan Ranch, Whiteaker wondered?

The name Charles Fleming appeared with a middle name written to read something like "Linil." The date there was May 11, and the next date was May 12 with the name Jona (Jonah?) R. Smallwood written opposite it.

Paul B. Allen was listed with the date May 15 in front of the name and the number "71" following the last name. John H. Jackson also appeared, and under the name was the date April 15, 1971

There were twenty-three other names or sets of initials listed, and the next move by the sheriff was to try first to find those whose names could be read and then to identify the initials and implications of the Spanish notations if possible.

One of the names on the list was that of William Earl Vaughan. The date April 5, 1971, was written under his name.

A check at the Day Center turned up the information that

Vaughan was a frequent visitor there and often attended the religious services. Ira Hall, a seventy-five-year-old part-time preacher, was able to provide a clue as to what might have happened to Vaughan.

Hall said that he preached at the mission early in April and, at the conclusion of his sermon, he was approached by Vaughan.

"He asked me to pray for him," Hall said. "He told me that he was going to a farm labor camp the next day and said, 'you know, it is very difficult to be a good Christian in such a place'. I promised him that I would do what he asked and he left. I have never seen him since that time."

Despite an intensive search by the sheriff's department, Vaughan was never found.

If the ledger was, truly, a "death list" as was widely publicized, then Muchache was also listed, if not by name, at least by designation. The third from the last entry on page 52 said, "May 18 Indio (Indian) 1971."

If Corona actually wrote the list—and Hawk vigorously denied that he ever did—he was a little more meticulous when he began than he was several months later. With the exception of two names, the entries on page 50 were neatly numbered "1" through "12," the top and bottom names being unnumbered.

The bottom name was that of Vaughan, but it was the first name on the page that created the most interest.

At the very top of the sheet was written, "Fev. 24, 1970," and beneath that, "Jose Romero R"; and following a word that began with "Med. . ." but which could not be fully deciphered. Teja and Whiteaker both assumed that the entry referred to Jose Romero Raya and the date of February 24, 1970 was the night on which Raya was cut in the Guadalajara Cafe. The police reports on the incident showed that the victim was found after midnight on February 25, but the occurrence was listed as having happened on the night of February 24.

Name number six on page 50 was written as "Joe E. Dollar" and beneath it the date, "Febrero 15—1971." The seventh name was "Billy Boy" followed by the date "15—1971." Although the name of the month was missing, the investigators believed the 15 referred to February as had the date listed with Dollar's name.

The months-long search for those two men was unsuccessful although in the case of Billy Boy, some significant information was obtained.

The inquiry led the investigators to the Golden Star Cafe, which was operated by Jerry Gibson and which served as a mail drop for some of the transients. Among Gibson's customers was Billy Cellen, described as being mentally retarded and referred to occasionally as "Billy Boy." Cellen had suffered a back injury in an industrial accident and was waiting for a compensation settlement.

Because Cellen could work very little and was often broke, Gibson frequently loaned him small amounts of cash, which he said Cellen always repaid. He recalled having loaned Cellen thirty to forty cents early in May, 1971, and then he never saw him again.

No trace could be found of Dollar, either. Here and there, as the investigation continued, a transient would recall having heard of a man with that name either at the mission or in Wino Park, but nobody could recall anything significant about him or when he had last been seen.

Raul Manuel Silva had worked in Roseville for the Pacific Fruit Express Company for more than wenty years before he discovered a skeleton in the family closet that literally drove him to drink. Relatives would never tell the police exactly what the disclosure was, but it was enough to cause Silva to quit his job and take to the wine.

An aunt told the officers that the last she had heard of Raul he was working in the harvests and she had heard that he was going to Marysville in the spring of 1971.

Silva dropped completely out of sight, and except for one clue he was never heard of again.

That clue was located on page 50 of the ledger found in Corona's home: "Raul Manuel Silva—March 18, 1971."

There were other names in the ledger that the officers attempted to trace without success. "Doctor Silver" was one, and with it was the date of April 3, 1971, and then the initials S.R., the same as had followed Kelley's name in the book. John Espidy was listed on April 10, 1971, and Higgen J. General was entered on April 14 of that year. Mr. Bacarfild's name was dated May 10, and on May 13 there were two entries of initials only. One was "D-D-M" and the other was "M D-M" with illegible scribblings tailing away from the last "M."

The legible names were followed up by the persevering deputies but with no results at all. The initials were also checked in an effort to find on the rolls of the mission or in the registers of the rundown hotels names of men whose names might correspond and who had dropped from sight. That, too, was unsuccessful.

Of the twenty-five bodies found in the orchard and riverbank graves, all but four had been positively identified. It was possible that the names of those four men might be hidden somewhere in the undecipherable scrawlings in the ledger, or they might be represented by some of the readable names. The bodies of the four victims had so deteriorated by the time they were found that not even the sophisticated equipment of the C.I.I. could produce identifiable fingerprints or other body markings.

The more the ledger was studied, the more interesting it became. There were, for instance, a number of names of Mexican-Americans included in the three pages. Those names were "Maldonado, Fev. 10, 1970"; "Mario Guizan, Junio 5, 1970"; "Dario Maran, March 7, 1971"; "Dinedo Chaket, March 22, Sullivan Ranch, 12 PM"; "Guiguies [sic] Lario, April 22, 1971"; "Mano Talumea [sic], April 29, 1971"; and "Sarto, May 19, 1971."

Some of the names were almost impossible to decipher and had to be guessed at, but they all had one thing in common. They were all of Mexican extraction and, despite a vigorous investigation that continued for almost two years—and never really stopped—none of the men were ever located.

Whiteaker developed a theory which he continues to maintain. He has always insisted that those men also were killed and their bodies separated from the American victims. "Somewhere around here there is a Mexican graveyard," Whiteaker claims.

The ledger became even more puzzling when some of the other entries were studied. The fourth entry on the first page was

"Guadalajara Jalisco, Dec. 27, 1970." Corona was in Mexico at that time visiting his mother, Candida. It is the sheriff's contention that somewhere in that beautiful Mexican city there is a body thus far undiscovered.

Item number five was written "Enero Americano uba," and directly below that line was written "Enero 28, 1972." *Enero* in Spanish means *January* and the sheriff concluded that the first "Enero" was written inadvertently and the word "Americano" meant a body. "Uba" was probably an abbreviation of "Yuba."

On April 27, 1971, was "Otro Amec," meaning, the sheriff surmised, another American, since *otro* means *another*.

A May 15 entry was written "Otro" and an illegible scrawl followed, and a May 16 listing was "Alli Otro" which the sheriff interpreted to mean "here is another." The last entry was written on May 21 or possibly 22 and the single word American. That may have been Sample.

It was also interesting to note that the writings in the ledger were in three different colors of ink: blue, green, and red. When he saw that, Whiteaker realized that the identification of the six-colored pen that was found in Corona's desk in the Sullivan ranch mess hall in the early morning hours of May 26 was going to be of utmost importance. The pen was now in the possession of the C.I.I. experts who were going to try to match the inks with the writings in the book. Other experts in Sacramento were even then studying the handwriting and comparing it with that found on Corona's check stubs and other business papers.

For Whiteaker the ledger held one more riddle that was yet to be solved. He had already set those wheels in motion. It was going to take awhile, but he got the answer eventually.

The sheriff was vitally interested in the report from the Tehama County Sheriff's Department. The telephone call had been somewhat sketchy. More than a year before, the body of a man had been fished from the Sacramento River near Corning. The Tehama County sheriff had told Whiteaker that the condition of the body indicated that the man had been killed much in the manner of the Yuba City victims. He promised to send the official report in the mail.

It proved to be enlightening when Whiteaker read it.

On January 1, 1970, two young men were walking along the banks of the Sacramento near a slough that was formed by backwater when they spotted a body floating face down in the water. The sheriff was notified and deputies retrieved the corpse.

It proved to be a body of a male, six feet tall and weighing about 190 pounds. The man had been murdered. There were deep wounds on the back and side of the head, apparently caused by a heavy, sharp knife of some kind, and he had been stabbed in the left chest.

The arms were raised and folded over the face and the victim's shirt had been pulled up over them, hiding the face. According to the pathologist who conducted the autopsy, the body had been in the water for as long as 2½ months. There was no identification on the body except an almost unidentifiable check stub, $21.22 in currency, and change found in one corner of the trouser pockets, and a ring with five keys, one of them apparently being the key to an apartment or a hotel room, judging by the identification markings stamped on it.

It was impossible at the time to determine whether the body was that of a black, a mulatto, or a Latin, but it definitely was not that of a white man, according to the report.

Whiteaker wasted no time. He immediately dispatched Purcell and two deputies to Tehama County with instructions to check every possible angle to the murder.

Purcell quickly learned that in the fall of 1969 Juan Corona had provided a crew to pick olives on the Johnston ranch, which was located adjacent to the slough where the body was found. During the season a dispute had arisen between the workers and Corona over the price to be paid for the work, and the men threatened to quit. Corona had become very angry with some of the men but, when the owner of the ranch ordered him to pay the men the price that was agreed on, he complied. The job was finished on October 29, 1969.

It had not been Corona's first contract in the area. He had been supplying crews to ranches there for several years, and was pretty well known. He had a good reputation for the quality of his work.

Tiso Ramos, a farm worker who had lived in the vicinity of

Corning for several years, knew Corona well. When he was interviewed, he told Purcell that Corona had a vicious temper and he was not surprised to learn that he was in jail. He knew about Corona's mental problems of 1956 and he had also heard that Juan had cut up a man in the Guadalajara Cafe. He did not believe that Corona was mentally sound.

Purcell decided to check the orchards near the river for possible gravesites, and he and his men found two of them. However, as had occurred along the Feather River earlier, the suspected graves turned out to be holes that extended only a couple of feet to hardpan and then were covered up.

After the body had been found on that New Year's Day, the Tehama sheriff's deputies had attempted to identify the victim but were unsuccessful. It was impossible to get fingerprints or find identifying marks. After a time, they stopped trying and the case was tucked away in the "unsolved" file.

At the urging of Whiteaker they now reopened the file and made an all-out attempt to identify the victim. It took several weeks but, through that almost obliterated check stub, they found out who the man was.

The check had been issued to a Frederick Sanchez, and when Whiteaker heard that, he took another look at the ledger.

There it was! The second name on the first page right under the name of Jose Romero R,—"Sanchez—Oct. 12, 1969."

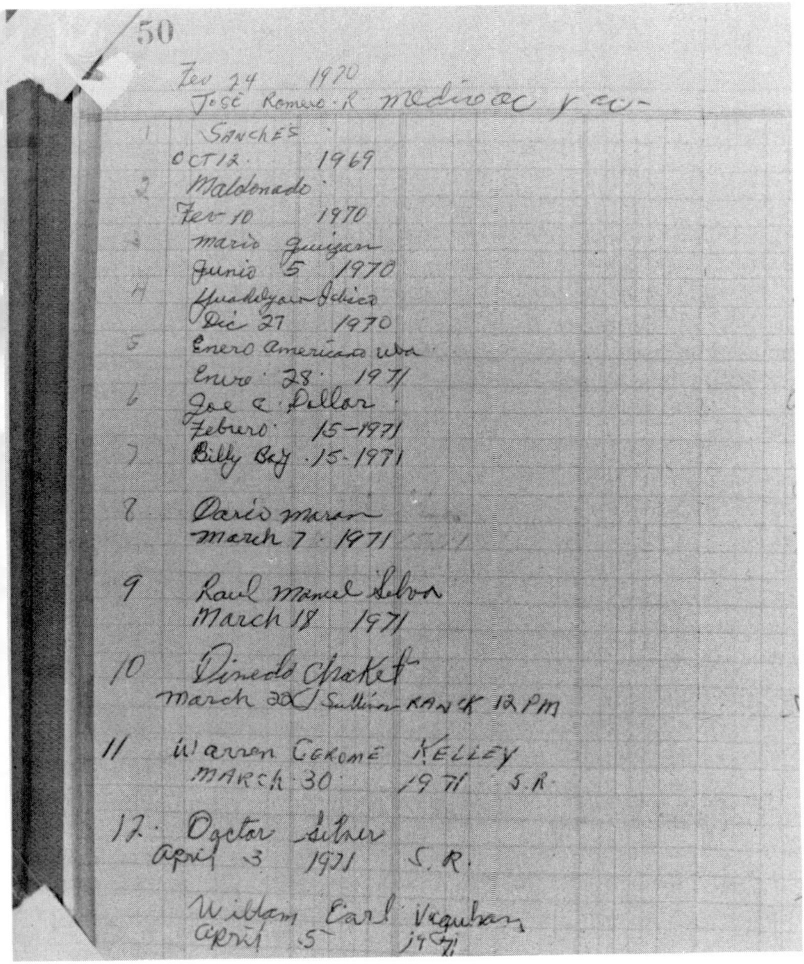

Part of the "Death List." The handwriting experts said it was Corona's. The jury said it was not a normal business record.

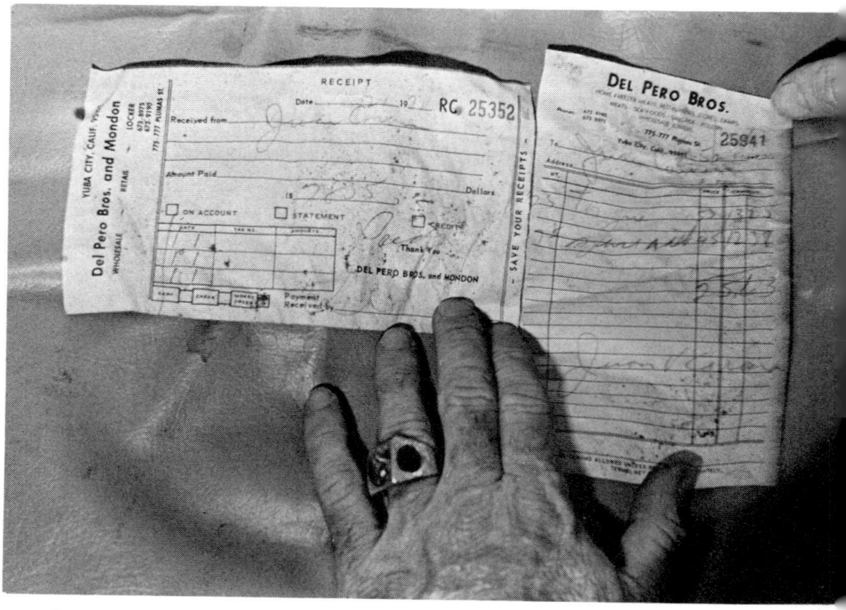

The meat receipts. They were found in grave number three with the nine-fingered man.

The bank deposit slips. They were found in grave number 25, the last victim discovered.

A victim. Most of them were found with arms raised and heads covered by their shirts.

The tire track at grave number one. The mold was lost for 17 months.

The brown van. Three types of human blood were found inside it despite frequent washings.

The Impala. Four types of human blood were found in its trunk.

The posthole digger. The human hairs could have come from any one of six victims.

Richard E. Hawk. The defense attorney was at his best during his press conferences. (Photo courtesy of Jim Skjelstad)

Juan Vallejo Corona. The security was strict and constant. (Photo courtesy of Jim Skjelstad)

Sheriff Roy Whiteaker. He "fired" the special prosecutor.

G. Dave Teja. The District Attorney refused to quit.

Ron Fahey. The "special" special prosecutor saved the day.

The confrontation. The jury met the Corona family but not willingly.

Judge Richard Patton. He met a tough situation head-on.

Chapter 15

The investigation extended into the Corona neighborhood where the investigators interviewed the residents of the quiet, tree-lined street.

Mrs. Baerbel Belew was a next-door neighbor of the Coronas and had been for the past two years. Mrs. Belew worked as a nurse on the night shift at the Sutter Community Hospital and went to work at 10:45 each night. She told officers that Corona kept odd hours and she often saw him coming or going when she left her home at night.

Jim and Wilma Huff were also neighbors and had lived on the street for two years. Mrs. Huff said she was a light sleeper and was often awakened by Corona at late hours. She never went to bed before 11 P.M. and often stayed up until midnight. Even so, she said, his coming and going at odd hours woke her on many occasions.

She distinctly remembered that about a year and a half before she was awakened at 4 A.M. by the smell of burning cloth and looked out to see the Corona trash barrel burning.

Her husband said he saw Corona on many weekends washing his vehicles in the driveway of the Corona home.

Mrs. Beatrice Valdez, who lived a block away from Corona, told investigators that she often saw him washing out the interior of the van. She said he performed that chore several times each week, but she thought it was odd that he only washed out the interior of the van rather than the outside. He used a garden hose to do the washing. "I thought he was an exceptionally clean man," she said. However, she never noticed anything like blood running down the gutters.

Mrs. Valdez said she also saw Corona wash out the inside of a blue van and his red and white pickup truck in the same manner, though it was the brown van that got the most frequent washing.

Chapter 16

Still following up leads that were coming in by telephone, Purcell sent Duncan to see Melvin Hodge, foreman of the California Packing Corporation ranch near Yuba City. Hodges wanted to talk about one of his men who had suddenly quit his job and left the ranch without stopping to get his pay.

The man was Juan Mosqueda, a good worker and normally very steady. On May 26 he had left his thinning crew and had told Hodges he was leaving for San Bernardino. The forty-five dollars that was due him could be sent to him general delivery in that city.

He wouldn't tell Hodges why he was leaving, but one of the other workmen told the foreman that the crew had been listening to a transistor radio when the news of Corona's arrest was announced. Mosqueda immediately became extremely nervous and upset. He told his fellow workman that about two months before he had met Corona in Marysville and then the two of them had picked up a wino in Marysville and driven him to the Sullivan ranch. Mosqueda said Corona dropped him off at the bunkhouse and took the wino in an easterly direction toward the levee. Corona was gone "quite awhile" and then came back alone.

Hodges said he doubted that Mosqueda would be in San Bernardino because he had mentioned something about picking apricots when he left. The foreman guessed that his errant employee would head for Stockton.

With the aid of the Stockton police, Mosqueda was finally picked up at the post office in that city when he called at the general delivery window. He was brought back to Yuba City and booked as a material witness. He denied ever being with Corona in the latter's pickup and denied ever saying that he had.

Duncan got permission to take Mosqueda to Oroville, where Larry Dansby was a polygraph expert for the Butte County district attorney.

Having just been questioned for five hours straight by the Yuba City officers after the long ride from Stockton, Mosqueda was "tired and nervous," Dansby said. However, he agreed to take the lie detector test.

The test lasted for three hours and twenty minutes and at the conclusion Dansby submitted a report to the Sutter County authorities. Dansby wrote:

"Subject's answers to the following questions produced answers indicative of deception: 'Did you ever see Juan Corona pick up a wino? Did you ever tell anyone that Juan Corona picked up a wino? Do you know if Juan Corona left camp with a wino? Did you lie to the police officers?"

Mosqueda's answers convinced Dansby that the farm worker was lying, and therefore Hodges' story to Duncan had been true. However Dansby asked Mosqueda two other questions and said that the test showed he was telling the truth when he answered "No" to each of them. The questions were: "Did Juan Corona leave camp with a wino and come back without him?" and, "Do you know who killed the winos?"

Mosqueda was released after he promised to keep Teja informed as to his whereabouts. He went from Yuba City to Oregon and, when the grand jury was called into session later, he traveled at his own expense back to Yuba City to testify. Mosqueda's story was to become even more interesting.

Corona himself created the next headline when he began to suffer chest pains in his cell in the Yuba County jail on June 18. The attack occurred at 11 A.M. Corona was rushed by ambulance to the Sutter General Hospital in Yuba City. Dr. Thomas Leavenworth, the medical director, took personal charge of the patient.

The headlines blared that Corona had suffered a heart attack and there were even some reports that his condition was critical and speculation as to what might happen to the investigation if he should die. Would the case be marked "closed" or would the sheriff continue his efforts to unravel the mystery?

A tight security ring was immediately placed around the hospital by the sheriff to control the fresh influx of newspeople who soon filled the lobby. The switchboard lit up with several dozen calls from out-of-county and out-of-state papers, television, and radio stations.

Guards were placed at the door to Corona's room and Whiteaker insisted that only people with direct authorization from him be admitted.

Dr. Leavenworth's first press release merely said that Corona's condition indicated a "possible" heart attack and that a definite diagnosis would not be made until specialists had a chance to look at the electrocardiograms that were being taken.

The doctors never were able to be certain that Corona had had a heart attack. He was given massive doses of thorazine, a tranquilizer used to quiet the nerves and relax tensions. He was admitted to the hospital where he was to remain for three weeks while doctors tried to figure whether he had actually had a heart attack or was suffering from hypertension.

In the end the doctors could only say that in view of some irregularities shown in the cardiograms and other symptoms, "We must assume that Mr. Corona has had a heart attack."

The situation created even more problems for Whiteaker and his overworked staff. Now it would be necessary to provide around-the-clock guards at the hospital to prevent unauthorized persons from getting in to see the prisoner.

Hawk added to the problem by attempting to crack the security by getting people other than those given clearance by the sheriff admitted to Corona's room. The incidents caused friction between Hawk and Whiteaker that grew in intensity as the weeks wore on.

If Hawk had his differences with the sheriff, he had none at all with Dr. Leavenworth. The doctor, who had been at the Sutter General Hospital since 1960, was content with his somewhat obscure job. It gave him plenty of time for personal activities and at the same time provided an active, interesting medical practice. He was a casual, quiet person by nature and managed to remain out of the limelight.

Now, overnight, he was an international celebrity, turned into a medical Moses by the power of the press. He was the source of "the word" insofar as the physical condition of the world's best-known prisoner was concerned. It was a heady experience. Hawk sensed it and was shrewd enough to take advantage of the opportunity to find an ally in the enemy camp. He and

Leavenworth became fast friends, and the doctor and lawyer spent many evenings together.

Chapter 17

Teja, on the other hand, was having his troubles. His case was not developing as well as he wished, and the flaws were quickly noticed by Hawk.

He was faced with a preliminary hearing that was scheduled for July 13 at which time he was going to have to produce enough evidence to warrant Corona's being held for a Superior Court trial. Legally, during a preliminary hearing, the defense has the right to challenge the evidence that the district attorney presents. If the prosecution cannot offer sufficient evidence to convince the judge that there is grounds for a trial in the higher court, the judge must dismiss the case.

As things stood, Teja's case was just not well enough organized to take into open court. The reports from the C.I.I. concerning the evidence had not come in except for some minor opinions. The lack of physical evidence was critical, and the circumstantial evidence thus far collected could be ripped to shreds by an experienced advocate such as Hawk.

There was one out left for the district attorney, and he took it. On July 1 he summoned the county grand jury into session. By getting an indictment from the grand jury, Teja could eliminate the scheduled preliminary hearing.

There was another advantage also. A grand jury would hear only one side of the story, and that side would be the prosecution's. It would only be necessary for the district attorney to provide the jury with enough evidence to prove that a crime had been committed and that the suspect in custody could have committed the offense. The defendant could testify if he wished, but he wouldn't. If he chose to testify, he would appear alone with no lawyer to represent him. He would be asked only those questions that the prosecutor wished to ask—questions designed to damn him rather than to protect him. No lawyer in his right mind would allow his client to appear before such a forum.

Hawk complained loudly and vigorously about Teja's tactic, but his histrionics were only for effect. He knew Teja was being smart, but he didn't want to admit it in public. Instead, he took the opportunity to hammer his message home to the press. The district attorney didn't dare go to the preliminary hearing because he would lose the first round, he said. It was a damn shame that a guy like Juan Corona, a family man, respected member of the community, a man with a spotless reputation for truth and honesty, should be held in jail on such a trumped-up charge. There was no evidence to connect Corona with the crimes, he bellowed, but Dave Teja was bound and determined to kill somebody, and he had picked Juan Corona.

Teja paraded some fifty-seven witnesses before the grand jury in outlining the people's case against the labor contractor. His only problem came in trying to keep the bodies numbered three and four in the correct order. The whole case was going to depend on that.

Cartoscelli had straightened out the numbering some time before.

Jody Ulrey, the Sacramento County deputy coroner, had come to Yuba City to see Teja because he was puzzled. He had received the two bodies from Sutter County and had recorded them according to the numbers that had been placed on them in the Yuba City mortuary. However, when he read the reports that had been written by Gregory at the gravesites, the descriptions of the clothing the victims were wearing did not match the numbers. Ulrey realized that a mistake had been made, a mistake that had to be rectified.

It had been Cartoscelli's job during the search for the graves to keep track of the sites and Purcell the order in which the victims were found. In the case of bodies three and four, he had been a passenger in the jeep when Rodemaker spotted the telltale trail of earth mounds and blood on the evening of May 25. The undersheriff was unaware of the body mixup that occurred later.

Cartoscelli had a photographic memory, and he was a stickler for details. He was an eleven-year veteran of the sheriff's department and had gone through the ranks to become a lieutenant by the time Whiteaker was elected sheriff. Cartoscelli was named undersheriff by his new boss on January 4, 1971.

The new second in command had lived most of his life in Yuba City. Born in the mountain mining town of Nevada City, his family moved when he was a small child. He had been educated in the Yuba City schools and then had gone on to Yuba College to study police science. His credentials also included a certificate from the National Academy of the F.B.I., where he completed a special course in police science.

He was young, tough, and experienced, and he had the extraordinary gift of being able to remember minute details of a case long after it had been completed.

Teja called Cartoscelli to his office where Ulrey asked him, "Do you remember what the victim in grave number three was wearing?"

With no hesitation the undersheriff replied, "Sure, that was Sample. He was wearing a green shirt with orange stripes and. . . ."

Ulrey stopped him. "That's it! That explains it. He was the one who was tagged number four when we got him."

Cartoscelli's memory had rescued a critical situation, critical because the two accusing meat receipts had been found in grave number three. The victim had been dead only a short time, and the meat receipts were dated May 21, four days before he was found. Gregory's report had listed the receipts as part of the evidence found in grave number three. The other man had been dead for at least two weeks and, had that body been allowed to continue to be labeled number four, the meat receipts could not possibly have been buried at the same time as the body.

Unless, as Hawk had already been quick to point out to the press, the grave had been partially uncovered and the meat receipts planted to frame his client.

Teja corrected the body chart in time to present it to the grand jury, but the damage had already been done. Hawk had already seen the original autopsy reports, and he was going to take full advantage of the error.

The other witnesses, all of whom had been interviewed by investigators earlier, told essentially the same stories they had told the officers. The jury heard from the men who had been offered jobs by Corona, the men who saw him drive away from Marysville with men who were never seen alive again, and the people who saw the labor contractor in the vicinity of several of the graves prior to their being discovered.

Shannon's testimony added a new flicker of interest to the investigation when he testified about seeing Corona and another Mexican drive away from Wino Park with three of the victims and also identified a picture of Mosqueda as the man who was with Corona. The next day Shannon was called again, and this time he said the man who was with Corona in the pickup was even then sitting out in the hallway waiting to testify.

Mosqueda had returned from Oregon to appear before the grand jury.

Mosqueda took the witness stand and said he spoke English slightly but he could understand better if there was an interpreter present. Teja told the jury that he thought Mosqueda could understand well enough to answer the questions The farm worker then proceeded to deny that he had been with Corona when Riley, Allen, and Smallwood were picked up. He did not tell anybody on the CPC ranch that he had ridden to the Sullivan ranch with Corona and a wino.

Teja believed Mosqueda was lying, but there was no way of proving it. Hodges had had no reason to tell the story he did unless it was the truth. Dansby's report on the lie detector test indicated there was something wrong with the farm worker's testimony, but there was no way of proving it. The lie detector test would not be admissible in court. Reluctantly, Teja dismissed Mosqueda from the stand.

Hodges also testified even though he didn't want to. He had been told by one of the company officials to stay out of the Corona thing. The official had said, "We are a packing company, not a police agency." He told Duncan and Cochran that the official had hinted that if Hodges talked to the police further, he could be replaced as foreman of the ranch.

In front of the grand jury Hodges told the same story he had told Duncan the first time about Mosqueda. However, his testimony would never be allowed during a court trial. It was hearsay evidence and therefore would not be admissible.

Walton testified as to his connection with Smith and the offer of work by Corona as did Pervis, Brboro, and the others. Without the defense attorney there to cross-examine them, their stories went smoothly and in the direction Teja pointed them.

Dr. William J. Vasquez, the Corona physician, testified that Corona had no history of heart trouble. However, he said Corona had a serious infection of his right foot which had incapacitated him for about two weeks during April.

Don Stottlemyer, the C.I.I. criminalist, was also called as a witness. His testimony was to give a hint of things to come, things that were not going to be good for the prosecution. However, in this particular hearing, there was nothing in Stottlemyer's answers to raise a question in the minds of the grand jurors. He was there only to relate the results of a preliminary study of the evidence.

Stottlemyer said he had found a human bloodstain on one of the sleeves of the denim jacket found in Corona's garage and on one of the two pairs of shorts found under the seat of the van. He couldn't determine the type of blood because of what he described as the "age of the stains."

There was blood on both knives found in Corona's desk, the Tennessee Toothpick and the hunting knife that was found in a sheath. Some blood had been found on a headband and two floor mats found in the trunk of the Impala and eight separate stains had been found in the van. They were all small stains, Stottlemyer testified, except for a large stain found on the inside of the rear bumper of the van.

Some of the stains appeared to have been washed by water, but most of them had not. He had also found blood on the boots that were taken from the rear of the van.

His examination of the bullet taken from Kamp's head showed that it was of nine-millimeter caliber, but because of deterioration caused by body acids, it was impossible to tell whether it had been fired from the pistol found in the desk. However, he added, there were human bloodstains on the muzzle and under the slide on the barrel.

Ruby Lillard was called to repeat the story that she had told Whiteaker six weeks before. Teja had not talked to Mrs. Lillard prior to her appearance before the grand jury, although he had listened to a tape recording of the statement she gave to two investigators who visited her at her home in Santa Rosa where she had recently moved.

There were parts of the story that were really wild, but when the jury heard it they were impressed. She told about her frightening experience that night on the banks of the Feather River. She also told of her association with the Corona family for a period of more than thirteen years.

The grand jury had heard enough. Late in the evening of July 12, after six separate sessions during the preceding twelve days, they indicted Corona on twenty-five counts of first-degree murder.

Chapter 18

Corona's condition continued to improve at the hospital, and he was able to walk from his room to the clinic for his daily examinations. Each time, as Whiteaker had ordered, he was accompanied by a deputy sheriff. Near the end of his stay he complained of stomach pains and Sizelove, who was on duty, walked him through the hallway to see the doctor.

The doctor asked him, "Have you ever had stomach pains before?"

"Yes," replied Corona.

"When do you have these pains?"

"When I do a lot of hard work like digging holes, shoveling dirt, and digging ditches."

"Have you had very many pains, Juan?"

Corona answered, "Yes."

Sizelove wrote a report on the conversation and turned it into the sheriff.

Within a short time after that, Dr. Leavenworth pronounced Corona sufficiently recovered to leave the institution.

When Corona was released from the hospital, he was not returned to the Yuba County jail but was instead hauled to the Sutter County jail, where the two-cell women's quarters were prepared for him. It was isolated from the other prisoners and it was roomy enough to provide him with such homey accommodations as a color television set, a radio, and a small library of Spanish language books. Dr. Leavenworth had made arrangements for a registered nurse to visit three times a week in order to keep track of his blood pressure, pulse, weight, and other vital functions.

In some ways it was a relief for Whiteaker, and in others it was a pain in the neck. For one thing, it was no longer necessary to maintain armed guards around the clock at the hospital, and that saved the county $200 a day. For another, it was better to have the prisoner close at hand so that the people who got in to see him could be more closely checked.

At the same time, human decency required the sheriff to allow the family to have almost unlimited visitors' privileges but there were so many family members that it took an extra jailer just to keep track of them. Corona's mother, Candida, had come up from Mexico and would remain for the duration of the trial. Pedro, who could be about as abrasive as a sharp cob on a cold morning, was hard to get along with. He despised the cops and he made no secret of it. He was convinced that his brother was being framed, and he chafed at the jail regulations. In no time at all he had every officer in the place hating his guts. Most of them would rather have seen him in the jug than Juan.

Hawk was still talking to the press at every opportunity, and he was getting his story across pretty well. He was the only source of news around and he played the newsies like a bunch of violins.

He was hoping to maintain a high level of interest in the story in order to encourage continuing contributions to the Corona Defense Fund. Things hadn't been going too well and the money had not rolled in as he had anticipated. He even made a trip to Fresno, where he spoke at a convention of MAPA in defiance of the court's gag order. There he went over the case in detail, disparaging the evidence that had been collected against his client and reserving a few choice invectives for Teja. For Whiteaker and his department, he had nothing but contempt and ridicule.

He already had an airtight alibi for Juan, he said, and nobody was going to convict his client—and his friend—of murder!

He drew a fine and a jail sentence for contempt of court from Judge Hauck for that one, imposition of sentence to be stayed until the end of the trial.

He was back in Yuba City in time for Corona's arraignment on the indictment in the Sutter County Superior Court. It had been set for July 27 to allow Hawk time to study the transcript of the grand jury proceedings and it also gave him time to take another jab at Whiteaker.

This time Hawk was demanding the right to have Corona interviewed by members of the press. The gag order had stipulated that only Hawk and his official associates might have access to the suspect and Hawk attempted to have some specific news representatives, whom he would choose, listed as "associates" in order to get them into the cell. Whiteaker refused. He told Hawk that he would allow an interview only if the defense attorney secured a court order approving it.

On July 18, 1971, Whiteaker returned a telephone call that Hawk had placed to him the previous day. The sheriff recorded the conversation.

After the opening amenities Hawk told the sheriff that he had selected three newsmen whom he wanted to have appointed as his official associates and who would accompany him to the Sutter County jail to talk to Corona. Whiteaker reminded him of the gag order and said that he would not take it upon himself to accredit the men.

Hawk argued that Corona had the right to tell his story to the public and reminded the sheriff that he could be the subject of bad publicity if he refused to allow the interview. He told Whiteaker, "Jerry Cohen of the Los Angeles *Times* is here with me. Would you like to talk to him?"

The next voice Whiteaker heard was that of a man who introduced himself as Cohen. He argued that the press had the right to talk to the accused and, he said, if permission was not granted, the sheriff could find himself getting real bad press.

The angry sheriff failed to react to the threats as had been anticipated. He flatly refused the request and cut off the conversation.

Three days later the persistent Hawk obtained an order from Judge Hauck, allowing the interview with the provision that Corona's doctor would have to be present. Leavenworth was taking a few days off at a lakeshore resort in the nearby mountains and Hawk flew up there in his own airplane to pick him up. The obliging Leavenworth returned to Yuba City, saw to it that Corona was given a heavy injection of thorazine, and then stood by in the jail cell while the interview was conducted.

The media representatives were Cohen of the *Times*, Vic Biondi of KCRA television of Sacramento, and Wayne Kint of the Sacramento *Union*. Before they talked to Corona they agreed to some stringent ground rules laid down by Hawk.

Hawk was to write the questions that could be asked and he reserved the right to stop the interview at any time. More importantly, he also reserved the right to read the reporters' stories that were to be written and to refuse to allow them to be published if he failed to approve the content.

Cohen, Biondi, and Kint agreed, and the interview proceeded on television. It consisted of Corona denying that he committed the murders with a positive "No!" in answer to the question. There was little else of importance, but the interview did result in some valuable publicity for Corona. He had at last been given the opportunity to stand up in public and assert his innocence.

Prior to the arraignment, Hawk had another chance to talk to the press, this time about the sheriff's security measures. He was particularly incensed, he said, that his client had never been allowed to show his face in public. The practice of covering Corona's head with a coat or a blanket every time he had to be taken from his cell was another example of Whiteaker's doubts about Corona's guilt.

"He has arrested the wrong man, and he knows it," Hawk told the press. "Now he wants to make him look like some monster from the swamp who shouldn't be allowed to be seen in public. Well, from now on Juan Corona is going to be seen as he really is, a clean, decent human, an innocent man who has nothing to hide!"

That remark sent Littlejohn into a rage The captain, who had been in sole charge of Corona's security, angrily declared, "That's a lie! Why the hell should we want to hide his face? The fact is he wouldn't even get up from his bunk without grabbing something to put over his head! I didn't give a damn whether he wanted to be seen or not. It was my job to keep some nut from shooting him, and that's what I did!"

On the twenty-seventh a new Corona took the short walk from his cell to the elevator and up to the second floor of the old courthouse where Hauck's court was located. Leaving the elevator, the neatly dressed, well-groomed suspect walked the gauntlet of television cameras and news representatives who jammed the narrow corridor from wall to wall. Surrounded by a corps of deputies, and with his hands cuffed in front of him, he was led into the newly remodeled courtroom with its stained oak walls.

Outside on the sidewalk which bordered the neatly cropped lawn, the parade of Corona supporters had formed. It was a strange sight in staid Yuba City. The old courthouse, a landmark of nineteenth-century dignity with its plump cupola towering over the Feather River bridge in the background, had become a hippodrome.

The Corona family, young and old alike, walked slowly back and forth in front of the building carrying signs which read, "Justicia para Juan Corona." There were other signs, too, accusing signs directed at Whiteaker and Teja. Richard Lopez had done his work well. Dressed in his Pancho Villa outfit and carrying a rustic cross upon which was fastened a figure of the Crucifixion, he stood at the crosswalk leading to the courthouse steps. Interspersed in the line of march were young men, strangers to the Yuba City area, and representing MAPA, the Brown Berets, and other Mexican societies.

Not generally known was the fact that an undercover agent of the sheriff was also marching, proudly carrying a sign which condemned his boss for having arrested Juan. He reported later that during the march he had asked one of the young men, "Is this guy guilty or not?" The reply was, "We don't give a damn. This is a chance for some good publicity."

Uniformed deputies guarded the several doors that led into the long, rambling building. Those who had been allowed to enter had been searched with the aid of electronic metal detectors and had received the regular police patdown. It was a procedure that was to be continued during the forthcoming hearings in Yuba City and then was to carry on in Fairfield.

Cameras were prohibited in the courtroom, but the artists employed by the various newspapers and television stations occupied the jury box, which extended down the left side of the room to the railing which separated the principals in the trial from the spectators.

The Corona family occupied almost half of the sixty-six-seat room, leaving the reporters to scramble for the remaining seats in competition with curious local residents. Those who could not find seats were not allowed to remain in the room. The sheriff and the judge had ruled that there would be no standees.

Judge Hauck painstakingly read off each of the twenty-five murder counts in the indictment, and to each one Corona pleaded innocent. The Corona case had at last begun to move through the judicial system, but it was to be many, many months before it was to reach a jury.

Following the arraignment, Hawk met with the press on the steps of the courthouse. He wanted to get the case to trial as soon as possible, he said, but not in Sutter County. Corona wouldn't have a chance if he was tried in Yuba City. Teja and the sheriff had already convinced everybody in Sutter County that Juan was guilty.

Once away from the confines of that county it would be a cinch to get an acquittal, he said. There had already been so many mistakes made by the sheriff and his investigators that no jury would ever convict.

During the ensuing days Hawk pointed out the delinquencies of the officers every time he had a chance to talk to newsmen. They had mixed up the bodies so badly that nobody knew now which was which. They had even mixed up the finger tips that had been delivered to the C.I.I. for ieentification, and now they couldn't tell which prints belonged to which body. They couldn't even prove that the possible weapons that were found actually belonged to Corona. They had handled them like amateurs and hadn't even tried to lift fingerprints from them. In fact, Hawk charged, there hadn't been one single effort made to lift prints from any item of evidence that was found.

Everything he said made news. It had to. Hawk was the only one who was talking to the press. Despite Teja's protests that the defense attorney was violating the court rule of silence, he continued to talk. He was making good copy and, significantly, he was planting in the minds of the press and the public, the implication that the case against Corona was not as conclusive as most people had believed.

On August 7 Corona again complained of chest pains and was returned to the hospital where Dr. Leavenworth diagnosed the problem as a coronary insufficiency—his heart muscles were not getting enough blood.

While it was not a heart attack in the true sense, it was serious enough to require hospitalization so that his heart could be closely monitored. Leavenworth prescribed nitroglycerin shots for the heart and large doses of thorazine for his nerves. The thorazine would relax him so he could sleep, something he had not been able to do in jail. Whiteaker was back to an around-the-clock security routine.

While Corona was in the hospital, Leavenworth was off sick

for a week and another doctor was placed in charge of the case. He ordered a psychiatric examination as part of his treatment and asked Dr. Valentine Andres to evaluate the patient.

The full text of Andres' report was never to be made public. Leavenworth returned to duty before the report could be turned over to the district attorney. He immediately demanded that he be served with a court order before he would surrender it.

Andres had already told Whiteaker that his report would show that Corona was psychotic and should be in a mental institution rather than in a jail. The district attorney was anxious to get his hands on it, and he was angry when Leavenworth prevented its release. He was even angrier when he learned that Leavenworth had told Hawk about it.

From the minute he took over the case, Hawk had steadfastly refused to allow any head shrinkers to see his client. He was convinced that Corona was a completely sane individual. "As sound as a dollar with an I.Q. higher than most of the people in the courthouse," he asserted.

The thought of having a psychiatric report on Corona being made public infuriated the defense attorney. Teja tried to go by way of Hogan's barn to get the report released when he went to a Yuba County judge who was sitting temporarily in the Sutter County court and obtained a court order. Then he attempted to subpoena Andres to testify at the change of venue hearing. However, when he discussed that intention in the judge's chambers a week before the hearing, Hauck angrily refused to allow the doctor to testify. The judge didn't appreciate the district attorney's attempt to circumvent his court.

Hawk filed for his change of venue and the hearing was set for September 8.

Meanwhile, Teja had gotten himself some help.

Chapter 19

Bartley C. Williams, young, brisk, and ambitious, had been an attorney since 1965.

He had served for a time as a deputy district attorney in Santa Clara County and then had moved north to the Butte County community of Gridley, about seventeen miles north of Yuba City. Private practice in that small town had not been a profitable venture for Williams, and he jumped at the chance to become a special prosecutor for Teja.

It was going to be up to him to organize the case that would eventually be presented in court. Teja would handle the preliminary skirmishes such as the motion for change of venue and the other actions that would precede the actual trial.

Things had not been going too well for Teja, and they didn't go much better for Williams. If there was a reason for it, it had to be a lack of communication.

It was almost three months since the last of the twenty-five victims had been found, and there had been only one meeting between law enforcement and the prosecution. That session, an informal one, had been set up late in June in an effort to organize what facts and evidence had already been discovered and to determine future moves by the investigators to fill in any loopholes that might appear.

Williams was not satisfied with the organization of the evidence by the sheriff's department. He wanted an expert called in to make an inventory of the evidence and to establish a chain of possession that would stand up in court. George Roche, a criminology professor at California State University at Sacramento, was hired for that task.

Roche's work involved primarily the identification of the fingertips that had been removed from the bodies. He eventually was able to clear up the discrepancies that had occurred between the time the fingers were excised and the time they reached the C.I.I. Some of the mistakes had been made by mislabeling, typographical errors on reports, and lack of proper identification of the persons who did the excising.

Roche was able to straighten the mess out in time and sent the report to Williams. The latter sent a copy to the C.I.I. fingerprint section along with a covering letter in which he said of the report, "You will also note it summarizes some of the mistakes, errors and omissions that have been made concerning primarily the chain-of-possession of this evidence."

The letter, with its damaging admission that the investigators had goofed, was leaked to Hawk by someone in the C.I.I. The defense attorney gleefully allowed the press in on the secret.

On September 8, Hawk went into court to seek a change of venue for Corona. Corona's murder trial was already set to begin on October 5 in the Sutter County Superior Court.

Hawk argued that it would be impossible for Corona to get a fair and unbiased hearing in the county. There were only 40,000 people living in the county, and those that weren't related to each other knew each other by name or reputation, he asserted. It would be impossible to find twelve people in the county who had not already formed an opinion about the case. To prove that point, he hired the prestigious Field Research Corporation to take a sample poll of potential jurors.

Norris Robert Heyer, vice-president of the firm, spent several days on the witness stand explaining that his telephone interviewers had the information developed by contacting 10 percent of the population. He produced figures which he said indicated that an overwhelming percentage of the population had not only read and talked about the crime, but more than 70 percent had already formed a prejudicial opinion.

Heyer asserted that in his opinion a move to a large city would improve Corona's chances for a fair trial.

Hawk produced witnesses to prove that contention, but when he attempted to insert the issue of racial prejudice into the hearing, Hauck stopped him. Said the judge, "The Court is married to a Mexican, the sheriff is married to a Panamanian, the Jury Commissioner is Hawaiian, and the district attorney is an East Indian. I do not believe the issue of racial prejudice is a valid one here."

Teja, using his own staff, conducted his own poll of the county's residents, using the same number of prospective jurors as Heyer. His results, predictably, diametrically opposed those of the Field Corporation.

The hearing dragged on intermittently for three weeks while the two or three bored reporters who were present drowsily tried to stay awake. It finally ended on October 1 when Hauck said he would take the matter under submission and announce his decision in a week.

The outcome was pretty predictable too, in view of the fact that the judge was an elected official of the county and had a fine ear for public sentiment. The motion was denied.

Hawk immediately filed for a write of mandate in the District Court of Appeal to force the removal of the case from Sutter County.

Corona came back to the Sutter County jail from the hospital and was again placed in the former women's section. The sheriff's department settled down to the routine of shepherding the Corona family in and out of the cell block four at a time and squabbling with the quarrelsome Pedro every so often.

Whiteaker, who spoke fluent Spanish, periodically visited Corona to check on his welfare and to relay any requests for books or any item that might help him while away his time. After the second attack, Whiteaker thought that perhaps a bit of therapy might be of value. Therefore, he contacted Mrs. Eva Moss, a trained therapeutic nurse and a painter of some talent, and asked for help.

Mrs. Moss suggested that Corona might spend an hour a day, two days a week, learning finger painting, and that she would teach him. The sheriff would provide the painting materials from the prisoner welfare fund.

For several weeks Mrs. Moss visited the prisoner regularly and Corona caught on to the technique quickly. Mrs. Moss enjoyed the assignment. She found Corona to be polite, very considerate, and even friendly although withdrawn and somber. That wasn't unusual for a man in his position.

However, there was one curious characteristic of her student's painting that she found perplexing. In a report to the doctors one day she mentioned it, "When he paints pictures with men in them he will not fill in the eyes," she said.

Whiteaker, after learning of the report, thought back to his conversation with Ruby Lillard when the murders were first discovered. She too had remarked that Corona drew pictures of men but had never filled in the eyes. Whiteaker was not a psychiatrist, but he figured it had to mean something. The guy just didn't want to look at the eyes of other men, and there had to be a reason for it.

Chapter 20

The case dragged on through the fall and winter months with only an occasional skirmish between Hawk and Teja. Hawk's main complaint was that Teja consistently refused to surrender evidence collected by the prosecution which the defense was entitled to under the discovery order issued months before.

The case was going badly for Teja. In fact, it was falling apart.

DeLong, one of his strongest witnesses, the man who reported Beierman missing and who had seen him drive away in Juan Corona's van from Marysville, was dead.

He got into a fight with Walter Taylor, a room clerk at the Golden West Hotel in Marysville's skid row on October 30 and wound up in the Yuba General Hospital. While he was recovering from the lumps and bruises he got from his thirty-seven-year-old antagonist, he suffered a heart attack and died on November 16. Taylor was questioned briefly after the fight and then released.

Chavella Vasquez was not going to be available either. She was a close friend of Raya and had served as his interpreter when he sued Natividad. There was no doubt that she knew a lot about the Guadalajara Cafe affair. She dropped out of sight after Raya's lawsuit, and Whiteaker had been wanting to talk to her.

She was eventually located—in the morgue in Marysville. A jealous boyfriend with whom she had been living in a town across the valley got all upset when she moved out. He followed her to Marysville and pumped nine .22-caliber bullets into her in a Marysville dive.

Ismael Kenneth Walton was not going to be around to testify, it seemed. Right after the grand jury hearing, he dropped out of sight and couldn't be located. The sheriff got word that he had hopped a freighter out of San Francisco and was headed for somewhere in the Pacific.

Whiteaker used every police agency he could think of to help him in the search, but Walton was gone. Apparently he was not coming back, thus the link between Corona and Donald Ray Smith, victim number five, was lost.

The reports from the C.I.I. were pretty dismal. Terrance Pascoe, the expert who had been assigned to make the handwriting comparisons, wasn't very encouraging. He couldn't definitely tie Corona in with the writing in the ledger when he compared it to handwriting found on check stubs, receipts and other records found in the suspect's home and office.

Stottlemyer's reports on the blood weren't conclusive, either. He still couldn't type the bloodstains to tie them in with any of the victims or to determine whether they had come from one person or several persons.

The tire track comparison was even more of a disaster. After studying the rolled impression of the tire from Corona's van and then likening it to the plaster of paris cast which had been sent to the laboratory from Yuba City, he stated flatly that there was no similarity.

It would have been a miracle if the impressions had matched. The wrong plaster of paris cast had been sent for analysis. Instead of the impression that Cochran had made at Whitacre's grave, and which was still sitting in the sheriff's evidence locker, Stottlemyer had been sent the one that Rodemaker had made six days later at one of the river-bottom graves.

Nobody, it seemed, had read the reports written by Cochran

and Rodemaker. Neither were they aware that investigators had traced the river-bottom tire track to a vehicle belonging to the California Department of Water Resources. The track had been made when Compton and his men were surveying in the bottoms during the month the bodies were found.

Whiteaker soon became aware of the fact that there was an apparent leak somewhere in the department of the C.I.I. Hawk, in his frequent talks with the press, was revealing information that could only have come from such a source. The sheriff relayed his feelings to Teja and Williams.

Also the sheriff noticed a distinct change in the attitude of the experts. Whereas earlier in the investigations they had expressed confidence in the evidence they were studying, they now became uncertain in their evaluations.

Williams made his most significant contribution to the prosecution at that time. Because of his experience in the Santa Clara County district attorney's office he had learned the whereabouts of people who were experts in the various fields associated with the science of criminology.

Dr. Ruth Guy was one. She was an immunohematologist who was associated with the Parkland General Hospital in Dallas, Texas. She had perfected a method of typing bloodstains even though they might be very old or even contaminated.

Another expert was John Harris of Los Angeles who was recognized around the world as one of the best of handwriting examiners. He was in business for himself and had successfully testified in hundreds of court cases.

There was also the Alcohol, Tobacco and Firearms Division of the Internal Revenue Service which maintained laboratories in Washington, D. C.

The prosecution began to line up a new team.

Dr. Guy agreed to come to Yuba City to discuss the evidence and to decide whether she could be of any assistance. She met with Teja, Williams, Whiteaker, and Stottlemyer. Dr. Guy, educated at Stanford University—Hawk's alma mater—was now a professor at the University of Texas' Southwestern Medical School in Dallas and was also associate director of the blood bank at

Parkland. She was said to be about the best there was in the fields of blood typing and hemotology.

By way of introduction to her skills, Dr. Guy suggested that a preliminary test of stains on some of the evidence be made. Smith and Mason took four items of the evidence to the jury room where Dr. Guy conducted a quick test with test tubes and chemicals she had brought with her from Texas. While the prosecutors, the sheriff, the deputies, and Stottlemyer watched, she removed stains from clothing fibers, swirled them in chemicals she had placed in test tubes, and within minutes pointed out three different types of blood found on articles of clothing taken from the victims more than six months before.

Stottlemyer questioned her technique, saying that it was a method he had never heard of before. She replied that many of the people who claimed to be experts in blood still had a lot to learn. It was a rebuke that Stottlemyer was not going to forget.

She was retained on the spot and, before leaving, asked that samples from the stains found in the Corona vehicles and other pieces of evidence be delivered to her. Before she left the Sacramento Airport the next day she had in her possession a total of thirty-seven specimens as well as pieces of skin or muscle removed from twenty-four of the victims by Dr. Rooney.

Harris, in his Los Angeles office, was studying the ledger and comparing the handwriting to samples of Corona's handwriting. He soon notified Williams that there was reason to believe that the writing had been done by one person but that he would have to have more samples in order to be certain. Teja promised to get them for him.

The hair fibers that were found on the posthole digger and in the trunk of the Impala were sent to the ATF laboratories in Washington where specialists were trying to compare them with samples taken from Corona and the victims. The ATF was to be called upon for much more assistance before the end of the trial.

The report on the machete that was found in Corona's van was not good for the prosecution. Stottlemyer had been given a section of bone taken from Whitacre's skull to compare with the blade but found that the striations did not match. Unless the machete blade had been altered between the time Whitacre died and the time the machete was taken from the Corona van, it definitely was not the weapon, the report said.

Chapter 21

The change of venue hearing was followed by a lull that lasted through the holiday season. Hawk took the few opportunities that were offered to belittle the sheriff and the prosecution in the press and to hint at the surprise he was going to hand Teja when the case got to trial.

He also took time to look after his own interest in the case.

The Corona Defense Fund had apparently not been growing as he would have liked to have seen it. The money just wasn't coming in and he was anxious to assure himself an adequate fee for his services. Therefore, on January 14, 1972, he and his wife, Geneva, called on Corona at the jail.

Hawk brought along an agreement that he wanted his client to sign. Under its terms, Hawk would be given the exclusive book, television, movie, and all other rights to the "Juan Corona Story."

There wasn't any doubt that the interest in America's "crime of the century" would continue long after the principals were gone and forgotten. Already there were rumors of books being planned for publication once the court's gag order was lifted. Hawk wanted to make certain that he had the inside track on the source of revenue.

The contract was signed by Corona and Hawk and was witnessed by Geneva.

There was no official announcement that the contract had been made, but the rumors soon began to circulate that it existed, and it caused a flurry of speculation.

There were some skeptics who suggested that the defense

counsel's desire to acquire the rights to the potential story might have precluded a defense plea of not guilty by reason of insanity.

They reasoned that if Corona were to be convicted and then found to be insane, such a contract would not be valid because legally a contract could not be made with a mentally incompetent person.

Pedro was also being active in his brother's behalf. He was carrying a substantial load that was rapidly wearing away at his nerves. He had taken Gloria and the four girls into his home where he and his wife were caring for them. His brother's arrest and imprisonment had had an adverse effect on his labor contracting business, thus seriously curtailing his income.

He may not have been the most pleasant man to be around with his hair-trigger temper and continually bitter disposition, but his family loyalty could not be questioned. He was firmly convinced that his brother was innocent and further, that he was being unjustly accused solely because of his race.

He had tried hard to whip up public sentiment for Juan and had had some success among the Mexican organizations and some college students. In an effort to apply even more public pressure on the prosecution, Pedro went to Mexico.

He asked the Mexican authorities to contribute to Corona's defense fund and was turned down. An attempt to get an audience with the president failed.

He did find a sympathetic newspaper reporter who interviewed him for *El Sol*, a Mexico City daily. In the story Pedro was quoted as charging that Juan was being used "as a scapegoat to discredit Mexican-American workers" in the United States.

Pedro's journey was not very productive from a pecuniary standpoint, but the junket did allow him to let off some steam in an atmosphere he considered to be friendlier than that of Yuba City.

Hawk took another shot at the prosecution—and the taxpayers of Sutter County—by filing a civil suit on behalf of Corona and his family.

In it he asked for a total of $350 million, $100 million for Juan and $50 million for Gloria and each of the four girls. Named as defendants were Teja, Whiteaker, the County of Sutter, and a whole covey of John Does. The suit charged the defendants with false arrest and slander, among other things. The amount asked was exactly twice the total assessed valuation of all Sutter County, its orchards, its rice fields, its homes—rich and poor alike—and its commercial and public buildings.

Actually, Hawk never figured to win the lawsuit or even get it into court. However, the action was a shot in the arm to the Corona family, who had begun to believe that Juan's attorney was not the greatest after all. The press turned out a lot of copy on the lawsuit thus keeping the Corona story and the defense attorney in the headlines.

Then an action that took place 150 miles away in San Francisco gave the Corona case a whole new dimension.

For several years the National Association for the Advancement of Colored People and other civil rights groups had been trying to get the death penalty outlawed. The pivotal argument came in a lawsuit filed by the NAACP on behalf of an obscure death row inmate named Anderson. A decision on the litigation had been expected any day.

On February 18, 1972, the California Supreme Court ruled that capital punishment was cruel and unusual, thus setting the stage for Hawk's next excursion to court. Because of the ruling, it was generally agreed among the legal fraternity that prisoners accused of capital crimes, such as murder, would become eligible for bail. It wasn't long after the decision that Angela Davis, a black militant who was accused of conspiring to free prisoners from the Marin County Courthouse, an incident that resulted in the murder of a judge and two other persons, was granted bail. Hawk immediately appealed to the court for bail for Corona.

His first move was to challenge Hauck, a petition that was automatically granted. In a criminal case the defendant has the right to challenge one judge without offering proof of cause. Hawk believed that the local judge, subject to public censure for decisions that were not popular with his constituents, would not grant bail under any circumstances. Hauck's action in denying the change of venue had convinced him of that.

The state's Judicial Council thereupon appointed Judge Richard E. Patton, of nearby Colusa County, to hear the motion for bail and any subsequent actions that might arise. The appointment locked Patton into the case until its very end.

Patton was fifty-two years old and a native of Colusa County where his family had been farmers. He had been on the Superior Court bench for ten years and was familiar with the courts of the Valley, having been assigned to them on occasion during the past several years. He had also been assigned to the Appellate Court bench several times in the past.

He had gained the reputation of being a student of the law and a fair and completely impartial jurist. He was respected by attorneys for his ability to get right to the "meat" of an action and to render a speedy, incisive decision. He was stern and demanding in court and a thorough gentleman both on and off the bench.

Hawk began the hearing on his motion for bail with full confidence that he would soon have his client out of jail. If the court were to follow the precedent set in the Angela Davis case, it would be merely a matter of proving that his client was not likely to become a menace to the community once he was free and to provide the necessary money or bond to warrant the release.

The defense attorney claimed that the Corona family and his friends had been able to secure property bond guarantees amounting to $200,000 which would justify the $100,000 bail that Hawk anticipated would be required by the court. That would be no great problem, the press was told.

The defense presented medical evidence to show that Corona had suffered from ill health ever since he had been in jail. His two seizures, if not actual heart attacks, were close enough to them to indicate that a critical attack could come at any time.

Dr. Leavenworth testified that Corona would be much better off, from a health standpoint, out of jail. He would be freed of the anxiety that came with being locked up and he would be able to think more clearly and thereby be better able to assist in his own defense.

Hawk introduced several character witnesses to testify as to the excellent standing of Corona as a citizen of the community.

Father Bishop, Fred Montez, Jack Sullivan, and realtor Tom Nevis all agreed that Corona, if freed on bail, would surely show up for any court hearings scheduled in the future. It was easy for the three of them to answer the key question put by Teja: "If the court were to order Mr. Corona freed on $100,000 bail, would you put up the money?"

Father Bishop, Nevis, and Montez, none of whom had that kind of money, said they would. Sullivan, who had the money and much more besides, said, "I make it a practice never to lend money to anyone."

Hawk added even more weight to his argument that Corona was a fit subject for bail. He told the court that if the people of Sutter County were worried about Juan being freed among them, he would take him to his own home in Concord and house him there. Once he mentioned that idea, Hawk really began to like it.

It would be a fine solution, he told the judge. He had plenty of room in his home for the Corona family and besides, Juan would be instantly available to work with his attorney on his defense. Even better, he told Patton, if Corona were living with his own lawyer, there would be no question about his appearing in court whenever he was supposed to.

Teja fought the bail motion doggedly. He was prevented from presenting any evidence that Corona was not mentally sound and therefore not eligible for bail. His attempt to circumvent Judge Hauck's authority and Hauck's subsequent ruling, prevented him from having gotten Dr. Andres' psychiatric testimony on the record previously. Thus, it could not be introduced now.

In addition, Patton ruled at the very beginning of the session that any question of the defendant's mental condition would have to be put before the court in a separate hearing. The district attorney was reduced to oral argument and cross-examination in his attempt to prevent Corona's release.

He needn't have worried. The attorney general of the state had been given thirty days in which to appeal the Supreme Court's decision of February 18. On the last day of the period, the high court amended its ruling to provide for the denial of bail to defendants in capital cases.

Despite an impassioned plea by Hawk that his client be given his liberty, if only temporarily, Judge Patton denied the bail motion.

Hawk again turned to the press, this time to convince them that Juan Corona was being illegally and unjustly kept in jail. He became even more vociferous in stating that the real killer was still at large and that he was going to make his name public before it was all over. He again claimed that Juan had an alibi for the day that Whitacre was killed and that he would account for his whereabouts all during that day.

He became so vigorous in his statements to the press that Teja complained to Patton and the latter set a hearing on the matter. In court the judge again instructed all participants in the case to refrain from discussing "any facts or presumed facts of this case." He ordered all of the files closed to public inspection with the exception of the attorneys and court personnel.

Chapter 22

Whiteaker's jailers, who were instructed to keep an eye on their prize prisoner at all times, began to make some disquieting reports to the sheriff. There were times, they said, when they found Corona crying in his cell for no apparent reason and there were other times when he failed to respond to the simplest of questions. His appetite was good, and despite the constant claims by Hawk that his health was steadily deteriorating, he gained twenty pounds of weight. However, his general attitude was one of severe depression.

Whiteaker would like to see Corona moved. He didn't want to have anything happen to one of his prisoners, especially one as notorious and important as Corona.

The sheriff discussed the matter with Teja, saying that he wanted the prisoner examined by a psychiatrist to determine whether he might harm himself if given the chance. Whiteaker claimed that as sheriff he alone was responsible for the health and well-being of all of the prisoners in his jail and that obligation gave him the right to have a prisoner examined by any accredited doctor.

Hawk had made it clear, both in court and out, that he didn't want *anybody* talking to Corona without his permission. Above all, he didn't want any shrinks examining him. He would never allow it to be suggested that his client was not mentally sound.

Teja got a ruling from the attorney general that gave Whiteaker the authority to have the prisoner examined. He contacted Dr. Stephen Sheppard, a psychiatrist who was on the staff of the Napa State Hospital.

Dr. Sheppard visited Corona in the jail and spent slightly more than an hour with him. At the conclusion of the interview he issued a report that said he found Corona to be "cooperative and affable, conventionally oriented and has a memory for both recent and remote events." He wrote that the prisoner denied hallucinations and there was no evidence of delusional thinking. His sense of humor was impaired and his mood was decidedly depressive. There was no evidence of psychosis, but he was in need of medication that would offset the heavy doses of thorazine that he was being given.

In his diagnosis, Dr. Sheppard wrote: "In view of the current depression it is my opinion based upon reasonable medical probability that Juan Corona does presently constitute a hazard to himself or others. It is my further opinion that he would benefit from a 1203.03 Penal Code commitment for 90 days observation at the California Medical Facility."

In the light of the diagnosis by the psychiatrist, Whiteaker attempted to have Corona transferred to the facility at Vacaville as recommended but the state was reluctant to take on the responsibility for any prisoners except those formally sentenced to the institution by a judge. Teja and Whiteaker were not willing to take the issue to court.

The sheriff ran into another problem about that time, this one involving the most prestigious of all police agencies, the Federal Bureau of Investigation.

An informer told the investigators that a man by the name of John LeMay had had a homosexual relationship with Juan Corona some years before. LeMay, the informant said, was somewhere in the vicinity of Los Angeles.

The information would have to be run down because of its importance to the case. There had never been a motive established for the twenty-five murders but because some of the victims had been found partially unclothed and exposed, there definitely was a homosexual angle. Even Hawk agreed with that. In fact, the defense attorney had already hinted that that very angle was going to be part of his defense.

The sheriff wanted his detectives to talk to LeMay, and he asked the Los Angeles Police Department for help. He told Gregory and Leonard Brunelle, an investigator in Teja's office, to try to talk to the confidential informant who had called from Los Angeles. There was a chance the man had some information the sheriff could use.

Gregory and Brunelle called the F.B.I. in Los Angeles and got Mike Williamson on the telephone. He told the two investigators that the confidential informant was working undercover for the F.B.I., and the agent in charge of the particular investigation would not allow him to be interviewed.

Williamson said the name of the informant could not be released, nor could the federal agency be of any further assistance to the Sutter County authorities.

The Los Angeles officers reported that they had talked to LeMay and they were of the opinion that he was willing to assist in a "full and truthful manner." However, the failure of the F.B.I. to cooperate with Whiteaker effectively blocked any follow-up investigation of the lead.

Closer to home Mrs. Thelma Broadnax of Marysville called

the sheriff's office about her friend Ruby Lillard. She said Ruby was having real mental problems and she wasn't getting any better. Her stories about Corona were getting wilder and wilder. Now she was talking about a five-year-old child being killed by Corona and she was also talking about how the Coronas, Juan and Natividad, had kidnapped her seven times. On top of that, Ruby said, she was held in a Sacramento apartment and was forced to marry Juan in Reno.

There was a lot more, and Gregory, who was taking the call, asked if Ruby had been drinking. Mrs. Broadnax said Ruby was drinking a lot more than she used to and only the week before she had said, "I think I'm losing my mind."

Mrs. Broadnax thought the sheriff ought to have Ruby examined by a psychiatrist. She had changed so much in the past several months since the Corona arrest that she just had to have some help, Mrs. Broadnax said.

Teja learned that Hawk had already had his own investigator talk to Mrs. Lillard and had learned the same things that Mrs. Broadnax told Gregory. Ruby Lillard wasn't in any condition to be a witness and, according to a doctor who examined her, she wasn't going to be. Her connection with the Corona case ended with that examination.

On the thirteenth of April the Court of Appeals granted Hawk's writ of mandate and ordered the trial to be moved out of Sutter County. The justices held that because of the small population and the widespread interest in the case among the 40,000 residents, it would not be possible for the defendant to receive a fair trial in Yuba City.

Chief Justice Leonard Friedman, writing the unanimous decision, referred to the massive publicity that was generated and stated, "In the minds of many, the media have stripped the defendant of the presumption of innocence and and he must now disprove his guilt." The case should be moved, he wrote, to a larger county where the effect of the publicity would be diminished through the lapse of time between the arrest and the trial.

The Judicial Council had recommended either Sacramento or

Stockton as possible locations for the trial, principally because both were located in predominantly agricultural areas as was Yuba City. It would be up to the attorneys to agree on a location before a definite move could be made. Judge Patton scheduled a hearing in the Sutter County Superior Court to resolve the question.

Teja preferred Sacramento because the state capital was only forty miles from Yuba City. Having the trial there would allow him and his witnesses to commute and it would not be necessary to move all of the files from Sutter County.

Hawk didn't like either location and he set out to eliminate both. His argument was based on his contention that there was a strong prejudice against farm workers and Mexicans in both areas. He produced witnesses to prove it and their testimony was enough to convince the court. Judge Patton ruled out both Stockton and Sacramento as possible sites, and the judge took the prorogative, allowed by law, of selecting three alternate counties. Patton chose Solano, Alameda, and Contra Costa, and the attorneys finally chose Solano.

He also set September 5 as the trial date.

Chapter 23

The county seat of Solano was Fairfield, eighty miles south and just a bit west of Yuba City. The county itself, with its population of just over 170,000 was one of the original twenty-seven that were carved out when California became a state in 1850. Its largest city was Vallejo, where one-third of the population lived and which had, for a short time many years before, served as the state capitol. The Mare Island Navy Shipyards provided jobs for several thousand residents and was one of the nation's most important naval bases.

Nearby Benicia, also a state capitol for a time in 1853, had been the site of a huge federal arsenal which had supplied much of the country's military firepower for more than seventy-five years. Right next door to Fairfield was Travis Air Force Base with its several thousand air force personnel and an almost equal number of civilian employees.

The county also had a substantial agricultural economy based on the production of fruits, nuts, and grain from its nearly half-million acres of farm lands. It had acquired its name from an Indian chief who had in turn taken the name of a Franciscan missionary upon his conversion to Christianity early in the nineteenth century.

Fairfield itself was a city of 47,500 residents and the newest of the county's incorporated communities, having become a city in 1903. It was only fifteen miles from the California Medical Facility at Vacaville where Corona would be kept by order of the court during the trial, and where doctors could keep a close watch on his health. The trial would be held in the old three-story courthouse which had recently been remodeled.

On July 1, 1972, Juan Corona was moved from the old Yuba County jail to get him "out of the clutches of Whiteaker," as Hawk put it. He was moved to the modern, sterile penal facility at Vacaville to await the beginning of the trial.

Hawk had one more chance to talk to the press in Yuba City and he took the opportunity to be even more positive in his assertion that the wrong man had been arrested. When the time came, he said, he would solve the crime right in the courtroom. "I'll pull a Perry Mason on them," he bragged.

He would also prove conclusively that it would have been physically impossible for Corona to have killed Kenneth Whitacre, whose body had been buried in Goro Kagehiro's peach orchard more than thirteen months before.

If Hawk was glad to get out of Yuba City, Whiteaker was equally as overjoyed to see the aggressive defense attorney leave. The sheriff issued a statement saying, "Mr. Hawk has been one of the most obnoxious attorneys that has even been in contact with this office and the sheriff. His attitude and approach to a difficult situation and in regard to this office has been similar to the actions of a small child."

Although more than a year had passed since the murders were discovered, the prosecution was not even close to being ready for trial. There had been a surprising lack of communication between the prosecutors and the investigators. There had been a meeting in June, 1972, to discuss the evidence that had been accumulated, but nothing had been accomplished. Neither Williams nor Teja had ever discussed with individual officers the reports they had written or the evidence they had cataloged either at the gravesites or at Corona's home or the labor camp.

The plans of the prosecution were the best-kept secret in Sutter County. Even the sheriff had no idea what Williams and Teja intended to do. They weren't talking; at least they weren't talking to the men who had investigated the murders.

Once the case reached Solano County and a definite trial date was established, the tempo picked up. Patton was assigned to go along to Fairfield and he quickly set up the ground rules. The gag order would remain in force and Sheriff Albert Cardoza was asked to organize security procedures for the protection of the principals during court sessions. The sheriff employed extra deputies and prepared to handle the most sensational trial that the county had ever seen.

While Williams and Teja were having trouble getting organized, Hawk was already laying the ground work for his trial strategy.

The first thing he was going to do was establish a motive. He intended to prove that the murders were committed by a homosexual and then he was going to show conclusively that Juan Corona was not one. In fact, he pointed out to the press, there was already a pervert in the picture. Natividad, Juan's half-brother, was a well-known homosexual and he had plenty of opportunity to commit the crimes.

He dropped the hint that his wife, Geneva, had seen Natividad in Marysville in June, 1971, just after Hawk took over the defense. He did not pursue that statement further, preferring to let his listeners draw their own conclusions.

Whiteaker immediately investigated that report and discovered that, as far as was known, Geneva had never been in Marysville prior to that time and therefore had no way of knowing

Natividad Corona. She wouldn't have been able to recognize him if she had seen him, which was highly unlikely.

Whiteaker had gone a step further. He had sent Dave Perales to Mexico where the Sacramento officer talked to the state prosecutor of Jalisco who had interrogated Natividad in Guadalajara in 1971. Natividad was questioned after a woman had accused him of kidnapping her teenage son and taking him to the United States early that year. Natividad denied any knowledge of the whereabouts of the youth, although he admitted paying fifty dollars to the boy to engage in an abnormal sex act.

More importantly, Natividad swore under oath—and apparently proved—that he had not left Mexico at any time after December, 1970.

The prosecutors had heard from both Harris and Pascoe who reported they would need exemplars of Corona's handwriting to compare with the writing in the ledger. Teja and Williams went into court where they got an order instructing Hawk to provide them.

Legally, such examplars must be taken under court supervision, but Hawk had refused to follow that procedure. Instead, he obtained a set of forms used by the C.I.I. to take such exemplars and had Corona fill them out in his cell under his own supervision.

In view of the fact that Harris had already notified the prosecutors that he was practically certain that Corona had written the names in the ledger, Teja refused to accept Hawk's offer. He went back to court. The people had a right, he argued, not only to suggest the material to be used in the exemplars but also to be present when they were completed. The prosecution wanted the exemplars to include names from the ledger both in script and black printing. In that way Pascoe, Harris, and Sidney Goldblatt of the ATF would have adequate material to compare.

Aligning Goldblatt with the prosecution had been Williams' idea. The treasury expert was a heavy-set native New Yorker who had established a reputation in the East. For the past twenty-one years he had been a documents examiner in the Treasury Department's New York office. He was qualified to serve as an expert witness in any court in the country.

It was going to be necessary to have another expert available to testify in view of Pascoe's latest comments. The C.I.I. man had become more and more vague in his reports and only recently had made a comment that depressed the prosecution. Some of the handwriting in the ledger, he said, was definitely not done by Corona. He also commented that if the prosecution "thought this (the ledger) was Juan Corona's handwriting, you are in trouble."

Hawk however, had another ace in the hole. He was about to spring it but didn't get the opportunity at that particular hearing. Patton, who was determined to maintain the authority of his court, gave the defense attorney and his client one last chance to comply with his order. When both Hawk and Corona refused, the judge sentenced Hawk to two days in the Solano County jail and fined them each $250.

Hawk did his two days, entering the jail while the television cameras recorded the event. When he emerged the press was waiting and quoted him as saying, "Corona is innocent. Both Dave Teja and I know who killed these people and this will be apparent after the trial begins."

A week later he was back in court and this time he produced his ace. At the same time, he revealed one of the leaks in the C.I.I.

Sherwood Morrill was the head of the C.I.I.'s handwriting laboratory and had assigned Pascoe to the Corona investigation. Morrill, with thirty-nine years of experience, was even then in the process of branching out on his own. It was his plan to go into business for himself as a private handwriting expert such as Harris already was in Los Angeles. Morrill had taken the first step toward that goal by becoming a partner in such a firm.

It was a surprise—even a shock—to the district attorney and his deputy when Hawk called Morrill as a defense witness to bolster his contention that the handwriting examples he had gotten from Corona at Vacaville, were authentic. Everybody in the courtroom was aware that Morrill and Hawk had reached some kind of a mutual agreement prior to the expert's appearance in court. He had been subpoenaed by the defense but it was apparent the summons had not been served until after he and Hawk had privately conferred. It explained where Hawk got the official

C.I.I. forms which he used to take the handwriting exemplars from Corona at Vacaville.

Morrill looked at the Corona exemplars and was asked by Hawk, "Do you have any opinion as to whether or not Mr. Corona made any attempt to disguise his handwriting?" It brought immediate objection from Teja which was just as quickly overruled by the judge. Morrill replied, "Your honor, in my opinion, and I examined the exhibits, the handwriting which purports to be that of one person is that of one person with no attempt to disguise whatsoever any place along the line."

It was one of several torpedoes the C.I.I. was to fire for the defense.

Despite Morrill's testimony, Patton refused to budge. He insisted on maintaining the integrity of his ruling of a week before saying, "The Court had previously held and now holds that the People are entitled to the exemplars, to be given under such methods as to assure their authenticity."

Hawk again refused to comply with the order. His client, reading the answer that his attorney had written for him, also refused. The sentence was three days in jail for the attorney and a $300 fine for counsel and client alike.

Hawk next attempted to have Corona qualified to act as co-counsel in his defense. Under questioning by Patton, Corona assured the court that he had a good understanding of the English language and was prepared to waive the services of an interpreter. Hawk said his client's activities as co-counsel would be limited, but he felt that Juan should have the right to prove to the jury that he is a "sane, intelligent, sympathetic, fine human being."

Patton denied the motion. He assured Hawk that Corona would be given the opportunity to impress the jury with his intelligence and demeanor if and when he chose to testify.

Teja and Williams were determined to get the exemplars prior to the start of the trial, and they therefore asked for the September 5 date to be vacated. Hawk's objections were long and furious.

He accused Teja and Williams of being afraid to try the case because they lacked the evidence to get a conviction. He insisted that the trial begin on the day scheduled and pointed out that his client had already spent sixteen months in jail.

Patton denied the motion and Teja announced that he would immediately file an appeal. The district attorney went into the District Court of Appeals and won his point. The high court ordered the trial date vacated. The writ of mandate stated that the delay in the start of the trial was caused by the defense attorney refusing to comply with Patton's order to supply the handwriting specimen.

Hawk agreed to provide the exemplars because, he said, to refuse would mean that his client would have to remain in jail several months longer while he appealed Patton's order. Patton set a new trial date of September 11 to allow time for the handwriting samples to be taken under court supervision.

A final pretrial court skirmish took place on September 7, just four days prior to the trial date. Both sides had issues to present to Patton.

Hawk had studied the letter which Williams had written to the C.I.I. some months before in which he made mention of the "mistakes, omissions and errors" in connection with the delivery of excised fingertips of some of the victims to the Sacramento laboratories. George Roche had spent two months trying to straighten out the chain of evidence. He had managed to match the exhibits with the victims but Hawk wanted copies of the reports the prosecution had received.

It had been Hawk's contention since he first took the case that Teja had consistently failed to surrender prosecution evidence to the defense as required by the discovery order. It had been Teja's claim that all of the material had been given to the defense, but he had failed to obtain receipts for much of it. Therefore, when Hawk claimed that he had not received the reports he was entitled to, Teja didn't have a leg to stand on.

Patton granted Hawk's motion and ordered the Roche report turned over to him. As it turned out, the report didn't have much of an effect on the outcome of the trial, but it gave Hawk a lot to talk about during his daily meeting with members of the press.

He enlivened the news stories with references to the sheriff's evidence locker, which he called a "Goodwill Store" and to the "phony" evidence that "Roy Whiteaker was braying about on the banks of the Feather River."

Teja and Williams also had a pitch to make to the judge. They wanted to exclude the Guadalajara Cafe incident from the trial.

Chapter 24

The district attorney and Williams had been counting on producing evidence that Juan Corona had been the one who attacked Raya as a means of demonstrating a "common plan, scheme and design" tying in the Raya cutting with the twenty-five murders. They had expected to show that the similarity of the wounds inflicted on Raya and the twenty-five dead men, together with the fact that Raya's name topped the ledger which they were now in the habit of referring to as "the death list," proved that Corona was the perpetrator of all of the crimes. Thus the common plan, scheme, design, theory.

However, Raya failed to cooperate. Although Perales had been trying for months to get Raya to change his story that it was Natividad who had cut him, the scarred farm worker refused. Unless they could not get the Raya incident excluded from the trial, they were going to give Hawk a chance to use their own ammunition to convince the jury that Natividad killed the twenty-five transients. Williams knew better than to give the bellicose defense lawyer that kind of leeway. He was having enough trouble with his prosecution as it was.

Hawk, on the other hand, saw the opening he was looking for. He reminded the judge that the Guadalajara Cafe affair had been mentioned in the search warrant that Whiteaker had obtained on May 26, 1971, and which had led to Corona's arrest. That, he claimed, made the Raya assault a part of the overall case, and it could not be elminated now. "What they're in effect saying, at one point the evidence shows that Juan was a killer. Now they're saying, well, we can't prove it so we don't want it in this trial at all," Hawk said. He continued, "Does this mean that if I can produce evidence of somebody killing these twenty-five people I can't get it in because it doesn't go toward Juan? That's in effect what they're saying to you."

Patton ruled that the incident could not be admitted, and he went a step further by admonishing Hawk that, if he had any thought of referring to it in his opening argument to the jury, he would be stopped. Patton issued an order that before Hawk made his opening argument, he discuss its contents with the judge out of the presence of the jury. That way Patton could rule in advance on its admissibility.

The judge pointed out that Corona was charged only with twenty-five murders in the present action and the Raya case had been settled in a civil suit two years before. Including it in the forthcoming trial could only add to the length of the hearing without contributing materially to its determination.

The ruling seemed to make the cafe attack a dead issue, but Perales was not ready to give up. When he was first assigned to talk to Raya he had been pretty well briefed by Whiteaker. He learned that when Raya originally filed his civil suit he had named both Natividad and Juan as being responsible for the attack. Juan was never served with the complaint but Whiteaker always figured that Raya must have had a good reason for naming Juan as a defendant. Perales decided to talk to Raya some more.

On the following Monday morning the long-awaited trial got under way.

Chapter 25

It was an unprecedented event in Fairfield, and it drew an overflow crowd. The narrow hallways of the second floor where the courtroom was located were filled with prospective jurors, members of the news media, the Corona family and spectators who were hoping to get a seat in the small courtroom number four. Sheriff Cardoza had set up a security checkpoint through which everyone had to pass. Spectators were required to sign in, submit to a search, and then have their pictures taken. When the courtroom was full, the overflow was asked to leave the building.

Outside the building the Corona supporters straggled along the sidewalk in a disorganized line carrying the familiar signs asking justice for Corona. Television cameramen and newspaper photographers, their equipment excluded from the building, loitered with nothing to do until recess or noon break.

It was anticipated that the trial would last for at least six months. The district attorney had established an office within two blocks of the courthouse and had moved the files there from Yuba City along with the necessary clerical help. Hawk, whose home and office were much closer to Fairfield, was able to commute each day, although packing his files in and out of the court was to become an increasingly heavy chore.

Hawk had acquired an associate to work with him during the trial; not to help with the defense but rather to collaborate with the attorney after the trial had ended. The associate was Edward Cray, a Los Angeles writer. It would be his job to follow the action and then to write a book which he and Hawk would copyright as the result of Hawk's contract with Corona.

The defense attorney had one other person at the table for help during the selection of the jury. He was Harvey Ross, a Los Angeles psychologist who would listen to the answers given by prospective jurors and then advise Hawk as to whether they would be beneficial or adverse to the defense. It was a procedure that had been used by defense attorneys in many major trials in recent years.

At 10:01 A.M. the bailiff called the court to order and Patton took the bench. There were 62 potential jurors present out of the 100 who had been summoned to appear. Another 200 had been notified that they might be summoned if necessary to choose the 12 who would hear the testimony and evaluate the evidence.

The names of all of the prospective jurors were placed in the jury wheel from which their names would be drawn one by one. It took only a couple of minutes to pick the first 12, who were then questioned under the system of voir dire, meaning the legal oath requiring jurors to make true answers to questions regarding competency to serve.

Both sides had checked the backgrounds of the people who had been called, trying to determine their age occupations, political and religious persuasions, financial condition, the neighborhoods they lived in, their personal feelings toward law enforcement, their racial prejudices, and any personality traits that might affect their judgments. Teja had the slight advantage of being able to check police records in case any of the veniremen had ever been involved in crimes of any kind.

The background checks were important. It was necessary to try to determine in advance whether a juror was going to lean over backward to favor law enforcement or would be defense-minded. It was also important to select jurors who would be levelheaded, thoughtful, and have the ability to withstand pressure from jurors with conflicting opinions.

Each side was assigned twenty-five peremptory challenges, meaning that they could excuse that many persons from the jury box without stating any reason. Jurors could also be excused for cause if they indicated they had already formed an opinion as to the guilt or innocence of the defendant or for other prejudicial feelings.

The voir dire sessions could also be used by opposing attorneys to instruct the jurors in basic features of the law. They could remind jurors that the defendant did not have to prove his innocence, that he did not have to testify if he chose not to, and that he was entitled to the benefit of any reasonable doubt. The law was specific on that latter point. A defendant had to be proven guilty "to a moral certainty and beyond a reasonable doubt." It meant that if a juror were to reach two conclusions, one favoring the defense and one favoring the prosecution, he had to choose in favor of the defendant.

The voir dire was a trying time for the judge, particularly in a capital criminal action. It was his duty to prevent the attorneys from attempting to unduly influence the jurors by inserting comments that were outside the scope of permissible questioning.

Hawk was a master of that technique, and Patton knew it. Even so, he was not prepared for the defense attorney's scandalous attempts to discredit the prosecution and influence the jury before the trial was even under way.

Hawk ran afoul of the court during questioning of the second prospective juror, Mrs. Phyllis L. Bailey of Fairfield. He asked her, "Do you believe that if the prosecution has evidence pointing to some else's guilt they ought to suppress it?"

Williams objected on the grounds that Hawk was asking the woman to make a legal decision on the duties of a prosecutor. Patton sustained the objection and Hawk asked the same question again, worded differently but conveying the same meaning. Again an objection and again the judge sustained.

It was apparent that the defense attorney was bent on planting in the minds of the jurors his contention that Teja and Williams were going to prevent any evidence that might point to Natividad's guilt.

After Mrs. Bailey came the other ten people in the box, and Hawk continued his attack. Patton, rapidly losing patience, called the attorneys into his chambers and admonished Hawk. He accused the defense attorney of speaking for the benefit of the press rather than attempting to question the panel members in an orderly manner. The judge made no attempt to hide his anger at Hawk's conduct in the courtroom.

By the end of the second day the judge was interjecting his own objections to many of Hawk's questions. He again called the attorneys into chambers and this time he vented his anger on Teja and Williams. He accused the prosecutors of failing to place objections at proper points during Hawk's questioning and said, "I think the People are not performing their proper function in this case."

It got worse instead of better. Hawk's questions wandered further and further afield, and the judge's comments became more frequent and acrimonious. Hawk persisted in making snide remarks about the prosecutors and in trying to confuse the jurors with insinuations that the defendant was the wrong man on trial. Frequent citations for contempt of court, accompanied by fines, failed to cool Hawk's enthusiasm. He had told the press that he was going to be just as nasty as he had to be in order to get his point across, and nothing was going to stop him.

He continued his daily sessions with the press, meeting them outside the courtroom at the close of each session. He was making good copy, and he never lacked for an audience.

It took ten court days extending over two weeks to select a jury from the more than sixty veniremen who were summoned to the box. During that time Hawk collected five more contempt citations and a total of $1,200 in fines.

At the same time he had demonstrated to the prosecutors that he was going to be a tough, contentious adversary. Judicial rules and courtroom decorum meant nothing to him. He was there to defend Juan Corona and, if he had to go to jail to do it, he was willing. He had served notice on the prosecutors that it was going to be a no-holds-barred fight to the end.

On September 28 Williams, with nine peremptory challenges left, announced that he was satisfied with the jury of ten men, two women, and four alternates. Hawk had six challenges left, but he too said he was willing to accept the jury.

It was a pretty good cross-section of the population of Solano County which had been chosen to hear the case of the People of the State of California versus Juan Vallejo Corona.

The number one juror was the only black on the regular panel. He was Calvin Williams, a custodian for the Vallejo Unified School District. A veteran of World War II, he was married and had a son in the service.

Number two was James R. Owens, a metals inspector at the Mare Island Shipyard. He was thirty-nine years old and was the father of four children. He was a religious man, a member of a church which had built a home for a Mexican family in Baja, California.

Number three was Victor Lorenzo, a forty-five-year-old produce man in a local market. He had three children.

Matthew Johnson was the fourth juror. He had served thirty years in the U.S. Marine Corps before retiring. He had been born in England and wore a beard. He was fifty-four years old.

George Muller, forty-eight, the fifth juror, was retired from the air force after twenty-nine years of service and was now employed as a jet engine mechanic at Travis Air Force Base. He was married and had two daughters.

The youngest member of the panel was Bill Hicks, who occupied seat number six. He was twenty-three years old and had been a helicopter gunner in Viet Nam. He was now employed by the Solano Irrigation District. His tenure on the jury was to be short.

Number seven was the only one of the original twelve who had been called into the box on the first day. He was Ernest Phillips, who had retired from the air force in 1969 after serving twenty-nine years. His home was in Vacaville, where he lived with his wife and five children.

By far the best educated among the jurors was number eight, Fay M. Blazek. She was also the oldest at sixty-six and was a retired school teacher and speech therapist. She had a master's degree from New York University and lived in Vallejo with her husband, also a retired teacher.

Donald Rogers, sixty, was number nine and the last juror selected. A retired machinist from Mare Island, his home was in Vallejo.

The tenth juror was Frank Broksell, also retired from Mare Island. He lived with his wife in Vallejo.

The second woman on the panel was juror number eleven, Mrs. Naomi Underwood, sixty-one, a semiretired salesclerk. She lived alone, except for her cats, in Vallejo.

Laurent Gallipeo, number twelve, was also a shipyard worker, but his job was across San Francisco Bay at the Hunters Point Shipyard. His home was in Vallejo, and he commuted each day.

There were also four alternate jurors, selected to take the places of any of the regular jurors who might become ill or be otherwise incapacitated. They were:

Lloyd Shanks, a thirty-eight-year-old employee of Union Carbide Company; Richard Bremen, twenty-four, a welder at Mare Island; Edward Johnson, sixty-two, black and a Vallejo service station owner, and David Campbell, forty-eight, a quality control inspector for a local manufacturing plant.

They were the jury who would decide the guilt or innocence of Corona.

Chapter 26

The opening statement is a traditional and important part of the American judicial system. Although defense attorneys sometimes decline to take advantage of the opportunity to outline their proposed defense to the jury, the prosecution rarely fails to, particularly in cases involving murder.

Traditionally also, the prosecution is the first to face the jury because it has the burden of proving the crime and the defendant's guilt. Williams, therefore, began the main body of the trial on September 29 with the opening statement for the people.

The length of the statement demonstrated the length of time he had spent in its preparation. For more than six hours, extending into the second day, he laboriously and monotonously read some 50,000 words which detailed all of the elements of the crime.

The prosecution had a huge map of the area in which the bodies were found painted by an artist and at twenty-five separate locations they had placed twenty-five electric light globes, each with its own switch. It would be possible, during the forthcoming testimony concerning the finding of the cadavers, to graphically demonstrate the exact spot where each body was found. Hawk, throughout the trial, sneeringly referred to the map as "the whiz-bang board."

Williams also discussed at length the testimony that he expected his witnesses to offer and promised to produce physical evidence that would point to Corona as the perpetrator of the murders. Occasionally he would stop speaking to show photographs or other items of evidence to the jury. During several of those pauses Hawk rose to object, protesting that he had not seen the evidence before, despite the discovery orders that were supposed to make them available to the defense. He made notations of the evidentiary material that he claimed had been withheld from him.

Williams' statement was not completed when Judge Patton recessed the court for the day. When the session began just before 10 A.M. the courtroom had been crowded to capacity, but by the time Patton called a halt, there were only a handful of reporters and members of the Corona family still present. The monotony of the special prosecutor's delivery had not only all but emptied the courtroom, it had also put a couple of jurors to sleep and made the sheriff drowsy.

When the trial resumed the following Monday morning, the attorneys met in Patton's chambers. Hawk produced his list of photographs and other items of evidence that he claimed had been withheld from him. He demanded that because they had been withheld in defiance of the court order that they be suppressed. Besides the photographs, Hawk said, other items such as investigators' reports, lists of the victims' clothing, and statements of potential witnesses had been concealed. In all, Hawk listed forty-six items.

Teja maintained that hawk had received the evidence, but the district attorney's staff had failed to obtain receipts for them. Williams, on the other hand, informed the judge that because the case was still being investigated and new leads were being followed up within the last thirty days, it had not been possible for his staff to reduce all of the information to writing. Patton was dumbfounded to learn for the first time that the prosecution's case was not organized by the time the trial began.

Patton denied Hawk's motion to suppress the evidence because, he said, the trial would be so lengthy that the defense would have plenty of time to study the evidence and to be able to use it to their advantage when it came time for them to present their case.

The principals then moved into the courtroom where Williams resumed his statement in front of the jury. Hawk continued his objections, now accusing the prosecutor of making false statements to the jury and distorting the facts. His objections were overruled in every instance, but the defense attorney wasn't disturbed. He was continuing to let the jury know that once given the opportunity, he was going to expose the People's case as being totally without substance.

Williams finally finished his resumé just before noon, and the judge dismissed the jury for the day. The slight delay was beneficial to Hawk. It was going to allow him to go over the notes he had written while Williams was exposing the various facets of his plan of attack. The defense attorney could use a lot of those details in framing the statement that he would make the next day.

This was what Hawk had been waiting for since he first went into the case sixteen months before. It was going to be his chance to tell the jury about the mistakes the investigators made, and, even better, to explain the defense he had so carefully constructed.

He had been the only person who had ever talked to Corona about the killings. Juan had refused to talk to the sheriff or his deputies when he was arrested and, after Hawk took over the defense, the attorney had made sure that his client said nothing. Except for the interview with the press, when Corona denied the murders, there had been no statements of any kind from the defendant.

It was the toughest kind of case for the prosecution. No confession, no eye witnesses to the actual murders, no motive that could reasonably implicate Juan; and, on the other side of the coin, lots of room to plant that all-important reasonable doubt in the minds of the jurors.

In Hawk's opinion, there *was* a motive but it was one that would shift the blame to somebody else—namely Natividad. Williams, in his opening statement, had talked about the homosexual aspect, pointing to the partially unclothed victims and to the exposure of the sexual organs of others. Whereas Williams had been unable even to hint that the prosecution was going to prove that Corona was a homosexual, Hawk, if given the chance, was actually going to name Natividad as one. Then by proving that Juan was not sexually abnormal, he was going to show that his client couldn't possibly have killed the victims. At the same time, if he could, he was going to conclusively prove that Natividad was the murderer.

Hawk had spent a lot of time talking to experts on blood, on handwriting, on homosexuality, and on ballistics. He intended to use the knowledge he had gained to challenge the prosecution experts. His defense was going to consist principally of two tactics that had worked well in the past.

First, he was going to insert as much confusion into the hearing as was possible in the hope that the uproar would prevent the jury from concentrating on any facts the prosecution might produce during testimony.

Secondly, he would employ a strategy that had been used for many years by attorneys who were called upon to defend unpopular causes. In lieu of a valid, logical defense, he would attack the police, thus making law enforcement the real villains in the action.

He had carefully laid his groundwork for his stratagem in his daily meetings with the press. Although the judge had been very explicit in his instructions to the jurors not to read, listen to, or watch TV reports of the trial, Hawk was a realist. He knew human nature and he was absolutely certain that at least some, if not all of the members of the panel would be following the coverage of the case in the seclusion of their own homes. If he could continue to coerce the press into publicizing his out-of-court comments, he might be able to distract them from publishing what they had heard in the courtroom.

After all, by meeting with the newsies at the end of the daily sessions, he would get in the last words of the day, and without being interrupted by shouted objections from his adversaries.

On October 3 the attorneys met in the judge's chambers at the beginning of the day. As had been ordered by Patton, Hawk was to go over his opening statement in order that the judge might rule in advance on the admissibility of his remarks.

Hawk said he intended to inform the jury that Corona himself would present an alibi that would account for all of his time on the day that Kenneth Whitacre was murdered. He would further prove that the murders were committed by a homosexual and that Juan was not one.

He would tell the jury that he could prove that Natividad was not only a homosexual but also that he was the man who killed the farm workers. In order to present that evidence, he said, he would have to discuss the Guadalajara Cafe cutting with the jurors.

Patton ruled that the cafe incident could not be one of the points of the argument despite Hawk's insistence that it was the one sure way of demonstrating Juan's innocence. His argument became so emotional that he suggested at one point that the judge was denying his client a fair trial. The patient Patton bristled at that remark and angrily retorted that he was vitally interested in seeing that Corona received a fair and unbiased hearing.

Williams, who had spent much time during his opening statement informing the jury of the homosexual aspects of the murders, made a right about-face and asked Patton to exclude any reference to abnormal sexual behavior in connection with the crime. The judge brusquely refused and gave Hawk permission to raise the issue both in his opening statement and with whatever evidence he could produce when it came time to put on his defense.

The courtroom was jammed when Hawk began his remarks to the jury. He had promised the press some fireworks and they were there in force to see and listen. His attack on the sheriff and his investigators was both vitriolic and demeaning, but there was also substance to it in some areas.

He spoke contemptuously of a "young, green sheriff" who went into a panic and "snapped an innocent man out of his home at four o'clock in the morning." He also ridiculed the lack of professionalism on the part of the deputies who conducted the searches of the Corona home and labor camp, pointing out that the evidence had been handled practically by everyone on the scene with not a single attempt to lift fingerprints from any of it.

He talked of the tire tracks that didn't match and of the mix-up in the bodies and the fingerprints of the victims. The sheriff's officers had botched the investigation from its very beginning and had made mistakes at every turn.

He would prove, he said, that the only motive for the murders was the homosexuality of a homicidal maniac, the type that Mexicans referred to as *passivo* homosexual. That description could not fit his client, he said, because Juan, with four children, had a normal sex life at home.

Hawk said that his expert witness would testify that Juan was "hopelessly heterosexual," a phrase that the members of the news media immediately picked up.

In that statement, Hawk was not exactly telling the truth. It was a fact that he had discussed the crime with Dr. Evelyn Hooker, a professor of psychology at the University of California Los Angeles Medical School. Dr. Hooker had listened to Hawk's descriptions of the murders and activities of both Juan and Natividad and then had told him she thought Natividad was more apt to be the killer than his younger half-brother. During the course of their discussion Dr. Hooker, who was an acknowledged expert on the subject of abnormal sexual behavior, jokingly described herself as being "hopelessly heterosexual." It was a fine, catchy phrase, and Hawk incorporated it in his statement to the jury. The press, in turn, picked it up as a weighty pronouncement and blared to the world that Juan was "hopelessly heterosexual."

Hawk tangled with Patton again before he ended his statement. He wandered too far afield in an attempt to elicit sympathy for his client despite an effort by the judge to restrain him. The result was another trip into the judge's chambers and a five-day sentence for contempt of court.

When the trial resumed, he finished his remarks on a lower key but with one final jab at the sheriff and his men. Emphasizing the fact that no motive had been established, he told the jury,

"I defy you or anybody else to make any sense out of a few fragments of circumstantial evidence without a motive."

Chapter 27

Undersheriff Frank Cartoscelli drew the dubious honor of being the first law enforcement witness in the trial.

He quickly became the target of Hawk's intention to put the police on trial.

As the second ranking officer in the department, he was technically responsible for the activities of the men in the field. He was familiar with all of the gravesites and had been present when all but four of the twenty-five bodies had been retrieved. Of all of the people involved in the discovering and investigation of the murders, Cartoscelli was the most familiar with the actual locations.

Before the body location map was created, Cartoscelli accompanied the civil engineer who was to make the drawing on a tour of the gravesites. The undersheriff pointed out each location and the engineer measured the distances from specific landmarks. He then drew a preliminary map which was checked by Cartoscelli and Sizelove, both of whom agreed that the sites as shown were correct. The final map, which covered much of one wall of the courtroom, was then constructed.

It would not be possible for the jury to travel to the orchards and the riverbank for a personal look because most of the gravesites had been eradicated. Disking, irrigating, plowing, and other farming operations had caused the holes to be filled in and any telltale marks to be erased.

Cartoscelli himself had written no reports of his activities during the early part of the investigation. As each body was found, the task of recording the time, the place, and the items of evidence fell to Gregory as the recording officer or to other officers if Gregory was not at the particular spot at the time.

It had been Cartoscelli who had straightened out the mix-up in bodies three and four and again when numbers five and six became misnumbered for a time. Under direct examination by Williams he was able to testify as to the grave locations, relying on his memory and on the reports of the officers.

However, under cross-examination by the nimble-witted, sharp-tongued Hawk, Cartoscelli was thrown to the wolves. Using the map with its lighted bulbs, the defense attorney attempted to prove that the locations of the graves were incorrect in several cases.

At one point in his testimony the undersheriff described a road alongside which some of the graves were found as running in a southerly direction. Actually the road ran south for much of its length and then turned to the east toward the river. When Cartoscelli attempted to correct his error, Hawk cut him off abruptly without objection from the prosecution.

Hawk then forced the undersheriff to draw a line from grave to grave according to his first description of the road. The result was that two graves appeared to be located in the river and one on the opposite side in Yuba County. Hawk suggested that if Cartoscelli could not tell south from east he should not take up flying.

While the undersheriff was taking the verbal lacing from Hawk, the prosecutors sat silently at their table. Only rarely did they voice an objection to Hawk's questions, many of which were so blatantly inadmissible that Patton himself complained.

Had Williams and Teja studied the original reports of the officers earlier in the case, they could have saved Cartoscelli and themselves much embarrassment. It was not until Cartoscelli was off the witness stand that the prosecutors discovered a report made by Steve Sizelove on June 5, 1971. The young deputy had submitted a pencil sketch he had made of the exact locations of graves twelve through twenty-five, but the prosecutors didn't discover it until Hawk had had his field day.

It got even worse before Cartoscelli left the witness stand. Hawk, noting that Cartoscelli was one of the officers on the scene when Whitacre's body was found, asked him to describe the activities. The undersheriff reviewed the circumstances as he recalled them and Hawk then asked about the tire track that was located eight feet from the grave, "Those are the ones that didn't match Mr. Corona's vehicle, is that correct?"

Suddenly the bewildered Cartoscelli found himself testifying about tire tracks that he had had no part in examining. While the prosecutors sat mute, the caustic Hawk hammered away at the tire track that didn't match and Cartoscelli was forced to admit that he had been informed that it didn't.

Again it had been the failure of the prosecutors adequately to study the original crime reports that led to a near disaster. Had either Teja or Williams checked the reports that followed the finding of the first body, they would have seen that Cochran had made the tire impression. It would have taken only a simple objection accompanied by the suggestion that the proper witness as to the validity of the tire tracks would be the deputy who made the impression. Once Cochran got to the stand and had he been shown the plaster of paris mold, he would have pointed out immediately that everybody was talking about the wrong exhibit. After all, his name was etched into the impression that was taken near the Whitacre grave and that one definitely was not the one that had been examined by Stottlemyer of the C.I.I.

However, no objection was forthcoming and Cartoscelli was forced to endure several hours of biting, acerbic cross-examination by Hawk. It was not much consolation for Cartoscelli to learn later that Hawk drew jail sentences of two and three days respectively for his harsh treatment. Nor did it help a lot to know that Patton also angrily accused Teja and Williams of failing to protect their own witnesses.

Patton had another reason for being upset with the prosecution. During the chambers session that followed Cartoscelli's second day of testimony, Williams and Teja sheepishly turned over to Hawk the pencil sketch that was made by Sizelove at the gravesites. In addition, they surrendered some supplemental reports by officers and some reports from the C I.I., none of which the defense had seen before.

Teja told the judge that he believed the defense now had

copies of everything in the prosecution files, but Patton wasn't convinced. He cited both prosecutors for contempt of court although only Teja was sentenced to jail for five days.

The trial resumed with Hawk continuing to point out the errors of the sheriff's men, emphasizing the mix-up of the excised fingers of the victims. This time it was Deputy Seth Reynolds' turn on the stand. Reynolds, under direct examination, testified to having delivered six sets of excised fingertips to the C.I.I. in Sacramento very early in the case.

Reynolds braced himself for Hawk's cross-examination, already having heard of Cartoscelli's tribulations. The first question was a request to see Reynolds' report of his trip to Sacramento. The deputy had none.

When asked why he had not written a report, Reynolds harkened back to the day of his trip and told of being ordered to report to Purcell in the field as soon as he returned to Yuba City. He hadn't made a report, he said, because "things were pretty hectic and I just plain forgot. I guess it was stupid."

It was pretty hard for Hawk to argue with that explanation. Therefore, he asked, "Well, did you get a receipt?" Reynolds replied that he had and explained that he had later given the receipt to Purcell, who immediately made copies and sent them on to the district attorney's office.

At that point Hawk acidly informed Patton that he had never been given a copy of the receipt; another case, he said, of the prosecution withholding evidence from him.

Williams rose from his seat and informed Patton that he had never seen such a receipt and had no record of one having been received.

Reynolds was perturbed. He had not only been made to look like an incompetent but a liar as well. He finished his stint as a witness and at the noon recess went directly to the prosecution's temporary office in Fairfield where he found Williams at his desk.

Reynolds said, "I got a receipt for those fingers from the C.I.I. and it was forwarded to the district attorney." Looking down at Williams' desk, Reynolds added, "In fact, here it is right in front of you." Williams glanced at the receipt and then told Reynolds, "I know it."

Even the deputies began to believe that Hawk might be right in his charges that he was being shortchanged.

The defense continued to peck away at the prosecuion witnesses, ridiculing some, lashing out at others, and, in the cases of Purcell and Duncan, handling them with extreme care.

Mason, who was the evidence officer and who also took the photographs, spent some nervous hours on the stand under cross-examination. His failure to label properly some of the pictures taken, particularly those in connection with graves two, three, four, five, and six, was seized upon by Hawk as another example of the delinquencies of the sheriff's department.

Purcell, who had been promoted from sergeant to captain during the time since the case began, was questioned briefly about the finding of Whitacre's body and the taking of the tire impression. The captain had asked Stottlemyer to make the inked impression of the tire on Corona's van and compare them to the tracks found at the gravesite. He was unaware that the wrong comparison had been made. When he received Stottlemyer's report he had concluded that the clue had fizzled.

Duncan, slight, muscular, and with a pair of intense, boring blue eyes, was ready for Hawk when he took the stand, and the defense attorney sensed it. The deputy's answers to questions about the search of the river bottoms were crisp and direct. Hawk was unable to shake him with any of the verbal shots he had fired at other witnesses, and Duncan finished his testimony without incident.

Hawk was so impressed with Duncan that he attempted to hire him as an investigator midway through the trial, but Duncan refused.

Williams and Teja were becoming more and more uncertain as the testimony continued. The People's case, under continuous bombardment by Hawk, appeared to be falling apart. The prosecution's position was not helped by the inability of Williams and Teja to contend with the defense attorney's keen and caustic attack on the credibility of their witnesses.

When it came time for Chain Singh Khera to testify, Teja was fit to be tied. The rancher, who had been so positive in July, 1971, that he had seen Corona near the site of Whitacre's grave within "two or three days" of May 20 when the body was found, now had a lapse of memory.

Khera told the jury that he had met Corona on an access road, the latter driving his van. He said he walked into his orchard with the labor contractor to discuss thinning the trees, and then Corona left.

Teja inadvertently gulped when Khera said the time was "around the first week of May." Under continued questioning by Teja, Khera said it might have been the eleventh or twelfth, or even the fifteenth. "I don't know what date." Teja read the testimony Khera had given the grand jury when he told them it was around the seventeenth or eighteenth and asked if that was what he had said. Khera told Teja that it was and then under cross-examination by Hawk, agreed that his testimony before the judge and jury was also correct. When he left the stand, nobody in the courtroom was sure of when, or even if, Khera had seen Corona on that orchard road.

At the conclusion of the day's testimony, Teja, Williams and some of the officers met in the temporary office to discuss the debacle that had overcome the prosecution. Williams was especially disturbed about the testimony involving the tire tracks at the Whitacre grave and the failure of the plaster of paris impression to match them.

Mason, who was listening to the conversation, told them that the reason was because they had probably compared the wrong exhibits. It wasn't until then that the startled Williams realized that there was another mold, that one still sitting in the sheriff's evidence locker in Yuba City.

Mason was dispatched to Yuba City to pick up the other tracks and return with them to Fairfield. The embarrassed Williams took one look at the writing Cochran had impressed into the plaster of paris and realized for the first time that a king-sized goof had occurred.

Teja wasted no time in ordering Leonard Brunelle to hop an airplane in San Francisco and head for Washington, D. C. with the inked impression of the Corona tire, the mold from Whitacre's grave, and other items of evidence including the six-colored pen, the machete, and the chunk of Whitacre's skull, the pistol along with the bullets found in the van, and the ledger. His instructions were to deliver the material to the ATF laboratories and to get a report on the tire tracks as quickly as possible.

The incident served to further dampen Williams' enthusiasm for his job. It had been more than fourteen months since Williams had been hired to organize the prosecution, and in less than a month Hawk had been able to show the world that there was no organization at all. Even the judge was disgusted with the lack of planning and the obvious disorder of the evidence.

Chapter 28

The crumbling of the case led to a collapse of the alliance between Teja and Williams. The latter had obviously lost confidence in the case and the former had certainly become disenchanted with his special deputy. Teja headed for Yuba City and a meeting with the Sutter County Board of Supervisors He wanted to tell them that he was going to have to hire a new deputy prosecutor in an effort to bail out the sagging prosecution

While Teja was meeting with the supervisors on Monday, Williams went alone into Patton's chambers to meet with the judge and Hawk. There the young attorney was forced to tell the judge about the mix-up in the tire tracks and inform him of Brunelle's trip to Washington with the mold that had been located in Yuba City. Williams told Patton that he had thought the impression that was located in the evidence locker was the one taken by Rodemaker in the river bottom orchard sixteen months before. Actually, Williams had not seen the set in the locker because he had not gone to the sheriff's department to inspect the evidence.

The normally even-tempered Patton was outraged. He became even angrier when Williams confessed to him that he had only then begun to catalogue the evidence that had been in the possession of the sheriff since June of 1971. Patton cited both Teja and Williams for contempt of court.

That was bad enough, but the worst was yet to come. Before the judge and attorneys returned to the presence of the jury, Williams abjectly told the judge that he had a reasonable doubt as to Corona's guilt. Because of the errors that had been made in assembling and studying the evidence, he was led to believe that "there could very well have been somebody else involved in this thing."

Hawk couldn't believe his good fortune. The case had hardly gotten under way and already the prosecution was suggesting that maybe the charge against his client should be dismissed! He could hardly wait to get to the members of the press.

Back in the courtroom Steve Sizelove was called to the stand to testify about the finding of the damaging meat receipts in grave number three. The young deputy explained that he found the receipts, handed them to Cartoscelli, who then handed them to Gregory. There was no attempt made to dust the papers for fingerprints because of fear of damaging the receipts to the point where they could not be used for evidence.

Russell Parmer, head of the fingerprint division of the C.I.I., was called as a prosecution witness to testify that he had attempted to lift fingerprints off a bottle found in one of the graves but was unable to because of the mud. Hawk, who was not interested in the bottle, got Parmer to admit under cross-examination that it might have been possible to take prints from the two meat receipts using special chemicals. He would not, however, say that such a procedure would be certain.

Parmer also testified under cross-examination that he had dusted Corona's vehicles for prints and found none that matched any of those taken from the victims.

Hawk used the testimony to get before the jury the fact that the sheriff's deputies had made no effort to take fingerprints from any of the evidence, particularly the meat receipts. For some reason, Williams did not ask the question that would have brought the response that it had been Teja who had decided against trying for prints for fear of damaging the paper evidence.

At Williams' request, court was adjourned early in order that he could attend a special meeting that was to be held that evening. The purpose was to allow the sheriff, Teja, Williams, and Larry Cilley, the administrative officer of Sutter County to discuss the status of the People's case. Williams wanted to throw in the towel and admit that the evidence was not sufficient to convict Corona.

Teja had already talked to Cilley and the county supervisors about getting a prosecutor to replace Williams. The supervisors, concerned about the rising costs of the case, were reluctant to put any more money into it. However, they were protected to some extent. Months before Assemblyman Ray Johnson had sponsored a bill in the state legislature which would reimburse the county for part of the costs. Under the measure, the state would pay all of the expenses over an amount that would be raised by a tax assessment of five cents per hundred-dollar valuation.

However, the frugal representatives first thought of turning to the company which carried Sutter County's insurance policies. The firm was reminded of the $350 million civil suit that had been filed. If Corona should be found innocent, there was a possibility that he might be able to collect on the lawsuit. With the possibility looming, perhaps the insurance company might want to aid the county by paying the wages of a special prosecutor.

The idea was considered by the company and then dropped.

Hawk met with the press within minutes of the court's adjournment and gleefully let them in on Williams admission. He also let slip the news of the scheduled meeting, and the headlines became live with speculation. Hawk was in his glory. He was dreaming of the biggest victory he had ever experienced, and was thinking of ways to make it happen quicker.

The meeting that night was a stormy one. The sheriff was astounded that Williams would consider dropping the charges against Corona. Whiteaker was absolutely convinced that Corona was guilty. Some of his anguished deputies were close to tears when they learned that the labor contractor might go free. The thoroughly angry Whiteaker assured them "it will never happen."

He would never agree, he said, that there might be another person involved in the slayings.

When the meeting convened, Whiteaker bluntly told Williams that he should be replaced immediately and the subdued special prosecutor meekly agreed. He said he would remain at his post until another attorney could be hired. When Whiteaker relayed the news to his staff everyone was elated.

Teja, too, was against quitting. He realized that he had made a mistake in hiring Williams and he also realized that he himself had not paid the proper attention to the case. However, he wanted to fight it through and let the jury decide.

The solution, as he saw it, was to find a prosecutor who could handle Hawk in the courtroom, somebody who could meet barb with barb and insult with insult.

Cilley, as the chief of the county's government, agreed with Teja. He gave Teja permission to find and hire the man he wanted.

Teja failed to appear for the next day's session, once more leaving Williams alone to face the hectic day ahead. As Williams called his first witness, the brash defense attorney rose and said, "Your honor, in view of Mr. Williams' statement yesterday that he has a reasonable doubt as to Juan Corona's guilt. . ." That was as far as he got. The nettled Patton called both attorneys into his chambers where he sentenced Hawk to five days in jail and fined him $500 for making the remark in front of the jury.

Williams, apparently hoping to salvage something from the rout that he could foresee, demanded the judge declare a mistrial. He pointed out that the members of the jury panel had heard Hawk's comment which he described as "prejudicial."

Hawk on the other hand made a motion that the charges against Corona be dismissed. The prosecution, he said, had no right to insist that his client continue to be held in jail in view of their own statement that they now doubted his guilt.

Williams told the judge that he could not enter into such a dismissal because he did not have the authority. Teja, as district attorney, was the only man who could make such a decision.

Patton refused to consider either Williams's or Hawk's motions. He said, "Just because Mr. Williams may express some reasonable doubt, that doesn't mean the case cannot be proven or otherwise." He said he wanted to hear the rest of the evidence. After all, he pointed out, there were twenty-five murders at issue in the trial and the hearing had really only just begun.

Patton was thoroughly exasperated with the prosecution. He was distrubed by the fact that after sixteen months and more, there was still no continuity to the prosecution's case and the investigation had not been completed.

"I would say at this point it appears that the investigation was inept, the preparation inefficient, and the prosecution inadequate," the irritated jurist snapped.

Williams continued the day's session much like a man in a dream. He allowed Hawk to wander so far from the points at issue in questioning beleaguered witnesses that Patton was forced to interpose objections on his own. The judge scolded Williams for not maintaining control of his case, but it was no use. The special prosecutor was a worried, uncertain man.

Hawk, high-spirited and smelling victory with every passing minute, continued to peck away at the mistakes he was discovering as the witnesses testified. Gregory, the recording officer at the gravesites, spent a worrisome hour on the stand while the defense attorney pointed out typographical errors in reports, lack of proper measurements between the graves, and similar mistakes. His penetrating cross-examination was impressive to the news media, and he was convinced that it was having a lasting effect on the jury.

He couldn't wait for the end of the day to let the media people in on another scoop. He had asked Patton to fix bail for Corona.

After all, he pointed out, the prosecution had admitted that they could not convict his client so why continue to hold him in jail? The fact that the judge had refused the bail request didn't dampen Hawk's enthusiasm. The way things were going, it was only a matter of a day or two until the judge came around.

That afternoon in chambers he renewed his request for bail and Patton said he would consider it. He told Hawk and Williams that he would wait until the next morning and then set a date for a bail hearing.

That in itself was another win for the defense. Nobody had ever heard of such a hearing being scheduled during the course of a murder trial.

By the time the day's session was over the afternoon papers were on the streets and Hawk never looked better. According to the press, the People's case was collapsing and a deal was even then in the works. In return for a promise to drop the civil suit against Sutter County, the charges against Corona would be dropped. It wasn't really true, but it made interesting reading.

In response to a call that something big was about to break in the most sensational trial of the day, Jerry Cohen, the Los Angeles *Times* reporter who had interviewed Corona in his cell those many months ago, arrived in Fairfield.

Hawk wanted to make certain that the prosecution's predicament was properly broadcast in the hope that members of the jury might see it or read about it in their homes. He therefore invited another contempt citation by releasing to Cohen a transcript of the in-chambers session wherein Williams had admitted his doubts. Included in the transcript were the scathing comments of the judge about the shortcomings of the investigators and the prosecution.

The headline writers called for the big type. Newspapers all over the nation shouted the news that the trial was all but over. Television and radio commentators held a like view. It was a foregone conclusion that Juan Corona was going to be a free man just as soon as the formalities could be taken care of.

If there had been any lingering doubts in the minds of the press up to that time, Hawk's release of the transcript had erased them. In the minds of most of the newspeople Corona's innocence had been established.

Only Eric Grunder, reporter for the Marysville *Appeal-Democrat*, failed to succumb to Hawk's blandishments. While most of the newspeople were listening to the very loquacious defense attorney, young Grunder was listening to the evidence as it was presented to the jury. As a result, when the trial ended, Grunder was the least surprised of all at the verdict.

Chapter 29

Teja, however, was not about to quit. He had looked around the area and had found a man to assist in the prosecution. In neighboring Sonoma County he had located Ron Fahey, chief prosecutor for the Sonoma County district attorney, who had agreed to take the job. Fahey was an experienced lawyer, forty years old with nine years of trial experience behind him. He had a wife and three children, and the $10,000 contract from Sutter County was just what the family needed for those extras that his salary didn't allow for. The district attorney of Sonoma County gave him a five-month leave of absence and Fahey headed for Fairfield. He had a lot of studying to do before he was ready to enter the arena against Hawk.

It had been decided that rather than have Williams leave the case and cause the jury to wonder, it would be better to have him stay on until the end. However, his part in the action would be almost that of a spectator rather than a participant.

Williams was alone again when the trial resumed. Teja was busy briefing Fahey and preparing for the appearances of the expert witnesses who were yet to testify.

The trial settled down to testimony surrounding the finding of the bodies one by one. As the deputies were called by Williams to detail their activities, Hawk used his chances for cross-examination to belittle each of the law enforcement witnesses in turn. There had been many mistakes made along the way, mistakes that had little to do with the eventual outcome, as it turned out, but Hawk was turning them into major blunders in the eyes of the press.

He struck hardest at the testimony of the deputies who had exhumed the body of Maczak in grave number twenty-five. The evidence found there was more damaging to the defense than that found in any of the other graves except that of Samples which was number three.

The diggers had found the two bank deposit slips bearing Corona's name as well as the broken religious candle holder and other household rubbish.

Purcell testified that Perales had taken the deposit slips to his Sacramento office in December, 1971, in an attempt to find fingerprints on them. Under cross-examination Purcell was unable to tell whether any other attempts to lift prints had been made. Purcell was wary and nervous, although he did not show it to Hawk. Therefore, the defense attorney's cross-examination was brief and he made little attempt to shake the captain's testimony.

He had already, without any serious objections from Williams, managed to embarrass most of the witnesses in one way or another.

When Wilbur Terry showed up in court to testify about his part in finding the bodies, he had with him several reports that Hawk claimed he had never seen before. The defense attorney demanded a session in chambers.

Patton had been faced with the same situation so many times in the trial that he finally lost his patience. There had been practically no communication with the sheriff by the district attorney's staff, and the judge was aware of it. He pointed out to Williams that it was the responsibility of the prosecution to work closely with the sheriff in keeping track of the evidence and added that the present situation was ridiculous, even "outrageous."

When Williams admitted that there apparently were reports in the sheriff's possession that the prosecutors didn't even know existed, Patton ordered the complete files in the sheriff's hands be hauled into court for Hawk's inspection. He recessed the trial to give the defense time to complete the survey, and Hawk went to work.

It took three days, and at the end of that time Hawk informed the judge that he had discovered more than 1,600 items in the files that he had never seen before. Much of the material was worthless to either side, but the discovery made good stuff for Hawk to use as he talked to the members of the press. It was useless for Williams to argue that most of the reports had already been turned over to the defense because there were no receipts to show for it.

Before the judge and the attorneys left Patton's chambers, a hearing on the issue of bail for Corona was scheduled for October 20.

The hearing took place on a Friday afternoon with the courtroom jammed and the jury absent. The press was there in force, as was the Corona family and several spectators who were clearly on the side of the defendant. A super-confident Hawk opened the proceedings.

He accused the district attorney of outright dishonesty in his original presentation to the grand jury in July of 1971 and pointed to the continual withholding of evidence from the defense as a further example of Teja's unwillingness to be fair. Hawk referred to the confusion in the numbering of the bodies, the tire tracks that didn't match, and a lack of any other evidence that would indicate guilt.

He also reminded the judge of Williams' declaration of his own doubt as to Corona's guilt and added that Corona had been held in jail for seventeen months "based upon what I consider to be the poorest investigation I have ever heard of."

He ended his argument by calling for Corona's release on bail "in the name of human decency."

Teja argued that the People had not yet presented the evidence which he believed would be sufficiently conclusive to warrant a conviction. He asserted also that a release on bail in the middle of a trial would constitute an outright invitation for the jury to bring in a verdict of innocent without paying any further attention to the evidence.

He agreed that there had been inconsistencies in the testimony already heard but added that the trial was actually only in the preliminary stage. Regardless of Williams' expression of doubt, he said, he himself had never wavered in his opinion that Juan Corona was guilty.

Williams, also given a chance to argue the motion, told the judge that his opinion had again changed and that he was again confident that Corona was guilty. He also revealed that a preliminary report from the ATF laboratories had indicated that the tire impression now appeared to match the tire from the Corona van. Testimony on that point would be forthcoming, he said.

Williams said, "I think the People's case would be extremely prejudiced by granting bail."

Judge Patton had a hard decision to make, and he had spent

several days researching the law. He resented the pressure that had been placed on him by the failure of the prosecution to adequately organize and present its case. He was also upset by Hawk's antics, and his complete disregard for the rules of the court. A judge with less fortitude would have lost control of the case long before the bail question arose.

However, now that he was faced with one of the knottiest legal problems of his career, Patton was able to make his decision without hesitation.

He first took the prosecution to task for having allowed the trial to become so confused and said the case "almost approaches dereliction of duty."

Then he denied bail.

The courtroom erupted in shouts of despair from the Corona family. A man shouted, "You are no judge! There is no justice here!" Two women stood and shrieked at the judge before they were removed from the courtroom by bailiffs. One of Corona's sisters collapsed and was taken by ambulance to a nearby hospital where she was revived and released.

Patton adjourned the court for the day while the courtroom was cleared. The members of the press, most of whom were now convinced that Corona was innocent, gathered around Hawk. The latter, visibly angry, railed at the injustice of it all and promised that he would see Corona exonerated regardless of the fact that he now realized that he was not only fighting the prosecution but the judge as well.

He was in a bitter, vengeful mood as he entered the courtroom on the following Monday. The defeat he had suffered in the bail hearing was a festering sore. He had also lost face with the Corona family, who had been assured that Juan would be released from jail. If he had been abrasive and intolerable before, he was now obstreperous, quarrelsome, and corrosive to a degree that surprised even his friends in the press row.

Witnesses who were called by Williams to testify to minor facts involving the discovery of the bodies, suddenly found themselves answering questions about totally unrelated matters under cross-examination. Hawk raged about the courtoom virtually unchecked. Williams' objections went almost unnoticed by the furious defense attorney.

Byron Shannon, who had told the grand jury that he saw Corona drive away from Marysville with four of the victims, was the first of the state's important witnesses. He spent several hours on the stand over a period of two days and courtroom observers felt that Hawk made a serious error in his attempt to discredit the black farm labor recruiter.

Shannon was not the fastest thinker in town, and his speech was not only slow but also ungrammatical to the point where it was difficult to understand him at times. He repeated the story he had told the grand jury—that he had seen Riley, Smallwood, and Allen get into a pickup truck driven by Corona at Wino Park in Marysville, and that later he had seen Jackson drive away with Corona. He was shown photos of clothing by Williams and identified the articles as belonging to Jackson. Hawk immediately challenged their introduction as evidence charging that he had never seen them before—another example of evidence being withheld. Williams admitted that the defense attorney had never been given copies of the photos.

During cross-examination, Hawk snapped, snarled, and sneered at Shannon's attempt to make himself understood. He accused the witness of being a convicted criminal, and when Williams objected declared in front of the jury, "He is a thief. He is doing time in jail. I am entitled to show that." When Williams replied that Shannon's crime was a misdemeanor, Patton ruled that Hawk could not refer to it.

As Shannon continued to be cross-examined by Hawk, the latter's questions became more scathing. The witness in turn became more and more confused until he was testifying that it was 1970, a full year before the murders, that he saw Jackson get into Corona's pickup truck. He was almost incoherent by the time Hawk was finished, but had stuck stubbornly to his statement that he had, indeed, seen the four victims with the labor contractor just prior to their disappearance.

Shannon's testimony resulted in another session in the judge's chambers. This time the irritated Patton handed out five-day jail sentences to both Hawk and Williams, Hawk's for referring to Shannon's criminal record and Williams' for failing to deliver the photographs of the victim's clothing to the defense prior to the witness' testimony.

Chapter 30

Ron Fahey actively entered the case on November 3, and Hawk's days of browbeating the prosecution ended. Fahey could be just as nasty as the defense attorney, and he proved it the first morning. The witnesses were all but forgotten as the fascinated jurors watched the two attorneys spar like a pair of banty roosters. With Purcell on the stand to relate again the story of the finding of the deposit slips in grave number twenty-five, Hawk began his cross-examination. When he attempted to ask the captain what Mason, the evidence officer, had done with the deposit slips, Fahey was on his feet to object. The judge upheld the objection and Hawk offered to argue the matter in chambers, "if Mr. Fahey is going to get all excited." Fahey snapped, "If counsel wants to testify I would ask that he be sworn in if he feels he has any evidence that should come before the jury." The judge suggested that they refrain from personalities, but the sniping continued until Patton called both attorneys into his chambers to insist that they maintain decorum in his court.

The trial dragged on through the first week in November as witnesses were called one after the other to describe the search of Corona's home and labor camp on the morning when he was arrested. Littlejohn told of serving the search warrant on Corona at his home and the officers who were with him at the time testified as to the search that followed. They described finding of the items of evidence that were taken and the bloodstains that were found in the van and the Impala. Those officers who had searched the mess hall and the contractor's desk in the building at the labor camp also described what they had done and what they had found.

The testimony was needed to lay the groundwork for the expert witnesses who were yet to be called. Hawk doggedly interrogated each in turn in an effort to remind the jury of the mistakes that had been made by the officers in failing to look for fingerprints, failing to write detailed reports, and failing to properly catalog the evidence. By this time the officers had grown wary of the defense lawyer's biting techniques and were harder to trap.

Too, whereas before the prosecution had never spoken to any of the witnesses before they took the stand, they were now briefing the officers before they were called. The line of communication that had never existed before had finally been established and was functioning.

The prosecution continued to tie up the loose ends of the evidence by calling witnesses who added a piece here and a piece there to the chain of circumstantial evidence.

James Pervis told the jury what he had told the grand jury the year before. On April 10, 1971, Corona had asked him if he would like to perform a few hours work as a handyman around the labor camp, but he had refused, he said. In reply to a specific question, he said he had observed Corona picking up casual laborers in Marysville's skid-row section prior to that time—mostly Mexican workers, he said, but occasionally a white man.

Hawk tried to discredit Pervis by bringing out the fact that he could not positively identify the color of the vehicle Corona was driving, but Pervis explained that away saying that he was color blind.

The jury had to be reshuffled the last week in November when Bill Hicks, the Vietnam veteran, suffered a broken arm in a motorcycle accident. Richard Bremen, the young Vallejo welder who was the first of the four alternates chosen, was placed in the box to take Hicks' place when Patton learned that Hicks would have to remain in the hospital for several days and then be confined at home at least two weeks.

Teja, who had regained much of his confidence, resumed his questioning of key witnesses. Mr. and Mrs. David Schmidl, who had seen Corona in the river bottoms before the bodies were found, repeated their grand jury testimony as did farm workers Joseph Breceda and Ernesto Garcia, both of whom had seen the labor contractor on an orchard road in January, 1971.

Breceda related that he had not told his foreman, Ray Duron, of the incident until after Corona's arrest at which time he and Garcia were told to search a section of the orchard near the road for indentations in the earth. They had found such an indentation and a body had been dug up there later.

Jose Ramirez testified as to having seen Corona's vehicle parked near where body number twenty-four was found later and also recalled having seen the suspect in another section of the orchard late one night.

Hawk tried desperately to break the stories, but the best he could do was to get the witness to testify that Corona was not acting strangely on any of the occasions.

James Cummings, the ranch carpenter, testified that he had seen the blue van backed up near the levee on May 17, 1971. He also testified that Corona had driven the blue van in the past, although the vehicle belonged to Juan's brother, Pedro. Corona, Cummings testified, was often seen in the orchard areas early in the morning prior to 6 A.M.

Hawk chipped away at the testimony of each witness, finding minor discrepancies in each case, but was unable to uncover any major errors that would serve to impeach the witnesses.

His big chance came, he thought, when Mrs. Sarah Vallejo was called to the witness stand. Mrs. Vallejo, the occupant of the home Corona owned in Live Oak, was called to verify the authenticity of a rent receipt which had been written for her by Corona in May 1971. Speaking through an interpreter, Mrs. Vallejo identified the receipt which was written in brown ink as the one her landlord had given her.

Hawk asked for and was given permission to make Mrs. Vallejo a defense witness so she wouldn't have to be recalled later in the trial. It was important to Hawk because Mrs. Vallejo was the ironclad alibi that he had promised to produce.

In a jail conversation months previously, Corona had explained to his lawyer that on May 19, 1971, the day when Whitacre was killed, he spent most of the day working on the Live Oak house. He had painted the place, he said, and had also replaced a screen door with a new one he had purchased in Yuba City the day before. Hawk had checked with the store where the screen door was bought and found that the purchase had indeed been made on May 18. Corona had also purchased a quantity of house paint previously from the same store.

Mrs. Vallejo had verified Corona's story with a couple of exceptions. First, he hadn't painted the house and, second, she wasn't sure of the day he hung the door. In talking with Hawk, who was a master at getting his own point across, she had said it was the nineteenth. Now she was in court to provide the alibi that Hawk had been talking about for months.

Whiteaker, too, had heard about Mrs. Vallejo's story and he had sent deputies to talk to her. The sheriff had formed his own opinion of what happened and when at the Vallejo home.

Mrs. Vallejo, under questioning by Hawk, testified that Corona and his wife had arrived at her home on a morning shortly after she had paid the rent. Juan had worked on the door for a time during the morning, and then the Coronas had left for a time. Juan and Gloria came back shortly after noon and he had worked until about 3:30 P.M. before the door was fixed. At no time during the day did she ever see him out of the company of Gloria, the witness said. Neither did he leave the house without Gloria going with him.

Hawk figured that it would have been impossible for Corona to leave Live Oak at 3:30, drive to Yuba City and drop Gloria off, then pick Whitacre up, murder him, and bury him, all in the space of 2½ hours before Kagehiro found the filled-in grave at 6 P.M.

Williams took over the questioning and asked Mrs. Vallejo how she could be sure that the screen door was hung on the nineteenth. She replied that she was not certain whether it was the nineteenth or the twentieth, and she was also vague as to the time of day. The court adjourned for the day at that point and she was told to return the next morning.

Williams had had time to go over the reports of Duncan and Fred Smith, each of whom had talked to Mrs. Vallejo on separate occasions.

Duncan, a former orchardist himself, reasoned that Corona could not have been at the Vallejo house on the morning of the nineteenth because at that time he had a crew thinning Kagahiro's peach trees. Even if he had only put the men to work and then left, he would still have had to return to pay them off when the job ended at noon. In talking to Mrs. Vallejo, Duncan, who understood Spanish, became convinced that Corona would have had to hang the new door on the twentieth.

He also learned that Corona did no painting at all. He had purchased the paint for Mr. Vallejo, who was to do the painting himself.

Fred Smith had visited Mrs. Vallejo with Mrs. Terry Arechar, a Sutter County sheriff's matron, who served as interpreter. Both Smith and Mrs. Arechar, called to testify, said Mrs. Vallejo had told them that the Coronas had left the house in the morning and had not returned until 3:30 or 4 o'clock in the afternoon to finish hanging the door.

Hawk was unable to shake the stories of Smith and Mrs. Arechar, nor was he able to improve on Mrs. Vallejo's memory as to the exact date or time when the work was done.

The alibi was an uncertain one at best.

For the next four days the trial was immersed in the medical testimony by the doctors who had examined the bodies. The doctors testified one by one that the wounds on the victim's heads could have been caused by a machete, but none could say that was definitely the case. The prosecution was attempting to prove that the machete found in Corona's van could have been one of the murder weapons, while Hawk was just as determined to show that any instrument with a heavy blade could have been used.

During his cross-examination, Hawk kept referring to the numbers that were given the bodies as a means of reminding the jury of the mix-ups that had occurred. He was successful despite objections by the prosecution.

The most critical phase of the medical testimony involved the body of Melford Sample, in whose grave the meat receipts were found. Although Hawk tried to establish that the body was buried before the meat receipts were issued, he was unsuccessful. Each doctor questioned said the body had been in the ground anywhere from two days to a few weeks. All agreed that the estimate of a "few days" would be closer to the truth. They agreed also that trying to fix the time of death when a body had been buried and then exhumed was at best "an educated guess."

The most puzzling factor that Hawk developed during his cross-examination of the physicians was the lack of large amounts of blood found near the gravesites. Had the men been killed at those spots, the doctors insisted, the type of wounds inflicted would have caused large amounts of blood. No substantial amounts had ever been found in any one place, leading to speculation that the men had been killed some place else.

However, despite an intensive search that extended into every corner of the county and reached into Yuba County as well, no evidence of a "slaughterhouse" as was suggested in many of the early news stories was ever found.

Along with a lack of motive, it remained among the curious unanswered questions that have continued to surround the "crime of the century."

Chapter 31

No sooner had the last of the doctors testified than the Guadalajara Cafe cutting once more became a cause for new argument in the trial.

Perales, who had been working in the Mexican community and sticking close to Jose Raya for the past several months, had finally made some headway. The Sacramento detective informed Teja that Raya had changed his story and was willing now to say that Juan Corona was the man who cut him. The break came,

Perales said, when Mrs. Paula Raynosa, sister-in-law of Ray Duron, reported that she heard Raya say, when he was released from the hospital, "Juan assaulted me." Perales said he talked to Raya about Mrs. Raynosa's remark and Raya admitted that his story of Natividad doing the cutting was untrue. According to Perales, Raya said, "I wanted to seek my own vengeance against Corona, and that is why I have been giving law enforcement the runaround." Raya was also said to have told Perales, "If Juan gets out of jail, one of us will be dead in a week."

With Perales' report in hand, Teja and Williams asked for a session in the judge's chambers. There they asked Patton to allow them to introduce the Guadalajara Cafe incident into the trial. With the information they now had, along with Raya willing to testify that Juan had cut him, they wanted to use it to show "a common scheme or plan."

Their idea was to show the jury that Juan had inflicted on Raya the same type of wounds that were inflicted on twenty-four of the twenty-five victims. Thus, they reasoned, the jury would have to come to the conclusion that Corona was a slayer. They would also point out that Juan was named in Raya's original civil suit, and although he did not actually become a defendant, Raya had a valid reason for naming him.

Hawk strenuously opposed the move by the prosecution. He reminded the judge that when he wanted to interject the cafe cutting in order to incriminate Natividad in the murders, the prosecution's objections had stopped him. At that time, he told the judge, they had admitted that they had been unable to tie Corona to the Raya cutting.

Williams replied that the new evidence, together with the fact that Raya's name was the first one listed in the ledger, would identify Corona not only as the Raya assailant, but also as the murderer of the twenty-five farm workers. There was also the fact that Corona had offered Raya work on the Sullivan ranch.

Patton agreed to take the matter under submission and instructed the attorneys to submit briefs to back up their oral arguments. Eventually, Patton ruled that the Guadalajara Cafe incident itself would not be admitted. However, he ruled that Raya could be called as a witness by the prosecution to testify that he and his friend, Nick Ramirez, had been offered work by Corona.

While Raya was not able to accuse Juan in front of a jury, he eventually got his new story out to the public. It was only a short time later that a nationally distributed newspaper came out with a story supposedly authored by him.

The title was, "I Survived a Machete Attack by the Man Who Killed 25 Farm Workers."

The press was kept abreast of what went on in the sessions in the judge's chambers by the accommodating defense counsel. They were aware of the fact that Raya wanted to change his story and that the prosecution now wanted to reopen the cafe incident. They were also reminded constantly of the contradictions in the testimony by the People's witnesses. In his daily sessions with them, Hawk was willing and even anxious to explain any technical points that might have cone up in the courtroom and which had not been fully understood by the media.

As the trial proceeded past the middle of November, the prosecution began to call its expert witnesses to the stand. The climactic sessions lay just ahead.

Don Stottlemyer, the C.I.I. criminalist who had examined most of the evidence, was going to testify about a variety of things.

As an expert laboratory technician, Stottlemyer had spent several months trying to group and type blood specimens taken from Corona's vehicles, the two knives, the pistol, and the stained clothing, all obtained from the Corona home or the labor camp.

He had found human bloodstains in the van and the Impala, on the sleeve of the denim jacket, on a pair of rubber boots found in the van, on a pair of shorts, and on both knives and the pistol. Because of the age of the stains and the fact that they were contaminated, he was unable to type the blood, he said.

As for the bullet taken from Kamp's skull, it was not possible to say that it had been fired from Corona's pistol because the grooves normally used by ballistics' experts for comparisons were gone. The decomposition of the body had created chemicals which had erased the marks, Stottlemyer testified.

The markings on the blade of the machete did not match the markings on the section of Whitacre's skull, therefore it could not be assumed that it was the murder weapon.

Hawk scored heavily during his cross-examination. Harking back to the conversations that he had held with Corona in the jail, he presented an explanation that Stottlemyer couldn't argue with.

Hawk had early been concerned about the bloodstains in the van and the automobile. Corona had explained the stains in the van by relating how one of his workers, Carlos Leone Sierra, had fallen from a tree on May 12, 1971, and had cut his head. Corona had hauled him to the doctor in the van for treatment. The records of Dr. Vasquez confirmed that Sierra had been treated for a head laceration on that date.

As for the bloodstains on the floor mats and the headband found in the trunk of the Impala, Corona had explained that his daughter, Yolanda, had frequent nosebleeds and no doubt that was where the blood came from. The stained mats had been tossed into the trunk for later washing.

Stottlemyer agreed in his answers that the stains would be consistent with those explanations. He couldn't do otherwise in view of his admission that he had found it impossible to type the blood.

Stottlemyer had not been much help to the prosecution but he hadn't hurt them either—up to that point.

Dr. Guy had flown up from Texas to give her opinions about the bloodstains and to explain her somewhat revolutionary method of typing blood.

Hawk was given the opportunity to question her as to her qualifications, and he spent a great deal of time on it. That Dr. Guy was qualified as an expert, there was no doubt. She presented an impressive list of qualifications that the defense could not find fault with, but he did question her methods. As his interrogation continued, it became apparent that Hawk had done his homework.

In an effort to destroy the witness' creditability, Hawk led her into a long, technical discussion of various blood types other than the usual A, O, B, end AB types that are so common. He asked her to explain why she did not "isoenzyme-type" the bloodstains that she worked with, and she replied that the samples were not adequate for that kind of test. There were many more technical questions, some of them ranging far away from the subject at hand and only a few of them of interest to the spectators until, finally, Dr. Guy was allowed to respond to queries from Williams.

She testified that by using a technique known to only half a dozen blood experts in the world, she was able to type the blood of each of the victims. She was also able, she said, to type the blood samples supplied her from the Corona vehicles, the weapons, and the various items of clothing.

She found, she said, four different types of human blood in the Impala and three distinct types in the van.

That meant seven different people had left bloodstains in the two vehicles. Even if the daughter's nosebleeds and the injured Carlos Leone Sierra's head laceration were included as sources, that still left five humans to be accounted for.

It was damning testimony, and Hawk should have been worried, but he continued to exude an air of supreme confidence. He seemed not the least concerned about Dr. Guy's shattering testimony. He acted like a man who had an ace up his sleeve, as indeed he did have.

Hawk had to challenge Dr. Guy's testimony if he hoped to save his case. He felt that he was far ahead of the opposition, and there were others who agreed with him. Jerry Cohen had returned to Los Angeles where he wrote a story for the *Times* in which he expressed the opinion that the best the prosecution could hope for was a hung jury. He also speculated that at least eight of the jurors were ready to acquit Corona if a vote were to be taken now.

Dr. Guy's testimony had tended to dampen the optimism of the Corona supporters, and it was going to take a real blockbuster to overcome it.

It appeared from an unexpected quarter. Stottlemyer had

appeared in court the day after Dr. Guy completed her direct testimony. He was there merely as one of the several witnesses who were going to establish a chain-of-possession by those who had handled some of the physical evidence. While he was on the stand, Hawk seized the chance to bring up Dr. Guy's testimony of the day before. Stottlemyer had watched her experiment in the jury room in Yuba City early in the year and had formed an opinion as to their validity.

In short, he told Hawk that Dr. Guy didn't know what she was talking about. He didn't frame his opinion in language that crude, but he got his point across nevertheless.

After a few preliminary questions, Hawk asked Stottlemyer if he wanted to make any observations about Dr. Guy's method of typing blood. The state's criminalist was more than willing. In his opinion, Dr. Guy's technique "would lead to inadequate results." He asserted that she had improperly handled the testing equipment and she based her conclusions on factors that were completely new to him. Stottlemyer didn't stop there. He also took a jab at the district attorney.

He said he had waited six months before receiving any request from Teja to make tests on the blood samples. "I believe the district attorney was interested in whether or not the material on the various items was blood, and if it was human blood, and that was important to him at the time. I asked him how about grouping of the stains and I got the indication that that wasn't important at the time."

Although he had been called by the prosecution, Stottlemyer had become the defense's best witness to date. Fahey was livid. Angrily he told Patton in chambers, "I hope it is the first and last time I ever see a criminalist who is supposed to be testifying for law enforcement walk into court apparently prepared to testify for the defense, and how that was arranged I don't know, but I have my own opinion."

Hawk vigorously denied that he had ever talked to Stottlemyer prior to his appearance on the stand, but Fahey remained unconvinced.

A telephone call brought Dr. Guy back from Texas and,

when she arrived, she was given a copy of Stottlemyer's testimony to read. Hawk complained bitterly that that was in violation of the court's gag order which, he claimed, did not allow witnesses to read the testimony of those who preceded them to the stand. He demanded that all of Dr. Guy's testimony be stricken from the record, but Patton, after considering the request, denied it.

Dr. Guy returned to the stand and said that Stottlemyer had based his opinion of her methods on the basis of the test she had made in the jury room many months before. She explained that that test had been made under adverse conditions and that none of the results of that experiment entered into her final tests which were made in her Texas laboratory. She reiterated her previous findings of seven distinct types of human blood found in the two Corona vehicles.

She explained that it had not been possible to use a typing method that would trace specific bloodstains to specific people because she had gotten into the case too late. Had she been called within the first two weeks, she said, she might have been able to be even more specific in her tests.

Strangely, the testimony of the seven different blood types failed to create any interest in the news media. It could have been because Hawk, in his daily meeting with the press, belittled the doctor's testimony and bragged instead about the sharp cross-examination that all but destroyed its worth.

The mixed-up tire tracks were another matter altogether. It was a confusing situation that had to be straightened out, and Fahey undertook to do it.

His first move was to call Jacob Compton back to the witness stand. Compton, the Department of Water Resources engineer, had been driving a pickup truck when his crew was surveying the riverbanks on the Sullivan ranch in the spring of 1971. It was a tire track from that pickup that Rodemaker had made an impression of when the nineteenth and twentieth bodies were found. The comparison of the tire and the mold had finally been made after Stottlemyer had declared that the impression did not match the tire on the Corona van.

Fahey next called Harold Cochran to identify the plaster of paris mold he had made at Whitacre's grave. That was the exhibit that had been mislaid for almost seventeen months. He explained how he had picked the clearest part of the tire track to cast the impression from and pointed to his signature on the exhibit.

That brought Roland Wilder to the witness stand. Wilder was a technician for the ATF laboratories and had examined the tire mold and the inked impression that Brunelle had delivered to Washington during the first month of the trial.

He told Fahey that in his opinion the impressions were very similar to the tire on the Corona vehicle. He had checked the inked impression against the plaster of paris mold first, he said, and then had checked both against the same brand of tire that had been on the Corona van when it was purchased only a short time before the murders were discovered.

Hawk complained to the judge that Wilder's report had been withheld from him until that very day, but he elected to proceed with his cross-examination rather than seek a delay while he studied Wilder's conclusions.

The defense attorney tried to pick Wilder's testimony apart but had very little success. He did, however, force the expert witness to admit that he had checked only one source of tires in reaching his decision. He also admitted that many other tire companies sold tires of similar size and design. He also admitted to Hawk that somewhere in the world there might be other tires that might have made the same track.

The winter rains had come to California's great valley, and with them chill, dank temperatures. The skies were continually overcast and the roadside ditches flowed full. Inside the big, white courthouse, the lights were turned on early in the day and the spectators left small puddles behind them as they filed into the courtroom. The small cafeteria in the basement was filled each recess by people who would normally have walked outside in better weather for a bit of fresh air.

Thanksgiving had come and gone and the Christmas shopping season was well under way in the town. Late in the day the multicolored holiday lights could be seen gleaming dimly through the fog that rolled in from the nearby bay.

There was no Christmas spirit in the courtroom, though. The atmosphere was grim and heavy with tension. The long trial was about to reach a climax, and everybody sensed it. Hawk outwardly maintained his air of effervescent confidence. Williams was ostensibly worried and subdued while Teja was somber and intense. On the prosecution team only Fahey seemed to be calm and composed.

Charles Michael Hoffman was another of the ATF criminalists who had been assigned to the Yuba City murders by his superiors. Hoffman was a forensic chemist, and his specialty was neutron activation analysis, which was a new wrinkle in crime detection. It was a sophisticated way of weighing the elements in such items as bullets as a means of establishing comparisons.

Hoffman had been given the nine-millimeter bullet that was found in Kamp's skull and two of the bullets from the partial box of ammunition found in Corona's desk at the labor camp.

Hoffman testified that there was no significant difference in the composition of the bullets when they were tested by the neutron method. He also said there was a possibility that the bullet taken from Kamp came from the same batch of Remington ammunition as the unfired bullets. While he couldn't state precisely that they were from the same box of cartridges, he had to believe that it was possible.

Hoffman had also analyzed hair that was taken from each of the victims and compared it to that which was found in the vehicles and on the posthole digger. It was also compared to hair taken from Corona by court order earlier in the month.

Using the neutron activation analysis Hoffman determined that none of the hair found on the victims' clothing matched Corona's. However, he found some similarity when he matched with hairs taken from the automobile to the hair of six of the murdered men. Also, hairs found on the posthole digger were similar to hair from the heads of several of the victims.

Hoffman testified that the hairs found on the posthole digger were human and had actively growing follicles, indicating that they had been forcibly removed.

Fahey asked if the person had been living when the hairs were removed and Hoffman replied, "Well, either living or it was removed before the tissue had decomposed to any extent. It could be a dead person as well."

Hoffman admittedly had difficulty with his hair analysis because the samples had been poorly handled by the investigators who found them in the vehicles and on the clothing.

Hawk took full advantage of the uncertainties that Hoffman expressed to minimize the importance of the hair. He was able to cast doubt on the importance of the testimony when Hoffman admitted that there was no absolute connection between Corona and the victims established by the hair samples.

The handwriting experts, Pascoe, Harris, and Goldblatt, had all studied the "death list" and all had compared the writing in it to the exemplars and other samples of Corona's handwriting. Now, with the trial approaching its fourth month, they were prepared to express their opinions to the jury.

Chapter 32

Hawk had prepared for the handwriting phase of the case by having specimens of Natividad's writing compared to that in the ledger by a member of the criminology faculty at the University of California at Berkeley. While the professor was not a handwriting expert, he agreed with Hawk that there was some similarity.

In addition, Hawk had his leak in the C.I.I. to fall back on for some information that was not included in any of the written reports.

On December 4 the ledger and its contents became the focal point of the trial. It was one of the more tangible pieces of evidence the prosecution had, and it was going to be important to tie the writing to the defendant to the satisfaction of the jury.

Pascoe, the C.I.I. expert, was the first witness called to the stand. He had first been handed the three pages of the ledger on which the incriminating names of the victims had been found on

July 1, 1971. In the seventeen months since that time he had not been able to make up his mind as to whether or not Corona had done all the writing.

Questioned by Teja he could only say that he found some of the writing "within the range" of the defendant, based on samples and on the exemplars he had been given to study. However, there were also some letters and combinations of letters that he said could have been written by some other writer.

There were still other letters that he could not make any decision on. He said, "I don't know whether this author produced them. I think they were well within the range of this writer, he could produce them. But I was unable to locate areas which would conclusively resolve these difficulties in my mind."

He didn't say yes, and he didn't say no. The best opinion he could give was a weak "Maybe."

On cross-examination by Hawk, Pascoe was of even less help to the prosecution. The wily Hawk, having apparently been tipped off in advance to Pascoe's uncertainties, first got Pascoe to admit that as late as December, 1971, he had told both Whiteaker and Williams that he could not identify the handwriting in the ledger as Corona's. He then produced a report written by the expert in April, 1972, in which he wrote that it would not be possible to say that all of the writing was by one person.

Hawk then threw his best punch of the day. He got Pascoe, the state's questioned-documents examiner, to testify that he had told the Sutter County officials, in effect, that if they thought the writing in the ledger was Corona's, they were in trouble.

Like Stottlemyer and Merrill before him, Pascoe had become a witness for the defense.

Next up was Harris, the Los Angeles expert who had learned his trade from his father. Harris had gone on his own in 1948 and had had extensive experience in several hundred criminal cases.

Harris was firm and concise in his answers and left no doubt that his opinion could not be easily shaken. He had examined the original samples of Corona's handwriting and, in comparing them with the writing in the ledger, had formed an opinion that the same person had done all of the writing. Having been handed the exemplars that were taken by court order on September 5, 1972, he was even more firm in his judgment.

Hawk's attempt to discredit Harris was intense and persistent. The best he could accomplish was to get Harris to admit that he could not evaluate some of the scribbling or "squiggles" that he found on the pages. Harris explained that such marks could not be considered handwriting and therefore he was unable to analyze them.

Hawk went over the ledger sheets line by line in trying to break through Harris' calm recitation of his opinions but failed. Harris tenaciously stuck to his personal judgment that the handwriting in the ledger and that on the samples and the exemplars were produced by one and the same person.

Sidney Goldblatt had flown out from New York to testify for the prosecution. It had been tough to get him to agree. He had been asked by Gregory when the deputy first visited the ATF laboratories with some of the evidence. At that time Gregory discussed the ledger with him and Goldblatt had examined it and had given a horseback opinion that the handwriting appeared to be that of one man. However, the expert said, since the sheriff had already contacted the C.I.I., he would not want to become involved. It was his department's policy, he said, not to become a part of any action in which another government agency was taking part. In that way, he said, there was no danger of becoming involved in a conflict of interest.

When the C.I.I. experts began to waver in their assessments of the handwriting, it became apparent that more expert help was going to be needed. Goldblatt finally agreed to join the prosecution team.

Hawk had also heard of Goldblatt, and he wanted desperately to prevent him from testifying, if possible. The stocky New Yorker was known to be a hard-nosed witness whose reaction to pressure was to apply some of the same himself. Hawk wasn't anticipating a cakewalk if Goldblatt was allowed to become a witness.

The defense attorney therefore entered an objection before Goldblatt was even sworn in. The expert had not filed a written report and intended to testify using only his own notes. Hawk demanded that he be given the notes and time to study them before Goldblatt was allowed to take the stand. He accused the prosecution of again withholding evidence from him.

Patton took the parties into chambers to resolve the dispute. He was obviously angry at Teja and Williams for not having provided the defense with some kind of a report involving Goldblatt's study of the handwriting. He decided to allow Goldblatt's direct testimony and then to allow Hawk to call him later for cross-examination after the defense had had time to study Goldblatt's notes.

The burly New Yorker was abrupt and positive as he asserted that he believed the handwriting in the ledger and that on the exemplars was that of one person. There was no question in his mind as he crisply explained to the jury why he believed the handwriting to be Corona's. He based his opinion he said, on the repeated characteristics of the handwriting, "which are individualized and pecular to one person."

Hawk decided to cross-examine Goldblatt immediately rather than to take advantage of Patton's permission to wait. Hawk had studied the books on the techniques of comparing handwriting and he had learned a lot in a short time. All he had learned, however, was not enough to dispute Goldblatt's testimony. At the close of the day he broke off the cross-examination and decided not to recall the expert. He still believed that he was far ahead of the prosecution and he was going to leave well enough alone.

Tracing the six-color pen that had been found in Corona's desk in the mess hall had been a long and tedious job, but Whiteaker accomplished it with some help.

Using the brand name to identify the manufacturer, the detectives learned that the pen had been made in Italy. The San Francisco Police Department, anxious to cooperate, sent two Italian-speaking detectives to visit the factory. There they learned that the pens were never intended to be sold in California but that two gross had been shipped by mistake to Macy's Department Store in Sacramento. The pens were purchased in May, 1970, but they did not sell well. Of the 288 in the original shipment, 173 were still in stock in October, 1971.

The factory also supplied the ink formulas to the investigators and the information was turned over to Richard Brunelle of the ATF.

Called to testify, Brunelle was able to state that the pen found in Corona's desk was not used to write the Biblical quotations in the notebook found on Kamp's body.

However, Brunelle did testify that the pen was definitely used to write the rent receipt that had been given to Mrs. Vallejo, several of the cancelled checks found in Corona's filing cabinet, and seven of the entries in the ledger using several different colors of ink. The ink formula used by the Italian manufacturer differed from that used in America and, Brunelle said, was only used in making the Italian ballpoint pens.

With the testimony of the expert witnesses completed, the prosecution's case was all but finished. Almost, but not quite. Teja was still determined to get the Guadalajara Cafe cutting before the jury. He was going to make a last attempt to get Patton to admit it, and if that didn't work, he intended to appeal to a higher court. It would delay the end of the trial for a time, but it was worth the risk.

The sheriff also had something that he wanted to air. Hawk wasn't the only one who could claim that evidence had been withheld or concealed from him. Whiteaker had learned of a second list of names that had been found among Corona's personal papers. The list, it was said, contained the names of at least two of the victims. Whiteaker wanted to see it.

He had learned of the list late in the case and now he talked to the district attorney about it. The list was among the papers that had been turned over to Roy Van den Heuval when the latter had been appointed to defend Corona on May 26, 1971. When Whiteaker asked Van den Heuval whether the list had ever existed, the public defender vaguely recalled having seen it, but it had left his possession when the case was turned over to Hawk. Van den Heuval had given Hawk all of the files he had on Corona at that time. Hawk denied that he had ever seen the list.

Teja and Whiteaker wanted a hearing before the judge so

everybody concerned with the missing ledger could testify under oath.

Teja filed a motion for discovery with Patton, who agreed to take the matter up at the first opportunity.

First, though, it would be best to finish the prosecution's section of the trial, and that was quickly done since there were only two more witnesses to call.

The first of those was Jose Raya, who was called only for the purpose of telling how Corona had offered him a job. Judge Patton, despite persistent attempts by Teja, Williams, and Fahey, refused to allow any mention of the attack on the farm worker to be mentioned.

Raya testified that he and Ramirez had met Corona on the evening of February 24, 1970, in downtown Marysville and Corona had offered them jobs. He said, as he had told the grand jury more than a year before, that Corona had wanted to drive them to the Sullivan ranch that night so they would be ready for work early the next morning. When he and Ramirez refused to go, he said, Corona tried to persuade them to get into his pickup truck and again they refused.

Raya had given statements to Gregory, Perales, and other officers following Corona's arrest. His statements were slightly awry. He had told Perales he met Corona in front of a theater and he had told Gregory that the job offer had been made in a tavern.

Hawk concentrated on the inconsistencies of Raya's statements to the officers, and on his confusion as to the color of the vehicle Corona was driving. In spite of discrepancies involving the location of the meeting and the description of the vehicle, Raya stuck grimly to his story of the job offer. Hawk tripped him up time after time on the occurrence, but he was unable to shake his story that Corona asked him to go with him to the Sullivan ranch.

It was a frustrating day for Hawk. Every time he seemed to have maneuvered Raya into a position where the witness seemed on the verge of becoming trapped, Raya pleaded either a failure to understand the questions or a lapse of memory.

Hawk finally gave up, but in his meeting with the press after the session he accused the prosecution of brainwashing Raya in order to keep from exposing Natividad as the real killer.

Mrs. Beatrice Valdez was the final witness for the prosecution. A cook at the Rideout Hospital in Marysville, Mrs. Valdez was the neighbor who had told the grand jury about Corona's practice of washing the inside of his vehicles on frequent occasions. Never on the outside, always the inside; and always with a garden hose. He never washed his car like the other men on the block with soap and sponge. Never the hood and the fenders and the sides. Only the inside and always with a garden hose.

Hawk's cross-examination was brief. Had she ever seen any bits of flesh or stains of blood running down the gutter? No, she was never that curious, she said. But she couldn't help but notice that her neighbor washed his vehicles at least three times a week, far more often than any of the others on the street.

It was December 21 and Christmas was just four days away. Judge Patton adjourned the court until December 27 after wishing everyone a most happy and joyous Christmas.

It had been expected that the People would rest their case when the trial resumed, but Teja had other ideas. He notified Judge Patton that he had filed an appeal from the judge's ruling on the Guadalajara Cafe affair and was even then waiting for a decision. Patton had no alternative but to continue the trial until January 3.

The appeals court put an end to the Guadalajara Cafe incident once and for all when it upheld Patton's ruling that it be excluded from the trial.

Patton chose to hold the hearing on the missing "death list" during the interval and convened court on December 29 for that purpose.

It took two days, December 29 and January 2, to hear the testimony, but nothing was really accomplished. Van den Heuval's memory was no better than Raya's had been ten days before. He vaguely remembered the list, but he couldn't remember what had happened to it. He did remember that it contained the names of two of the victims, but he couldn't remember which two. He had not listed the material he had turned over to Hawk, nor had he obtained a receipt for it.

As for Hawk, he said he had never seen the list. It was not among the Corona papers that had been given him in June, 1971.

Whiteaker was not convinced, but he had to accept the judge's decision to close the hearing without making any decision. However, the fact that the public defender never did deny outright that such a document existed served only to convince Whiteaker that his original information had been correct.

The prosecution had spent most of the holiday recess and the expected postponement that followed preparing to contest the defense that Hawk had promised he would present. Based on what Hawk had told the jury in his opening statement, they expected a bitter fight. Teja and Fahey had therefore worked to perfect answers to whatever evidence Hawk might produce.

Williams had done what he could but had been handicapped. He had gone skiing during the holidays and had broken an ankle. It cost him two or three days away from the case, but he was still able to assist with the research.

When court convened on January 3 the prosecution immediately rested its case and then sat back in anticipation. They had plugged every loophole they could think of, and now they nervously awaited the promised attack.

Hawk rose from his seat and asked for an immediate verdict of acquittal. He argued that the People had failed to prove its case against the defendant and he described the mistakes made by the investigators, the inconsistencies in the testimony of key witnesses, and lack of any motive for the murders. His argument was forceful, but the judge disagreed. The motion was denied.

While the full courtroom sat in complete silence, Hawk then quietly announced that he would rest his case without presenting a single witness!

He couldn't have created more of a sensation if he had tossed a hand grenade into the room. Reporters rushed from the press row to get to a telephone. One of the weirdest criminal cases in history had become even more weird.

The prosecution was caught completely off guard; they were

in no way prepared to begin closing arguments. They would need time in which to draft their recapitulation of the case for the jury.

Hawk, seeking to take advantage of his surprise move, objected to any further postponement of the trial. He demanded that the People proceed with their argument without delay.

Patton ruled that the prosecution should have five days in which to prepare their closing arguments and postponed the trial until January 8.

Chapter 33

The rule of law requires that the prosecution make the first of the final arguments to the jury and the defense the second. The prosecution then gets a final chance to summarize its case before the judge instructs the jury and then sequesters them for their deliberations.

Teja elected to open the final arguments when court convened on January 8.

His summary was as much an attack on Hawk as it was a resumé of the evidence. He reminded the jury of Hawk's opening statement at the very beginning of the trial. He recalled that the defense attorney had said he would produce witnesses who would explain such things as the bloodstains in the Corona vehicles and the other circumstantial evidence that the sheriff had used as a reason for taking Corona into custody.

He questioned the lack of expert testimony that Hawk had said would prove that homosexuality was the motive for the slayings, and he pointed out that none of those witnesses had appeared to testify that Corona was not a homosexual.

Hawk bounced to his feet when Teja asked, "Ladies and gentlemen, where is any evidence whatsoever that the defendant didn't kill those twenty-five people and bury their bodies in and about the Sullivan ranch?"

Hawk's objection was an angry one. He snapped, "Your Honor, I will object to that statement on the basis that he has been standing here for half an hour trying to shift off the burden of proof onto me, and I don't have it, and that last statement is just rank!"

It was the first of many objections by Hawk during Teja's summary, all of them accusing the district attorney of trying to shift the burden of proof to the defense. Patton was forced to remind the jury on many occasions that it was the duty of the prosecution to prove the guilt of the defendant while the latter had no responsibility to establish his innocence.

Teja spent the entire day and a portion of the next in his flat, unemotional voice, detailing the evidence that had been put before the jury. Beginning with the finding of Whitacre's body, he went step by step through the entire case. At intervals he commented on the fact that the defense had failed to introduce evidence that would challenge the people's case. Hawk met every one of the comments with an objection that Teja was violating the Constitutional provision that a defendant need not testify in a criminal case in order to prove his innocence. The objections became so frequent and so stormy that Patton was forced to halt the trial and call the attorneys into chambers. There the judge warned the district attorney that he was edging dangerously close to a mistrial or, in the case of a conviction, a reversal by a higher court later on.

Teja resumed his slow, tedious review of the prosecution's case until the judge recessed court for the day. By that time several of the jurors and most of the spectators were either asleep or nodding.

The next morning the stolid Teja picked up his argument of the day before, continuing to insinuate that because the defense had made no attempt to present contradictory evidence it was, in effect, admitting guilt. Hawk's protests became more indignant, but the district attorney nevertheless plodded on. On several occasions Patton was compelled to order Teja's remarks to be stricken from the record and reiterated that the defendant was presumed to be innocent until the jury decided otherwise.

Teja finally closed his argument by telling the jury, "I submit after you perform your jobs in the jury room dispassionately and thoroughly that you will return to this courtroom, ladies and gentlemen, with a verdict of guilty as charged against the defendant, Juan Vallejo Corona."

Patton held another session in chambers with the attorneys prior to Hawk's final argument. Had the defense attorney wished, he might have been granted a mistrial at that point. The judge was upset and angry over some of Teja's remarks to the jury, particularly his reference to the failure of the defense to call specific witnesses as promised. Hawk refused to move for a mistrial. His client had been in jail for almost two years, and a mistrial would only result in another hearing that could stretch on for another year.

The defense attorney was convinced that he was going to win the case. He had already shared with the press his guess that at least eleven of the jurors were on his side, and he figured that the other one could be swung over by the others. With his final argument to the jury all prepared, he was eager to get the trial over.

Before Hawk began his address, Judge Patton again reminded the jury that in the eyes of the law Corona was still presumed innocent.

He told the jury, "The burden of proof in this matter is upon the People, and the reference to his (the defense's) possible witness and to what he may or might not have testified to had he been called is not a proper subject of argument, not a proper matter to be considered by the jury, and you are ordered to completely put that comment and the argument out of mind."

Hawk's argument was brief considering the length of the trial, and consisted in the main of an attack on the flimsiness of the evidence and the importance of "reasonable doubt." The prosecution, he scathingly declared, spent more than $500,000 to produce what he described as "this pitiful amount of evidence" and still had been unable to produce any proof of Corona's guilt.

He mentioned by name the investigators and the mistakes they had made along the way, especially in mixing-up the numbers of the bodies and the misplacing of the tire tracks in the evidence locker. He scornfully asserted, "You know, if you just read 'Dick Tracy' and looked at 'Crime Stoppers' you ought to know more about how to investigate a crime than Sutter County did."

Because the prosecution could not prove their case against Corona, he said, they had tried desperately to relieve themselves of the responsibility of proving guilt. They now wanted to convince the jury that Corona should have proved his innocense. The concealing of vital evidence by the prosecution, which he claimed occurred time after time both before and during the trial, was a flagrant abuse of his client's right to a fair trial. He obliquely suggested that the meat receipts, the broken candle holder, and other items of evidence could well have been planted in order to incriminate Corona.

Hawk did not complete his argument on that day. He asked for an early recess and then resumed his summation the next morning. He reminded the jury that the investigators had failed to try for fingerprints on evidence which he said would have produced such prints.

"What they did in this case is they picked their man and arrested him and then set out to prove him guilty," he barked. He discounted the testimony of the handwriting experts, of Dr. Guy and the other experts, and declared that Corona's innocence had been established by the very men who were determined to convict him.

With a plea to the jury to remember the importance of "reasonable doubt" and to apply it to the evidence that had been presented, he asked that they also consider the lack of motive. No motive had been established, he asserted, other than the one that he himself had suggested, one involving homosexuality. Juan Corona, a man with a wife and four children whom he loved, was definitely not such a person, he declared.

As to his not having put on any defense, he explained that the case against his client had been so flimsy and so ridden with inconsistencies and untruths that it did not warrant a reply.

His closing words were, "The final sentence, I guess, of the chapter in Juan Corona's case will be written by you with your verdict. And I know that and I believe in my heart, that you will treat Juan fairly. And I know that we wound up in the right place with the right twelve jurors."

It was Ron Fahey's duty to present the rebuttal, or final argument. The shortness of Hawk's summation caught him unprepared, but he proved to be able. For the next three hours he ad libbed from the few notes he had scribbled on his tablet while Hawk was talking.

Since the prosecution's case was wholly circumstantial, Fahey proposed to define the phrase "circumstantial evidence" by giving the jury examples to ponder.

Speaking directly to the twelve jurors and the three alternates, he said, "You are home. You go to the mailbox and find a letter. You take the letter, return to the house and tell your wife that the mailman was there. If you were put on the witness stand and asked if you saw the postman, you would have to say that you didn't. However, you would say that you got a letter therefore you knew that the postman had been there. That is circumstantial evidence."

He then ranged over a wide variety of subjects connected with the evidence in an obvious effort to kill time until the adjournment hour. That would give him time to organize his thoughts and outline the balance of his argument before the court reconvened the next morning.

Hawk objected several times, urging the judge to force Fahey to speed up his argument. Patton could do no more than keep the session going until a half-hour after the regular 4:30 P.M. quitting time, but Fahey was able to continue speaking slowly and quietly.

He spoke of the social status of the victims, saying, "They walked the streets of Marysville and the surrounding area, and there is no evidence to indicate that they were bothering anybody. Maybe they lived in an element that was not the same as yours or mine. Maybe they worked when they could. Maybe they slept outside some of the time, but the fact of the matter is there was no justification or excuse for their deaths.

"They are a long time dead; they are not coming back. They are not walking around anymore, and that's what this case is all about."

At five o'clock the judge adjourned court for the day, giving Fahey the time he needed.

The next morning when the jury filed into the courtroom they brought with them personal articles and extra clothing. They had already been told that barring unforeseen happenings they would not be returning home until they had either reached a verdict or had been dismissed as a deadlocked panel.

Fahey proceeded with his closing statement, touching twice on the failure of the defense to produce any evidence that would indicate innocence. Hawk objected each time, and the judge again reminded the jury that the presumption of innocence extended throughout the entire proceedings.

He reminded the jury of the testimony of witnesses who saw some of the victims in the company of the defendant prior to their disappearances. He mentioned Jose Raya, and called him the only man whose name was in the ledger and who was still walking the streets; a man who was asked by Corona to go with him to the Sullivan ranch for work when Corona had no work on the ranch. There were also James Pervis and Byron Shannon, whose testimony had not been refuted, he said—Pervis, who was offered work, and Shannon, who had seen Corona drive away from Marysville with four of the victims.

Fahey covered the failure to establish a motive for the killings by telling the jury, "I defy you or anyone to know what is going through the mind of a man who systematically chops and stabs twenty-five men to death and then buries them in a remote area in an orchard over a period of time."

Shortly before 11 A.M. Fahey finished by saying, "Look at this evidence, examine it. Examine the fact that there has been no evidence that contradicts it or rebuts it, and you will arrive at the one inescapable conclusion, the only man living in the area of Marysville having access to the Sullivan ranch, having access to the lower end of Marysville, being seen with the people down there, having a virtual conglomerate of weapons consistent with the way these men met their deaths, having vans, vehicles, clothing, all stained with blood, being in areas all over the ranch where bodies were found, leaving evidence of his identity there, and you will arrive at one inescapable conclusion:

"That there is only one explanation that this evidence gives you. And that explanation is that only one man in that area could have committed these crimes, and that man is Juan Vallejo Corona."

After a short recess Judge Patton began to instruct the jury, reading from a set of instructions the attorneys had agreed to submit to the panel. He advised them as to the definitions of murder in its various phases, the weight of circumstantial evidence, and the doctrine of reasonable doubt. It took thirty minutes to read the legal ground rules the jury would be required to follow and at the end of that time the judge ordered the twelve members of the main panel to be turned over to six bailiffs who would escort them to the jury room. The three remaining alternates were placed off by themselves since they would have no part in the deliberations.

It was Thursday, January 11, 1973. It had been 603 days since Goro Kagehiro found the hole in his orchard.

Chapter 34

The press corps had been augmented by the addition of correspondents of national and international publications who had drifted in a few at a time as the trial neared its end. The persistent rain had driven them to the basement of the courthouse where they filled the small cafeteria.

At 1 P.M. the jury asked to talk to the judge and the court was reconvened. Phillips, the number seven juror and the only one remaining of the original two whose names had been drawn first, had been elected foreman. It was he who rose and asked the judge, "If we find him innocent or guilty on one count, do we have to find him innocent of all?

Patton explained that Corona had been charged with all twenty-five of the murders which the prosecution claimed had been committed by one man alone. Thus, the verdict on one of the counts would mean the same verdict for all twenty-five.

The jury returned to their deliberations and continued until 5:45 P.M. when they called it a day. They boarded their chartered bus and were transported to a nearby motel where they would sleep until they were dismissed from the trial

The ballots taken by the jury during their eight-day ordeal were done in the privacy of the jury room, but an informal record of each vote was written down by a member. The record later found its way into the files of the case and is revealed here for the first time.

On Friday they drove through the rain back to the old white courthouse to begin another day of discussion, argument and study. At 1 P.M. they took their first vote, and the result was seven for acquittal and five for conviction. Within two hours the majority had swung toward the prosecution as shown by a ballot taken at 3 P.M. It was nine to three for conviction that time, and by 4 P.M. when the panel was canvassed for the third time it was eleven to one for conviction.

Naomi Underwood, the semiretired salesclerk, was the lone holdout but, as the discussions went on, others began to disagree wih the majority. Just before they quit for the day, they took another ballot and this one came out eight to four for a guilty verdict.

Hawk was in high spirits and was bubbling over with optimism. He let the press know that he felt he had the jury in his hip pcket. It wouldn't take too many ballots, he said, to get the acquittal he was confidently expecting.

The jury returned to its work at 9 A.M. Saturday, and at 9:20 the judge called the attorneys into his chambers. He told them he had just received a telephone call from the prison at Vacaville informing him that Corona had suffered a possible heart attack.

Hawk was quick to let the press know of the latest development, and the word spread through the courthouse. Corona's wife and mother became distraught and were taken by Pedro to the community hospital for sedatives. The defense attorney, anxious to get as much headline play as possible—hopefully some of the members of the jury might hear of the incident—told the news media that it would be a shame for Corona to die right when the jury was on the verge of setting him free.

The jury, unaware of what was happening, continued to deliberate. That they were seriously studying the evidence and arguing it pro and con was seen by the fact that only two ballots were taken that day.

At 10:45 A.M. the vote stood seven to five for conviction, and by 4:45 P.M., when they took their sixth vote, it was nine guilty and three not guilty.

The rain had stopped temporarily and the jury left the courthouse after 5 p.m., walking toward their bus between the lines of Corona family members and friends who were gathered outside the courtroom.

Judge Patton decided to give the jury the next day off. It was Sunday, January 14, and the Super Bowl was to be played. Those who wanted to watch it would be able to see it on television sets in their rooms. It would give them a chance to relax and prepare for their next session on Monday.

Doctors at the prison hospital had reported that Corona had experienced a coronary insufficiency and had not had a heart attack. He had been given medication and would be able to return to the courtroom after a couple of days' rest.

On Monday the jury deliberated briefly and then asked to speak to the judge. Patton ordered the court to convene in the prison at Vacaville where the visitors' room was turned into a temporary courtroom. Corona was dressed in the clothing he had been wearing during the trial in Fairfield, and the wheelchair he was sitting in was camouflaged to conceal it from the eyes of the jury. Hawk would have preferred otherwise, but Patton was anxious not to generate a sympathy vote among the jurors.

The jury was transported by bus and the other principals went by their own automobiles. Members of the press and the

Corona family were admitted to the makeshift courtroom where tables were arranged for the judge's bench and the counsel tables.

Phillips informed the judge that the jury was deadlocked and wanted to know, "If we can't decide on guilt or innocence, does this constitute a hung jury?"

Without saying how the jury was leaning, he told Patton that they stood eight to four. It had been an impromptu vote and not a regular ballot, but the foreman said there appeared to be no hope of reaching a unanimous decision as required by law in criminal cases.

At that time the jury had deliberated less than three full court days. In a private discussion with the attorneys, Patton reminded them that the trial had lasted four months and, even counting Sunday when they did not meet, the jury had been out only four days altogether. He said he would order the jury to continue their deliberations and attempt to reach a unanimous agreement.

It was raining as the jurors left the prison to return to court. Shortly after they arrived they took another formal ballot at 11 A.M. and the result was ten to two for conviction. Another ballot at noon showed a similar vote, and one at 4:30 P.M. was the same. They continued in session until 5:45 P.M. and voted for the tenth time. The count was nine guilty and three not guilty.

There were not as many reporters present on Tuesday because there was no point in loitering about the courthouse. Those who left asked the few who remained to telephone them if a break in the deadlock appeared to be imminent.

Tuesday was a full day for the jury, with most of the time spent in rehashing the evidence and arguing individual points of view. The eleventh ballot was taken at 9:15 A.M., with the result being nine to three for conviction. At 10:30 A.M. it had swung back to ten to two for the prosecution, and by noon it was eleven to one against the defendant. The fourteenth vote was at 2:30 P.M. and it remained eleven to one. Mrs. Underwood was tenaciously holding out for a not guilty verdict.

Somehow the word had filtered through to the waiting attorneys that a verdict would be coming soon, and the crowd gathered early on Wednesday. They were going to be disappointed.

Some of the jurors had been short-tempered with Mrs. Underwood on Tuesday, and the only effect was to make her more determined in her viewpoint. Phillips, therefore, suggested that there be no voting on Wednesday. Instead, he suggested that the holdout juror be given the entire day to rest and think. Discussions would be maintained at low key and no attempt would be made to make her change her mind.

The jury remained in session throughout the day and then left for their motel. The members of the news media also drifted away, several of them to a nearby tavern where Hawk customarily held forth at the end of the trial day and where many of the news stories that accompanied the trial were developed.

It began to rain during the night, and the skies were wet and gray Thursday morning when the jury arrived at the courthouse. It was a short session with little discussion. The fifteenth ballot was taken by Phillips at 10:05 A.M., and the result was unanimous. Corona had been found guilty.

It was a solemn, subdued jury that entered the courtroom to turn over its verdict to the judge. In the weeks that had passed since the trial began they had become more than just friendly. The trial recesses had become convivial coffee klatches during which they had come to know the intimate details of personality generally reserved for sharing with only the closest of friends. They had joked with each other, confided in each other, and had faithfully promised to continue their new friendships at happier times and in happier places once the fraternal restrictions of the trial were behind them.

The past eight days had changed the friendly, uninhibited attitude of the jurors. Their somber expressions as they gravely marched back into the courtroom clearly indicated that they had wrestled long and hard with a distasteful assignment and had arrived at a decision they would remember forever. There were no smiles as they filed through the doorway and into the courtroom, which was still dominated by the large map showing the locations of the graves. They looked neither at the spectators nor at each other. They stared rigidly at the far wall

It had taken more than two hours to reconvene the court after the jury foreman notified the bailiff that a verdict had been reached. The lawyers had been summoned by telephone and Corona had been brought into the courtroom from the adjacent room where he had been waiting. The sheriff dispatched extra officers to the courthouse, and the security check was even more stringent. Members of the press hurried to the courthouse bounding up the two flights of stairs and rapidly filling the press section.

Finally, at 12:15 P.M., Phillips handed the verdict to the bailiff, who gave it to the judge. The latter read it to a courtroom which was hushed as a matter of traditional restraint; but as the reading went on the hush was one of stunned disbelief.

The family tears came then, along with the muttering and grumbling from the Corona supporters to be quickly silenced by the bailiffs. The judge thanked the jurors for their services and ordered everyone in the courtroom to remain in place until the members of the panel had left the room. They returned to the jury room to collect their personal belongings and then were escorted from the building thus vacating their briefly occupied place in the sun—all but Naomi Underwood, who would have much to say.

Hawk immediately moved for a new trial, and Patton said he would hear the motion on February 5, the same day on which he would pass sentence.

Outside the building where the news media people had gathered, the prosecutors had little to say other than the usual platitudes about justice being served before they got into their automobiles and headed for Yuba City and an impromptu celebration involving huge pizzas, many hamburgers, and several belts of "the creature."

Hawk was not so reticent. With very little of his former air of supreme confidence left, he said, "I was completely fooled by the jury's level of intelligence." He had harsh words for the judge, the prosecution, and the sheriff, all of whom, he broadly hinted, had deprived Corona of his right to a fair trial in order to achieve a conviction.

To add to his troubles, he had been fined fourteen times for contempt of court during the trial and had received a like number of jail sentences totaling seventy-four days, two days of which he had already served. The fines alone amounted to more than $4,000. His own personal fight to overturn the citations loomed in the future.

Phillips, the jury foreman, was cornered by the press and made his few remarks alluding to "the string or continuity" that led to the conviction. He and two others suggested that the lack of defense bothered them but had not influenced their decisions.

Naomi Underwood, once she was freed from the judge's admonition not to discuss the trial in public, wanted to talk to the press, and she did. She had been forced to agree with a verdict that she did not believe in, she said. In her mind, Corona's guilt was still not established and she thought he should have another trial.

She accused Georgia Wallis, a temporary sheriff's matron who had been assigned to watch over the women members of the jury during the trial, of trying to influence her vote.

It had happened on the night before the verdict had been rendered, she told the reporters. She had asked permission to call her sister to inquire about the condition of her pet cats which the sister was caring for. Mrs. Wallis placed the call, she said, and listened while she told her sister, "I'll be home tomorrow." Then she and the matron sat on her bed and talked. Mrs. Wallis told her, "If you have any doubts about your vote, I'll tell you some things about Corona after the trial is over that will ease your mind." Mrs. Underwood said she asked the matron, "If Corona committed the crimes, where were his bloody clothes?" Mrs. Wallis replied, "His wife probably washed them."

The interview only served to further confuse an already fouled-up case. The impact of Mrs. Underwood's statement almost overshadowed the verdict. Some members of the press freely predicted that a mistrial would be declared.

Hawk was elated and Patton was visibly disturbed. Mrs.

Underwood was suddenly the most publicized woman in the entire State of California. She was receiving requests for interviews from all segments of the news media. The Columbia Broadcasting System wanted her to be the guest of the company at San Francisco's finest hotel while she told her story to the world via their facilities.

Instead, she told her story to the judge and to Hawk in separate interviews which were officially recorded.

Judge Patton summoned both Mrs. Underwood and Mrs. Wallis to the court, and in the presence of a court reporter, questioned both women closely. He was concerned mainly with the activities of the matron rather than with any quarrels that might have occurred in the jury room. At the end of his session he declared that he was "not convinced that Mrs. Underwood was telling the truth or that the matron was lying." He did not consider the indiscretion of the matron sufficiently important to warrant a new trial because, it turned out, Mrs. Underwood had already made and announced her decision to vote for a conviction before she ever talked to the matron.

Hawk's interrogation of Mrs. Underwood was also done with a court reporter present in his office in Concord eight days after the verdict. Although what she told the lawyer had no effect on the validity of the conviction, it did give a pretty good insight into what had gone on in the jury room during the eight days of deliberation.

She had steadfastly voted against a guilty verdict from the very outset and, when the first ballot was taken, there were six others who felt the same way. However, when Phillips suggested that they begin a step-by-step review of the evidence, the majority of the panel members swung against the defendant.

By Tuesday the tension in the jury room had thickened to the point where the friendliness that had existed at the start of deliberations had all but evaporated. Mrs. Underwood was proving to be a very trying obstacle for the majority. By noon of that day she was the lone holdout, and the tempers of some of the others were noticeably frayed.

Richard Breman, the young welder who had taken the injured Hick's place, began to take the initiative. He could see no reason why the agitated widow couldn't see what to him was completely obvious.

As the hours went on several of the men became angrier. Finally Laurent Gallipeo reprimanded the others and told them that they would never get anywhere if they continued to shout at her.

As for Mrs. Underwood, her doubts were legitimate in her own mind. She posed some questions to the other jurors but got no satisfactory answers. Why, she asked, did not Sheriff Whiteaker testify? Why couldn't she send a personal note to the judge asking him for some guidance? The bloodstains in the trunk of the Impala were never fully explained to her. There were so few of them and there was no evidence to show that they could not have been put there after the murders were discovered. She wanted to see the evidence from the Kagehiro ranch, but the foreman refused to send for it. None of the jurors were able to adequately explain the theory of reasonable doubt to her.

She was disturbed because Phillips insisted that the vote of the jury had to be unanimous, either guilty or not guilty. When she showed the foreman three pages of notes she had written on her own doubts, he brusquely informed her that all of her arguments had already been covered and explained.

On Wednesday the session began with George Muller telling the other jurors to stop quarreling with Mrs. Underwood. "She has a right to her opinion," he told them. The others didn't agree, but the day was at least a little less hectic for her than Tuesday had been. Late in the afternoon she told her fellow jurors, "All right, I'll make my decision tonight and you can all go home tomorrow." They quit for the day right after that and she went to make her telephone call. She told the matron at that time that she had decided to vote for a guilty verdict but she wanted to think about it overnight.

Before the final ballot was taken on Thursday morning, both Gallipeo and James Owen urged her not to change her vote unless she was sincere. However, she maintained later, she was mentally and physically exhausted and she had been away from her home and her cats for seven full days.

At 10:05 A.M., against her better judgment and in defiance of her principles, she threw the last stone.

On February 5 the courtroom was again filled to capacity. Hawk had argued his case well with the news media people, and they were there in force. If, on the basis of Mrs. Underwood's revelations, Patton was to grant a new trial, the Corona story would be good for several more months of headlines.

Patton listened courteously to Hawk's plea for a new trial. The defense attorney, still somewhat subdued by the shock of the unexpected conviction, based most of his argument on the interference of the matron at the end of the deliberations. He also insisted that the evidence presented did not warrant a guilty verdict and the actions of the prosecution at various stages of the hearing effectively deprived Corona of a fair and unbiased trial.

The prosecution's argument was brief, and the decision of the judge was even shorter. The motion for a new trial was summarily denied.

Patton then sentenced Corona to prison on each count. The sentences were prescribed to run concurrently, meaning that the defendant would be technically eligible for parole at the end of seven years.

The crowd filed out into the street where the Corona supporters staged a brief but noisy demonstration. The marchers shouted that Corona had been betrayed, and there were harsh words for the sheriff, the prosecutors, and the judge. At the height of the tumult someone threw a rock through a window of the courthouse and the deputies who were on the scene radioed for help. The show of force was all that was needed to disperse the crowd and end the tantrum.

The momentum was running down. There was a brief mention on February 7 that the defendant had filed a notice of appeal. It rated no more than a couple of paragraphs by the wire services, and some papers didn't even use it.

On March 1 Patton put it in writing. The findings of fact did not warrant another trial.

For the moment, at least, the Corona story was at an end.

Chapter 35

There were still a lot of puzzled people in the country, however. Based on what they had read in the newspapers and heard on the electronic media, it didn't seem possible that enough evidence had been produced to justify a conviction. Certainly the members of the jury were not listening to the same evidence that the public was reading and hearing. A few magazine articles that were printed in prestigious publications decrying the verdict further implanted doubt in the minds of a lot of people. Just what the hell did the jurors base their verdict on, anyway?

When the deliberations became serious because of a definite possibility that there could be a deadlock, the jurors began to list on paper what they considered to be important facets of the evidence. By the time they completed their deliberations, they had compiled sixteen points. Although the reading and listening public never heard of many of them, the jury heard them all and remembered.

Studied one by one the sixteen points amount to a condensed recapitulation of the evidence that was compiled by the sheriff's investigators during their probe of the twenty-five murders.

The sixteen points were never made public, and until now were seen by only a few of the principals in the trial. They did not become a part of the official trial record and it is doubtful that even the judge was aware of them.

Nevertheless, they were all derived from the evidence that was presented in open court, heard by the jurors but apparently overlooked for the most part by the press. Considered one by one, as the members of the panel must have studied them, they presented a chain of circumstantial evidence that was devastating to the defendant.

Blood, the amounts of it and the several types found on Corona's possessions, dominated the list. The worth of Dr. Guy's testimony was emphasized by point number one, the four types of human blood found in the trunk of the Impala. The second point listed the three types found in the back of the van and also the distinctive stains that ran down the inside of the rear bumper.

Number four in importance was the blood that was found on the knives and the pistol, all of which was successfully typed by Dr. Guy. Number seven dealt with even more blood, all of it human and found on the boots and the shovel taken from the van and one pair of men's shorts found under the seat of the vehicle. The jurors also listed under number seven the bolo machete and the nine-milimeter cartridges that were also located under the seat. Point number eight was the blood that was found on the denim jacket which was found stuffed in the rafters of the Corona garage.

There was just too much blood for the jurors to believe that the stains were acquired casually. Neither could they believe that the evidence was planted as Hawk had suggested. Even Stottlemyers's attempt to discredit Dr. Guy failed to change the opinion that a substantial number of people had shed quite a lot of blood on Corona's personal property.

Corona's beige-colored van figured in the deliberations that surrounded the third point on the list. They recalled the testimony of Juan Sanchez, who reported seeing the van parked near the levee for a period of two hours or more prior to the bodies' being discovered. The body of Sam Bonifide, victim number twenty-four, was found in that vicinity, and the jurors noted that the incident remained unexplained by the defense.

The famous ledger or "death list" figured in point number five. The jurors decided that the ledger, containing the names of seven of the victims, was not a normal business record. They accepted the testimony of Goldblatt and Harris, the handwriting experts, that the names were written by the defendant.

The jurors were also impressed by the testimony of the several witnesses who saw Corona in the Sullivan orchards and along the riverbank on many occasions prior to the bodies' being found. Point number six stressed that seven bodies were found in the north river bottoms where Corona had been seen by the Schmidls, Jacob Compton, and the Sullivan farm workers who testified at the trial. They decided that Corona's presence in those areas was more than just a coincidence, especially since Sullivan had testified that the defendant had no business being there.

The blue van that Natividad had sold to Pedro just before fleeing to Mexico a step ahead of Raya's lawsuit dominated points nine and ten. They recalled the testimony of James Cummings, the ranch carpenter, who saw the blue van in the orchard about the middle of May. In number nine they recalled the fact that the van was in the orchard early in the morning despite the fact that Corona had no work going on at that time. The body of John Henry Jackson, victim number twenty-one, was located near that spot.

The jurors then noted in point number ten that testimony had revealed that Corona not only had access to his brother's blue van but had been seen driving it on several occasions including the morning when he was seen by Cummings.

The testimony of Corona's neighbors who saw Juan washing out the inside of his vehicles was considered in point number eleven. Jim Huff and Mrs. Beatrice Vasquez had told the jury that they had observed Corona washing the interior of the blue van, the beige van, and the pickup truck. The panel was impressed by the fact that Corona only washed the inside of the vehicles but was never seen washing them on the outside.

Byron Shannon, the black labor recruiter, had suffered for hours under the penetrating, often vicious, cross-examination by Hawk and had become so confused and inarticulate that his testimony had been considered worthless by many members of the press. The jury, however, believed that Shannon had, as he testified, seen four of the victims ride away from Marysville with Corona. Riley, Smallwood, Allen, and Jackson were the men that Shannon named, and the jurors were convinced he told the truth. Point number twelve remarked that Corona had been seen picking up the four victims who were never seen alive again.

The incriminating meat receipts that were found in the grave of Melford Sample, victim number three, were considered such vital evidence that the jurors listed them thirteenth in importance. In recognizing the receipts as valid evidence, the jurors also demonstrated that they had resolved in their own minds the early mix-up of the body numbers. Point number thirteen listed the receipts as having been found in the grave of the nine-fingered man, who was Sample. Their action also indicated that they believed that Sample, the last man killed, was murdered either on May 21, the day the receipts were written by the butcher, or shortly thereafter.

The bank deposit slips bearing Corona's name also drew the attention of the jurors. Point number fourteen noted that the slips had been found in the grave of Joseph Maczak, victim number twenty-five. They therefore concluded that the deposit slips, together with the broken candle holder and other household trash, had indeed been dumped in the grave by the defendant as he buried his last victim.

Points number fifteen and sixteen involved the testimony of James Pervis and Jose Raya. The jurors, despite the uncertainties of both witnesses as to the times and the color of the pickup trucks involved, did not doubt the contentions of both men that they had been offered work by Corona and had been asked to go with him to the Sullivan ranch. They remembered the testimony of Jack Sullivan who told them that Corona had no business being on his ranch at the times he made the job offers. In their minds, therefore, the job offers had an unsavory odor about them.

Whether or not an aggressive defense might have refuted the sixteen points or at least answered them in such a way as to create a reasonable doubt in the minds of the panel would not be known short of a whole new trial being granted. The evidence that Hawk had belittled as being unworthy of any consideration had certainly impressed the jury. Its members also disagreed with the defense attorney's contention that the investigation had been incompetent. In the flood of rhetoric that inundated the trial, they were able to fish out what they believed were enough hard facts to justify the conviction.

In spite of the verdict, an air of controversy and uncertainty will always surround the Corona case. The lack of a definite motive for the murders, the necessity for the prosecution as well as the jury to rely wholly on circumstantial evidence to pursue the case and reach a conclusion, and the inadequacies and delinquencies of both the defense and the prosecution will forever provide fuel for argument.

However, if Juan Corona did not commit the murders for which he was charged and convicted, it must be said that he was the victim of one of the damnedest set of coincidences that ever put a man behind bars.

THEORY OF MARKOV PROCESSES

E. B. DYNKIN

Translated from the Russian by
D. E. BROWN

Edited by
T. KÖVÁRY

DOVER PUBLICATIONS, INC.
Mineola, New York

Bibliographical Note

This Dover edition, first published in 2006, is an unabridged republication of the work originally published by Prentice-Hall, Inc., Englewood Cliffs, New Jersey, in 1961.

International Standard Book Number: 0-486-45305-7

Manufactured in the United States of America
Dover Publications, Inc., 31 East 2nd Street, Mineola, N.Y. 11501

CONTENTS

CONTENTS

Set by Vi Leach

PREFACE

The present book aims at investigating the logical foundations of the theory of Markov random processes.

The theory of Markov processes has developed rapidly in recent years. The properties of the trajectories of such processes and their infinitesimal operators have been studied, and intimate connexions have been discovered between the behaviour of the trajectories and the properties of the differential equations corresponding to the process. These connexions are useful for studying differential equations as well as Markov processes. The material thus accumulated has made necessary a critical survey of the fundamentals of the theory. In particular, the usual statement of the Markov principle of "absence of after-effects" has been found to be inadequate and various authors have proposed different forms for a strengthened principle whereby a process is "strictly Markov." It has become obvious that the most natural subject for study is presented by Markov processes cut off at a random instant. All these and other ideas were originally introduced by different authors in different forms, according to the specific purposes of their specialized works - in which stationary Markov processes are considered almost exclusively.

A general theory is built up in the present book which also covers non-stationary processes. Stationary processes are regarded as an important special case. Non-stationary processes are well known to be reducible to the stationary type by an artificial method requiring the passage to a more complicated phase space*). However, the stationary processes thus obtained are in a certain sense degenerate, so that this type of reduction is by no means always suitable. Then again, a concept of the Markov process that is more general in essence is closer to first principles than the concept of stationary Markov process. There is a canonical time scale for stationary Markov processes. In the general process there is no such scale and all the definitions have to be

---

*See article 3 of Chapter 4 .

invariant with respect to any monotonic continuous transformation of time.

The theory cannot be adequately developed by extending the concept of a Markov process as a random function of a special type.

For we are usually concerned, when studying Markov processes, not with a single probability measure but with a whole collection of such measures, corresponding to all the possible initial instants and all the possible initial states; in other words, we are concerned, not with one random function, but with a whole collection of such functions, with definite inter-relationships. This is one of the reasons why the theory of Markov processes has to possess its familiar autonomy with respect to the general theory of probability processes. The theory of Markov processes is built up in the present book without any reference whatever to the general theory of probability processes.

This book cannot be used by the student to make his first acquaintance with the theory of Markov processes. Although we have not assumed formally any previous acquaintance with the theory of probability, in fact a reading of the book can only prove of value to someone already acquainted with an elementary exposition of the theory of Markov processes, such as is contained, for instance, in Feller's "Introduction to probability theory and its applications," Vol. 1 (Vvedenie v teoriyu veroyatnostei i ee prilozheniya), or Gnedenko's "Course of probability theory" (Kurs teorii veroyatnostei).

The first introductory chapter contains a brief survey of the necessary concepts and theorems from measure theory. Any proofs that can be found in text-books are omitted here. The second chapter gives a general definition of Markov process and investigates the operations that make possible an inspection of the class of Markov processes corresponding to a given transition function. The more complicated operation of generating a subprocess is studied in Chapter 3. The connexion is revealed between the subprocesses of a Markov process and the multiplicative functionals of its trajectory. The most important classes of multiplicative functionals and subprocesses are investigated. Chapter 4 is concerned with the construction of Markov processes with given transition functions. The concept of strictly Markov process is discussed in Chapter 5. Finally, Chapter 6 is devoted to a study of the conditions to be imposed on the transition function so that among the Markov processes corresponding to this function, there should be at least one, all the trajectories of which possess some type of continuity or boundedness. The supplement describes some of Choquet's results concerning the general theory of capacities. Measurability theorems for the instants of first departure are deduced from these results. A historical and bibliographical index will be found at the end of the book.

The present work is closely allied to a monograph now in the press entitled "Infinitesimal operators of Markov processes" (Infinitezimalnye operatory markovskikh protsessov), which is devoted to the task of classifying Markov processes. The two works should be regarded as the two parts of a single monograph on the theory of Markov processes.

The present material comes from a series of papers and special courses given by the author at Moscow and Pekin universities. The author is grateful to his audience for a number of observations which he made use of during the final preparation of the manuscript.

I must express my indebtedness and sincere gratitude to Mr. A.A. Yushkevich for his careful reading of the manuscript and various comments that made it possible to eliminate a number of inaccuracies and obscurities.

E.B. Dynkin

THEORY OF MARKOV PROCESSES

CHAPTER 1

INTRODUCTION

1. Measurable Spaces and Measurable Sets

1.1. Let $\mathcal{M}$ be a system of subsets of a set Ω satisfying the following conditions:

1.1.A_1. If $A \in \mathcal{M}$, then $\bar{A} \in \mathcal{M}$ *).

1.1.A_2. If $A_i \in \mathcal{M}$ $(i = 1, 2, \ldots)$, then $\bigcup_1^\infty A_i \in \mathcal{M}$ and $\bigcap_1^\infty A_i \in \mathcal{M}$.

We say in this case that the system of subsets $\mathcal{M}$ is a σ-algebra in the space Ω. Let $\mathcal{C}$ be any system of subsets of Ω. The intersection of all the σ-algebras in the space Ω that contain $\mathcal{C}$ is also a σ-algebra. We refer to it as the σ-algebra generated by $\mathcal{C}$, and write it as $\sigma(\mathcal{C})$.

If $\mathcal{M}$ is a σ-algebra in the space Ω and $\tilde{\Omega} \in \mathcal{M}$, the aggregate of all sets $A \in \mathcal{M}$ that are contained in $\tilde{\Omega}$ forms a σ-algebra in the space $\tilde{\Omega}$. We shall denote this σ-algebra by $\mathcal{M}[\tilde{\Omega}]$.

We shall call the system of subsets $\mathcal{C}$ of the space Ω a π-system if:

1.1.B_1. It follows from $A_1, A_2 \in \mathcal{C}$ that $A_1 \cap A_2 \in \mathcal{C}$ **).

We shall call a system $\mathcal{F}$ a λ-system if it satisfies the following conditions:

1.1.C_1. $\Omega \in \mathcal{F}$.

---

*$\bar{A}$ denotes the complement of A in Ω, i.e. $\Omega \setminus A$

**The intersection of sets A and B will generally be written as $A \cap B$.

1.1.C$_2$. If $A_1, A_2 \in \mathcal{F}$ and $A_1 \cap A_2 = \emptyset$ *), then $A_1 \cup A_2 \in \mathcal{F}$.

1.1.C$_3$. If $A_1, A_2 \in \mathcal{F}$ and $A_1 \supseteq A_2$, then $A_1 \setminus A_2 \in \mathcal{F}$.

1.1.C$_4$. If $A_1, \ldots, A_n, \ldots \in \mathcal{F}$ and $A_n \uparrow A$ **) then $A \in \mathcal{F}$.

It may be noticed that, if a system of sets $\mathcal{M}$ is simultaneously a π-system and a λ-system, it is a σ-algebra. For 1.1.A$_1$ follows from 1.1.C$_1$ and 1.1.C$_3$. Moreover, it follows from the relationship $A \cup B = A \cup (B \setminus AB)$ and properties 1.1.B$_1$, 1.1.C$_3$ and 1.1.C$_2$ that, if $A, B \in \mathcal{M}$, then $A \cup B = A \cup (B \setminus AB) \in \mathcal{M}$, and consequently, if $A_1, A_2, \ldots, A_n \in \mathcal{M}$ then $\bigcup_1^n A_i \in \mathcal{M}$. Now let $A_n \in \mathcal{M}$ $(n = 1, 2, \ldots)$. Then $A_n' = \bigcup_1^n A_k \in \mathcal{M}$, and inasmuch as $A_n' \uparrow \bigcup_1^\infty A_n$, we have $\bigcup_1^\infty A_n \in \mathcal{M}$ by 1.1.C$_4$. It follows from the relationship

$$\bigcap_1^\infty A_n = \overline{\bigcup_1^\infty \bar{A}_n}$$

that $\bigcap_1^\infty A_n \in \mathcal{M}$. Condition 1.1.A$_2$ is therefore satisfied.

Lemma 1.1. If the λ-system $\mathcal{F}$ contains the π-system $\mathcal{C}$ then $\mathcal{F}$ contains $\sigma(\mathcal{C})$.

Proof. The intersection $\mathcal{F}'$ of all the λ-systems containing the π-system $\mathcal{C}$ is obviously a λ-system. We shall show that this intersection is at the same time a π-system. The assertion of the lemma will follow from this.

The class $\mathcal{F}_1$ of all the sets A such that $A \cap B \in \mathcal{F}'$ for all $B \in \mathcal{C}$ is readily seen to be a λ-system. Since $\mathcal{F}_1 \supseteq \mathcal{C}$, we have $\mathcal{F}_1 \supseteq \mathcal{F}'$. This means that, if $A \in \mathcal{F}', B \in \mathcal{C}$, then $A \cap B \in \mathcal{F}'$.

We now put $B \in \mathcal{F}_2$ if $B \cap A \in \mathcal{F}'$ for all $A \in \mathcal{F}'$. It may readily be seen that $\mathcal{F}_2$ is a λ-system. By what has been proved,

---

*The symbol $\emptyset$ denotes the empty set.
** $A_n \uparrow A$ means that $A_1 \subseteq A_2 \subseteq \ldots \subseteq A_n \subseteq \ldots$ and $A = \bigcup_{n=1}^\infty A_n$. Similarly, $A_n \downarrow A$ means that $A_1 \supseteq A_2 \supseteq \ldots \supseteq A_n \supseteq \ldots$ and $A = \bigcap_1^\infty A_n$.

$\mathcal{F}_2 \supseteq \mathcal{C}$, so that $\mathcal{F}_2 \supseteq \mathcal{F}'$. This means that, if $A, B \in \mathcal{F}'$, then $A \cap B \in \mathcal{F}'$. Consequently $\mathcal{F}'$ is a π-system.

1.2. The pair $(\Omega, \mathcal{A})$, consisting of a set Ω and a σ-algebra $\mathcal{A}$ of subsets of Ω is called a measurable space.

An important example of a measurable space is provided by the space $(I_t^s, \mathcal{B}_t^s)$, where $I_t^s = [s, t]$ is a segment of the real line and $\mathcal{B}_t^s$ is the σ-algebra of subsets of this segment which is generated by all the intervals contained in I_t^s. The values of s and t can be infinite as well as finite, and we put $I_{+\infty}^{-\infty} = (-\infty, +\infty)$, $I_t^{-\infty} = (-\infty, t)$, $I_{+\infty}^s = [s, +\infty)$.

Let $(\Omega_1, \mathcal{A}_1)$ and $(\Omega_2, \mathcal{A}_2)$ be two measurable spaces. The mapping of the space Ω_1 into Ω_2 is said to be measurable if the complete pre-image of any set from $\mathcal{A}_2$ belongs to $\mathcal{A}_1$. This definition is likewise applicable when the mapping is defined only on a subset $\tilde{\Omega}_1 \subset \Omega$.

It may be noted that, if $\sigma(\mathcal{C}) = \mathcal{A}_2$, the only requirements that need to be satisfied by the mapping for the reflection α to be measurable are that the complete pre-image of any set from $\mathcal{C}$ belongs to $\mathcal{A}_1$ and that $\Omega_2 = \bigcup_{n=1}^{\infty} C_n$, where $C_n \in \mathcal{C}$ (this is proved simply by observing that the sets whose complete pre-image belongs to $\mathcal{A}_1$ from a σ-algebra in Ω_2).

Obviously, if α is the measurable mapping of $(\Omega_1, \mathcal{A}_1)$ into $(\Omega_2, \mathcal{A}_2)$ and β is the measurable mapping of $(\Omega_2, \mathcal{A}_2)$ into $(\Omega_3, \mathcal{A}_3)$, then $\beta\alpha$ is the measurable mapping of $(\Omega_1, \mathcal{A}_1)$ into $(\Omega_3, \mathcal{A}_3)$, provided only that the domain of definition of β contains $\alpha(\Omega_1)$.

The most important particular case of mappings is provided by numerical functions, i.e. mappings into the real line $I_{+\infty}^{-\infty}$.

Let $\mathcal{A}$ be a σ-algebra of subsets of Ω. We shall say that the numerical functions $\xi(\omega)(\omega \in \Omega)$ is measurable with respect to $\mathcal{A}$ or is $\mathcal{A}$-measurable, if the mapping defined by it of $(\Omega, \mathcal{A})$ into $(I_{+\infty}^{-\infty}, \mathcal{B}_{+\infty}^{-\infty})$, is measurable, i.e. if for any $\Gamma \in \mathcal{B}_{+\infty}^{-\infty}$:

$$\{\omega : \xi(\omega) \in \Gamma\} \in \mathcal{A}.$$

Since the intervals $(t, +\infty)$ generate the σ-algebra $\mathcal{B}_{+\infty}^{-\infty}$, the requirement for the function $\xi(\omega)$ to be $\mathcal{A}$-measurable is simply that, for any t,

$$\{\omega : \xi(\omega) > t\} \in \mathcal{A}.$$

The concept of $\mathcal{A}$-measurable function extends automatically to the case when the system of sets $\mathcal{A}$ is a σ-algebra in some subspace $\tilde{\Omega}$ of the space Ω instead of in the whole of Ω. It may easily be seen that in this case the domain of definition of any $\mathcal{A}$-measurable function ξ coincides with $\tilde{\Omega}$.

Let $\mathcal{L}$ be any system of real functions in Ω, satisfying the condition

1.2.A. If $\xi \in \mathcal{L}$ and

$$\eta(\omega) = \begin{cases} \xi(\omega) & \text{with } \xi(\omega) \geqslant 0, \\ 0 & \text{with } \xi(\omega) < 0, \end{cases}$$

then η and $\xi - \eta$ belong to $\mathcal{L}$.
A system of numerical functions $\mathcal{H}$ is called an $\mathcal{L}$-system if the following conditions are fulfilled:

1.2.B$_1$. $1 \in \mathcal{H}$.

1.2.B$_2$. A linear combination of any two functions of $\mathcal{H}$ also belongs to $\mathcal{H}$.

1.2.B$_3$. If $\xi_n \in \mathcal{H}$, $0 \leqslant \xi_n(\omega) \uparrow \xi(\omega)$ *) and $\xi(\omega)$ is bounded or belongs to $\mathcal{L}$, then $\xi \in \mathcal{H}$.

Lemma 1.2. If an $\mathcal{L}$-system $\mathcal{H}$ contains the characteristic**) functions of all the sets belonging to some π-system $\mathcal{C}$, then $\mathcal{H}$ contains all the functions of $\mathcal{L}$ which are measurable with respect to $\sigma(\mathcal{C})$.

Proof. The class of all sets whose characteristic functions belong to $\mathcal{H}$ forms the λ-system $\mathcal{F}$. Since $\mathcal{F} \supseteq \mathcal{C}$, we have $\mathcal{F} \supseteq \sigma(\mathcal{C})$ by lemma 1.1.

---

*We write $a_n \uparrow a$ if $a_n \to a$ and $a_1 \leqslant a_2 \leqslant \dots \leqslant a_n \leqslant \dots$. Similarly, $a_n \downarrow a$ means that $a_n \to a$ and $a_1 \geqslant a_2 \geqslant \dots \geqslant a_n \geqslant \dots$.
**The characteristic function of a set A is the function

$$\chi_A(\omega) = \begin{cases} 1, & \text{if } \omega \in A, \\ 0, & \text{if } \omega \overline{\in} A. \end{cases}$$

Let ξ be a non-negative function belonging to $\mathscr{L}$ and measurable with respect to $\sigma(\mathcal{C})$. We put

$$\Gamma_{kn}=\left\{\frac{k}{2^n}\leqslant\xi(\omega)<\frac{k+1}{2^n}\right\};$$

$$\xi_n=\sum_{k=0}^{2^{2n}}\frac{k}{2^n}\chi_{\Gamma_{kn}}$$

Obviously, $0\leqslant\xi_n\uparrow\xi$ and, in accordance with 1.2.B$_3$, $\xi\in\mathscr{H}$.

In view to 1.2.A an arbitrary $\sigma(\mathcal{C})$-measurable function $\eta\in\mathscr{L}$ can be represented as the difference between two $\sigma(\mathcal{C})$ -measurable non-negative functions of $\mathscr{L}$. The latter belong to $\mathscr{H}$, as already pointed out. Consequently, we also have $\eta\in\mathscr{H}$.

1.3. Let $\mathcal{A}_i$ be a σ-algebra of subsets of sets Ω_i $(i=1, 2, \ldots, n)$. We shall write $\Omega_1\times\ldots\times\Omega_n$ for the set of vectors $(\omega_1, \ldots, \omega_n)$, where $\omega_i\in\Omega_i$, and $\mathcal{A}_1\times\ldots\times\mathcal{A}_n$ for the σ-algebra generated by subsets of the form $A_1\times\ldots\times A_n$, where $A_i\in\mathcal{A}_i$ (it may be noticed that the sets $A_1\times\ldots\times A_n$ form a π-system). In the case when $\Omega_1=\ldots=\Omega_n=\Omega$, we shall write Ω^n instead of $\Omega_1\times\ldots\times\Omega_n$, and similarly $\mathcal{A}^n$ instead of $\mathcal{A}_1\times\ldots\times\mathcal{A}_n$, when $\mathcal{A}_1=\ldots=\mathcal{A}_n=\mathcal{A}$.

Now let an infinite sequence of spaces Ω_i be given and a σ-algebra of subsets $\mathcal{A}_i$ in each Ω space. We shall write $\Omega_1\times\ldots\times\Omega_n\times\ldots$ for the space of sequences $(\omega_1, \omega_2, \ldots, \omega_n, \ldots)$, where $\omega_i\in\Omega_i$, and $\mathcal{A}_1\times\ldots\times\mathcal{A}_n\times\ldots$ for the σ-algebra in this space generated by the subsets

$$A_1\times A_2\times\ldots\times A_n\times\Omega_{n+1}\times\Omega_{n+2}\times\ldots \quad (n=1, 2, \ldots;\ A_i\in\mathcal{A}_i). \tag{1.1}$$

When the factors are the same we shall write Ω^∞ and $\mathcal{A}^\infty$ for brevity. It may be noticed that the class of subsets of type (1.1) is a π-system.

Lemma 1.3. Let α_i be the measurable mapping of $(\Omega, \mathcal{A})$ into $(\Omega_i, \mathcal{A}_i)$ (i can run either through the values $1, 2, \ldots, n$, or through all natural numbers). Then the mapping α of the space $(\Omega, \mathcal{A})$ into $(\Omega_1\times\Omega_2\times\ldots, \mathcal{A}_1\times\mathcal{A}_2\times\ldots)$, defined by the expression

$$\alpha(\omega)=\{\alpha_1(\omega), \alpha_2(\omega), \ldots\},$$

is measurable.

Proof. Suppose for clarity that i runs through all natural numbers. The class of all the sets of $\mathcal{A}_1 \times \mathcal{A}_2 \times \cdots$, whose complete pre-images with mapping α belong to $\mathcal{A}$, clearly forms a σ-algebra. This σ-algebra contains all the sets of type (1.1). It therefore contains $\mathcal{A}_1 \times \mathcal{A}_2 \times \cdots$.

<u>Lemma 1.4</u>. Let $\mathcal{A}_i$ be a σ-algebra of subsets of the space Ω_i $(i = 1, 2)$ and let $f(\omega_1, \omega_2)(\omega_1 \in \Omega_1, \omega_2 \in \Omega_2)$ be an $\mathcal{A}_1 \times \mathcal{A}_2$-measurable function. Then for any fixed $\omega_2 \in \Omega_2$ $f(\omega_1, \omega_2)$ is an $\mathcal{A}_1$-measurable function of ω_1.

Proof. Let $\mathcal{L}$ denote the class of all functions in the space $\Omega_1 \times \Omega_2$. The system $\mathcal{H}$ of all functions $f(\omega_1, \omega_2)$ for which our lemma holds is evidently an $\mathcal{L}$-system. This system contains the characteristic function of any set $A_1 \times A_2$. By lemma 1.2, it contains all functions measurable with respect to the σ-algebra $\mathcal{A}_1 \times \mathcal{A}_2$.

<u>Lemma 1.5</u>. For each t of some set T let there be associated a function $x_t(\omega)$ $(\omega \in \Omega)$ with values in the measurable space $(E, \mathcal{B})$. The necessary and sufficient condition for a function $\xi(\omega)$ $(\omega \in \Omega)$ to be measurable with respect to the σ-algebra $\mathcal{N}_T$ generated by the sets $\{\omega : x_t(\omega) \in \Gamma\}$ $(t \in T, \Gamma \in \mathcal{B})$ is that

$$\xi(\omega) = f[x_{t_1}(\omega), x_{t_2}(\omega), \ldots, x_{t_n}(\omega), \ldots], \tag{1.2}$$

where $t_1, t_2, \ldots, t_n, \ldots \in T$ and $f(x_1, x_2, \ldots, x_n, \ldots)$ is a $\mathcal{B}^\infty$-measurable function in the space E^∞.

Proof. The mapping of Ω into the real line $I_{+\infty}^{-\infty} = (-\infty, +\infty)$ given by expression (1.2) can be written as the product $f\alpha$, where

$$\alpha(\omega) = \{x_{t_1}(\omega), x_{t_2}(\omega), \ldots, x_{t_n}(\omega), \ldots\}.$$

For any $t \in T$ $x_t(\omega)$ defines a measurable mapping of $(\Omega, \mathcal{N}_T)$ into $(E, \mathcal{B})$. By lemma 1.3, α is the measurable mapping of $(\Omega, \mathcal{N}_T)$ in $(E^\infty, \mathcal{B}^\infty)$. By hypothesis, f defines the measurable mapping of $(E^\infty, \mathcal{B}^\infty)$ into $(I_{+\infty}^{-\infty}, \mathcal{B}_{+\infty}^{-\infty})$. Consequently $\xi = f\alpha$ is the measurable mapping of $(\Omega, \mathcal{N}_T)$ into $(I_{+\infty}^{-\infty}, \mathcal{B}_{+\infty}^{-\infty})$. Hence all the functions that can be written in the form (1.2) are $\mathcal{N}_T$-measurable.

Now let $\mathcal{L}$ denote the class of all functions $\xi(\omega)$ $(\omega \in \Omega)$, let $\mathcal{H}$ be the set of functions ξ that can be written in the form (1.2), and let $\mathcal{C}$ be the system of all ω-sets of the form

$$\{x_{t_1} \in \Gamma_1, \ldots, x_{t_n} \in \Gamma_n\}$$
$$(n = 1, 2, \ldots; t_1, \ldots, t_n \in T; \Gamma_1, \ldots, \Gamma_n \in \mathscr{B}). \quad (1.3)$$

The characteristic function of the set (1.3) is equal to

$$\chi_{\Gamma_1}[x_{t_1}(\omega)] \cdots \chi_{\Gamma_n}[x_{t_n}(\omega)].$$

Thus it can be written in the form (1.2) and belongs to $\mathscr{H}$. Obviously, $\mathscr{H}$ is an $\mathscr{L}$-system, and $\mathcal{C}$ a π-system, and by lemma 1.2, $\mathscr{H}$ contains all the functions $\xi(\omega)$ measurable with respect to $\sigma(\mathcal{C}) = \mathscr{N}_T$.

2. Measures and Integrals

1.4. Let $(\Omega, \mathscr{M})$ be a measurable space. The non-negative numerical function $\varphi(A)$ $(A \in \mathscr{M})$ is called a measure*) if, for any finite or denumerable collection of mutually disjoint sets $A_1, A_2, \ldots$ of $\mathscr{M}$, $\varphi(\bigcup A_k) = \Sigma\varphi(A_k)$. The measure satisfying the condition $\varphi(\Omega) = 1$ is known as the probability measure.

Let φ be a measure given on the σ-algebra $\mathscr{M}$. Let f be an $\mathscr{M}$-measurable numerical function, given on some subset Ω_f of the space Ω, and let A be contained in Ω_f. We shall say that the function f is φ-summable in the set A if the finite limits exist,

$$\lim_{n\to\infty} \sum_{0}^{+\infty} \frac{k}{n} \varphi\left\{\omega : \omega \in A, \quad \frac{k}{n} < f(\omega) \leqslant \frac{k+1}{n}\right\}$$

*All the statements and definitions contained in section 1.4 can be translated without difficulty to the case when the function $\varphi(A)$ is allowed the value $+\infty$ as well as finite values. (A particular example of such a function is the ordinary Lebesgue measure on an infinite numerical straight line.) We shall only encounter such functions in a few examples, however, so that, unless there is some special proviso to the contrary, the measure φ will always be understood to be a function that takes only finite values.

and

$$\lim_{n\to\infty}\sum_{1}^{-\infty}\frac{k+1}{n}\varphi\left\{\omega:\omega\in A,\quad \frac{k}{n}<f(\omega)\leqslant\frac{k+1}{n}\right\}^{*)}.$$

The sum of these limits is called the (Lebesgue) <u>integral</u> of the function f on the set A with respect to the measure φ and is written as

$$\int_A f(\omega)\,\varphi(d\omega).$$

If one limit is infinite but the other finite, the integral is ascribed the value $\pm\infty$ ($+\infty$ if the first limit is infinite, and $-\infty$ if the second limit is infinite).

We shall assume that the reader is familiar with the basic properties of Lebesgue integrals. The properties that we shall use most frequently are as follows:

1.4.A. If $0\leqslant f_n(\omega)\uparrow f(\omega)$ for all $\omega\in A$, then

$$\lim\int_A f_n(\omega)\,\varphi(d\omega)=\int_A f(\omega)\,\varphi(d\omega). \tag{1.4}$$

1.4.B. If for all $\omega\in A$ $f_n(\omega)\to f(\omega)$, $|f_n(\omega)|<g(\omega)$ and g is φ-summable in A, then

$$\lim\int_A f_n(\omega)\,\varphi(d\omega)=\int_A f(\omega)\,\varphi(d\omega). \tag{1.5}$$

1.4.C. (Fubini's theorem.) Let $\mathcal{M}_i$ be a σ-algebra in Ω_i and φ_i a measure in $\mathcal{M}_i$ $(i=1, 2)$. Let $f(\omega_1, \omega_2)$ be an $\mathcal{M}_1\times\mathcal{M}_2$--measurable function in $\Omega_1\times\Omega_2$ such that

$$\int_{\Omega_1}\left[\int_{\Omega_2}|f(\omega_1, \omega_2)|\,\varphi_2(d\omega_2)\right]\varphi_1(d\omega_1)<\infty.$$

Then

$$\int_{\Omega_1}\left[\int_{\Omega_2}f(\omega_1, \omega_2)\,\varphi_2(d\omega_2)\right]\varphi_1(d\omega_1)=$$
$$=\int_{\Omega_2}\left[\int_{\Omega_1}f(\omega_1, \omega_2)\,\varphi_1(d\omega_1)\right]\varphi_2(d\omega_2)^{**)}. \tag{1.6}$$

*When a φ-summable function is referred to without mentioning on which set A, it will be a question of a function which is φ-summable throughout its domain of definition.
**If f is non-negative, the proviso regarding the absolute convergence of the integral on the left-hand side of (1.6) is unnecessary.

The following property is a particular case of 1.4.A:

1.4.A$_1$. If $A_n \uparrow A$, then $\varphi(A_n) \uparrow \varphi(A)$.

1.5. We shall prove two useful lemmas.

Lemma 1.6. Let α be the measurable mapping of $(\Omega_1, \mathcal{A}_1)$ into $(\Omega_2, \mathcal{A}_2)$ and let φ be a measure on $\mathcal{A}_1$. Then the expression

$$\psi(\Gamma) = \varphi\{\alpha(\omega) \in \Gamma\} \qquad (\Gamma \in \mathcal{A}_2) \tag{1.7}$$

defines a measure in $\mathcal{A}_2$. We have for any $\mathcal{A}_2$-measurable function f:

$$\int_{\Omega_2} f(\omega_2)\,\psi(d\omega_2) = \int_{\Omega_1} f[\alpha(\omega_1)]\,\varphi(d\omega_1) \tag{1.8}$$

(more precisely, if one of these integrals exists the other exists and the two are equal).

Proof. The first part of the lemma is obvious.

Let $\mathcal{L}$ denote the class of all ψ-summable functions. The class of all functions for which equation (1.8) is satisfied is clearly an $\mathcal{L}$-system. This system contains the characteristic function of any set of $\mathcal{A}_2$. By lemma 1.2, it contains all the $\mathcal{A}_2$-measurable functions of $\mathcal{L}$. Consequently, if the integral on the left-hand side of (1.8) exists for f, f satisfies (1.8). It can be shown similarly that (1.8) is satisfied for any function f for which the integral on the right-hand side of (1.8) exists.

Lemma 1.7. Let U, V, Z be three spaces and $\mathcal{A}_U$, $\mathcal{A}_V$, $\mathcal{A}_Z$ σ-algebras in these spaces; let $F(u, z)(u \in U, z \in Z)$ be a real function measurable with respect to $\mathcal{A}_U \times \mathcal{A}_Z$; and let $\mathbf{P}_v\,(v \in V)$ be measures in the σ-algebra $\mathcal{A}_Z$, the numerical function $\mathbf{P}_v(\Gamma)$ being $\mathcal{A}_V$-measurable for any $\Gamma \in \mathcal{A}_Z$. If the integral

$$G(u, v) = \int_Z F(u, z)\,\mathbf{P}_v(dz) \tag{1.9}$$

converges for all $u \in U$, $v \in V$, it defines an $\mathcal{A}_U \times \mathcal{A}_V$-

measurable function*).

Proof. Let $\mathscr{L}$ denote the system of all $\mathcal{A}_U \times \mathcal{A}_Z$-measurable functions $F(u, z)$ for which $\int_Z F(u, z)\mathbf{P}_v(dz)$ converges for all $u \in U$, $v \in V$. The system $\mathscr{H}$ of all the functions $F(u, z)$ for which $G(u, v)$ is $\mathcal{A}_U \times \mathcal{A}_V$-measurable is evidently an $\mathscr{L}$-system. It contains the characteristic function of any set $A_U \times A_Z (A_U \in \mathcal{A}_U, A_Z \in \mathcal{A}_Z)$. Since these sets form a π-system, $\mathscr{H}$ contains all $\mathcal{A}_U \times \mathcal{A}_Z$-measurable functions of $\mathscr{L}$ by lemma 1.2.

3. Conditional Probabilities and Mathematical Expectations

1.6. The triple $(\Omega, \mathscr{M}, \mathbf{P})$, where Ω is a set, $\mathscr{M}$ is a σ-algebra of its subsets, and $\mathbf{P}$ is a probability measure in $\mathscr{M}$, is called a probability space. The points of Ω are called elementary events, the elements of $\mathscr{M}$ are events, and the values of $\mathbf{P}(A)$ are their probabilities. Every $\mathscr{M}$-measurable function $\xi(\omega)$ $(\omega \in \Omega)$ is called a random variable. The integral $\int_\Omega \xi(\omega)\mathbf{P}(d\omega)$ (if it has a meaning) is called the expectation of ξ and is denoted by $\mathbf{M}\xi$. We shall also describe as random variables $\mathscr{M}$-measurable functions ξ which are only defined in some subset Ω_ξ of Ω instead of throughout the space Ω (it follows from the $\mathscr{M}$-measurability of ξ that $\Omega_\xi \in \mathscr{M}$). The expectation of such a ξ is given by the expression.

$$\mathbf{M}\xi = \int_{\Omega_\xi} \xi(\omega)\mathbf{P}(d\omega).$$

Let $\widetilde{\Omega} \subseteq \Omega$ and let $\varphi(\omega)$ and $\psi(\omega)$ be two functions whose domains of definition contain $\widetilde{\Omega}$. We shall say that $\varphi = \psi$ almost certainly in $\widetilde{\Omega}$ (in the sense of the measure $\mathbf{P}$) and write

$$\varphi = \psi \qquad (\text{a.c.}\, \widetilde{\Omega}, \mathbf{P}),$$

if $\mathbf{P}(\widetilde{\Omega}, \varphi \neq \psi) = 0$. Similar meanings attach to the expressions

$$\varphi < \psi \qquad (\text{a.c.}\, \widetilde{\Omega}, \mathbf{P}), \qquad \varphi_n \to \varphi \qquad (\text{a.c.}\, \widetilde{\Omega}, \mathbf{P})$$

and so on.

---

*In the case of a non-negative function F the requirement of convergence of the integral is unnecessary.

Let $\mathcal{A}$ be a σ-algebra in $\tilde{\Omega} \subseteq \Omega$, where $\mathcal{A} \subseteq \mathcal{M}$. Let the function $\xi(\omega)$ be $\mathbf{P}$-summable on the set $\tilde{\Omega}$. Every $\mathcal{A}$-measurable function satisfying the relationship

$$\int_A \xi(\omega)\,\mathbf{P}(d\omega) = \int_A \mathbf{M}(\xi \mid \mathcal{A})\,\mathbf{P}(d\omega). \tag{1.10}$$

for any $A \in \mathcal{A}$ is known as a <u>conditional expectation</u> of ξ with respect to $\mathcal{A}$ (written as $\mathbf{M}(\xi \mid \mathcal{A})$).

Such a function may be shown always to exist. It may easily be seen to be defined only up to an arbitrary set of the σ-algebra $\mathcal{A}$ having $\mathbf{P}$-measure zero. Since it is impossible to conclude from the equations $\mathbf{M}(\xi \mid \mathcal{A}) = \varphi$, $\mathbf{M}(\xi \mid \mathcal{A}) = \psi$ that $\varphi(\omega) = \psi(\omega)$ for all ω, the only conclusion that may be drawn being that $\varphi = \psi$ (a.c. $\tilde{\Omega}$, $\mathbf{P}$), we shall avoid paradoxes by writing $\mathbf{M}(\xi \mid \mathcal{A}) = \varphi$ (a.c. $\tilde{\Omega}$, $\mathbf{P}$) instead of $\mathbf{M}(\xi \mid \mathcal{A}) = \varphi$.

It should be noticed that the function $\mathbf{M}(\xi \mid \mathcal{A})$ is unaffected by the values of the function ξ outside $\tilde{\Omega}$.

If $B \in \mathcal{M}$, the characteristic function $\chi_B(\omega)$ is an $\mathcal{M}$-measurable function. The function $\mathbf{M}(\chi_B \mid \mathcal{A})$ is called the <u>conditional probability</u> of the event B with respect to the σ-algebra $\mathcal{A}$ and is denoted by $\mathbf{P}(B \mid \mathcal{A})$. This function can also be characterized as the $\mathcal{A}$-measurable function satisfying for any $A \in \mathcal{A}$:

$$\mathbf{P}(AB) = \int_A \mathbf{P}(B \mid \mathcal{A})\,\mathbf{P}(d\omega). \tag{1.11}$$

(It is defined only as far as an ω-set of $\mathcal{A}$ having $\mathbf{P}$-measure zero.)

We shall mention a few examples*).

1.6.1. Let $\mathcal{A}_0$ be an algebra consisting of two elements: the empty set $\emptyset$ and the whole of the space Ω. Then constants are the only $\mathcal{A}_0$-measurable functions and we have from relationship (1.10) with $A = \Omega$.

$$\mathbf{M}(\xi \mid \mathcal{A}_0) = \mathbf{M}\xi$$

---

*The σ-algebra $\mathcal{A}$ does not contain non-empty sets of measure zero in examples 1.6.1 and 1.6.2, so that the function $\mathbf{P}(\xi \mid \mathcal{A})$ is uniquely defined for any ξ.

1.6.2. Let $A \in \mathcal{M}$ and let $0 < \mathbf{P}(A) < 1$. The four sets $\{0, A, \overline{A}, \Omega\}$ form a σ-algebra $\mathcal{A}$. We have

$$\mathbf{M}(\xi \mid \mathcal{A}) = \begin{cases} \frac{1}{\mathbf{P}(A)} \int\limits_A \xi(\omega)\, \mathbf{P}(d\omega) & \text{for } \omega \in A, \\ \frac{1}{\mathbf{P}(\overline{A})} \int\limits_{\overline{A}} \xi(\omega)\, \mathbf{P}(d\omega) & \text{for } \omega \in \overline{A}, \end{cases}$$

$$\mathbf{P}(B \mid \mathcal{A}) = \begin{cases} \frac{\mathbf{P}(BA)}{\mathbf{P}(A)} & \text{for } \omega \in A, \\ \frac{\mathbf{P}(B\overline{A})}{\mathbf{P}(\overline{A})} & \text{for } \omega \in \overline{A}. \end{cases}$$

These expressions establish the connexion between the general concepts of conditional mathematical expectation and conditional probability with respect to a given σ-algebra and the popular elementary concepts of mathematical expectation and probability that some event A might occur.

We shall deduce the fundamental properties of conditional mathematical expectations and conditional probabilities. In the statement of these properties, $\mathcal{A}$ denotes a σ-algebra in $\widetilde{\Omega} \subseteq \Omega$, it being assumed that $\mathcal{A} \subseteq \mathcal{M}$.

1.6.A. If ξ is $\mathcal{A}$-measurable and $\mathbf{P}$-summable in $\widetilde{\Omega}$, then

$$\mathbf{M}(\xi \mid \mathcal{A}) = \xi \qquad (\text{a.c.}\ \Omega, \mathbf{P}).$$

1.6.A_1. For any constant c,

$$\mathbf{M}(c \mid \mathcal{A}) = c \qquad (\text{a.c.}\ \widetilde{\Omega}, \mathbf{P}).$$

1.6.B. If ξ and η are $\mathbf{P}$-summable in $\widetilde{\Omega}$ and

$$\xi \geqslant \eta \qquad (\text{a.c.}\ \widetilde{\Omega}, \mathbf{P}), \tag{1.12}$$

then

$$\mathbf{M}(\xi \mid \mathcal{A}) \geqslant \mathbf{M}(\eta \mid \mathcal{A}) \qquad (\text{a.c.}\ \widetilde{\Omega}, \mathbf{P}). \tag{1.13}$$

1.6.B_1. For every $A \in \mathcal{M}$

$$0 \leqslant \mathbf{P}(A \mid \mathcal{A}) \leqslant 1 \qquad (\text{a.c.}\ \widetilde{\Omega}, \mathbf{P}). \tag{1.14}$$

If $P(\tilde{\Omega} \setminus A\tilde{\Omega}) = 0$, then

$$P(A \| \mathcal{A}) = 1 \qquad (\text{a.c.}\, \tilde{\Omega},\, P). \tag{1.15}$$

1.6.C. If ξ_1 and ξ_2 are P-summable in $\tilde{\Omega}$, c_1 and c_2 being arbitrary constants, then

$$M(c_1\xi_1 + c_2\xi_2 | \mathcal{A}) = c_1 M(\xi_1 | \mathcal{A}) + c_2 M(\xi_2 | \mathcal{A}) \qquad (\text{a.c.}\, \tilde{\Omega},\, P).$$

1.6.D. If ξ is P-summable in $\tilde{\Omega}$ and

$$0 \leqslant \xi_n \uparrow \xi \qquad (\text{a.c.}\, \tilde{\Omega},\, P),$$

then

$$M(\xi_n \| \mathcal{A}) \uparrow M(\xi \| \mathcal{A}) \qquad (\text{a.c.}\, \tilde{\Omega},\, P).$$

1.6.D_1. If $A_n \uparrow A$, then

$$P(A_n \| \mathcal{A}) \uparrow P(A \| \mathcal{A}) \qquad (\text{a.c.}\, \tilde{\Omega}\; P).$$

1.6.E. If η is P-summable in $\tilde{\Omega}$ and

$$|\xi_1| < \eta, \; \ldots, \; |\xi_n| \leqslant \eta, \; \ldots; \; \xi_n \to \xi \qquad (\text{a.c.}\, \tilde{\Omega},\, P),$$

then

$$M(\xi_n | \mathcal{A}) \to M(\xi | \mathcal{A}) \qquad (\text{a.c.}\, \tilde{\Omega},\, P).$$

1.6.F. If $\xi\eta$ and η are P-summable in $\tilde{\Omega}$ and ξ is $\mathcal{A}$-measurable, then

$$M(\xi\eta | \mathcal{A}) = \xi M(\eta | \mathcal{A}) \qquad (\text{a.c.}\, \tilde{\Omega},\, P).$$

1.6.G. Let $\Omega \supseteq \tilde{\Omega}_1 \supseteq \tilde{\Omega}_2$, let $\mathcal{A}_1$ be a σ-algebra in $\tilde{\Omega}_1$ and $\mathcal{A}_2$ a σ-algebra in $\tilde{\Omega}_2$, where $\mathcal{A}_1 \subseteq \mathcal{M}$, $\mathcal{A}_2 \subseteq \mathcal{M}$ and $A_1\tilde{\Omega}_2 \in \mathcal{A}_2$ for all $A_1 \in \mathcal{A}_1$ *) . If the functions $\xi\eta$ and η are P-summable in $\tilde{\Omega}_2$ and the function ξ is equal to zero in $\tilde{\Omega}_1 \setminus \tilde{\Omega}_2$ and induces an $\mathcal{A}_2$-measurable function in $\tilde{\Omega}_2$, we have

$$M(\xi\eta | \mathcal{A}_1) = M[\xi M(\eta \| \mathcal{A}_2) \| \mathcal{A}_1] \qquad (\text{a.c.}\, \tilde{\Omega}_1,\, P) \;{}^{**}). \tag{1.16}$$

If $A \in \mathcal{A}_2$, $B \in \mathcal{M}$, then

$$P(AB | \mathcal{A}_1) = M\{\chi_A P(B \| \mathcal{A}_2) \| \mathcal{A}_1\} \qquad (\text{a.c.}\, \tilde{\Omega}_1,\, P). \tag{1.17}$$

---

*That is, $\mathcal{A}_1[\tilde{\Omega}_2] \subseteq \mathcal{A}_2$; in the case when $\tilde{\Omega}_1 = \tilde{\Omega}_2$, this requirement reduces to the simpler condition $\mathcal{A}_1 \subseteq \mathcal{A}_2$.
**The first factor in the product $\xi M(\eta \| \mathcal{A}_2)$ vanishes whilst the second is not defined in $\tilde{\Omega}_1 \setminus \tilde{\Omega}_2$. The product is reckoned to be defined and equal to zero in $\tilde{\Omega}_1 \setminus \tilde{\Omega}_2$.

1.6.H. If the functions $\xi\eta$ and η are $\mathbf{P}$-summable in $\tilde{\Omega}$ and the function ξ is $\mathcal{A}$-measurable and equal to zero (or not defined) outside $\tilde{\Omega}$, then

$$\mathbf{M}\xi\eta = \mathbf{M}[\xi\mathbf{M}(\eta \mid \mathcal{A})].$$

1.6.I. Let $\mathcal{A}$ be a σ-algebra in the space Ω. If η is $\mathbf{P}$-summable in Ω, then

$$\mathbf{M}\eta = \mathbf{M}[\mathbf{M}(\eta \mid \mathcal{A})]. \tag{1.18}$$

If $A \in \mathcal{M}$, then

$$\mathbf{P}(A) = \mathbf{M}[\mathbf{P}(A \mid \mathcal{A})]. \tag{1.19}$$

We now turn to the proof of properties 1.6.A-1.6.I.

Property 1.6.A is an obvious consequence of the definition of conditional mathematical expectation. On putting $\xi = c$, in 1.6.A, we get 1.6.A$_1$.

Proof of 1.6.B.-1.6.B$_1$. We have by (1.10) and (1.12), for any $A \in \mathcal{A}$:

$$\int_A \mathbf{M}(\xi \mid \mathcal{A})\,\mathbf{P}(d\omega) = \int_A \xi\mathbf{P}(d\omega) \geqslant \int_A \eta\mathbf{P}(d\omega) = \int_A \mathbf{M}(\eta \mid \mathcal{A})\,\mathbf{P}(d\omega). \tag{1.20}$$

We put

$$A_n = \left\{\omega : \mathbf{M}(\xi \mid \mathcal{A}) < \mathbf{M}(\eta \mid \mathcal{A}) - \frac{1}{n}\right\}.$$

Obviously $A_n \in \mathcal{A}$ and

$$\int_{A_n} \mathbf{M}(\xi \mid \mathcal{A})\,\mathbf{P}(d\omega) \leqslant \int_{A_n} \mathbf{M}(\eta \mid \mathcal{A})\,\mathbf{P}(d\omega) - \frac{1}{n}\mathbf{P}(A_n). \tag{1.21}$$

It follows from a comparison of (1.20) and (1.21) that $\mathbf{P}(A_n) = 0$. But

$$\{\mathbf{M}(\xi \mid \mathcal{A}) < \mathbf{M}(\eta \mid \mathcal{A})\} \subset \bigcup A_n,$$

whence (1.13) follows.

To deduce (1.14), we only need to notice that $0 \leqslant \chi_A \leqslant 1$, and to make use of properties 1.6.B and 1.6.A$_1$ already proved.

Finally, if $\mathbf{P}(\widetilde{\Omega} \setminus A\widetilde{\Omega}) = 0$, then $\chi_A \geqslant 1$ (a.c. $\widetilde{\Omega}$, $\mathbf{P}$) and, by (1.13) and 1.6.A, $\mathbf{P}(A \mid \mathcal{A}) = \mathbf{M}(\chi_A \mid \mathcal{A}) \geqslant 1$ (a.c. $\widetilde{\Omega}$, $\mathbf{P}$). Taken in conjunction with (1.14), this gives expression (1.15).

Proof of 1.6.C. In view of (1.10), we have for any $A \in \mathcal{A}$:

$$\int_A \xi_1 \mathbf{P}(d\omega) = \int_A \mathbf{M}(\xi_1 \mid \mathcal{A}) \mathbf{P}(d\omega);$$

$$\int_A \xi_2 \mathbf{P}(d\omega) = \int_A \mathbf{M}(\xi_2 \mid \mathcal{A}) \mathbf{P}(d\omega),$$

so that

$$\int_A (c_1\xi_1 + c_2\xi_2) \mathbf{P}(d\omega) = \int_A [c_1 \mathbf{M}(\xi_1 \mid \mathcal{A}) + c_2 \mathbf{M}(\xi_2 \mid \mathcal{A})] \mathbf{P}(d\omega),$$

which is equivalent to proposition 1.6.C.

Proof of 1.6.D-1.6.D_1. In accordance with 1.6.B, it follows from the relationship

$$0 \leqslant \xi_1 \leqslant \dots \leqslant \xi_n \leqslant \dots \quad (\text{a.c. } \widetilde{\Omega}, \mathbf{P}), \tag{1.22}$$

that

$$0 \leqslant \mathbf{M}(\xi_1 \mid \mathcal{A}) \leqslant \dots \leqslant \mathbf{M}(\xi_n \mid \mathcal{A}) \leqslant \dots \quad (\text{a.c. } \Omega, \mathbf{P}). \tag{1.23}$$

By (1.10), for any $A \in \mathcal{A}$,

$$\int_A \mathbf{M}(\xi_n \mid \mathcal{A}) \mathbf{P}(d\omega) = \int_A \xi_n \mathbf{P}(d\omega). \tag{1.24}$$

By 1.4.A, it follows from (1.22), (1.23) and (1.24) that

$$\int_A \lim \mathbf{M}(\xi_n \mid \mathcal{A}) \mathbf{P}(d\omega) = \int_A \lim \xi_n \mathbf{P}(d\omega)$$

and therefore

$$\mathbf{M}(\xi_n \mid \mathcal{A}) = \mathbf{M}(\xi \mid \mathcal{A}) \quad (\text{a.c. } \widetilde{\Omega}, \mathbf{P}).$$

We can prove 1.6.D_1 simply by applying 1.6.D to the quantities χ_{A_n}.

Proof of 1.6.E. We put

$$\zeta_n^+ = \sup_{k \geqslant 0} \xi_{n+k}, \quad \zeta_n^- = \inf_{k \geqslant 0} \xi_{n+k}.$$

Obviously,

$$0 \leqslant \eta - \zeta_n^+ \uparrow \eta - \xi \quad \& \quad 0 \leqslant \eta + \zeta_n^- \uparrow \eta + \xi \quad (\text{a.c. } \widetilde{\Omega}, \mathbf{P}).$$

Therefore, by 1.6.D,

$$\mathbf{M}(\eta-\zeta_n^+|\mathcal{A})\uparrow\mathbf{M}(\eta-\xi|\mathcal{A}) \quad \& \quad \mathbf{M}(\eta+\zeta_n^-|A)\uparrow\mathbf{M}(\eta+\xi|A)$$
$$(\text{a.c.}\ \tilde{\Omega},\ \mathbf{P}).$$

Thus

$$\mathbf{M}(\zeta_n^+|\mathcal{A})\downarrow\mathbf{M}(\xi|\mathcal{A}) \quad \& \quad \mathbf{M}(\zeta_n^-|\mathcal{A})\uparrow\mathbf{M}(\xi|\mathcal{A}) \qquad (\text{a.c.}\ \tilde{\Omega},\ \mathbf{P}).$$

It remains to remark that, by 1.6.B,

$$\mathbf{M}(\zeta_n^-|\mathcal{A})\leqslant\mathbf{M}(\xi_n|\mathcal{A})\leqslant\mathbf{M}(\zeta_n^+|\mathcal{A}).$$

Proof of 1.6.F. We fix any function η. P-summable in $\tilde{\Omega}$ and put $\xi\in\mathcal{L}$, if $\xi\eta$ is P-summable in $\tilde{\Omega}$. By 1.6.C and 1.6.D, the class $\mathcal{H}$ of all ξ for which 1.6.F is satisfied forms an $\mathcal{L}$-system in $\tilde{\Omega}$. It follows readily from (1.10) that $\mathcal{H}$ contains the characteristic functions of all the sets of $\mathcal{A}$. By lemma 1.2, $\mathcal{H}$ contains all the $\mathcal{A}$-measurable functions of $\mathcal{L}$.

Proof of 1.6.G. We have by (1.10) and 1.6.F for every $A\in\mathcal{A}_1$:

$$\begin{aligned}\int_A \mathbf{M}\{\xi\mathbf{M}(\eta|\mathcal{A}_2)|\mathcal{A}_1\}\,\mathbf{P}(d\omega)&=\int_A \xi\mathbf{M}(\eta|\mathcal{A}_2)\,\mathbf{P}(d\omega)=\\ =\int_{A\tilde{\Omega}_2}\xi\mathbf{M}(\eta|\mathcal{A}_2)\,\mathbf{P}(d\omega)&=\int_{A\tilde{\Omega}_2}\mathbf{M}(\xi\eta|\mathcal{A}_2)\,\mathbf{P}(d\omega)=\\ &=\int_{A\tilde{\Omega}_2}\xi\eta\mathbf{P}(d\omega)=\int_A\xi\eta\mathbf{P}(d\omega).\end{aligned} \tag{1.25}$$

Since the function $\mathbf{M}\{\xi\mathbf{M}(\eta|\mathcal{A}_2)|\mathcal{A}_1\}$ is $\mathcal{A}_1$-measurable, (1.16) follows from (1.25). On putting $\xi=\chi_A$, $\eta=\chi_B$, we get (1.17).

We prove property 1.6.H simply by applying 1.6.G to the case $\tilde{\Omega}_1=\Omega$, $\mathcal{A}_1=\mathcal{M}$, $\tilde{\Omega}_2=\tilde{\Omega}$, $\mathcal{A}_2=\mathcal{A}$. We get (1.18) on putting $\tilde{\Omega}=\Omega$, $\xi=1$ in 1.6.H, and (1.19) by putting $\eta=\chi_A$ in (1.18).

4. Topological Measurable Spaces

1.7. A topological space is a pair $(E, \mathcal{C})$, where E is a set and $\mathcal{C}$ a system of subsets of E such that:

1.7.A_1. The empty set and the whole of space E belong to $\mathcal{C}$.

1.7.A_2. The intersection of a finite number, and the sum of any number, of subsets of $\mathcal{C}$ again belongs to $\mathcal{C}$.

The elements of the system $\mathcal{C}$ are called <u>open sets</u> of the space E. Every open set containing a point x is called a <u>neighbourhood</u> of x.

We describe $A \subseteq E$ as <u>closed</u> if $\bar{A} \in \mathcal{C}$. The intersection of all the closed sets containing a set B is called the <u>closure</u> of B. The closure of B is the least closed set containing B.

Let x_n be a sequence of points of the space $(E, \mathcal{C})$. If every neighbourhood of the point x contains all the elements of the sequence x_n apart from a finite number, x_n is said to be <u>convergent</u> to x and we write $x_n \to x$.

The topological space $(E, \mathcal{C})$ is said to be <u>compact</u> if a convergent subsequence can be chosen from every sequence. It may easily be shown that a finite covering can be chosen from every denumerable covering of a compact space E by open sets*). If this condition is satisfied for any (not merely denumerable) covering of E by open sets, $(E, \mathcal{C})$ is said to be a <u>bicompact</u> topological space.

We refer to $(E, \mathcal{C})$ as a <u>Hausdorff</u> topological space if, for any two distinct points $x, y \in E$ disjoint sets $U, V \in \mathcal{C}$ can be found such that $x \in U, y \in V$. A bicompact Hausdorff space is called a <u>bicompact</u>.

A subset A of a topological space $(E, \mathcal{C})$ is said to be <u>everywhere dense</u> in E if, for every non-empty $C \in \mathcal{C}$, the intersection $A \cap C$ is non-empty. If a denumerable everywhere dense set exists in E, $(E, \mathcal{C})$ is described as a <u>separable</u> space.

Let E' be an arbitrary subset of E and let $\mathcal{C}'$ be the class of all subsets E' expressible as intersections $E' \cap C$, where $C \in \mathcal{C}$. Evidently, $\mathcal{C}'$ satisfies conditions 1.7.A_1-1.7.A_2, so that $(E', \mathcal{C}')$ is a topological space. Every subset of a topological space can thus be regarded as in turn a topological

*)A system of sets $\tilde{\mathcal{C}}$ is said to form a covering of E if each point $x \in E$ belongs to at least one set of $\tilde{\mathcal{C}}$.

space. In particular, it is meaningful to speak of the compactness or bicompactness of a subset E'.

If E can be expressed as the sum of a denumerable number of compact (bicompact) subsets, the space $(E, \mathcal{C})$ is said to be σ-compact (σ-bicompact). If there is an open set U and a compact (bicompact) set K for every point such that $x \in U \subseteq K$, E is said to be locally compact (locally bicompact).

Let $(E_1, \mathcal{C}_1)$ and $(E_2, \mathcal{C}_2)$ be two topological spaces. Let $\mathcal{C}_1 \times \mathcal{C}_2$ be the class of subsets of the set $E_1 \times E_2$ expressible as sums of "rectangles" $C_1 \times C_2$ $(C_1 \in \mathcal{C}_1, C_2 \in \mathcal{C}_2)$. The topological space $(E_1 \times E_2, \mathcal{C}_1 \times \mathcal{C}_2)$ is said to be the topological product of spaces $(E_1, \mathcal{C}_1)$ and $(E_2, \mathcal{C}_2)$.

It should be noticed that $(x_n, y_n) \to (x, y)$ in $(E_1 \times E_2, \mathcal{C}_1 \times \mathcal{C}_2)$ when and only when $x_n \to x$ in $(E_1, \mathcal{C}_1)$ and $y_n \to y$ in $(E_2, \mathcal{C}_2)$.

A metric space is defined as a pair (E, ρ), where E is a set and ρ a non-negative function in $E \times E$, satisfying the following conditions:

1.7.B_1. $\rho(x, y) = \rho(y, x)$

1.7.B_2. $\rho(x, y) + \rho(y, z) \geqslant \rho(x, z)$

1.7.B_3. $\rho(x, y) = 0$ when and only when $x = y$.

The set of all points y satisfying the condition $\rho(x, y) < \varepsilon$ is called an ε-neighbourhood of the points x and is written $U_\varepsilon(x)$. A set U is said to be open if, for every point $x \in U$, there is an $\varepsilon > 0$ such that $U_\varepsilon(x) \subseteq U$. The class $\mathcal{C}$ of all open sets U satisfies conditions 1.7.A_1-1.7.A_2. Every metric space can therefore be regarded as a topological space and all the concepts introduced for topological spaces can be applied to it. Topological spaces which can be got with the aid of the above construction from some metric space are described as metrizable.

A sequence of points x_n of a metric space (E, ρ) converges to a point x when and only when $\rho(x_n, x) \to 0$.

A metric space is said to be complete if every sequence x_n satisfying the condition $\lim\limits_{m, n \to \infty} \rho(x_m, x_n) = 0$ is convergent.

The simplest example of a metric space is the set of all

real numbers R with distance $\rho(x, y)=|y-x|$. This space is complete, separable, σ-bicompact and locally bicompact.

1.8. Let $(E_1, \mathcal{C}_1)$ and $(E_2, \mathcal{C}_2)$ be two topological spaces. The mapping α of E_1 into E_2 is said to be continuous if the complete pre-image of any set $C \in \mathcal{C}_2$ belongs to $\mathcal{C}_1$. If α is the continuous mapping of $(E_1, \mathcal{C}_1)$ into $(E_2, \mathcal{C}_2)$ and β is the continuous mapping of $(E_2, \mathcal{C}_2)$ into $(E_3, \mathcal{C}_3)$, $\beta\alpha$ is the continuous mapping of $(E_1, \mathcal{C}_1)$ into $(E_3, \mathcal{C}_3)$.

If α is the continuous mapping of $(E_1, \mathcal{C}_1)$ in $(E_2, \mathcal{C}_2)$, it follows from $x_n \to x$ that $\alpha(x_n) \to \alpha(x)$. The question arises as to whether the fact that $\alpha(x_n) \to \alpha(x)$ as $x_n \to x$ implies the continuity of the mapping α. Although this is not in general true, it is true in the case of metrizable spaces.

It follows from 1.7.B$_2$ that, if $x_n \to x, y_n \to y$, then $\rho(x_n, y_n) \to \rho(x, y)$. The function $\rho(x, y)$ is therefore continuous in the topological space $(E \times E, \mathcal{C} \times \mathcal{C})$ ($\mathcal{C}$ being the system of all open sets of (E, ρ))*).

Let Γ be a subset of the metric space (E, ρ). We write $\rho(x, \Gamma)$ for the lower bound of $\rho(x, y)$ over all $y \in \Gamma$. It follows from 1.7.B$_1$-1.7.B$_2$ that

$$|\rho(x, \Gamma)-\rho(y, \Gamma)| \leqslant \rho(x, y),$$

so that $\rho(x, \Gamma)$ is a continuous function of x.

1.9. A topological measurable space is a triple $(E, \mathcal{C}, \mathcal{B})$, where the pair $(E, \mathcal{C})$ is a topological space and the pair $(E, \mathcal{B})$ is a measurable space.

The simplest and most important particular case of a topological measurable space is provided by spaces of the form $(E, \mathcal{C}, \sigma(\mathcal{C}))$. We shall sometimes write these as $(E, \mathcal{C})$ for brevity. The elements of the σ-algebra $\sigma(\mathcal{C})$ are known as Borel sets of the topological space $(E, \mathcal{C})$.

Let $(E_1, \mathcal{C}_1, \mathcal{B}_1)$ and $(E_2, \mathcal{C}_2, \mathcal{B}_2)$ be two topological measurable spaces and α the mapping of E_1 into E_2. It is meaningful to speak of α as being measurable or continuous. We shall show that the continuity of α implies its measurability if $\mathcal{B}_1=\sigma(\mathcal{C}_1)$ and $\mathcal{B}_2=\sigma(\mathcal{C}_2)$. For let $\mathcal{F}$ denote the class of all subsets of E_2 whose complete pre-images belong to $\sigma(\mathcal{C}_1)$.

---

*)The space $(E \times E, \mathcal{C} \times \mathcal{C})$ is obviously metrizable.

Obviously, $\mathscr{F}$ is a λ-system and contains the π-system $\mathcal{C}_2$. By lemma 1.1, $\mathscr{F} \supseteq \sigma(\mathcal{C}_2)$.

There is no point in confining ourselves to topological measurable spaces for which $\mathscr{B}=\sigma(\mathcal{C})$, since this considerably restricts the possible applications of the theory. Various assumptions will be made regarding the connexion between $\mathscr{B}$ and $\mathcal{C}$, depending on the circumstances. The most important of these assumptions are stated below.

1.9.A. $\mathscr{B}$ is a σ-algebra generated by some sub-system of the system $\mathcal{C}$, or what amounts to the same thing, $\mathscr{B}=\sigma(\mathscr{B}\cap\mathcal{C})$

1.9.B. For every $U\in\mathscr{B}\cap\mathcal{C}$ there is a $\mathscr{B}$-measurable continuous function $f(x)$ such that $f(x)\neq 0$ when and only when $x\in U$.

Lemma 1.8. Let the topological measurable space $(E, \mathcal{C}, \mathscr{B})$ satisfy conditions 1.9.A-1.9.B. If the $\mathscr{L}$-system $\mathscr{H}$ contains all the bounded continuous measurable functions in E, it also contains all the measurable functions belonging to $\mathscr{L}$.

Proof. The system of sets $\mathscr{B}\cap\mathcal{C}$ is a π-system, where, by 1.9.A, $\sigma(\mathscr{B}\cap\mathcal{C})=\mathscr{B}$. In accordance with lemma 1.2, we only need to show that the characteristic function of any set $U\in\mathscr{B}\cap\mathcal{C}$ belongs to $\mathscr{H}$. We take the function $f(x)$ defined by condition 1.9.B and put

$$q_n(u)=\begin{cases} 1, & \text{if } |u|\geqslant\frac{1}{n}, \\ n|u|, & \text{if } |u|<\frac{1}{n}, \end{cases} \qquad f_n(x)=q_n[f(x)].$$

The functions f_n are continuous, bounded and measurable; they thus belong to $\mathscr{H}$. Since $0\leqslant f_n\uparrow\chi_U$, we have $\chi_U\in\mathscr{H}$.

Lemma 1.9. Let $\alpha_1, \ldots, \alpha_n, \ldots$ be measurable mappings of a measurable space $(\Omega, \mathscr{M})$ into a topological measurable space $(E, \mathcal{C}, \mathscr{B})$, satisfying conditions 1.9.A-1.9.B. If $\alpha_n(\omega)\to\alpha(\omega)$ for any $\omega\in\Omega$, the mapping α is also measurable.

Proof. Let $U\in\mathcal{C}\cap\mathscr{B}$ and let f be the function defined in condition 1.9.B. We have

$$\{\alpha(\omega)\in U\}=\bigcup_{m=1}^{\infty}\bigcup_{k=1}^{\infty}\bigcap_{n=m}^{\infty}\left\{|f[\alpha_n(\omega)]|>\frac{1}{k}\right\}.$$

The function $f[\alpha_n(\omega)]$ is measurable, so that $\{|f[\alpha_n(\omega)]| > \frac{1}{k}\} \in \mathscr{M}$. Consequently $\{\alpha(\omega) \in U\} \in \mathscr{M}$. It may easily be deduced from this, by 1.9.A, that $\{\alpha(\omega) \in \Gamma\} \in \mathscr{M}$ for every $\Gamma \in \mathscr{B}$.

A term may be introduced that we shall occasionally find useful below.

We shall say that the points t_k^n define a canonical sequence of subdivisions $\{\Delta_k^n\}$ of the interval Δ if:

1) for any n, $\Delta = \bigcup_k \Delta_k^n, \Delta_i^n$ and Δ_j^n being disjoint for $i \neq j$;

2) the points t_k^n is the right-hand end of the interval Δ_k^n; all the points t_k^n belong to Δ;

3) $\lim_{n\to\infty} \sup_k |\Delta_k^n| = 0$ where $|\Delta_k^n| = |t_k^n - t_{k-1}^n|$ is the length of the interval Δ_k^n.

Lemma 1.10. Let Δ be a numerical interval, $(\Omega, \mathscr{M})$ a measurable space, and $(E, \mathscr{C}, \mathscr{B})$ a topological measurable space satisfying conditions 1.9.A-1.9.B. Let the mapping F of the product $\Delta \times \Omega$ into E satisfy the conditions:

a) for any $t \in \Delta$, the mapping F is a the measurable mapping of $(\Omega, \mathscr{M})$ into $(E, \mathscr{B})$;

b) for any $\omega \in \Omega$, the mapping F is the mapping, continuous from the right, of Δ into $(E, \mathscr{C})$*).

Then F is the measurable mapping of $(\Delta \times \Omega, \mathscr{B}_\Delta \times \mathscr{M})$ into $(E, \mathscr{B})$.

Proof. Let the points t_k^n define a canonical sequence of subdivisions $\{\Delta_k^n\}$ of the interval Δ. In view of a), the mappings F_n of the space $\Delta \times \Omega$ into E are given by

$$F_n(t, \omega) = F(t_k^n, \omega), \qquad \text{if } t \in \Delta_k^n,$$

and are measurable. In view of b),

$$F_n(t, \omega) \to F(t, \omega)$$

as $n \to \infty$ and F is measurable by lemma 1.9.

A metric measurable space is the triple $(E, \rho, \mathscr{B})$, where

*) That is, for any $\omega \in \Omega$ and $t_0 \in \Delta$ $F(t, \omega) \to F(t_0, \omega)$, if $t \downarrow t_0$.

the pair (E, ρ) is a metric space and the pair $(E, \mathscr{B})$ a measurable space. When the σ-algebra $\mathscr{B}$ is generated by the system of all open sets of the space (E, ρ) we shall write (E, ρ) for brevity instead of $(E, \rho, \mathscr{B})$. It may be noticed that conditions 1.9.A and 1.9.B are satisfied in this case: $\rho(x, \bar{U})$ can be taken as the function $f(x)$.

5. The Construction of Probability Measures

1.10 The following general theorem is usually taken as the basis for constructing probability measures.

Theorem 1.1. Let $\mathcal{C}$ be a system of subsets of a set E satisfying the conditions:

1.10.A$_1$. $E \in \mathcal{C}$.

1.10.A$_2$. If $A \in \mathcal{C}$, then $\bar{A}$ can be expressed as the sum of a finite number of disjoint elements of $\mathcal{C}$.

1.10.A$_3$. If $A, B \in \mathcal{C}$, then $AB \in \mathcal{C}$.

Let $\Phi(A)$ be a function in system $\mathcal{C}$ such that:

1.10.B$_1$. $\Phi(A) \geqslant 0$ for every $A \in \mathcal{C}$.

1.10.B$_2$. If $A = \bigcup_1^\infty A_n$, where $A, A_1, A_2, \ldots \in \mathcal{C}$ and $A_i A_j = \emptyset$ for $i \neq j$, then

$$\Phi(A) = \sum_{n=1}^{\infty} \Phi(A_n).$$

1.10.B$_3$. $\Phi(E) = 1$.

Then there exists a unique probability measure $\mathbf{P}(A)$ on the σ-algebra $\sigma(\mathcal{C})$ such that

$$\mathbf{P}(A) = \Phi(A) \qquad (A \in \mathcal{C}). \tag{1.26}$$

The uniqueness of the measure $\mathbf{P}$ follows directly from lemma 1.1. For let $\tilde{\mathbf{P}}$ be a measure in $\sigma(\mathcal{C})$ which, like $\mathbf{P}$, satisfies condition (1.26). We put $B \in \mathscr{F}$ if $\tilde{\mathbf{P}}(B) = \mathbf{P}(B)$. Obviously $\mathscr{F} \supseteq \mathcal{C}$ and is a λ-system. Since $\mathcal{C}$ is a π-system, $\mathscr{F} \supseteq \sigma(\mathcal{C})$ by lemma 1.1.

In order to construct at least one measure $\mathbf{P}$ satisfying condition (1.26) we put for each $B \subseteq E$

$$\mathbf{P}(B) = \inf \sum_{n=1}^{\infty} \mathbf{P}(A_n),$$

where $A_1, \ldots, A_n, \ldots \in \mathcal{C}$ and the lower bound runs over all the systems $\{A_n\}$ such that $\bigcup_{n=1}^{\infty} A_n \supseteq B$. We consider the system $\mathscr{B}$ of all sets B for which $P(B) + P(\bar{B}) = 1$. It may be shown that the system $\mathscr{B}$ contains $\mathcal{C}$ and is a σ-algebra and that the function $\mathbf{P}(B)$, if it is considered only in the σ-algebra $\mathscr{B}$, is a measure satisfying conditions (1.26). This is all the more true if $\mathbf{P}$ is considered only in the σ-algebra $\sigma(\mathcal{C})$, which is contained in $\mathscr{B}$.

1.11 We take an important example. Let $E = [a, b]$*) and let the function $F(u)$ $(u \in [a, b])$ satisfy the following conditions:

1.11.A. $F(u)$ is non-decreasing;

1.11.B. $F(u)$ is continuous from the right;

1.11.C. $F(b) = 1$

We write $\mathcal{C}$ for the aggregate of all intervals $(s, t]$ $(a \leqslant s < t \leqslant b)$ and $[a, t]$ $(a \leqslant t \leqslant b)$ and put

$$\Phi(s, t] = F(t) - F(s), \quad \Phi[a, t] = F(t).$$

It may easily be seen that $\mathcal{C}$ satisfies conditions $1.10.A_1$-$1.10.A_3$, and Φ the conditions $1.10.B_1$-$1.10.B_3$. The probability measure $\mathbf{P}(A)$, the existence of which is asserted in theorem 1.1, obviously satisfies the condition

$$\mathbf{P}[a, t] = F(t). \tag{1.27}$$

1.12. Theorem 1.2. Let T be an arbitrary set, $\widetilde{T}$ a subset of T, $(E, \mathcal{C}, \mathscr{B})$ a σ-compact topological space satisfying condition 1.9.A. We write E^T for the class of all functions $\varphi(t)$ on the set T with values from E and $\mathcal{N}_{\widetilde{T}}$ for the σ-algebra in the space E^T generated by the sets $\{\varphi : \varphi(t) \in \Gamma\}$ $(t \in \widetilde{T}, \Gamma \in \mathscr{B})$. Let the function $\Phi_{t_1, \ldots, t_n}(\Gamma_1, \ldots, \Gamma_n)$ $(\Gamma_1, \ldots, \Gamma_n \in \mathscr{B})$ be given for every $n = 1, 2, \ldots$ u and any $t_1, \ldots, t_n \in \widetilde{T}$, and let this function be subject to the following requirements:

*) a and b can take either finite or infinite values.

1.12.A. $\Phi_{t_{i_1}, \ldots, t_{i_n}}(\Gamma_{i_1}, \ldots, \Gamma_{i_n}) = \Phi_{t_1, \ldots, t_n}(\Gamma_1, \ldots, \Gamma_n)$ for any permutation $(i_1, \ldots, i_n)$ of the numbers $1, 2, \ldots, n$.

1.12.B. If the values of all the arguments except one of the function $\Phi_{t_1, \ldots, t_n}(\Gamma_1, \ldots, \Gamma_n)$ are fixed in an arbitrary manner, the function is a measure with respect to the remaining argument.

1.12.C. $\Phi_t(E) = 1$;

$$\Phi_{t_1, \ldots, t_{n-1}, t_n}(\Gamma_1, \ldots, \Gamma_{n-1}, E) = \Phi_{t_1, \ldots, t_{n-1}}(\Gamma_1, \ldots, \Gamma_{n-1}) \quad (n > 1).$$

Then there exists the unique probability measure $\mathbf{P}$ in the σ-algebra $\mathcal{N}_{\widetilde{T}}$ such that, for any $t_1, \ldots, t_n \in \widetilde{T}$, $\Gamma_1, \ldots, \Gamma_n \in \mathscr{B}$:

$$\mathbf{P}\{\varphi(t_1) \in \Gamma_1, \ldots, \varphi(t_n) \in \Gamma_n\} = \Phi_{t_1, \ldots, t_n}(\Gamma_1, \ldots, \Gamma_n). \tag{1.28}$$

We prove this theorem by observing that the subsets of the space E^T that have the form

$$A = \{\varphi : \varphi(t_1) \in \Gamma_1, \ldots, \varphi(t_n) \in \Gamma_n\}$$
$$(n = 1, 2, \ldots; \quad t_1, \ldots, t_n \in \widetilde{T}; \ \Gamma_1, \ldots, \Gamma_n \in \mathscr{B}),$$

form a system $\mathcal{C}$ that satisfies conditions 1.10.A_1-1.10.A_3. It may further be verified that the function Φ, defined in the system $\mathcal{C}$ by the expression

$$\Phi\{\varphi(t_1) \in \Gamma_1, \ldots, \varphi(t_n) \in \Gamma_n\} = \Phi_{t_1, \ldots, t_n}(\Gamma_1, \ldots, \Gamma_n),$$

satisfies requirements 1.10.B_1-1.10.B_3 (the assumptions regarding the topology of the space $(E, \mathscr{B})$, introduced in the statement of the theorem, are employed in verifying property 1.10.B_2). After this, theorem 1.2 follows from theorem 1.1.

CHAPTER 2

MARKOV PROCESSES

1. The Definition of Markov Process

2.1 The clearest picture of a Markov process may be got from the following description. Suppose a particle is in random motion in a space E during the interval of time $[0, \zeta)$. If the position of the particle is known at the instant t, supplementary information regarding the phenomena observed up till the instant t (and in particular, regarding the nature of the motion until t) has no effect on prognosis of the motion after the instant t (for a known "present", the "future" and the "past" are independent of each other). The instant ζ at which the motion is cut off may be random.

The accurate definition is as follows. Given:

a) a function $\zeta(\omega)$ in a space Ω, taking non-negative values (including the value $+\infty$);

b) a function $x(t, \omega) = x_t(\omega)$, defined for $\omega \in \Omega$, $t \in [0, \zeta(\omega))$ and taking values from a measurable space $(E, \mathscr{B})$ (the σ-algebra $\mathscr{B}$ is assumed to contain all the subsets consisting of a single point);

c) for each $0 \leqslant s \leqslant t$, a σ-algebra $\mathscr{M}_t^s$ in the space $\Omega_t = \{\omega : \zeta(\omega) > t\}$;

d) for each $s \geqslant 0$, $x \in E$ a function $\mathbf{P}_{s,x}(A)$ on a σ-algebra $\mathscr{M}^s$ in the space Ω containing $\mathscr{M}_t^s$ for all $t \geqslant s$.

We shall say that these elements define a Markov process $X = (x_t, \zeta, \mathscr{M}_t^s, \mathbf{P}_{s,x})$ if the following conditions are satisfied:

2.1.A. $s \leqslant t \leqslant u$ and $A \in \mathscr{M}_t^s$, then $\{A, \zeta > u\} \in \mathscr{M}_u^s$.

2.1.B. $\{x_t \in \Gamma\} \in \mathscr{M}_t^s$ for any $0 \leqslant s \leqslant t$, $\Gamma \in \mathscr{B}$*).

*) We find, in particular, on setting $\Gamma = E$ that $\{\zeta > t\} \in \mathscr{M}_t^s$ for any $0 \leqslant s \leqslant t$.

2.1.C. $\mathbf{P}_{s,x}$ is a probability measure on the σ-algebra $\mathcal{M}^s$.

2.1.D. For any $0 \leqslant s \leqslant t$, $\Gamma \in \mathcal{B}$

$$P(s, x; t, \Gamma) = \mathbf{P}_{s,x}\{x_t \in \Gamma\} \tag{2.1}$$

is a $\mathcal{B}$-measurable function of x.

2.1.E. $P(s, x; s, E \setminus x) = 0$.

2.1.F. If $0 \leqslant s \leqslant t \leqslant u$, $x \in E$, $\Gamma \in \mathcal{B}$, then

$$\mathbf{P}_{s,x}\{x_u \in \Gamma \mid \mathcal{M}_t^s\} = P(t, x_t; u, \Gamma) \quad (\text{a.c. } \Omega_t, \mathbf{P}_{s,x}). \tag{2.2}$$

The set Ω is called the space of elementary events. The measurable space $(E, \mathcal{B})$ is called the phase space, the quantity ζ the instant of cut-off (or the life), the function $P(s, x; t, \Gamma)$ the transition function of the process X. With ω fixed the function $x_t(\omega)$ $(t \in [0, \zeta(\omega)))$ defines the trajectory of the process in the space E corresponding to the elementary event ω.

The σ-algebra $\mathcal{M}_t^s$ can be pictured as the class of events which are observed during the interval of time $[s, t]$. The value of $\mathbf{P}_{s,x}(A)$ $(A \in \mathcal{M}^s)$ is interpreted as the probability of event A on condition that the particle is at the point x at the instant s.

Condition 2.1.F can be replaced by the following:

2.1.F'. If $0 \leqslant s \leqslant t \leqslant u$, $x \in E$, $A \in \mathcal{M}_t^s$, then

$$\mathbf{P}_{s,x}(A, x_u \in \Gamma) = \int_A P(t, x_t; u, \Gamma)\,\mathbf{P}_{s,x}(d\omega). \tag{2.3}$$

For by definition of conditional probability (see sec. 1.6), 2.1.F is equivalent to the combination of 2.1.F' and the requirement that $P(t, x_t; u, \Gamma)$ be an $\mathcal{M}_t^s$-measurable function of ω. But this latter requirement follows from condition 2.1.D. In fact, the mapping of Ω_t into the segment $I_1^0 = [0, 1]$ defined by the function $P(t, x_t; u, \Gamma)$ is the product of the measurable mapping of $(\Omega_t, \mathcal{M}_t^s)$ into $(E, \mathcal{B})$ defined by the function $x_t(\omega)$ and the measurable mapping of $(E, \mathcal{B})$ in $(I_1^0, \mathcal{B}_1^0)$ defined by the function $P(t, x; u, \Gamma)$.

An important class of Markov processes is provided by those for which $\zeta(\omega) = +\infty$ for all $\omega \in \Omega$. We shall refer to these as non-cut-off processes and write them as $(x_t, \mathcal{M}_t^s, \mathbf{P}_{s,x})$.

__Remark.__ The above definition of Markov processes can be somewhat widened. We fix a set T of real numbers and assume that:

a) $\zeta(\omega)$ can take only values from T and the improper value $+\infty$;

b) the function $x_t(\omega)$ is defined for values of $t \in T$ less than $\zeta(\omega)$;

c) the σ-algebras $\mathcal{M}_t^s$ and $\mathcal{M}^s$ and the functions $\mathbf{P}_{s,x}$ are defined only for $s, t \in T$.

If this assemblage satisfies conditions 2.1.A-2.1.F, it is said to define a __Markov process in the time set__ T*). On putting $T = [0, +\infty)$, we return to the fundamental case considered at the beginning of sec. 2.1. If T coincides with the set of all non-negative integers (or positive integers), we speak of a __discrete Markov process__ or __Markov chain.__ We shall save ourselves unnecessary complexity in the future by confining ourselves to the fundamental case $T = [0, +\infty)$, since the case of an arbitrary set T does not differ from this in any essentials.

Some further concepts related to Markov processes may usefully be introduced.

We shall describe as a __Markov random function__ in the phase space $(E, \mathscr{B})$ and in the time interval $I = [a, b]$ the aggregate of the following objects:

a) the function $\zeta(\omega)$ in some set Ω with values from the segment $[a, b]$;

b) the function $x_t(\omega) = x(t, \omega)$ defined for $\omega \in \Omega$, $t \in [a, \zeta(\omega))$ and taking values from E;

c) for each $t \in I$ the σ-algebra $\mathcal{M}_t$ in the space $\Omega_t = \{\zeta > t\}$;

d) the probability measure $\mathbf{P}$ on the σ-algebra $\mathcal{M}$ in space Ω, containing $\mathcal{M}_t$ for all $t \in I$.

It is required here that:

---

*)The concept obviously remains meaningful in the case of any ordered, or even partially ordered, set T.

2.1. α_1. $\{x_t \in \Gamma\} \in \mathcal{M}_t$ for any $\Gamma \in \mathcal{B}$, $t \in I$.

2.1. α_2. $\mathcal{M}_t[\Omega_u] \subseteq \mathcal{M}_u$ for any $t \leqslant u \in I$.

2.1. α_3. $\mathbf{P}\{x_u \in \Gamma \mid \mathcal{M}_t\} = \mathbf{P}\{x_u \in \Gamma \mid x_t\}$ (a.c. Ω_t, $\mathbf{P}$)*) for any $t \leqslant u \in I$ and $\Gamma \in \mathcal{B}$.

We shall speak of a <u>Markov family of random functions</u> if there is associated with each pair $s \geqslant 0$, $x \in E$ a Markov random function $X^{s,x} = \{x_t^{s,x}, \zeta^{s,x}, \mathcal{M}_t^{s,x}, \mathbf{P}^{s,x}\}$ in the phase space $(E, \mathcal{B})$ and in the time interval $[s, \infty)$. The following conditions must be fulfilled here:

2.1. β_1. $P(s, x; t, \Gamma) = \mathbf{P}^{s,x}\{x_t^{s,x} \in \Gamma\}$ is a $\mathcal{B}$-measurable function of x.

2.1. β_2. $P(s, x; s, E \setminus x) = 0$.

2.1. β_3. $\mathbf{P}^{s,x}\{x_u^{s,x} \in \Gamma \mid x_t^{s,x}\} = P(t, x_t^{s,x}; u, \Gamma)$ (a.c. $\Omega_t^{s,x}, \mathbf{P}^{s,x}$), for any $0 \leqslant s \leqslant t \leqslant u$, $\Gamma \in \mathcal{B}$.

Let $X = (x_t, \zeta, \mathcal{M}_t^s, \mathbf{P}_{s,x})$ be an arbitrary Markov process. We fix an $s \geqslant 0$ and $x \in E$ and put

$$\zeta^{s,x}(\omega) = \max(\zeta(\omega), s),$$

$$x_t^{s,x}(\omega) = x_t(\omega) \qquad (t \in [s, \infty),\ \omega \in \Omega_t),$$

$$\mathcal{M}_t^{s,x} = \mathcal{M}_t^s \qquad (t \in [s, \infty)),$$

$$\mathbf{P}^{s,x}(A) = \mathbf{P}_{s,x}(A) \qquad (A \in \mathcal{M}^s).$$

The elements $(\zeta^{s,x}, x_t^{s,x}, \mathcal{M}_t^{s,x}, \mathbf{P}^{s,x})$ are easily seen to define a Markov random function in the time interval $[s, \infty)$. The aggregate of these functions for all $s \geqslant 0$, $x \in E$ is clearly a Markov family.

On the other hand, a Markov process may readily be associated with each Markov family of random functions $X^{s,x} = (x_t^{s,x}, \zeta^{s,x}, \mathcal{M}_t^{s,x}, \mathbf{P}^{s,x})$. For let $\tilde{\Omega}$ be the class of triples (s, x, ω), where $s \geqslant 0$, $x \in E$, $\omega \in \Omega^{s,x}$, and let

$$\tilde{\zeta}(s, x, \omega) = \zeta^{s,x}(\omega),$$

$$\tilde{x}_t(s, x, \omega) = x_t^{s,x}(\omega), \qquad \text{if } t \in [s, \zeta^{s,x}(\omega))$$

---

*) $\mathbf{P}\{-\mid x_t\}$ denotes the conditional probability with respect to the σ-algebra in the space Ω_t generated by the sets $\{x_t \in B\}$ $(B \in \mathcal{B})$.

[we define the function $\widetilde{x}_t(s, x, \omega)$ in an arbitrary manner for $t\in[0, s)$]. For each $A\subseteq\widetilde{\Omega}$ we put

$$A^{s,x}=\{\omega:(s, x, \omega)\in A\}.$$

We write $\widetilde{\mathcal{M}}^s$ for the class of all sets $A\subseteq\widetilde{\Omega}$, such that $A^{s,x}\in\mathcal{M}^{s,x}$ for any $x\in E$, and $\widetilde{\mathcal{M}}_t^s$ for the class of all $A\subseteq\Omega$ such that $A^{s,x}\in\mathcal{M}_t^{s,x}$ for any $x\in E$. It can easily be seen that $\widetilde{\mathcal{M}}_t^s$ is a σ-algebra in the space $\widetilde{\Omega}_t=\{\widetilde{\zeta}>t\}$ and $\widetilde{\mathcal{M}}^s$ a σ-algebra in the space $\widetilde{\Omega}$, where $\widetilde{\mathcal{M}}^s\supseteq\widetilde{\mathcal{M}}_t^s$ for all $t\geqslant s$. Finally, for every $A\in\widetilde{\mathcal{M}}^s$ we put

$$\widetilde{\mathbf{P}}_{s,x}(A)=\mathbf{P}^{s,x}(A^{s,x}).$$

We leave it to the reader to verify that the system $(\widetilde{x}_t, \widetilde{\zeta}, \widetilde{\mathcal{M}}_t^s, \widetilde{\mathbf{P}}_{s,x})$ satisfies conditions 2.1.A-2.1.F and is therefore a Markov process.

2.2. We shall use the notation $\mathcal{N}_t^s$ for the σ-algebra in the space Ω_t generated by the sets $\{\omega:x_u(\omega)\in\Gamma\}\cap\Omega_t$ $(u\in I_t^s,\ \Gamma\in\mathscr{B})$, and $\mathcal{N}^s$ for the σ-algebra in the space generated by the sets $\{\omega:x_u(\omega)\in\Gamma\}$ $(u\in I^s,\ \Gamma\in\mathscr{B})$.

In view of conditions 2.1.A and 2.1.B, $\mathcal{N}_t^s\subseteq\mathcal{M}_t^s$, and $\mathcal{N}^s\subseteq\mathcal{M}^s$. Obviously, $(x_t, \zeta, \mathcal{N}_t^s, \mathbf{P}_{s,x})$ is a Markov process as well as $(x_t, \zeta, \mathcal{M}_t^s, \mathbf{P}_{s,x})$.

Furthermore, we put $A\in\overline{\mathcal{M}}^s$ if there exist sets B_1 and B_2 of $\mathcal{M}^s$ for every $x\in E$ such that $B_1\subseteq A\subseteq B_2$ and $\mathbf{P}_{s,x}(B_1)=\mathbf{P}_{s,x}(B_2)$.

On putting $\mathbf{P}_{s,x}(A)=P_{s,x}(B_1)=\mathbf{P}_{s,x}(B_2)$, we extend the probability measures $\mathbf{P}_{s,x}$ to the σ-algebra $\overline{\mathcal{M}}^s$. This evidently does not affect the fact of $(x_t, \zeta, \mathcal{M}_t^s, \mathbf{P}_{s,x})$ being a Markov process; it is not affected even by replacing the σ-algebras $\mathcal{M}_t^s$ by the wider σ-algebras $\overline{\mathcal{M}}_t^s$, which are constructed as follows: we put $A\in\overline{\mathcal{M}}_t^s$ if $A\in\overline{\mathcal{M}}^s$, $A\subseteq\Omega_t$ and for every $x\in E$ there exists $B\in\mathcal{M}_t^s$ such that

$$\mathbf{P}_{s,x}(A\setminus AB)=\mathbf{P}_{s,x}(B\setminus AB)=0.$$

<u>Theorem 2.1</u>. Let $(x_t, \zeta, \mathcal{M}_t^s, \mathbf{P}_{s,x})$ be a Markov process and let $0\leqslant s\leqslant t$. If $B\in\mathcal{N}^t$, then

$$\mathbf{P}_{s,x}(B\,|\,\mathcal{M}_t^s)=\mathbf{P}_{t,x_t}(B)\qquad(\text{a.c. }\Omega_t,\ \mathbf{P}_{s,x})\ ^{*)}. \tag{2.4}$$

---

*)It is clear from (2.4) that, for any $B\in\mathcal{N}^t$ the function $\mathbf{P}_{s,y}(B)$ can be constructed in accordance with $\mathbf{P}_{0,x}$ as far as a y-set Γ', for which $P(0, x; s, \Gamma')=0$.

If ξ is $\mathcal{N}^t$ measurable and $\mathbf{P}_{s,x}$-summable, then

$$\mathbf{M}_{s,x}(\xi\,|\,\mathcal{M}_t^s) = \mathbf{M}_{t,x_t}\xi \qquad (\text{a.c. } \Omega_t,\ \mathbf{P}_{s,x}). \tag{2.5}$$

Proof. Expressions (2.4) and (2.5) will be proved simultaneously. We start by showing that (2.5) is satisfied for $\xi = f(x_u)$, where $u \geqslant t$ and f is a bounded $\mathcal{B}$-measurable function in space E. Let $\mathcal{L}$ be the class of all bounded functions $f(x)$ $(x \in E)$ and $\mathcal{H}$ the class of all $\mathcal{B}$-measurable functions f such that $f(x_u)$ satisfies (2.5). Clearly, $\mathcal{H}$ is an $\mathcal{L}$-system. In view of 2.1.F, $\mathcal{H}$ contains the characteristic functions of all sets $\Gamma \in \mathcal{B}$. By lemma 1.2, $\mathcal{H}$ contains all bounded $\mathcal{B}$-measurable functions.

We now prove that (2.4) is satisfied for every set

$$B = \{x_{u_1} \in \Gamma_1, \ldots, x_{u_n} \in \Gamma_n\}\ (t \leqslant u_1, \ldots, u_n;\ \Gamma_1, \ldots, \Gamma_n \in \mathcal{B}). \tag{2.6}$$

If $n = 1$, this is true in view of 2.1.F. We now use induction. Let

$$B_1 = \{x_{u_1} \in \Gamma_1\};\quad B_2 = \{x_{u_2} \in \Gamma_2, \ldots, x_{u_n} \in \Gamma_n\}.$$

Obviously, $B = B_1 B_2$, and by 1.6.H,

$$\mathbf{P}_{s,x}(B\,|\,\mathcal{M}_t^s) = \mathbf{M}_{s,x}\{\chi_{B_1}\mathbf{P}_{s,x}[B_2\,|\,\mathcal{M}_{u_1}^s]\,|\,\mathcal{M}_t^s\}\ (\text{a.c. } \Omega_t, \mathbf{P}_{s,x}).$$

We have by induction:

$$\mathbf{P}_{s,x}(B_2\,|\,\mathcal{M}_{u_1}^s) = \mathbf{P}_{u_1, x_{u_1}}(B_2) \qquad (\text{a.c. } \Omega_{u_1},\ \mathbf{P}_{s,x}).$$

Therefore

$$\begin{aligned}\mathbf{P}_{s,x}(B\,|\,\mathcal{M}_t^s) &= \mathbf{M}_{s,x}\{\chi_{B_1}\mathbf{P}_{u_1, x_{u_1}}(B_2)\,|\,\mathcal{M}_t\} = \\ &= \mathbf{M}_{s,x}\{f(x_{u_1})\,|\,\mathcal{M}_t^s\} \qquad (\text{a.c. } \Omega_t,\ \mathbf{P}_{s,x}),\end{aligned}$$

where

$$f(x) = \chi_{\Gamma_1}(x)\,\mathbf{P}_{u_1,x}(B_2).$$

On applying the particular case of (2.5) already proved, we have

$$\mathbf{M}_{s,x}\{f(x_{u_1})\,|\,\mathcal{M}_t^s\} = \mathbf{M}_{t,x_t} f(x_{u_1}) \qquad (\text{a.c. } \Omega_t,\ \mathbf{P}_{s,x}). \tag{2.7}$$

On the other hand, by 1.6.H and our inductive assumption,

$$\mathbf{P}_{t, y}(B) = \mathbf{M}_{t, y}\{\chi_{B_1}\mathbf{P}_{t, y}[B_2 \| \mathcal{M}^t_{u_1}]\} =$$
$$= \mathbf{M}_{t, y}[\chi_{B_1}\mathbf{P}_{u_1, x_{u_1}}(B_2)] = \mathbf{M}_{t, y} f(x_{u_1}). \tag{2.8}$$

On comparing (2.7) and (2.8), we conclude that (2.4) is satisfied for all sets of the type (2.6).

We now write $\mathcal{L}$ for the class of all $\mathbf{P}_{s, x}$-summable functions $\xi(\omega)$ $(\omega \in \Omega)$. Obviously, the set $\mathcal{H}$ of all functions for which condition (2.5) is satisfied is an $\mathcal{L}$-system. By what has been proved, $\mathcal{H}$ contains the characteristic functions of all sets (2.6). The latter form a π-system generating the σ-algebra $\mathcal{N}^t$. By lemma 1.2, $\mathcal{H}$ contains all $\mathcal{N}^t$-measurable $\mathbf{P}_{s, x}$-summable functions. Relationship (2.5) is now fully proved. If B is any set of $\mathcal{N}^t$, on putting $\xi = \chi_B$ in (2.5) we get (2.4).

Corollary. If $A \in \mathcal{M}^s_t$, $B \in \mathcal{N}^t$, then

$$\mathbf{P}_{s, x}(AB) = \int_A \mathbf{P}_{t, x_t}(B)\, \mathbf{P}_{s, x}(d\omega). \tag{2.9}$$

If ξ is $\mathcal{N}^s_t$-measurable η $\mathcal{N}^t$-measurable and $\xi\eta$ $\mathbf{P}_{s, x}$-summable then

$$\mathbf{M}_{s, x}\xi\eta = \mathbf{M}_{s, x}[\xi \mathbf{M}_{t, x_t}\eta] \text{ *)}. \tag{2.10}$$

Expression (2.9) follows from a comparison of (2.4) and (1.11), and (2.10) from a comparison of (2.5) and 1.6.I.

2.3. We put

$$P(s, x; A; t, \Gamma) = \mathbf{P}_{s, x}\{A, x_t \in \Gamma\}$$
$$(0 \leqslant s \leqslant t,\ A \in \mathcal{M}^s_t,\ \Gamma \in \mathcal{B}).$$

On the basis of lemma 1.6, we can write condition 2.1.F′ in the following form.

2.1.F′′. $0 \leqslant s \leqslant t \leqslant u$, $\Gamma \in \mathcal{B}$, $A \in \mathcal{M}^s_t$, then

$$P(s, x; A; u, \Gamma) = \int_E P(s, x; A; t, dy)\, P(t, y; u, \Gamma). \tag{2.11}$$

*) The functions $\xi\eta$ and $\xi\mathbf{M}_{t, x_t}\eta$ are defined only on the set Ω_t. In accordance with sec. 1.6, their mathematical expectations are understood to imply integration over the set Ω_t.

We notice that, with $A = \Omega_t$ $P(s, x; A; u, \Gamma) = P(s, x; u, \Gamma)$ and equation (2.11) becomes

$$P(s, x; u, \Gamma) = \int_E P(s, x; t, dy) P(t, y; u, \Gamma) \quad (0 \leqslant s \leqslant t \leqslant u, \ \Gamma \in \mathscr{B}). \tag{2.12}$$

This relationship for the transition function of the process is usually known as the Kolmogorov-Chepmen equation *).

We put

$$P(s, x; t_1, \Gamma_1, \ldots, t_n, \Gamma_n) = \mathbf{P}_{s, x}(x_{t_1} \in \Gamma_1, \ldots, x_{t_n} \in \Gamma_n) \quad (x \in E; \ 0 \leqslant s \leqslant t_1, \ldots, t_n; \ \Gamma_1, \ldots, \Gamma_n \in \mathscr{B}). \tag{2.13}$$

Let $s \leqslant t_1 \leqslant \ldots \leqslant t_n$. On putting

$$A = \{x_{t_1} \in \Gamma_1, \ldots, x_{t_{n-1}} \in \Gamma_{n-1}\}, \quad t = t_{n-1}, \ u = t_n, \ \Gamma = \Gamma_n,$$

in relationship (2.11), we get

$$P(s, x; t_1, \Gamma_1, \ldots, t_n, \Gamma_n) = \int_{\Gamma_{n-1}} P(s, x; t_1, \Gamma_1, \ldots, t_{n-1}, dy) P(t_{n-1}, y; t_n, \Gamma). \tag{2.14}$$

Hence we find by induction that

$$P(s, x, t_1, \Gamma_1, \ldots, t_n, \Gamma_n) = \int_{\Gamma_1} \cdots \int_{\Gamma_{n-1}} P(s, x; t_1, dy_1) \times \times P(t_1, y_1; t_2, dy_2) \ldots P(t_{n-1}, y_{n-1}, t_n, \Gamma_n) \quad (s \leqslant t_1 \leqslant t_2 \leqslant \ldots \leqslant t_n; \ \Gamma_1, \ldots, \Gamma_n \in \mathscr{B}). \tag{2.15}$$

Lemma 2.1. If $\mathscr{M}_t^s = \mathscr{N}_t^s$, condition 2.1.F in the definition of Markov process can be replaced by the requirement that (2.14) be satisfied for any $n = 1, 2, \ldots, 0 \leqslant s \leqslant t_1 \leqslant t_2 \leqslant \ldots \leqslant t_n, \ \Gamma_1, \ldots, \Gamma_n \in \mathscr{B}$.

Proof. It follows at once from (2.14) that condition 2.1.F'' is satisfied for any

$$A = \{\Omega_t, x_{t_1} \in \Gamma_1, \ldots, x_{t_n} \in \Gamma_n\} \quad (n = 1, 2, \ldots; t_1, \ldots, t_n \in [s, t], \ \Gamma_1, \ldots, \Gamma_n \in \mathscr{B}). \tag{2.16}$$

*) On putting in particular $\Gamma = E$, $s = t = u$ and taking 2.1.E into account, $P(s, x; s, E)$ is seen to equal 0 or 1 for any $s \geqslant 0$, $x \in E$.

Sets (2.16) form a π-system $\mathcal{C}$ in Ω_t. On the other hand, the class $\mathcal{F}$ of all sets A for which condition 2.1.F'' is satisfied is a λ-system (in Ω_t). By lemma 1.1, since $\mathcal{F} \supseteq \mathcal{C}$ we have $\mathcal{F} \supseteq \sigma(\mathcal{C}) = \mathcal{N}_t^s$, and the lemma is proved.

Lemma 2.2. For any $s \geqslant 0$, $A \in \mathcal{N}^s$ $\mathbf{P}_{s,x}(A)$ is a $\mathcal{B}$-measurable function of x.

Proof. We show by induction over n that all the functions $P(s, x; t_1, \Gamma_1, \ldots, t_n, \Gamma_n)$ are measurable with respect to x. Our assertion follows for $n = 1$ from condition 2.1.D. The passage from $n-1$ to n is accomplished by means of lemma 1.7 and equation (2.14).

We now remark that the class $\mathcal{F}$ of all $A \in \mathcal{N}^s$ for which the assertion of the lemma holds is a λ-system. By what has been proved, $\mathcal{F}$ contains the π-system $\mathcal{C}$, consisting of the sets

$$A = \{x_{t_1} \in \Gamma_1, \ldots, x_{t_n} \in \Gamma_n\}$$
$$(n = 1, 2, \ldots; t_1, \ldots, t_n \geqslant s;$$
$$\Gamma_1, \ldots, \Gamma_n \in \mathcal{B}).$$

In view of lemma 1.1, $\mathcal{F} \supseteq \sigma(\mathcal{C}) = \mathcal{N}^s$. The lemma is proved.

2.4. Let μ be an arbitrary measure on the σ-algebra $\mathcal{B}$. In accordance with lemma 2.2, the integral

$$\mathbf{P}_{s,\mu}(A) = \int_E \mathbf{P}_{s,x}(A)\,\mu(dx).$$

has a meaning for any $A \in \mathcal{N}^s$.

It may readily be seen that this integral defines a measure on the σ-algebra $\mathcal{N}^s$ and that (2.3) [and therefore also (2.2)] remains true on replacing $\mathbf{P}_{s,x}$ by $\mathbf{P}_{s,\mu}$*). If μ is a probability measure, $\mathbf{P}_{s,\mu}$ is also a probability measure, and the

---

*) It may easily be verified, on the basis of lemma 1.2, that

$$\int_E \int_\Omega f(\omega)\,\mathbf{P}_{s,x}(d\omega)\,\mu(dx) = \int_\Omega f(\omega)\,\mathbf{P}_{s,\mu}(d\omega).$$

for any $\mathcal{N}^s$-measurable bounded function $f(\omega)$. Expression (2.3) soon follows from this.

value $\mathbf{P}_{s,\mu}(A)$ is naturally interpreted as the probability of event A if the moving particle has a probability distribution μ at the instant s.

We write $A \in \overline{\mathcal{N}}^s$ if, for every measure μ on the σ-algebra $\mathcal{B}$, an A_1, A_2 of $\mathcal{N}^s$ can be constructed such that $A_1 \subseteq A \subseteq A_2$ and $\mathbf{P}_{s,\mu}(A_1) = \mathbf{P}_{s,\mu}(A_2)$. Obviously, $\overline{\mathcal{N}}^s \subseteq \overline{\mathcal{M}}^s$. The measures $\mathbf{P}_{s,\mu}$ can be extended to the σ-algebra $\overline{\mathcal{N}}^s$ in precisely the way the measures $\mathbf{P}_{s,x}$ were extended in sec. 2.2 to the σ-algebra $\overline{\mathcal{M}}^s$.

Theorem 2.1′. Expressions (2.4) and (2.5) remain valid for any $B \in \overline{\mathcal{N}}^t$ and any $\overline{\mathcal{N}}^t$-measurable $\mathbf{P}_{s,x}$-summable function ξ. Expressions (2.9) and (2.10) remain valid for any $A \in \mathcal{M}_t^s$, $B \in \overline{\mathcal{N}}^t$ and any functions ξ, η, such that ξ is $\mathcal{M}_t^s$-measurable, η $\overline{\mathcal{N}}^t$-measurable, and η and $\xi\eta$ $\mathbf{P}_{s,x}$-summable*).

Proof. Let $A \in \mathcal{M}_t^s$, $B \in \overline{\mathcal{N}}^t$. The expression

$$\mu(\Gamma) = \mathbf{P}_{s,x}(A,\ x_t \in \Gamma) \quad (\Gamma \in \mathcal{B})$$

defines a measure in $\mathcal{B}$. We choose B_1 and B_2 from $\mathcal{N}^t$ such that $B_1 \subseteq B \subseteq B_2$ and $\mathbf{P}_{t,\mu}(B_1) = \mathbf{P}_{t,\mu}(B_2)$. By the corollary of theorem 2.1,

$$\mathbf{P}_{s,x}(AB_i) = \int_A \mathbf{P}_{t,x_t}(B_i)\,\mathbf{P}_{s,x}(d\omega) = \int_E \mu(dy)\,\mathbf{P}_{t,y}(B_i) = \mathbf{P}_{t,\mu}(B_i).$$

It follows from $AB_1 \subseteq AB \subseteq AB_2$ that

$$\mathbf{P}_{t,\mu}(B_1) = \mathbf{P}_{s,x}(AB_1) \leqslant \mathbf{P}_{s,x}(AB) \leqslant \mathbf{P}_{s,x}(AB_2) = \mathbf{P}_{t,\mu}(B_2).$$

The extreme terms of this inequality are equal, so that

$$\mathbf{P}_{s,x}(AB) = \mathbf{P}_{t,\mu}(B_i) = \int_A \mathbf{P}_{t,x_t}(B_i)\,\mathbf{P}_{s,x}(d\omega). \tag{2.16′}$$

Furthermore, it follows from $B_1 \subseteq B \subseteq B_2$ that, for all $\omega \in \Omega_t$:

$$\mathbf{P}_{t,x_t}(B_1) \leqslant \mathbf{P}_{t,x_t}(B) \leqslant \mathbf{P}_{t,x_t}(B_2).$$

The integrals of the extreme terms over set A with respect to

---

*)We assume that all the measures $\mathbf{P}_{s,x}$ are extended to the σ-algebra $\overline{\mathcal{M}}^s$ as described in sec. 2.2.

the measure $\mathbf{P}_{s,x}$ are equal, therefore

$$\mathbf{P}_{t,x_t}(B_1)=\mathbf{P}_{t,x_t}(B)=\mathbf{P}_{t,x_t}(B_2) \qquad (\text{a.c. } A, \ \mathbf{P}_{s,x}).$$

Comparison of this expression with equation (2.16′) shows that (2.9) is satisfied. Hence it follows, by the definition of conditional probability, that equation (2.4) holds for every $B\in\overline{\mathcal{N}}^t$. We deduce (2.5) from (2.4) by making standard use of lemma 1.2. Finally, (2.10), follows from a comparison of (2.5) and 1.6.3.

<u>Remark</u>. As mentioned in sec. 2.2, the Markov nature of a process is not affected by replacing $\mathcal{M}_t^s$ by $\overline{\mathcal{M}}_t^s$. We can therefore write $\overline{\mathcal{M}}_t^s$ for $\mathcal{M}_t^s$ in the statements of theorems 2.1 and 2.1′.

2. <u>Stationary Markov Processes</u>

2.5. Let $\mathcal{N}^*$ denote the minimal system of subsets of the space $\Omega_0=\{\zeta>0\}$ that contains all the sets $\{x_t\in\Gamma\}$ $(t\geqslant 0,\ \Gamma\in\mathscr{B})$ and is closed with respect to the operations of addition and intersection of any number of sets and with respect to the operation of taking complements. The Markov process $X=(x_t,\ \zeta,\ \mathcal{M}_t^s,\ \mathbf{P}_{s,x})$ is said to be <u>stationary</u> if a subset $\theta_t A\subseteq\Omega$ can be associated with any $t\geqslant 0$ and any subset $A\in\mathcal{N}^*$ such that the following conditions are fulfilled:

2.5.A. $\theta_t\Omega_0=\Omega_t;\quad \theta_t(A\setminus B)=\theta_t A\setminus\theta_t B;$

$$\theta_t\Big(\bigcup A_\alpha\Big)=\bigcup\theta_t A_\alpha;\quad \theta_t\Big(\bigcap A_\alpha\Big)=\bigcap\theta_t A_\alpha$$

(the index α runs through an arbitrary set of values.)

2.5.B. $\theta_t\{x_h\in\Gamma\}=\{x_{t+h}\in\Gamma\} \qquad (h\geqslant 0,\ \Gamma\in\mathscr{B}).$

2.5.C. For any $A\in\mathcal{N}=\mathcal{N}^0[\Omega_0]$ $\mathbf{P}_{t,x}(\theta_t A)=\mathbf{P}_{0,x}(A).$

It may be observed that, if operators θ_t and $\widetilde{\theta}_t$ satisfy conditions 2.5.A-2.5.C, the system of sets $\mathcal{A}$ for which $\theta_t A=\widetilde{\theta}_t A$ contains the sets $\{x_h\in\Gamma\}$ $(h\geqslant 0,\ \Gamma\in\mathscr{B})$ and is invariant with respect to all set operations. It follows from this that operators θ_t are defined uniquely for the process X. The following properties of the θ_t are readily derived from 2.5.A-2.5.C:

2.5.D. $\theta_t \mathcal{N}_h^0 = \mathcal{N}_{t+h}^t$.

2.5.E. If $B \in \overline{\mathcal{N}}$, then $\theta_t B \in \overline{\mathcal{N}}$ and $\mathbf{P}_{t,x}(\theta_t B) = \mathbf{P}_{0,x}(B)$ (we assume that the measures $\mathbf{P}_{s,x}$ are extended to $\overline{\mathcal{M}}_s$ as indicated in sec. 2.2, and put $B \in \overline{\mathcal{N}}$ if $B \in \mathcal{N}^*$ and for every measure μ in $\mathscr{B}$ there are sets B_1 and B_2 of $\mathcal{N}$ such that $B_1 \subseteq B \subseteq B_2$ and $\mathbf{P}_{0,\mu}(B_1) = \mathbf{P}_{0,\mu}(B_2)$.

2.6. Let the function $\xi(\omega)$ $(\omega \in \Omega_0)$ be $\mathcal{N}^*$-measurable. The sets $\{\xi(\omega) = a\}$ are mutually disjoint and form the sum Ω_0. The sets $\theta_t\{\xi(\omega) = a\}$ are therefore also mutually disjoint and form the sum $\theta_t\Omega_0 = \Omega_t$. We put $\theta_t\xi(\omega) = a$ if $\omega \in \theta_t\{\xi = a\}$. Hence for every $\mathcal{N}^*$-measurable function $\xi(\omega)$ $(\omega \in \Omega_0)$ there is an associated function $\theta_t\xi(\omega)$ defined on the set Ω_t.

We can readily deduce the following properties of operators θ_t.

2.6.A. For any numerical set Γ:

$$\theta_t\{\xi \in \Gamma\} = \{\theta_t\xi \in \Gamma\}.$$

(it is clear from this that the function $\theta_t(\xi)$ is $\theta_t\mathcal{N}^*$-measurable.)

2.6.B. The necessary and sufficient condition for $\eta = \theta_t\xi$ is that, for any a,

$$\theta_t\{\xi = a\} = \{\eta = a\},$$

or that for any a,

$$\theta_t\{\xi > a\} = \{\eta > a\}.$$

2.6.C. $\theta_t\zeta = \zeta - t$ $(\omega \in \Omega_t)$. (This follows from 2.5.B and 2.6.B).

2.6.D. $\theta_t\chi_B = \chi_{\theta_t B}$ $(B \in \mathcal{N}^*)$.

2.6.E. If $f(x_1, \ldots, x_n, \ldots)$ is any function in the space R^∞ and $\xi_1, \ldots, \xi_n, \ldots$ are arbitrary $\mathcal{N}^*$-measurable ω-functions, we have

$$\theta_t f(\xi_1, \ldots, \xi_n, \ldots) = f(\theta_t\xi_1, \ldots, \theta_t\xi_n, \ldots).$$

In particular, the operators θ_t preserve all the algebraic operations and the operation of passage to the limit.

2.6.F. For every $\overline{\mathcal{N}}$-measurable function ξ:

$$\mathbf{M}_{t,x}\theta_t\xi = \mathbf{M}_{0,x}\xi. \tag{2.17}$$

The definition of operator $\theta_t\xi$, as also properties 2.6.A, 2.6.D, 2.6.E and the first half of 2.6.B are readily extended to functions whose values, instead of being numerical, are points of any measurable space $(E, \mathscr{B})$. (The main thing is simply that $\mathscr{B}$ should contain all sets consisting of a single point.) The functions $\xi(\omega)$ can in this case be defined in some subset $\widetilde{\Omega} \in \mathcal{N}^*$ instead of throughout the set Ω_0 ($\theta_t\xi$ being now defined in $\theta_t\widetilde{\Omega}$). If follows from 2.5.B and 2.6.A that

2.6.G. $\theta_t x_h = x_{t+h}$.

Theorem 2.2. Let $(x_t, \zeta, \mathcal{M}_t^s, \mathbf{P}_{s,x})$ be a stationary Markov process. Let $0 \leqslant s \leqslant t$. If $B \in \overline{\mathcal{N}}$, then

$$\mathbf{P}_{0,x}(\theta_t B \,\|\, \mathcal{M}_t^0) = \mathbf{P}_{0,x_t}(B) \qquad (\text{a.c. } \Omega_t, \mathbf{P}_{0,x}). \tag{2.18}$$

If ξ is $\overline{\mathcal{N}}$-measurable and $\mathbf{P}_{0,x}$-summable, then

$$\mathbf{M}_{0,x}(\theta_t\xi \,|\, \mathcal{M}_t^0) = \mathbf{M}_{0,x_t}\xi \qquad (\text{a.c. } \Omega_t, \mathbf{P}_{0,x}). \tag{2.19}$$

This is proved simply by comparing theorem 2.1′ with expressions 2.5.E and 2.6.F.

Corollary. If $A \in \mathcal{M}_t^0$, $B \in \overline{\mathcal{N}}$, then

$$\mathbf{P}_{0,x}(A\theta_t B) = \int_A \mathbf{P}_{0,x_t}(B)\,\mathbf{P}_{s,x}(d\omega). \tag{2.20}$$

If ξ is $\mathcal{M}_t^0$-measurable, η $\overline{\mathcal{N}}$-measurable and η and $\xi\theta_t\eta$ $\mathbf{P}_{0,x}$-summable, then

$$\mathbf{M}_{0,x}(\xi\theta_t\eta) = \mathbf{M}_{0,x}(\xi\mathbf{M}_{0,x_t}\eta). \tag{2.20′}$$

2.7. We have already seen in sec.2.5 that the operators θ_t are uniquely defined by the process X. The conditions will now be discussed in which we can assert the existence of such operators θ_t, i.e. stationarity of the process $X = (x_t, \zeta, \mathcal{M}_t^s, \mathbf{P}_{s,x})$.

Theorem 2.3. The necessary and sufficient condition for the Markov process $X = (x_t, \zeta, \mathcal{M}_t^s, \mathbf{P}_{s,x})$ to be stationary is that it satisfy the following conditions:

2.7.A. $P(h, x; t+h, \Gamma) = P(0, x; t, \Gamma)$.

2.7.B. For any $0 < t < \zeta(\omega)$ there exists $\omega' \in \Omega_0$ such that

2.7.B$_1$. $\zeta(\omega') = \zeta(\omega) - t$.

2.7.B$_2$. $x_{t+h}(\omega) = x_h(\omega')$ for all $0 \leqslant h < \zeta(\omega') = \zeta(\omega) - t$.

Suppose that the process X is stationary.

We shall write $\omega' = c_t(\omega)$ if ω' and ω are connected by relationships 2.7.B$_1$-2.7.B$_2$. Now

$$\theta_t A = \{\omega : c_t\omega \in A\} \qquad (A \in \mathscr{N}^*); \tag{2.21}$$

$$\theta_t \xi(\omega) = \xi(c_t\omega) \tag{2.22}$$

(ξ is an $\mathscr{N}^*$-measurable function, $\omega \in \Omega_t$).)

Proof. Necessity. Condition 2.7.A follows from 2.5.B and 2.5.C. We show that condition 2.7.B holds. For every $\omega \in \Omega_t$ let A_ω be the intersection of all sets $A \in \mathscr{N}^*$ such that $\omega \in \theta_t A$. Obviously, $A_\omega \in \mathscr{N}^*$ and $\omega \in \theta_t A_\omega$. We notice that, if $\omega' \in A_\omega$, conditions 2.7.B$_1$-2.7.B$_2$ are satisfied. In fact, let $\zeta(\omega) = u$, $x_{t+h}(\omega) = a$. Then

$$\omega \in \{\zeta = u,\ x_{t+h} = a\} = \theta_t \{\zeta = u - t,\ x_h = a\}.$$

Therefore $\omega' \in A_\omega \subseteq \{\zeta = u - t,\ x_h = a\}$ and $\zeta(\omega') = u - t$, $x_h(\omega') = a$.

Sufficiency. We show first of all that, if $A \in \mathscr{N}^*$, either all or else none of the values of $c_t\omega$ belong to A. The class of all sets A having the property in question is in fact closed with respect to all set operations and contains (by 2.7.B$_1$-2.7.B$_2$) the sets $\{x_h \in \Gamma\}$ $(h \geqslant 0,\ \Gamma \in \mathscr{B})$. The aggregate thus contains $\mathscr{N}^*$.

It remains to show that condition 2.5.C holds. Let $\mathscr{F}$ be the system of all sets A for which 2.5.C is satisfied. Let $\mathscr{C}$ denote the system of all sets

$$A = \{x_{h_1} \in \Gamma_1, \ldots, x_{h_n} \in \Gamma_n\} \qquad (0 \leqslant h_1 \leqslant \ldots \leqslant h_n). \tag{2.23}$$

Obviously, $\mathscr{F}$ is a λ-system and $\mathscr{C}$ a π-system in the space Ω_0 .

Moreover, for sets (2.23), we have

$$\mathbf{P}_{0,x}(A) = P(0,\ x;\ h_1,\ \Gamma_1,\ \ldots,\ h_n,\ \Gamma_n),$$

$$\mathbf{P}_{t,x}(\theta_t A) = P(t,\ x;\ t+h_1,\ \Gamma_1,\ \ldots,\ t+h_n,\ \Gamma_n).$$

We observe on comparing 2.7.A and (2.15) that $\mathbf{P}_{0,x}(A) = \mathbf{P}_{t,x}(\theta_t A)$. Therefore $\mathscr{F} \supseteq \mathcal{C}$ and by lemma 1.1, $\mathscr{F} \supseteq \sigma(\mathcal{C}) = \mathscr{N}^0[\Omega_0]$.

Operators θ_t thus satisfy all the requirements 2.5.A-2.5.C.

Relationship (2.22) follows from (2.21) and 2.6.D.

2.8. Let $(x_t,\ \zeta,\ \mathscr{M}_t^s,\ \mathbf{P}_{s,x})$ be a stationary Markov process and let θ_t be operators satisfying conditions 2.5.A-2.5.C. We consider the system $(x_t, \zeta, \mathscr{M}_t, \mathbf{P}_x, \theta_t)$, where $\mathscr{M}_t = \mathscr{M}_t^0;\ \mathbf{P}_x = \mathbf{P}_{0,x}$. Evidently this system has the following properties:

2.8.A. If $t \leqslant u$ and $A \in \mathscr{M}_t$, then $\{A, \zeta > u\} \in \mathscr{M}_u$

2.8.B. $\{x_t \in \Gamma\} \in \mathscr{M}_t\ (t \geqslant 0,\ \Gamma \in \mathscr{B})$

2.8.C. $\mathbf{P}_x$ is a probability measure on the σ-algebra $\mathscr{M}^0$.

2.8.D. For any $t \geqslant 0,\ \Gamma \in \mathscr{B}$:

$$P(t,\ x,\ \Gamma) = \mathbf{P}_x\{x_t \in \Gamma\}$$

is a $\mathscr{B}$-measurable function of x.

2.8.E. $P(0,\ x,\ E \setminus x) = 0.$

2.8.F. For any $t \geqslant 0,\ A \in \mathscr{N}$

$$\mathbf{P}_x\{\theta_t A \mid \mathscr{M}_t\} = \mathbf{P}_{x_t}(A) \qquad (\text{a.c.}\ \Omega_t,\ \mathbf{P}_x).$$

2.8.G. $$\theta_t\Omega_0 = \Omega_t,\ \ \theta_t(A \setminus B) = \theta_t A \setminus \theta_t B,$$
$$\theta_t\{\cup A_\alpha\} = \cup\, \theta_t A_\alpha,\ \ \theta_t\{\cap A_\alpha\} = \cap\, \theta_t A_\alpha$$

(α runs through an arbitrary set of values).

2.8.H. $\theta_t\{x_h \in \Gamma\} = \{x_{t+h} \in \Gamma\} \qquad (t > 0,\ h \geqslant 0,\ \Gamma \in \mathscr{B}).$

<u>Theorem 2.4</u>. Given:

a) a function $\zeta(\omega)$ $(\omega \in \Omega)$ taking values from the interval $[0, +\infty]$;

b) a function $x_t(\omega)$ defined for $\omega \in \Omega$, $t \in [0, \zeta(\omega))$ and taking values from the measurable space $(E, \mathscr{B})$;

c) for any $t \geqslant 0$ a σ-algebra $\mathscr{M}_t$ in the space $\Omega_t = \{\zeta > t\}$;

d) for each $x \in E$ a function $\mathbf{P}_x(A)$ in a σ-algebra $\mathscr{M}^0$ in the space Ω containing $\mathscr{M}_t$ for all $t \geqslant 0$;

e) for each $t > 0$ and $A \in \mathscr{N}^*$ a set $\theta_t A \subseteq \Omega$ (the system $\mathscr{N}^*$ is defined in accordance with $x_t(\omega)$ and ζ as in sec. 2.5).

We suppose that the system $(x_t, \zeta, \mathscr{M}_t, P_x, \theta_t)$ satisfies conditions 2.8.A-2.8.H. Then there exists a stationary Markov process $X = (x_t, \zeta, \mathscr{M}_t^s, \mathbf{P}_{s,x})$ for which $\mathscr{M}_t = \mathscr{M}_t^0$, $\mathbf{P}_x = \mathbf{P}_{0,x}$ and θ_t is a system of operators satisfying requirements 2.5.A-2.5.C.

Proof. We put $\mathscr{M}_t^0 = \mathscr{M}_t$, $\mathbf{P}_{0,x} = \mathbf{P}_x$. With $s > 0$, let $\mathscr{M}^s$ denote the class of all sets of the form $\theta_s A$ and $\overline{\Omega}_s \cup \theta_s A$, where $A \in \mathscr{N}^0$, and let

$$\mathbf{P}_{s,x}(\theta_s A) = \mathbf{P}_x(A),$$

$$\mathbf{P}_{s,x}(\overline{\Omega}_s \cup \theta_s A) = 1 - \mathbf{P}_x(\Omega_0) + \mathbf{P}_x(A),$$

$$\mathscr{M}_t^s = \theta_s \mathscr{N}_{t-s}{}^{*)}.$$

It may easily be verified that the system $(x_t, \zeta, \mathscr{M}_t^s, \mathbf{P}_{s,x})$ possesses all the properties 2.1.A-2.1.F, whilst the operators θ_t possess all the properties 2.5.A-2.5.C. The only property whose proof requires a certain amount of working is 2.1.F.

To start with, a function $\theta_t\xi$ can easily be defined for every $\mathscr{N}^*$-measurable function as in sec. 2.6. Properties 2.6.A-2.6.G are soon seen to hold here.

We have to verify that, for any $s \leqslant t \leqslant u$, $\Gamma \in \mathscr{B}$, $A \in \mathscr{M}_t^s$,

$$\mathbf{P}_{s,x}\{A, x_u \in \Gamma\} = \int_A P(t, x_t; u, \Gamma)\,\mathbf{P}_{s,x}(d\omega) = \mathbf{M}_{s,x}[\chi_A P(t, x_t; u, \Gamma)]. \tag{2.24}$$

*) $\mathscr{N}_t$ denotes the σ-algebra in $\Omega_t = \{\zeta > t\}$ generated by the sets $\{x_u \in \Gamma, \zeta > t\}$ $(0 \leqslant u \leqslant t, \Gamma \in \mathscr{B})$, and $\mathscr{N}^0$ the σ-algebra in Ω generated by the sets $\{x_u \in \Gamma\}$ $(u \geqslant 0, \Gamma \in \mathscr{B})$.

This relationship is obvious if $s=0$. If $s>0$, we have by definition of $\mathcal{M}_t^s$ $A=\theta_s B$, where $B\in\mathcal{M}_{t-s}$. By 2.8.G, 2.8.H, 2.6.D and 2.6.E,

$$\theta_t\{B, x_{u-s}\in\Gamma\}=\{A, x_u\in\Gamma\},$$
$$\theta_s[\chi_B P(t, x_{t-s}; u, \Gamma)]=\chi_A P(t, x_t; u, \Gamma)$$

and by 2.5.C and (2.17), relationship (2.24) is equivalent to the equation

$$\mathbf{P}_x\{B, x_{u-s}\in\Gamma\}=\mathbf{M}_x\chi_B P(t, x_{t-s}; u, \Gamma)= \\ =\int_B P(t, x_{t-s}; u, \Gamma)\,\mathbf{P}_x(d\omega). \quad (2.25)$$

To prove (2.25), we only need to verify that

$$\mathbf{P}_x\{x_{u-s}\in\Gamma\,|\,\mathcal{M}_{t-s}\}=P(t, x_{t-s}; u, \Gamma).$$

But, by 2.8.F and 2.8.H,

$$\mathbf{P}_x\{x_{u-s}\in\Gamma\,|\,\mathcal{M}_{t-s}\}=\mathbf{P}_x\{\theta_{t-s}[x_{u-t}\in\Gamma]\,|\,\mathcal{M}_{t-s}\}= \\ =\mathbf{P}_{x_{t-s}}\{x_{u-t}\in\Gamma\}=P(u-t, x_{t-s}, \Gamma)\,(\text{a.c.}\,\Omega_{t-s}, \mathbf{P}_x).$$

It remains to observe that, by 2.5.C and 2.8.H, for every $y\in E$

$$P(t, y; u, \Gamma)=\mathbf{P}_{t,y}\{x_u\in\Gamma\}=\mathbf{P}_y\{x_{u-t}\in\Gamma\}=P(u-t, y, \Gamma).$$

The theorem is thus proved.

We shall employ the term "stationary Markov process" below in two different senses, either for the system $(x_t, \zeta, \mathcal{M}_t^s, \mathbf{P}_{s,x})$ subject to conditions 2.1.A-2.1.F, for which a system of operators θ_t exists satisfying requirements 2.5.A-2.5.C, or for the system $(x_t, \zeta, \mathcal{M}_t, \mathbf{P}_x, \theta_t)$ subject to conditions 2.8.A-2.8.H. Writing $X=(x_t, \zeta, \mathcal{M}_t^s, \mathbf{P}_{s,x})$ denotes a stationary Markov process in the first sense, whilst $X'=(x_t, \zeta, \mathcal{M}_t, \mathbf{P}_x, \theta_t)$ denotes a stationary Markov process in the second sense. If $\mathcal{M}_t^0=\mathcal{M}_t$, $\mathbf{P}_{0,x}=\mathbf{P}_x$ and operators θ_t satisfy conditions 2.5.A-2.5.C in regard to the process X, we shall say that X corresponds to X' (or X' corresponds to X) and write $X\longleftrightarrow X'$. For every stationary Markov process in the first sense there is a corresponding stationary Markov process in the second sense. The converse is true by theorem 2.4: for every stationary Markov process in the second sense there is a corresponding stationary Markov process in the first sense. The two meanings of the term "stationary Markov process" are thus very closely related. The difference between them amounts to this: when it is a question of a stationary Markov process in the first sense, our knowledge of $x_t, \zeta, \mathcal{M}_t^s, \mathbf{P}_{s,x}$ is essentially complete, whereas when it is a question of a stationary Markov process in the second sense our knowledge of $x_t, \zeta, \mathcal{M}_t^0, \mathbf{P}_{0,x}, \theta_t$ is essentially complete but there is some arbitrariness in the choice of σ-algebras $\mathcal{M}_t^s$ and measures $\mathbf{P}_{s,x}$ for $s>0$.

3. Equivalent Markov Processes

2.9. Let $X=(x_t, \zeta, \mathcal{M}_t^s, \mathbf{P}_{s,x})$ and $\widetilde{X}=(\widetilde{x}_t, \widetilde{\zeta}, \widetilde{\mathcal{M}}_t^s, \widetilde{\mathbf{P}}_{s,x})$ be two Markov processes in the same phase space $(E, \mathcal{B})$. We shall say that $\widetilde{X}$ is got from X by means of the transformation of the space of elementary events $\gamma: \widetilde{\Omega} \to \Omega$ (Ω is the space of elementary events for X, $\widetilde{\Omega}$ the similar space for $\widetilde{X}$, and γ the mapping of $\widetilde{\Omega}$ into Ω), if the following requirements are satisfied:

2.9.A. $\widetilde{\zeta}(\widetilde{\omega})=\zeta[\gamma(\widetilde{\omega})] \qquad (\widetilde{\omega}\in\widetilde{\Omega})$.

2.9.B. $\widetilde{x}_t(\widetilde{\omega})=x_t[\gamma(\widetilde{\omega})] \quad (\widetilde{\omega}\in\widetilde{\Omega},\ 0\leqslant t<\widetilde{\zeta}(\widetilde{\omega})=\zeta[\gamma(\widetilde{\omega})])$.

2.9.C. $\widetilde{\mathcal{M}}_t^s=\gamma^{-1}(\mathcal{M}_t^s)$ *).

2.9.D. $\widetilde{\mathcal{M}}^s=\gamma^{-1}(\mathcal{M}^s)$ and $\widetilde{\mathbf{P}}_{s,x}(\gamma^{-1}A)=\mathbf{P}_{s,x}(A) \qquad (A\in\mathcal{M}^s)$.

Evidently the process $\widetilde{X}$ is uniquely defined, given the process X, by the transformation γ. Now what conditions must be imposed on the mapping γ for a Markov process satisfying conditions 2.9.A-2.9.D to exist? The answer to this question is supplied by the following theorem.

Theorem 2.5. The necessary and sufficient condition for a mapping $\gamma:\widetilde{\Omega}\to\Omega$ to give a transformation of the space of elementary events of a process X is that:

2.9.α. For any $s\geqslant 0,\ x\in E,\ A\in\mathcal{M}^s$, it follows from $A\supseteq\gamma(\widetilde{\Omega})$ that $\mathbf{P}_{s,x}(A)=1$ **).

---

*) $\gamma^{-1}(A)$ denotes the complete pre-image of A for the mapping γ, i.e. the set $\{\widetilde{\omega}:\gamma(\widetilde{\omega})\in A\}$. If $\mathcal{A}$ is a system of subsets of the space Ω, $\gamma^{-1}(\mathcal{A})$ denotes the system of all sets $\gamma^{-1}(A)$ $(A\in\mathcal{A})$.

**) In other words, no matter what measures $\mathbf{P}_{s,x}$ we start from, the corresponding outer measure of the set $\gamma(\widetilde{\Omega})$ is equal to unity.

<u>Proof</u>. If $A \supseteq \gamma(\widetilde{\Omega})$, then $\gamma^{-1}(A)=\widetilde{\Omega}$ and by expression 2.9.D $\mathbf{P}_{s,x}(A)=\widetilde{P}_{s,x}(\widetilde{\Omega})=1$. We have thus proved the necessity of the condition. Turning to the proof of sufficiency, we consider the elements $\widetilde{\zeta}, \widetilde{x}_t, \mathcal{M}_t^s, \widetilde{\mathcal{M}}^s$ and $\widetilde{\mathbf{P}}_{s,x}$ defined by expressions 2.9.A-2.9.D. We show first of all that the function $\widetilde{\mathbf{P}}_{s,x}(B)$ is defined uniquely for any $B \in \widetilde{\mathcal{M}}^s$. This is done simply by verifying that, if

$$B=\gamma^{-1}(A_1)=\gamma^{-1}(A_2), \tag{2.26}$$

then

$$\mathbf{P}_{s,x}(A_1)=\mathbf{P}_{s,x}(A_2).$$

In fact, it follows from (2.26) that

$$\gamma^{-1}\ \overline{(A_1\setminus A_1A_2)}=\overline{\gamma^{-1}(A_1)\setminus\gamma^{-1}(A_1)\,\gamma^{-1}(A_2)}=\widetilde{\Omega}.$$

Consequently $\overline{A_1\setminus A_1A_2}\supseteq\gamma(\widetilde{\Omega})$ and by 2.9.α, $\mathbf{P}_{s,x}(A_1\setminus A_1A_2)=1$ and therefore $\mathbf{P}_{s,x}(A_1\setminus A_1A_2)=0$, $\mathbf{P}_{s,x}(A_1)=\mathbf{P}_{s,x}(A_1A_2)$. It may similarly be shown that $\mathbf{P}_{s,x}(A_2)=\mathbf{P}_{s,x}(A_1A_2)$.

The proof of the fact that the system $(\widetilde{x}_t, \widetilde{\zeta}, \widetilde{\mathcal{M}}_t^s, \widetilde{\mathbf{P}}_{s,x})$ satisfies conditions 2.1.A-2.1.E and 2.1.F′ presents no difficulties and is left to the reader.

We shall take two particular cases of transormation of the space of elementary events.

a) If γ is a one-to-one mapping of $\widetilde{\Omega}$ into Ω, $\widetilde{\Omega}$ can be identified with some subset of set Ω. The passage from process X to process $\widetilde{X}$ reduces in this case to restricting the domains of definition of functions $\zeta(\omega)$ and $x_t(\omega)$, to replacing each set A of $\mathcal{M}^s$ (or of $\mathcal{M}_t^s$) by its intersection with $\widetilde{\Omega}$ and to a natural transfer of measures $\mathbf{P}_{s,x}$ to these intersections. We shall speak in this special case of the process $\widetilde{X}$ being got from X by a <u>restriction of the space of elementary events</u>. Given X, the process $\widetilde{X}$ is uniquely defined by the set $\widetilde{\Omega}$. By theorem 2.5, this latter is subject to the single requirement:

2.9.α'. For any $s\geqslant 0$, $x\in E$, $A\in\mathcal{M}^s$, it follows from $A\supseteq\widetilde{\Omega}$ that $\mathbf{P}_{s,x}(A)=1$.

b) If γ is the mapping of $\widetilde{\Omega}$ into Ω, each point $\omega\in\Omega$ can be visualized as being "split" into the set of points $\gamma^{-1}(\omega)=\{\widetilde{\omega}:\gamma(\widetilde{\omega})=\omega\}$. In this case we shall say that $\widetilde{X}$ is got from X by <u>splitting the elementary events</u>.

It may readily be seen that a general transformation of the space of elementary events can be got by successively purging the space of elementary events (when Ω is restricted to $\gamma(\widetilde{\Omega})$) and splitting the elementary events (signifying passage from $\gamma(\widetilde{\Omega})$ to $\widetilde{\Omega}$).

2.10. Let $X=(x_t,\ \zeta,\ \mathcal{M}_t^s,\ \mathbf{P}_{s,x})$ and $\widetilde{X}=(x_t,\ \zeta,\ \widetilde{\mathcal{M}}_t^s,\ \widetilde{\mathbf{P}}_{s,x})$ be two Markov processes in the same phase space and with the same space of elementary events, and let

2.10.A. $\widetilde{\mathcal{M}}_t^s \supseteq \mathcal{M}_t^s$.

2.10.B. $\widetilde{\mathcal{M}}^s \supseteq \mathcal{M}^s$ and $\widetilde{\mathbf{P}}_{s,x}(A)=\mathbf{P}_{s,x}(A)\ (A\in\mathcal{M}^s)$.

We shall speak here of $\widetilde{X}$ being got from X by a <u>widening</u> (or of X being got from $\widetilde{X}$ by a <u>narrowing</u>) <u>of the basic</u> σ-algebras.

The operation of supplementing the measures described in sec. 2.2 can be quoted as an example of widening the basic σ-algebras. As an example of narrowing these algebras, we may mention the passage from σ-algebras $\mathcal{M}_t^s,\ \mathcal{M}^s$ to σ-algebras $\mathcal{N}_t^s,\ \mathcal{N}^s$, which was also discussed in sec. 2.2.

2.11. We shall speak of the Markov process $\widetilde{X}$ being <u>subordinate</u> to the Markov process X if $\widetilde{X}$ can be got from X by carrying out successively a transformation of the space of elementary events and a widening of the basic σ-algebras. The necessary and sufficient condition for this is that some mapping $\gamma:\widetilde{\Omega}\to\Omega$ satisfy the following requirements

2.11.A. $\widetilde{\zeta}(\widetilde{\omega})=\zeta[\gamma(\widetilde{\omega})]\quad(\widetilde{\omega}\in\widetilde{\Omega})$

2.11.B. $\widetilde{x}_t(\widetilde{\omega})=x_t[\gamma(\widetilde{\omega})]\quad(\widetilde{\omega}\in\widetilde{\Omega},\ 0\leqslant t<\widetilde{\zeta}(\widetilde{\omega}))$.

2.11.C. $\widetilde{\mathcal{M}}_t^s \supseteq \gamma^{-1}(\mathcal{M}_t^s)$.

2.11.D. $\widetilde{\mathcal{M}}^s \supseteq \gamma^{-1}(\mathcal{M}^s)$ and $\widetilde{\mathbf{P}}_{s,x}(\gamma^{-1}A)=\mathbf{P}_{s,x}(A)\ (A\in\mathcal{M}^s)$.

If process $\widetilde{X}$ is subordinate to process X, every trajectory of $\widetilde{X}$ is at the same time a trajectory of X. The transition functions of processes $\widetilde{X}$ and X are the same.

We shall consider every possible interval $[0, \lambda)$ and every possible function $\varphi(t)$ defined in these intervals with values in the space E. The class of all these functions will be denoted by Ω_E. Let $\varphi \in \Omega_E$. We shall write $\hat{\zeta}(\varphi)$ for the right-hand end of the interval in which the function φ is given. Two elements φ and ψ of Ω_E will be reckoned identical when and only when $\hat{\zeta}(\varphi) = \hat{\zeta}(\psi)$ and $\varphi(t) = \psi(t)$ for all $0 \leqslant t < \hat{\zeta}(\varphi) = \hat{\zeta}(\psi)$ *).

We put $\hat{x}_t(\varphi) = \varphi(t)$ $(0 \leqslant t < \hat{\zeta}(\varphi))$ and write $\hat{\mathcal{N}}^s$ for the σ-algebra in space Ω_E generated by the sets $\{\varphi : \hat{x}_u(\varphi) \in \Gamma\}$ $(u \geqslant s,\ \Gamma \in \mathscr{B})$ and $\hat{\mathcal{N}}_t^s$ for the σ-algebra in space $\{\varphi : \hat{\zeta}(\varphi) > t\}$, generated by the sets $\{\varphi : \hat{x}_u(\varphi) \in \Gamma,\ \hat{\zeta}(\varphi) > t\}$ $(u \in [s, t],\ \Gamma \in \mathscr{B})$. The Markov process $(x_t, \zeta, \mathcal{M}_t^s, \mathbf{P}_{s,x})$ in the phase space $(E, \mathscr{B})$ will be said to be <u>canonical</u> if we have for the process $\Omega = \Omega_E$, $x_t = \hat{x}_t$, $\zeta = \hat{\zeta}$, $\mathcal{M}_t^s = \hat{\mathcal{N}}_t^s$, $\mathcal{M}^s = \hat{\mathcal{N}}^s$.

<u>Lemma 2.3</u>. Every Markov process $X = (x_t, \zeta, \mathcal{M}_t^s, \mathbf{P}_{s,x})$ is subordinate to some canonical process $\hat{X} = (\hat{x}_t, \hat{\zeta}, \hat{\mathcal{N}}_t^s, \hat{\mathbf{P}}_{s,x})$.

Proof. Let Ω be the space of elementary events of the process X. We associate each $\omega \in \Omega$ with a function $\varphi(t)$ having values from E and defined in the interval $[0, \zeta(\omega))$ by the expression

$$\varphi(t) = x_t(\omega) \qquad (0 \leqslant t < \zeta(\omega)). \tag{2.27}$$

Expression (2.27) defines the mapping $\gamma : \Omega \to \Omega_E$ **).

We evidently have here

$$\hat{\zeta}[\gamma(\omega)] = \zeta(\omega),$$
$$\hat{x}_t[\gamma(\omega)] = x_t(\omega),$$
$$\gamma^{-1}(\hat{\mathcal{N}}^s) \subseteq \mathcal{M}^s,\quad \gamma^{-1}(\hat{\mathcal{N}}_t^s) \subseteq \mathcal{M}_t^s.$$

For every $A \in \hat{\mathcal{N}}^s$ we put

$$\hat{\mathbf{P}}_{s,x}(A) = \mathbf{P}_{s,x}(\gamma^{-1}A).$$

The system $(\hat{x}_t, \hat{\zeta}, \hat{\mathcal{N}}_t^s, \hat{\mathbf{P}}_{s,x})$ satisfies conditions 2.1.A-2.1.F

*)One of the elements of the space Ω_E is the function φ_0 which is nowhere defined. For this, $\hat{\zeta}(\varphi_0) = 0$.

**)If $\zeta(\omega) = 0$, we put $\gamma\omega = \varphi_0$, where φ_0 is the element of Ω_E defined in the previous foot-note.

and therefore yields some Markov process $\hat{X}$. This process is canonical and the process X is subordinate to it.

The canonical process $\hat{X}$ constructed in lemma 2.3 will be called the <u>canonical form</u> of the process X.

<u>Remark</u>. All the concepts and results given in sec. 2.9-2.11 for Markov processes may be carried over directly to Markov random functions. In particular, we can assert the following, which will be useful later.

<u>The necessary and sufficient condition for the space of elementary events of the Markov random function</u> $X=(x_t, \zeta, \mathcal{M}_t, \mathbf{P})$ <u>to be reducible by restriction to the subset</u> $\tilde{\Omega}\subseteq\Omega$ <u>is that, for every</u> $A\in\mathcal{M}$, <u>it follows from</u> $A\supseteq\tilde{\Omega}$ <u>that</u> $\mathbf{P}(A)=1$.

2.12. We shall speak of the Markov processes X' and X'' being <u>equivalent</u> if they are defined in the same phase space and have the same transition function.

<u>Theorem 2.6</u>. Every class of equivalent Markov processes contains one and only one canonical process $\hat{X}$ and consists of all the processes subordinate to $\hat{X}$.

Proof. By lemma 2.3, it is a matter of proving that, if two canonical processes $X'=(\hat{x}_t, \hat{\zeta}, \hat{\mathcal{N}}_t^s, \mathbf{P}'_{s,x})$ and $X''=(\hat{x}_t, \hat{\zeta}, \hat{\mathcal{N}}_t^s, \mathbf{P}''_{s,x})$ have the same transition functions they must coincide. We thus need to show that, for any $A\in\hat{\mathcal{N}}^s$,

$$\mathbf{P}'_{s,x}(A)=\mathbf{P}''_{s,x}(A). \tag{2.28}$$

By (2.15), this relationship is satisfied at least for the sets

$$A=\{\hat{x}_{t_1}\in\Gamma_1, \ldots, \hat{x}_{t_n}\in\Gamma_n\}$$
$$(n=1, 2, \ldots; s\leqslant t_1, \ldots, t_n; \Gamma_1, \ldots, \Gamma_n\in\mathcal{B}). \tag{2.29}$$

The sets for which equation (2.28) is satisfied form a λ-system $\mathcal{F}$, whilst the sets of form (2.29) form a π-system $\mathcal{C}$. By lemma 1.1, it follows from $\mathcal{F}\supseteq\mathcal{C}$ that $\mathcal{F}\supseteq\sigma(\mathcal{C})=\hat{\mathcal{N}}^s$.

We shall discuss in detail in Chapter 4 the question of what sort of functions are transition functions for Markov processes.

2.13. Let $\mathscr{L}$ be a subset of the set Ω_E. Let $\mathscr{K}_{P,\mathscr{L}}$ denote the aggregate of all Markov processes corresponding to the transition function $P(s, x; t, \Gamma)$ and such that all their trajectories belong to the set $\mathscr{L}$. The aggregate $\mathscr{K}_{P,\mathscr{L}}$ may be empty. If it is non-empty, we can conclude on the basis of theorem 2.5 that:

a) the set $\mathscr{L}$ satisfies condition 2.9.α with respect to the corresponding transition function $P(s, x; t, \Gamma)$ for the canonical process $\hat{X}$;

b) the space of elementary events of the process $\hat{X}$ can be contracted by means of a restriction to the set $\mathscr{L}$.

We shall describe the Markov process obtained as a result of such a purge as $\mathscr{L}$-canonical. The following variant of theorem 2.6 admits of a simple proof which we shall leave to the reader.

<u>Theorem 2.7</u>. If the class $\mathscr{K}_{P,\mathscr{L}}$ is non-empty, it contains one and only one $\mathscr{L}$-canonical Markov process $\tilde{X}$ and consists of all the Markov processes subordinate to $\tilde{X}$.

In particular, on choosing as $\mathscr{L}$ the class E^I of all functions defined in the interval $I=[0, \infty)$, we arrive at the following result.

<u>Corollary</u>. Every class of equivalent non-cut-off Markov processes contains one and only one canonical non-cut-off process $\tilde{X}$ and consists of all non-cut-off Markov processes subordinate to $\tilde{X}$.

We shall now prove an important theorem which enables us to judge whether some class of equivalent non-cut-off Markov processes contains a process whose trajectories possess certain previously assigned properties.

<u>Theorem 2.8</u>. Let $X=(x_t, \mathscr{M}_t^s, \mathrm{P}_{s,x})$ be a non-cut-off*) Markov process in the phase space $(E, \mathscr{B})$ and let $\mathscr{L}\subseteq E^I$ We shall assume the existence of a non-negative function

$$q(t_1, x_1, \ldots, t_n, x_n, \ldots)$$
$$(0 \leqslant t_1, \ldots, t_n, \ldots; x_1, \ldots, x_n, \ldots \in E),$$

*) A similar theorem for cut-off processes is proved in sec. 6.1.

which, for any $s \geqslant 0$ and for any denumerable everywhere dense subset $\{t_1, \ldots, t_n, \ldots\}$ of the interval $[s, \infty)$ is a $\mathscr{B}^\infty$-measurable function of $x_1, \ldots x_n, \ldots$, and satisfies the following conditions:

2.13.A. If $q(t_1, x_1, \ldots, t_n, x_n, \ldots) = 0$, there exists $\varphi \in \mathscr{L}$ such that $\varphi(t_k) = x_k$ $(k = 1, 2, \ldots, n, \ldots)$.

2.13.B. $\mathbf{M}_{s,x} q(t_1, x_{t_1}, \ldots, t_n, x_{t_n}, \ldots) = 0$ (or what amounts to the same thing, $\mathbf{P}_{s,x}\{q(t_1, x_{t_1}, \ldots, t_n, x_{t_n}, \ldots) \neq 0\} = 0$).

Then there exists for the process X an equivalent Markov process, all the trajectories of which belong to the set $\mathscr{L}$.

Proof. We shall take the canonical form of the non-cut-off process X: $\widetilde{X} = (\widetilde{x}_t, \widetilde{\mathscr{N}}^s_t, \widetilde{\mathbf{P}}_{s,x})$. The theorem will be proved if we can show that condition 2.9.α is satisfied for process $\widetilde{X}$ and set $\mathscr{L}$, i.e. that it follows from $A \supseteq \mathscr{L}$ that $\widetilde{\mathbf{P}}_{s,x}(A) = 1$ no matter what $s \geqslant 0$, $x \in E$ and $A \in \widetilde{\mathscr{N}}^s$.

Thus let $A \in \widetilde{\mathscr{N}}^s$ and $A \supseteq \mathscr{L}$. On the basis of lemma 1.5, we can write the characteristic function of A in the form

$$\chi_A(\varphi) = f[\widetilde{x}_{t_1}(\varphi), \ldots, \widetilde{x}_{t_n}(\varphi), \ldots] = \\ = f[\varphi(t_1), \ldots, \varphi(t_n), \ldots] \quad (\varphi \in E^I), \tag{2.30}$$

where $t_1, \ldots, t_n, \ldots$ is some sequence of points of $[s, \infty)$. We can obviously suppose without loss of generality that $t_1, \ldots, t_n, \ldots$ is everywhere dense in $[s, \infty)$.

We show that, if $\psi \overline{\in} A$, then

$$q[t_1, \psi(t_1), \ldots, t_n, \psi(t_n), \ldots] \neq 0.$$

If in fact we had

$$q[t_1, \psi(t_1), \ldots, t_n, \psi(t_n), \ldots] = 0,$$

there would exist a function $\varphi \in \mathscr{L}$ by 2.13.A such that $\psi(t_k) = \varphi(t_k)$ for $k = 1, \ldots, n, \ldots$ By (2.30), $\chi_A(\psi) = \chi_A(\varphi)$, and $\psi \in A$ inasmuch as $\varphi \in \mathscr{L} \subseteq A$. It now remains for us to observe that, in view of the equivalence of X and $\widetilde{X}$,

$$\widetilde{\mathbf{M}}_{s,x} q(t_1, \widetilde{x}_{t_1}, \ldots, t_n, \widetilde{x}_{t_n} \ldots) = \mathbf{M}_{s,x} q(t_1, x_{t_1}, \ldots, t_n, x_{t_n}, \ldots) \tag{2.31}$$

(this is proved by conventional use of lemma 1.2).

It follows from (2.31), 2.13.B and the fact that the function q is non-negative, that

$$\widetilde{\mathbf{P}}_{s,x}\{q(t_1, \widetilde{x}_{t_1}, \ldots, t_n, \widetilde{x}_{t_n}, \ldots) = 0\} = 1$$

so that all the more,

$$\widetilde{\mathbf{P}}_{s,x}(A) = 1.$$

<u>Remark</u>. Let all the trajectories of the non-cut-off process X belong to the set $\mathscr{L}_0 \subseteq E^T$ and let the function $q(t_1, x_1, \ldots, t_n, x_n, \ldots)$ satisfy 2.13.B and the following condition:

2.13.A′. If $\psi \in \mathscr{L}_0$ and $(t_1, \psi(t_1), \ldots, t_n, \psi(t_n), \ldots) = 0$, the function $\varphi \in \mathscr{L} \cap \mathscr{L}_0$ exists such that $\varphi(t_k) = \psi(t_k)$.

Then there exists an equivalent of X, all the trajectories of which belong to $\mathscr{L} \cap \mathscr{L}_0$.

In fact, let $\widetilde{X}$ be the canonical form of process X. Let $A \in \mathscr{N}^s$ and $A \supseteq \mathscr{L} \cap \mathscr{L}_0$. We put $\psi \in B$ if $q(t_1, \psi(t_1), \ldots, t_n, \psi(t_n), \ldots) \neq 0$. We show, as in the proof of theorem 2.8, that $\mathscr{L}_0 \cap \bar{A} \subseteq B$. Therefore $\mathscr{L}_0 \subseteq A \cup B$ and by theorem 2.5, $\mathbf{P}_{s,x}(A \cup B) = 1$. By condition 2.13.B, $\mathbf{P}_{s,x}(B) = 0$, so that $\mathbf{P}_{s,x}(A) = 1$.

2.14. We shall give an illustration of the application of theorem 2.8.

Let Γ and G be measurable sets in the space $(E, \mathscr{B})$. We shall speak of Γ being <u>inaccessible from</u> G if, for any $0 \leqslant s \leqslant t$

$$\{x_s(\omega) \in G\} \subseteq \{x_t(\omega) \overline{\in} \Gamma\}.$$

If set Γ is inaccessible from $E \setminus \Gamma$, we shall simply say that Γ is inaccessible.

<u>Lemma 2.4</u>. If the transition function of a non-cut-off process X satisfies the condition

2.14.A. $P(s, x; t, \Gamma) = 0$ for all $x \in G$, $0 \leqslant s \leqslant t$, a process equivalent to X exists for which the set Γ is inaccessible from G.

Proof. We write $\mathscr{L}$ for the set of all functions $\varphi(t)$ $(0 \leqslant t < \infty)$ for which the following condition is satisfied: if $\varphi(s) \in G$ for a certain s, then $\varphi(t) \bar{\in} \Gamma$ for any $t \geqslant s$. By theorem 2.8, our assertion will be proved if we can construct a function $q(t_1, x_1, \ldots, t_n, x_n, \ldots)(t_i \geqslant 0, x_i \in E)$ that satisfies conditions 2.13.A-2.13.B.

We put

$$q(t_1, x_1, \ldots, t_n, x_n, \ldots) = \sum_{t_i < t_j} \chi_G(x_i) \chi_\Gamma(x_j).$$

Obviously, the function q is $\mathscr{B}^\infty$-measurable and non-negative and satisfies condition 2.13.A. Furthermore,

$$\begin{aligned} \mathbf{M}_{s, x} q(t_1, x_{t_1}, \ldots, t_n, x_{t_n}, \ldots) = \\ = \sum_{t_i < t_j} \mathbf{P}_{s, x}\{x_{t_i} \in G, x_{t_j} \in \Gamma\} = \\ = \sum_{t_i < t_j} \int_G P(s, x; t_i, dy) P(t_i, y; t_j, \Gamma) = 0. \end{aligned}$$

Thus the function q also satisfies condition 2.13.B.

2.15. The following theorem is also useful in investigating the properties of the trajectories of Markov processes.

Theorem 2.9. Let $X = (x_t, \zeta, \mathscr{M}_t^s, \mathbf{P}_{s, x})$ be a Markov process in the phase space $(E, \mathscr{B})$ and let $\mathscr{L}$ be an arbitrary subset of space Ω_E. We suppose that there is associated with each pair $s \geqslant 0$, $x \in E$ a set $\Omega^{s, x} \subseteq \Omega_s$ having the following properties:

2.15.A. For each $\omega \in \Omega^{s, x}$ there exists a function $\varphi(t)(t \in [0, \lambda))$ of $\mathscr{L}$ such that $\lambda = \zeta(\omega)$ and $\varphi(t) = x_t(\omega)$ for all $t \in [s, \zeta(\omega))$.

2.15.B. If $A \in \mathscr{M}^s$ and $A \supseteq \Omega^{s, x}$, then $\mathbf{P}_{s, x}(A) = 1$. Then a Markov process $\widetilde{X}$ equivalent to X exists, all the trajectories of which belong to $\mathscr{L}$.

Proof. We put

$$\zeta^{s, x}(\omega) = \max(\zeta(\omega), s),$$
$$x_t^{s, x}(\omega) = x_t(\omega) \quad (t \in [s, \infty), \ \omega \in \Omega_t).$$

In accordance with sec. 2.1, the elements $(x_t^{s, x}, \zeta^{s, x}, \mathscr{M}_t^s, \mathbf{P}_{s, x})$

define a Markov random function $X^{s,x}$ in the time interval $[s, \infty)$. Let $\widetilde{X}^{s,x}$ denote the Markov random function obtained from $X^{s,x}$ by a restriction of the space of elementary events to the set $\Omega^{s,x}$ (by the remark at the end of sec. 2.11, the existence of such a function is guaranteed by condition 2.15.B). The system $\widetilde{X}^{s,x}$ $(s \geqslant 0, x \in E)$ is easily seen to be a Markov family. By using the construction described in sec. 2.1, we can build up from this family a Markov process $\widetilde{X}$ in such a way (in view of condition 2.15.A) that all the trajectories of $\widetilde{X}$ belong to $\mathscr{L}$. It may readily be seen that X and $\widetilde{X}$ are equivalent.

2.16. We shall dwell in conclusion on some special problems connected with the subordination and equivalence of Markov processes.

Let $X=(x_t, \zeta, \mathscr{M}_t^s, \mathbf{P}_{s,x})$ and $\widetilde{X}=(\widetilde{x}_t, \widetilde{\zeta}, \widetilde{\mathscr{M}}_t^s, \widetilde{\mathbf{P}}_{s,x})$ be stationary Markov processes, the process $\widetilde{X}$ being subordinate to X. Let θ_t and $\widetilde{\theta}_t$ be the corresponding operators satisfying conditions 2.5.A-2.5.C. Then

$$\widetilde{\theta}_t \gamma^{-1} A = \gamma^{-1} \theta_t A \qquad (A \in \mathscr{N}^*). \tag{2.32}$$

For,

$$\gamma^{-1}\{x_h \in \Gamma\} = \{\widetilde{x}_h \in \Gamma\}. \tag{2.33}$$

The events A, for which relationship (2.32) holds, form an invariant system with respect to all set operations. By (2.33) and 2.5.B, this system contains all the sets $\{x_h \in \Gamma\}$. It thus contains $\mathscr{N}^*$.

<u>Theorem 2.10.</u> Let $\mathscr{K}$ be the class of equivalent Markov processes having the transition function $P(s, x; t, \Gamma)$. The necessary and sufficient condition for class $\mathscr{K}$ to contain a stationary process is that

$$P(s, x; t, \Gamma) = P(0, x; t-s, \Gamma) \qquad (0 \leqslant s \leqslant t,\ x \in E,\ \Gamma \in \mathscr{B}). \tag{2.34}$$

If condition (2.34) is fulfilled, the canonical*) process $\widetilde{X}$ belonging to $\mathscr{K}$ is stationary.

---

*)As is clear from the proof, any $\mathscr{L}$-canonical process is stationary, provided only that $\mathscr{L}$ satisfy condition 2.7.B.

Proof. The necessity of condition (2.34) follows from 2.5.B and 2.5.C. On the other hand, the canonical process $\widetilde{X}$ always satisfies condition 2.7.B. If (2.34) is satisfied, $\widetilde{X}$ also satisfies condition 2.7.A and, by theorem 2.3, is a stationary process.

2.17. We shall now look on a stationary Markov process as a system $(x_t, \zeta, \mathcal{M}_t, \mathbf{P}_x, \theta_t)$ satisfying conditions 2.8.A-2.8.H. We shall describe the stationary process $\widetilde{X}=(\widetilde{x}_t, \widetilde{\zeta}, \widetilde{\mathcal{M}}_t, \widetilde{\mathbf{P}}_x, \widetilde{\theta}_t)$ as subordinate to the stationary process $X=(x_t, \zeta, \mathcal{M}_t, \mathbf{P}_x, \theta_t)$ if we can construct a mapping γ of the space of elementary events $\widetilde{\Omega}$ of process $\widetilde{X}$ into the space of elementary events Ω of process X such that:

2.17.A. $\widetilde{\zeta}(\widetilde{\omega})=\zeta[\gamma(\widetilde{\omega})] \quad (\widetilde{\omega}\in\widetilde{\Omega})$.

2.17.B. $\widetilde{x}_t(\widetilde{\omega})=x_t[\gamma(\widetilde{\omega})] \quad (\widetilde{\omega}\in\widetilde{\Omega},\ 0\leqslant t<\widetilde{\zeta}(\widetilde{\omega}))$.

2.17.C. $\gamma^{-1}\mathcal{M}_t\subseteq\widetilde{\mathcal{M}}_t$.

2.17.D $\widetilde{\mathcal{M}}^0\supseteq\gamma^{-1}\mathcal{M}^0$ and $\widetilde{\mathbf{P}}_x(\gamma^{-1}A)=\mathbf{P}_x(A)$ for $A\in\mathcal{M}^0$ *).

Theorem 2.11. The process $\widetilde{X}=(\widetilde{x}_t, \widetilde{\zeta}, \widetilde{\mathcal{M}}_t, \widetilde{\mathbf{P}}_x, \widetilde{\theta}_t)$ is subordinate to process $X=(x_t, \zeta, \mathcal{M}_t, \mathbf{P}_x, \theta_t)$ when and only when there exist stationary Markov processes $\widetilde{X}'=(\widetilde{x}_t, \widetilde{\zeta}, \widetilde{\mathcal{M}}_t^s, \widetilde{\mathbf{P}}_{s,x})$ and $X'=(x_t, \zeta, \mathcal{M}_t^s, \mathbf{P}_{s,x})$ such that $\widetilde{X}'\longleftrightarrow\widetilde{X}$, $X'\longleftrightarrow X$ and $\widetilde{X}'$ is subordinate to X'.

Proof. The sufficiency of the condition is obvious. The necessity is proved with the aid of the construction used in proving theorem 2.4 (sec. 2.8).

We shall say that a process $X'=(x_t, \zeta, \mathcal{M}_t, \mathbf{P}_x, \theta_t)$ is <u>canonical</u> if $X'\longleftrightarrow X$, where $X=(x_t, \zeta, \mathcal{M}_t^s, \mathbf{P}_{s,x})$ is a canonical process in the sense of sec. 2.11. Two processes $X=(x_t, \zeta, \mathcal{M}_t, \mathbf{P}_x, \theta_t)$ and $\widetilde{X}=(\widetilde{x}_t, \widetilde{\zeta}, \widetilde{\mathcal{M}}_t, \widetilde{\mathbf{P}}_x, \widetilde{\theta}_t)$ will be called equivalent if their transition functions coincide, i.e. for all $t\geqslant 0$, $x\in E$, $\Gamma\in\mathcal{B}$

$$\mathbf{P}_x\{x_t\in\Gamma\}=\widetilde{\mathbf{P}}_x\{\widetilde{x}_t\in\Gamma\}.$$

Theorems 2.6 and 2.11 readily yield the following result.

Theorem 2.12. Every class of equivalent stationary Markov processes $X=(x_t, \zeta, \mathcal{M}_t, \mathbf{P}_x, \theta_t)$ contains one and only one canonical process $\widetilde{X}=(\widetilde{x}_t, \widetilde{\zeta}, \widetilde{\mathcal{M}}_t, \widetilde{\mathbf{P}}_x, \widetilde{\theta}_t)$ and consists of all stationary processes subordinate to $\widetilde{X}$.

---

*) Relationship (2.32) follows obviously from these conditions.

CHAPTER 3

SUBPROCESSES

1. Definition of Subprocess. The Connexion Between Subprocesses and Multiplicative Functionals

3.1. We discussed in article 3 of Chapter 2 some constructions (transformations of the space of elementary events, widening of the basic σ-algebras) whereby further Markov processes could be built up from a given process. All these Markov processes have the same transition function as the initial process.

The present chapter is concerned with a type of transformation in which the transfer function is altered. The essence of such transformations consists in a shortening of the life ζ of the process.

Let $X=(x_t, \zeta, \mathcal{M}_t^s, \mathrm{P}_{s,x})$ and $\widetilde{X}=(\widetilde{x}_t, \widetilde{\zeta}, \widetilde{\mathcal{M}}_t^s, \mathrm{P}_{s,x})$ be two Markov processes, where $\widetilde{\zeta}(\omega)\leqslant\zeta(\omega)$ for any $\omega\in\Omega$, $\widetilde{x}_t(\omega)=x_t(\omega)$ for $0\leqslant t<\widetilde{\zeta}(\omega)$ and $\widetilde{\mathcal{M}}_t^s=\mathcal{M}_t^s[\widetilde{\Omega}_t]$ $(\widetilde{\Omega}_t=\{\widetilde{\zeta}>t\})$. We shall speak in this case of $\widetilde{X}$ being got from X by a <u>shortening of the life</u>.

We shall speak of a Markov process $\widetilde{X}$ being a <u>subprocess</u> of Markov process X if $\widetilde{X}$ can be obtained by shortening the life of some Markov process subordinate to X.

We note that every trajectory of subprocess $\widetilde{X}$ is part of some trajectory of process X. Hence, if process X is given in a topological measurable space and is continuous or continuous from the right*), the subprocess $\widetilde{X}$ possesses the same properties.

Let Ω be the space of elementary events of process

---

*)Process X is said to be continuous if all its trajectories are continuous, i.e. if for every $\omega\in\Omega$ $x_t(\omega)$ is a continuous function of t in the interval $[0,\zeta(\omega))$. Continuity of X from the right is similarly defined.

$X=(x_t, \zeta, \mathcal{M}_t^s, \mathbf{P}_{s,x})$ and $\widetilde{\Omega}$ the space of elementary events of process $\widetilde{X}=(\widetilde{x}_t, \widetilde{\zeta}, \widetilde{\mathcal{M}}_t^s, \widetilde{\mathbf{P}}_{s,x})$. In view of sec. 2.11, the necessary and sufficient condition for $\widetilde{X}$ to be a subprocess of X is that there exist a mapping $\gamma: \widetilde{\Omega} \to \Omega$ satisfying the following requirements (cf. 2.11.A-2.11.D).

3.1.A. $\widetilde{\zeta}(\widetilde{\omega}) \leqslant \zeta[\gamma(\widetilde{\omega})] \quad (\widetilde{\omega} \in \widetilde{\Omega})$.

3.1.B. $\widetilde{x}_t(\widetilde{\omega}) = x_t[\gamma(\widetilde{\omega})] \quad (\widetilde{\omega} \in \widetilde{\Omega},\ 0 \leqslant t < \widetilde{\zeta}(\widetilde{\omega}))$.

3.1.C. If $A \in \mathcal{M}_t^s$, then $\{\gamma^{-1}(A), \widetilde{\zeta} > t\} \in \widetilde{\mathcal{M}}_t^s$.

3.1.D. $\widetilde{\mathcal{M}}^s \supseteq \gamma^{-1}(\mathcal{M}^s)$ and $\widetilde{\mathbf{P}}_{s,x}(\gamma^{-1}A) = \mathbf{P}_{s,x}(A)$ for $A \in \mathcal{M}^s$.

We agree to identify every function $\xi(\omega)$ in space Ω with a function $\xi[\gamma(\widetilde{\omega})]$ in space $\widetilde{\Omega}$, every subset A of space Ω with the subset $\gamma^{-1}A$ of space $\widetilde{\Omega}$, and every system of subsets $\mathcal{F}=\{A\}$ of space Ω with the system of subsets $\gamma^{-1}\mathcal{F}=\{\gamma^{-1}A\}$ of space $\widetilde{\Omega}$. In these circumstances conditions 3.1.A-3.1.D can be rewritten as

3.1.A'. $\widetilde{\zeta} \leqslant \zeta$.

3.1.B'. $\widetilde{x}_t = x_t \quad (0 \leqslant t < \widetilde{\zeta})$.

3.1.C'. If $A \in \mathcal{M}_t^s$, then $\{A, \widetilde{\zeta} > t\} \in \widetilde{\mathcal{M}}_t^s$.

3.1.D'. $\widetilde{\mathcal{M}}^s \supseteq \mathcal{M}^s$ and $\widetilde{\mathbf{P}}_{s,x}(A) = \mathbf{P}_{s,x}(A)$ for $A \in \mathcal{M}^s$.

Our definition of subprocess is so far unnecessarily general. We narrow it down by requiring the following condition to be satisfied in addition.

3.1.E. For every $x \in E$ and any $0 \leqslant s \leqslant t$

$$\widetilde{\mathbf{P}}_{s,x}\{\widetilde{\zeta} > t \mid \mathcal{M}^s\} = \alpha_t^s \qquad (\text{a.c.}\ \Omega_t, \mathbf{P}_{s,x})\ ^{*)},$$

---

*)This relationship can be written in more detail as

$$\widetilde{\mathbf{P}}_{s,x}\{\widetilde{\zeta} > t \mid \gamma^{-1}\mathcal{M}^s\} = \alpha_t^s[\gamma(\widetilde{\omega})] \qquad (\text{a.c.}\ \gamma^{-1}\Omega_t, \widetilde{\mathbf{P}}_{s,x}).$$

In the formula in the text, $\gamma^{-1}\mathcal{M}^s$ is equated with $\mathcal{M}^s$, $\gamma^{-1}\Omega_t$ with Ω_t, measures $\widetilde{\mathbf{P}}_{s,x}$ on $\gamma^{-1}\mathcal{M}^s$ with measures $\mathbf{P}_{s,x}$ on $\mathcal{M}^s$ and finally, functions $\alpha_t^s[\gamma(\widetilde{\omega})]\ (\widetilde{\omega} \in \widetilde{\Omega})$ with functions $\alpha_t^s(\omega)$ $(\omega \in \Omega)$.

where $\alpha_t^s(\omega)$ is an $\mathcal{N}_t^s$-measurable function*).

The last condition may be pictured in the following way. When calculating the probability of the event $\zeta > t$, a knowledge of the total aggregate of phenomena connected with process X and observed during time $[s, \infty)$ yields no more than a knowledge of the trajectories of the process during time $[s, t]$. In other words, given a knowledge of the course of X during time $[s, t]$ an event $\zeta > t$ is independent of the remaining phenomena observed during time $[s, \infty)$.

We shall put $A \in \mathcal{R}_t^s$ if $A \in \mathcal{N}^s$, $A \subseteq \Omega_t$ and there exists $B \in \mathcal{N}_t^s$ such that $\mathbf{P}_{s, x}(A \setminus AB) = \mathbf{P}_{s, x}(B \setminus AB) = 0$ for all $x \in E$. Obviously, $\mathcal{R}_t^s$ is a σ-algebra in space Ω_t. It may easily be verified that condition 3.1.E is equivalent to the following:

3.1.E'. For every $x \in E$

$$\widetilde{\mathbf{P}}_{s, x}\{\zeta > t \mid \mathcal{M}^s\} = \alpha_t^s(\omega) \qquad (\text{a.c. } \Omega_t, \mathbf{P}_{s, x}),$$

where $\alpha_t^s(\omega)$ is an $\mathcal{R}_t^s$-measurable function of ω**).

We note that it follows from $\mathcal{M}^s \supseteq \mathcal{M}_t^s \supseteq \mathcal{N}_t^s$, $\mathcal{M}^s \supseteq \mathcal{N}^s \supseteq \mathcal{N}_t^s$, $\mathcal{M}^s \supseteq \mathcal{R}_t^s \supseteq \mathcal{N}_t^s$ and condition 3.1.E that, for every $x \in E$,

$$\begin{aligned} \widetilde{\mathbf{P}}_{s, x}\{\zeta > t \mid \mathcal{M}^s\} &= \mathbf{P}_{s, x}\{\zeta > t \mid \mathcal{M}_t^s\} = \widetilde{\mathbf{P}}_{s, x}\{\zeta > t \mid \mathcal{N}^s\} = \\ &= \widetilde{\mathbf{P}}_{s, x}\{\zeta > t \mid \mathcal{R}_t^s\} = \widetilde{\mathbf{P}}_{s, x}\{\zeta > t \mid \mathcal{N}_t^s\} \quad (\text{a.c. } \Omega_t, \mathbf{P}_{s, x}). \end{aligned} \tag{3.1}$$

We notice further that, for any $0 \leqslant s \leqslant t$, $x \in E$,

$$\widetilde{\mathbf{P}}_{s, x}\{\zeta > t \mid \mathcal{M}^s\} = 0 \qquad (\text{a.c. } \bar{\Omega}_t, \mathbf{P}_{s, x}). \tag{3.2}$$

---

*)Condition 3.1.E presupposes that function α_t^s is independent of x. It would be sufficient to require that $\alpha_t^s(\omega, x)$ be an $\mathcal{N}_t^s \times \mathcal{B}$-measurable function of ω and x. For in this case the function $\alpha_t^s(\omega, x_s(\omega))$ is $\mathcal{N}_t^s$-measurable, does not depend on x and for every x differs from $\alpha_t^s(\omega, x)$ only on a set of $\mathbf{P}_{s, x}$-measure zero.

**)We put $A \in \overline{\mathcal{N}}_t^s$ if, for every measure μ on the σ-algebra $\mathcal{B}$ we can choose A_1, A_2 of $\mathcal{N}_t^s$ such that $A_1 \subseteq A \subseteq A_2$ and $\mathbf{P}_{s, \mu}(A_1) = \mathbf{P}_{s, \mu}(A_2)$. We put $A \in \overline{\mathcal{N}}_{t+0}^s$ if $A\Omega_t \in \overline{\mathcal{N}}_v^s$ for every $v > t$. We leave it to the reader to show that the whole of our theory of subprocesses remains valid if the σ-algebra $\mathcal{R}_t^s$ is defined by $\mathcal{R}_t^s = \overline{\mathcal{N}}_{t+0}^s \cap \mathcal{M}_t^s$. The set of subprocesses is considerably widened with this definition and includes several important new examples.

For, since $\{\zeta > t\} \in \mathcal{N}^s$, we have from 3.1.A and 1.6.H:

$$\widetilde{\mathbf{P}}_{s,x}\{\widetilde{\zeta} > t \mid \mathcal{M}^s\} = \widetilde{\mathbf{P}}_{s,x}\{\zeta > t, \widetilde{\zeta} > t \mid \mathcal{M}^s\} =$$
$$= \chi_{\Omega_t}\widetilde{\mathbf{P}}_{s,x}\{\widetilde{\zeta} > t \mid \mathcal{M}^s\} \qquad (\text{a.c. } \Omega, \mathbf{P}_{s,x}).$$

3.2. Lemma 3.1. Let $\widetilde{X} = (\widetilde{x}_t, \widetilde{\zeta}, \widetilde{\mathcal{M}}_t^s, \widetilde{\mathbf{P}}_{s,x})$ be a subprocess of Markov process $X = (x_t, \zeta, \mathcal{M}_t^s, \mathbf{P}_{s,x})$ and let functions α_t^s be defined by condition 3.1.E (or 3.1.E′). Then for any $B \in \mathcal{M}^s$

$$\widetilde{\mathbf{P}}_{s,x}\{B, \widetilde{\zeta} > t\} = \mathbf{M}_{s,x}\chi_B\alpha_t^s; \tag{3.3}$$

for any $\mathcal{M}^s$-measurable function ξ:

$$\widetilde{\mathbf{M}}_{s,x}\xi\chi_{\widetilde{\zeta} > t} = \mathbf{M}_{s,x}\xi\alpha_t^s. \tag{3.4}$$

The transition function of subprocess $\widetilde{X}$ is given by

$$\widetilde{P}(s, x; t, \Gamma) = \mathbf{M}_{s,x}\alpha_t^s\chi_\Gamma(x_t). \tag{3.5}$$

Proof. By 1.6.F and (3.2),

$$\widetilde{\mathbf{M}}_{s,x}\xi\chi_{\widetilde{\zeta} > t} = \widetilde{\mathbf{M}}_{s,x}\{\xi\widetilde{\mathbf{P}}_{s,x}(\widetilde{\zeta} > t \mid \mathcal{M}^s)\} = \widetilde{\mathbf{M}}_{s,x}\xi\alpha_t^s = \mathbf{M}_{s,x}\xi\alpha_t^s$$

and expression (3.4) is proved. On putting $\xi = \chi_B$ in this, we get (3.3). We remark further that, by 3.1.B,

$$\{\widetilde{x}_t \in \Gamma\} = \{x_t \in \Gamma, \widetilde{\zeta} > t\}. \tag{3.6}$$

Expression (3.5) follows from (3.3) and (3.6).

Lemma 3.2. The necessary and sufficient condition for two subprocesses

$$\widetilde{X} = (\widetilde{x}_t, \widetilde{\zeta}, \widetilde{\mathcal{M}}_t^s, \widetilde{\mathbf{P}}_{s,x}) \;\&\; \overline{X} = (\overline{x}_t, \overline{\zeta}, \overline{\mathcal{M}}_t^s, \overline{\mathbf{P}}_{s,x})$$

to be equivalent is that, for any $0 \leqslant s \leqslant t$, $x \in E$,

$$\widetilde{\mathbf{P}}_{s,x}\{\widetilde{\zeta} > t \mid \mathcal{M}^s\} = \overline{\mathbf{P}}_{s,x}\{\overline{\zeta} > t \mid \mathcal{M}^s\} \qquad (\text{a.c. } \Omega_t, \mathbf{P}_{s,x}). \tag{3.7}$$

Proof. The sufficiency of (3.7) follows directly from lemma 3.1. The proof of necessity reduces to showing that

$$\widetilde{\alpha}_t^s = \overline{\alpha}_t^s \qquad (\text{a.c. } \Omega_t, \mathbf{P}_{s,x}), \tag{3.8}$$

where $\widetilde{\alpha}_t^s$ and $\overline{\alpha}_t^s$ are $\mathcal{N}_t^s$-measurable functions corresponding to subprocesses $\widetilde{X}$ and $\overline{X}$ by virtue of condition 3.1.E. We remark that, for any $s \leqslant t_1 < t_2 < \ldots < t_n = t$, $\Gamma_1, \ldots, \Gamma_n \in \mathscr{B}$ by (3.3) and (3.6):

$$\widetilde{\mathbf{P}}_{s,x}(s, x; t_1, \Gamma_1, \ldots, t_n, \Gamma_n) = \widetilde{\mathbf{P}}_{s,x}\{\widetilde{x}_{t_1} \in \Gamma_1, \ldots, \widetilde{x}_{t_n} \in \Gamma_n\} = \\ = \widetilde{\mathbf{P}}_{s,x}\{x_{t_1} \in \Gamma_1, \ldots, x_{t_n} \in \Gamma_n, \widetilde{\zeta} > t\} = \\ = \mathbf{M}_{s,x}[\chi_{\Gamma_1}(x_{t_1}) \cdots \chi_{\Gamma_n}(x_{t_n}) \widetilde{\alpha}_t^s].$$

Similarly,

$$\overline{P}(s, x; t_1, \Gamma_1, \ldots, t_n, \Gamma_n) = \mathbf{M}_{s,x}[\chi_{\Gamma_1}(x_{t_1}) \cdots \chi_{\Gamma_n}(x_{t_n}) \overline{\alpha}_t^s].$$

But it follows by (2.15) from the equivalence of $\widetilde{X}$ and $\overline{X}$ that $\widetilde{P}(s, x; t_1, \Gamma_1, \ldots, t_n, \Gamma_n) = \overline{P}(s, x; t_1, \Gamma_1, \ldots, t_n, \Gamma_n)$, and therefore

$$\mathbf{M}_{s,x}[(\overline{\alpha}_t^s - \widetilde{\alpha}_t^s)\chi_{\Gamma_1}(x_{t_1}) \cdots \chi_{\Gamma_n}(x_{t_n})] = 0. \tag{3.9}$$

We write $\mathscr{L}$ for the class of all functions $\xi(\omega)$ $(\omega \in \Omega_t)$, $\mathscr{C}$ for the class of ω-sets of the form

$$\{x_t \in \Gamma_1, \ldots, x_{t_n} \in \Gamma_n\}$$
$$(n = 1, 2, \ldots; s \leqslant t_1 < \ldots < t_n = t; \Gamma_1, \ldots, \Gamma_n \in \mathscr{B})$$

and $\mathscr{H}$ for the class of functions $\xi(\omega)$ $(\omega \in \Omega_t)$ such that

$$\mathbf{M}_{s,x}[(\widetilde{\alpha}_t^s - \overline{\alpha}_t^s)\xi] = 0.$$

Obviously, $\mathscr{C}$ is a π-system, and $\mathscr{H}$ an $\mathscr{L}$-system in space Ω_t. By (3.9), $\mathscr{H}$ contains the characteristic functions of all sets of $\mathscr{C}$, and by lemma 1.2, $\mathscr{H}$ contains all functions measurable with respect to $\sigma(\mathscr{C}) = \mathscr{N}_t^s$. In particular, $\mathscr{H}$ contains $\widetilde{\alpha}_t^s - \overline{\alpha}_t^s$. Thus $\mathbf{M}_{s,x}[\widetilde{\alpha}_t^s - \overline{\alpha}_t^s]^2 = 0$ so that relationship (3.8) is satisfied.

3.3. The subprocess $\widetilde{X} = (\widetilde{x}_t, \widetilde{\zeta}, \widetilde{\mathscr{M}}_t^s, \widetilde{\mathbf{P}}_{s,x})$ of a Markov process $X = (x_t, \zeta, \mathscr{M}_t^s, \mathbf{P}_{s,x})$ will be described as <u>canonical</u> if:

3.3.A. The space of elementary events $\widetilde{\Omega}$ of process $\widetilde{X}$ is connected with the space of elementary events Ω of process X as follows: $\widetilde{\Omega} = \Omega \times I$, where $I = [0, +\infty]$ and $\gamma(\omega, \lambda) = \omega$ $(\omega \in \Omega, \lambda \in I)$.

3.3.B. $\widetilde{\zeta}(\omega, \lambda) = \min[\zeta(\omega), \lambda]$.

3.3.C. $\widetilde{x}_t(\omega, \lambda) = x_t(\omega)$ for $0 \leqslant t < \widetilde{\zeta}(\omega, \lambda)$.

3.3.D. $\widetilde{\mathscr{M}}_t^s$ consists of all sets of the type $A \times (t, \infty]$, where $A \in \mathscr{M}_t^s$. .

3.3.E. $\widetilde{\mathscr{M}}^s$ is a σ-algebra in space $\widetilde{\Omega}$, generated by the sets

$$\{A, \widetilde{\zeta} > t\} = [A, \zeta > t] \times (t, \infty] \quad (A \in \mathscr{M}^s, t \geqslant s).$$

Theorem 3.1. Every class of equivalent subprocesses of process X contains precisely one canonical subprocess $\widetilde{X}$ and coincides with the class of all Markov processes subordinate to $\widetilde{X}$.

Proof. a) We show first of all that equivalent canonical subprocesses coincide. Let $\widetilde{X} = (\widetilde{x}_t, \widetilde{\zeta}, \widetilde{\mathscr{M}}_t^s, \widetilde{\mathbf{P}}_{s,x})$ and $\overline{X} = (\overline{x}_t, \overline{\zeta}, \overline{\mathscr{M}}_t^s, \overline{\mathbf{P}}_{s,x})$ be two equivalent canonical subprocesses of process X. By 3.3.A-3.3.E, these processes have the same space of elementary events $\Omega \times I$ and we have for them $\widetilde{\zeta} = \overline{\zeta}$, $\widetilde{x}_t = \overline{x}_t$, $\widetilde{\mathscr{M}}_t^s = \overline{\mathscr{M}}_t^s$ and $\widetilde{\mathscr{M}}^s = \overline{\mathscr{M}}^s$.

It remains to show that, for any $B \in \widetilde{\mathscr{M}}^s$,

$$\widetilde{\mathbf{P}}_{s,x}(B) = \overline{\mathbf{P}}_{s,x}(B). \qquad (3.10)$$

The sets B for which (3.10) holds form a λ-system $\mathscr{F}$ in the space $\widetilde{\Omega} = \overline{\Omega} = \Omega \times I$. On the other hand, sets $B = [A, \zeta > t] \times (t, \infty]$ $(A \in \mathscr{M}^s, t \geqslant s)$ form a π-system $\mathcal{C}$, where $\sigma(\mathcal{C}) = \widetilde{\mathscr{M}}^s$. By lemma 1.1, it is a question of proving that $\mathscr{F} \supseteq \mathcal{C}$, i.e. that (3.10) holds for sets $B = [A, \zeta > t] \times (t, \infty]$ $(A \in \mathscr{M}^s, t \geqslant s)$. By (3.3), we have with any $A \in \mathscr{M}^s$, $t \geqslant s$ and $x \in E$,

$$\widetilde{\mathbf{P}}_{s,x}\{[A, \zeta > t] \times (t, \infty]\} = \widetilde{\mathbf{P}}_{s,x}\{A, \widetilde{\zeta} > t\} = \mathbf{M}_{s,x}\chi_A \widetilde{\alpha}_t^s,$$
$$\overline{\mathbf{P}}_{s,x}\{[A, \zeta > t] \times (t, \infty]\} = \overline{\mathbf{P}}_{s,x}\{A, \overline{\zeta} > t\} = \mathbf{M}_{s,x}\chi_A \overline{\alpha}_t^s,$$

where $\widetilde{\alpha}_t^s$ and $\overline{\alpha}_t^s$ are functions satisfying condition 3.1.E for $\widetilde{X}$ and $\overline{X}$ respectively. Since subprocesses $\widetilde{X}$ and $\overline{X}$ are equivalent, (3.8) is satisfied and therefore

$$\widetilde{\mathbf{P}}_{s,x}\{[A, \zeta > t] \times (t, \infty]\} = \overline{\mathbf{P}}_{s,x}\{[A, \zeta > t] \times (t, \infty]\}.$$

b) Obviously, if $\widetilde{X}$ is a subprocess of process X, all the Markov processes subordinate to $\widetilde{X}$ must also be subprocesses of X and equivalent to $\widetilde{X}$.

It remains to show that every subprocess $\overline{X} = (\overline{x}_t, \overline{\zeta}, \overline{\mathscr{M}}_t^s, \overline{\mathbf{P}}_{s,x})$ of process X is subordinate to some canonical subprocess $\widetilde{X}$.

Let us suppose that the space of elementary events $\overline{\Omega}$ of subprocess $\overline{X}$ is connected with the space of elementary events Ω of process X by a mapping $\bar{\gamma}: \bar{\Omega} \to \Omega$. Then the expression

$$\tilde{\gamma}(\bar{\omega}) = (\bar{\gamma}(\bar{\omega}), \bar{\zeta}(\bar{\omega})) \tag{3.11}$$

gives the mapping of $\bar{\Omega}$ in $\tilde{\Omega} = \Omega \times I_1$. We write $\tilde{\zeta}, \tilde{x}_t, \tilde{\mathcal{M}}_t^s$ and $\tilde{\mathcal{M}}^s$ for the elements defined by conditions 3.3.B-3.3.E. If we take into account the fact that elements $\bar{\zeta}, \bar{x}_t, \bar{\mathcal{M}}_t^s$ and $\bar{\mathcal{M}}^s$ are connected with elements $\zeta, x_t, \mathcal{M}_t^s, \mathcal{M}^s$ by expressions 3.1.A-3.1.D, we can deduce the following relationships between $\tilde{\zeta}, \tilde{x}_t, \tilde{\mathcal{M}}_t^s, \tilde{\mathcal{M}}^s$ and $\bar{\zeta}, \bar{x}_t, \bar{\mathcal{M}}_t^s, \bar{\mathcal{M}}^s$:

$$\left.\begin{array}{l} \tilde{\zeta}[\tilde{\gamma}(\bar{\omega})] = \bar{\zeta}(\bar{\omega}) \\ \tilde{x}_t[\tilde{\gamma}(\bar{\omega})] = \bar{x}_t(\bar{\omega}) \quad \text{for } t < \tilde{\zeta}[\tilde{\gamma}(\bar{\omega})] \\ \tilde{\gamma}^{-1}(\tilde{\mathcal{M}}_t^s) \subseteq \bar{\mathcal{M}}_t^s \\ \tilde{\gamma}^{-1}(\tilde{\mathcal{M}}^s) \subseteq \bar{\mathcal{M}}^s \end{array}\right\} \tag{3.12}$$

We put for each $A \in \tilde{\mathcal{M}}^s$:

$$\tilde{\mathbf{P}}_{s,x}(A) = \bar{\mathbf{P}}_{s,x}[\tilde{\gamma}^{-1}(A)]. \tag{3.13}$$

It may easily be shown that all the conditions 2.1.A-2.1.F are satisfied for $(\tilde{x}_t, \tilde{\zeta}, \tilde{\mathcal{M}}_t^s, \tilde{\mathbf{P}}_{s,x})$. These elements thus define some Markov process $\tilde{X}$. Obviously, $\tilde{X}$ is a canonical subprocess of process X. On combining (3.12)-(3.13) with conditions 2.11.A-2.11.D, we observe that the Markov process $\bar{X}$ is subordinate to process $\tilde{X}$.

3.4. In view of condition 3.1.E′, for every subprocess of a Markov process X there is a corresponding system of functions $\alpha_t^s(\omega)$ $(0 \leqslant s \leqslant t,\ \omega \in \Omega_t)$ (functions α_t^s are measurable with respect to the σ-algebra $\mathfrak{R}_t^s$). Here, every function α_t^s can be varied as desired over any set belonging to $\mathfrak{R}_t^s$ and having $\mathbf{P}_{s,x}$-measure zero for any $x \in E$. We shall speak of two systems $\{\alpha_t^s\}$ and $\{\bar{\alpha}_t^s\}$ as being equivalent if $\alpha_t^s = \bar{\alpha}_t^s$ (a.c. $\Omega_t, \mathbf{P}_{s,x}$) for any $0 \leqslant s \leqslant t, x \in E$. By lemma 3.2, there is a one-to-one correspondence between classes of equivalent subprocesses of a Markov process X and classes of equivalent systems of functions $\{\alpha_t^s\}$ (if we consider only systems that correspond to some subprocess). Our main purpose is now to discover what sort of systems $\{\alpha_t^s\}$ correspond to subprocesses of a Markov process X. The first step in this direction is provided by the following lemma.

<u>Lemma 3.3</u>. Let $\tilde{X} = (\tilde{x}_t, \tilde{\zeta}, \tilde{\mathcal{M}}_t^s, \tilde{\mathbf{P}}_{s,x})$ be a subprocess of the

Markov process $X=(x_t, \zeta, \mathscr{M}_t^s, \mathbf{P}_{s,x})$. The functions α_t^s defined by condition 3.1.E (or 3.1.E′), possess the following properties:

3.4.A. For any $s\leqslant t\leqslant u$, $x\in E$

$$\alpha_u^s=\alpha_t^s\alpha_u^t \qquad (\text{a.c. } \Omega_u, \mathbf{P}_{s,x}).$$

3.4.B. For any $s\leqslant t$, $x\in E$

$$0\leqslant \alpha_t^s\leqslant 1 \qquad (\text{a.c. } \Omega_t, \mathbf{P}_{s,x}),$$

3.4.C. For any $s\leqslant t$, $x\in E$

$$\lim_{t_n\downarrow t} \alpha_{t_n}^s=\alpha_t^s \qquad (\text{a.c. } \Omega_t, \mathbf{P}_{s,x}).$$

Proof. Property 3.4.B follows from 1.6.B_1, and property 3.4.C from 1.6.D. It remains to prove 3.4.A.

We shall show that, if $A\in \mathscr{N}_t^s$, $B\in \mathscr{N}_u^t$, then

$$\widetilde{\mathbf{P}}_{s,x}\{AB, \widetilde{\zeta}> u\}=\mathbf{M}_{s,x}[\chi_{AB}\alpha_t^s\alpha_u^t]. \tag{3.14}$$

We note first of all that

$$\{B, \widetilde{\zeta}> u\}\in \widetilde{\mathscr{N}}_u^t, \tag{3.15}$$

where $\widetilde{\mathscr{N}}_u^t$ is the σ-algebra in space $\widetilde{\Omega}_u$ generated by sets $\{\widetilde{x}_v\in \Gamma, \ \widetilde{\zeta}> u\}$ $(v\in [t, u], \Gamma\in \mathscr{B})$. For the class of all subsets B of set Ω_u that satisfy (3.15) is a σ-algebra in Ω_u. By (3.6), this σ-algebra contains all sets $\{x_v\in\Gamma, \zeta>u\}$ $(v\in [t, u]$, $\Gamma\in \mathscr{B})$. It thus contains $\mathscr{N}_u^t$.

Since $\{A, \widetilde{\zeta}>t\}\in \widetilde{\mathscr{M}}_t^s$, $\{B, \widetilde{\zeta}> u\}\in \widetilde{\mathscr{N}}_u^t$, we have on applying (2.9) to the process $\widetilde{X}$:

$$\begin{aligned}\widetilde{\mathbf{P}}_{s,x}\{AB, \widetilde{\zeta}> u\}=\widetilde{\mathbf{P}}_{s,x}\{A, \widetilde{\zeta}> t, B, \widetilde{\zeta}> u\}=\\ =\widetilde{\mathbf{M}}_{s,x}\{\chi_{A,\widetilde{\zeta}>t}\mathbf{P}_{t,\widetilde{x}_t}(B, \widetilde{\zeta}> u)\}.\end{aligned} \tag{3.16}$$

Moreover, by (3.3),

$$\mathbf{P}_{t,y}(B, \widetilde{\zeta}> u)=\mathbf{M}_{t,y}(\chi_B\alpha_u^t). \tag{3.17}$$

We have from (3.4), (3.16) and (3.17),

$$\widetilde{\mathbf{P}}_{s,x}(AB, \widetilde{\zeta}> u)=\mathbf{M}_{s,x}[\alpha_t^s\chi_A\mathbf{M}_{t,x_t}(\chi_B\alpha_u^t)]. \tag{3.18}$$

On the other hand, we find on applying (2.10) to the

process X:

$$\mathbf{M}_{s,x}[\chi_A \alpha_t^s \chi_B \alpha_u^t] = \mathbf{M}_{s,x}[\chi_A \alpha_t^s \mathbf{M}_{t,x_t}(\chi_B \alpha_u^t)]. \tag{3.19}$$

On comparing (3.19) and (3.18), we get (3.14).

Let $\mathscr{F}$ be the class of events $D \subseteq \Omega_u$, for which

$$\widetilde{\mathbf{P}}_{s,x}(D, \widetilde{\zeta} > u) = \mathbf{M}_{s,x}[\chi_D \alpha_t^s \alpha_u^t]. \tag{3.20}$$

and let $\mathscr{C}$ be the class of all events AB, where $A \in \mathscr{N}_t^s$, $B \in \mathscr{N}_u^t$. We have already shown that $\mathscr{F} \supseteq \mathscr{C}$. It is clear that $\mathscr{C}$ is a π-system and $\mathscr{F}$ a λ-system in Ω_u, and by lemma 1.1, $\mathscr{F} \supseteq \sigma(\mathscr{C})$. But obviously, $\sigma(\mathscr{C}) = \mathscr{N}_u^s$. Hence $\mathscr{F} \supseteq \mathscr{N}_u^s$. Since (3.20) holds for any $D \in \mathscr{N}_u^s$ and since function $\alpha_t^s \alpha_u^t$ is clearly $\mathscr{N}_u^s$-measurable, we have

$$\widetilde{\mathbf{P}}_{s,x}\{\widetilde{\zeta} > u \,|\, \mathscr{N}_u^s\} = \alpha_t^s \alpha_u^t \qquad (\text{a.c. } \Omega_u, \mathbf{P}_{s,x}). \tag{3.21}$$

On the other hand, by (3.1),

$$\widetilde{\mathbf{P}}_{s,x}\{\widetilde{\zeta} > u \,|\, \mathscr{N}_u^s\} = \alpha_u^s \qquad (\text{a.c. } \Omega_u, \mathbf{P}_{s,x}). \tag{3.22}$$

Expressions (3.21) and (3.22) yield 3.4.A, and the lemma is proved.

3.5. We now take the equivalent systems $\{\alpha_t^s\}$ connected with a given subprocess $\widetilde{X}$ of process X by condition 3.1.E′ and attempt to distinguish the one for which conditions 3.4.A-3.4.C are satisfied in a stronger form (not for almost all, but for all ω).

We shall speak of the system of functions $\alpha_t^s(\omega)$ $(0 \leqslant s \leqslant t$, $\omega \in \Omega_t)$ as defining a multiplicative functional α of the Markov process $X = (x_t, \zeta, \mathscr{M}_t^s, \mathbf{P}_{s,x})$ if the $\alpha_t^s(\omega)$ satisfy the following conditions.

3.5.A. $\alpha_t^s(\omega)$ is $\mathscr{R}_t^s$-measurable.

3.5.B. $\alpha_t^s(\omega)\alpha_u^t(\omega) = \alpha_u^s(\omega)$ $(s \leqslant t \leqslant u,\ \omega \in \Omega_u)$.

3.5.C. $0 \leqslant \alpha_t^s(\omega) \leqslant 1$ $(s \leqslant t,\ \omega \in \Omega_t)$.

3.5.D. $\lim_{t_n \downarrow t} \alpha_{t_n}^s(\omega) = \alpha_t^s(\omega)$ $(s \leqslant t,\ \omega \in \Omega_t)$.

We shall say that the subprocess $\widetilde{X}$ of Markov process X corresponds to the multiplicative functional α if, for any

$s \leqslant t,\ x \in E$

$$\mathbf{P}_{s,x}\{\tilde{\zeta} > t \mid \mathscr{M}^s\} = \alpha_t^s(\omega) \qquad (\text{a.c. } \Omega_t,\ \mathbf{P}_{s,x}). \tag{3.23}$$

Theorem 3.2. The sufficient condition for the subprocess $\tilde{X} = (\tilde{x}_t, \tilde{\zeta}, \tilde{\mathscr{M}}_t^s, \tilde{\mathbf{P}}_{s,x})$ of Markov process X to correspond to some multiplicative functional is that either of the following two conditions be satisfied:

3.5.α. $\tilde{P}(s, x; s, E) = \tilde{\mathbf{P}}_{s,x}(\tilde{\zeta} > s) = 1$ for any $s \geqslant 0,\ x \in E$.

3.5.β. The functions α_t^s defined by condition 3.1.E′ are subject to the convergence

$$\lim_{s_n \downarrow s} \alpha_t^{s_n} = \alpha_t^s \qquad (\text{a.c. } \Omega_t,\ \mathbf{P}_{s,x})$$

for any $s < t,\ x \in E$.

Proof. a) If $\tilde{\mathbf{P}}_{s,x}\{\tilde{\zeta} > s\} = 1$, then by 1.6.$B_1$,

$$\alpha_s^s = \mathbf{P}_{s,x}\{\tilde{\zeta} > s \mid \mathscr{M}^s\} = 1 \qquad (\text{a.c. } \Omega_s,\ \mathbf{P}_{s,x}). \tag{3.24}$$

Let $s_n \downarrow s$. By 3.4.A, 3.4.C and (3.24), we have for almost all $\omega \in \Omega_t$ (in the sense of $\mathbf{P}_{s,x}$) $\alpha_t^s = \alpha_{s_n}^s \alpha_t^{s_n},\ \alpha_{s_n}^s \to \alpha_s^s$ and $\alpha_s^s = 1$. Condition 3.5.β follows from this.

b) We now show that, as a consequence of 3.5.β, the subprocess corresponds to some multiplicative functional α. We shall start from any system of functions α_t^s defined by condition 3.1.E′ and construct an equivalent system of functions yielding the multiplicative functional α.

The set

$$A_t^s = \{\alpha_t^s < 0\} \cup \{\alpha_t^s > 1\}$$

belongs to $\mathscr{R}_t^s$ and, by 3.4.B, $\mathbf{P}_{s,x}(A_t^s) = 0$. We replace the values of functions $\alpha_t^s(\omega)$ on the set A_t^s by zero. We get the equivalent system of functions which satisfies condition 3.5.C. (Naturally, it also satisfies condition 3.1.E′ and conditions 3.4.A-3.4.C.) Our initial functions will be denoted by α_t^s again.

We put

$$Q_{s,t,u} = \{\alpha_u^s \neq \alpha_t^s \alpha_u^t\} \qquad (s \leqslant t \leqslant u).$$

Obviously, $Q_{s,t,u} \in \mathcal{N}^s$. By (2.9), for any $q \leqslant s$ we have

$$\mathbf{P}_{q,x}(Q_{s,t,u}) = \int_{\Omega_s} \mathbf{P}_{s,x_s}(Q_{s,t,u}) \mathbf{P}_{q,x}(d\omega).$$

In view of 3.4.A, $P_{s,y}(Q_{s,t,u}) = 0$ for any y, and therefore $\mathbf{P}_{q,x}(Q_{s,t,u}) = 0$ for any x.

Let $\eta(\omega)$ denote the exact upper bound of rational numbers such that $\omega \in Q_{s,t,u}$ for certain rational $u \geqslant t \geqslant s$. Clearly, $\eta(\omega) \leqslant \zeta(\omega)$ and

$$\{\eta > q\} = \bigcup_{q < s \leqslant t \leqslant u} Q_{s,t,u}$$

(summation over rational s, t, u). Hence it follows that, for any $x \in E$,

$$\mathbf{P}_{q,x}\{\eta > q\} = 0. \tag{3.25}$$

Condition 3.5.B is evidently satisfied for any rational $u \geqslant t \geqslant s$ of (η, ζ). Hence for any $\omega \in \Omega_t$ and any rational $t \in (\eta, \zeta)$, $\alpha_t^s(\omega)$ is a non-decreasing function of s (if s runs through rational numbers of the interval $(\eta(\omega), t)$). Thus the limit exists for any real $s \geqslant \eta(\omega)$:

$$\alpha_t^{s+0}(\omega) = \lim_{p \downarrow s} \alpha_t^p(\omega) \quad (p \text{ rational}). \tag{3.26}$$

It is clear that

$$\alpha_q^{s+0} = \alpha_{q'}^{s+0} \alpha_q^{q'} \quad (\eta(\omega) \leqslant s < q' \leqslant q < \zeta(\omega),\ q \text{ and } q' \text{ rational}). \tag{3.27}$$

Hence α_t^{s+0} is a non-increasing function of t (for rational values of $t \in (s, \zeta)$). We put

$$\alpha_{t+0}^{s+0} = \lim_{q \downarrow t} \alpha_q^{s+0} \quad (q \text{ rational},\ \eta \leqslant s \leqslant t < \zeta). \tag{3.28}$$

If $s \leqslant t \leqslant u$ are any real numbers from $[\eta, \zeta)$, we obtain by putting first $q' \downarrow t$ then $q \downarrow u$ in (3.27):

$$\alpha_{u+0}^{s+0} = \alpha_{t+0}^{s+0} \alpha_{u+0}^{t+0}.$$

Let $s \leqslant t < \zeta(\omega)$. We put

$$\widetilde{\alpha}_t^s(\omega) = \begin{cases} \alpha_{t+0}^{s+0}(\omega), & \text{if } \eta(\omega) \leqslant s, \\ 0, & \text{if } \eta(\omega) > s. \end{cases}$$

These functions may easily be seen to satisfy conditions 3.5.B-3.5.D. Furthermore,

$$\{\widetilde{\alpha}_t^s \neq \alpha_t^s\} \subseteq C_1 \cup C_2,$$

where

$$C_1 = \{\eta > s\}, \qquad C_2 = \{\eta \leqslant s,\ \alpha_{t+0}^{s+0} \neq \alpha_t^s\}.$$

By (3.25), for any $x \in E$,

$$\mathbf{P}_{s,x}(C_1) = 0.$$

By (3.28) and (3.26),

$$C_2 \subseteq \left\{\bigcup_q \left[\Omega_s,\ \lim_{p\downarrow s} \alpha_q^p \neq \alpha_q^s\right]\right\} \cup \left\{\lim_{q\downarrow t} \alpha_q^s \neq \alpha_t^s\right\}$$

($p \leqslant q$ are rational numbers). By 3.5.β and 3.4.C, we now conclude that $\mathbf{P}_{s,x}(C_2) = 0$ and therefore

$$\mathbf{P}_{s,x}\{\widetilde{\alpha}_t^s \neq \alpha_t^s\} = 0. \tag{3.29}$$

Function $\widetilde{\alpha}_t^s$ is clearly $\mathcal{N}^s$-measurable. In view of (3.29) it is $\mathcal{R}_t^s$-measurable and satisfies relationship (3.23).

The theorem is thus proved.

3.6. Theorem 3.3. For every multiplicative functional α of the Markov process $X = (x_t, \zeta, \mathcal{M}_t^s, \mathbf{P}_{s,x})$ there is a corresponding subprocess $\widetilde{X}$ of X.

Proof. It follows from theorem 3.1 that, if one subprocess corresponds to the functional α, there is a canonical subprocess corresponding to α. We shall therefore construct subprocess $\widetilde{X}$ in the canonical form. We define $\widetilde{\Omega}, \widetilde{\zeta}, \widetilde{x}_t, \widetilde{\mathcal{M}}_t^s$ and $\widetilde{\mathcal{M}}^s$ by means of conditions 3.3.A-3.3.E. It remains to assign the measures $\widetilde{\mathbf{P}}_{s,x}$.

We fix $\omega \in \Omega$ and $s \geqslant 0$ and consider the function

$$F^s(t) = \begin{cases} 0 & \text{for } 0 \leqslant t < s, \\ 1 - \alpha_t^s(\omega) & \text{for } s \leqslant t < \zeta(\omega), \\ 1 & \text{for } t \geqslant \zeta(\omega). \end{cases}$$

In view of 3.5.B-3.5.D this function satisfies conditions 1.11.A-1.11.C, and in accordance with sec. 1.11, there exists on the segment $[0, \infty]$ the probability measure α^s_Γ $(\Gamma \in \mathscr{B}^0)$ *) such that $\alpha^s_{[0,t]} = F^s(t)$ and therefore $\alpha^s_{[t,\infty]} = \alpha^s_t$ for $\omega \in \Omega_t$.

Let $A \in \tilde{\mathscr{M}}^s$. Then $A \in \mathscr{M}^s \times \mathscr{B}^s$, and in accordance with lemma 1.4, the set

$$A_\omega = \{\lambda : (\omega, \lambda) \in A\}$$

belongs to $\mathscr{B}^s \subseteq \mathscr{B}^0$ for every $\omega \in \Omega$. We put

$$\alpha^s_A(\omega) = \alpha^s_{A_\omega}(\omega). \tag{3.30}$$

Obviously, for $A = [C, \zeta > t] \times (t, \infty]$ $(C \in \mathscr{M}^s,\ t \geqslant s)$

$$\alpha^s_A(\omega) = \chi_C(\omega)\, \alpha^s_t(\omega) \qquad (\omega \in \Omega_t). \tag{3.31}$$

Hence we easily deduce by conventional use of lemma 1.2 that the function $\alpha^s_A(\omega)$ is $\mathscr{M}^s$-measurable for any $A \in \tilde{\mathscr{M}}^s$. We put

$$\tilde{\mathbf{P}}_{s,x}(A) = \mathbf{M}_{s,x}\alpha^s_A. \tag{3.32}$$

Clearly, for every $A \in \mathscr{M}^s$,

$$\tilde{\mathbf{P}}_{s,x}(A \times I) = P_{s,x}(A).$$

It follows from (3.31) that

$$\tilde{\mathbf{P}}_{s,x}\{C, \tilde{\zeta} > t\} = \tilde{\mathbf{P}}_{s,x}\{[C, \zeta > t] \times (t, \infty]\} = \\ = \mathbf{M}_{s,x}\chi_C\alpha^s_t \qquad (C \in \mathscr{M}^s,\ t \geqslant s). \tag{3.33}$$

The system of elements $(\tilde{x}_t, \tilde{\zeta}, \tilde{\mathscr{M}}^s_t, \tilde{\mathbf{P}}_{s,x})$ evidently satisfies conditions 3.1.A-3.1.D. It follows from expression (3.33) that

$$\tilde{\mathbf{P}}_{s,x}\{\tilde{\zeta} > t \,\|\, \mathscr{M}^s\} = \alpha^s_t \qquad (\text{a.c. } \Omega_t,\ \mathbf{P}_{s,x}),$$

so that condition 3.1.E′ and relationship (3.23) are satisfied.

We also want to show that elements $(\tilde{x}_t, \tilde{\zeta}, \tilde{\mathscr{M}}^s_t, \tilde{\mathbf{P}}_{s,x})$ satisfy conditions 2.1.A-2.1.F. It is obvious that 2.1.A, 2.1.B and

*) $\mathscr{B}^s$ denotes the σ-algebra in the space $[s, +\infty]$ generated by all intervals.

2.1.C hold. It follows from (3.33) that $\widetilde{P}(s, x; t, \Gamma) = \mathbf{M}_{s,x}\alpha_t^s\chi_\Gamma(x_t)$. Since the function $\chi_\Gamma(x_t)\alpha_t^s$ is $\mathscr{N}^s$-measurable, it readily follows from lemma 2.2 that $\widetilde{P}(s, x; t, \Gamma)$ is a $\mathscr{B}$-measurable function of x, so that condition 2.1.D is fulfilled. It is obvious that 2.1.E holds. It remains to prove condition 2.1.F.

We can more conveniently prove this last condition in the form 2.1.F'. In accordance with 3.3.D, every set A of $\widetilde{\mathscr{M}}_t^s$ has the form $A = C \times (t, \infty]$ $(C \in \mathscr{M}_t^s)$. By (3.33),

$$\widetilde{\mathbf{P}}_{s,x}(A, \widetilde{x}_u \in \Gamma) = \widetilde{\mathbf{P}}_{s,x}\{[C, x_u \in \Gamma] \times (u, \infty]\} = \\ = \mathbf{M}_{s,x}[\chi_C\chi_\Gamma(x_u)\alpha_u^s]. \tag{3.34}$$

We have on the basis of 3.5.B and 1.6.H,

$$\mathbf{M}_{s,x}[\chi_C\chi_\Gamma(x_u)\alpha_u^s] = \mathbf{M}_{s,x}[\alpha_t^s\chi_C\chi_\Gamma(x_u)\alpha_u^t] = \\ = \mathbf{M}_{s,x}\{\chi_C\alpha_t^s\mathbf{M}_{s,x}[\alpha_u^t\chi_\Gamma(x_u) \mid \mathscr{M}_t^s]\}. \tag{3.35}$$

The function $\alpha_u^t\chi_\Gamma(x_u)$ is $\mathscr{N}^t$-measurable. We therefore have, on applying theorem 2.1 to the process X:

$$\mathbf{M}_{s,x}[\alpha_u^t\chi_\Gamma(x_u) \mid \mathscr{M}_t^s] = \mathbf{M}_{t,x_t}[\alpha_u^t\chi_\Gamma(x_u)] = \\ = \widetilde{P}(t, x_t; u, \Gamma) \qquad (\text{a.c. } \Omega_t, \mathbf{P}_{s,x}). \tag{3.36}$$

We have from (3.34), (3.35) and (3.36):

$$\widetilde{\mathbf{P}}_{s,x}(A, \widetilde{x}_u \in \Gamma) = \mathbf{M}_{s,x}\{\chi_C\alpha_t^s\widetilde{P}(t, x_t; u, \Gamma)\}. \tag{3.37}$$

It may easily be seen from (3.33) that (3.4) holds. Relationship (3.37) can therefore be rewritten as

$$\widetilde{P}_{s,x}(A, \widetilde{x}_u \in \Gamma) = \widetilde{\mathbf{M}}_{s,x}\{\chi_C\chi_{\zeta > t}\widetilde{P}(t, x_t; u, \Gamma)\} = \\ = \widetilde{\mathbf{M}}_{s,x}[\chi_A\widetilde{P}(t, \widetilde{x}_t; u, \Gamma)],$$

and condition 2.1.F' is satisfied.

The theorem is now proved.

3.7. We can connect with every multiplicative functional α of a process X a system of random variables ξ_s which are defined as follows:

$$\xi_s(\omega) = \begin{cases} \inf\{t : \alpha_t^s(\omega) = 0\} & (\omega \in \Omega_s), \\ s \quad (\omega \,\overline{\in}\, \Omega_s) \end{cases} \tag{3.38}$$

(if $\alpha_t^s > 0$ for all $t \in [s, \zeta)$, we put $\xi_s(\omega) = \zeta$). In view of 3.5.D, the lower bound is attained in (3.38), so that $\alpha_{\xi_s}^s = 0$.

Some obvious properties of the functions ξ_s may be noted.

3.7.A. $s \leqslant \xi_s(\omega) \leqslant \zeta(\omega)$.

3.7.B. $\{\xi_s > t\} \in \mathcal{R}_t^s \qquad (0 \leqslant s \leqslant t)$.

3.7.C. $\{\xi_s > t\} \subseteq \{\xi_s = \xi_t\} \quad (0 \leqslant s \leqslant t)$.

<u>Lemma 3.4</u>. If $\widetilde{X}$ is any subprocess of process X corresponding to the multiplicative functional α, we have for all $s \geqslant 0,\ x \in E$,

$$\widetilde{\mathbf{P}}_{s,x}\{\widetilde{\zeta} \leqslant \xi_s\} = 1. \tag{3.39}$$

Proof. By 3.7.B, 1.6.F, (3.2), (3.23) and (3.38),

$$\widetilde{\mathbf{P}}_{s,x}\{\widetilde{\zeta} > t \geqslant \xi_s \,|\, \mathcal{M}^s\} = \chi_{t \geqslant \xi_s} \widetilde{\mathbf{P}}_{s,x}\{\widetilde{\zeta} > t \,|\, \mathcal{M}^s\} = 0 \quad (\text{a.c. } \Omega,\ \mathbf{P}_{s,x}). \tag{3.40}$$

Consequently

$$\widetilde{\mathbf{P}}_{s,x}\{\widetilde{\zeta} > t \geqslant \xi_s\} = 0. \tag{3.41}$$

Let Λ be a denumerable set everywhere dense in the interval $[s, \infty)$. Then

$$\{\widetilde{\zeta} > \xi_s\} = \bigcup_{t \in \Lambda} \{\widetilde{\zeta} > t \geqslant \xi_s\}. \tag{3.42}$$

Equation (3.39) follows from a comparison of (3.41) and (3.42).

We shall consider in detail the important particular case when the functions α_t^s defining the multiplicative functional α take only two values: zero and unity. In this case the functional α is expressed in terms of functions ξ_s by

$$\alpha_t^s(\omega) = \chi_{\xi_s > t}(\omega). \tag{3.43}$$

If $\{\xi_s\}$ is any system of functions satisfying conditions 3.7.A-3.7.C, the functions $\alpha_t^s = \chi_{\xi_s > t}$ will satisfy requirements 3.5.A-3.5.D. Formulae (3.38) and (3.43) thus define a one-to-one correspondence between multiplicative functionals with values zero and unity and all the possible systems of functions ξ_s subject to conditions 3.7.A-3.7.C.

A comparison of (3.5) and (3.43) shows that the transition function of the subprocess is expressed in terms of ξ_s by

$$\widetilde{\mathbf{P}}(s, x; t, \Gamma) = \mathbf{P}_{s, x}\{x_t \in \Gamma, \xi_s > t\}. \tag{3.44}$$

Lemma 3.4 can be strengthened as follows in the case in question.

<u>Lemma 3.5</u>. If $\widetilde{X}$ is any subprocess of process X corresponding to the system $\{\xi_s\}$, we have for all $s \leqslant 0, x \in E$

$$\widetilde{\mathbf{P}}_{s, x}\{\xi_s > s, \quad \widetilde{\zeta} \neq \xi_s\} = 0 \tag{3.45}$$

and for all $x \in E$

$$\widetilde{\mathbf{P}}_{0, x}\{\widetilde{\zeta} \neq \xi_0\} = 0. \tag{3.46}$$

Proof. For any $t \geqslant s$,

$$\begin{aligned}\widetilde{\mathbf{P}}_{s, x}\{\widetilde{\zeta} \leqslant t < \xi_s \,|\, \mathscr{M}^s\} &= \chi_{t < \xi_s} \widetilde{\mathbf{P}}_{s, x}\{\widetilde{\zeta} \leqslant t \,|\, \mathscr{M}^s\} = \\ &= \chi_{t < \xi_s}[1 - \chi_{\xi_s > t}] = 0 \qquad (\text{a.c.}\,\Omega, \mathbf{P}_{s, x}).\end{aligned} \tag{3.47}$$

If Λ is a denumerable, everywhere dense subset of the interval $[s, \infty)$, we have

$$\{\xi_s > s, \widetilde{\zeta} < \xi_s\} = \bigcup_{t \in \Lambda} \{\widetilde{\zeta} \leqslant t < \xi_s\}. \tag{3.48}$$

It follows from (3.47) and (3.48) that

$$\widetilde{\mathbf{P}}_{s, x}\{\xi_s > s, \widetilde{\zeta} < \xi_s\} = 0,$$

and we get (3.45) on taking into account (3.39).

If $s = 0$, the set $\{\xi_s \leqslant s, \widetilde{\zeta} < \xi_s\} = \{\xi_0 = 0, \widetilde{\zeta} < 0\}$ is empty, and equation (3.46) therefore holds.

2. Subprocesses Corresponding to Admissible Subsets. The Formation of Parts of a Process

3.8. Let Γ be a subset of the phase space $(E, \mathscr{B})$. We put *)

*)Writing $x_t(\omega) \overline{\in} \Gamma$ indicates that the value of $x_t(\omega)$ is either not defined or else belongs to $E \setminus \Gamma$.

$$\left.\begin{array}{c}\xi_s(\Gamma)=\xi_s(\Gamma,\omega)=\inf\{t: t\geqslant s,\ x_t(\omega)\bar{\in}\Gamma\}\ (\omega\in\Omega)\\ \xi(\Gamma)=\xi_0(\Gamma)\end{array}\right\}. \quad (3.49)$$

Let $t<\zeta(\omega)$. The segment of trajectory x_u $(s\leqslant u\leqslant t)$ is contained in Γ if $t<\xi_s(\Gamma)$, and is not contained in Γ if $t>\xi_s(\Gamma)$. It is therefore natural to speak of $\xi_s(\Gamma)$ as the instant of first departure after s of the trajectory from set Γ. The functions $\xi_s=\xi_s(\Gamma)$ always satisfy conditions 3.7.A and 3.7.C. If they also satisfy condition 3.7.B, we shall describe the set Γ as <u>admissible</u>. Some subprocess of process X corresponds to each admissible set.

The question as to whether a given set is admissible for a process X has to be considered on its merits in each case.

<u>Lemma 3.6</u>. The sufficient conditions for a set Γ to be admissible for a process X are that:

3.8.A. $\Psi_t^s=\bigcap\limits_{u\in[s,t]}\{x_u\in\Gamma\}\in\mathfrak{N}_t^s$.

3.8.B. $\{\xi_t(\Gamma)>t\}\in\mathcal{N}^t$ and

$\widetilde{P}(t,x;t,E)=\mathbf{P}_{t,x}\{\xi_t(\Gamma)>t\}=1$ for all $t\geqslant 0$, $x\in\Gamma$.

The transfer function of the subprocess corresponding to set Γ is given by

$$\widetilde{P}(s,x;t,G)=\mathbf{P}_{s,x}\{\Psi_t^s,\ x_t\in G\}. \quad (3.50)$$

Proof. We have

$$\{\xi_\Gamma^s>t\}=\{\Psi_t^s,\ \xi_t(\Gamma)>t\}.$$

Hence by theorem 2.1,

$$\mathbf{P}_{s,x}\{\xi_s(\Gamma)>t\}=\int\limits_{\Psi_t^s}\mathbf{P}_{t,x_t}\{\xi_t(\Gamma)>t\}\,\mathbf{P}_{s,x}(d\omega)=\mathbf{P}_{s,x}(\Psi_t^s).$$

Thus

$$\mathbf{P}_{s,x}\{\Psi_t^s\setminus[\xi_s(\Gamma)>t]\}=0 \quad (3.51)$$

and $\{\xi_s(\Gamma)>t\}\in\mathfrak{N}_t^s$. Formula (3.50) follows from (3.44) and (3.51).

We note that, if process X is continuous, $x_{\xi_s(\Gamma,\omega)}(\omega)$ belongs to the boundary of Γ*) for every ω satisfying the inequality $s<\xi_s(\Gamma,\omega)<\zeta(\omega)$. If G is an open set, the boundary of G does not intersect with G and therefore

$$\{\omega:\xi_s(G,\omega)<\zeta(\omega)\}=\{\omega:x_{\xi_s(G,\omega)}\in E\setminus G\}. \tag{3.52}$$

Let η be an arbitrary ω-function. It is natural to speak of $\xi_\eta(\Gamma)=\xi_{\eta(\omega)}(\Gamma,\omega)$ as the first instant of departure after η from set Γ. The reader will easily prove that

$$\{\xi_s(\Gamma)\geqslant\eta\geqslant s\}\subseteq\{\xi_s(\Gamma)=\xi_\eta(\Gamma)\}. \tag{3.53}$$

If $G\subseteq\Gamma$, we have $s\leqslant\xi_s(G)\leqslant\xi_s(\Gamma)$, and it is clear from (3.53) that

$$\xi_s(\Gamma)=\xi_{\xi_s(G)}(\Gamma)\qquad(\omega\in\Omega). \tag{3.54}$$

The question as to whether set Γ is admissible is closely bound up with the question of the measurability of events $\Psi_t^s(\Gamma)=\{$segment of trajectory $x_u(s\leqslant u\leqslant t)$ is contained in $\Gamma\}$.

If process X is given in a topological measurable space, it is important for us to investigate, in addition to events $\Psi_t^s(\Gamma)$, the events: $\hat{\Psi}_t^s(\Gamma)=\{$closure of segment of trajectory $x_u(s\leqslant u\leqslant t)$ is contained in $\Gamma\}$.

A general investigation of the conditions of measurability of events $\hat{\Psi}_t^s(\Gamma)$ and $\Psi_t^s(\Gamma)$ requires the use of the theory of continuation of capacities. The subject is therefore treated separately in a special supplement.

3.9. When we construct a subprocess of a Markov process to correspond to an admissible set $\widetilde{E}$, the phase space remains unchanged. This naturally suggests a modification to the construction so that the phase space is shortened to the set $\widetilde{E}$.

Let $X=(x_t,\zeta,\mathscr{M}_t^s,\mathbf{P}_{s,x})$ be a Markov process in the measurable space $(E,\mathscr{B})$ and let $\widetilde{E}\in\mathscr{B}$ and $\widetilde{\mathscr{B}}=\mathscr{B}[\widetilde{E}]$. We shall describe the Markov process $\widetilde{X}=(\widetilde{x}_t,\widetilde{\zeta},\widetilde{\mathscr{M}}_t^s,\widetilde{\mathbf{P}}_{s,x})$ in the phase space $(\widetilde{E},\widetilde{\mathscr{B}})$ as <u>part of process</u> X if there exists a mapping $\gamma:\widetilde{\Omega}\to\Omega$ ($\widetilde{\Omega}$ and Ω are the spaces of elementary events for $\widetilde{X}$ and X respectively) such that:

*)The boundary of a set Γ is defined as the intersection of the closure of Γ with the closure of $E\setminus\Gamma$.

3.9.A. $\tilde{\zeta}(\tilde{\omega})=\xi[\tilde{E}, \gamma(\tilde{\omega})] \quad (\tilde{\omega}\in\tilde{\Omega})$.

3.9.B. $\tilde{x}_t(\tilde{\omega})=x_t[\gamma(\tilde{\omega})] \quad (\tilde{\omega}\in\tilde{\Omega},\ 0\leqslant t<\tilde{\zeta}(\tilde{\omega}))$.

3.9.C. If $A\in\mathscr{M}_t^s$, then $\{\gamma^{-1}A, \tilde{\zeta}>t\}\in\tilde{\mathscr{M}}_t^s$.

3.9.D. $\tilde{\mathscr{M}}^s\supseteq\gamma^{-1}(\mathscr{M}^s)$ and $\tilde{\mathbf{P}}_{s,x}(\gamma^{-1}A)=\mathbf{P}_{s,x}(A)$ for $A\in\mathscr{M}^s,\ x\in\tilde{E}$.

The transition function of process $\tilde{X}$ is given by

$$\tilde{P}(s, x; t, \Gamma)=\mathbf{P}_{s,x}\{x_t\in\Gamma, \xi_s>t\} \quad (x\in\tilde{E},\ 0\leqslant s\leqslant t). \tag{3.55}$$

Theorem 3.4. A part of process X can be generated on every non-accessible set satisfying condition 3.8.B.

Proof. Since

$$\Psi_t^s=\{x_t\in\tilde{E}\}\in\mathfrak{R}_t^s,$$

the set $\tilde{E}$ satisfies condition 3.8.A. It is admissible by lemma 3.6. We now consider the subprocess $\overline{X}=(\overline{x}_t, \overline{\zeta}, \overline{\mathscr{M}}_t^s, \overline{\mathbf{P}}_{s,x})$ of process X corresponding to the admissible set $\tilde{E}$. We put

$$\xi_s=\xi_s(\tilde{E}),\ \xi=\xi(\tilde{E}),\ \tilde{\Omega}=\{\overline{\zeta}=\xi\},\ \tilde{\gamma}(\tilde{\omega})=\tilde{\omega}\ (\tilde{\omega}\in\tilde{\Omega}).$$

Since $\tilde{E}$ is non-accessible, we have

$$\{\xi_s>s\}\subseteq\{\xi=\xi_s\}.$$

Thus

$$\tilde{\Omega}\supseteq\{\overline{\zeta}=\xi,\ \xi_s>s\}=\{\overline{\zeta}=\xi_s>s\}. \tag{3.56}$$

Let $A\in\overline{\mathscr{M}}^s$ and $A\supseteq\tilde{\Omega}$. We now have, in view of (3.56),

$$A\supseteq\{\overline{\zeta}=\xi_s>s\}=\{\xi_s>s\}\setminus\{\overline{\zeta}\neq\xi_s,\ \xi_s>s\}$$

and, by 3.8.B and (3.45), $\overline{\mathbf{P}}_{s,x}(A)=1$ for every $x\in\tilde{E}$. Hence the probability measures $\overline{\mathbf{P}}_{s,x}(x\in\tilde{E})$ defined in the σ-algebra $\overline{\mathscr{M}}^s$ induce the probability measures $\tilde{\mathbf{P}}_{s,x}$ in the σ-algebra $\tilde{\mathscr{M}}^s=\tilde{\gamma}^{-1}\overline{\mathscr{M}}^s$ (in space $\tilde{\Omega}$) (cf. the proof of theorem 2.5). We put

$$\tilde{\mathscr{M}}_t^s=\tilde{\gamma}^{-1}\overline{\mathscr{M}}_t^s,\ \tilde{\zeta}(\tilde{\omega})=\overline{\zeta}[\tilde{\gamma}(\tilde{\omega})],\ \tilde{x}_t(\tilde{\omega})=\overline{x}_t[\tilde{\gamma}(\tilde{\omega})].$$

The elements $(\tilde{x}_t, \tilde{\zeta}, \tilde{\mathscr{M}}_t^s, \tilde{\mathbf{P}}_{s,x})$ obviously form a Markov process in space $(\widetilde{E}, \widetilde{\mathscr{B}})$. This process is readily seen to be a part of process X.

The theorem is thus proved.

3.10. If $\widetilde{E}$ is any admissible set for process X and if $\overline{X}$ is any subprocess corresponding to $\widetilde{E}$, there exists by virtue of (3.44) and lemma 2.4 a process $\overline{\overline{X}}$ equivalent to $\overline{X}$ for which the set $\widetilde{F}$ is inaccessible (lemma 2.4 is easily rewritten for cut-off processes). Suppose that $\widetilde{E}$ satisfies condition 3.8.B. Then by theorem 3.4 we can form a part $\widetilde{X}$ of process $\overline{\overline{X}}$ on $\widetilde{E}$. Process $\widetilde{X}$ will not in general be a part of process X, however, since the passage from $\overline{X}$ to the equivalent $\overline{\overline{X}}$ will generally involve a widening of the space of elementary events (and the set of trajectories) and a narrowing of the basic σ-algebras $\mathscr{M}^s_t, \mathscr{M}^s$. In order to generate a part of process X on the set $\widetilde{E}$, certain restrictions need to be imposed on X, viz we must require that its set of elementary events be not too narrow, or its basic σ-algebras too wide.

<u>Theorem 3.5</u>. Let the Markov process $X=(x_t, \zeta, \mathscr{M}^s_t, \mathbf{P}_{s,x})$ in the measurable space $E \in \mathscr{B}$ and the set $(E, \mathscr{B})$ satisfy conditions 3.8.A and 3.8.B and the following conditions:

3.10.A. $\mathscr{M}^s = \mathscr{N}^s$.

3.10.B. If $x_s(\omega) \in \widetilde{E}$, there exists an ω' such that $x_u(\omega') \in \widetilde{E}$ for all $u \in [0, s]$ and $\zeta(\omega') = \zeta(\omega), x_u(\omega') = x_u(\omega)$ for all $u \in [s, \zeta(\omega)$.

A part of process X can now be generated on set $\widetilde{E}$.

Proof. The set $\widetilde{E}$ is admissible by reason of lemma 3.6. Let $\overline{X}=(\overline{x}_t, \overline{\zeta}, \overline{\mathscr{M}}^s_t, \overline{\mathbf{P}}_{s,x})$ be the canonical subprocess of X corresponding to $\widetilde{E}$. As in the proof of theorem 3.4, it amounts to showing that the set $\widetilde{\Omega}=\{\overline{\zeta}=\xi\}$ satisfies the condition: If $A \in \overline{\mathscr{M}}^s$ and $A \supseteq \widetilde{\Omega}$, then $\overline{\mathbf{P}}_{s,x}(A)=1$ for all $x \in \widetilde{E}$. In our present case, $\overline{\Omega}=\Omega \times I, \overline{\zeta}=\min(\lambda, \zeta), \overline{\mathscr{M}}^s \subseteq \mathscr{M}^s \times \mathscr{B}^s = \mathscr{N}^s \times \mathscr{B}^s$.

We put $\omega \in A_\lambda$ if $(\omega, \lambda) \in A$. By lemma 1.4, $A_\lambda \in \mathscr{N}^s$. The inclusion $A \supseteq \widetilde{\Omega}$ is equivalent to the system of inclusions

$$A_\lambda \supseteq \{\min(\lambda, \zeta)=\xi\} \qquad (\lambda \in I). \tag{3.56'}$$

We put $C \in \mathscr{F}$ if C possesses the following property: as soon as $\omega \in C$, $\zeta(\omega)=\zeta(\omega')$ and $x_u(\omega)=x_u(\omega')$ for all $u \in [s, \zeta(\omega))$, then $\omega' \in C$. Evidently $\mathcal{F}$ contains all sets $\{x_t \in \Gamma\}$ $(t \geqslant s,$ $\Gamma \in \mathscr{B})$ and is a σ-algebra. Therefore $\mathcal{F} \supseteq \mathcal{N}^s$.

Let $\lambda > s$ and let $\xi_s(\omega) = \xi_s(\widetilde{E}, \omega) = \min[\lambda, \zeta(\omega)]$. By virtue of condition 3.10.B, an ω' exists such that $\zeta(\omega') = \zeta(\omega)$, $x_u(\omega') = x_u(\omega)$ for all $u \in [s, \zeta(\omega))$ and $x_u(\omega') \in \widetilde{E}$ for all $u \in [0, s]$. Evidently $\xi(\omega') = \xi(\widetilde{E}, \omega') = \xi_s(\widetilde{E}, \omega) = \min[\lambda, \zeta(\omega)]$. By (3.56'), $\omega' \in A_\lambda$ and since $A_\lambda \in \mathcal{N}^s$ we have $\omega \in A_\lambda$. We have shown that, for all $\lambda > s$,

$$A_\lambda \supseteq \{\xi_s = \min[\lambda, \zeta(\omega)]\}. \tag{3.57}$$

It follows from the system of inclusions (3.57) that

$$A \supseteq \{\overline{\zeta} = \xi_s > s\}.$$

Therefore

$$\overline{\mathbf{P}}_{s,x}(A) \geqslant \overline{\mathbf{P}}_{s,x}\{\overline{\zeta} = \xi_s > s\} = \overline{\mathbf{P}}_{s,x}\{\xi_s > s\} - \overline{\mathbf{P}}_{s,x}\{\overline{\zeta} \neq \xi_s,\ \xi_s > s\} = 1$$

[by 3.8.B and (3.45)].

3. Subprocesses Corresponding to Admissible Systems of Subsets

3.11. Let $\mathcal{F}$ be a system of subsets of the measurable space $(E, \mathscr{B})$. We put

$$\begin{aligned} \xi_s(\mathcal{F}) = \xi_s(\mathcal{F}, \omega) &= \sup_{\Gamma \in \mathcal{F}} \xi_s(\Gamma, \omega) \qquad (\omega \in \Omega), \\ \xi(\mathcal{F}) = \xi_0(\mathcal{F}) &= \sup_{\Gamma \in \mathcal{F}} \xi(\Gamma). \end{aligned} \tag{3.58}$$

Let $G_{\mathcal{F}}$ denote the sum of all sets of system $\mathcal{F}$. It is easily seen that

$$\xi_s(\mathcal{F}) \leqslant \xi_s(G_{\mathcal{F}}). \tag{3.59}$$

We shall call $\xi_s(\mathcal{F})$ the first instant of departure after s of a trajectory from the system of sets $\mathcal{F}$.

The functions $\xi_s(\mathcal{F}, \omega)$ always satisfy conditions 3.7.A and 3.7.C. If they also satisfy condition 3.7.B, we shall say that system $\mathcal{F}$ is <u>admissible</u>. In accordance with sec. 3.7, for every admissible system $\mathscr{F}$ there is a corresponding class of equivalent subprocesses $\tilde{X}$ of process X for which

$$\tilde{P}_{s,x}\{\tilde{\zeta}=\xi_s(\mathscr{F})\}=1. \tag{3.60}$$

We shall describe system $\mathscr{F}$ as <u>subordinate</u> to system $\mathscr{F}'$ if there exists for every set $\Gamma\in\mathscr{F}$ a set $\Gamma'\in\mathscr{F}'$ containing it. It is evident from this that $\xi_s(\mathscr{F})\leqslant\xi_s(\mathscr{F}')$ for any $s\geqslant 0$. It may be remarked that all subsystems of $\mathscr{F}$ are subordinate to $\mathscr{F}$. We shall refer to $\mathscr{F}$ and $\mathscr{F}'$ as <u>equivalent</u> systems if $\mathscr{F}$ is subordinate to $\mathscr{F}'$ and $\mathscr{F}'$ subordinate to $\mathscr{F}$. In this case, $\xi_s(\mathscr{F})=\xi_s(\mathscr{F}')$ for any s, so that equivalent systems define the same class of subprocesses of X.

On replacing s in $\xi_s(\mathscr{F},\omega)$ by any ω-function $\eta(\omega)$, we get a quantity $\xi_\eta(\mathscr{F})$ which it is natural to call the first instant of departure after η of the trajectory from system $\mathscr{F}$. We have from (3.53) and (3.58):

$$\begin{aligned}\{\xi(\mathscr{F})>\eta\}&=\bigcup_s\{\eta=s,\ \xi(\mathscr{F})>s\}\subseteq\\ &\subseteq\bigcup_s\{\eta=s,\ \xi(\mathscr{F})=\xi_s(\mathscr{F})\}=\{\xi(\mathscr{F})=\xi_\eta(\mathscr{F})\}.\end{aligned}\tag{3.61}$$

3.12. We shall describe the system of subsets $\mathscr{F}$ of a topological measurable space $(E,\mathscr{C},\mathscr{B})$ as <u>normal</u> if an equivalent system $\Gamma_1,\ldots\Gamma_n,\ldots$, can be found satisfying the following conditions:

3.12.A. $\Gamma_1,\ldots,\Gamma_n,\ldots\in\mathscr{B}$.

3.12.B. $\Gamma_1,\ldots,\Gamma_n,\ldots$ are closed.

3.12.C. For any n there exists $G_n\in\mathscr{C}$ such that $\Gamma_n\subseteq G_n\subseteq\Gamma_{n+1}$.

We observe that

$$\xi_s(\mathscr{F})=\lim_{n\to\infty}\xi_s(\Gamma_n). \tag{3.62}$$

Some important examples of normal systems will now be discussed.

3.12.1. Let $(E,\rho,\mathscr{B})$ be a metric measurable space and let $\mathscr{F}$ be the class of all bounded sets of this space. We choose any point a in E and put $\Gamma_n=\{x:\rho(x,a)\leqslant n\}$. The sequence $\{\Gamma_n\}$ is obviously equivalent to system $\mathscr{F}$ and satisfies requirement 3.12.B. We see on putting $G_n=\Big\{x:\rho(x,a)$

$< n+\frac{1}{2}\}$ that it also satisfies requirement 3.12.C. We can satisfy requirement 3.12.A simply by supposing that $\mathscr{B} \supseteq \mathscr{C}$ or that $\rho(x, a)$ is a $\mathscr{B}$-measurable function of x.

3.12.2. Let G be an open set in the metric measurable space $(E, \rho, \mathscr{B})$ and let $\mathscr{F}$ be the class of all sets Γ for which $\rho(\Gamma, E\setminus G) > 0$. The sequence $\Gamma_n = \left\{x : \rho(x, E\setminus G)\right\} \geqslant \frac{1}{n}$ is equivalent to $\mathscr{F}$ and satisfies conditions 3.12.B and 3.12.C($\left\{x : \rho(x, E\setminus G) > \frac{2}{2n+1}\right\}$) can be taken as G_n). If $\mathscr{B} \supseteq \mathscr{C}$, the continuity of the function $\rho(x, E\setminus G)$ (cf. sec. 1.8) implies that condition 3.12.A holds.

3.12.3. Let the topological measurable space $(E, \mathscr{C}, \mathscr{B})$ have the following properties:

3.12.3.A. For every point x a measurable bicompact set Q and a measurable open set U can be found such that $x \in U \subseteq Q$.

3.12.3.B. A sequence of measurable bicompact subsets E_n exists such that $E = \bigcup_{n=1}^{\infty} E_n$.*)

We shall write $\mathscr{F}$ for the system of all measurable bicompact subsets of the space $(E, \mathscr{C}, \mathscr{B})$.

We note that, for any set $\Gamma \in \mathscr{F} \cap \mathscr{B}$, there exist sets $U \in \mathscr{C} \cap \mathscr{B}$ and $Q \in \mathscr{F} \cap \mathscr{B}$ such that $\Gamma \subseteq U \subseteq Q$. For, by 3.12.3.A, for every $x \in \Gamma$ there exist $U(x) \in \mathscr{C} \cap \mathscr{B}$ and $Q(x) \in \mathscr{F} \cap \mathscr{B}$ such that $x \in U(x) \subseteq Q(x)$. Sets $U(x)$ form a covering of Γ, and a finite covering $U(x_1), \ldots, U(x_m)$ can be chosen from this. Sets $U = \bigcup_{1}^{m} U(x_k)$ and $Q = \bigcup_{1}^{n} Q(x_k)$ obviously have the properties that we require.

We start from the system E_n defined in condition 3.12.3.B and construct sequences Γ_n and G_n by the following recurrence method. We put $\Gamma_1 = E_1$. Assuming set Γ_n to be already constructed, we choose sets $G_n \in \mathscr{C}\mathscr{B}$ and $Q_n \in \mathscr{F}\mathscr{B}$ such that $\Gamma_n \subseteq G_n \subseteq Q_n$, and put $\Gamma_{n+1} = Q_n \cup E_{n+1}$. Sequences $\{\Gamma_n\}$ and $\{G_n\}$ obviously satisfy conditions 3.12.A-3.12.C. Sets G_n moreover form a covering for any $\Gamma \in \mathscr{F}$, and since a finite

*)Property 3.12.3.A is a strengthened type of local bicompactness, whilst 3.12.3.B is a strengthened type of σ-bicompactness (cf. sec. 1.7).

covering can be chosen from this, and $G_1 \subseteq \ldots \subseteq G_n \subseteq \ldots$, we have $\Gamma \subseteq G_n \subseteq \Gamma_{n+1}$ for any n. It is clear from this that $\{\Gamma_n\}$ is equivalent to $\mathscr{F}$.

3.12.4. Let G be a subset of the topological measurable space $(E, \mathscr{C}, \mathscr{B})$ satisfying the following conditions:

3.12.4.A. For every $x \in G$ a measurable open set $U \subseteq G$ and a measurable bicompact set $Q \subseteq G$ can be found such that $x \in G \subseteq Q$.

3.12.4.B. $G = \bigcup_{n+1}^{\infty} E_n$, where the E_n are measurable bicompact sets.

On repeating the arguments of example 3.12.3, the system of all measurable bicompact subsets of set G will be seen to be normal.

Lemma 3.7. Let $\mathscr{F}$ be a normal system of subsets of a topological measurable space $(E, \mathscr{C}, \mathscr{B})$. Now $G_{\mathscr{F}} \in \mathscr{B} \cap \mathscr{C}$. The converse holds if space $(E, \mathscr{C}, \mathscr{B})$ is subject to requirement 1.9.B: every set $G \in \mathscr{B} \cap \mathscr{C}$ can be written in the form $G = G_{\mathscr{F}}$, where $\mathscr{F}$ is a normal system.

Proof. The first assertion is obvious. To prove the second, we consider a measurable continuous function f such that

$$G = \{x : f(x) > 0\},$$

and put

$$\Gamma_n = \left\{x : f(x) \geqslant \frac{1}{n}\right\} \qquad (n = 1, 2, \ldots).$$

It is easily seen that $\mathscr{F} = \{\Gamma_n\}$ is a normal system that satisfies the condition $G_{\mathscr{F}} = G$ (we can take $\left\{x : f(x) > \frac{2}{2n+1}\right\}$ as G_n).

Lemma 3.8. If the system $\tilde{\mathscr{F}}$ consists of compact sets, it is subordinate to any normal system $\mathscr{F}$ satisfying the condition $G_{\tilde{\mathscr{F}}} \subseteq G_{\mathscr{F}}$.

Proof. Let Γ_n be a sequence equivalent to $\mathscr{F}$ and subject to conditions 3.12.A-3.12.C, and let G_n be the sets described in condition 3.12.C. The system $\{G_n\}$ is a denumerable covering for any set $\Gamma \in \tilde{\mathscr{F}}$. Hence a number n can be found such that $\Gamma \subseteq G_n \subseteq \Gamma_{n+1}$. System $\tilde{\mathscr{F}}$ is thus subordinate to the sequence $\{\Gamma_n\}$ and therefore also subordinate to $\mathscr{F}$.

Corollary. Let $G \in \mathscr{B} \cap \mathscr{C}$. All the normal systems $\mathscr{F}$ consisting of compact sets and satisfying the condition $G_{\mathscr{F}} = G$ are equivalent to each other.

3.13. Let X be a Markov process in the topological measurable space $(E, \mathscr{C}, \mathscr{B})$, where the space satisfies 1.9.B, and let $G \in \mathscr{C} \cap \mathscr{B}$. In accordance with lemma 3.7, a normal system $\mathscr{F}$ can be constructed for which $G_{\mathscr{F}} = G$. We agree to write

$$\tau_s(G) = \xi_s(\mathscr{F}) \tag{3.63}$$

and to call $\tau_s(G)$ the first instant after s of departure of the trajectory from the interior of the open set G. The value of $\tau_s(G)$ is dependent in general on the choice of system $\mathscr{F}$ as well as on G. As we have just seen, however, all systems $\mathscr{F}$ consisting of compact sets lead to the same value of $\tau_s(G)$. We shall see later (cf. lemma 3.10) that the proviso regarding compactness ceases to have any importance when the process X is continuous.

We shall write $\tau(G)$ instead of $\tau_0(G)$ and $\tau_\eta(G)$ instead of $\xi_\eta(\mathscr{F})$ $(G = G_{\mathscr{F}})$.

Lemma 3.9. Let X be a Markov process continuous from the right in the topological measurable space $(E, \mathscr{C}, \mathscr{B})$. If $U, G \in \mathscr{C} \cap \mathscr{B}$ and the closure of U is compact and contained in G, we have

$$\tau_{\tau_s(U)}(G) = \tau_s(G). \tag{3.64}$$

Proof. It follows from (3.61) that, for any function $\eta(\omega)$ $(\omega \in \Omega_s)$,

$$\{\tau_s(G) > \eta \geqslant s\} \subseteq \{\tau_s(G) = \tau_\eta(G)\}. \tag{3.65}$$

Let $\mathscr{F} = \{\Gamma_n\}$ be a sequence satisfying conditions 3.12.A-3.12.C and such that $G_{\mathscr{F}} = G$. Let G_n be the sets defined by condition 3.12.C. The same method as used in proving lemma 3.8 shows that, for a certain n_0, the set G_{n_0} contains the closure of U. Hence it follows that $U \subseteq \Gamma_n$ for all $n > n_0$. We note that $x_t \in U$ for $s \leqslant t < \tau_s(U)$. If $x_{\tau_s(U)} \in G$, we have $x_t \in G_n$ for some $n > n_0$ and, in view of the fact that the process is continuous from the right, there exists $\varepsilon > 0$ such that $x_t \in G_n \subseteq \Gamma_{n+1}$ for all $s \leqslant t < \tau_s(U) + \varepsilon$. Consequently

$$\{x_{\tau_s(U)} \in G\} \subseteq \{\tau_s(G) > \tau_s(U)\}. \tag{3.66}$$

On putting $\eta = \tau_s(U)$ in (3.65) and comparing with (3.66), we get

$$\{x_{\tau_s(U)} \in G\} \subseteq \{\tau_s(G) = \tau_{\tau_s(U)}(G)\}. \tag{3.67}$$

Expression (3.64) follows from (3.67) and the obvious inclusion

$$\{x_{\tau_s(U)} \overline{\in} G\} \subseteq \{\tau_s(G) = \tau_s(U),\ \tau_{\tau_s(G)}(G) = \tau_s(G)\}.$$

3.14. Lemma 3.10. A normal system of subsets $\mathscr{F}$ of a topological measurable space $(E, \mathscr{C}, \mathscr{B})$ is admissible for every Markov process X continuous from the right. If X is continuous, we have

$$\xi_s(\mathscr{F}) = \xi_s(G_{\mathscr{F}}) \qquad (s \geqslant 0). \tag{3.68}$$

Proof. a) We consider the sequence $\{\Gamma_n\}$, equivalent to $\mathscr{F}$ and satisfying conditions 3.12.A-3.12.C. We have from (3.62):

$$\{\xi_s(\mathscr{F}) > t\} = \bigcup_{n=1}^{\infty} \{\xi_s(\Gamma_n) > t\}. \tag{3.69}$$

In accordance with sec. 3.8, we put

$$\Psi_t^s(\Gamma) = \bigcap_{u \in [s,\, t]} \{x_u \in \Gamma\}.$$

If $\omega \in \Psi_t^s(\Gamma_n)$, and consequently $x_u(\omega) \in \Gamma_n$ for $u \in [s, t]$, the fact that X is continuous from the right means that a $\delta > 0$ exists such that $x_u(\omega) \in G_n$ for $u \in [s, t+\delta)$. Hence $\xi_s(\Gamma_{n+1}, \omega) > t$. Therefore $\Psi_t^s(\Gamma_n) \subseteq \{\xi_s(\Gamma_{n+1}) > t\}$. It follows from the inclusion

$$\Psi_t^s(\Gamma_n) \subseteq \{\xi_s(\Gamma_{n+1}) > t\} \subseteq \Psi_t^s(\Gamma_{n+1})$$

and formula (3.69) that

$$\{\xi_s(\mathscr{F}) > t\} = \bigcup_{n=1}^{\infty} \Psi_t^s(\Gamma_n). \tag{3.70}$$

If Λ is any denumerable everywhere dense subset of the segment $[s, t]$ containing the point t, we have

$$\Psi_t^s(\Gamma_n) = \bigcap_{u \in \Lambda} \{x_u \in \Gamma_n\} \in \mathscr{N}_t^s. \tag{3.71}$$

It follows from (3.70) and (3.71) that $\{\xi_s(\mathscr{F}) > t\} \in \mathscr{N}_t^s$.

The first assertion of the lemma is thus proved.

b) In view of (3.59), we can prove (3.68) simply by showing that

$$\xi_s(\mathcal{F}) \geqslant \xi_s(G). \tag{3.72}$$

This inequality is trivial in the case when $\xi_s(\mathcal{F}, \omega) \geqslant \zeta(\omega)$. If $\xi_s(\mathcal{F}, \omega) < \zeta(\omega)$, it follows from the fact that now $x_{\xi_s(\mathcal{F})} \bar{\in} G$. We show that

$$\{\xi_s(\mathcal{F}) < \zeta\} \subseteq \{x_{\xi_s(\mathcal{F})} \bar{\in} G\}.$$

On putting $t = s$ in (3.70), we get

$$\{\xi_s(\mathcal{F}) > s\} = \bigcup_{n=1}^{\infty} \Psi_s^s(\Gamma_n) = \bigcup_{n=1}^{\infty} \{x_s \in \Gamma_r\} = \{x_s \in G\}.$$

It is clear from this that $\{\xi_s(\mathcal{F}) = s\} \subseteq \{x_{\xi_s(\mathcal{F})} \bar{\in} G\}$. It remains to consider the case when $s < \xi_s(\mathcal{F}, \omega) < \zeta(\omega)$. By (3.62), starting from a certain n we have $s < \xi_s(\Gamma_n) < \zeta(\omega)$. It now follows, as shown in sec. 3.8, that $x_{\xi_s(\Gamma_n)}$ belongs to the boundary of Γ_n and, in view of 3.12.C, $x_{\xi_s(\Gamma_n)} \bar{\in} G_m$ for $m < n$. On letting $n \to \infty$ and taking into account the fact that $\lim_{n\to\infty} x_{\xi_s(\Gamma_n)} = x_{\xi_s(\mathcal{F})}$, we conclude that $x_{\xi_s(\mathcal{F})} \bar{\in} G_m$ for any m, so that $x_{\xi_s(\mathcal{F})} \bar{\in} G$.

Corollary. Let X be a continuous Markov process in the topological measurable space $(E, \mathcal{C}, \mathcal{B})$, where the space satisfies condition 1.9.B. Every set $G \in \mathcal{C} \cap \mathcal{B}$ is now admissible for process X.

For, in view of lemma 3.7, there exists a normal system $\mathcal{F}$ such that $G = G_{\mathcal{F}}$. By lemma 3.10, this system is admissible and $\xi_s(\mathcal{F}) = \xi_s(G_{\mathcal{F}})$. Therefore

$$\{\xi_s(G) > t\} = \{\xi_s(\mathcal{F}) > t\} \in \mathcal{R}_t^s,$$

which is what we wished to prove.

3.15. Let $X = (x_t, \zeta, M_t^s, \mathbf{P}_{s,x})$ be a Markov process in the measurable space $(E, \mathcal{B})$, $\mathcal{F}$ a system of subsets of the space E, $G = G_{\mathcal{F}}$ and $\tilde{\mathcal{B}} = \mathcal{B}[G]$. We shall describe the Markov process $\tilde{X} = (\tilde{x}_t, \tilde{\zeta}, \tilde{\mathcal{M}}_t^s, \tilde{\mathbf{P}}_{s,x})$ of space $(G, \tilde{\mathcal{B}})$ as the part of process X corresponding to the system $\mathcal{F}$ if there exists a mapping $\gamma : \tilde{\Omega} \to \Omega$ ($\tilde{\Omega}$ and Ω are spaces of elementary events for

$\widetilde{X}$ and X) such that:

3.15.A. $\widetilde{\zeta}(\widetilde{\omega})=\xi[\mathscr{F},\ \gamma(\widetilde{\omega})]$ $(\widetilde{\omega}\in\widetilde{\Omega})$.

3.15.B. $\widetilde{x}_t(\widetilde{\omega})=x_t[\gamma(\widetilde{\omega})]$ $(\widetilde{\omega}\in\widetilde{\Omega},\ 0\leqslant t<\widetilde{\zeta}(\widetilde{\omega}))$.

3.15.C. If $A\in\mathscr{M}_t^s$, then $\{\gamma^{-1}A,\ \widetilde{\zeta}>t\}\in\widetilde{\mathscr{M}}_t^s$.

3.15.D. $\widetilde{\mathscr{M}}^s\supseteq\gamma^{-1}(\mathscr{M}^s)$ and $\widetilde{\mathbf{P}}_{s,x}(\gamma^{-1}A)=\mathbf{P}_{s,x}(A)$ for $A\in\mathscr{M}^s$, $x\in G$.

When $\xi(\mathscr{F})=\xi(G_{\mathscr{F}})$, this definition becomes the definition of sec. 3.9 for a part of process X on the set $G_{\mathscr{F}}$.

The following theorem is based on lemma 3.10 and is got by repeating almost word for word the proof of theorem 3.5.

Theorem 3.6. Let $\mathscr{F}$ be a normal system of subsets of the topological measurable space $(E,\ \mathscr{C},\ \mathscr{B})$, where all sets of $\mathscr{F}$ satisfy condition 3.10.B. For every process X continuous from the right in the space $(E,\ \mathscr{C},\ \mathscr{B})$ and subject to condition 3.10.A, a part can be generated corresponding to the system $\mathscr{F}$.

4. The Integral Type of Multiplicative Functional and the Corresponding Subprocesses

3.16. Theorem 3.7. Let the Markov process $X=(x_t,\ \zeta,\ \mathscr{M}_t^s,\ \mathbf{P}_{s,x})$ in the measurable space $(E,\ \mathscr{B})$ satisfy the condition:

3.16.A. For any $0\leqslant s\leqslant t$, the mapping defined by the function $x_u(\omega)$ of $(I_t^s\times\Omega_t,\mathscr{B}_t^s\times\mathfrak{R}_t^s)$ in $(E,\ \mathscr{B})$ is measurable.

Let $V(u,\ x)$ $(u\geqslant 0,\ x\in E)$ be a non-negative $\mathscr{B}_\infty^0\times\mathscr{B}$-measurable function and μ a measure on the σ-algebra $\mathscr{B}_\infty^0$. The expression

$$\alpha_t^s(\omega)=\exp\left[-\int\limits_{(s,\ t]}V(u,\ x_u)\,\mu(du)\right]\qquad(\omega\in\Omega_t)\tag{3.73}$$

now defines a multiplicative functional of process X, provided only that the integral in the expression is convergent for any $0\leqslant s<t<\zeta(\omega)$.

Proof. The mapping defined by the function $V(u,\ x_u(\omega))$ of the space $(I_t^s\times\Omega_t,\mathscr{B}_t^s\times\mathfrak{R}_t^s)$ into $(I_\infty^0,\ \mathscr{B}_\infty^0)$ can be written as the product $V\alpha$, where α is the mapping of $(I_t^s\times\Omega_t,\ \mathscr{B}_t^s\times\mathfrak{R}_t^s)$ into

$(I_t^s \times E, \mathscr{B}_t^s \times \mathscr{B})$ given by

$$\alpha(u, \omega) = \{u, x_u(\omega)\}.$$

In view of 3.16.A and lemma 1.3, the mapping α is measurable. By hypothesis, the mapping V is also measurable. Thus $V\alpha$ is the measurable mapping of $(I_t^s \times \Omega_t, \mathscr{B}_t^s \times \mathscr{R}_t^s)$ in $(I_\infty^0, \mathscr{B}_\infty^0)$, i.e. the function $V(u, x_u(\omega))$ $(u \in I_t^s, \omega \in \Omega_t)$ is $\mathscr{B}_t^s \times \mathscr{R}_t^s$-measurable. It follows from this, by lemma 1.7, that the function $\int\limits_{(s,t]} V(u, x_u)\mu(du)$ is $\mathscr{R}_t^s$-measurable, so that the same can be said of the function α_t^s. The system α_t^s thus satisfies condition 3.5.A. It obviously also satisfies conditions 3.5.B, 3.5.C and 3.5.D. The theorem is thus proved.

The functionals defined by (3.73) will be described as <u>multiplicative functionals of the integral type</u>.

Let us consider the subprocess of process X corresponding to multiplicative function (3.73). We have for this:

$$\begin{aligned} &\mathbf{P}_{s,x}\{\zeta > s+h \,|\, \mathscr{N}^s\} = \\ &= \exp\left[-\int\limits_{(s,s+h]} V(s, x_s)\mu(ds)\right] \quad (\text{a.c. } \Omega_{s+h}, \mathbf{P}_{s,x}). \end{aligned} \tag{3.74}$$

Suppose that, for every $\omega \in \Omega$, $V(u, x_u)$ is a function of u continuous from the right in the interval $[0, \zeta(\omega))$. It now follows from (3.74) that

$$P_{s,x}\{\zeta > s+h \,|\, \mathscr{N}^s\} = 1 - V(s, x_s)\mu(s, s+h][1+\varepsilon(h)]$$
$$(\text{a.c. } \Omega_{s+h}, P_{s,x}),$$

where $\varepsilon(h) \to 0$ as $h \downarrow 0$.

Hence, on the assumption that the course of the process is known after the instant s, the probability that it will be cut off after a time $(s, s+h]$ is equal to $V(s, x_s)\mu(s, s+h]$ to an accuracy of higher order infinitesimals.

3.17. We now suppose that measure μ coincides with the Lebesgue measure *) and investigate the connexion between the transition functions of process X and its subprocess

*)The case when μ is absolutely continuous with respect to the Lebesgue measure with a density of $\rho(x)$ reduces to the case of Lebesgue measure by replacing V by ρV.

corresponding to functional (3.73).

Theorem 3.8. Let $X=(x_t, \zeta, \mathcal{M}_t^s, \mathbf{P}_{s,x})$ be a Markov process satisfying condition 3.16.A, and let $V(u, x)$ $(u \geqslant 0, x \in E)$ be a non-negative*) $\mathcal{B}_\infty^0 \times \mathcal{B}$-measurable function. We put

$$\alpha_t^s(\omega) = \exp\left[-\int_s^t V(u, x_u)\,du\right] \qquad (\omega \in \Omega_t). \tag{3.75}$$

If the integral in (3.75) is convergent for any $0 \leqslant s \leqslant t < \zeta(\omega)$ the function $\widetilde{P}(s, x; t, \Gamma) = \mathbf{M}_{s,x}[\alpha_t^s \chi_\Gamma(x_t)]$ is connected with the function $P(s, x; t, \Gamma) = \mathbf{P}_{s,x}(x_t \in \Gamma)$ by the integral equation

$$\widetilde{P}(s, x; t, \Gamma) + \int_s^t \int_E P(s, x; u, dy) V(u, y) \widetilde{P}(u, y; t, \Gamma)\,du = P(s, x; t, \Gamma). \tag{3.76}$$

Proof. For any $t > 0$ and any $\omega \in \Omega_t$ $\int_s^t V(u, x_u)$, and consequently α_t^s also, is an absolutely continuous function of s. Therefore

$$\alpha_t^s = 1 - \int_s^t \frac{d\alpha_t^u}{du}\,du = 1 - \int_s^t V(u, x_u)\,\alpha_t^u\,du.$$

On multiplying both sides by $\chi_\Gamma(x_t)$ and passing to the mathematical expectations, we have

$$\widetilde{P}(s, x; t, \Gamma) = P(s, x; t, \Gamma) - \mathbf{M}_{s,x}\left[\int_s^t V(u, x_u)\,\alpha_t^u \chi_\Gamma(x_t)\,du\right]. \tag{3.77}$$

---

*)The reader may observe on running through the proof that our proposition still holds when the function $V(u, x)$ takes complex values of any kind, provided only that, for all $x \in E$ and $0 \leqslant s \leqslant t$

$$\mathbf{M}_{s,x}|\alpha_t^s| < K_1 < \infty,$$

$$\int_s^t \left[\int_E P(s, x; u, dy)\,|V(u, y)|\right] du < K_2 < \infty.$$

By Fubini's theorem (see 1.4.C), the last term is equal to

$$\int_s^t \mathbf{M}_{s,x}[V(u, x_u)\alpha_t^u \chi_\Gamma(x_t)]\,du. \tag{3.78}$$

In view of (2.10) and lemma 1.6:

$$\begin{aligned}\mathbf{M}_{s,x}&[V(u, x_u)\alpha_t^u\chi_\Gamma(x_t)] = \\ &= \mathbf{M}_{s,x}\{V(u, x_u)\mathbf{M}_{u,x_u}[\alpha_t^u\chi_\Gamma(x_t)]\} = \\ &= \mathbf{M}_{s,x}[V(u, x_u)\widetilde{P}(u, x_u;\ t\ \Gamma)] = \\ &= \int_E P(s, x;\ u, dy)V(u, y)\widetilde{P}(u, y;\ t, \Gamma).\end{aligned} \tag{3.79}$$

A comparison of (3.77), (3.78) and (3.79) gives us (3.76).

5. Stationary Subprocesses of Stationary Markov Processes

3.18. Two variants of a theory of stationary subprocesses can be described, corresponding to the two meanings attached to the term "stationary Markov process" (cf. sec. 2.8). The first variant is discussed in secs. 3.18-3.20, the second in secs. 3.21-3.24.

We start in the first variant from the idea of a stationary process as the Markov process $(x_t, \zeta, \mathcal{M}_t^s, \mathbf{P}_{s,x})$ for which a system of operators θ_t exists, satisfying requirements 2.5.A-2.5.C.

Let $\widetilde{X}=(\widetilde{x}_t, \widetilde{\zeta}, \widetilde{\mathcal{M}}_t^s, \widetilde{\mathbf{P}}_{s,x})$ be a stationary subprocess of the stationary Markov process $X=(x_t, \zeta, \mathcal{M}_t^s, \mathbf{P}_{s,x})$ and let $\theta_t, \widetilde{\theta}_t$ be the operators corresponding to $X, \widetilde{X}$ and satisfying conditions 2.5.A-2.5.C. It may easily be seen that we now have (cf. the derivation of expression (2.32) on p. 51)

$$\widetilde{\theta}_t\{\gamma^{-1}A, \widetilde{\zeta} > 0\} = \{\gamma^{-1}\theta_t A, \widetilde{\zeta} > t\} \tag{3.80}$$

for every $A \in \mathcal{N}^*$.

On equating $\gamma^{-1}A$ to A and $\gamma^{-1}\theta_t A$ to $\theta_t A$, we can write (3.80) in the following more compact form:

$$\widetilde{\theta}_t\{A, \widetilde{\zeta} > 0\} = \{\theta_t A, \widetilde{\zeta} > t\} \qquad (A \in \mathcal{N}^*). \tag{3.81}$$

Theorem 3.9. Let $\widetilde{X}$ be a stationary subprocess of the stationary Markov process X and let α_t^s be functions defined by condition 3.1.E. Then for any $0 \leqslant s \leqslant t,\ x \in E$,

$$\theta_s \alpha_{t-s}^0 = \alpha_t^s \quad (\text{a.c. } \Omega_t,\ \mathbf{P}_{s,x}). \tag{3.82}$$

Conversely, if condition (3.82) is fulfilled, there are stationary subprocesses in the class of equivalent subprocesses corresponding to the system of α_t^s; or more precisely, a canonical subprocess belonging to the class in question is stationary.

Proof. a) Let $\widetilde{X} = (\widetilde{x}_t,\ \widetilde{\zeta},\ \widetilde{\mathcal{M}}_t^s,\ \widetilde{\mathbf{P}}_{s,x})$ be a stationary subprocess of the stationary process $X = (x_t,\ \zeta,\ \mathcal{M}_t^s,\ \mathbf{P}_{s,x})$. Let $B \in \mathcal{N}$. We have by 2.5.A, (3.81) and 2.6.C,

$$\widetilde{\theta}_s \{B,\ \widetilde{\zeta} > t-s\} = \widetilde{\theta}_s \{B,\ \widetilde{\zeta} > 0\} \widetilde{\theta}_s \{\widetilde{\zeta} > t-s\} =$$
$$= \{\theta_s B,\ \widetilde{\zeta} > s\} \{\widetilde{\zeta} > t\} = \{\theta_s B,\ \widetilde{\zeta} > t\}.$$

It follows from this, in accordance with 2.5.C, that

$$\widetilde{\mathbf{P}}_{s,x} \{\theta_s B,\ \widetilde{\zeta} > t\} = \widetilde{\mathbf{P}}_{0,x} \{B,\ \widetilde{\zeta} > t-s\}.$$

Using (3.3), the last relationship can be rewritten as

$$\mathbf{M}_{s,x} \chi_{\theta_s B} \alpha_t^s = \mathbf{M}_{0,x} \chi_B \alpha_{t-s}^0. \tag{3.83}$$

We have on the basis of 2.6.F and 2.6.D,

$$\mathbf{M}_{0,x} \chi_B \alpha_{t-s}^0 = \mathbf{M}_{s,x} \theta_s [\chi_B \alpha_{t-s}^0] = \mathbf{M}_{s,x} \chi_{\theta_s B} \theta_s \alpha_{t-s}^0. \tag{3.84}$$

Functions α_t^s and $\theta_s \alpha_{t-s}^0$ are $\mathcal{N}_t^s$-measurable. Since $\mathcal{N}_t^s = \theta_s \mathcal{N}_{t-s}^0 \subseteq \mathcal{N}^s \theta \Xi$, it follows from (3.83) and (3.84) that

$$\int_A \alpha_t^s \mathbf{P}_{s,x}(d\omega) = \int_A \theta_s \alpha_{t-s}^0 \mathbf{P}_{s,x}(d\omega)$$

for any $A \in \mathcal{N}_t^s$. We easily get (3.82) from this.

b) Let $\widetilde{X} = (\widetilde{x}_t,\ \widetilde{\zeta},\ \widetilde{\mathcal{M}}_t^s,\ \widetilde{\mathbf{P}}_{s,x})$ be a canonical subprocess of X and let functions α_t^s satisfy conditions 3.1.E and (3.82). We observe that

$$\widetilde{\mathcal{N}}^* \subseteq \mathcal{N}^* \times \mathcal{B}_{(0,+\infty]},$$

where $\mathcal{B}_{(0,+\infty]}$ is the σ-algebra in the space $(0, +\infty]$, generated by all intervals. Every set $A \in \widetilde{\mathcal{N}}^*$ can be written uniquely in the form

$$A = \bigcup_{0<\lambda\leqslant+\infty} A_\lambda \times \lambda, \tag{3.85}$$

where $A_\lambda \in \mathscr{N}^*$. We put

$$\widetilde{\theta}_t A = \bigcup_{0<\lambda\leqslant+\infty} \theta_t A_\lambda \times (\lambda + t). \tag{3.86}$$

In particular, for any $C \in \mathscr{N}^*$, $h \geqslant 0$,

$$\widetilde{\theta}_t \{C, \widetilde{\zeta} > h\} = \widetilde{\theta}_t \{[C, \zeta > h] \times (h, \infty]\} = \\ = [\theta_t C, \zeta > t + h] \times (t + h, \infty] = \{\theta_t C, \widetilde{\zeta} > t + h\}. \tag{3.87}$$

The operators $\widetilde{\theta}_t$ are easily seen to satisfy conditions 2.5.A-2.5.B. We shall prove that they also satisfy 2.5.C.

If

$$A = \{C, \widetilde{\zeta} > h\} \qquad (C \in \mathscr{N},\ h > 0), \tag{3.88}$$

we have by (3.87), (3.3), 2.5.C and (3.82),

$$\widetilde{\mathbf{P}}_{t,x}(\widetilde{\theta}_t A) = \widetilde{\mathbf{P}}_{t,x}\{\theta_t C, \widetilde{\zeta} > t + h\} = \mathbf{M}_{t,x} \chi_{\theta_t C} \alpha^t_{t+h} = \\ = \mathbf{M}_{t,x} \theta_t [\chi_C \alpha^0_h] = \mathbf{M}_{0,x} [\chi_C \alpha^0_h] = \\ = \widetilde{\mathbf{P}}_{0,x}\{C, \widetilde{\zeta} > h\} = \widetilde{\mathbf{P}}_{0,x}(A). \tag{3.89}$$

The sets of type (3.88) form a π-system $\mathscr{C}$. On the other hand, the class $\mathscr{F}$ of all sets A for which condition 2.5.C is fulfilled is a λ-system in the space $\widetilde{\Omega}_0$. In accordance with (3.89), $\mathscr{F} \supseteq \mathscr{C}$. By lemma 1.1, $\mathscr{F} \supseteq \sigma(\mathscr{C}) = \widetilde{\mathscr{N}}$. This proves the theorem.

3.19. Theorem 3.10. Let $\widetilde{X} = (\widetilde{x}_t, \widetilde{\zeta}, \widetilde{\mathscr{M}}^s_t, \widetilde{\mathbf{P}}_{s,x})$ be the stationary subprocess of the stationary process $X = (x, \zeta, \mathscr{M}^s_t, \mathbf{P}_{s,x})$ corresponding to the multiplicative functional $\alpha = \{\alpha^s_t\}$. The random variables ξ_s defined by (3.38) now satisfy the relationship

$$\xi_s = s + \theta_s \xi_0 \qquad (\text{a.c. } \Omega_s, \mathbf{P}_{s,x}). \tag{3.90}$$

If ξ_s is any system of random variables satisfying conditions 3.7.A-3.7.C and (3.90), the canonical subprocess corresponding to the multiplicative functional

$$\alpha^s_t = \chi_{\xi_s > t}, \tag{3.91}$$

is a stationary subprocess.

Proof. We have for every $r \geqslant 0$,

$$\{\xi_0 < r\} \subseteq \{\alpha_r^0 = 0\}$$

and therefore

$$\{\theta_s \xi_0 < r\} \subseteq \{\theta_s \alpha_r^0 = 0\} \subseteq \{\alpha_{s+r}^s = 0\} \cup \{\theta_s \alpha_r^0 \neq \alpha_{s+r}^s\}.$$

On the other hand,

$$\{\xi_s - s > r\} = \{\xi_s > s + r\} \subseteq \{\alpha_{s+r}^s > 0\}.$$

Hence

$$\{\xi_s - s > r > \theta_s \xi_0\} \subseteq \{\theta_s \alpha_r^0 \neq \alpha_{s+r}^s\}$$

and by (3.82),

$$\mathbf{P}_{s,x}\{\xi_s - s > r > \theta_s \xi_0\} = 0. \tag{3.92}$$

If Λ is the set of all non-negative rational numbers, it is obvious that

$$\{\xi_s - s > \theta_s \xi_0\} = \bigcup_{r \in \Lambda} \{\xi_s - s > r > \theta_s \xi_0\}.$$

It thus follows from (3.92) that

$$\mathbf{P}_{s,x}\{\xi_s - s > \theta_s \xi_0\} = 0. \tag{3.93}$$

It may be proved in the same way that

$$\mathbf{P}_{s,x}\{\xi_s - s < \theta_s \xi_0\} = 0. \tag{3.94}$$

We get (3.90) from (3.93) and (3.94).

Moreover, if the quantities ξ_s satisfy conditions 3.7.A-3.7.C, expression (3.91) defines, in accordance with sec. 3.7, a multiplicative functional of process X. If (3.90) is satisfied in addition, we have

$$\theta_s \alpha_{t-s}^0 = \theta_s \chi_{\xi_0 > t-s} = \chi_{\theta_s (\xi_0 > t-s)} = \chi_{\xi_s > t} = \alpha_t^s$$
$$(\text{a.c. } \Omega_t,\ \mathbf{P}_{s,x}),$$

i.e. condition (3.82) is fulfilled. It follows from this, by theorem 3.9, that the canonical subprocess corresponding to functional (3.91) is stationary.

3.20. We shall consider some examples.

3.20.1. Let Γ be a subset of the measurable space $(E, \mathscr{B})$ admissible for the stationary Markov process X, and let the random variables $\xi_s = \xi_s(\Gamma)$ be defined by expression (3.49). We have

$$\{\xi_0 > t\} = \bigcup_n \bigcap_{0 \leqslant u \leqslant t + \frac{1}{n}} \{x_u \in \Gamma\}.$$

Hence

$$\{\theta_s \xi_0 > t\} = \bigcup_n \bigcap_{0 \leqslant u \leqslant t + \frac{1}{n}} \{x_{u+s} \in \Gamma\} = \{\xi_s > s + t\}.$$

The random variables $\xi_s = \xi_s(\Gamma)$ thus satisfy condition (3.90) and, in accordance with theorem 3.10, we can in fact assume that the subprocess of X corresponding to the admissible set Γ is stationary.

We leave it to the reader to show that the same situation applies for any part of a stationary process X.

3.20.2. Let a system $\mathscr{F}$ of subsets of the phase space be admissible for a stationary Markov process X. Condition (3.90) is easily shown to be fulfilled for the quantities defined by expression (3.58). A subprocess of X corresponding to the admissible system $\mathscr{F}$ can therefore be chosen such that it is stationary. The same thing can be said as regards the part of a stationary process corresponding to some system of subsets $\mathscr{F}$.

3.20.3. We take a stationary Markov process $X = (x_t, \zeta, \mathscr{M}_t^s, \mathbf{P}_{s,x})$ satisfying condition 3.16.A, and let $\alpha = \{\alpha_t^s\}$ be the multiplicative functional of the integral type defined by formula (3.73). If μ coincides with the Lebesgue measure, whilst the function $V(u, x)$ is independent of u, we have

$$\alpha_t^s = \theta_t \alpha_{t-s}^0. \tag{3.95}$$

For suppose we put

$$\eta = \int_0^{t-s} V(x_u)\, du$$

and write L_a for the set of all $\mathscr{B}_{t-s}^0$-measurable μ-summable functions in the interval $[0, t-s]$, for which

$$\int_0^{t-s} \varphi(u)\, du = a.$$

We have

$$\{\eta = a\} = \bigcup_{\varphi \in L_a} \bigcap_{0 \leqslant u \leqslant t-s} \{V(x_u) = \varphi(u)\}$$

and by 2.5.A, 2.6.E and 2.6.G,

$$\begin{aligned} \{\theta_s \eta = a\} &= \bigcup_{\varphi \in L_a} \bigcap_{0 \leqslant u \leqslant t-s} \{V(x_{u+s}) = \varphi(u)\} = \\ &= \left\{ \int_0^{t-s} V(x_{u+s})\, du = a \right\} = \left\{ \int_s^t V(x_v)\, dv = a \right\}. \end{aligned} \tag{3.96}$$

It follows from (3.96), in accordance with 2.6.B, that

$$\theta_s \eta = \int_s^t V(x_v)\, dv. \tag{3.97}$$

We get (3.95) by comparing (3.73), (3.97) and 2.6.E.

We conclude from relationship (3.95), on the basis of theorem 3.9, that the functional α corresponds to a stationary subprocess of process X.

3.21. We now base our remarks on the concept of a stationary Markov process as a system $(x_t, \zeta, \mathcal{M}_t, \mathbf{P}_x, \theta_t)$ satisfying conditions 2.8.A-2.8.H. The theory of subprocesses admits a number of important simplifications from this point of view.

Let $X = (x_t, \zeta, \mathcal{M}_t, \mathbf{P}_x, \theta_t)$ and $\widetilde{X} = (\widetilde{x}_t, \widetilde{\zeta}, \widetilde{\mathcal{M}}_t, \widetilde{\mathbf{P}}_x, \widetilde{\theta}_t)$ be two stationary Markov processes in the same phase space $(E, \mathcal{B})$ and let Ω and $\widetilde{\Omega}$ be the spaces of elementary events of X and $\widetilde{X}$ respectively. We shall speak of $\widetilde{X}$ as a <u>subprocess</u> of X if there exists a mapping $\gamma: \widetilde{\Omega} \to \Omega$ such that:

3.21.A. $\widetilde{\zeta}(\widetilde{\omega}) \leqslant \zeta[\gamma(\widetilde{\omega})] \quad (\widetilde{\omega} \in \widetilde{\Omega})$.

3.21.B. $\widetilde{x}_t(\widetilde{\omega}) = x_t[\gamma(\widetilde{\omega})] \quad (\widetilde{\omega} \in \widetilde{\Omega},\ 0 \leqslant t < \widetilde{\zeta}(\widetilde{\omega}))$.

3.21.C. If $A \in \mathcal{M}_t$, then $\{\gamma^{-1}A, \widetilde{\zeta} > t\} \in \widetilde{\mathcal{M}}_t$.

3.21.D. $\widetilde{\mathcal{M}}^0 \supseteq \gamma^{-1}\mathcal{M}^0$ and $\widetilde{\mathbf{P}}_x(\gamma^{-1}A) = \mathbf{P}_x(A)$ for $A \in \mathcal{M}^0$.

3.21.E. $\widetilde{P}_x\{\widetilde{\zeta}>t\,|\,\gamma^{-1}\mathscr{M}^0\}=\alpha_t[\gamma(\widetilde{\omega})]$ (a.c. $\gamma^{-1}\Omega_t$, $\widetilde{\mathbf{P}}_x$), where $\alpha_t(\omega)$ is an $\mathscr{N}_t$-measurable function.

On equating as usual $\varphi(\gamma(\widetilde{\omega}))\,(\widetilde{\omega}\in\widetilde{\Omega})$ with $\varphi(\omega)$ $(\omega\in\Omega)$, $\gamma^{-1}A$ with $\mathscr{A}$, $\gamma^{-1}\mathscr{F}=\{\gamma^{-1}A\}$ with $\mathscr{F}=\{A\}$, we can rewrite the conditions as follows:

3.21.A′. $\widetilde{\zeta}\leqslant\zeta$.

3.21.B′. $\widetilde{x}_t=x_t$ $(0\leqslant t<\widetilde{\zeta})$.

3.21.C′. If $A\in\mathscr{M}_t$, then $\{A,\ \widetilde{\zeta}>t\}\in\widetilde{\mathscr{M}}_t$.

3.21.D′. $\widetilde{\mathscr{M}}^0\supseteq\mathscr{M}^0$ and $\widetilde{\mathbf{P}}_x(A)=\mathbf{P}_x(A)$ for $A\in\mathscr{M}^0$.

3.21.E′. $\widetilde{\mathbf{P}}_x\{\widetilde{\zeta}>t\,|\,\mathscr{M}^0\}=\alpha_t$ (a.c. Ω_t, $\mathbf{P}_x$), where α_t is an $\mathscr{N}_t$-measurable function.

If $\mathscr{R}_t$ denotes the class of all sets $A\in\mathscr{M}^0$ such that, for some $B\in\mathscr{N}_t$ $\mathbf{P}_x(A\setminus AB)=\mathbf{P}_x(B\setminus AB)=0$ for all $x\in E$, condition 3.21.E can be put in the following form:

3.21.E″. $\widetilde{\mathbf{P}}_x\{\widetilde{\zeta}>t\,|\,\mathscr{M}^0\}=\alpha_t$ (a.c. Ω_t, $\mathbf{P}_x$), where α_t is some $\mathscr{R}_t$-measurable function *).

We remark that, if $(\widetilde{x}_t,\ \widetilde{\zeta},\ \widetilde{\mathscr{M}}^s_t,\ \widetilde{\mathbf{P}}_{s,x})$ is a stationary subprocess of the stationary Markov process $(x_t,\ \zeta,\ \mathscr{M}^s_t,\ \mathbf{P}_{s,x})$ (in the sense of sec. 3.18) and if the operators θ_t, $\widetilde{\theta}_t$ are so chosen that conditions 2.5.A-2.5.C are fulfilled, $(\widetilde{x}_t,\ \widetilde{\zeta},\ \widetilde{\mathscr{M}}^0_t,\ \widetilde{\mathbf{P}}_{0,x},\ \widetilde{\theta}_t)$ is a subprocess of the process $(x_t,\ \zeta,\ \mathscr{M}^0_t,\ \mathbf{P}_{0,x},\ \theta_t)$. Is the converse true? Or more precisely, can we assert that, if $\widetilde{X}=(\widetilde{x}_t,\ \widetilde{\zeta},\ \widetilde{\mathscr{M}}_t,\ \widetilde{\mathbf{P}}_x,\ \widetilde{\theta}_t)$ is a subprocess of $X=(x_t,\ \zeta,\ \mathscr{M}_t,\ \mathbf{P}_x,\ \theta_t)$, there exist stationary Markov processes $\widetilde{X}'=(\widetilde{x}_t,\ \widetilde{\zeta},\ \widetilde{\mathscr{M}}^s_t,\ \widetilde{\mathbf{P}}_{s,x})$ and $X'=(x_t,\ \zeta,\ \mathscr{M}^s_t,\ \mathbf{P}_{s,x})$ such that $\widetilde{X}'\longleftrightarrow\widetilde{X}$, $X'\longleftrightarrow X$ and $\widetilde{X}'$ is a stationary subprocess of X' in the sense of sec. 3.18? This question can be answered in the affirmative at least if it is assumed that $\widetilde{\mathbf{P}}_x\{\widetilde{\zeta}>0\}=1$ for all $x\in E$. The proof is omitted since we shall make no use of the proposition.

3.22. We shall describe the subprocess $\widetilde{X}=(\widetilde{x}_t,\ \widetilde{\zeta},\ \widetilde{\mathscr{M}}_t,\ \widetilde{\mathbf{P}}_x,\ \widetilde{\theta}_t)$, of process $X=(x_t,\ \zeta,\ \mathscr{M}_t,\ \mathbf{P}_x,\ \theta_t)$ as a <u>canonical subprocess</u> if:

---

*) The whole of the theory still holds good if we put $\mathscr{R}_t=\mathscr{N}^*\cap\overline{\mathscr{N}}_{t+0}\cap\mathscr{M}_t$, where the definition of $\overline{\mathscr{N}}_{t+0}$ in terms of $\mathscr{N}_t$ is the same as that of $\overline{\mathscr{N}}^s_{t+0}$ in terms of $\mathscr{N}^s_t$ (see footnote on page 55).

3.22.A. The space of elementary events $\widetilde{\Omega}$ of process $\widetilde{X}$ is equal to $\Omega\times I$, where Ω is the space of elementary events of process X and $I=[0, +\infty]$; the mapping $\gamma:\widetilde{\Omega}\to\Omega$ is given by

$$\gamma(\omega; \lambda)=\omega \qquad (\omega\in\Omega, \lambda\in I).$$

3.22.B. $\widetilde{\zeta}(\omega, \lambda)=\min[\zeta(\omega), \lambda]$.

3.22.C. $\widetilde{x}_t(\omega, \lambda)=x_t(\omega)$ for $0\leqslant t<\widetilde{\zeta}(\omega, \lambda)$.

3.22.D. $\widetilde{\mathcal{M}}_t$ consists of all sets of the form $A\times(t, \infty]$ where $A\in\mathcal{M}_t$.

3.22.E. $\widetilde{\mathcal{M}}^0$ is the σ-algebra in space $\widetilde{\Omega}$ generated by sets $\{A, \widetilde{\zeta}>t\}=[A, \zeta>t]\times(t, \infty]$ $(A\in\mathcal{M}^0, t\geqslant 0)$.

We shall speak of the system of functions $\alpha_t(\omega)$ $(t\geqslant 0, \omega\in\Omega_t)$ as defining a multiplicative functional of Markov process $X=(x_t, \zeta, \mathcal{M}_t, \mathbf{P}_x, \theta_t)$ if:

3.22.α. α_t is $\mathcal{R}_t$-measurable.

3.22.β. $\alpha_s\theta_s\alpha_t=\alpha_{s+t}$ (a.c. Ω_{s+t}, $\mathbf{P}_x$) $(s, t\geqslant 0, x\in E)$.

3.22.γ. $0\leqslant\alpha_t\leqslant 1$ $(t\geqslant 0, \omega\in\Omega_t)$.

3.22.δ. $\lim\limits_{t_n\downarrow t}\alpha_{t_n}(\omega)=\alpha_t(\omega)$ $(t\geqslant 0, \omega\in\Omega_t)$.

Two stationary multiplicative functionals α and $\widetilde{\alpha}$ will be said to be equivalent if, for any $t\geqslant 0, x\in E$,

$$\alpha_t=\widetilde{\alpha}_t \qquad (\text{a.c. } \Omega_t, \mathbf{P}_x).$$

We shall say that the subprocess $\widetilde{X}=(\widetilde{x}_t, \widetilde{\zeta}, \widetilde{\mathcal{M}}_t, \widetilde{\mathbf{P}}_x, \widetilde{\theta}_t)$ of $X=(x_t, \zeta, \mathcal{M}_t, \mathbf{P}_x, \theta_t)$ corresponds to the multiplicative functional $\alpha=\{\alpha_t\}$ if functions α_t satisfy condition 3.21.E''.

Theorem 3.11. A one-to-one correspondence holds between all the classes of equivalent subprocesses of a stationary Markov process $X=(x_t, \zeta, \mathcal{M}_t, \mathbf{P}_x, \theta_t)$ and all the classes of equivalent multiplicative functionals of X. Each class of equivalent subprocesses contains one and only one canonical process $\widetilde{X}$ and consists of all the stationary processes subordinate to $\widetilde{X}$. The transition function of the process corresponding to the functional $\alpha=\{\alpha_t\}$ is equal to

$$\widetilde{P}(t, x, \Gamma)=\mathbf{M}_x\chi_\Gamma(x_t)\alpha_t. \tag{3.98}$$

Proof. a) It may be seen by repeating the arguments of lemma 3.3 with obvious modifications that, if $\tilde{X}=(\tilde{x}_t, \tilde{\zeta}, \tilde{\mathcal{M}}_t, \tilde{\mathbf{P}}_x, \tilde{\theta}_t)$ is a subprocess of the stationary process X, the functions α_t defined by condition 3.21.E satisfy the relationships

$$0 \leqslant \alpha_t \leqslant 1 \qquad (\text{a.c. } \Omega_t, \mathbf{P}_x), \tag{3.99}$$

$$\lim_{t_n \downarrow t} \alpha_{t_n} = \alpha_t \qquad (\text{a.c. } \Omega_t, \mathbf{P}_x) \tag{3.100}$$

together with relationship 3.22.β. We put

$$Q_{p,q} = \{\alpha_p \theta_p \alpha_q \neq \alpha_{p+q}\} \cup \{\alpha_p < 0\} \cup \{\alpha_p > 1\} \cup \cup \{\theta_p \alpha_q < 0\} \cup \{\theta_p \alpha_q > 1\}.$$

It follows from properties 3.22.β and (3.99) that $\mathbf{P}_x(Q_{p,q}) = 0$ for any $p, q \geqslant 0$ $x \in E$. Let Q denote the sum of sets $Q_{p,q}$ over all rational p and q. Obviously, $\mathbf{P}_x(Q) = 0$ for all $x \in E$.

If $\omega \in Q$, for any rational p, q of $[0, \zeta(\omega))$ we have the inequality

$$0 \leqslant \alpha_{p+q}(\omega) \leqslant \alpha_p(\omega).$$

Thus, for any $t \in [0, \zeta(\omega))$, a limit exists for α_p when p tends to t taking rational values greater than t. We put

$$\tilde{\alpha}_t(\omega) = \begin{cases} \lim\limits_{p \downarrow t} \alpha_p(\omega), & \text{if} \quad \omega \bar{\in} Q, \\ 1, & \text{if} \quad \omega \in Q. \end{cases}$$

We have for any $x \in E$, in view of (3.100),

$$\mathbf{P}_x\{\tilde{\alpha}_t \neq \alpha_t\} = 0. \tag{3.101}$$

The function $\tilde{\alpha}_t(\omega)$ is obviously $\mathcal{N}^0$-measurable; and by (3.101), it is $\mathfrak{R}_t$-measurable. It follows also from (3.101) that functions $\tilde{\alpha}_t$ satisfy conditions 3.22.β and 3.21.E''. They evidently also satisfy conditions 3.22.γ and 3.22.δ.

b) Let $\alpha = \{\alpha_t\}$ be any multiplicative functional of process X. We shall show that there is a canonical subprocess $\tilde{X} = (\tilde{x}_t, \tilde{\zeta}, \tilde{\mathcal{M}}_t, \tilde{\mathbf{P}}_x, \tilde{\theta}_t)$ of X corresponding to α. We find $\tilde{\Omega}, \tilde{\zeta}, \tilde{x}_t, \tilde{\mathcal{M}}_t, \tilde{\mathcal{M}}^0$ by means of conditions 3.22.A-3.22.E and associate with each $\omega \in \Omega$ the probability measure $\varkappa_\Gamma(\omega)$, on the σ-

algebra $\mathscr{B}_I$, given by the requirement that

$$\alpha_{(t,\infty]}(\omega)=\begin{cases}\alpha_t(\omega), & \text{if } t<\zeta(\omega),\\ 0, & \text{if } t\geqslant\zeta(\omega)\end{cases}$$

(the existence and uniqueness of this measure follows from properties 3.22.γ -3.22.δ of the functions α_t combined with the results of sec. 1.11.). We put for each $A\in\tilde{\mathscr{M}}^0$ and each $\omega\in\Omega$,

$$A_\omega=\{\lambda:(\omega,\lambda)\in A\},$$
$$\alpha_A(\omega)=\alpha_{A_\omega}(\omega),$$
$$\tilde{\mathbf{P}}_x(A)=\mathbf{M}_x\alpha_A.$$

In particular, for any $C\in\mathscr{M}^0$,

$$\tilde{\mathbf{P}}_x\{C,\tilde{\zeta}>t\}=\tilde{\mathbf{P}}_x\{[C,\zeta>t]\times(t,\infty]\}=\mathbf{M}_x\chi_C\alpha_t. \qquad (3.102)$$

We define the operators $\tilde{\theta}_t$ by the same formulae as in the proof of theorem 3.9 [see (3.85)-(3.86)]. The reader will easily verify that the system $(\tilde{x}_t,\tilde{\zeta},\tilde{\mathscr{M}}_x,\tilde{\mathbf{P}}_x,\tilde{\theta}_t)$ satisfies conditions 2.8.A-2.8.H and 3.21.A-3.21.E. It therefore defines the subprocess of X corresponding to the functional α.

c) The fact that (3.98) holds may be seen by repeating the argument of the proof of lemma 3.1. It follows from (3.98) that subprocesses corresponding to equivalent functionals are mutually equivalent. On the other hand, our arguments when proving lemma 3.2 show that, if two subprocesses of a process X are equivalent, they correspond to equivalent functionals. Finally, an almost word for word repetition of the proof of theorem 3.1 shows that each class of equivalent subprocesses of X contains one and only one canonical subprocess $\tilde{X}$ and consist of all the subprocesses subordinate to $\tilde{X}$.

The proof of the theorem is now complete.

3.23. Theorem 3.12. Given the stationary Markov process $X=(x_t,\zeta,\mathscr{M}_t,\mathbf{P}_x,\theta_t)$, let $\alpha=\{\alpha_t\}$ be a multiplicative functional of X, where $\alpha_s\theta_s\alpha_t=\alpha_{s+t}$ for any $s,t\geqslant0$. $\omega\in\Omega_{s+t}$ (a strengthened form of requirement 3.22.β). We put

$$\xi(\omega)=\begin{cases}\inf\{t:\alpha_t(\omega)=0\} & (\omega\in\Omega_0),\\ 0 & (\omega\overline{\in}\Omega_0)\end{cases} \qquad (3.103)$$

(if $\alpha_t(\omega) > 0$ for all $0 \leqslant t < \zeta(\omega)$, we put $\xi(\omega) = \zeta(\omega)$). The function $\xi(\omega)$ has the following properties:

3.23.A. $0 \leqslant \xi(\omega) \leqslant \zeta(\omega) \quad (\omega \in \Omega)$.

3.23.B. For every $t \geqslant 0$ $\{\xi > t\} \in \mathfrak{N}_t$.

3.23.C. For any $s > 0$

$$\{\xi > s\} \subseteq \{\theta_s \xi = \xi - s\}.$$

If $\xi(\omega)$ is any function subject to conditions 3.23.A-3.23.C, the formula $\alpha_t = \chi_{\xi > t}$ yields a multiplicative functional of X, and the subprocess $\widetilde{X} = (\widetilde{x}_t, \widetilde{\zeta}, \widetilde{\mathcal{M}}_t, \widetilde{\mathbf{P}}_x, \widetilde{\theta}_t)$ corresponding to this functional is defined by the formulae

$$\left.\begin{aligned} &\widetilde{\zeta}(\omega) = \xi(\omega) \qquad (\omega \in \Omega) \\ &\widetilde{x}_t(\omega) = x_t(\omega) \qquad (\omega \in \Omega, \quad 0 \leqslant t < \xi(\omega)) \\ &\widetilde{\mathcal{M}}_t = \mathcal{M}_t \; [\xi > t] \\ &\widetilde{\mathcal{M}}^0 = \mathcal{M}^0, \quad \widetilde{\mathbf{P}}_x = \mathbf{P}_x \\ &\widetilde{\theta}_t A = \{\theta_t A, \; \xi > t\} \qquad (A \in \mathcal{N}^*) \end{aligned}\right\} \tag{3.104}$$

(the space of elementary events for $\widetilde{X}$ is the same as for X).

Proof. The function ξ defined by (3.103), clearly satisfies inequality 3.23.A. The equation

$$\{\xi > t\} = \{\alpha_t > 0\}. \tag{3.105}$$

yields 3.23.B. Furthermore, by 3.22.β and (3.105),

$$\begin{aligned} \{\xi > s, \; \theta_s \xi > t\} &= \{\alpha_s > 0, \; \theta_s \alpha_t > 0\} = \\ &= \{\alpha_s \theta_s \alpha_t > 0\} = \{\alpha_{s+t} > 0\} = \{\xi > s + t\}, \end{aligned}$$

whence we easily obtain 3.23.C.

Now let ξ be any function subject to conditions 3.23.A-3.23.C. Clearly, $\alpha_t = \chi_{\xi > t}$ now satisfies conditions 3.22.α, 3.22.γ and 3.22.δ. Moreover

$$\begin{aligned} \alpha_s \theta_s \alpha_t = \chi_{\xi > s} \theta_s \chi_{\xi > t} = \chi_{\xi > s, \; \theta_s \xi > t} = \\ = \chi_{\xi > s, \; \xi - s > t} = \chi_{\xi > s + t} = \alpha_{s+t}, \end{aligned}$$

so that 3.22.β is also satisfied.

Finally, let ξ satisfy conditions 3.23.A-3.23.C. The system $(\widetilde{x}_t, \widetilde{\zeta}, \widetilde{\mathcal{M}}_t, \widetilde{\mathbf{P}}_x, \widetilde{\theta}_t)$ given by formulae (3.104) will obviously possess properties 2.8.A-2.8.E and 2.8.G-2.8.H. The series of equalities

$$\widetilde{\mathbf{P}}_x(\widetilde{\theta}_t A \mid \widetilde{\mathcal{M}}_t) = \mathbf{P}_x(\theta_t A,\ \xi > t \mid \mathcal{M}_t) = \chi_{\xi > t}\mathbf{P}_x(\theta_t A \mid \mathcal{M}_t) =$$
$$= \chi_{\xi > t}\mathbf{P}_{x_t}(A) = \mathbf{P}_{\widetilde{x}_t}(A) \qquad (\text{a.c. } \widetilde{\Omega}_t,\ \widetilde{\mathbf{P}}_x)$$

shows that it also possesses property 2.8.F. The system thus defines a stationary Markov process. It may readily be seen that $\widetilde{X}$ and X are connected by relationships 3.21.A-3.21.E (where $\gamma(\omega) = \omega$). Hence $\widetilde{X}$ is the subprocess of X corresponding to the functional $\{\alpha_t\}$.

3.24. Let $X = (x_t,\ \zeta,\ \mathcal{M}_t,\ \mathbf{P}_x,\ \theta_t)$ be a stationary Markov process in the measurable space $(E,\ \mathscr{B})$, such that $\mathfrak{R}_t \subseteq \mathcal{M}_t$, and let $\Gamma \subseteq E$. In accordance with (3.49) we put

$$\xi(\Gamma) = \inf\{t : x_t \overline{\in} \Gamma\}.$$

We shall call the set Γ admissible for the process X if $\xi(\Gamma)$ satisfies condition 3.23.B. Conditions 3.23.A and 3.23.C are easily seen to be also fulfilled in this case. Formulae (3.104) thus yield a subprocess of X. We shall refer to it as the subprocess corresponding to the admissible set Γ*).

The transition function of this subprocess is given by

$$\widetilde{P}(t,\ x,\ G) = \mathbf{P}_x\{x_t \in G,\ \xi(\Gamma) > t\}. \tag{3.106}$$

We now consider the system $(\widetilde{x}_t,\ \widetilde{\zeta},\ \widetilde{\mathcal{M}}_t,\ \widetilde{\mathbf{P}}_x,\ \widetilde{\theta}_t)$ defined by formula (3.104), the measure $\widetilde{\mathbf{P}}_x$ being considered for $x \in \Gamma$ only. This system evidently yields a stationary Markov process in the measurable space $(\Gamma,\ \mathscr{B}[\Gamma])$. We shall describe it as the part of process X in the admissible set Γ**).

Theorem 3.13. Let $E_n \in \mathscr{B}$ be a sequence of sets in the measurable space $(E,\ \mathscr{B})$ such that $E_n \uparrow E$. Suppose, further, that for every n a stationary Markov process $X^{(n)} = \{x_t^{(n)},\ \zeta^{(n)},\ \mathcal{M}_t^{(n)},\ \mathbf{P}_x^{(n)},\ \theta_t^{(n)}\}$ is given in the measurable space $(E_n,\ \mathscr{B}[E_n])$, $X^{(n)}$

---

*)It must be emphasised that X and Γ uniquely define the subprocess $\widetilde{X}$ of X corresponding to the admissible set Γ, the space of elementary events for $\widetilde{X}$ being the same as for X.

**)As distinct from the general case discussed in sec.3.9-3.10, a part of a stationary process $X = (x_t,\ \zeta,\ \mathcal{M}_t,\ \mathbf{P}_x,\ \theta_t)$ can be generated in every admissible subset.

being the part of $X^{(n+1)}$ in the set E_n. Then a stationary Markov process $X=(x_t, \zeta, \mathcal{M}_t, \mathbf{P}_x, \theta_t)$ exists in the space $(E, \mathcal{B})$ such that $\zeta(\omega)=\lim_{n\to\infty}\zeta^{(n)}(\omega)$ and $X^{(n)}$ is the part of X in the set E_n.

Proof. Since $X^{(n)}$ is the part of $X^{(n+1)}$ in the set E_n, we have in accordance with (3.104),

$$\zeta^{(n)}(\omega)\leqslant\zeta^{(n+1)}(\omega),$$
$$x_t^{(n)}(\omega)=x_t^{(n+1)}(\omega)\quad\text{for}\quad 0\leqslant t<\zeta^{(n)}(\omega),$$
$$\mathcal{M}_t^{(n)}=\mathcal{M}_t^{(n+1)}[\zeta^{(n)}(\omega)>t],$$
$$(\mathcal{M}^0)^{(n)}=(\mathcal{M}^0)^{(n+1)}\text{ and }\mathbf{P}_x^{(n)}=\mathbf{P}_x^{(n+1)}\quad\text{for}\quad x\in E_n,$$
$$\theta_t^{(n)}A=\{\theta_t^{(n+1)}A,\ \zeta^{(n)}>t\}.$$

Therefore the limit exists:

$$\zeta(\omega)=\lim_{n\to\infty}\zeta^{(n)}(\omega)$$

and a unique meaning, independent of the choice of n, attaches to the expressions

$$\left.\begin{aligned}&x_t(\omega)=x_t^{(n)}(\omega),\quad\text{if}\quad 0\leqslant t<\zeta^{(n)}(\omega)\\&\mathcal{M}_t=\mathcal{M}_t^{(n)}[\zeta(\omega)>t]\\&\mathcal{M}^0=(\mathcal{M}^0)^{(n)};\ \mathbf{P}_x=\mathbf{P}_x^{(n)},\quad\text{if}\quad x\in E_n\\&\theta_tA=\{\theta_t^{(n)}A,\ \zeta>t\},\quad\text{if}\quad A\in\mathcal{N}^*.\end{aligned}\right\}\tag{3.107}$$

The system $(x_t, \zeta, \mathcal{M}_t, \mathbf{P}_x, \theta_t)$ is easily seen to satisfy conditions 2.8.A-2.8.H, so that it defines a stationary Markov process X. For this process, the instant $\xi(E_n)$ of departure of the trajectory from set E_n coincides with $\zeta^{(n)}$, and the part of X in set E_n coincides with $X^{(n)}$ by virtue of (3.107)*).

All the definitions and propositions relating to subprocesses and parts of stationary processes corresponding to admissible sets are easily carried over to subprocesses and parts corresponding to admissible systems of sets.

---

*)It may be remarked that ζ coincides with the instant of first departure of the trajectory of X from the sequence $\{E_n\}$.

CHAPTER 4

THE CONSTRUCTION OF MARKOV PROCESSES WITH GIVEN TRANSITION FUNCTIONS

1. Definition of Transition Function. Examples.

4.1. We take any measurable space $(E, \mathscr{B})$. The function $P(s, x; t, \Gamma)$ $(0 \leqslant s \leqslant t,\ x \in E,\ \Gamma \in \mathscr{B})$ is said to be a transition function if the following conditions are satisfied:

4.1.A. $P(s, x; t, \Gamma)$ is a measure. (As a function of the set Γ.)

4.1.B. $P(s\ x; t, \Gamma)$ is a $\mathscr{B}$-measurable function of x.

4.1.C. $P(s, x; t, \Gamma) \leqslant 1$.

4.1.D. $P(s, x; s, E \setminus x) = 0$.

4.1.E. $P(s, x; u, \Gamma) = \int\limits_E P(s, x; t, dy) P(t, y; u, \Gamma)$ $(0 \leqslant s \leqslant t \leqslant u)$.

We shall describe the transition function $P(s, x; t, \Gamma)$ as normal if $P(s, x; s, E) = 1$ for all $s \geqslant 0$, $x \in E$, and as complete if $P(s, x; t, E) = 1$ for $t \geqslant s \geqslant 0$, $x \in E$.

There is a corresponding transition function for every Markov process:

$$P(s, x; t, \Gamma) = \mathbf{P}_{s, x}\{x_t \in \Gamma\}$$

(properties 4.1.A-4.1.D follow from 2.1.C, 2.1.D, 2.1.E; property 4.1.E follows from(2.12)). If the Markov process is non-cut-off, the corresponding transition function is complete.

The aim of the present chapter is to investigate under what conditions does the transition function $P(s, x; t, \Gamma)$ correspond to some Markov process. (The connexion between the various Markov processes having the same transition functions was discussed in article 3 of Chapter 2.)

4.2. We shall consider some examples of transition functions.

4.2.1. Let E be a numerical straight line, $\mathscr{B}$ the class of all Borel subsets of E, and v an arbitrary constant. The expression

$$P(s, x; t, \Gamma) = \chi_\Gamma[x + v(t-s)]$$

defines a complete transition function of $(E, \mathscr{B})$. We shall describe this function as corresponding to a determinate motion with velocity v.

4.2.2. Let E be the set of all natural numbers and $\mathscr{B}$ the class of all subsets of this set, and let $p_{ij}(s, t)$ $(i, j = 1, 2, \ldots, n, \ldots; 0 \leqslant s \leqslant t)$ be a system of functions satisfying the following conditions:

4.2.2.A. $p_{ij}(s, t) \geqslant 0.$

4.2.2.B. $\sum_{j=1}^{\infty} p_{ij}(s, t) \leqslant 1.$

4.2.2.C. $p_{ij}(s, s) = 0$ for $i \neq j$.

4.2.2.D. $\sum_{j=1}^{\infty} p_{ij}(s, t)\, p_{jk}(t, u) = p_{ik}(s, u)$ $(s \leqslant t \leqslant u).$

The expression

$$P(s, x; t, \Gamma) = \sum_{y \in \Gamma} p_{xy}(s, t) \qquad (x \in E,\ s \leqslant t,\ \Gamma \in \mathscr{B}) \tag{4.1}$$

now defines a transition function, and it may easily be seen that all the transition functions in the space $E = \{1, 2, \ldots, n, \ldots\}$ can be got by this method. The necessary and sufficient condition for the transition function to be normal is that $p_{ii}(s, s) = 1$. The condition for completeness is given by

$$\sum_{j=1}^{\infty} p_{ij}(s, t) = 1.$$

Everything that has been said is applicable also to the case when E consists of a finite number of points $\{1, 2, \ldots, n\}$.

4.2.3. Let E be the n-dimensional Euclidean space R^n and $\mathscr{B}$ the σ-algebra generated by all open sets of this space.

We write for each $x \in E$, $\Gamma \in \mathscr{B}$,

$$P(s, x; t, \Gamma) = \begin{cases} [2\pi(t-s)]^{-\frac{n}{2}} \int\limits_{\Gamma} \exp\left[-\frac{(y-x)^2}{2(t-s)}\right] dy & \text{for } 0 \leqslant s < t, \\ \chi_{\Gamma}(x) & \text{for } 0 \leqslant s = t, \end{cases} \tag{4.2}$$

where $(y-x)^2$ denotes the scalar square of the vector $y-x$ and integration is carried out with respect to the usual Lebesgue measure on R^n. It may easily be verified that the function $P(s, x; t, \Gamma)$ defined by this formula satisfies all the conditions 4.1.A-4.1.E and is consequently a transition function. This type of transition function is complete and is known as a <u>Wiener transition function</u>.

4.2.4. Let $E = (0, \infty)$ and $\mathscr{B}$ be the σ-algebra in the space E generated by all intervals. We shall consider a function closely connected with the one-dimensional Wiener function,

$$P(s, x; t, \Gamma) = \begin{cases} \frac{1}{\sqrt{2\pi(t-s)}} \int\limits_{\Gamma} \left\{ \exp\left[-\frac{(y-x)^2}{2(t-s)}\right] - \exp\left[-\frac{(y+x)^2}{2(t-s)}\right] \right\} dy & \text{for } 0 \leqslant s < t, \\ \chi_{\Gamma}(x) & \text{for } 0 \leqslant s = t. \end{cases} \tag{4.3}$$

This function clearly satisfies conditions 4.1.A-4.1.D. A certain amount of calculation shows that it satisfies 4.1.E. The transition function (4.3) is normal but not complete.

4.2.5. We keep the same values for E and $\mathscr{B}$ as in sec. 4.2.4 and put

$$P(s, x; t, \Gamma) = \begin{cases} \frac{1}{\sqrt{2\pi(t-s)}} \int\limits_{\Gamma} \left\{ \exp\left[-\frac{(y-x)^2}{2(t-s)}\right] + \exp\left[-\frac{(y+x)^2}{2(t-s)}\right] \right\} dy & \text{for } 0 \leqslant s < t, \\ \chi_{\Gamma}(x) & \text{for } 0 \leqslant s = t. \end{cases} \tag{4.4}$$

It is easy to verify that $P(s, x; t, \Gamma)$ is a complete transition function.

4.2.6. Let $(E, \mathscr{B})$ be any measurable space and $\Pi(x, \Gamma)$ $(x \in E, \Gamma \in \mathscr{B})$ a function satisfying the conditions:

a) $\Pi(x, \Gamma)$ is a probability measure on $\mathscr{B}$ for any $x \in E$;

b) $\Pi(x, \Gamma)$ is a $\mathscr{B}$-measurable function in E for any $\Gamma \in \mathscr{B}$.

We define functions $\Pi_n(x, \Gamma)$ as follows:

$$\Pi_0(x, \Gamma) = \chi_\Gamma(x),$$

$$\Pi_n(x, \Gamma) = \int_E \Pi(x, dy)\, \Pi_{n-1}(y, \Gamma) \qquad (n \geqslant 1).$$

It may readily be seen that:

1) $0 \leqslant \Pi_n(x, \Gamma) \leqslant 1$ for any $n \geqslant 0$, $x \in E$, $\Gamma \in \mathscr{B}$;

2) $\Pi_{n+m}(x, \Gamma) = \int_E \Pi_n(x, dy)\, \Pi_m(y, \Gamma)$.

We put

$$P(s, x; t, \Gamma) = \sum_{n=0}^{\infty} \frac{a^n (t-s)^n}{n!} e^{-a(t-s)} \Pi_n(x, \Gamma), \tag{4.5}$$

where a is a positive constant. In view of 1), the series on the right-hand side of (4.5) is convergent, whilst in view of 2), $P(s, x; t, \Gamma)$ satisfies condition 4.1.E. It is easily seen to satisfy conditions 4.1.A-4.1.D also. We thus have a transition function which is clearly complete. It will be described as a Poisson transition function.

2. The Construction of a Markov Process with Given Transition Function

4.3. Theorem 4.1. Let $(E, \mathscr{C}, \mathscr{B})$ be a σ-compact topological measurable space satisfying condition 1.9.A. Every complete transition function $P(s, x; t, \Gamma)$ $(0 \leqslant s \leqslant t,\ x \in E,\ \Gamma \in \mathscr{B})$, will now correspond to some non-cut-off Markov process in the phase space $(E, \mathscr{C}, \mathscr{B})$.

Proof. We shall construct the non-cut-off Markov process X in its canonical form, i.e. we take E^I $(I = [0, \infty))$ as the space of elementary events, put $x_t(\varphi) = \varphi(t)$ $(t \in I,\ \varphi \in E^I)$ and write $\mathscr{N}^s$ for the σ-algebra in the space E^I generated by sets $\{\varphi : \varphi(u) \in \Gamma\}$ $(u \geqslant s,\ \Gamma \in \mathscr{B})$ and $\mathscr{N}_t^s$ for the σ-algebra generated by sets $\{\varphi : \varphi(u) \in \Gamma\}$ $(s \leqslant u \leqslant t, \Gamma \in \mathscr{B})$ (see sec. 2.13). We still have to define the probability measures $\mathbf{P}_{s,x}$ in the σ-algebras $\mathcal{N}^s$; this is done by using theorem 1.2.

We first of all use (2.15) to construct in accordance with the transition function $P(s, x; t, \Gamma)$, the functions

$$P(s, x; t_1, \Gamma_1, \ldots, t_n, \Gamma_n)$$
$$(x \in E, s \leqslant t_1 \leqslant t_2 \leqslant \cdots \leqslant t_n, \quad \Gamma_1, \ldots, \Gamma_n \in \mathscr{B}).$$

We put, for any $t_1, \ldots, t_n \in [s, \infty)$,

$$\Phi_{t_1, \ldots, t_n}(\Gamma_1, \ldots, \Gamma_n) = P(s, x; t_{i_1}, \Gamma_1, \ldots, t_{i_n}, \Gamma_n),$$

where $t_{i_1} \leqslant t_{i_2} \leqslant \cdots \leqslant t_{i_n}$, and $(i_1, \ldots, i_n)$ is some permutation of the numbers $1, 2, \ldots, n$. The functions $\Phi_{t_1, \ldots, t_n}$ are easily seen to satisfy all the conditions 1.12.A-1.12.C. We use theorem 1.2 by putting $T = [0, \infty)$, $\widetilde{T} = (s, \infty)$. The theorem states that a probability measure $\mathbf{P}$ satisfying condition (1.28) exists on the σ-algebra $\mathcal{N}_{\widetilde{T}} = \mathcal{N}^s$. The measure $\mathbf{P}$ depends on parameters s and x, and we write it as $\mathbf{P}_{s,x}$. We have for any $x \in E$, $0 \leqslant s \leqslant t_1 \leqslant \cdots \leqslant t_n$, $\Gamma_1, \ldots, \Gamma_n \in \mathscr{B}$:

$$\mathbf{P}_{s,x}\{x_{t_1} \in \Gamma_1, \ldots, x_{t_n} \in \Gamma_n\} = P(s, x; t_1, \Gamma_1, \ldots, t_n, \Gamma_n).$$

The system $(x_t, \mathcal{N}_t^s, \mathbf{P}_{s,x})$ obviously satisfies conditions 2.1.A-2.1.E. Furthermore, the functions $P(s, x; t_1, \Gamma_1, \ldots, t_n, \Gamma_n)$ satisfy expression (2.14), and by lemma 2.1, condition 2.1.F is fulfilled. The system $(x_t, \mathcal{N}_t^s, \mathbf{P}_{s,x})$ thus defines a non-cut-off Markov process. The transition function of this process obviously coincides with $P(s, x; t, \Gamma)$.

4.4. Theorem 4.2. Let $(E, \mathcal{C}, \mathscr{B})$ be a σ-compact topological measurable space subject to condition 1.9.A. Every normal transition function $P(s, x; t, \Gamma)$ will now correspond to some Markov process. We can assert, furthermore, that the function corresponds to some part of a non-cut-off Markov process.

Proof. We write $\widetilde{E}$ for the set obtained from E by the addition of a single point a. Let $A \subseteq \widetilde{E}$. We put $A \in \widetilde{\mathcal{C}}$ if $A \cap E \in \mathcal{C}$, and $A \in \widetilde{\mathscr{B}}$ if $A \cap E \in \mathscr{B}$. It is easy to see that $(\widetilde{E}, \widetilde{\mathcal{C}}, \widetilde{\mathscr{B}})$ is a σ-compact topological measurable space satisfying condition 1.9.A. We define the function $\widetilde{P}(s, x; t, \Gamma)$ in the space $(\widetilde{E}, \widetilde{\mathcal{C}}, \widetilde{\mathscr{B}})$ as follows:

$$\widetilde{P}(s, x; t, \Gamma) = \\ = \begin{cases} P(s, x; t, \Gamma E) + \chi_\Gamma(a)[1 - P(s, x; t, E)], & \text{if } x \neq a, \\ \chi_\Gamma(a), & \text{if } x = a. \end{cases} \tag{4.6}$$

The function $\tilde{P}$ is easily seen to satisfy conditions 4.1.A-4.1.E, so that it is a transition function. This transition function is complete, and by theorem 4.1, a non-cut-off Markov process $\tilde{X}$ exists in the phase space $(E, \tilde{\mathscr{C}}, \tilde{\mathscr{B}})$ corresponding to $\tilde{P}$. Using lemma 2.4, an equivalent process X of the non-cut-off process $\tilde{X}$ can be constructed, for which the set E is inaccessible from a. Since the function $P(s, x; t, \Gamma)$ is normal, E satisfies condition 3.8.B. In accordance with theorem 3.4, we can generate a part of process $\tilde{X}$ on the set E. Taking into account (3.55) and (4.6), the transition function of the 'part' is seen to coincide with $P(s, x; t, \Gamma)$.

3. Stationary Transition Functions and the Corresponding Stationary Markov Processes

4.5. The transition function $P(s, x; t, \Gamma)$ is said to be stationary if it depends only on the difference $t-s$. We shall write in this case $P(t-s, x, \Gamma)$ instead of $P(s, x; t, \Gamma)$.

The functions constructed in 4.4.1, 4.2.3-4.2.6 may be mentioned as examples of stationary transition functions. The functions of 4.2.2 are stationary when, and only when, the functions $p_{ij}(s, t)$ depend only on the difference $t-s$. We shall write $p_{ij}(t-s)$ in this case instead of $p_{ij}(s, t)$.

If we take into account conditions 4.1.A-4.1.E, we can say that the function $P(h, x, \Gamma)$ $(h \geqslant 0, x \in E, \Gamma \in \mathscr{B})$ is a stationary transition function when, and only when:

4.5.A. $P(h, x, \Gamma)$ is a measure, (as a function of the set Γ).

4.5.B. $P(h, x, \Gamma)$ is a $\mathscr{B}$-measurable function of x.

4.5.C. $0 \leqslant P(h, x, \Gamma) \leqslant 1$.

4.5.D. $P(0, x, E \setminus x) = 0$.

4.5.E. $P(h_1+h_2, x, \Gamma) = \int_E P(h_1, x, dy) P(h_2, y, \Gamma)$ $(h_1, h_2, \geqslant 0)$.

The condition for a stationary transition function to be normal is

$$P(0, x, E) = 1 \qquad (x \in E). \tag{4.7}$$

The condition for completeness is

$$P(t, x, E)=1 \qquad (t \geqslant 0,\ x \in E). \tag{4.8}$$

In accordance with theorem 2.10, the class of equivalent Markov processes contains stationary processes when and only when the transition function corresponding to this class is stationary.

4.6. We shall indicate a method by which any transition function may be associated with a stationary transition function in a rather more complicated phase space. In view of the connexion between transition functions and Markov processes, this method enables us to reduce a discussion of non-stationary to a discussion of stationary processes.

Given the transfer function $P(s, x; t, \Gamma)$ $(0 \leqslant s \leqslant t,\ x \in \Gamma\ \Gamma \in \mathscr{B})$ let $(\widetilde{E}, \widetilde{\mathscr{B}})$ be a measurable space, where $\widetilde{E} = I \times E$, $\widetilde{\mathscr{B}} = \mathscr{B}^0_\infty \times \mathscr{B}$ $(I = [0, \infty)$ whilst $\mathscr{B}^0_\infty$ denotes the σ-algebra in space $I)$ generated by all intervals), and let the function $\widetilde{P}(h, y, B)$ $(h \geqslant 0,$ $y \in \widetilde{E}, B \in \widetilde{\mathscr{B}})$ be defined by

$$\widetilde{P}(h, y, B) = P(t, x; t+h, \Gamma), \tag{4.9}$$

where $y = (t, x)$ and the set Γ is defined by the condition $z \in \Gamma$ if $(t+h, z) \in B$. (It follows from lemma 1.4 that $\Gamma \in \mathscr{B}$, so that (4.9) has a meaning for any $h \geqslant 0$ and any $B \in \widetilde{\mathscr{B}}$.) It follows from 4.1.A-4.1.E that the function $\widetilde{P}(h, y, B)$ satisfies 4.5.A, 4.5.C, 4.5.D and 4.5.E. In order for 4.5.B also to be satisfied, the additional requirement is needed that $P(s, x; t, \Gamma)$ as a function of s, x and t should be measurable.

CHAPTER 5

STRICTLY MARKOV PROCESSES

1. Random Variables Independent of the Future and s-Past. Lemmas on Measurability

5.1 Among all Markov processes we shall distinguish an important class for which the principle of the independence of the future from the past for a known present is valid in a strengthened form. More precisely, in the statements of the condition for a process to be Markov it is a matter of a fixed instant t (one not depending on chance); for the process to be considered in the present chapter, a similar condition is also satisfied for a definite type of random variable (random variables independent of the future and s-past).

Let $X=(x_t, \zeta, \mathcal{M}_t^s, \mathrm{P}_{s,x})$ be any Markov process. We shall call the non-negative function $\tau(\omega)$ a random variable independent of the future and s-past if:

5.1.A. $s \leqslant \tau(\omega) \leqslant \max[s, \zeta(\omega)] \qquad (\omega \in \Omega)$.

5.1.B. $\{\omega : \tau(\omega) \leqslant t < \zeta(\omega)\} \in \mathcal{M}_t^s \qquad (s \leqslant t)$.

(Condition 5.1.B can be visualized as meaning that the answer to the question, which is the greater, τ or t, depends only on the phenomena observed in the time intervals $[s, \min(t, \zeta)]$.).

By 5.1.A, $\{\tau > t\} \cup \{\tau \leqslant t < \zeta\} = \{\zeta > t\} \in \mathcal{M}_t^s$, so that 5.1.B is equivalent to the following condition:

5.1.B′. $\{\omega : \tau(\omega) > t\} \in \mathcal{M}_t^s \qquad (s \leqslant t)$.

We put $\Omega_\tau = \{\omega : \tau(\omega) < \zeta(\omega)\}$.

The subsets $A \subseteq \Omega_\tau$, such that for any $t \geqslant s$, $\{A, \tau \leqslant t < \zeta\} \in \mathcal{M}_t^s$, may easily be seen to form a σ-algebra in the space Ω_τ. We shall denote this σ-algebra by $\mathcal{M}_\tau^s$. It is natural to regard $\mathcal{M}_\tau^s$ as the class of all events observed during the time interval $[s, \tau]$.

If the function τ satisfies 5.1.A and takes only a finite or denumerable set of different values $t_1, t_2, \ldots \in [s, \infty)$ in Ω_τ, it is a random variable independent of the future and the s-past when and only when $\{\tau = t_k < \zeta\} \in \mathcal{M}^s_{t_k}$ for $k = 1, 2, \ldots$ With this, $A \in \mathcal{M}^s_\tau$ when and only when $\{A, \tau = t_k < \zeta\} \in \mathcal{M}^s_{t_k}$ for all k.

An example of a random variable not depending on the future and s-past is given by the function

$$\tau(\omega) = \begin{cases} t, \text{ if } & \zeta(\omega) > t, \\ \zeta(\omega), \text{ if } & s < \zeta(\omega) \leqslant t, \\ s, \text{ if } & \zeta(\omega) \leqslant s. \end{cases}$$

For this function, $\Omega_\tau = \Omega_t$. Another example is the function $\tau(\omega) = \max[\zeta(\omega), s]$ (for which $\Omega_\tau = \emptyset$). Further examples are provided by the systems of random variables ξ_s satisfying conditions 2.7.A-3.7.C, on the assumption that $\mathcal{R}^s_t \subseteq \mathcal{M}^s_t$*); and in particular, by the instants of first departure after s of the trajectory from the admissible set Γ (see sec.3.8) or from the admissible system of sets $\mathcal{F}$ (sec. 3.11).

The function $\xi(\omega)$ defined in Ω_τ is measurable with respect to $\mathcal{M}^s_\tau$ when and only when for any $t \geqslant s$ the function induced from ξ in the set $\{\tau \leqslant t < \zeta\}$ is measurable with respect to $\mathcal{M}^s_t$. The measurability of the function ξ with respect to the σ-algebra $\mathcal{M}^s_\tau$ may be pictured as meaning that ξ depends only on phenomena which are observed during the time $[s, \tau]$.

It may be remarked that the function $\tau(\omega)$ satisfying condition 5.1.A is a random variable that does not depend on the future or s-past when and only when its restriction to the set Ω_τ is measurable with respect to $\mathcal{M}^s_\tau$.

<u>Lemma 5.1</u>. Let τ be a random magnitude independent of the future and s-past for the Markov process X, and let $\Omega' \in \mathcal{M}^s_\tau$. Moreover, let the function $\eta(\omega) (\omega \in \Omega_\tau)$ be $\mathcal{M}^s_\tau$-measurable and satisfy the inequality $\eta \geqslant \tau$. Then the function

$$\eta^*(\omega) = \begin{cases} \eta(\omega) \text{ for } \omega \in \Omega_{\eta^*} = \{\Omega', \eta < \zeta\}, \\ \max[s, \zeta(\omega)] \text{ for } \omega \in \overline{\Omega}_{\eta^*} \end{cases}$$

*) This assumption does not seriously affect the generality since by sec.2.2 we can always extend the σ-algebra $\mathcal{M}^s_t$ to $\mathcal{M}^s_t \supseteq \mathcal{R}^s_t$ without thereby transgressing requirements 2.1.A-2.1.E.

represents a random variable independent of the future and s-past, and $A\Omega_{\eta^*} \in \mathcal{M}^s_{\eta^*}$ for any $A \in \mathcal{M}^s_\tau$.

Proof. Since $\eta \geqslant \tau$, we have for any $t \geqslant s$,

$$\{\eta \leqslant t\} \subseteq \{\tau \leqslant t\}$$

and $$\{\eta^* \leqslant t < \zeta\} = \{\Omega', \tau \leqslant t < \zeta\}\{\eta \leqslant t, \tau \leqslant t < \zeta\} \in \mathcal{M}^s_t.$$

The first assertion of the lemma is proved. Furthermore, if $A \in \mathcal{M}^s_\tau$, we have

$$\{A\Omega_{\eta^*}, \eta^* \leqslant t < \zeta\} = \{A, \tau \leqslant t < \zeta\}\{\eta^* \leqslant t < \zeta\} \in \mathcal{M}^s_t,$$

which proves the lemma.

5.2. We put for brevity $I^s_t = [s, t], I^s = [s, \infty), I_t = [0, t]$ and write $\mathcal{B}^s_t, \mathcal{B}^s$ and $\mathcal{B}_t$ for the σ-algebras generated by all intervals in I^s_t, I^s and I_t respectively.

The function $x(u, \omega) = x_u(\omega)$ induces a mapping of the measurable space $(I^s_t \times \Omega_t, \mathcal{B}^s_t \times \mathcal{M}^s_t)$ into the measurable space $(E, \mathcal{B})$. The Markov process is said to be measurable if this mapping is measurable for any $0 \leqslant s \leqslant t$.

Lemma 5.2. Let $X = (x_t, \zeta, \mathcal{M}^s_t, \mathbf{P}_{s,x})$ be a measurable Markov process and $\tau(\omega)$ a random variable independent of the future and s-past. Then the function $\beta(\omega) = x[\tau(\omega), \omega]$ defines a measurable mapping of $(\Omega_\tau, \mathcal{M}^s_\tau)$ into $(E, \mathcal{B})$.

Proof. We put $C_t = \{\tau \leqslant t < \zeta\}$. We have to show that, for any $t \geqslant s$, the mapping of $(C_t, \mathcal{M}^s_t)$ into $(E, \mathcal{B})$ induced by β is measurable. Since τ defines a measurable mapping of $(C_t, \mathcal{M}^s_t)$ into $(I^s_t, \mathcal{B}^s_t)$, the expression $\alpha_1(\omega) = \{\tau(\omega), \omega\}$ defines a measurable mapping of $(C_t, \mathcal{M}^s_t)$ into $(I^s_t \times \Omega_t, \mathcal{B}^s_t \times \mathcal{M}^s_t)$ (lemma 1.3). On the other hand, in view of the measurability of the process, the mapping α_2 of $(I^s_t \times \Omega_t, \mathcal{B}^s_t \times \mathcal{M}^s_t)$ into $(E, \mathcal{B})$ induced by the function $x(t, \omega)$ is measurable. Consequently the mapping $\alpha_2\alpha_1$ of $(C_t, \mathcal{M}^s_t)$ in $(E, \mathcal{B})$ is measurable. But obviously, $\alpha_2\alpha_1$ coincides with the mapping induced by β in C_t.

Lemma 5.3. Let $X = (x_t, \zeta, \mathcal{M}^s_t, \mathbf{P}_{s,x})$ be a measurable Markov process and let the function

$$P(s, x; t, \Gamma) = \mathbf{P}_{s,x}\{x_t \in \Gamma\} \qquad (s \in I_t, x \in E)$$

be measurable for any $t \geqslant 0, \Gamma \in \mathcal{B}$ with respect to $\mathcal{B}_t \times \mathcal{B}$. Then

a) whatever the $r>0$ and $A\in\mathcal{N}^r$, the function

$$\mathbf{P}_{s,x}(A) \qquad (s\in I_r,\ x\in E)$$

is $\mathcal{B}_r\times\mathcal{B}$-measurable;

b) for any $n\geqslant 1$ and any $\Gamma_1,\ldots,\Gamma_n\in\mathcal{B}$, the function

$$P(s,x;\ t_1,\Gamma_1,\ldots,t_n,\Gamma_n)=\mathbf{P}_{s,x}\{x_{t_1}\in\Gamma_1,\ldots,x_{t_n}\in\Gamma_n\}$$
$$(s\leqslant t_1,\ldots,t_n,\ x\in E)$$

is $\mathcal{B}^0\times\mathcal{B}\times[\mathcal{B}^0]^n$-measurable.

Proof. Assertion a) can be proved simply by repeating the proof of lemma 2.2 with a few trivial changes.

We turn to the proof of assertion b). We take the function

$$\varphi(s,x,t)=\begin{cases}P(s,x;\ t,E)=\mathbf{P}_{s,x}\{\zeta>t\}, & \text{if} \quad s\leqslant t,\\ 0, & \text{if} \quad s>t.\end{cases}$$

With s and x fixed, $\varphi(s,x,t)$ is a function of t continuous from the right. With t fixed, it is a $\mathcal{B}^0\times\mathcal{B}$-measurable function of s,x. It follows from this, by lemma 1.10, that $\varphi(s,x,t)$, and consequently also $P(s,x;\ t,E)$ is a $\mathcal{B}^0\times\mathcal{B}\times\mathcal{B}^0$-measurable function of s, x and t. We complete the definition of function $\chi_\Gamma[x_t(\omega)]$ by putting $\chi_\Gamma[x_t(\omega)]=0$ with $\omega\,\bar{\in}\,\Omega_t$. Now clearly,

$$P(s,x;\ t_1,\Gamma_1,\ldots,t_n,\Gamma_n)=$$
$$=\int_\Omega \chi_{\Gamma_1}[x_{t_1}(\omega)]\ldots\chi_{\Gamma_n}[x_{t_n}(\omega)]\,\mathbf{P}_{s,x}(d\omega). \qquad (5.1)$$

We select an arbitrary $r\geqslant 0$. It follows from the measurability of the process that, for any $k=1,2,\ldots,n$, the function $\chi_{\Gamma_k}[x_{t_k}(\omega)]$ $(t_k\in I^r,\ \omega\in\Omega)$ is $\mathcal{B}^r\times\mathcal{M}^r$-measurable. The function

$$\chi_{\Gamma_1}[x_{t_1}(\omega)]\ldots\chi_{\Gamma_n}[x_{t_n}(\omega)] \qquad (t_1,\ldots,t_n\in I^r,\ \omega\in\Omega)$$

is therefore measurable with respect to $[\mathcal{B}^r]^n\times\mathcal{M}^r$. In view of a), the function $\mathbf{P}_{s,x}(A)$ is $\mathcal{B}_r\times\mathcal{B}$-measurable for any $A\in\mathcal{M}^r$. Therefore by lemma 1.7, the function defined by (5.1) in the set $s\in I_r,\ x\in E,\ t_1,\ldots,t_n\in I^r$ is $\mathcal{B}_r\times\mathcal{B}\times[\mathcal{B}^r]^n$-measurable.

We now observe that, if $C\in\mathcal{B}_1^0$ and A is the set of systems $(s,x,t_1,\ldots,t_n)$ for which

$$\{s \leqslant t_1, \ldots, t_n;\ P(s, x;\ t_1, \Gamma_1, \ldots, t_n, \Gamma_n) \in C\},$$

we have

$$A = \left[\bigcup_r \{A, I_r \times E \times [I^r]^n\}\right] \cup \{A, t_1 = s\} \cup \ldots \cup \{A, t_n = s\}, \quad (5.2)$$

where r runs through all non-negative rational numbers.

We have by what has been proved:

$$\{A, I_r \times E \times [I^r]^n\} \in \mathscr{B}_r \times \mathscr{B} \times [\mathscr{B}^r]^n \subseteq \mathscr{B}^0 \times \mathscr{B} \times [\mathscr{B}^0]^n. \quad (5.3)$$

We now notice that, by 2.1.E,

$$P(s, x;\ s, \Gamma) = \chi_\Gamma(x) P(s, x;\ s, E). \quad (5.4)$$

Hence with $n = 1$,

$$\{A, t_1 = s\} = \{t_1 = s, \chi_{\Gamma_1}(x) P(s, x;\ t_1, E) \in C\} \in \mathscr{B}^0 \times \mathscr{B} \times \mathscr{B}^0, \quad (5.5)$$

and assertion b) follows from (5.2), (5.3) and (5.5). With $n > 1$, we have by (2.14) and (5.4) for $k = 1, 2, \ldots, n$:

$$\{A, t_k = s\} = \{t_k = s;\ s \leqslant t_1, \ldots, t_{k-1}, t_{k+1}, \ldots, t_n;$$
$$\chi_{\Gamma_1}(x) P(s, x;\ t_k, E) P(s, x;\ t_1, \Gamma_1, \ldots, t_{k-1}, \Gamma_{k-1}, \ldots$$
$$\ldots, t_{k+1}, \Gamma_{k+1} \ldots, t_n, \Gamma_n) \in C\}.$$

If we assume that assertion b) has already been proved for the case $n-1$, it follows from this that

$$\{A, t_k = s\} \subseteq \mathscr{B}^0 \times \mathscr{B} \times [\mathscr{B}^0]^n \quad (5.6)$$

On combining (5.2), (5.3) and (5.6), we conclude that assertion b) is likewise satisfied for the case n.

Remark. The function $P(s, x;\ t, \Gamma)$ is always measurable with respect to x, and the arguments used in proving lemma 5.2 show that, for any measurable Markov process, the function $P(s, x;\ t, \Gamma)$ is measurable over the aggregate of x and t. For the stationary process $X = (x_t, \zeta, \mathscr{M}_t^s, P_{s,x})$ we have $P(s, x; t, \Gamma) = P(0, x, t-s, \Gamma)$ by theorem 2.9. Hence for any stationary measurable Markov process $P(s, x;\ t, \Gamma)$ is a measurable function of s, x, t.

2. Definition of Strictly Markov Process

5.3. Definition. The Markov process $X=(x_t, \zeta, \mathcal{M}_t^s, \mathbf{P}_{s,x})$ in the phase space $(E, \mathcal{B})$ is said to be strictly Markov if it is measurable and satisfies the following conditions:

5.3.A. With any $t \geqslant 0$, $\Gamma \in \mathcal{B}$,

$$P(s, x; t, \Gamma) = \mathbf{P}_{s,x}\{x_t \in \Gamma\}$$

is a $\mathcal{B}_t \times \mathcal{B}$-measurable function of s and x ($\mathcal{B}_t$ is the σ-algebra of the subsets of space $I_t = [0, t]$. generated by all intervals contained in I_t).

5.3.B. If τ is a random variable not dependent on the future and s-past, we have for any $\mathcal{M}_\tau^s$-measurable function $\eta(\omega) \geqslant \tau(\omega)$ and any $x \in E$, $\Gamma \in \mathcal{B}$,

$$\mathbf{P}_{s,x}\{x_\eta \in \Gamma \,|\, \mathcal{M}_\tau^s\} = P(\tau, x_\tau; \eta, \Gamma) \qquad (\text{a.c.}\,\Omega_\tau, \mathbf{P}_{s,x}). \tag{5.7}$$

Condition 5.3.B can take the following form:

5.3.B′. Whatever the $x \in E$, $s \geqslant 0$, $\Gamma \in \mathcal{B}$, the random variable τ independent of the future and s-past, and the $\mathcal{M}_\tau^s$-measurable function $\eta(\omega) \geqslant \tau(\omega)$, the following equation holds for any $A \in \mathcal{M}_\tau^s$:

$$\mathbf{P}_{s,x}(A, x_\eta \in \Gamma) = \int_A P(\tau, x_\tau; \eta, \Gamma)\, \mathbf{P}_{s,x}(d\omega). \tag{5.8}$$

For, by definition of conditional probability, requirement 5.3.B is equivalent to the combination of 5.3.B′ with the requirement that $P(\tau, x_\tau; \eta, \Gamma)$ be an $\mathcal{M}_\tau^s$-measurable function of ω. It follows from condition 5.3.A by lemma 5.3.b, that the function $P(s, x; t, \Gamma)$ is $\mathcal{B}^0 \times \mathcal{B} \times \mathcal{B}^0$-measurable. The $\mathcal{M}_\tau^s$-measurability of the function $P(\tau, x_\tau; \eta, \Gamma)$ therefore follows from lemmas 5.2 and 1.3.

5.4. Later on we shall construct examples of Markov processes which are not strictly Markov (see sec. 6.18). Conditions 5.3.B-5.3.B′ are not fulfilled for these processes. We now show, however, that a weakened from of the conditions is satisfied for any Markov process.

Lemma 5.4. No matter what the Markov process X, conditions 5.3.B and 5.3.B′ are satisfied if the random variables τ and η take only a finite or denumerable set of values in Ω_τ.

Proof. Let τ take the values $t_1, t_2, \ldots,$ and η the values $u_1, u_2, \ldots$. Let $A \in \mathcal{M}_\tau^s$, $\Gamma \in \mathcal{B}$.

Clearly,

$$A_{ik} = \{A, \tau = t_i, \eta = u_k\} = \\ = \{A, \tau = t_i\}\{\eta = u_k, \tau = t_i\} \in \mathcal{M}_{t_i}^s \quad (i, k = 1, 2, \ldots),$$

and by 2.1.F′, we have for $t_i \leqslant u_k$,

$$\mathbf{P}_{s,x}(A_{ik}, x_\eta \in \Gamma) = \mathbf{P}_{s,x}(A_{ik}, x_{u_k} \in \Gamma) = \\ = \int_{A_{ik}} P(t_i, x_{t_i}; u_k, \Gamma)\,\mathbf{P}_{s,x}(d\omega) = \int_{A_{ik}} P(\tau, x_\tau; \eta, \Gamma)\,\mathbf{P}_{s,x}(d\omega).$$

On summing these relationships over all pairs i, k for which $t_i \leqslant u_k$, we get equation (5.8).

We now notice that the function $\psi(\omega) = P(\tau, x_\tau; \eta, \Gamma)$ induces in the set A_{ik} the function $P(t_i, x_{t_i}; u_k, \Gamma)$, which is clearly $\mathcal{M}_{t_i}^s$-measurable. Therefore, whatever the number a, we have for $t_i \leqslant t$:

$$\{A_{ik}, \psi(\omega) < a, \tau \leqslant t < \zeta\} = \\ = \{P(t_i, x_{t_i}; u_k, \Gamma) < a, t < \zeta\} \cap \{A_{ik}, t < \zeta\} \in \mathcal{M}_t^s.$$

The sum of all these sets is equal to $\{\psi(\omega) < a, \tau \leqslant t < \zeta\}$. Hence this latter set also belongs to $\mathcal{M}_t^s$. The function $\psi(\omega)$ is thus $\mathcal{M}_\tau^s$-measurable, and (5.7) follows from (5.8).

5.5. Condition 5.3.B or 5.3.B′ for a process to be strictly Markov is to be regarded as a variant of the principle of independence of the "future" (x_η) from the "past" ($\mathcal{M}_\tau^s$) for a known "present" (x_τ). We now show that this principle remains valid for a wider conception of "future" (any event, defined by the values $x_{\eta_1}, \ldots, x_{\eta_n}$ where $\eta_1, \ldots, \eta_n$ are random variables depending only on the phenomena observed during the time $[s, \tau]$). A precise formulation is given in theorem 5.1, the proof of which follows the same lines as the proof of theorem 2.1 except that certain extra technical difficulties have to be overcome.

We shall first prove a lemma.

<u>Lemma 5.5.</u> Let $X = (x_t, \zeta, \mathcal{M}_t^s, \mathbf{P}_{s,x})$ be a strictly Markov process, τ a random variable independent of the future and s-past, $\eta \geqslant \tau$ an $\mathcal{M}_\tau^s$-measurable function, and $(\omega \in \Omega_\tau, x \in E)$ $\Phi(\omega, x)$ an $\mathcal{M}_\tau^s \times \mathcal{B}$-measurable function such that $\mathbf{M}_{s,x}\Phi(\omega, x_\eta)$ exists. Then

$$\mathbf{M}_{s,x}\{\Phi(\omega, x_\eta) \mid \mathscr{M}_\tau^s\} = \psi(\omega, \tau, x_\tau, \eta) \quad (\text{a.c. } \Omega_\tau, \mathbf{P}_{s,x}), \tag{5.9}$$

where

$$\psi(\omega_0, u, y, v) = \int_{\Omega_v} \Phi[\omega_0, x_v(\omega)] \mathbf{P}_{u,y}(d\omega). \tag{5.10}$$

Proof. We suppose first that

$$\Phi(\omega, x) = \chi_C(\omega)\chi_\Gamma(x) \quad (C \in \mathscr{M}_\tau^s, \Gamma \in \mathscr{B}).$$

Then by 1.6.F,

$$\mathbf{M}_{s,x}\{\Phi(\omega, x_\eta) \mid \mathscr{M}_\tau^s\} = \chi_C(\omega)\mathbf{M}_{s,x}\{\chi_\Gamma(x_\eta) \mid \mathscr{M}_\tau^s\} = \chi_C(\omega)\mathbf{P}_{s,x}\{x_\eta \in \Gamma \mid \mathscr{M}_\tau^s\} \quad (\text{a.c. } \Omega_\tau, \mathbf{P}_{s,x}) \tag{5.11}$$

and on taking (5.7) into account,

$$\mathbf{M}_{s,x}\{\Phi(\omega, x_\eta) \mid \mathscr{M}_\tau^s\} = \chi_C(\omega) P(\tau, x_\tau; \eta, \Gamma) \quad (\text{a.c. } \Omega_\tau, \mathbf{P}_{s,x}). \tag{5.12}$$

On the other hand,

$$\psi(\omega_0, u, y, v) = \chi_C(\omega_0) P(u, y; v, \Gamma). \tag{5.13}$$

Equation (5.9) follows from (5.12) and (5.13).

Let $\mathscr{L}$ denote the class of all functions $\Phi(\omega, x)$ $(\omega \in \Omega_\tau, \ x \in E)$ such that $\mathbf{M}_{s,x}\Phi(\omega, x_\eta)$ exists. The class $\mathscr{H}$ of all functions $\Phi(\omega, x)$ for which relationships (5.9) and (5.10) are satisfied is evidently an $\mathscr{L}$-system. The sets $C \times \Gamma$ form a π-system $\mathscr{C}$. By lemma 1.2, the $\mathscr{L}$-system $\mathscr{H}$ contains all functions Φ of $\mathscr{L}$ measurable with respect to the σ-algebra $\sigma(\mathscr{C}) = \mathscr{M}_\tau^s \times \mathscr{B}$. The lemma is proved.

5.6. Theorem 5.1. Let $X = (x_t, \zeta, \mathscr{M}_t^s, \mathbf{P}_{s,x})$ be a strictly Markov process, τ a random variable independent of the future and s-past and $\tau \leqslant \eta_1, \ldots, \eta_n$ a system of $\mathscr{M}_\tau^s$-measurable functions. Then for any $\Gamma_1, \ldots, \Gamma_n \in \mathscr{B}$,

$$\mathbf{P}_{s,x}\{x_{\eta_1} \in \Gamma_1, \ldots x_{\eta_n} \in \Gamma_n \mid \mathscr{M}_\tau^s\} = P(\tau, x_\tau; \eta_1, \Gamma_1, \ldots, \eta_n, \Gamma_n) \quad (\text{a.c. } \Omega_\tau, \mathbf{P}_{s,x}), \tag{5.14}$$

where $P(s, x; t_1, \Gamma_1, \ldots, t_n, \Gamma_n)$ is given by formula (2.13).

Proof. With $n=1$, (5.14) reduces to condition 5.3.B. We assume that (5.14) is satisfied for $n-1$, and prove it for n. We put

$$\eta(\omega)=\min(\eta_1(\omega), \ldots, \eta_n(\omega)),$$
$$A_k=\{\eta_1>\eta, \ldots, \eta_{k-1}>\eta, \eta_k=\eta\}.$$

We notice that $A_k \in \mathscr{M}^s_\tau$, $\tau \leqslant \eta \leqslant \eta_1, \eta_2, \ldots, \eta_n$ and η are measurable with respect to $\mathscr{M}^s_\tau$. We fix a value of $k (1 \leqslant k \leqslant n)$, put

$$\eta^*(\omega)=\begin{cases} \eta(\omega) \text{ for } \omega \in \Omega_{\eta^*}=\{A_k, \eta<\zeta\}, \\ \max(s, \zeta) \text{ for } \omega \overline{\in} \Omega_{\eta^*} \end{cases}$$

and denote the random variables $\eta_1, \ldots, \eta_n$ considered only in the set Ω_{η^*} by $\eta_1^*, \ldots, \eta_n^*$. It follows from lemma 5.1 that η^* is independent of the future and s-past and $\eta_1^*(\omega), \ldots, \eta_n^*(\omega)$ $(\omega \in \Omega_{\eta^*})$ are $\mathscr{M}^s_{\eta^*}$-measurable. Apart from this, the inequalities $\eta_i^* \geqslant \eta^*$ are satisfied, so that by our inductive assumption:

$$\begin{aligned} \mathbf{P}_{s,x}(C_k \,|\, \mathscr{M}^s_{\eta^*}) &= H_k(\eta^*, x_{\eta^*}; \eta_1^*, \ldots, \eta_{k-1}^*, \eta_{k+1}^*, \ldots, \eta_n^*)= \\ &= H_k(\eta, x_\eta; \eta_1, \ldots, \eta_{k-1}, \eta_{k+1}, \ldots, \eta_n) \quad (\text{a.c. } \Omega_{\eta^*}, \mathbf{P}_{s,x}), \end{aligned} \tag{5.15}$$

where

$$\left.\begin{aligned} C_k &= \{x_{\eta_1^*} \in \Gamma_1, \ldots, x_{\eta_{k-1}^*} \in \Gamma_{k-1}, \\ &\qquad x_{\eta_{k+1}^*} \in \Gamma_{k+1}, \ldots, x_{\eta_n^*} \in \Gamma_n\} \\ H_k&(u, y; v_1, \ldots, v_{n-1}) = \\ &= P(u, y; v_1, \Gamma_1, \ldots, v_{k-1}, \Gamma_{k-1}, v_k, \Gamma_{k+1}, \ldots, v_{n-1}, \Gamma_n). \end{aligned}\right\} \tag{5.16}$$

We put $B=\{x_{\eta_1} \in \Gamma_1, \ldots, x_{\eta_n} \in \Gamma_n\}$. Obviously

$$B=\bigcup_{k=1}^{n}\{A_k, x_{\eta_k} \in \Gamma_k, C_k. \tag{5.17}$$

By (5.15) and (5.17), we have for any $A \in \mathscr{M}^s_\tau$,

$$\mathbf{P}_{s,x}(AB)=\sum_{k=1}^{n}\mathbf{P}_{s,x}\{AA_k,\ x_{\tau_{\eta_k}}\in\Gamma_k,\ C_k\}=$$
$$=\sum_{k=1}^{n}\int\limits_{\{AA_k,\ x_{\tau_{\eta_k}}\in\Gamma_k\}}H_k(\eta,\ x_{\tau_i};\ \eta_1,\ \ldots$$
$$\ldots,\ \eta_{k-1},\ \eta_{k+1},\ \ldots,\ \eta_n)\,\mathbf{P}_{s,x}(d\omega)= \tag{5.18}$$
$$=\sum_{k=1}^{n}\mathbf{M}_{s,x}[\Phi_k(\omega,\ x_{\tau_i})\chi_A]=$$
$$=\sum_{k=1}^{n}\mathbf{M}_{s,x}\{\chi_A\mathbf{M}_{s,x}[\Phi_k(\omega,\ x_{\tau_i})\,|\,\mathcal{M}_\tau^s]\},$$

where

$$\Phi_k(\omega,\ x)=$$
$$=\chi_{A_k}(\omega)\chi_{\Gamma_k}(x)H_k(\eta,\ x;\ \eta_1,\ \ldots,\ \eta_{k-1},\ \eta_{k+1},\ \ldots,\ \eta_n). \tag{5.19}$$

The mapping $\Omega_\tau\times E\to I_1^0$ defined by the function $\Phi_k(\omega,x)$ can be written in the product form $\beta\alpha$, where the mappings $\alpha:\Omega_\tau\times E\to[I^0]^n\times E$ and $\beta:[I^0]^n\times E\to I_1^0$ are given by the expressions

$$\alpha(\omega,\ x)=$$
$$=\{\eta(\omega),\ \eta_1(\omega),\ \ldots,\ \eta_{k-1}(\omega),\ \eta_{k+1}(\omega),\ \ldots,\ \eta_n(\omega),\ x\},$$
$$\beta(v,\ v_1,\ \ldots,\ v_{n-1},\ x)=H_k(v,\ x;\ v_1,\ \ldots,\ v_{n-1}).$$

It follows from lemma 1.3 that α is the measurable mapping of $(\Omega_\tau\times E,\ \mathcal{M}_\tau^s\times\mathcal{B})$ in $([I^0]^n\times E,\ [\mathcal{B}^0]^n\times\mathcal{B})$. In accordance with lemma 5.3, β is the measurable mapping of $([I^0]^n\times E,$ $[\mathcal{B}^0]^n\times\mathcal{B})$ in $(I_1^0,\ \mathcal{B}_1^0)$. The function $\Phi_k(\omega,x)$ is therefore $\mathcal{M}_\tau^s\times\mathcal{B}$-measurable, and we are justified in applying lemma 5.5. In our case

$$\psi(\omega_0,\ u,\ y,\ v)=\int\limits_{\Omega_v}\Phi_k[\omega_0,\ x_v(\omega)]\,\mathbf{P}_{u,y}(d\omega)=$$
$$=\int\limits_{\Omega_v}\chi_{A_k}(\omega_0)\chi_{\Gamma_k}[x_v(\omega)]H_k[\eta(\omega_0),\ x_v(\omega);\ \eta_1(\omega_0),\ \ldots$$
$$\ldots,\ \eta_{k-1}(\omega_0),\ \eta_{k+1}(\omega_0),\ \ldots,\ \eta_n(\omega_0)]\,\mathbf{P}_{u,y}(d\omega)=$$
$$=\chi_{A_k}(\omega_0)\int\limits_{\Gamma_k}P(u,\ y;\ v,\ dz)H_k[\eta(\omega_0),\ z;\ \eta_1(\omega_0),\ \ldots$$
$$\ldots,\ \eta_{k-1}(\omega_0),\ \eta_{k+1}(\omega_0),\ \ldots,\ \eta_n(\omega)],$$

and by (5.16) and (2.14),

$$\psi(\omega_0, u, y, \eta(\omega_0)) = \chi_{A_k}(\omega_0) P(u, y; \eta(\omega_0), \Gamma_k, \eta_1(\omega_0), \Gamma_1, \ldots$$
$$\ldots, \eta_{k-1}(\omega_0), \Gamma_{k-1}, \eta_{k+1}(\omega_0), \Gamma_{k+1}, \ldots, \eta_n(\omega_0), \Gamma_n) =$$
$$= \chi_{A_k}(\omega_0) P(u, y; \eta_1(\omega_0), \Gamma_1, \ldots, \eta_n(\omega_0), \Gamma_n).$$

Hence

$$\psi(\omega, \tau, x_\tau, \eta) = \chi_{A_k}(\omega) P(\tau, x_\tau; \eta_1, \Gamma_1, \ldots, \eta_n, \Gamma_n). \tag{5.20}$$

On comparing (5.9) and (5.20), we find that

$$\mathbf{M}_{s, x}\{\Phi_k(\omega, x_{\tau_l}) | \mathcal{M}_\tau^s\} =$$
$$= \chi_{A_k}(\omega) P(\tau, x_\tau; \eta_1, \Gamma_1, \ldots, \eta_n, \Gamma_n) \quad (\text{a.c.}\,\Omega_\tau, \mathbf{P}_{s, x}). \tag{5.21}$$

It follows from (5.18) and (5.21) that

$$\mathbf{P}_{s, x}(AB) = M_{s, x}[\chi_A P(\tau, x_\tau; \eta_1, \Gamma_1, \ldots, \eta_n, \Gamma_n)]. \tag{5.22}$$

Since the function $P(\tau, x_\tau; \eta_1, \Gamma_1, \ldots, \eta_n, \Gamma_n)$ is $\mathcal{M}_\tau^s$-measurable (as follows from lemmas 5.2 and 5.3), (5.22) is equivalent to (5.14).

<u>Corollary</u>. Let X be a strictly Markov process. If $\tau, \eta_1, \ldots, \eta_n, \ldots$ is the system of ω-functions described in theorem 5.1, and $f(x_1, \ldots, x_n, \ldots)$ is any $\mathcal{B}^\infty$-measurable function in the space E^∞, such that $\mathbf{M}_{s, x} f(x_{\tau_{\eta_1}}, \ldots, x_{\tau_{\eta_n}}, \ldots)$ exists, then

$$\mathbf{M}_{s, x}\{f(x_{\tau_{\eta_1}}, \ldots, x_{\tau_{\eta_n}}, \ldots) | \mathcal{M}_\tau^s\} = F(\tau, x_\tau; \eta_1, \ldots, \eta_n, \ldots) \quad (\text{a.c.}\,\Omega_\tau, \mathbf{P}_{s, x}), \tag{5.23}$$

where

$$F(u, y; v_1, \ldots, v_n, \ldots) = \mathbf{M}_{u, y} f(x_{v_1}, \ldots, x_{v_n}, \ldots). \tag{5.24}$$

Proof. We write $\mathcal{L}$ for the class of all functions f for which $\mathbf{M}_{s, x} f(x_{\tau_{\eta_1}}, \ldots, x_{\tau_{\eta_n}}, \ldots)$ exists, and $\mathcal{H}$ for the class of all functions f for which equations (5.23)-(5.24) hold. By theorem 5.1, $\mathcal{H}$ contains the characteristic functions of sets $\Gamma_1 \times \ldots \times \Gamma_n$ $(n = 1, 2, \ldots; \Gamma_1, \ldots, \Gamma_n \in \mathcal{B})$. These sets form a π-system generating $\mathcal{B}^\infty$. Obviously, $\mathcal{H}$ is an $\mathcal{L}$-system, and by lemma 1.2, $\mathcal{H}$ contains all the $\mathcal{B}^\infty$-measurable functions of $\mathcal{L}$.

5.7. We shall give a further important formulation of the principle of independence of the "future" from the "past" for a known "present." Some new notation is first introduced.

We shall write $\mathfrak{F}^s$ for the σ-algebra in the space $\Omega \times I^s$ generated by sets $\Omega \times I_T^s (T \geqslant s)$ and

$$\{(\omega, t) : x_{\varphi(t)}(\omega) \in \Gamma\}$$

($\Gamma \in \mathscr{B}$, $\varphi(t)$ is an arbitrary $\mathscr{B}^s$-measurable function in the interval I^s such that $\varphi(t) \geqslant t$ for all t). Evidently, $\mathfrak{F}^s$ can also be described as the minimal σ-algebra in space $\Omega \times I^s$ with respect to which the functions

$$f(t, \omega) = t \text{ and } \Phi(t, \omega) = x_{\varphi(t)}(\omega),$$

are measurable.

<u>Lemma 5.6</u>. If $T \geqslant s$ and $\xi(\omega)$ is an arbitrary $\mathscr{N}^T$-measurable function, the function $\chi_{[s, T]}(t)\xi(\omega)$ is $\mathfrak{F}^s$-measurable. All sets of the form

$$\{x_u \in \Gamma\} \times [s, T] \qquad (u \geqslant T, \Gamma \in \mathscr{B}) \tag{5.25}$$

belong to the σ-algebra $\mathfrak{F}^s$. In conjunction with sets $\Omega \times I_T^s$ $(T \geqslant s)$ they generate the σ-algebra $\mathfrak{F}^s$ in the case when X is a process continuous from the right in the topological measurable space satisfying conditions 1.9.A-1.9.B.

Proof. In accordance with lemma 1.5,

$$\xi(\omega) = f(x_{t_1}, \ldots, x_{t_n}, \ldots),$$

where $t_1, \ldots, t_n, \ldots \geqslant T$ and f is a $\mathscr{B}^\infty$-measurable function in the space E^∞. We take any $\mathscr{B}_\infty^s$-measurable function $\varphi_i(t)$ satisfying the conditions

$$\begin{aligned} \varphi_i(t) &= t_i \quad \text{for } s \leqslant t \leqslant T, \\ \varphi_i(t) &\geqslant t \quad \text{for } t > T. \end{aligned}$$

Obviously,

$$\chi_{[s, T]}(t)\xi(\omega) = \chi_{[s, T]}(t) f(x_{\varphi_1(t)}, \ldots, x_{\varphi_n(t)}, \ldots),$$

so that $\chi_{[s, T]}(t)\xi(\omega)$ is $\mathfrak{F}^s$-measurable.

Putting $\xi=\chi_\Gamma(x_u)$ $(u\geqslant T)$, we conclude that

$$\{x_u\in\Gamma\}\times[s,\ T]\in\mathfrak{F}^s.$$

Now let X be a process continuous from the right in the topological measurable space $(E,\ \mathcal{C},\ \mathcal{B})$ subject to conditions 1.9.A-1.9.B. We write $\tilde{\mathfrak{F}}^s$ for the σ-algebra in $\Omega\times I^s$ generated by sets $\Omega\times I^s_T(T\geqslant s)$ and set (5.25). Let $\varphi(t)$ be any $\mathcal{B}^s_\omega$-measurable function satisfying the inequality $\varphi(t)\geqslant t$, and let the points t^n_k define a canonical sequence of subdivisions $\{\Delta^n_k\}$ of the interval I^s. We put

$$\varphi_n(t)=t^n_k,\quad \text{if}\quad \varphi(t)\in\Delta^n_k.$$

For any $\Gamma\in\mathcal{B}$

$$\{(t,\ \omega):x_{\varphi_n(t)}(\omega)\in\Gamma\}=\bigcup_k\{x_{t^n_k}\in\Gamma\}\times\{\varphi(t)\in\Delta^n_k\}\in\tilde{\mathfrak{F}}^s.$$

The function $x_{\varphi_n(t)}(\omega)$ is therefore $\tilde{\mathfrak{F}}^s$-measurable. As $n\to\infty$, $\varphi_n(t)\downarrow\varphi(t)$ and in view of the fact that X is continuous from the right, $x_{\varphi_n(t)}\to x_{\varphi(t)}$. By lemma 1.9, $x_{\varphi_n(t)}(\omega)$ is also $\tilde{\mathfrak{F}}^s$-measurable. Therefore $\tilde{\mathfrak{F}}^s=\mathfrak{F}^s$.

5.8. Theorem 5.2. Let X be a strictly Markov process, and τ a random variable independent of the future and s-past. Let $\Phi(\omega,\ t)(\omega\in\Omega,\ t\in I^s)$ be an $\mathfrak{F}^s$-measurable function such that $\Phi(\omega,\ \tau)$ is $\mathbf{P}_{s,\ x}$-summable. Then

$$\mathbf{M}_{s,\ x}\{\Phi(\omega,\ \tau)\,\|\,\mathcal{M}^s_\tau\}=F(\tau,\ x_\tau)\qquad(\text{a.c.}\ \Omega_\tau,\ \mathbf{P}_{s,\ x}),\tag{5.26}$$

where

$$F(t,\ y)=\mathbf{M}_{t,\ y}\Phi(\omega,\ t).\tag{5.27}$$

Proof. Let

$$B=\{(\omega,\ t):s\leqslant t\leqslant T,\ x_{\varphi_1(t)}\in\Gamma_1,\ \ldots\ x_{\varphi_n(t)}\in\Gamma_n\},\tag{5.28}$$

where $T\geqslant s,\ \Gamma_1,\ \ldots,\ \Gamma_n\in\mathcal{B}$ and $\varphi_1,\ \ldots,\ \varphi_n$ are $\mathcal{B}^s$-measurable functions such that $\varphi_i(t)\geqslant t$. If $\Phi(\omega,\ t)=\chi_B$, we have

$$\Phi(\omega,\ t)=\chi_{[s,\ T]}(t)\chi_{\Gamma_1}[x_{\varphi_1(t)}]\ldots\chi_{\Gamma_n}[x_{\varphi_n(t)}].$$

Hence (see 1.6.F)

$$\mathbf{M}_{s,\ x}\{\Phi(\omega,\ \tau)\,\|\,\mathcal{M}^s_\tau\}=$$
$$=\chi_{\tau\leqslant T}\mathbf{P}_{s,\ x}\{x_{\eta_1}\in\Gamma_1,\ \ldots,\ x_{\eta_n}\in\Gamma_n\,\|\,\mathcal{M}^s_\tau\}\qquad(\text{a.c.}\ \Omega_\tau,\ \mathbf{P}_{s,\ x}),$$

where $\eta_i = \varphi_i(\tau)$. By theorem 5.1 it follows from this that

$$\mathbf{M}_{s,x}\{\Phi(\omega,\tau)\,|\,\mathcal{M}_\tau^s\} = \chi_{\tau\leqslant T}P(\tau, x_\tau; \eta_1, \Gamma_1, \ldots, \eta_n, \Gamma_n). \quad (5.29)$$

On the other hand,

$$\mathbf{M}_{t,y}\Phi(\omega, t) = \chi_{[s,T]}(t)\,P(t, y; \varphi_1(t), \Gamma_1, \ldots, \varphi_n(t), \Gamma_n). \quad (5.30)$$

On comparing (5.29) and (5.30), we conclude that relationship (5.26) is satisfied for $\Phi(\omega, t) = \chi_B$. Sets B of the form (5.28) form a π-system $\mathcal{C}^{\cdot}$. The functions Φ for which (5.26) is satisfied form an $\mathcal{L}$-system ($\mathcal{L}$ denotes the class of all functions Φ such that $\Phi(\omega, \tau)$ is $\mathbf{P}_{s,x}$-summable). By lemma 1.2, this system contains all the functions of $\mathcal{L}$ which are measurable with respect to $\sigma(\mathcal{C}) = \mathcal{F}^s$.

Corollary. Let X be a strictly Markov process and let the random variable τ independent of the future and s-past satisfy the inequality $\tau \leqslant T$. Then for any $\mathcal{N}^T$-measurable and $\mathbf{P}_{s,x}$-summable function ξ,

$$\mathbf{M}_{s,x}(\xi\,|\,\mathcal{M}_\tau^s) = \mathbf{M}_{\tau, x_\tau}\xi \qquad (\text{a.c.}\ \Omega_\tau, \mathbf{P}_{s,x}). \quad (5.31)$$

This may be seen simply by applying theorem 5.2 to the $\mathcal{F}^s$-measurable function $\chi_{[s,T]}(t)\,\xi(\omega)$.

Remark. In an important particular case theorems 5.1 and 5.2 and their corollaries are applicable to any Markov, and not merely to strictly Markov, processes. This is the case when the functions $\tau, \eta_1, \ldots, \eta_n$ take only a finite or denumerable set of values in Ω_τ. For, in accordance with lemma 5.4, conditions 5.3.B-5.3.B′ are fulfilled for these functions, so that all the proofs contained in sec. 5.5-5.8 remain valid.

5.9. As an application of the general theorems just proved we shall mention some properties of the random variables $\xi_s(\Gamma), \xi_s(\mathcal{F}), \tau_s(G)$ defined in articles 2-3 of Chapter 3.

Lemma 5.7. Let X be a strictly Markov process continuous from the right in the topological measurable space $(E, \mathcal{C}, \mathcal{B})$ and satisfying conditions 1.9.A-1.9.B. Let $\mathcal{F}$ be a normal system of subsets of $(E, \mathcal{C}, \mathcal{B})$ and $\xi_t(\mathcal{F})$ the instant of first departure after 't' of the trajectory of the process from the system $\mathcal{F}$ (see sec. 3.11). Then the functions $\xi_t(\mathcal{F}, \omega)$ $(\zeta(\omega) > t \geqslant s)$ and $x_{\xi_t(\mathcal{F},\omega)}(\omega)$ are $\mathcal{F}^s$-measurable.

Proof. Let $\{\Gamma_n\}$ be a sequence satisfying conditions 3.12.A-3.12.C and equivalent to $\mathscr{F}$. We observe that

$$\xi_t(\mathscr{F}, \omega) = \lim_{n\to\infty} \inf_{r\in\Lambda} (t+r) f_{n,r}(\omega, t) \qquad (\zeta(\omega) > t \geqslant s),$$

where Λ is the set of all non-negative rational numbers and

$$f_{n,r}(\omega, t) = \begin{cases} +\infty, & \text{if } x_{r+t}(\omega) \in \Gamma_n, \\ 1 & \text{for the remaining } (\omega, t). \end{cases}$$

The functions $f_{n,r}(\omega, t)$ are easily seen to be $\mathfrak{F}^s$-measurable. This means that the functions $(t+r) f_{n,r}(\omega, t)$, and hence also the functions $\xi_t(\mathscr{F}, \omega)$ are $\mathfrak{F}^s$-measurable.

Since the mapping of the space $(\Omega\times I^s, \mathfrak{F}^s)$ into $(E, \mathscr{B})$ defined by the function $x_t(\omega)$ is measurable, we can prove that $x_{\xi_t(\mathscr{F}, \omega)}(\omega)$ is measurable simply by showing the measurability of the mapping β of the space $(\Omega\times I^s, \mathfrak{F}^s)$ into itself given by the expression

$$\beta(\omega, t) = (\omega, \xi_t(\mathscr{F}, \omega)).$$

By lemma 5.6, we can show this simply by verifying that

$$\beta^{-1}\{\Omega\times I_T^s\} \in \mathfrak{F}^s \qquad (T \geqslant s)$$

$$\beta^{-1}\{[x_u\in\Gamma]\times I_T^s\} \in \mathscr{F}^s \qquad (u \geqslant T \geqslant s).$$

The first of these inclusions follows from the $\mathfrak{F}^s$-measurability of the function $\xi_t(\mathscr{F}, \omega)$ proved above; the second inclusion follows from

$$\beta^{-1}\{[x_u\in\Gamma]\times I_T^s\} = \{x_u\in\Gamma, \xi_t(\mathscr{F}) \leqslant T\} = \\ = \{x_u\in\Gamma\times I_T^s\} \cap \{\xi_t(\mathscr{F}) \leqslant T\}.$$

This proves the lemma.

Theorem 5.3. Let X be a strictly Markov process continuous from the right in the topological measurable space $(E, \mathcal{C}, \mathscr{B})$ and satisfying conditions 1.9.A-1.9.B. We put

$$\Pi_G(s, x; \Delta, \Gamma) = \mathbf{P}_{s,x}\{\tau_s(G)\in\Delta, \quad x_{\tau_s(G)}\in\Gamma\}, \tag{5.32}$$

where $G\in\mathcal{C}\cap\mathscr{B}$ and $\tau_s(G)$ is the random magnitude defined in sec. 3.13. Then we have for any random magnitude η not depending on the future and the s-past:

$$\mathbf{P}_{s,x}\{\tau_\eta(G)\in\Delta,\ x_{\tau_\eta(G)}\in\Gamma\,|\,\mathcal{M}^s_\eta\}=\Pi_G(\eta,\ x_\eta;\ \Delta,\ \Gamma)\quad (\text{a.c.}\,\Omega_\eta,\ \mathbf{P}_{s,x}). \tag{5.33}$$

If $U\in\mathcal{C}\cap\mathcal{B}$, the closure of U being compact and contained in G, we have

$$\mathbf{P}_{s,x}\{\tau_s(G)\in\Delta,\ x_{\tau_s(G)}\in\Gamma\,|\,\mathcal{M}^s_{\tau_s(U)}\}= =\Pi_G(\tau_s(U),\ x_{\tau_s(U)};\ \Delta,\ \Gamma)\quad (\text{a.c.}\,\Omega_{\tau_s(U)}\mathbf{P}_{s,x}) \tag{5.34}$$

and

$$\Pi_G(s,\ x;\ \Delta,\ \Gamma)=\int_E\int_0^\infty \Pi_U(s,\ x;\ dt,\ dy)\,\Pi_G(t,\ y;\ \Delta,\ \Gamma). \tag{5.35}$$

When the process X is continuous, relationships (5.34) and (5.35) are satisfied for any open measurable sets $U\subseteq G$.

Proof. In view of lemma 5.7, the function

$$\Phi(t,\ \omega)=\chi_\Delta[\tau_t(G,\ \omega)]\,\chi_\Gamma\left[x_{\tau_t(G,\ \omega)}(\omega)\right]$$

is $\mathcal{F}^s$-measurable. If we apply theorem 5.2 to this, we arrive at relationship (5.33). Equation (5.34) follows from lemma 3.9 and (5.33). In the case of a continuous process, we can use lemma 3.10 and relationship (3.54) instead of lemma 3.9.

3. Stationary Strictly Markov Processes

5.10. Let $X=(x_t,\zeta,\mathcal{M}^s_t,\mathbf{P}_{s,x})$ be a stationary Markov process and let θ_t be operators satisfying conditions 2.5.A-2.5.C. We take any non-negative function $\tau(\omega)$ and put for any $A\in\mathcal{N}^*$:

$$\theta_\tau A=\bigcup_{t\geqslant 0}\{\theta_t A,\ \tau(\omega)=t\}. \tag{5.36}$$

It follows from 2.5.A-2.5.B that operators θ_τ possess the following properties:

5.10.A. $\theta_\tau\Omega_0=\Omega_\tau,\ \theta_\tau(A\setminus B)=\theta_\tau A\setminus\theta_\tau B,$
$\theta_\tau(\bigcup A_\alpha)=\bigcup\theta_\tau A_\alpha,\ \theta_\tau(\bigcap A_\alpha)=\bigcap\theta_\tau A_\alpha$

(α runs through an arbitrary set of values).

5.10.B. $\theta_\tau \{x_h \in \Gamma\} = \{x_{\tau+h} \in \Gamma\}$.

Let $\xi(\omega)$ be an $\mathcal{N}^*$-measurable function. We define the function $\theta_\tau \xi$ by the expression

$$\theta_\tau \xi(\omega) = \theta_t \xi(\omega), \quad \text{if} \quad \tau(\omega) = t. \tag{5.37}$$

It may readily be seen that properties 2.6.A-2.6.E and 2.6.G of operators θ_t still hold when t is replaced by τ. In particular,

$$\theta_\tau \zeta = \zeta - \tau. \tag{5.38}$$

<u>Lemma 5.8</u>. Let X be a stationary Markov process and let $\xi(\omega)(\omega \in \Omega_0)$ be an arbitrary $\mathcal{N}^0$-measurable function. Then the function $\varphi(\omega, t) = \theta_t \xi(\omega)$ is $\mathcal{F}^0$-measurable.

Proof. Let $\mathcal{L}$ denote the class of all functions $\xi(\omega)(\omega \in \Omega_0)$. Obviously, the class $\mathcal{H}$ of all functions ξ for which the assertion of the lemma is satisfied is an $\mathcal{L}$-system. Furthermore, the characteristic function χ_B of any set $B = \{x_{t_1} \in \Gamma_1, \ldots, x_{t_n} \in \Gamma_n\}$ $(t_1, \ldots, t_n \geqslant 0;\ \Gamma_1, \ldots, \Gamma_n \in \mathcal{B})$ belongs to $\mathcal{H}$. These sets form a π-system generating the σ-algebra $\mathcal{N}$. The statement of the lemma therefore follows from lemma 1.2.

On combining lemma 5.8 and theorem 5.2 and taking 2.5.C into account, we arrive at the theorem:

<u>Theorem 5.4</u>. Let $X = (x_t, \zeta, \mathcal{M}_t^s, \mathbf{P}_{s,x})$ be a stationary strictly Markov process, and τ a random variable independent of the future and s-past. Let ξ be an $\mathcal{N}$-measurable function such that $\mathbf{M}_{s,x}\theta_\tau\xi$ exists. Then

$$\mathbf{M}_{s,x}(\theta_\tau \xi \,|\, \mathcal{M}_\tau^s) = \mathbf{M}_{x_\tau} \xi \ ^{*)} \qquad (\text{a.c.}\ \Omega_\tau, \mathbf{P}_{s,x}). \tag{5.39}$$

We have for any $B \in \mathcal{N}$:

$$\mathbf{P}_{s,x}(\theta_\tau B \,|\, \mathcal{M}_\tau^s) = \mathbf{P}_{x_\tau}(B) \qquad (\text{a.c.}\ \Omega_\tau, \mathbf{P}_{s,x}). \tag{5.40}$$

<u>Corollary 1</u>. Let the assumption of theorem 5.4 be fulfilled. Then for any $A \in \mathcal{M}_\tau^s$, $B \in \mathcal{N}$:

$$\mathbf{P}_{s,x}(A, \theta_\tau B) = \int_A \mathbf{P}_{x_\tau}(B)\, \mathbf{P}_{s,x}(d\omega). \tag{5.41}$$

---

*) We write $\mathbf{M}_x\xi$ instead of $\mathbf{M}_{0,x}\xi$ and $\mathbf{P}_x(B)$ instead of $\mathbf{P}_{0,x}(B)$.

If the function $\xi(\omega)$ is $\mathcal{N}$-measurable, the function $\eta(\omega)$ $\mathcal{M}_\tau^s$-measurable and $\eta\theta_\tau\xi$ and $\theta_\tau\xi$ are $\mathbf{P}_{s,x}$-summable, then

$$\mathbf{M}_{s,x}(\eta\theta_\tau\xi) = \mathbf{M}_{s,x}(\eta\mathbf{M}_{x_\tau}\xi). \tag{5.42}$$

Corollary 2. If $\psi(\omega, t)$ $(\omega \in \Omega_0, t \in [0, \infty))$ is an arbitrary $\mathcal{N} \times \mathcal{B}_\infty^0$-measurable function and if $\Phi(\omega, t) = \theta_t\psi(\omega, t)$, we have for any random variable τ independent of the future and s-past:

$$\mathbf{M}_{s,x}\{\Phi(\omega, \tau) \,|\, \mathcal{M}_\tau^s\} = F(\tau, x_\tau) \quad (\text{a.c.}\,\Omega_\tau, \mathbf{P}_{s,x}),$$

where

$$F(t, y) = \mathbf{M}_y\psi(\omega, t).$$

These expressions are deduced from (5.39) by normal use of lemma 1.2.

<u>Theorem 5.4′</u>. Expressions (5.39), (5.40), (5.41) and (5.42) likewise hold in the case when $B \in \overline{\mathcal{N}}$ and ξ is $\overline{\mathcal{N}}$-measurable. (Measure $\mathbf{P}_x$ is to be continued into $\overline{\mathcal{M}}^0$ as described in sec. 2.2).

The proof of this theorem is very similar to that of theorem 2.1. We shall therefore omit the details and just give the broad outlines. Let $A \in \mathcal{M}_\tau^s$, $B \in \overline{\mathcal{N}}$. We take the measure in $\mathcal{B}$:

$$\mu(\Gamma) = \mathbf{P}_x(A, x_\tau \in \Gamma) \qquad (\Gamma \in \mathcal{B})$$

and choose B_1, B_2 from $\mathcal{N}$ such that $B_1 \subseteq B \subseteq B_2$ and $\mathbf{P}_\mu(B_1) = \mathbf{P}_\mu(B_2)$. On applying formula (5.41) to A, B_i we get

$$\mathbf{P}_x(A\theta_\tau B_i) = \int_A \mathbf{P}_{x_\tau}(B_i)\,\mathbf{P}_x(d\omega) = \int_E \mathbf{P}_y(B_i)\,\mu(dy) = \mathbf{P}_\mu(B_i).$$

This gives us

$$\mathbf{P}_x(A\theta_\tau B) = \mathbf{P}_\mu(B_i).$$

On the other hand,

$$\mathbf{P}_\mu(B_i) = \int_A P_{x_\tau}(B)\,\mathbf{P}_x(d\omega),$$

and (5.41) is proved for sets A, B. Expressions (5.39), (5.40) and (5.42) are deduced from (5.41) with the aid of arguments which will by now be familiar.

5.11. Let ξ_s be random variables satisfying conditions 3.7.A-3.7.C and (3.90). We have

$$\theta_\tau \xi_0 = \xi_\tau - \tau \qquad (\omega \in \Omega_\tau). \tag{5.43}$$

Moreover, for any $a \in E$:

$$\theta_\tau \{x_{\xi_0} = a\} = \theta_\tau \bigcup_u \{\xi_0 = u,\ x_u = a\} =$$
$$= \bigcup_u \{\theta_\tau \xi_0 = u, \theta_\tau x_u = a\} = \bigcup_u \{\xi_\tau - \tau = u, x_{\tau+u} = a\} = \{x_{\xi_\tau} = a\}$$

so that

$$\theta_\tau x_{\xi_0} = x_{\xi_\tau}. \tag{5.44}$$

Let $f(t, x)$ $(t \geqslant 0,\ x \in E)$ be an arbitrary $\mathscr{B}_{[0,\infty)} \times \mathscr{B}$-measurable function. It follows from (5.43)-(5.44) and 2.6.E that

$$\theta_\tau f(\xi_0, x_{\xi_0}) = f(\xi_\tau - \tau, x_{\xi_\tau}). \tag{5.45}$$

We now make the assumptions that process X is strictly Markov, that τ is a random variable independent of the future and s-past, and that the function $\mathbf{M}_{s,x} f(\xi_\tau - \tau, x_{\xi_\tau})$ is $\mathbf{P}_{s,x}$-summable. On applying theorem 5.4, (5.45) now gives us

$$\mathbf{M}_{s,x} \{f(\xi_\tau - \tau, x_{\xi_\tau}) \mid \mathscr{M}_\tau^s\} = \mathbf{M}_{x_\tau} f(\xi_0, x_{\xi_0}) \tag{5.46}$$
$$(\text{a.c. } \Omega_\tau, \mathbf{P}_{s,x})^{*)}.$$

Let G be an admissible set for process X.

---

*) In order to apply theorem 5.4, we have to verify that function $f(\xi_0, x_{\xi_0})$ $(\omega \in \Omega_0)$ is $\mathscr{N}$-measurable. In view of 3.7.B, $\{\xi_0 > t\} \in \mathscr{R}_t^0$ for any $t \geqslant 0$. The function $\xi_0(\omega)$ $(\omega \in \Omega_0)$ is therefore a random variable independent of the future and 0-past for the process $(x_t, \xi, \mathscr{R}_t^s, \mathbf{P}_{s,x})$. By lemma 5.2, x_{ξ_0} is measurable with respect to $\mathscr{R}_t^0$. Since $\mathscr{R}_t^0$ and $\mathscr{R}_\tau^0$ are contained in $\mathscr{N}^0$, it follows that ξ_0 and x_{ξ_0} are measurable with respect to $\mathscr{N} = \mathscr{N}^0[\Omega_0]$, whence we may readily deduce the $\mathscr{N}$-measurability of $f(\xi_0, x_\xi)$.

We introduce the following notation:

$$\pi_G^\lambda(x, \Gamma) = \int_{x_{\xi(G)} \in \Gamma} e^{-\lambda\xi(G)} \mathbf{P}_x(d\omega) \quad (\lambda \geqslant 0),$$

$$\Pi_G^\lambda f(x) = \mathbf{M}_x e^{-\lambda\xi(G)} f[x_{\xi(G)}] = \int_E \pi_G^\lambda(x, dy) f(y),$$

$$\pi_G(x, \Gamma) = \pi_G^0(x, \Gamma) = \mathbf{P}_x\{x_{\xi(G)} \in \Gamma\},$$

$$\Pi_G f(x) = \Pi_G^0 f(x) = \mathbf{M}_x f[x_{\xi(G)}] = \int_E \pi_G(x, dy) f(y),$$

$$m_G(x) = \mathbf{M}_x \xi(G).$$

Theorem 5.5. Let U, G be admissible sets for the stationary strictly Markov process X, where $U \subseteq G$. Then the following relationships hold:

$$\Pi_G^\lambda f(x) = \Pi_U^\lambda \Pi_G^\lambda f(x) \tag{5.47}$$

(if $e^{-\lambda\xi(G)} f[x_{\xi(G)}]$ is $\mathbf{P}_x$-summable),

$$\pi_G^\lambda(x, \Gamma) = \int_E \pi_U^\lambda(x, dy) \pi_G^\lambda(y, \Gamma), \tag{5.48}$$

$$m_G(x) = m_U(x) + \mathbf{M}_x m_G[x_{\xi(U)}] =$$

$$= m_U(x) + \int_E m_G(y) \pi_U(x, dy) \tag{5.49}$$

(if $m_G(x) < \infty$).

Proof. We put in formula (5.46): $s = 0$, $f(t, x) = e^{-\lambda t} f(x)$, $\xi_t = \xi_t(G)$, $\tau = \xi(U)$. On taking into account the fact that $\xi_\tau = \xi(G)$ by virtue of (3.54), we have

$$\mathbf{M}_x\{e^{-\lambda[\xi(G) - \xi(U)]} f[x_{\xi(G)}] \,|\, \mathcal{M}^0_{\xi(U)}\} = \Pi_G^\lambda f[x_{\xi(U)}] \text{ a.c. } \Omega_{\xi(U)}, \mathbf{P}_x).$$

Since the function $e^{\lambda\xi(U)}$ is $\mathcal{M}^0_{\xi(U)}$-measurable, it now follows that

$$\mathbf{M}_x\{e^{-\lambda\xi(G)} f[x_{\xi(G)}] \,|\, \mathcal{M}^0_{\xi(U)}\} = e^{-\lambda\xi(U)} \Pi_G^\lambda f[x_{\xi(U)}]$$
$$(\text{a.c. } \Omega_{\xi(U)}, \mathbf{P}_x)$$

On taking the mathematical expectation of both sides, we get (5.47). With $f(x) = \chi_\Gamma(x)$, relationship (5.47) becomes (5.48).

Relationship (5.49) follows from the series of equations:

$$\mathbf{M}_x\xi(G) - \mathbf{M}_x\xi(U) = \int_{\Omega_{\xi(U)}} [\xi(G) - \xi(U)]\, \mathbf{P}_x(d\omega) =$$
$$= \int_{\Omega_{\xi(U)}} \theta_{\xi(U)}\xi(G)\, \mathbf{P}_x(d\omega) = \mathbf{M}_x \mathbf{M}_{x_{\xi(U)}} \xi(G).$$

<u>Remark</u>. Let X be a stationary strictly Markov process continuous from the right in the topological measurable space $(E, \mathcal{C}, \mathscr{B})$ and satisfying condition 1.9.B, and let U, G be open measurable sets in $(E, \mathcal{C}, \mathscr{B})$, the closure of U being compact and contained in G. If we replace $\xi_s(G)$ by $\tau_s(G)$ in the definition of functions $\Pi_G^\lambda f(x)$, $\pi_G^\lambda(x, \Gamma)$, and $m_G(x)$, relationships (5.47)-(5.49) remain valid. (This follows from lemmas 3.7 and 3.9.)

5.12. We shall now indicate briefly how our definitions and results are modified if the stationary process is understood as the system $(x_t, \zeta, \mathscr{M}_t, \mathbf{P}_x, \theta_t)$ subject to conditions 2.8.A-2.8.H.

We shall describe the process $X = (x_t, \zeta, \mathscr{M}_t, \mathbf{P}_x, \theta_t)$ as measurable if the mapping of the space $(\Omega_t \times I_t, \mathscr{M}_t \times \mathscr{B}_t)$ into $(E, \mathscr{B})$ defined by the function $x_u(\omega)$ is measurable for any t. We shall describe the non-negative function $\tau(\omega)$ $(\omega \in \Omega)$ as a <u>random variable independent of the future</u> if $\tau(\omega) \leqslant \zeta(\omega)$ and $\{\tau \leqslant t < \zeta\} \in \mathscr{M}_t$ for any t. If $A \subseteq \Omega_\tau = \{\tau < \zeta\}$ and $\{A, \tau \leqslant t < \zeta\} \in \mathscr{M}_t$ for any t, we shall put $A \in \mathscr{M}_\tau$. All the lemmas of article 1 are easily carried over to the present case. In particular, we can assert (see the remark at the end of sec. 5.2) that, for any measurable stationary process, the transition function $P(t, x, \Gamma)$ is always a measurable function of $\{t, x\}$.

The process $X = (x_t, \zeta, \mathscr{M}_t, \mathbf{P}_x, \theta_t)$ will be described as <u>strictly Markov</u> if we have for any random variable τ independent of the future, for any non-negative $\mathscr{M}_\tau$-measurable function $\delta(\omega)$ $(\omega \in \Omega_\tau)$ and for any $\Gamma \in \mathscr{B}$:

$$\mathbf{P}_x\{x_{\tau+\delta} \in \Gamma \,|\, \mathscr{M}_\tau\} = P(\delta, x_\tau, \Gamma) \qquad (\text{a.c. } \Omega_\tau, \mathbf{P}_x). \tag{5.50}$$

It follows from this that, for any $B \in \mathscr{N}$:

$$\mathbf{P}_x\{\theta_\tau B \,|\, \mathscr{M}_\tau\} = \mathbf{P}_{x_\tau}(B) \qquad (\text{a.c. } \Omega_\tau, \mathbf{P}_x) \tag{5.51}$$

and for any $\mathscr{N}$-measurable function ξ such that $\theta_\tau\xi$ is $\mathbf{P}_x$-summable:

$$\mathbf{M}_x\{\theta_\tau\xi \,|\, \mathscr{M}_\tau\} = \mathbf{M}_{x_\tau}\xi \qquad (\text{a.c. } \Omega_\tau, \mathbf{P}_x). \tag{5.52}$$

We remark in conclusion that all the expressions deduced in article 3 for stationary strictly Markov processes hold for all stationary Markov processes if the random variable τ takes only a finite or denumerable set of values.

4. Weakening the Form of the Condition for Processes Continuous from the Right to be Strictly Markov

5.13. Throughout the remainder of Chapter 5 we shall consider Markov processes continuous from the right in the topological measurable space $(E, \mathcal{C}, \mathcal{B})$ and satisfying conditions 1.9.A-1.9.B. We can weaken for these processes the formulation of the strictly Markov property 5.3.B by limiting the classes of random magnitudes τ and η appearing in the statement; also, we can conveniently introduce the random variables $f(x_t)$ instead of the events $\{x_t \in \Gamma\}$. We agree to write C for the class of all bounded continuous measurable functions $f(x)$ in the space $(E, \mathcal{C}, \mathcal{B})$.

Lemma 5.9. The Markov process continuous from the right $X=(x_t, \zeta, \mathcal{M}_t^s, \mathbf{P}_{s,x})$ is measurable.

To prove this, we simply apply lemma 1.10 to the interval $\Delta=[s, t]$, the measurable space $(\Omega_t, \mathcal{M}_t^s)$, the topological measurable space $(E, \mathcal{C}, \mathcal{B})$ and the mapping $x_u(\omega)$.

Theorem 5.6. Let $X=(x_t, \zeta, \mathcal{M}_t^s, \mathbf{P}_{s,x})$ be a Markov process continuous from the right satisfying condition 5.3.A and the following condition:

5.13.A. Whatever the $x \in E$, $0 \leqslant s \leqslant t$, $f \in C$, the equation holds for any random variable $\tau \leqslant t$ independent of the future and s-past:

$$\mathbf{M}_{s,x}\{f(x_t) \mid \mathcal{M}_\tau^s\} = \mathbf{M}_{\tau, x_\tau} f(x_t) \quad (\text{a.c.}\, \Omega_\tau, \mathbf{P}_{s,x}). \tag{5.53}$$

Then X is a strictly Markov process.

Proof. The process is measurable by lemma 5.9. Let $f \in C$, let τ be any random variable independent of the future and s-past and η an $\mathcal{M}_\tau^s$-measurable function satisfying the inequality $\eta \geqslant \tau$. Let the points t_k^n define a canonical sequence of subdivisions $\{\Delta_k^n\}$ of the interval $[s, \infty)$. We put

$$\tau_i^n(\omega) = \begin{cases} \tau(\omega), & \text{if } \tau(\omega) \leqslant t_i^n, \\ t_i^n, & \text{if } \tau(\omega) > t_i^n. \end{cases}$$

In view of condition 5.13.A, we have for any $i \leqslant k$:

$$\mathbf{M}_{s,x}\left\{f\left(x_{t_k^n}\right) \Big\| \mathscr{M}^s_{\tau_i^n}\right\} = F\left[\tau_i^n,\ x_{\tau_i^n},\ t_k^n\right] \text{ (a.c. } \Omega_{\tau_i^n}, \mathbf{P}_{s,x}). \qquad (5.54)$$

where

$$F(u, y, v) = \mathbf{M}_{u,y} f(x_v). \qquad (5.55)$$

Let $A \in \mathscr{M}^s_\tau$. Then the ω-set

$$A^n_{ik} = \{A,\ \tau \in \Delta^n_i,\ \eta \in \Delta^n_k\}$$

belongs to $\mathscr{M}^s_{\tau_i^n}$. For obviously, $A^n_{ik} \in \mathscr{M}^s_\tau$ and $\tau^n_i(\omega) = \tau(\omega)$ for $\omega \in A^n_{ik}$. Therefore

$$\{A^n_{ik},\ \tau^n_i \leqslant t < \zeta\} = \{A^n_{ik},\ \tau \leqslant t < \zeta\} \in \mathscr{M}^s_t.$$

Since $A^n_{ik} \in \mathscr{M}^s_{\tau_i^n}$, it follows from (5.54) that

$$\int_{A^n_{ik}} f\left(x_{t_k^n}\right) \mathbf{P}_{s,x}(d\omega) = \int_{A^n_{ik}} F\left(\tau^n_i,\ x_{\tau_i^n},\ t^n_k\right) \mathbf{P}_{s,x}(d\omega). \qquad (5.56)$$

We put $\eta_n(\omega) = t^n_k$ if $\eta(\omega) \in \Delta^n_k$. Obviously, $\eta_n(\omega) = t^n_k$, $\tau(\omega) = \tau^n_i(\omega)$ for $\omega \in A^n_{ik}$. Relationship (5.56) can therefore be rewritten as

$$\int_{A^n_{ik}} f(x_{\eta_n}) \mathbf{P}_{s,x}(d\omega) = \int_{A^n_{ik}} F(\tau,\ x_\tau,\ \eta_n) \mathbf{P}_{s,x}(d\omega).$$

On summing over all pairs of values $i \leqslant k$, we get

$$\int_A f(x_{\eta_n}) \mathbf{P}_{s,x}(d\omega) = \int_A F(\tau,\ x_\tau,\ \eta_n) \mathbf{P}_{s,x}(d\omega). \qquad (5.57)$$

We now observe that, since the process is continuous from the right whilst $f(x)$ is continuous and bounded, the function of (5.55) must be continuous from the right with respect to v.

On the other hand, $\eta_n \downarrow \eta$ as $n \to \infty$ so that

$$f(x_{\eta_n}) \to f(x_\eta).$$

On passing to the limit in (5.57) as $n \to \infty$, we get

$$\int_A f(x_\eta) \mathbf{P}_{s,x}(d\omega) = \int_A F(\tau,\ x_\tau,\ \eta) \mathbf{P}_{s,x}(d\omega). \qquad (5.58)$$

Let $\mathscr{L}$ denote the class of all bounded $\mathscr{B}$-measurable functions and let $f \in \mathscr{H}$ if relationships (5.55) and (5.58) are satisfied for f. It follows from lemma 1.8 that $\mathscr{H} \supseteq \mathscr{L}$. Relationships (5.55) and (5.58) therefore hold for every function $f \in \mathscr{L}$. If we put, in particular, $f = \chi_\Gamma$, we get equation (5.8).

5.14. Theorem 5.7. Let $X = (x_t, \zeta, \mathscr{M}^s, \mathbf{P}_{s,x})$ be a Markov process continuous from the right satisfying condition 5.3.A and the following condition:

5.14.A. Whatever the $x \in E$, $s \geqslant 0$, $h \geqslant 0$, $f \in C$ and the random variable τ independent of the future and s-past, the equation holds:

$$\mathbf{M}_{s,x}\{f(x_{\tau+h}) \mid \mathscr{M}_\tau^s\} = F(\tau, x_\tau, \tau + h) \qquad (\text{a.c.}\, \Omega_\tau, \mathbf{P}_{s,x}), \tag{5.59}$$

where

$$F(u, y, v) = \mathbf{M}_{u,y} f(x_v). \tag{5.60}$$

Then the process X is strictly Markov.

Proof. It is sufficient to show that condition 5.13.A follows from 5.14.A. Let $f \in C$ and let τ be a random variable independent of the future and s-past satisfying the inequality $\tau \leqslant t$. We take the canonical sequence of subdivisions $\{\Delta_k^n\}$ of the interval $[s, t]$ defined by the points

$$t_k^n = s + \frac{k}{n}(t - s) \quad (k = 1, 2, \ldots, n; \qquad n = 1, 2, \ldots).$$

We put

$$h_k^n = t - t_{k-1}^n,$$
$$\beta_n(u) = u + h_k^n, \quad \text{if} \quad u \in \Delta_k^n.$$

By (5.59),

$$\mathbf{M}_{s,x}\left\{f\left(x_{\tau + h_k^n}\right) \Big| \mathscr{M}_\tau^s\right\} = F(\tau, x_\tau, \tau + h_k^n) \quad (\text{a.c.}\, \Omega_\tau, \mathbf{P}_{s,x}). \tag{5.61}$$

Let $A \in \mathscr{M}_\tau^s$. Then $A_k^n = \{A, \tau \in \Delta_k^n\} \in \mathscr{M}_\tau^s$, and by (5.61):

$$\int_{A_k^n} f\left(x_{\tau + h_k^n}\right) \mathbf{P}_{s,x}(d\omega) = \int_{A_k^n} F(\tau, x_\tau, \tau + h_k^n) \mathbf{P}_{s,x}(d\omega). \tag{5.62}$$

But $\beta_n(\tau) = \tau + h_k^n$ for $\omega \in A_k^n$. On substituting this value in

(5.62) and summing over k, we get

$$\int_A f[x_{\beta_n(\tau)}]\, \mathbf{P}_{s,x}(d\omega) = \int_A F[\tau, x_\tau, \beta_n(\tau)]\, \mathbf{P}_{s,x}(d\omega). \qquad (5.63)$$

We now notice that $\beta_n(u) \downarrow t$ as $n \to \infty$. On passing to the limit in (5.63), we get

$$\int_A f(x_t)\, \mathbf{P}_{s,x}(d\omega) = \int_A F(\tau, x_\tau, t)\, \mathbf{P}_{s,x}(d\omega). \qquad (5.64)$$

It follows from property 5.3.A that for any t $F(u, y, t)$ is a measurable function of $\{u, y\}$ so that $F(\tau, x_\tau, t) = \mathbf{M}_{\tau, x_\tau} f(x_t)$ is an $\mathcal{M}^s_\tau$-measurable function of ω. Relationship (5.64) is therefore equivalent to (5.53).

<u>Remark</u>. Let Q be an arbitrary family of monotonic transformations of the interval $[0, \infty)$ into itself, satisfying the following conditions.

5.14.α. $\varphi(t) \geqslant t$ for any $\varphi \in Q, t \geqslant 0$.

5.14.β. The constant K exists, such that, for any $\varphi \in Q$, $s, t, \geqslant 0$,

$$|\varphi(t) - \varphi(s)| < K|t - s|.$$

5.14.γ. For any $0 \leqslant s < t$ there can be found a $\varphi \in Q$ such that $\varphi(s) = t$.

Theorem 5.7 remains completely valid, and no substantial changes are needed in the proof if we replace condition 5.14.α by the following more general condition:

5.14.α'. For every $\varphi \in Q$:

$$\mathbf{M}_{s,x}\{f[x_{\varphi(\tau)}] \,|\, \mathcal{M}^s_\tau\} = F(\tau, x_\tau, \varphi(\tau)) \qquad (\text{a.c.}\, \Omega_\tau, \mathbf{P}_{s,x})$$

(τ, f, F have the same meanings as in the statement of condition 5.14.α).

Condition 5.14.α' reduces to 5.14.α when the family Q consists of the functions $\varphi(t) = t + h$ (h being any non-negative constant).

It may also be noticed that condition 5.14.α' is equivalent to the requirement that condition 5.3.B be satisfied for the random variables $\eta = \varphi(\tau)$ $(\varphi \in Q)$.

5. Strictly Markov Subprocesses

5.15. Is the strictly Markov property preserved when processes are transformed as described in Article 3 of Chapter 2 and in Chapter 3? It is easily verified that, if a strictly Markov process $\tilde{X}$ is subordinate to a measurable Markov process X (see sec. 2.11), X is also strictly Markov. The converse does not hold: a non-strictly Markov process will be constructed in 5.22 by widening the basic σ-algebras of a strictly Markov process. We are still less entitled to expect the strictly Markov property from arbitrary subprocesses of a strictly Markov process. It will be shown, however, that given very broad assumptions, the class of equivalent subprocesses of a strictly Markov process contains a strictly Markov process (this being the canonical subprocess described in sec. 3.3).

The fundamental result of the present article is stated in theorem 5.8. We shall first prove some lemmas.

5.16. Lemma 5.10. If the strictly Markov process X satisfies condition 5.3.A, this condition is satisfied by every subprocess of X subject to requirement 3.5.β.

Proof. Let $\Gamma \in \mathscr{B}$, $0 \leqslant s \leqslant u$; $s \leqslant t$, $x \in E$. We put

$$F(s, x, t) = \begin{cases} \mathbf{M}_{s,x} \alpha_u^t \chi_\Gamma(x_u), & \text{if } t \leqslant u, \\ \mathbf{M}_{u,x} \alpha_u^u \chi_\Gamma(x_u), & \text{if } t > u. \end{cases}$$

Let h be any positive number. We select points $r_0 = 0$, $r_1, \ldots, r_k = u$ such that

$$r_2 - r_1 = r_3 - r_2 = \ldots = r_k - r_{k-1} = h, \quad 0 < r_1 - r_0 \leqslant h.$$

We consider the function $F(s, x, t)$ in the set $I_{r_{i+1}}^{r_i} \times E \times I_{r_{i+2}}^{r_{i+1}}$ *). It is continuous from the right in t (by virtue of 3.5.β) and $\mathscr{B}_{r_{i+1}}^{r_i} \times \mathscr{B}$-measurable with respect to s and x (by lemma 5.3). It is consequently (see lemma 1.10) $\mathscr{B}_{r_{i+1}}^{r_i} \times \mathscr{B} \times \mathscr{B}_{r_{i+2}}^{r_{i+1}}$-measurable on the product set (whose elements are the triples) $\{s, x, t\}$. We conclude from this, on the basis of lemma 1.3, that $F(s, x, s+h)$ is a $\mathscr{B}_{r_{i+1}}^{r_i} \times \mathscr{B}$-measurable function of s and x on the set $I_{r_{i+1}}^{r_i} \times E$ $(i = 0, 1, 2, \ldots, k-2)$.

*) We put $I_t^s = [s, t)$ and write $\mathscr{B}_t^s$ for the σ-algebra in the space I_t^s generated by all the intervals contained in I_t^s.

This function is independent of s on the set $I_{r_k}^{r_{k-1}} \times E$ and is clearly also measurable (see lemma 2.2). Hence $F(s, x, s+h)$ is a $\mathscr{B}_u^0 \times \mathscr{B}$-measurable function throughout the set $I_u^0 \times E$. By lemma 3.1,

$$\tilde{P}(s, x; u, \Gamma) = F(s, x, s) = \lim_{h \downarrow 0} F(s, x, s+h) \quad (s \in I_u^0, x \in E).$$

Hence $\tilde{P}(s, x; u, \Gamma)$ is a $I_u^0 \times \mathscr{B}$-measurable function of s and x, and the subprocess satisfies condition 5.3.A.

Let $\tilde{X}$ be a subprocess of the Markov process X. Let τ be a random variable independent of the future and s-past for process X. We shall show that $\tilde{\tau} = \min(\tau, \tilde{\zeta})$ is a random variable independent of the future and s-past for the subprocess $\tilde{X}$. In fact, by 3.1.C′,

$$\{\tilde{\tau} \leqslant t < \tilde{\zeta}\} = \{\tau \leqslant t < \zeta, t < \tilde{\zeta}\} \in \tilde{\mathscr{M}}_t^s,$$

so that condition 5.1.B is satisfied. Condition 5.1.A is obviously also satisfied. We observe that $A\Omega_{\tilde{\tau}} \in \tilde{\mathscr{M}}_{\tilde{\tau}}^s$ if $A \in \mathscr{M}_\tau^s$. For we have for any $t \geqslant 0$:

$$\{A, \Omega_{\tilde{\tau}}, \tilde{\tau} \leqslant t < \zeta\} = \{A, \tau \leqslant t > \zeta, \tilde{\zeta} > t\} \in \tilde{\mathscr{M}}_t^s.$$

Lemma 5.11. Let $\tilde{X}$ be the canonical subprocess of the Markov process X (see sec. 3.3). Then an arbitrary random variable $\tilde{\tau}$ independent of the future and s-past for the subprocess $\tilde{X}$ is equal to min $(\tau, \tilde{\zeta})$, where τ is a random variable independent of the future and s-past for process X. Any event $\tilde{A} \in \tilde{\mathscr{M}}_{\tilde{\tau}}^s$ may be written in the form $\tilde{A} = A \cap \Omega_{\tilde{\tau}}$, where $A \in \mathscr{M}_\tau^s$.

Proof. Conditions 3.3.A-3.3.E define $\tilde{\Omega}, \tilde{\zeta}, \tilde{x}_t, \tilde{\mathscr{M}}_t^s$ and $\tilde{\mathscr{M}}^s$ for the canonical subprocess. We write C_ω for the aggregate of $\lambda \in [0, \infty)$ such that $(\omega, \lambda) \in \Omega_{\tilde{\tau}}$, and Ω_τ for the set of all $\omega \in \Omega$ for which C_ω is non-empty. We put

$$\tau(\omega) = \begin{cases} \sup\limits_{\lambda \in C_\omega} \tilde{\tau}(\omega, \lambda) \text{ for } \omega \in \Omega_\tau, \\ \max[s, \zeta(\omega)] \text{ for } \omega \in \bar{\Omega}_\tau. \end{cases} \tag{5.65}$$

We have for every $t \geqslant s$:

$$\{\tilde{\tau} \leqslant t < \tilde{\zeta}\} \in \tilde{\mathscr{M}}_t^s$$

so that

$$\{\tilde{\tau} \leqslant t < \tilde{\zeta}\} = B \times (t, \infty], \qquad (5.66)$$

where $B \in \mathcal{M}_t^s$. On comparing this equation with the obvious inclusion

$$\{\tau \leqslant t < \zeta\} \times (t, \infty] \subseteq \{\tilde{\tau} \leqslant t < \tilde{\zeta}\},$$

we get

$$\{\tau \leqslant t < \zeta\} \subseteq B.$$

On the other hand, it is clear from (5.66) that, if $\omega_0 \in B'$, we have $\tilde{\tau}(\omega_0, \lambda) \leqslant t < \tilde{\zeta}(\omega_0, \lambda)$ for all $\lambda > t$. Hence it follows, in view of (5.65) and 3.3.B, that $\tau(\omega_0) \leqslant t < \zeta(\omega_0)$. Thus

$$\{\tau \leqslant t < \zeta\} = B \in \mathcal{M}_t^s. \qquad (5.67)$$

We have from (5.66) and (5.67), for any $t \geqslant s$,

$$\{\tilde{\tau} \leqslant t < \tilde{\zeta}\} = \{\tau \leqslant t < \zeta,\ t < \lambda\} = \{\tau \leqslant t < \tilde{\zeta}\}. \qquad (5.68)$$

It follows from this that

$$\Omega_{\tilde{\tau}} = \{\tilde{\tau} < \tilde{\zeta}\} = \bigcup_{t \geqslant s} \{\tilde{\tau} \leqslant t < \tilde{\zeta}\} = \bigcup_{t \geqslant s} \{\tau \leqslant t < \tilde{\zeta}\} = \{\tau < \tilde{\zeta}\}$$

and

$$\tilde{\tau} = \min(\tau, \tilde{\zeta}).$$

It is evident from (5.65) that τ satisfies condition 5.1.A. In view of (5.67), τ satisfies condition 5.1.B.

The function τ is thus a random variable independent of the future and s-past.

Moreover, if $\tilde{A} \in \tilde{\mathcal{M}}^s_{\tilde{\tau}}$, we have for any $t \geqslant s$:

$$\{\tilde{A}, \tilde{\tau} \leqslant t < \tilde{\zeta}\} \in \tilde{\mathcal{M}}_t^s$$

so that

$$\{\tilde{A}, \tilde{\tau} \leqslant t < \tilde{\zeta}\} = D \times (t, \infty], \qquad (5.69)$$

where $D \in \mathcal{M}_t^s$. From (5.68) and (5.69):

$$\{\widetilde{A},\ \tau \leqslant t < \zeta,\ t < \lambda\} = \{D,\ t < \lambda\}. \tag{5.70}$$

We put $\omega \in A$ if $(\omega, \lambda) \in \widetilde{A}$ for all sufficiently large values of λ. It is clear from (5.70) that, for $\omega_0 \in D, (\omega_0, \lambda) \in \{\widetilde{A},\ \tau \leqslant t < \zeta\}$ for all $\lambda > t$ so that $\omega_0 \in \{A,\ \tau \leqslant t < \zeta\}$. Thus

$$D \subseteq \{A,\ \tau \leqslant t < \zeta\}.$$

On the other hand, if $\omega_0 \in \{A,\ \tau \leqslant t < \zeta\}$, we have $(\omega_0, \lambda) \in \{\widetilde{A},\ \tau \leqslant t < \zeta,\ t < \lambda\} = \{D,\ t < \lambda\}$ for all sufficiently large λ, so that $\omega_0 \in D$. Therefore

$$\{A,\ \tau \leqslant t < \zeta\} = D \in \mathcal{M}_t^s. \tag{5.71}$$

This shows that $A \in \mathcal{M}_\tau^s$. It is clear from (5.69) and (5.71) that

$$\{\widetilde{A},\ \widetilde{\tau} \leqslant t < \widetilde{\zeta}\} = \{A,\ \tau \leqslant t < \widetilde{\zeta}\}$$

so that

$$\widetilde{A} = \bigcup_{t \geqslant s} \{\widetilde{A},\ \widetilde{\tau} \leqslant t < \widetilde{\zeta}\} =$$

$$= \bigcup_{t \geqslant s} \{\widetilde{A},\ \tau \leqslant t < \widetilde{\zeta}\} = \{A,\ \tau < \widetilde{\zeta}\} = A\Omega_{\widetilde{\tau}}.$$

Lemma 5.12. If $\alpha = \{\alpha_t^s\}$ is a multiplicative functional and τ a random variable independent of the future and s-past for the Markov process X, the function α_τ^s is $\overline{\mathcal{M}}_\tau^s$-measurable*). If $\widetilde{X} = (\widetilde{x}_t,\ \widetilde{\zeta},\ \mathcal{M}_t^s,\ \widetilde{\mathbf{P}}_{s,x})$ is the canonical subprocess of X corresponding to the functional α, we have

$$\widetilde{\mathbf{P}}_{s,x}\{\tau < \widetilde{\zeta} \,|\, \mathcal{M}\} = \alpha_\tau^s \qquad (\text{a.c. } \Omega_\tau,\ \mathbf{P}_{s,x}). \tag{5.72}$$

Proof. Let $s \leqslant t$. The function $\alpha_u^s(\omega)\,(u \in I_t^s, \omega \in \Omega_t)$ is continuous from the right in u for any $\omega \in \Omega_t$ and is $\overline{\mathcal{M}}_t^s$-measurable in ω for any $u \in I_t^s$. By lemma 1.10, this function is $\mathcal{B}_t^s \times \overline{\mathcal{M}}_t^s$-measurable on the product-set (u, ω). On the

*) The σ-algebra $\overline{\mathcal{M}}_\tau^s$ is constructed in accordance with the σ-algebra $\mathcal{M}_\tau^s$ just as $\overline{\mathcal{M}}_t^s$ is constructed in accordance with $\mathcal{M}_t^s$ (see sec. 2.2). It is easily seen that $A \in \overline{\mathcal{M}}_\tau^s$ when and only when $\{A, \tau \leqslant t < \zeta\} \in \overline{\mathcal{M}}_t^s$ for any t.

other hand, the restriction of the function $\tau(\omega)$ to the set $\{\tau(\omega) \leqslant t < \zeta(\omega)\}$ defines an $\overline{\mathcal{M}}_t^s$-measurable mapping of this set into the segment I_t^s. The restriction of $\alpha_{\tau(\omega)}^s(\omega)$ to the set $\{\tau(\omega) \leqslant t < \zeta(\omega)\}$ is thus $\overline{\mathcal{M}}_t^s$-measurable, which proves the first assertion of the lemma.

Further, let $A \in \mathcal{M}^s$. We put $B = \{A, \tau < \zeta\}$. Then in the notation of sec. 3.6:

$$B_\omega = \begin{cases} (\tau(\omega), \infty] & \text{for } \omega \in A \cap \Omega_\tau, \\ 0 & \text{for } \omega \overline{\in} A \cap \Omega_\tau. \end{cases}$$

Therefore

$$\alpha_B^s = \alpha_{B_\omega}^s = \alpha_{\tau(\omega)}^s \chi_A \qquad (\omega \in \Omega_\tau)$$

and

$$\mathbf{P}_{s,x}(B) = \mathbf{M}_{s,x} \alpha_B^s = \mathbf{M}_{s,x} \alpha_\tau^s \chi_A,$$

which is equivalent to relationship (5.72).

<u>Lemma 5.13</u>. If $\alpha = \{\alpha_t^s\}$ is a multiplicative functional satisfying the condition

5.16.A. $\lim\limits_{u \downarrow s} \alpha_t^u(\omega) = \alpha_t^s(\omega)$ for all $0 \leqslant s < t < \zeta(\omega)$,

then the function

$$f(u, \omega) = \alpha_t^u(\omega) \qquad (u \in [s, t], \ \omega \in \Omega_t)$$

is $\mathcal{F}^s$-measurable.

Proof. Let the points t_k^n define a canonical sequence of subdivisions $\{\Delta_k^n\}$ of the interval $[s, t]$ (see sec. 1.9). We put

$$\varphi_n(u) = t_k^n, \text{ if } u \in \Delta_k^n.$$

By virtue of condition 5.16.A,

$$\lim_{n \to \infty} \alpha_t^{\varphi_n(u)}(\omega) = \alpha_t^u(\omega) = f(u, \omega).$$

It is readily seen that

$$\alpha_t^{\varphi_n(u)}(\omega) = \sum_k \chi_{\Delta_k^n}(u) \alpha_t^{t_k^n}(\omega).$$

It follows from this, in view of lemma 5.6, that the function $\alpha_t^{\varphi_n(u)}(\omega)$ is $\mathcal{F}^s$-measurable. The limit function $f(u, \omega)$ is therefore also $\mathcal{F}^s$-measurable.

5.17 Theorem 5.8. Let X be a strictly Markov process continuous from the right in the topological measurable space $(E, \mathcal{C}, \mathcal{B})$ and let $\alpha = \{\alpha_t^s\}$ be a multiplicative functional for process X satisfying condition 5.16.A. Then the canonical subprocess $\widetilde{X}$ of X corresponding to functional α is a strictly Markov process.

Proof. Since the subprocess $\widetilde{X}$ is continuous from the right and, in view of lemma 5.10, satisfies condition 5.3.A, we only need to show that it also satisfies condition 5.13.A (see theorem 5.6). Let $f \in C$, $\widetilde{\tau} \leqslant t$ be a random variable independent of the future and s-past for $\widetilde{X}_t$, and $\widetilde{A} \in \mathcal{M}^s_{\widetilde{\tau}}$. We consider the corresponding random variable τ and event A constructed in lemma 5.11. It is clear from (5.65) that $\tau \leqslant t$. We have by lemma 3.1:

$$\widetilde{\mathbf{M}}_{s, x} \chi_{\widetilde{A}} f(\widetilde{x}_t) = \widetilde{\mathbf{M}}_{s, x} \chi_A f(x_t) \chi_{\widetilde{\zeta} > t} = \mathbf{M}_{s, x} \chi_A f(x_t) \alpha_t^s. \tag{5.73}$$

By 3.5.B, $\alpha_t^s = \alpha_\tau^s \alpha_t^\tau$, and we obtain on taking lemma 5.12 and 1.6.H into account:

$$\mathbf{M}_{s, x} \chi_A f(x_t) \alpha_t^s = \mathbf{M}_{s, x} \{\chi_A \alpha_\tau^s \mathbf{M}_{s, x} [f(x_t) \alpha_t^\tau \,|\, \mathcal{M}_\tau^s]\}. \tag{5.74}$$

It follows from lemma 5.13 that the function $f(x_t)\alpha_t^u$ ($u \in [s, t]$, $\omega \in \Omega_t$) is $\mathcal{F}^s$-measurable, and by theorem 5.2:

$$\mathbf{M}_{s, x} \{f(x_t) \alpha_t^\tau \,|\, \mathcal{M}_\tau^s\} = F(\tau, x_\tau) \quad (\text{a.e. } \Omega_\tau, \mathbf{P}_{s, x}), \tag{5.75}$$

where

$$F(u, y) = \mathbf{M}_{u, y} f(x_t) \alpha_t^u = \widetilde{\mathbf{M}}_{u, y} f(\widetilde{x}_t). \tag{5.76}$$

We conclude from (5.73), (5.74) and (5.75) that

$$\widetilde{\mathbf{M}}_{s, x} \chi_{\widetilde{A}} f(\widetilde{x}_t) = \mathbf{M}_{s, x} \chi_A \alpha_\tau^s F(\tau, x_\tau). \tag{5.77}$$

On the other hand, in view of lemma 5.12:

$$\begin{aligned} \widetilde{\mathbf{M}}_{s, x} \chi_{\widetilde{A}} F(\widetilde{\tau}, \widetilde{x}_{\widetilde{\tau}}) &= \widetilde{\mathbf{M}}_{s, x} \chi_A F(\tau, x_\tau) \chi_{\widetilde{\zeta} > \tau} = \\ &= \widetilde{\mathbf{M}}_{s, x} \{\chi_A F(\tau, x_\tau) \widetilde{\mathbf{P}}_{s, x} [\widetilde{\zeta} > \tau \,|\, \mathcal{M}^s]\} = \mathbf{M}_{s, x} \chi_A F(\tau, x_\tau) \alpha_\tau^s. \end{aligned} \tag{5.78}$$

Comparison of (5.76), (5.77) and (5.78) gives us (5.53).

The reader will easily prove the following variant of theorem 5.8 for stationary processes in the sense of sec. 2.8.

Theorem 5.8′. Let $X=(x_t, \zeta, \mathcal{M}_t, \mathbf{P}_x, \theta_t)$ be a stationary strictly Markov process (see sec. 5.12) and let α_t be a multiplicative functional of X for which condition 3.22.β is satisfied in the following strengthened form: $\alpha_s\theta_s\alpha_t = \alpha_{s+t}$ for all $s, t \geqslant 0$ and $\omega \in \Omega_{s+t}$. Then the canonical subprocess corresponding to α_t is strictly Markov.

6. Criteria for a Process to be Strictly Markov

5.18. Theorem 5.9. A sufficient condition for a Markov process continuous from the right to be strictly Markov is that its transition function satisfy the following condition:

5.18.A. Whatever the $f \in C$, the function

$$F(u, y) = \int_E P(u, y; t, dz) f(z) \tag{5.79}$$

possesses the following continuity property:

$$\lim_{\substack{y \to x \\ u \downarrow s}} F(u, y) = F(s, x). \tag{5.80}$$

Proof. We write $\mathcal{L}$ for the class of all $\mathcal{B}$-measurable bounded functions in E and $\mathcal{H}$ for the class of all functions $f \in \mathcal{L}$ such that

$$F(u, y) = \int_E P(u, y; t, dz) f(z)$$

is a $\mathcal{B}_{[0,\infty)} \times \mathcal{B}$-measurable function of u and y. We note first of all that, by lemma 1.7, $F(u, y)$ is a $\mathcal{B}$-measurable function of y for any $f \in \mathcal{L}$ and any $u \geqslant 0$. If $f \in C$, condition (5.80) is satisfied in addition, and by lemma 1.10, $F(u, y)$ is a $\mathcal{B}_{[0,\infty)} \times \mathcal{B}$-measurable function of u and y. Thus $\mathcal{H} \supseteq C$. But $\mathcal{H}$ is obviously an $\mathcal{L}$-system, and by lemma 1.8, $\mathcal{H} \supseteq \mathcal{L}$. We see on putting $f = \chi_\Gamma (\Gamma \in \mathcal{B})$ that the function $P(u, y;, t, \Gamma)$ is measurable with respect to u, y. Condition 5.3.A is thus fulfilled. In view of theorem 5.6, it remains to verify that 5.13.A is also fulfilled. Let $f \in C$, and let τ be a random variable independent of the future and s-past such that $\tau \leqslant t$. Let the points t_k^n define a canonical sequence of subdivisions $\{\Delta_k^n\}$ of the segment $[s, t]$. We put

$$\tau_n(\omega) = t_k^n, \quad \text{if} \quad \tau(\omega) \in \Delta_k^n.$$

The random variable τ_n takes only a finite number of values. Expression (5.31) is thus applicable to it, in accordance with the remark at the end of sec. 5.8, and

$$\mathbf{M}_{s,x}\{f(x_t) \mid \mathcal{M}_{\tau_n}^s\} = F(\tau_n, x_{\tau_n}) \quad (\text{a.c. } \Omega_{\tau_n}, \mathbf{P}_{s,x}),$$

where $F(u, y)$ is given by (5.79). The restrictions of τ_n to Ω_τ are clearly $\mathcal{M}_\tau^s$-measurable, and by lemma 5.1, $\{A, \tau_n < \zeta\} \in \mathcal{M}_{\tau_n}^s$ for any $A \in \mathcal{M}_\tau^s$. We therefore have for all n and any $A \in \mathcal{M}_\tau^s$:

$$\mathbf{M}_{s,x}\chi_A\chi_{\tau_n<\zeta}f(x_t) = \mathbf{M}_{s,x}\chi_A\chi_{\tau_n<\zeta}F(\tau_n, x_{\tau_n}). \tag{5.81}$$

We observe that $\tau_n \downarrow \tau$ for $n \to \infty$. Obviously, $\chi_{\tau_n<\zeta} \to \chi_{\tau<\zeta} = \chi_{\Omega_\tau}$. Using condition 5.18.A and the fact that the process is continuous from the right, we have $F(\tau_n, x_{\tau_n}) \to F(\tau, x_\tau)$. On passing to the limit in (5.81), we get

$$\mathbf{M}_{s,x}\chi_A f(x_t) = \mathbf{M}_{s,x}\chi_A F(\tau, x_\tau).$$

Since the function $F(\tau, x_\tau)$ is $\mathcal{M}_\tau^s$-measurable, this relationship is equivalent to (5.53).

<u>Remark</u>. As is clear from the proof, the assertion of theorem 5.9 still holds if the transition function satisfies condition 5.3.A and the following weakened variant of condition 5.18.A.

5.18.A′. For every $f \in C$ and $\omega \in \Omega$, the function

$$\Phi(\omega, u) = F(u, x_u) = \int_E P(u, x_u; t, dz) f(z)$$

is continuous from the right in regard to u.

5.19. In the stationary case it is advantageous to modify slightly the continuity condition 5.18.A and to replace it by the following:

5.19.A. Whatever the $f \in C$, the function

$$F(y) = \int_E P(h, y, dz) f(z) \tag{5.82}$$

is continuous with respect to y for any h.

Condition 5.19.A was first discussed by Feller, and we shall refer to stationary Markov processes satisfying this condition as <u>Feller processes</u>. In general, if condition 5.19.A is fulfilled for a stationary transition function, we shall speak of this as a <u>Feller transition function</u>.

<u>Theorem 5.10</u>. A Feller process continuous from the right is strictly Markov.

Proof. In view of lemma 5.9 and the remark on lemma 5.3, condition 5.3.A is satisfied. By theorem 5.7, we only need to prove that condition 5.14.A is also fulfilled. The proof follows the same lines as that of theorem 5.9.

Let $f \in C$ and let τ be a random variable independent of the future and s-past. Let the points t_k^n specify a canonical sequence of subdivisions $\{\Delta_k^n\}$ of the interval $[s, \infty)$.

We put $\tau_n(\omega) = t_k^n$ if $\tau(\omega) = \Delta_k^n$. In accordance with the remark at the end of sec. 5.12, we are justified in applying expression (5.39) to τ_n, so that

$$\mathbf{M}_{s,x}\{f(x_{\tau_n+h}) \,|\, \mathcal{M}_{\tau_n}^s\} = \mathbf{M}_{x_{\tau_n}} f(x_h) = F(x_{\tau_n}) \quad (\text{a.c.}\,\Omega_{\tau_n}, \mathbf{P}_{s,x}),$$

where $F(y)$ is given by formula (5.82). If $A \in \mathcal{M}_\tau^s$, then $A \in \mathcal{M}_{\tau_n}^s$, and

$$\int_A f(x_{\tau_n+h}) \mathbf{P}_{s,x}(d\omega) = \int_A F(x_{\tau_n}) \mathbf{P}_{s,x}(d\omega). \tag{5.83}$$

As $n \to \infty$ $\tau_n \downarrow \tau$. On passing to the limit in (5.83) and using condition 5.19.A and the fact that the process is continuous from the right, we get

$$\int_A f(x_{\tau+h}) \mathbf{P}_{s,x}(d\omega) = \int_A F(x_\tau) \mathbf{P}_{s,x}(d\omega), \tag{5.84}$$

whence (5.59) follows.

<u>Remark</u>. The above proof of theorem 5.10 remains unchanged if we replace the Feller condition 5.19.A by the weaker condition:

5.19.A′. For any $f \in C$, $\omega \in \Omega$, the function

$$F(x_t) = \int_E P(h, x_t, dz) f(z)$$

is continuous from the right with respect to t.

5.20. We shall say in future that the Markov process $X = (x_t, \zeta, \mathcal{M}_t^s, \mathbf{P}_{s,x})$ is <u>continuous from the right at the point</u> x if $\{x_t = x\} \subseteq \{\lim_{u \downarrow t} x_u = x\}$ for any $t \geqslant 0$. We shall say that the stationary Markov process X is <u>of Feller's type at the point</u> x if, for any $f \in C$, the function $F(y)$ given by (5.82) is continuous at the point x. A word for word repetition of the arguments used in proving theorem 5.10 leads to the following variant of this theorem.

<u>Theorem 5.10'</u>. If a stationary Markov process is continuous from the right and of Feller's type at every point x of some subset G of the phase space E, condition 5.3.B for being strictly Markov is satisfied for any random variable τ such that $x_\tau \in G$ for all $\omega \in \Omega_\tau$. Theorem 5.9 can be similarly localized.

5.21. The conditions imposed on the process in theorems 5.9 and 5.10 remain valid for any widening of the basic σ-algebras. Hence if these conditions are satisfied, not only the process X, but any process obtained from X by a widening of the basic σ-algebras, is strictly Markov, and the same can be said of any process subordinate to X (see sec. 5.15).

We put $A \in \mathcal{M}_{t+0}^s$ if $A \subseteq \Omega_t$ and $\{A, \zeta > v\} \in \mathcal{M}_v^s$ for any $v > t$. Obviously, $\mathcal{M}_{t+0}^s$ is a σ-algebra in the space Ω_t.

<u>Theorem 5.11</u>. Let $X = (x_t, \zeta, \mathcal{M}_t^s, \mathbf{P}_{s,x})$ be a Markov process continuous from the right in the topological measurable space $(E, \mathcal{C}, \mathcal{B})$. Let X satisfy condition 5.18.A and be a stationary Feller process. Then $X' = (x_t, \zeta, \mathcal{M}_{t+0}^s, \mathbf{P}_{s,x})$ is also a Markov, and indeed a strictly Markov, process.

Proof. In view of the remark just made, we only need to prove that X' is a Markov process. The system X' clearly satisfies conditions 2.1.A-2.15.E, so that it only remains to prove condition 2.1.F'.

We start by supposing that X satisfies condition 5.18.A. Let $f \in C$, $0 \leqslant s \leqslant t < u$ and let $v \in (t, u]$. By (2.5),

$$\mathbf{M}_{s,x}\{f(x_u) \mid \mathcal{M}_v^s\} = F(v, x_v) \quad (\text{a.c. } \Omega_v, \mathbf{P}_{s,x}).$$

where

$$F(v, y) = \mathbf{M}_{v, y} f(x_u).$$

If $A \in \mathcal{M}_{t+0}^s$, then $\{A, \zeta > v\} \in \mathcal{M}_v^s$, and

$$\int_{\{A, \zeta > v\}} f(x_u) \mathbf{P}_{s, x}(d\omega) = \int_{\{A, \zeta > v\}} F(v, x_v) \mathbf{P}_{s, x}(d\omega).$$

On passing to the limit here as $v \downarrow t$ and taking into account 5.18.A and the facts that x_u is continuous from the right and f continuous, we find for any $t < u$:

$$\int_A f(x_u) \mathbf{P}_{s, x}(d\omega) = \int_A F(t, x_t) \mathbf{P}_{s, x}(d\omega). \tag{5.85}$$

On letting $u \downarrow t$, we find that this equation is also valid for $u = t$. Moreover, it may easily be deduced, on the basis of lemma 1.8, from the fact that (5.85) is satisfied for all $f \in C$, that these relationships are satisfied for every $\mathscr{B}$-measurable bounded function f (cf. the end of the proof of theorem 5.6).

Putting $f = \chi_\Gamma$, we get

$$\mathbf{P}_{s, x}(A, x_u \in \Gamma) = \int_A P(t, x_t; u, \Gamma) \mathbf{P}_{s, x}(d\omega),$$

which is what we wanted to prove.

Now let X be stationary and satisfy condition 5.19.A. Let $f \in C, 0 \leqslant s \leqslant t < u$. In accordance with (2.5), 2.6.F and 2.5.B, we have for every $\varepsilon > 0$:

$$\mathbf{M}_{s, x}\{f(x_{u+\varepsilon}) \,|\, \mathcal{M}_{t+\varepsilon}\} = F(x_{t+\varepsilon}) \qquad (\text{a.c.}\, \Omega_{u+\varepsilon}, \mathbf{P}_{s, x}),$$

where

$$F(y) = \mathbf{M}_{t+\varepsilon, y} f(x_{u+\varepsilon}) = \mathbf{M}_y f(x_{u-t}).$$

Let $A \in \mathcal{M}_{t+0}^s$. Then $\{A, \zeta > t+\varepsilon\} \in \mathcal{M}_{t+\varepsilon}^s$ and

$$\int_A f(x_{u+\varepsilon}) \mathbf{P}_{s, x}(d\omega) = \int_A F(x_{t+\varepsilon}) \mathbf{P}_{s, x}(d\omega). \tag{5.86}$$

On letting $\varepsilon \downarrow 0$, we have

$$\int_A f(x_u) \mathbf{P}_{s, x}(d\omega) = \int_A F(x_t) \mathbf{P}_{s, x}(d\omega). \tag{5.87}$$

Just as in the first half of the proof, we can show that (5.87) is satisfied for all $\mathscr{B}$-measurable bounded functions f. We have with $f=\chi_\Gamma$:

$$\mathbf{P}_{s,x}(A, x_u\in\Gamma)=\int_A P(t, x_t; u, \Gamma)\mathbf{P}_{s,x}(d\omega),$$

and we have now established that condition 2.1.F′ is satisfied.

<u>Corollary</u>. (The law of zero or unity.) If the assumptions of theorem 5.11 hold, $\mathbf{P}_{s,x}(A)$ is either zero or unity for any $A\in\mathscr{M}^s_{s+0}\cap\overline{\mathscr{N}^s}$.

For, in accordance with theorem 2.1′ and 2.1.E, we have

$$\mathbf{P}_{s,x}(A\,|\,\mathscr{M}^s_{s+0})=\mathbf{P}_{s,x_s}(A)=\mathbf{P}_{s,x}(A) \qquad (\text{a.c.}\,\Omega_s,\ \mathbf{P}_{s,x}).$$

On the other hand, in view of 1.6.A,

$$\mathbf{P}_{s,x}(A\,|\,\mathscr{M}^s_{s+0})=\chi_A(\omega) \qquad (\text{a.c.}\,\Omega_s,\ \mathbf{P}_{s,x}).$$

Our assertion follows on combining these two equations.

<u>Remark</u>. The necessary and sufficient condition for a function $\tau(\omega)$ satisfying condition 5.1.A to be a random variable independent of the future and s-past for the process $X'=(x_t, \zeta, \mathscr{M}^s_{t+0}, \mathbf{P}_{s,x})$ is that $\{\omega\ \tau(\omega)<t<\zeta(\omega)\}\in\mathscr{M}^s_t$ for any $t>s$.

It is also necessary and sufficient for this that, for any $\varepsilon>0$ the function $\tau+\varepsilon$ be a random variable independent of the future and s-past for the process $X=(x_t, \zeta_t, \mathscr{M}^s_t, \mathbf{P}_{s,x})$. (We leave the proof of these statements to the reader). It seems natural to describe such functions τ as random variables independent of the distant future and s-past (for process X). If X satisfies the conditions of theorem 5.11, we can apply to variables independent of the distant future and s-past all the formulae proved in Chapter 5 for random variables independent of the future and s-past.

5.22. In order to apply the criteria obtained in the present article for a process to be strictly Markov, we need suitable tests for continuity of the process from the right. These tests will be deduced in the next chapter. By using these in conjunction with theorems 5.9-5.10, we shall construct in Chapter 6 a number of important examples of strictly Markov processes (see articles 4 and 7).

One instructive example may be considered here, however*).

We suppose that a particle can either move uniformly to the right on the half-line $[0, \infty)$ or remain at rest at the point 0. Further, if it is situated at the point 0 at some instant t, it remains there until the instant $t+h$ with a probability of e^{-h} independently of the time which it has already spent at 0. We have here a non-cut-off stationary Markov process $X=(x_t, \mathcal{N}_t^s, \mathbf{P}_{s,x})$ with the transition function

$$P(s, x; t, \Gamma)=P(t-s, x, \Gamma)= \\ =\begin{cases}\chi_\Gamma(t-s+x), & \text{if } x>0, \\ \int\limits_0^t e^{-(t-s-u)}\chi_\Gamma(u)\,du+\chi_\Gamma(0)\,e^{-(t-s)}, & \text{if } x=0.\end{cases} \tag{5.88}$$

It is clear from this that, for $x>0$,

$$F(x)=\int\limits_0^\infty P(t, x, dy)\, f(y)=f(x+t) \tag{5.89}$$

so that the process is of Feller's type for all points $x>0$.

Let τ be any random variable independent of the future and s-past. As in the proof of theorem 5.10, we construct random variables $\tau_n \downarrow \tau$ satisfying condition (5.83). To prove that X is a strictly Markov process, we only need to show that (5.83) becomes (5.84) as $n\to\infty$ (assuming that $f\in C$). By (5.89), we can do this simply by proving that

$$\mathbf{P}_{s,x}\{x_\tau=0,\ x_{\tau_n}>0 \text{ for } n=1, 2, \ldots\}=0. \tag{5.90}$$

We put

$$D=\{\omega: x_\tau=0\}.$$

Suppose that $\omega_1, \omega_2\in D$ and $\tau(\omega_1)=t<\tau(\omega_2)$. We have

$$C=\{D, \tau=t\}=\{\tau=t,\ x_t=0\}\in\mathcal{N}_t^s$$

and by lemma 1.5,

$$\chi_C(\omega)=f(x_{t_1}, \ldots, x_{t_n}, \ldots). \tag{5.91}$$

*)We leave it to the reader to give a strict statement of this example, i.e. to construct the space Ω, the function $x_t(\omega)$ and the measures $\mathbf{P}_{s,x}$.

where $f(x_1, \ldots, x_n, \ldots)$ is a $\mathscr{B}^\infty$-measurable function in the space E^∞ and $t_1, \ldots, t_n \ldots \in [s, t]$. Evidently $x_u(\omega_1) = x_u(\omega_2) = 0$ for all $u \in [s, t]$, and $\chi_C(\omega_1) = \chi_C(\omega_2)$ by virtue of (5.91). But this contradicts the fact that $\omega_1 \in C$, $\omega_2 \bar{\in} C$. The contradiction proves that the function $\tau(\omega)$ takes only one value in set D. If this value is equal to t, we have

$$D = \{x_\tau = 0\} = \{x_t = 0, \ \tau = t\}.$$

Hence, for any $\delta > 0$,

$$\{x_\tau = 0, \ x_{\tau_n} > 0 \ \text{for} \ n = 1, 2, \ldots\} \subseteq \{x_t = 0, \ x_{t+\delta} > 0\}.$$

But in view of (2.15) and (5.88),

$$\begin{aligned} \mathbf{P}_{s,x}\{x_t = 0, \ x_{t+\delta} > 0\} &= P(s, x; t, 0, t+\delta, (0, \infty)) = \\ = P(s, x; t, 0) P(t, 0; t+\delta, (0, \infty)) &\leqslant P(t, 0; t+\delta, (0, \infty)) = \quad (5.92) \\ &= \int_0^\delta e^{-(\delta-u)} du \to 0 \end{aligned}$$

as $\delta \downarrow 0$, which proves (5.90).

We notice that $X' = (x_t, \mathscr{N}^s_{t+0}, \mathbf{P}_{s,x})$ is also a Markov process. For we can deduce relationship (5.85) precisely as in the proof of theorem 5.11. In view of (5.88) and (5.92), (5.85) becomes (5.86) as $\varepsilon \downarrow 0$. At the same time, X' is not a strictly Markov process. For the instant $\tau = \xi_0$ of first departure of the trajectory from the set $\{0\}$ is a random variable independent of the future for X'. We put $A = \Omega_\tau$, $\eta = \tau + 1$, $\Gamma = \{1\}$. The left-hand side of equation (5.8) is now equal to unity, whilst the right-hand side is equal to zero.

CHAPTER 6

CONDITIONS FOR BOUNDEDNESS AND CONTINUITY OF A MARKOV PROCESS

1. Introduction

6.1. The present chapter aims at deducing the conditions in which the processes corresponding to a given transition function include at least one of the trajectories which possess definite properties of boundedness or continuity.

The fundamental results will be obtained on the assumption that the initial transition function $P(s, x; t, \Gamma)$ is normal, i.e. satisfies the condition $P(s, x; s, E) = 1$ for all $s \geqslant 0$, $x \in E$. The processes corresponding to a normal transition function will be described as normal.

We shall take as our basis the following general theorem.

Theorem 6.1. Let $X = (x_t, \zeta, \mathcal{M}_t^s, \mathbf{P}_{s,x})$ be a normal Markov process in the measurable space $(E, \mathcal{B})$ and let $\mathcal{L} \subseteq \Omega_E$ *). We assume the existence of the non-negative function

$$q(\lambda; t_1, x_1, \ldots, t_n, x_n, \ldots)$$
$$(\lambda \in [0, +\infty]; t_1, \ldots, t_n, \ldots \in [0, +\infty); \quad x_1, \ldots, x_n, \ldots \in E),$$

which is a $\mathcal{B}_\infty^0 \times \mathcal{B}^\infty$-measurable function of $\lambda, x_1, \ldots, x_n, \ldots$ and which satisfies the following conditions for any denumerable everywhere dense subset $\{t_1, t_2, \ldots, t_n, \ldots\}$ of interval $[s, \infty)$:

6.1.A. $$q(\lambda; t_1, x_1, \ldots, t_n, x_n, \ldots) = q(\lambda; t_1, x_1', \ldots, t_n, x_n', \ldots),$$

if $x_i = x_i'$ for all indices i for which $t_i < \lambda$.

*) The space Ω_E is defined in sec. 2.11.

6.1.B. If $\lambda \in [s, +\infty]$ and $q(\lambda, t_1, x_1, \ldots, t_n, x_n, \ldots) = 0$, a definite function φ can be found in the interval $[0, \lambda)$ and belonging to $\mathscr{L}$ such that $\varphi(t_i) = x_i$ for all $t_i \in [0, \lambda)$ *).

6.1.C. $\mathbf{M}_{s,x} q(\zeta; t_1, x_{t_1}, \ldots, t_n, x_{t_n}, \ldots) = 0$ **).

Then there exists a Markov process equivalent to X such that all its trajectories belong to $\mathscr{L}$.

Proof. We write $\widetilde{E}$ for the set got from E by adding the extra point a, and $\widetilde{\mathscr{B}}$ for the σ-algebra composed from all sets of the form $B, B \cup \{a\}$ $(B \in \mathscr{B})$.

We put

$$\widetilde{\zeta}(\omega) = +\infty,$$

$$\widetilde{x}_t(\omega) = \begin{cases} x_t(\omega), & \text{if } t < \zeta(\omega), \\ a, & \text{if } t \geqslant \zeta(\omega), \end{cases}$$

$$\widetilde{\mathbf{P}}_{s,x}(A) = \mathbf{P}_{s,x}(A) \qquad (x \in E,\ A \in \mathscr{N}^s).$$

We use $\widetilde{\mathscr{N}}_t^s$ to denote the σ-algebra in the space Ω generated by the sets $\{\omega : \widetilde{x}_u(\omega) \in \Gamma\}$ $(u \in [s, t], \Gamma \in \widetilde{\mathscr{B}})$. It still remains to define $\widetilde{\mathbf{P}}_{s,a}(A)$. It is easily shown that every set $A \in \mathscr{N}^s$ either does not intersect with $\overline{\Omega}^s = \{\zeta \leqslant s\}$, or else contains $\overline{\Omega}^s$. We put

$$\widetilde{\mathbf{P}}_{s,a}(A) = \begin{cases} 0, & \text{if } A \cap \overline{\Omega}^s = \emptyset, \\ 1, & \text{if } A \supseteq \overline{\Omega}^s \end{cases} \text{***}).$$

---

*) To fulfil condition 6.1.B with $\lambda = s$ we simply require $\mathscr{L}$ to contain any function with $[0, s]$ as its domain of definition.

**) The function $q(\zeta; t_1, x_{t_1}, \ldots, t_n, x_{t_n} \ldots)$ can be regarded as uniquely defined for all $\omega \in \Omega$. For, although the values of the x_{t_n} are not defined for $t_n \geqslant \zeta$, the expression $q(\zeta; t_1, x_{t_1}, \ldots, t_n, x_{t_n}, \ldots)$ does not depend on x_{t_n} for $t_n \geqslant \zeta$ by virtue of 6.1.A. We can therefore assign arbitrary values to x_{t_n} for $t_n \geqslant \zeta$ without their choice being reflected in the value of $q(\zeta; t_1, x_{t_1}, \ldots, t_n, x_{t_n}, \ldots)$.

***) This definition is incorrect if $\overline{\Omega}^s = \emptyset$, since for every $A \in \mathscr{N}^s$ we now have simultaneously $A \supseteq \overline{\Omega}^s$ and $A \cap \overline{\Omega}^s = \emptyset$. But we can suppose without loss of generality that $\zeta(\omega_0) = 0$ for some $\omega_0 \in \Omega$, so that $\overline{\Omega}^s$ is non-empty for any s. For, if there is no element ω_0 with this property in the space Ω, we can enlarge Ω with the single point ω_0 and put $\zeta(\omega_0) = 0$, $\mathbf{P}_{s,x}(\{\omega_0\}) = 0$ $(s \geqslant 0, x \in E)$, whilst retaining the previous values for the symbols $x_t(\omega)$ and $\mathscr{M}_t^s$. It is clear that, with this, a Markov process is obtained which is equivalent to the initial process X and which satisfies, along with X, the conditions of theorem 6.1.

We have for any $0 \leqslant s \leqslant t$, $x \in \widetilde{E}$, $\Gamma \in \widetilde{\mathscr{B}}$:

$$\widetilde{P}(s, x; t, \Gamma) = \widetilde{\mathbf{P}}_{s,x}\{\widetilde{x}_t \in \Gamma\} = \\ = \begin{cases} P(s, x; t, \Gamma \cap E) + \chi_\Gamma(a)[1 - P(s, x; t, E)], & \text{if} \quad x \neq a, \\ \chi_\Gamma(a), & \text{if} \quad x = a. \end{cases}$$

The system $(\widetilde{x}_t, \widetilde{\zeta}, \widetilde{\mathscr{N}}^s_t, \widetilde{\mathbf{P}}_{s,x})$ may readily be seen to satisfy all the conditions 2.1.A-2.1.E and 2.1.F', so that it defines a (non-cut-off) Markov process $\widetilde{X}$. (When proving property 2.1.F' we have to use the relationship $\widetilde{\mathscr{N}}^s_t[\Omega_t] = \mathscr{N}^s_t$.)

We define the mapping $\alpha: \Omega_E \to \widetilde{E}^{[0,\infty)}$ as follows: if $\varphi(t)$ $(t \in [0, \lambda))$ is a function of Ω_E, we put

$$\alpha\varphi(t) = \begin{cases} \varphi(t) & \text{for} \quad t \in [0, \lambda), \\ a & \text{for} \quad t \in [\lambda, +\infty). \end{cases}$$

We bring in the following notation:

$$\widetilde{\mathscr{L}} = \alpha(\mathscr{L}); \qquad \hat{\lambda} = \inf\{t_n : x_n = a\};$$

$$\Phi_i(t_1, x_1, \ldots, t_n, x_n, \ldots) = \begin{cases} 1, & \text{if} \quad t_i \geqslant \hat{\lambda} \text{ and } x_i \in E, \\ 0 & \text{in remaining cases;} \end{cases}$$

$$\widetilde{q}(t_1, x_1, \ldots, t_n, x_n, \ldots) = q(\hat{\lambda}; t_1, x_1, \ldots, t_n, x_n, \ldots) + \\ + \sum_{i=1}^{\infty} \Phi_i(t_1, x_1, \ldots, t_n, x_n, \ldots).$$

The function $\widetilde{q}$ is clearly measurable with respect to $x_1, \ldots x_n, \ldots$ Let $\{t_1, \ldots, t_n, \ldots\} \subseteq [s, +\infty)$. If $\widetilde{q}(t_1, x_1, \ldots, t_n, x_n, \ldots) = 0$ then $q(\hat{\lambda}; t_1, x_1, \ldots, t_n, x_n, \ldots) = 0$ and $x_i = a$ for all $t_i \geqslant \hat{\lambda}$. In view of 6.1.B, there is a function φ of $\mathscr{L}$, defined in the interval $[0, \hat{\lambda})$ and such that $\varphi(t_i) = x_i$ for all $t_i < \hat{\lambda}$. The function $\widetilde{\varphi} = \alpha\varphi \in \widetilde{\mathscr{L}}$ evidently satisfies $\widetilde{\varphi}(t_i) = x_i$ for all i. Condition 2.13.A is thus fulfilled for the process $\widetilde{X}$ and the space $\widetilde{\mathscr{L}}$. Moreover, for all $\omega \in \Omega$,

$$\hat{\lambda}(t_1, \widetilde{x}_{t_1}, \ldots, t_n, \widetilde{x}_{t_n}, \ldots) = \zeta,$$
$$\Phi_i(t_1, \widetilde{x}_{t_1}, \ldots, t_n, \widetilde{x}_{t_n}, \ldots) = 0.$$

Therefore

$$\widetilde{q}(t_1, \widetilde{x}_{t_1}, \ldots, t_n, \widetilde{x}_{t_n}, \ldots) = q(\zeta, t_1, \widetilde{x}_{t_1}, \ldots, t_n, \widetilde{x}_{t_n}, \ldots)$$

and by 6.1.C, condition 2.13.B is fulfilled. By theorem 2.8, a process X' equivalent to $\tilde{X}$ exists such that all its trajectories are contained in $\tilde{\mathscr{L}}$. The set E is obviously inaccessible for this process. In view of the normality of process X, the set E satisfies condition 3.8.B with respect to the process X'. By theorem 3.4, we can form a part X'' of process X on the set E. It can readily be seen that X'' has the same transition function as the initial process X, and all the trajectories of X'' belong to $\mathscr{L}$. The theorem is proved.

Remark. Let all the trajectories of process X belong to the set $\mathscr{L}_0 \subseteq \Omega_E$ and let the function $q(\lambda; t_1, x_1, \ldots, t_n, x_n, \ldots)$ satisfy conditions 6.1.A, 6.1.C and the following condition:

6.1.B′. If $\psi(t)\,(t \in [0, \lambda))$ is an element of space $\mathscr{L}_0$ and

$$q(\lambda;\ t_1, \psi(t_1), \ \ldots,\ t_n, \psi(t_n), \ldots) = 0,$$

there exists a function $\varphi \in \mathscr{L} \cap \mathscr{L}_0$ defined in the interval $[0, \lambda)$ such that $\varphi(t_i) = \psi(t_i)$ for all $t_i \in [0, \lambda)$.

Then there exists a Markov process equivalent to X such that all its trajectories belong to $\mathscr{L} \cap \mathscr{L}_0$.

Proof. We take the process $\tilde{X}$, the mapping $\alpha : \Omega_E \to \tilde{E}^{[0,\infty)}$ and the function $\tilde{q}$ constructed in the proof of theorem 6.1. Conditions 2.13.A′ and 2.13.B are fulfilled for the process $\tilde{X}$, the function $\tilde{q}$ and the spaces $\tilde{\mathscr{L}} = \alpha(\mathscr{L})$, $\tilde{\mathscr{L}}_0 = \alpha(\mathscr{L}_0)$. Hence, in accordance with the remark on theorem 2.8, a Markov process X' equivalent to $\tilde{X}$ exists, all the trajectories of which belong to $\tilde{\mathscr{L}} \cap \tilde{\mathscr{L}}_0$. The part X'' of this process on the (inadmissible) set E is equivalent to X, and all the trajectories of X'' belong to $\mathscr{L} \cap \mathscr{L}_0$.

2. Conditions for Boundedness

6.2. Let $\mathscr{F}$ be an arbitrary system of subsets of the set E. We shall describe the function $\varphi(t)\,(t \in [0, \lambda))$ with values from E as $\mathscr{F}$-bounded if, for any $T < \lambda$, there exists $\Gamma \in \mathscr{F}$ such that $\varphi(t) \in \Gamma$ for all $t \in [0, T]$. The Markov process $X = (x_t, \zeta, \mathscr{M}_t^s, P_{s,x})$ in the measurable space $(E, \mathscr{B})$ will be described as $\mathscr{F}$-bounded if all its trajectories are $\mathscr{F}$-bounded.

We shall assume that the system $\mathscr{F}$ is subject to the following condition:

6.2.A. A sequence $\Gamma_1 \subseteq \Gamma_2 \subseteq \ldots \subseteq \Gamma_n \subseteq \ldots$ exists, consisting of elements of the σ-algebra $\mathscr{B}$ and equivalent to $\mathscr{F}$ (see sec. 3.11)*).

It may be remarked that a Markov process X is $\mathscr{F}$-bounded when and only when $\zeta = \xi(\mathscr{F})$ (the function $\xi(\mathscr{F})$ is defined by formula (3.58)). If the system $\mathscr{F}$ satisfies condition 6.2.A, this equation can be written as follows:

$$\zeta = \lim_{n \to \infty} \xi(\Gamma_n) \tag{6.1}$$

(the function $\xi(\Gamma)$ is given by (3.49)).

Let $\Gamma \in \mathscr{B}$ and let Λ be a subset of the interval $[0, \infty)$.

We put

$$\Psi_\Lambda(\Gamma) = \bigcap_{t \in \Lambda} \{x_t \in \Gamma\}; \quad \Phi_\Lambda(\Gamma) = \bigcup_{t \in \Lambda} \{x_t \in E \setminus \Gamma\}. \tag{6.2}$$

The sets $\Psi_\Lambda(\Gamma)$ and $\Phi_\Lambda(\Gamma)$ are obviously disjoint. For a non-cut-off process their sum forms the space Ω. This is not generally true for a cut-off process.

Lemma 6.1. If X is a Markov process in the space $(E, \mathscr{B})$, $\Gamma \in \mathscr{B}$, and Λ is a finite or denumerable subset of the interval $[s, b]$, containing the right-hand end b, we have for any $G \in \mathscr{B}$:

$$\mathbf{P}_{s, x}[\Psi_\Lambda(\Gamma)] \geqslant P(s, x; b, G) - \sup_{y \bar{\in} \Gamma,\, u \in \Lambda} P(u, y; b, G). \tag{6.3}$$

Proof. We suppose first that the set Λ is finite, and put

$$\tau = \begin{cases} \inf\{t : t \in \Lambda,\ x_t \bar{\in} \Gamma\}, & \text{if} \quad \omega \bar{\in} \Psi_\Lambda(\Gamma), \\ b, & \text{if} \quad \omega \in \Psi_\Lambda(\Gamma). \end{cases}$$

Obviously, τ is a random variable independent of the future and s-past $(\Omega_\tau = \Phi_\Lambda(\Gamma) \cup \Psi_\Lambda(\Gamma))$. Lemma 5.4 justifies us in applying expression (5.8), so that

*)This condition is satisfied by all normal systems and in particular, by systems 3.12.1-3.12.4 (see sec. 3.12).

$$P(s, x; b, G) = \mathbf{P}_{s,x}\{\Omega_\tau, x_b \in G\} = \int_{\Omega_\tau} P(\tau, x_\tau; b, G)\, \mathbf{P}_{s,x}(d\omega) =$$
$$= \int_{\Psi_\Lambda(\Gamma)} P(\tau, x_\tau; b, G)\, \mathbf{P}_{s,x}(d\omega) + \int_{\Phi_\Lambda(\Gamma)} P(\tau, x_\tau; b, G)\, \mathbf{P}_{s,x}(d\omega). \quad (6.4)$$

Expression (6.3) follows from (6.4).

If Λ is denumerable, we consider the sequence of finite sets $\Lambda_n \uparrow \Lambda$ (we choose the Λ_n here so that they contain b). We can apply (6.3) to each set Λ_n, and on passing to the limit we find that (6.3) is applicable to the set Λ.

6.3. Theorem 6.2. Let the system $\mathcal{F} \subseteq \mathcal{B}$ in the space $(E, \mathcal{B})$ satisfy condition 6.2.A and let the normal Markov process $X = (x_t, \zeta, \mathcal{M}_t^s, \mathbf{P}_{s,x})$ satisfy the following condition:

6.3.A. There exists $\delta > 0$ and a sequence of sets $E_n \in \mathcal{B}$ such that $E_n \uparrow E$ and for any n:

$$\inf_{\Gamma \in \mathcal{F}} \sup_{\substack{y \overline{\in} \Gamma \\ 0 < v - u < \delta}} P(u, y; v, E_n) = 0. \quad (6.5)$$

Then an $\mathcal{F}$-bounded Markov process exists, equivalent to X.

Proof. We write $\mathcal{L}$ for the set of all $\mathcal{F}$-bounded functions. By theorem 6.1, the problem amounts to constructing a function $q(\lambda; t_1, x_1, \ldots, t_n, x_n, \ldots)$ satisfying conditions 6.1.A-6.1.C.

We take the sequence of Γ_n which is equivalent to $\mathcal{F}$ and for which condition 6.2.A is satisfied, and introduce the following notation:

$$h(x) = \sup\{k : x \overline{\in} \Gamma_k\} \text{ *)},$$

$$h_\varepsilon(\lambda; t_1, x_1, \ldots, t_n, x_n, \ldots) = \begin{cases} \sup\{h(x_k) : t_k < \lambda - \varepsilon\} & \text{for } \lambda < \infty, \\ \sup\left\{h(x_k) : t_k < \frac{1}{\varepsilon}\right\} & \text{for } \lambda = +\infty. \end{cases}$$

We put $q(\lambda; t_1, x_1, \ldots, t_n, x_n, \ldots) = 0$ if $h_\varepsilon(\lambda; t_1, x_1, \ldots, t_n, x_n, \ldots) < \infty$ for all ε. If the opposite is the case we put $q(\lambda; t_1, x_1, \ldots, t_n, x_n) = 1$. This function is clearly measurable with respect to $\lambda, x_1, \ldots, x_n, \ldots$ and satisfies condition 6.1.A.

*) We put $h(x) = 0$ if $x \in \Gamma_k$ for all k.

Let $\Lambda = \{t_1, \ldots, t_n, \ldots\}$ be any sequence of numbers and $x_1, \ldots, x_n, \ldots$ any sequence of points of E. We consider the function $\varphi(t)$ $(t \in [0, \lambda))$ given by

$$\varphi(t) = \begin{cases} x_i, & \text{if } t = t_i,\ t < \lambda, \\ y_0, & \text{if } t \bar{\in} \Lambda,\ t < \lambda, \end{cases} \tag{6.6}$$

where y_0 is an arbitrary fixed point of Γ_1. It may easily be seen that $\varphi \in \mathscr{L}$ if $q(\lambda; t_1, x_1, \ldots, t_n, x_n, \ldots) = 0$. Condition 6.1.B is thus fulfilled.

We now show that condition 6.1.C is satisfied. Let $\Lambda = \{t_1, \ldots, t_n, \ldots\}$ be an everywhere dense subset of the interval $[s, \infty)$. We put for brevity $q^* = q(\zeta; t_1, x_{t_1}, \ldots, t_n, x_{t_n}, \ldots)$, and define h_ε^* similarly. Let ε be any positive number. We take a sequence tending to $+\infty$: $u_1 < u_2 < \ldots < u_k < \ldots \in \Lambda$, such that each of the numbers $u_1 - s,\ u_2 - u_1, \ldots, u_{k+1} - u_k, \ldots$ is less than $\varepsilon/2$. We put

$$\begin{aligned} &\Delta_1 = [s, u_1],\ \Delta_2 = [u_1, u_2], \ldots, \Delta_k = [u_{k-1}, u_k], \ldots \\ &\Lambda_k = \Lambda\Delta_k, \\ &\Psi_k = \Psi_{\Lambda_k}(E) = \{\zeta > u_k\},\ \Psi_k^{(m)} = \Psi_{\Lambda_k}(\Gamma_m). \end{aligned}$$

It will be observed that

$$\{h_\varepsilon^* = \infty\} \subseteq \bigcup_{k=0}^{\infty} \bigcap_{m=1}^{\infty} \{\Psi_k \setminus \Psi_k^{(m)}\}. \tag{6.7}$$

In view of lemma 6.1, we have for each E_n:

$$\mathbf{P}_{s,x}(\Psi_k^{(m)}) \geqslant P(s, x; u_k, E_n) - \sup_{\bar{y \in} \Gamma_m,\ u \in \Lambda_k} P(u, y; u_k, E_n).$$

If $\frac{\varepsilon}{2} < \delta$, it follows from (6.5) that

$$\lim_{m \to \infty} \sup_{\bar{y \in} \Gamma_m,\ u \in \Lambda_k} P(u, y; u_k, E_n) = 0.$$

Hence for any n,

$$\lim_{m \to \infty} \mathbf{P}_{s,x}\{\Psi_k^{(m)}\} \geqslant P(s, x; u_k, E_n)$$

and therefore

$$\begin{aligned} \lim_{m \to \infty} \mathbf{P}_{s,x}\{\Psi_k \setminus \Psi_k^{m}\} &= \mathbf{P}_{s,x}\{\Psi_k\} - \lim_{m \to \infty} \mathbf{P}_{s,x}\{\Psi_k^{(m)}\} \leqslant \\ &\leqslant P(s, x; u_k, E) - P(\bar{s}, x; u_k, E) = 0. \end{aligned} \tag{6.8}$$

It follows from (6.7) and (6.8) that

$$\mathbf{P}_{s,x}\{h_s^* = \infty\} = 0,$$

provided that $\frac{\varepsilon}{2} < \delta$. It remains to notice that

$$\{q^* > 0\} \subseteq \bigcup_{n=1}^{\infty} \left\{h_{\frac{1}{n}}^* = \infty\right\}$$

so that

$$\mathbf{P}_{s,x}\{q^* > 0\} \leqslant \lim_{n \to \infty} \mathbf{P}_{s,x}\{h_{\frac{1}{n}}^* = \infty\} = 0.$$

3. Conditions for Continuity from the Right and Absence of Discontinuities of the Second Kind

6.4. Let $X = (x_t, \zeta, \mathscr{M}_t^s, \mathbf{P}_{s,x})$ be a Markov process in the topological measurable space $(E, \mathcal{C}, \mathscr{B})$ and let $\eta(\omega)$ be any function subject to the inequality $\eta \leqslant \zeta$. We shall say that <u>the process X has no discontinuities of the second kind up to the instant</u> η if the limits $x_{t+0}(\omega) = \lim_{u \downarrow t} x_u(\omega)$ and $x_{t-0}(\omega) = \lim_{u \uparrow t} x_u(\omega)$. exist for any $\omega \in \Omega$, $t \in [0, \eta(\omega))$. To say that "<u>the process X has no discontinuities of the second kind</u>" is the same as saying that "X has no discontinuities of the second kind up to the instant ζ". Let Γ be any subset of E and $\mathscr{F}$ any system of subsets of E. We define $\xi(\Gamma)$ by expression (3.49) and $\xi(\mathscr{F})$ by (3.58). If the process X has no discontinuities of the second kind up to the instant $\xi(\Gamma)(\xi(\mathscr{F}))$, we say that it <u>has no discontinuities of the second kind up to departure from</u> Γ (from $\mathscr{F}$). Analogous meanings attach to the statements: "process X is continuous from the right up to the instant η", "process X is continuous up to the instant η", "process X is continuous from the right up to departure from Γ ", and so forth.

6.5. <u>Lemma 6.2</u>. If the Markov process X is continuous from the right in the topological measurable space $(E, \mathcal{C}, \mathscr{B})$, we have for any $U \in \mathcal{C}\mathscr{B}$ and any $x \in U$, $t \geqslant 0$:

$$\lim_{h \downarrow 0} P(t, x; t+h, \overline{U}) = 0. \tag{6.9}$$

Proof. If $h_n \downarrow 0$, we have

$$\bigcap_{m=1}^{\infty} \bigcup_{n=m}^{\infty} \{x_t = x,\ x_{t+h_n} \in \overline{U}\} = \emptyset.$$

Consequently, as $m \to \infty$,

$$\mathbf{P}_{t,x}\left\{\bigcup_{n=m}^{\infty} [x_{t+h_n} \in \overline{U}]\right\} \to 0.$$

But

$$\mathbf{P}_{t,x}\{x_{t+h_m} \in \overline{U}\} \leqslant \mathbf{P}_{t,x}\left\{\bigcup_{n=m}^{\infty} x_{t+h_n} \in \overline{U}\right\}.$$

Therefore $\mathbf{P}_{t,x}\{x_{t+h_m} \in \overline{U}\} = P(t, x; t+h_m, \overline{U})$ also tends to zero, which proves the lemma.

6.6. We shall now suppose that the process is given in the metric measurable space $(E, \rho, \mathscr{B})$, the distance $\rho(x, y)$ being $\mathscr{B} \times \mathscr{B}$-measurable*). It follows from this condition (see lemma 1.4) that $\rho(x, y)$ is a $\mathscr{B}$-measurable function of y for any fixed x. The σ-algebra $\mathscr{B}$ therefore contains the ε-neighbourhood $U_\varepsilon(x)$ of any point x.

We put

$$\alpha_\Gamma^\varepsilon(\delta) = \sup_{\substack{0 \leqslant s \leqslant t \leqslant s+\delta \\ x \in \Gamma}} P(s, x; t, \overline{U_\varepsilon(x)}) \tag{6.10}$$

(here $\Gamma \subseteq E$, $\varepsilon, \delta > 0$).

We bring in the following condition.

The $M(\Gamma)$ condition. For any $\varepsilon > 0$,

$$\lim_{\delta \downarrow 0} \alpha_\Gamma^\varepsilon(\delta) = 0. \tag{6.11}$$

Our main purpose is to prove the following theorem.

<u>Theorem 6.3</u>. Let $(E, \rho, \mathscr{B})$ be a complete metric measurable

---

*)In accordance with sec. 18, $\rho(x, y)$ is always a continuous function of the pair (x, y). Hence $\rho(x, y)$ is $\mathscr{B} \times \mathscr{B}$-measurable if $\mathscr{B}$ contains all open sets of the space (E, ρ) (see sec. 1.9).

space, the function $\rho(x, y)$ being $\mathscr{B}\times\mathscr{B}$-measurable. Let $\mathscr{T}$ be a system of subsets of E satisfying condition 6.2.A. If a normal Markov process in the space $(E, \rho, \mathscr{B})$ is subject to the $M(\Gamma)$ condition for every set $\Gamma\in\mathscr{T}$, an equivalent of this process exists which is continuous from the right and has no discontinuities of the second kind up to departure from $\mathscr{T}$.

6.7. We shall first of all prove a few lemmas.

Lemma 6.3. Let $X=(x_t, \zeta, \mathscr{M}_t^s, \mathbf{P}_{s,x})$ be a Markov process in the metric measurable space $(E, \rho, \mathscr{B})$. Let $\rho(x, y)$ be a $\mathscr{B}\times\mathscr{B}$-measurable function. Let $\Gamma\in\mathscr{B}$. Then for any $\varepsilon>0$, $0\leqslant s\leqslant t\leqslant u$:

$$\mathbf{P}_{s,x}\{x_t\in\Gamma,\ \rho(x_t, x_u)\geqslant\varepsilon\}\leqslant\alpha_\Gamma^\varepsilon(u-t). \tag{6.12}$$

Furthermore, if Λ is any given finite or denumerable subset of the interval $[a, b]$ $(s\leqslant a\leqslant b)$ and

$$D=D_\Gamma^\varepsilon(\Lambda)=\bigcup_{t,u\in\Lambda}\{x_a\in\Gamma,\ x_t\in\Gamma,\ x_u\in\Gamma,\ \rho(x_t, x_u)\geqslant 4\varepsilon\}, \tag{6.13}$$

we have

$$\mathbf{P}_{s,x}(D)\leqslant 2\alpha_\Gamma^\varepsilon(b-a). \tag{6.14}$$

Proof. By (2.9),

$$\mathbf{P}_{s,x}\{x_t\in\Gamma, \rho(x_t, x_u)\geqslant\varepsilon\}=\int_{x_t\in\Gamma}\mathbf{P}_{t,x_t}\{\rho(x_t, x_u)\geqslant\varepsilon\}\,\mathbf{P}_{s,x}(d\omega)=$$
$$=\int_{x_t\in\Gamma}P(t, x_t; u, \overline{U_\varepsilon(x_t)}]\,\mathbf{P}_{s,x}(d\omega)\leqslant\alpha_\Gamma^\varepsilon(u-t),$$

and expression (6.12) is proved.

We turn to the proof of (6.14). First, let the set Λ be finite and consist of the points $t_1<t_2<\ldots<t_n$. We write τ for the least among the numbers $t\in\Lambda$, satisfying the conditions $x_t\in\Gamma$, $\rho(x_a, x_t)\geqslant 2\varepsilon$ (if there are no such numbers, we put $\tau=\max(s, \zeta)$). We put

$$B=\{x_a\in\Gamma,\ \rho(x_a, x_b)\geqslant\varepsilon\},\quad C=\{\rho(x_\tau, x_b)\geqslant\varepsilon\}.$$

Clearly, $D\subseteq B\cup C$, so that

$$\mathbf{P}_{s,x}(D)\leqslant\mathbf{P}_{s,x}(B)+\mathbf{P}_{s,x}(C). \tag{6.15}$$

The random variable τ is independent of the future and s-past.

We apply the corollary of theorem 5.1 to the quantities $\tau(\omega)$, $\eta_1(\omega)=\tau(\omega)$, $\eta_2(\omega)=b\ (\omega\in\Omega_\tau)$ and to the function

$$f(y_1, y_2)=\begin{cases} 1, & \text{if } \rho(y_1, y_2)\geqslant\varepsilon, \\ 0, & \text{if } \rho(y_1, y_2)<\varepsilon \end{cases}$$

(in accordance with the remark at the end of sec. 5.9, this is justifiable because τ, η_1 and η_2 take only a finite number of values in Ω_τ). We have

$$\mathbf{P}_{s,x}(C\,|\,\mathcal{M}_\tau^s)=\mathbf{M}_{s,x}\{f(x_{\eta_1}, x_{\eta_2})\,|\,\mathcal{M}_\tau^s\}=F(\tau, x_\tau;\ \eta_1, \eta_2)= \\ =F(\tau, x_\tau;\ \tau, b) \qquad (\text{a.c.}\,\Omega_\tau, \mathbf{P}_{s,x}),$$

where

$$F(u, y;\ v_1, v_2)=\mathbf{M}_{u,y}f(x_{v_1}, x_{v_2})=\mathbf{P}_{u,y}\{\rho(x_{v_1}, x_{v_2})\geqslant\varepsilon\},$$

so that

$$F(u, y;\ u, b)=P(u, y;\ b, \overline{U_\varepsilon(y)}).$$

Obviously, $F(u, y;\ u, b)\leqslant\alpha_\Gamma^\varepsilon(b-a)$ for any $u\in[a, b]$, $y\in\Gamma$.

Consequently

$$\mathbf{P}_{s,x}(C\,|\,\mathcal{M}_\tau^s)\leqslant\alpha_\Gamma^\varepsilon(b-a) \qquad (\text{a.c.}\,\Omega_\tau, \mathbf{P}_{s,x})$$

and

$$\mathbf{P}_{s,x}(C)\leqslant\alpha_\Gamma^\varepsilon(b-a).$$

Moreover, in view of (6.12), $\mathbf{P}_{s,x}(B)\leqslant\alpha_\Gamma^\varepsilon(b-a)$. On substituting these inequalities in (6.15), we get (6.14).

If Λ is denumerable, we can choose a sequence of finite sets $\Lambda_n\uparrow\Lambda$. Then $D_\Gamma^\varepsilon(\Lambda_n)\uparrow D_\Gamma^\varepsilon(\Lambda)$, and we get inequality (6.14) for the set Λ by a passage to the limit.

Lemma 6.4. Let X be a Markov process in the metric measurable space $(E, \rho, \mathscr{B})$ with a $\mathscr{B}\times\mathscr{B}$-measurable function $\rho(x, y)$. Let $\Gamma\in\mathscr{B}$, and let Λ be a finite or denumerable subset of the segment $[a, b]\subseteq[s, \infty)$. We put

$$A_k = A_k^\varepsilon(\Lambda, \Gamma) = \{\text{there exist } s_1 < s_2 < \dots < s_{2k-1} < \\ < s_{2k} \text{ of } \Lambda \text{ such that } x_{s_{2i-1}} \in \Gamma,\ x_{s_{2i}} \in \Gamma,\ \rho(x_{s_{2i-1}}, x_{s_{2i}}) \geqslant \\ \geqslant 4\varepsilon \text{ for } i = 1, 2, \dots, k\}. \tag{6.16}$$

Then

$$\mathbf{P}_{s,x}(A_k) \leqslant [2\alpha_\Gamma^\varepsilon(b-a)]^k. \tag{6.17}$$

Proof. We suppose first that the set Λ is finite and consists of the points $t_1 < t_2 < \dots < t_n$. We take the random variable τ_k , equal to max (s, ζ) outside A_k and given in A_k by the equation

$$\tau_k(\omega) = \inf\{t_m : \omega \in A_k^\varepsilon[t_1, \dots, t_{m-1}]\}.$$

We put

$$\eta_i = \max(t_i, \tau_k) \qquad (i = 0, 1, \dots, n).$$

Obviously,

$$A_{k+1} = \bigcup_{i,j=1}^{n} \{x_{\eta_1} \in \Gamma,\ x_{\eta_i} \in \Gamma,\ x_{\eta_j} \in \Gamma, \rho(x_{\eta_i}, x_{\eta_j}) \geqslant 4\varepsilon\}.$$

The characteristic function of A_{k+1} is therefore equal to $f(x_{\eta_1}, \dots, x_{\eta_n})$, where

$$f(y_1, \dots, y_n) = \begin{cases} 1, & \text{if } y_1 \in \Gamma \text{ and there exist } y_i, y_j \in \Gamma, \\ & \text{for which } \rho(y_i, y_j) \geqslant 4\varepsilon, \\ 0 & \text{otherwise.} \end{cases}$$

The quantities τ_k are independent of the future and s-past, whilst the $\eta_1, \dots, \eta_n$ are $\mathcal{M}_{\tau_k}^s$-measurable. We have by the corollary of theorem 5.1.:

$$\mathbf{P}_{s,x}(A_{k+1} \,|\, \mathcal{M}_{\tau_k}^s) = F(\tau_k, x_{\tau_k}; \eta_1, \dots, \eta_n) \quad (\text{a.c. } \Omega_{\tau_k}, \mathbf{P}_{s,x}), \tag{6.18}$$

where

$$F(u, y; v_1, \dots, v_n) = \mathbf{M}_{u,y} f(x_{v_1}, \dots, x_{v_n}) = \\ = \mathbf{P}_{u,y}[D_\Gamma^\varepsilon(v_1, \dots, v_n)].$$

We conclude from lemma 6.3 that

$$F(u, y; v_1, \dots, v_n) \leqslant 2\alpha_\Gamma^\varepsilon(v_n - v_1) \leqslant 2\alpha_\Gamma^\varepsilon(b-a). \tag{6.19}$$

From (6.18) and (6.19):

$$\begin{aligned} \mathbf{P}_{s,x}(A_{k+1}) &= \mathbf{P}_{s,x}(A_k A_{k+1}) = \\ &= \int\limits_{A_k} \mathbf{P}_{s,x}\left(A_{k+1} \,\middle|\, \mathcal{M}^s_{\tau_k}\right) \mathbf{P}_{s,x}(d\omega) \leqslant 2\alpha^\varepsilon_\Gamma (b-a)\, \mathbf{P}_{s,x}(A_k). \end{aligned} \tag{6.20}$$

Expression (6.17) follows readily from (6.20).

If Λ is a denumerable set, we choose a sequence of finite sets $\Lambda_n \uparrow \Lambda$ and observe that $A^\varepsilon_k(\Lambda_n, \Gamma) \uparrow A^\varepsilon_k(\Lambda, \Gamma)$. A passage to the limit shows that (6.17) likewise holds in this case.

Lemma 6.5. Let the Markov process $X = (x_t, \zeta, \mathcal{M}^s_t, \mathbf{P}_{s,x})$ in the space $(E, \mathcal{C}, \mathcal{B})$ satisfy the $M(\Gamma)$ condition $(\Gamma \in \mathcal{B})$. If $x_t \in \Gamma$ for all $t \in [0, \eta)$ and process X has no discontinuities of the second kind up to the instant η, a Markov process $\widetilde{X}$ equivalent to X exists which has no discontinuities of the second kind and which is continuous from the right up to the instant η.

Proof. We put

$$y_t = \begin{cases} x_{t+0} & \text{when } t < \eta, \\ x_t & \text{when } \eta \leqslant t < \zeta. \end{cases}$$

We have for any $s \leqslant t$:

$$\{y_t \neq x_t\} = \{\eta > t,\ x_t \neq x_{t+0}\} \subseteq \{x_t \in \Gamma,\ x_t \neq x_{t+0}\}. \tag{6.21}$$

We notice that, if $\varepsilon > 0,\ s \leqslant t < u$, then by theorem 2.1 and 2.1.D,

$$\begin{aligned} \mathbf{P}_{s,x}\{x_t \in \Gamma,\ \rho(x_t, x_u) \geqslant \varepsilon\} &= \int\limits_{x_t \in \Gamma} \mathbf{P}_{t,x_t}\{\rho(x_t, x_u) \geqslant \varepsilon\}\, \mathbf{P}_{s,x}(d\omega) = \\ &= \int\limits_{x_t \in \Gamma} P(t, x_t;\ u, \overline{U_\varepsilon(x_t)})\, \mathbf{P}_{s,x}(d\omega), \end{aligned}$$

and in view of the $M(\Gamma)$ condition:

$$\lim_{u \downarrow t} \mathbf{P}_{s,x}\{x_t \in \Gamma,\ \rho(x_t, x_u) \geqslant \varepsilon\} = 0.$$

But $\rho(x_t, x_u) \to \rho(x_t, x_{t+0})$ as $u \downarrow t$, so that

$$\{\rho(x_t, x_{t+0}) > \varepsilon\} \subseteq \bigcup_{n=1}^{\infty} \bigcap_{k=n}^{\infty} \left\{\rho\left(x_t, x_{t+\frac{1}{k}}\right) \geqslant \varepsilon\right\}.$$

Hence

$$\mathbf{P}_{s,x}\{x_t \in \Gamma,\ \rho(x_t, x_{t+0}) > \varepsilon\} \leqslant$$
$$\leqslant \lim_{n\to\infty} \mathbf{P}_{s,x}\left\{x_t \in \Gamma,\ \bigcap_{k=n}^{\infty}\left[\rho\left(x_t, x_{t+\frac{1}{k}}\right) \geqslant \varepsilon\right]\right\} \leqslant$$
$$\leqslant \overline{\lim_{n\to\infty}}\, \mathbf{P}_{s,x}\left\{x_t \in \Gamma,\ \rho\left(x_t, x_{t+\frac{1}{n}}\right) \geqslant \varepsilon\right\} = 0.$$

Since this is true for any $\varepsilon > 0$, we have

$$\mathbf{P}_{s,x}\{x_t \in \Gamma,\ x_t \neq x_{t+0}\} = 0$$

and in view of (6.21), $\mathbf{P}_{s,x}\{y_t \neq x_t\} = 0$. An obvious consequence of this relationship is that $\widetilde{X} = (y_t, \zeta, \overline{\mathcal{N}}_t^s, \mathbf{P}_{s,x})$ (the σ-algebras $\overline{\mathcal{N}}_t^s$ are defined in sec. 2.2) is a Markov process equivalent to process X. Evidently, $\widetilde{X}$ has no discontinuities of the second kind and is continuous from the right up to the instant η.

6.8. Proof of theorem 6.3. In view of lemma 6.5, we simply need to construct a process $\widetilde{X}$ equivalent to X and having no discontinuities of the second kind up to departure from $\mathcal{F}$. We make use of theorem 6.1 for this construction.

Let $\varphi(t)$ be a function in the interval $[0, \lambda)$ with values from E. We put

$$\left.\begin{aligned} \xi(\Gamma, \varphi) &= \inf\{t : \varphi(t) \bar{\in} \Gamma\} \\ \xi(\mathcal{F}, \varphi) &= \sup_{\Gamma\in\mathcal{F}} \xi(\Gamma, \varphi) \end{aligned}\right\} \tag{6.22}$$

(if $\varphi(t) \in \Gamma$ for all $t \in [0, \lambda)$, we put $\xi(\Gamma, \varphi) = \lambda$). We shall consider φ belonging to the system $\mathcal{L}$ if the limits $\varphi(t+0)$ and $\varphi(t-0)$ exist for each $t \in [0, \xi(\mathcal{F}, \varphi))$.

Let $\varepsilon > 0,\ \Lambda = \{t_1, \ldots, t_n, \ldots\} \subseteq [0, \infty),\ x_1, \ldots x_n, \ldots \in E$, and let Δ be some interval. We put

$$\xi_\Lambda^\lambda(\Gamma) = \begin{cases} \inf\{t_n : t_n < \lambda,\ x_n \bar{\in} \Gamma\}, & \text{if } t_n < \lambda,\ x_n \bar{\in} \Gamma \text{ for some } n, \\ \lambda & \text{in the remaining cases,} \end{cases} \tag{6.23}$$

$$\xi = \xi_\Lambda^\lambda(\mathcal{F}) = \sup_{\Gamma\in F} \xi_\Lambda^\lambda(\Gamma), \tag{6.24}$$

$$h_\varepsilon(x, y)=\begin{cases}1, & \text{if } x\in\Gamma \text{ and } \rho(x, y)\geqslant 4\varepsilon,\\ 0 & \text{otherwise},\end{cases}$$

and we define $h_{\varepsilon,\Delta}(\lambda;\ t_1, x_1, \ldots, t_n, x_n, \ldots)$ as the upper bound of the values of the sum

$$h_\varepsilon(x_{i_1}, x_{i_2})+h_\varepsilon(x_{i_3}, x_{i_4})+\cdots+h_\varepsilon(x_{i_{2n-1}}, x_{i_{2n}}),$$

when n runs through all natural numbers, the indices $i_1, \ldots, i_{2n}$ being only subject to the condition that $t_{i_1}<t_{i_2}<\cdots<t_{i_{2n}}\in\Delta\cap[0, \xi)$ *). We put $q(\lambda; t_1, x_1, \ldots, t_n, x_n, \ldots)=0$ if $h_{\varepsilon,\Delta}(\lambda; t_1, x_1, \ldots, t_n, x_n, \ldots)<\infty$ for any $\varepsilon>0$ and any finite interval Δ. Otherwise, we put $q(\lambda;\ t_1, x_1, \ldots, t_n, x_n, \ldots)=1$. We note that the function q is measurable with respect to $\lambda, x_1, \ldots, x_n, \ldots$ This follows from the fact that $h_{\varepsilon,\Delta}$ depends monotonically on ε and Δ, and we can therefore consider only ε and Δ running through certain denumerable sequences when defining q.

The function q clearly satisfies condition 6.1.A. We shall verify that it also satisfies conditions 6.1.B-6.1.C. Let $\Lambda=\{t_1, \ldots, t_n, \ldots\}$ be an everywhere dense subset of the interval $[s, \infty)$. If $q(\lambda;\ t_1, x_1, \ldots, t_n, x_n, \ldots)=0$, whatever the monotonic bounded subsequence $t_{i_1}, t_{i_2}, \ldots, t_{i_n}, \ldots<\xi$ of the sequence $t_1, \ldots, t_n, \ldots$ the corresponding sequence of points $x_{i_1}, \ldots, x_{i_n}, \ldots$ satisfies the condition: for any $\varepsilon>0$ there exists $n(\varepsilon)$ such that $\rho(x_{i_n}, x_{i_m})<\varepsilon$ for $m, n>n(\varepsilon)$. In view of the completeness of space E, the sequence $x_{i_1}, \ldots, x_{i_n}, \ldots$ is convergent.

We define the function $\varphi(t)$ $(t\in[0, \lambda))$ by the formulae

$$\varphi(t)=\begin{cases}x_i, & \text{if } t=t_i\in\Lambda\cap[0, \lambda),\\ \lim\limits_{u\downarrow t,\ u\in\Lambda}\varphi(u), & \text{if } t\in[s, \xi)\cap\bar{\Lambda},\\ \varphi(s), & \text{if } t\in[0, s) \text{ or if } t\in[\xi, \lambda)\cap\bar{\Lambda}.\end{cases}\tag{6.25}$$

It is easily seen that $\xi(\mathscr{F}, \varphi)\leqslant\xi$, and if $t_1', \ldots, t_n', \ldots$ is any monotonic bounded sequence of points of $[0, \xi)$, the limit $\lim\limits_{n\to\infty}\varphi(t_n')$ exists. The function φ therefore belongs to the class $\mathscr{L}$. Condition 6.1.B is satisfied.

---

*) If such indices can not be found, we put $h_{\varepsilon,\Delta}=0$.

We now show that q satisfies condition 6.1.C. Let $\delta > 0$, $\Lambda = \{t_1, \ldots, t_n, \ldots\} \subset [s, \infty)$. We put

$$q^* = q(\zeta;\ t_1,\ x_{t_1}, \ldots, t_n,\ x_{t_n}, \ldots),$$
$$h^*_{\varepsilon, \Delta} = h_{\varepsilon, \Delta}(\zeta;\ t_1,\ x_{t_1}, \ldots, t_n,\ x_{t_n}, \ldots),$$
$$\Delta_m = [s + m\delta,\ s + (m+1)\delta] \qquad (m = 0, 1, 2, \ldots).$$

Clearly,

$$\{q^* > 0\} \subseteq \bigcup_{n=1}^{\infty} \bigcup_{m=0}^{\infty} \left\{h^*_{\frac{1}{n}, \Delta_m} = \infty\right\}. \tag{6.26}$$

Let $\Gamma_1 \subseteq \ldots \subseteq \Gamma_l \subseteq \ldots$ be a sequence of sets as described in condition 6.2.A. Then $\xi^{\lambda}_{\Delta}(\Gamma_l) \uparrow \xi$ and therefore, for any $\varepsilon > 0$ and any k,

$$\{h^*_{\varepsilon, \Delta_m} = \infty\} \subseteq \bigcup_{l=1}^{\infty} A^{\varepsilon}_k(\Lambda \cap \Delta_m,\ \Gamma_l),$$

where A^{ε}_k is defined by expression (6.16). It follows from this that

$$\mathbf{P}_{s, x}\{h^*_{\varepsilon, \Delta_m} = \infty\} \leqslant \lim_{l \to \infty} \mathbf{P}_{s, x}\{A^{\varepsilon}_k(\Lambda \cap \Delta_m,\ \Gamma_l)\}.$$

By lemma 6.4,

$$\mathbf{P}_{s, x}\{A^{\varepsilon}_k(\Lambda \cap \Delta_m,\ \Gamma_l)\} \leqslant [2\alpha^{\varepsilon}_{\Gamma}(\delta)]^k.$$

Consequently,

$$\mathbf{P}_{s, x}\{h^*_{\varepsilon, \Delta_m} = \infty\} \leqslant [2\alpha^{\varepsilon}_{\Gamma}(\delta)]^k.$$

By the hypothesis of the theorem, for any $\varepsilon > 0$ there exists a $\delta > 0$ such that $\alpha^{\varepsilon}_{\Gamma}(\delta) < \frac{1}{4}$. We have with this choice of δ,

$$\mathbf{P}_{s, x}\{h^*_{\varepsilon, \Delta_m} = \infty\} \leqslant \left(\frac{1}{2}\right)^k,$$

and, since this is true for any k,

$$\mathbf{P}_{s, x}\{h^*_{\varepsilon, \Delta_m} = \infty\} = 0.$$

On combining this equation with inclusion (6.26), it may be seen that $\mathbf{P}_{s, x}(q^* > 0) = 0$, and the theorem is proved.

6.9. Remark 1. Let $(E, \rho, \mathscr{B})$ be a metric measurable space satisfying the conditions of theorem 6.3, and let $\mathcal{F}$ be a system of subsets of E equivalent to a sequence of closed sets $\Gamma_1 \subseteq \Gamma_2 \subseteq \ldots \subseteq \Gamma_n \subseteq \ldots$. If the normal Markov process X in the space $(E, \rho, \mathcal{B})$ is $\mathcal{F}$-bounded and satisfies the $M(\Gamma)$ condition for all $\Gamma \in \mathcal{F}$, a Markov process equivalent to X exists which is $\mathcal{F}$-bounded, continuous from the right and devoid of discontinuities of the second kind.

Proof. We define $\mathcal{L}$ as in the proof of theorem 6.3, and write $\mathcal{L}_0$ for the class of all $\mathcal{F}$-bounded functions of Ω_E. We notice that, if $\psi \in \mathcal{L}_0$ and $x_i = \psi(t_i)$, the function $\varphi(t)$ given by (6.25) belongs to $\mathcal{L} \cap \mathcal{L}_0$. It may be concluded from this, in view of the remark on theorem 6.1, that a process $\widetilde{X}$ equivalent to X exists, all the trajectories of which belong to $\mathcal{L} \cap \mathcal{L}_0$. We have $\xi(\mathcal{F}) = \zeta$ for this process, which proves our statement.

<u>Remark 2</u>. Let (E, ρ) be a σ-compact complete metric space, $\mathcal{B}$ the σ-algebra generated by all open sets of (E, ρ) and $P(s, x; t, \Gamma)$ the normal transition function in the space $(E, \rho, \mathcal{B})$. We assume the existence of a sequence of closed sets $\Gamma_n \uparrow E$ such that:

a) the $M(\Gamma_n)$ condition is fulfilled for each Γ_n;

b) there exists $0 < \varrho$ such that, for all m,

$$\lim_{n \to \infty} \sup_{\substack{y \overline{\in} \Gamma_n \\ |v-u| < \delta}} P(u, y; v, \Gamma_m) = 0.$$

Then there is a Markov process with the transition function $P(s, x; t, \Gamma)$ which is $\{\Gamma_n\}$-bounded, continuous from the right, and devoid of discontinuities of the second kind*).

If condition 5.18.A is satisfied, or if $P(s, x; t, \Gamma) = P(t-s, x, \Gamma)$, where $P(t, x, \Gamma)$ satisfies requirement 5.19.A, this process is strictly Markov.

Proof. By theorem 4.2, a Markov process X exists with the transition function $P(s, x; t, \Gamma)$. We put $\mathcal{F} = \{\Gamma_n\}$. By theorem 6.2, we can construct an $\mathcal{F}$-bounded Markov process X' equivalent to X. This process satisfies the $M(\Gamma_n)$ condition for every n. In accordance with remark 1, a process $\widetilde{X}$

---

*)Needless to say, it is sufficient to require that the $M(E)$ condition be fulfilled instead of condition a)-b).

equivalent to X' exists which is $\mathcal{F}$-bounded and continuous from the right and which has no discontinuities of the second kind. When condition 5.18.A or 5.19.A holds, this process is strictly Markov by theorems 5.9 and 5.10.

4. Jump-Type and Step Processes

6.10. The Markov process $X = (x_t, \zeta, \mathcal{M}_t^s, \mathbf{P}_{s,x})$, in the measurable space $(E, \mathcal{B})$ is said to be a *jump-type process* if, for each $\omega \in \Omega$, $t \in [0, \zeta(\omega))$ there exists $\delta > 0$ such that $x_{t+h}(\omega) = x_t(\omega)$ for all $0 \leqslant h < \delta$. The number t is called the *instant of jump* of the trajectory $x_t(\omega)$ if the sequence $t_n \uparrow t$ exists such that $x_{t_n}(\omega) \neq x_t(\omega)$ $(n = 1, 2, \ldots)$. The instants of jump may easily be seen to form a denumerable set. If, for any ω, this set has no limit points inside the interval $[0, \zeta(\omega))$, we shall describe X as a *step process*.

We introduce a discrete topology in the space $(E, \mathcal{B})$, taking for $\mathcal{C}$ the class of all subsets of E. The class of jump-type processes in $(E, \mathcal{B})$ is easily seen to coincide with the class of processes continuous from the right in $(E, \mathcal{C}, \mathcal{B})$; the class of step processes coincides with the class of processes continuous from the right and devoid of discontinuities of the second kind. It follows from theorem 5.10 that *every stationary jump-type Markov process is strictly Markov*.

The topological space $(E, \mathcal{C})$ is metrizable. The corresponding metric is given by

$$\rho(x, y) = \begin{cases} 0, & \text{if } x = y, \\ 1, & \text{if } x \neq y. \end{cases}$$

The following is a sufficient condition for the function $\rho(x, y)$ to be measurable with respect to $\mathcal{B} \times \mathcal{B}$:

6.10.A. The subset of space $E \times E$ consisting of points of the type (x, x) $(x \in E)$ belongs to the σ-algebra $\mathcal{B} \times \mathcal{B}$.

The following theorem is obtained by applying the results of article 3.

Theorem 6.4. Let $(E, \mathcal{B})$ be a measurable space satisfying condition 6.10.A, and let X be a Markov process in $(E, \mathcal{B})$ subject to the condition:

6.10.B. The convergence is uniform over $t \geqslant 0$, $x \in E$:

$$\lim_{h \downarrow 0} P(t, x; t+h, E \setminus x) = 0.$$

Then a step process exists which is the stochastic equivalent of process X.

We suggest that the reader define a process which is jump-type (or is a step process) until departure from the system $\mathcal{F}$, and state the analogue of theorem 6.4 for such processes.

6.11. Examples. 6.11.1. Let $E=\{1, 2, \ldots, n, \ldots\}$ and let $\mathcal{B}$ be the system of all subsets of E. In accordance with 4.2.2, every transition function in the space $(E, \mathcal{B})$ can be specified with the aid of a system of functions $p_{ij}(s, t)$ $(0 \leqslant s \leqslant t)$. Condition 6.10.B is expressed in terms of the $p_{ij}(s, t)$ as

$$\lim_{h \downarrow 0} \sup_{t, i} \sum_{j \neq i} p_{ij}(t, t+h) = 0. \tag{6.26'}$$

In the stationary case, this amounts to requiring the uniform convergence (in regard to i) of:

$$\lim_{h \downarrow 0} \sum_{j \neq i} p_{ij}(h) = 0.$$

Furthermore, if the set E is finite, the uniformity requirement is satisfied automatically, and condition 6.10.B is equivalent to the requirement that $p_{ij}(h) \to 0$ as $h \downarrow 0$ for any $i \neq j$.

We can conclude, on taking into account the fact that the conditions of theorem 4.2 and condition 6.10.A are fulfilled in the present case, that there is a corresponding step process for every transition function subject to condition (6.26′) in the finite or denumerable set E.

6.11.2. The Poisson transition function (example 4.2.6) is readily seen to be complete and to satisfy condition 6.10.B. There will therefore be a non-cut-off step process corresponding to the Poisson transition function, if the phase space is subject to condition 6.10.A and a topology satisfying the requirements of theorem 4.2 can be introduced into it. We shall term this a Poisson process.

5. Continuity Conditions

6.12. The $N(\Gamma)$ condition formulated below will be shown to play the same role in investigating the continuity of a Markov process as is played by the $M(\Gamma)$ condition in criteria for continuity from the right and absence of discontinuities of the second kind.

The $N(\Gamma)$ condition. For any $\varepsilon > 0$,

$$\lim_{\delta \downarrow 0} \frac{\alpha_{\Gamma}^{\varepsilon}(\delta)}{\delta} = 0.$$

We shall make use of the following lemma when deducing criteria for continuity.

Lemma 6.6. Let $X = (x_t, \zeta, \mathcal{M}_t^s, \mathbf{P}_{s,x})$ be a Markov process in the metric measurable space $(E, \rho, \mathscr{B})$ (with a $\mathscr{B} \times \mathscr{B}$-measurable function ρ), let the set $\Gamma \in \mathscr{B}$, and let the subset Λ of the segment $[s, T]$ be finite or denumerable. We write $\xi = \xi_\Lambda$ for the strict lower bound of elements t of set Λ for which $x_t \bar{\in} \Gamma$, and put

$$Q = Q_{\Gamma}^{\delta, \varepsilon}(\Lambda) = \bigcup_{\substack{t, u \in \Lambda \\ |t-u| < \delta}} \{t < \xi,\ u < \xi,\ \rho(x_t, x_u) \geqslant 4\varepsilon\}. \tag{6.27}$$

Then

$$\mathbf{P}_{s,x}(Q) \leqslant 2[T - s] \frac{\alpha_{\Gamma}^{\varepsilon}(2\delta)}{\delta}. \tag{6.28}$$

Proof. We choose the points $u_1 < u_2 < \ldots < u_k \in [s, T]$ such that

$$u_1 - s = u_2 - u_1 = \ldots = u_k - u_{k-1} = \delta, \quad 0 \leqslant T - u_k < \delta, \tag{6.29}$$

and put

$$\Delta_0 = [s, u_2],\ \Delta_1 = [u_1, u_3],\ \Delta_2 = [u_2, u_4],\ \ldots,\ \Delta_{k-1} = [u_{k-1}, T],$$
$$D_i = D_{\Gamma}^{\varepsilon}(\Lambda \cap \Delta_i) \qquad (i = 1, \ldots, k-1),$$

where the event D_{Γ}^{ε} is given by expression (6.13). Clearly, $Q \subseteq \bigcup_{i=1}^{k-1} D_i$. Therefore

$$\mathbf{P}_{s,x}(Q) \leqslant \sum_{i=1}^{k-1} \mathbf{P}_{s,x}(D_i). \tag{6.30}$$

Since each of the sets $\Lambda \cap \Delta_i$ is situated on a segment of length 2δ, we have by lemma 6.3:

$$\mathbf{P}_{s,x}(D_i) \leqslant 2\alpha_\Gamma^s(2\delta),$$

and in view of (6.30):

$$\mathbf{P}_{s,x}(Q) \leqslant 2(k-1)\alpha_\Gamma^s(2\delta). \tag{6.31}$$

But, by (6.29), $k\delta \leqslant T-s$. Therefore $k-1 < k \leqslant \frac{T-s}{\delta}$, and (6.28) follows from (6.31).

6.13. Theorem 6.5. Let $(E, \rho, \mathscr{B})$ be a complete metric measurable space with $\mathscr{B}\times\mathscr{B}$-measurable metric ρ. Let Γ be a measurable set in the space $(E, \rho, \mathscr{B})$ and X a normal Markov process subject to the $N(\Gamma)$ condition. Then a Markov process equivalent to X can be constructed which is continuous up to departure from Γ and is such that, for every $\omega \in \Omega$, either $\xi(\Gamma, \omega) = \zeta(\omega)$ or $\lim\limits_{t \uparrow \xi(\Gamma,\omega)} x_t(\omega)$ exists and belongs to the boundary Γ' of the set Γ.

Proof. Let $\varphi(t)$ be a function in the interval $[0, \lambda)$ with values from E. We define the quantity $\xi(\varphi) = \xi(\Gamma, \varphi)$ by expression (6.22) and we shall say that the function φ belongs to the system $\mathscr{L}$ if:

a$_1$) $\varphi(t)$ is continuous in the interval $[0, \xi(\varphi))$;

a$_2$) either $\xi(\varphi) = \lambda$, or $\lim\limits_{t \uparrow \xi(\varphi)} \varphi(t)$ exists and belongs to Γ'.

Let $T > 0$, $\delta > 0$, $\Lambda = \{t_1, \ldots, t_n, \ldots\} \subseteq [0, \infty)$, $x_1, \ldots x_n, \ldots \in E$. We define the function $\xi = \xi_\Lambda^\lambda(\Gamma)$ by expression (6.23) and put $\xi^T = \min(\xi, T)$;

$$h_{\delta, T}(\lambda; t_1, x_1, \ldots, t_n, x_n, \ldots) = \sup_{\substack{t_i, t_j < \xi^T \\ |t_i - t_j| < \delta}} \rho(x_i, x_j)\ ^{*});$$

$$h_T = \lim_{\delta \downarrow 0} h_{\delta, T}, \quad h = \lim_{T \uparrow \infty} h_T,$$

$$g(\lambda; x, t, y) = \begin{cases} \rho(x, y), & \text{if } t < \lambda,\ x \in \Gamma,\ y \bar{\in} \Gamma, \\ +\infty & \text{in the remaining cases;} \end{cases}$$

---

*) If the set for which the upper bound is taken is empty, we put

$$h_{\delta, T}(\lambda; t_1, x_1, \ldots, t_n, x_n, \ldots) = 0.$$

$$g_\beta(\lambda; t_1, x_1, \ldots, t_n, x_n, \ldots) = \begin{cases} \inf\limits_{\beta < t_i < \xi} g(\lambda; x_i, t_j, x_j), & \text{if } \xi < \lambda, \\ C, & \text{if } \xi = \lambda. \end{cases}$$

$$g(\lambda; t_1, x_1, \ldots, t_n, x_n, \ldots) = \lim_{\beta \downarrow 0} g_\beta(\lambda; t_1, x_1, \ldots, t_n, x_n, \ldots).$$

The function $q = h + g$ satisfies condition 6.1.A and is measurable with respect to $\lambda, x_1, \ldots, x_n, \ldots$ We prove that it also satisfies conditions 6.1.B-6.1.C.

Let $\Lambda = \{t_1, \ldots, t_n, \ldots\}$ be an everywhere dense subset of the interval $[s, \infty), \lambda \in (s, \infty)$ and let $q(\lambda; t_1, x_1, \ldots t_n, x_n, \ldots) = 0$. We suppose first that $\xi < \lambda$; we choose $T \in (\xi, \lambda)$. It follows from the equation $h_T(\lambda; t_1, x_1, \ldots, t_n, x_n, \ldots) = 0$ that, for any $\varepsilon > 0$, there is a $\delta > 0$ such that $\rho(x_i, x_j) < \varepsilon$ for $t_i, t_j < \xi^T = \xi$ and $|t_i - t_j| < \delta$. This means that the function φ given by $\varphi(t_i) = x_i$ in the set $\Lambda \cap [s, \xi)$ is uniformly continuous in this set and may therefore be extended (uniquely) to the continuous function $\varphi(t)$ in $[s, \xi)$, which has a limit as $t \uparrow \xi$. We complete the definition of this function by putting

$$\varphi(t) = \begin{cases} \varphi(s) & \text{for } 0 \leqslant t < s, \\ x_i, & \text{if } t = t_i \in [\xi, \lambda), \\ x_1, & \text{if } t \in [\xi, \lambda) \cap \overline{\Lambda}. \end{cases}$$

The function $\varphi(t)$ satisfies the condition $\varphi(t_i) = x_i$ for all $t_i < \lambda$, and condition a_1). Moreover, $\xi(\varphi) \leqslant \xi$ and condition a_2) is obviously satisfied if $\xi(\varphi) < \xi$. On the other hand, if $\xi(\varphi) = \xi$, it follows from the relationship $g(\lambda; t_1, x_1, \ldots, t_n, x_n, \ldots) = 0$ that $\inf\limits_{\xi - \beta < t < \xi} \rho(\varphi(t), \overline{\Gamma}) = 0$ for any $\beta > 0$. We put $z = \lim\limits_{t \uparrow \xi} \varphi(t)$. Evidently, $\rho(z, \overline{\Gamma}) = \rho(z, \Gamma) = 0$. Consequently $z \in \Gamma'$. This proves, in fact, that the function ψ satisfies condition a_2) and therefore belongs to $\mathscr{L}$.

We now suppose that $\xi = \lambda$. Since

$$h_T(\lambda; t_1, x_1, \ldots, t_n, x_n, \ldots) = 0$$

for all T, the function φ, defined in the set Λ by the expression $\varphi(t_i) = x_i$ is uniformly continuous in the intersection of this set with any segment $[s, T] \subset [s, \lambda)$. The function may be extended uniquely to a continuous function in $[s, \lambda)$. On extending it to the interval $[0, s)$ in accordance with the expression $\varphi(t) = \varphi(s)(t \in [0, s))$, we evidently get a function of $\mathscr{L}$.

Turning to the proof of condition 6.1.C. we write for brevity $\xi^* = \xi_{\Lambda}^{\zeta}(\Gamma)$, $g^* = g(\zeta; t_1, x_{t_1}, \ldots, t_n, x_{t_n}, \ldots)$ and similarly define h^*, h_T^*, $h_{\delta,T}^*$ and q^*.

Let $\Lambda = \{t_1, \ldots, t_n, \ldots\}$ be an everywhere dense subset of the interval $[s, \infty)$. It will be observed that, for any positive ε, δ, T:

$$\{h_T^* > 4\varepsilon\} \subseteq \{h_{\delta,T}^* > 4\varepsilon\} \subseteq Q_\Gamma^{\delta,\varepsilon}\{\Lambda \cap [s, T]\},$$

where $Q_\Gamma^{\delta,\varepsilon}$ is defined by expression (6.27). It follows from this, in accordance with lemma 6.6, that

$$\mathbf{P}_{s,x}\{h_T^* > 4\varepsilon\} \leqslant 2(T-s)\frac{\alpha_\Gamma^\varepsilon(2\delta)}{\delta}.$$

If we let $\delta \to 0$, we have from the $N(\Gamma)$ condition: $\mathbf{P}_{s,x}(h_T^* > 4\varepsilon) = 0$.

Since $h_T^* \uparrow h^*$ as $T \uparrow \infty$, we have

$$\{h^* > 0\} \subseteq \bigcup_{n=1}^{\infty}\bigcup_{T=1}^{\infty}\left\{h_T^* > \frac{1}{n}\right\},$$

whence it is clear that $\mathbf{P}_{s,x}(h^* > 0) = 0$.

We now represent the set Λ as the sum of finite sets $\Lambda^n = \{u_1^n < u_2^n < \ldots < u_{m_n}^n\}$ such that

b$_1$) $\Lambda^1 \subset \Lambda^2 \subset \ldots \subset \Lambda^n \subset \ldots$;

b$_2$) $\frac{\delta_n}{3} \leqslant u_{k+1}^n - u_k^n < \delta_n \quad (k = 1, 2, \ldots, m_n - 1)$, where $\delta_n \downarrow 0$ as $n \to \infty$.

We agree to write for brevity x_k^n instead of $x_{u_k^n}$.

We bring in the random variables:

$$\mu_n = \sup\{u_k^n : x_j^n \in \Gamma \text{ for } j = 1, 2, \ldots, k\},$$
$$\nu_n = \inf\{u_k^n : x_k^n \overline{\in} \Gamma\}.$$

We notice that, for any $T > 0$,

$$\{\rho(x_{\mu_n}, x_{\nu_n}) \geqslant \varepsilon, \mu_n < T\} \subseteq \bigcup_{u_l^n < T}\{x_l^n \in \Gamma, \rho(x_l^n, x_{l+1}^n) \geqslant \varepsilon\}. \quad (6.32)$$

But in view of (6.12) and b_2),

$$P_{s,x}\{x_l^n\in\Gamma,\ \rho(x_l^n,\ x_{l+1}^n)\geqslant\varepsilon\}\leqslant\alpha_\Gamma^\varepsilon(u_{l+1}^n-u_l^n)\leqslant\alpha_\Gamma^\varepsilon(\delta_n). \quad (6.33)$$

On the other hand, by b_2), the number of points of sets Λ^n located in the segment $[s, T]$ does not exceed $\frac{3(T-s)}{\delta_n}+1$. Therefore we have from (6.32) and (6.33):

$$P_{s,x}\{\rho(x_{\mu_n},\ x_{\nu_n})\geqslant\varepsilon,\ \mu_n<T\}\leqslant C\frac{\alpha_\Gamma^\varepsilon(\delta_n)}{\delta_n}, \quad (6.34)$$

where $C=3(T-s)+\delta_1$.

We now write π_n for the greatest of the elements of set Λ^n less than ξ^*. It is evident that $\pi_n\leqslant\mu_n<\xi^*\leqslant\nu_n$ and $\nu_n\downarrow\xi^*$, as $n\to\infty$. On the other hand, $\pi_n\uparrow\xi^*$ by virtue of b_2). Therefore $\nu_n-\pi_n\downarrow 0$, and all the more, $\mu_n-\pi_n\to 0$. We notice that, for any $T>0,\ \varepsilon>0,\ \delta>0$ and any sufficiently large n:

$$\begin{aligned}\{g^*>5\varepsilon\}&\subseteq\{\xi^*<\lambda,\ \rho(x_{\pi_n},\ x_{\nu_n})\geqslant 5\varepsilon\}\subseteq\\ &\subseteq\{T\leqslant\xi^*<\infty\}\cup\{\mu_n-\pi_n\geqslant\delta\}\cup\\ &\quad\cup\{\xi^*<T,\ \mu_n-\pi_n<\delta,\ \rho(x_{\pi_n},\ x_{\nu_n})\geqslant 5\varepsilon\}\subseteq\\ &\subseteq\{T\leqslant\xi^*<\infty\}\cup\{\mu_n-\pi_n\geqslant\delta\}\cup\\ &\qquad\cup Q_\Gamma^{\delta,\varepsilon}(\Lambda^n\cap[s,\ T))\cup\{\xi^*<T,\ \rho(x_{\mu_n},\ x_{\nu_n})\geqslant\varepsilon\}.\end{aligned}$$

This gives us, using lemma 6.6 and inequality (6.34):

$$\begin{aligned}P_{s,x}\{g^*>5\varepsilon\}&\leqslant P_{s,x}\{T\leqslant\xi^*<\infty\}+P_{s,x}(\mu_n-\pi_n\geqslant\delta)+\\ &\quad+2(T-s)\frac{\alpha_\Gamma^\varepsilon(2\delta)}{\delta}+C\frac{\alpha_\Gamma^\varepsilon(\delta_n)}{\delta_n}.\end{aligned}$$

If we first let n tend to infinity, then δ to zero, and finally T to infinity, we now get $P_{s,x}\{g^*>5\varepsilon\}=0$. Thus $P_{s,x}\{g^*>0\}=0$. The relationships proved above: $P_{s,x}\{h^*>0\}=P_{s,x}\{g^*>0\}=0$ show us that $P_{s,x}\{j^*>0\}=0$. Condition 6.2.C is fulfilled and the theorem is proved.

6.14. <u>Theorem 6.6</u>. Let X be a Markov process subject to the requirements of theorem 6.5 in the space $(E,\ \rho,\ \mathscr{B})$. Let $\mathscr{F}$ be a system of subsets of space $(E,\ \rho,\ \mathscr{B})$ such that the $N(\Gamma)$ condition is satisfied for each $\Gamma\in\mathscr{F}$.

Then a Markov process $\widetilde{X}$ can be constructed which is equivalent to X, is continuous up to departure from $\mathscr{F}$ and has the following properties: for every $\widetilde{\omega}\in\widetilde{\Omega}$ there is either a $\Gamma\in\mathscr{F}$ such that $\widetilde{x}_t(\widetilde{\omega})\in\Gamma$ for all $t\in[0,\ \widetilde{\zeta}(\widetilde{\omega}))$, or else for every $\Gamma\in\mathscr{F}$ there is a $t_n\uparrow\xi(\mathscr{F},\ \widetilde{\omega})$ such that $\widetilde{x}_{t_n}(\widetilde{\omega})\in\Gamma$.

If the process X is $\mathscr{F}$-bounded, $\tilde{X}$ can be chosen so that $\xi(\mathscr{F})=\zeta$.

Proof. Let Γ_m be a sequence of sets satisfying conditions 3.12.A-3.12.C. We say that $\varphi\in\mathscr{L}$ if φ is continuous until departure from $\mathscr{F}$ and either $x_t\in\Gamma_m$ for some m and all $t\in[0,\lambda)$, or there exists the sequence $t_m\uparrow\xi(\mathscr{F},\varphi)$ such that $\varphi(t_m)\bar{\in}\Gamma_m$.

We construct for each set Γ_m a function q_m as described in the proof of theorem 6.5. We shall write q_m^* for the result of substituting λ and x_{t_n} for x_n in q_m. We put $q=\sum_1^\infty q_m$, $q^*=\sum_1^\infty q_m^*$. The function q is clearly measurable with respect to $\lambda, x_1, \ldots, x_n, \ldots$ and satisfies condition 6.1.A. When proving theorem 6.5 we showed that $\mathbf{P}_{s,x}\{q_m^*>0\}=0$. Hence $\mathbf{P}_{s,x}\{q^*>0\}=0$ and condition 6.1.C is satisfied. It remains to prove condition 6.1.B.

Let $\Lambda=\{t_1, \ldots, t_n, \ldots\}\subseteq[s,\infty)$, $\lambda\in(s,\infty)$. We put

$$\xi_m=\xi_\Lambda^\lambda(\Gamma_m),\quad \xi=\xi_\Lambda^\lambda(\mathscr{F})=\lim\xi_m,$$

where $\xi_\Lambda^\lambda(\Gamma)$ is given by (6.23). We assume that $q(\lambda; t_1, x_1, \ldots, t_n, x_n, \ldots)=0$ so that $q_m(\lambda; t_1, x_1, \ldots, t_n, x_n, \ldots)=0$ for any m. We consider a function φ defined in the set Λ by the equation $\varphi(t_i)=x_i$. This function is uniformly continuous in $\Lambda\cap[s,K]$ for every $K\in[s,\xi)$ and can therefore be uniquely extended to a continuous function in the interval $[s,\xi)$. We put $\varphi(t)=\varphi(s)$ for $t\in[0,s)$ and define φ arbitrarily in the interval (ξ,λ), except for the proviso that $\varphi(t_i)=x_i$ for all i. Let $\xi_m'=\xi(\Gamma_m,\varphi)$, $\xi'=\xi(\mathscr{F},\varphi)$. We show in the same way as when proving theorem 6.5 that, if $\xi_m'<\lambda$, then $\lim_{t\uparrow\xi_{m+1}'}\varphi(t)$ exists and belongs to Γ_{m+1}'. It follows from condition 3.12.C that $\Gamma_{m+1}'\subseteq E\setminus\Gamma_m$. Therefore $\xi_m'<\xi_{m+1}'$. Hence either $\xi_m'=\lambda$ for a certain m, or $\xi_1'<\xi_2'<\ldots<\xi_m'<\ldots<\xi'$. It may easily be seen that in both cases the function φ that we have constructed belongs to $\mathscr{L}$. This completes the proof of the first assertion of the theorem.

It can further be seen that, if ψ is any $\mathscr{F}$-bounded function in Ω_E and if $x_i=\psi(t_i)$, the function constructed by us is also $\mathscr{F}$-bounded. The second assertion of our theorem follows from this in accordance with the remark on theorem 6.1.

6.15. Corollary. Let (E,ρ) be a σ-compact complete metric space, $\mathscr{B}$ the σ-algebra generated by all open sets, and

$P(s, x; t, \Gamma)$ a transition function in the space $(E, \rho, \mathscr{B})$.

Let $\mathscr{F}$ be a normal system of subsets of space $(E, \rho, \mathscr{B})$ satisfying condition 6.3.A, and let the $N(\Gamma)$ condition hold for every $\Gamma \in \mathscr{F}$. Then there exists a continuous $\mathscr{F}$-bounded Markov process with the transition function $P(s, x; t, \Gamma)$.

If condition 5.18.A holds, or if the transition function is stationary and satisfies requirement 5.19.A, the process is strictly Markov.

The proof of this corollary follows exactly the same lines as that of remark 2 on theorem 6.3.

Remark 1. The corollary obviously still holds in the case when the $N(E)$ condition is satisfied.

Remark 2. If the transition function $P(s, x; t, \Gamma)$ is complete, we can evidently choose a non-cut-off process as the process described in the corollary. Similarly, a stationary process can be chosen if the transition function is stationary.

6. A Continuity Theorem for Strictly Markov Processes

6.16. Theorem 6.7. Let $\mathscr{F}$*) be a system of open measurable sets $G_1 \subseteq G_2 \subseteq \ldots \subseteq G_n \subseteq \ldots$ in the metric measurable space $(E, \rho, \mathscr{B})$ with $\mathscr{B} \times \mathscr{B}$-measurable function $\rho(x, y)$, and let $X = (x_t, \zeta, \mathscr{M}_t^s, \mathbf{P}_{s,x})$ be a strictly Markov process in the space which is $\mathscr{F}$-bounded and continuous from the right**) and satisfies conditions $M(G_n)$ $(n = 1, 2, \ldots)$. Let $\tau_1 \leqslant \tau_2 \leqslant \ldots \leqslant \tau_n \leqslant \ldots$ be an arbitrary sequence of random variables independent of the future and s-past. We put

$$\left.\begin{aligned} \tau(\omega) &= \lim_{n \to \infty} \tau_n(\omega) \quad (\omega \in \Omega) \\ \Omega_\tau &= \{\tau < \zeta\}. \end{aligned}\right\} \qquad (6.35)$$

*)The theorem obviously still holds if $\mathscr{F}$ is any set system equivalent to the sequence $\{G_n\}$.

**)If process X were not continuous from the right it could be replaced by an equivalent process that was continuous from the right, in accordance with remark 1 on theorem 6.3.

Then

$$x_{\tau_n(\omega)} \to x_{\tau(\omega)} \qquad (\text{a.c.}\ \Omega_\tau,\ \mathbf{P}_{s,x}). \tag{6.36}$$

Proof. Let $\xi(G_k)$ be the instant of first departure of the trajectory from G_k (see sec. 3.8). Since process X is $\mathcal{F}$-bounded, we have $\{\tau < \xi(G_k)\} \uparrow \Omega_\tau$, and consequently

$$\{\tau < \xi(G_k),\ x_{\tau_n} \not\to x_\tau\} \uparrow \{\Omega_\tau,\ x_{\tau_n} \not\to x_\tau\}. \tag{6.37}$$

Furthermore,

$$\{\tau < \xi(G_k),\ x_{\tau_n} \not\to x_\tau\} = \bigcup_m C_m^k, \tag{6.38}$$

where

$$C_m^k = \bigcap_{N=1}^{\infty} \bigcup_{n=N}^{\infty} \left\{\rho(x_{\tau_n},\ x_\tau) > \frac{4}{m},\ \tau < \xi(G_k)\right\}.$$

We choose an arbitrary $h > 0$ and put

$$f(t,\ \omega) = \sup_{u \in [0,\ h)} \chi_{G_k}(x_t)\, \chi_{G_k}(x_{t+u})\, \rho(x_t,\ x_{t+u})$$
$$(t \in [s,\ \infty),\ \omega \in \Omega_t).$$

Obviously,

$$C_m^k \subseteq \bigcup_{M=1}^{\infty} \bigcap_{N=M}^{\infty} \left\{f(\tau_N,\ \omega) > \frac{4}{m}\right\}. \tag{6.39}$$

Since X is continuous from the right, whilst the sets G_k are open, we have

$$f(t,\ \omega) = \sup_{u \in \Lambda} \chi_{G_k}(x_t)\, \chi_{G_k}(x_{t+u})\, \rho(x_t,\ x_{t+u}),$$

where Λ is the set of all rational numbers of the interval $[0,\ h)$. It is clear from this that the function $f(t,\ \omega)$ is measurable with respect to the σ-algebra $\mathcal{F}^s$, and by theorem 5.2:

$$\mathbf{P}_{s,x}\left\{f(\tau_N,\ \omega) > \frac{4}{m}\right\} = \mathbf{M}_{s,x} F(\tau_N,\ x_{\tau_N}), \tag{6.40}$$

where

$$F(u,\ y) = \mathbf{P}_{u,y}\left\{f(u,\ \omega) > \frac{4}{m}\right\}.$$

By lemma 6.3, we have for any $y \in G_k$:

$$F(u, y) \leqslant 2\alpha_{G_k}^{\frac{1}{m}}(h). \tag{6.41}$$

We obtain by combining (6.39), (6.40) and (6.41):

$$\mathbf{P}_{s,x}(C_m^k) \leqslant 2\alpha_{G_k}^{\frac{1}{m}}(h).$$

In view of the $M(G_k)$ conditions, $\alpha_{G_k}^{\frac{1}{m}}(h) \to 0$ as $h \to 0$, so that $\mathbf{P}_{s,x}(C_m^k) = 0$. On taking into account (6.37) and (6.38), we get (6.36).

Remark. Theorem 6.5 holds for any strictly Markov process which is continuous from the right and satisfies the $M(E)$ condition. For we can put in this case $G_1 = \ldots = G_n = \ldots = E$.

6.17. We shall in future describe the Markov process $X = (x_t, \zeta, \mathscr{M}_t^s, \mathbf{P}_{s,x})$ as quasi-continuous from the left if, whatever the random variables $\tau_1, \tau_2, \ldots, \tau_n, \ldots$ independent of the future and s-past, and whatever the subset $\widetilde{\Omega}$ of set Ω, the relationship

$$\tau_n(\omega) \uparrow \tau(\omega) < \zeta(\omega) \qquad (\omega \in \widetilde{\Omega}), \tag{6.42}$$

leads (for every $x \in E$) to the relationship

$$x_{\tau_n} \to x_\tau \qquad (\text{a.c.} \ \widetilde{\Omega}, \ \mathbf{P}_{s,x}).$$

We arrive at the following proposition by using theorems 6.7 and 5.9 in conjunction with remark 2 on theorem 6.3 (sec. 6.9):

Theorem 6.8. Let (E, ρ) be a σ-compact complete metric space and $\mathscr{B}$ the σ-algebra of all Borel sets of the space (E, ρ). Let $\mathscr{F} = \{G_n\}$ be a sequence of open sets such that the closure of G_n is contained in G_{n+1} and $G_n \uparrow E$. The transition function $P(s, x; t, \Gamma)$ in the space $(E, \rho, \mathscr{B})$ will be assumed to satisfy conditions 5.18.A, 6.3.A and $M(G_n)$ $(n = 1, 2, \ldots)$.

Then a process can be constructed with the transition function $P(s, x; t, \Gamma)$ such that it is strictly Markov, continuous from the right, quasi-continuous from the left, devoid of discontinuities of the second kind and $\mathscr{F}$-bounded.

Remark. If the transition function $P(s, x; t, \Gamma)$ is stationary, conditions 5.18.A can be replaced by condition 5.19.A, i.e. the requirement that the transition function be of Feller's type.

7. Examples

6.18. The phase space in all the examples below is a σ-compact complete metric space, whilst the σ-algebra $\mathscr{B}$ is generated by the system of all open sets of this space. We can therefore base our discussion on the corollary of theorem 6.6.

6.18.1. We have for the transition function $P(s, x; t, \Gamma) = \chi_\Gamma[x+v(t-s)]$ (see sec. 4.2.1):

$$\alpha^\varepsilon(\delta) = \alpha_E^\varepsilon(\delta) = 0, \quad \text{if} \quad \delta < \frac{\varepsilon}{v}.$$

In accordance with the remarks at the end of sec. 6.15, there is a stationary non-cut-off continuous process on a straight line corresponding to this function. We shall describe this process as a determinate motion with velocity v. We can easily show that, for the process,

$$\mathbf{P}_x\{x_t = x+t \text{ for all } t \geqslant 0\} = 1.$$

6.18.2. We have for the Wiener transition function constructed in sec. 4.2.3:

$$P(t, x; t+h, \overline{U_\varepsilon(x)}) = [2\pi h]^{-\frac{n}{2}} \int\limits_{|z| \geqslant \varepsilon} e^{-\frac{z^2}{2h}} dz,$$

where z^2 denotes the scalar square, and $|z|$ the length of vector z. We get from this, after some simple calculation

$$P(t, x; t+h, \overline{U_\varepsilon(x)}) = c_n F\left(\frac{\varepsilon}{\sqrt{h}}\right), \tag{6.43}$$

where c_n is a constant, and

$$F(r) = \int\limits_r^\infty e^{-\frac{r^2}{2}} r^{n-1} dr.$$

It follows from (6.43) that

$$\alpha^\varepsilon(\delta) = c_n F\left(\frac{\varepsilon}{\sqrt{\delta}}\right).$$

By L'Hospital's rule, $F(r) \sim r^{n-2} e^{-\frac{r^2}{2}}$ as $r \to \infty$, so that, as $\delta \downarrow 0$:

$$\alpha^\varepsilon(\delta) \sim c_n \varepsilon^{n-2} \delta^{-\frac{n-2}{2}} e^{-\frac{\varepsilon^2}{2\delta}}.$$

It is clear from this expression that the $N(E)$ condition is fulfilled. In accordance with the remarks at the end of sec. 6.15, we can conclude from this that there is a stationary non-cut-off continuous Markov process which corresponds to the Wiener transition function. We describe it as a Wiener process. It may easily be seen to be of Feller's type. It is therefore strictly Markov (see theorem 5.10).

6.18.3. We shall now investigate the transition function described in sec. 4.2.4 in the interval $[0, \infty)$. We notice that, for any $a > 0,\ x > 0,\ t > 0,\ h \geqslant 0$:

$$P(t, x;\ t+h,\ (a, \infty)) = \\ = \frac{1}{\sqrt{2\pi}} \int\limits_{|y\sqrt{h}-a| \leqslant x} e^{-\frac{y^2}{2}}\, dy < \frac{1}{\sqrt{2\pi}} \cdot \frac{2x}{\sqrt{h}}. \qquad (6.44)$$

It follows easily from (6.44) that the system $\mathcal{F}$ of all sets $[a, \infty)$ $(a > 0)$ satisfies condition 6.3.A.($\left[\frac{1}{n}, \infty\right)$ can be taken as E_n). System $\mathcal{F}$ is obviously normal. Simple calculation similar to that of 6.18.2, shows that, for $\varepsilon < a$,

$$\alpha^{\varepsilon}_{[a, \infty)}(\delta) \sim c\varepsilon^{-1}\delta^{\frac{1}{2}} e^{-\frac{\varepsilon^2}{2\delta}}.$$

The $N(\Gamma)$ condition thus holds for any $\Gamma \in \mathcal{F}$, and by the corollary of theorem 6.6 (see also remark 2) an $\mathcal{F}$-bounded continuous stationary Markov process exists with transition probabilities 4.2.4. This process is clearly of Feller's type and is therefore strictly Markov. It can be shown that, for any $s \geqslant 0,\ x \in E$:

$$\lim_{t \uparrow \zeta(\omega)} x_t(\omega) = 0 \qquad (\text{a.c. } \Omega_s,\ \mathbf{P}_{s,x}).$$

We may describe the process as a one-dimensional Wiener process with a break at the point 0*).

6.18.4. For the transition function of sec. 4.2.5 we have $\alpha^{\varepsilon}(\delta) \sim c\varepsilon^{-1}\delta^{\frac{1}{2}} e^{-\frac{\varepsilon^2}{2\delta}}$, and some continuous Markov process therefore corresponds to the function. In accordance with remark 2 (sec. 6.15), we can choose a non-cut-off stationary process for the process. We shall refer to this as a <u>one-dimensional Wiener process with reflection at the point</u> 0.

6.18.5. We shall now construct an example of a continuous

---

*) What we have described is not in fact one process but a whole class of processes. For the sake of clarity we can choose from among these the canonical process which is subordinate to all the rest.

Markov process which is not strictly Markov.

We take a stationary transition function on the real line $E=(-\infty, +\infty)$ with the usual metric $\rho(x, y)=|y-x|$, the function being defined by

$$P(s, x; t, \Gamma)=\begin{cases}\frac{1}{\sqrt{2\pi(t-s)}}\int\limits_{\Gamma}\exp\left[-\frac{(x-y)^2}{2(t-s)}\right]dy, & \text{if } x\neq 0,\\ \chi_{\Gamma}(x), & \text{if } x=0.\end{cases}$$

This function is complete and satisfies the $N(E)$ condition. It therefore corresponds to some non-cut-off continuous stationary Markov process $X=(x_t, \mathscr{N}^s_t, \mathbf{P}_{s, x})$.

The instant $\tau=\xi(G)$ of first departure of the trajectory from the set $G=E\setminus\{0\}$ is a random variable independent of the future and 0-past. For, if Λ is a denumerable set everywhere dense in the segment $[0, t]$, we have

$$\{\tau>t\}=\bigcup_{m=1}^{\infty}\bigcap_{v\in\Lambda}\left\{|x_v|\geqslant\frac{1}{m}\right\}\in\mathscr{M}^0_t.$$

We put $\omega\in A$ if there exists a t such that $x_v(\omega)=0$ for all $v\geqslant t$. It may be observed that, if $x\neq 0$, $\mathbf{P}_{0, x}(A)=0$. This follows from the inclusion $A\subseteq\bigcup\limits_{n=1}^{\infty}\{x_n=0\}$ and the equation $\mathbf{P}_{0, x}\{x_n=0\}=P(0, x; n, x)=0.$

On the other hand, $\mathbf{P}_{0, 0}(A)=1$. For

$$A\supseteq\bigcap_{r\in\Lambda}\{x_r=0\},$$

where Λ is the set of all rational non-negative numbers. Since for every r:

$$\mathbf{P}_{0, 0}\{x_r=0\}=P(0, 0; r, 0)=1,$$

we have

$$P_{0, 0}\left\{\bigcap_{r\in\Lambda}(x_r=0)\right\}=1$$

and all the more:

$$P_{0, 0}(A)=1.$$

It may easily be seen, moreover, that $\theta_u A = A$ for any u, so that $\theta_\tau A = A$.

If the process X were strictly Markov, we should be able to write, in accordance with (5.40),

$$\mathbf{P}_{0,x}\{\theta_\tau A\} = \mathbf{M}_{0,x}\mathbf{P}_{0,x_\tau}(A). \tag{6.45}$$

But $x_\tau = 0$, so that the right-hand side of (6.45) is equal to unity for any x*). At the same time, the left-hand side is equal to zero for $x \neq 0$.

*)It is easily proved that $\mathbf{P}_{0,x}\{\Omega_\tau\} = 1$ for all x.

ADDENDUM

A THEOREM REGARDING THE PROLONGATION OF CAPACITIES AND THE PROPERTIES OF MEASURABILITY OF THE INSTANTS OF FIRST DEPARTURE

1. A Theorem Regarding the Extension of Capacities

1. A compact Hausdorff space with a denumerable base*) is referred to as a compact.

Locally compact Hausdorff spaces with denumerable bases will be described as semi-compacts. Some properties of such spaces will be listed.

1.A. A semi-compact is a σ-compact space.

1.B. A topological space is a semi-compact when and only when it can be got by discarding a point from a compact.

1.C. A complete metric can be introduced into any semi-compact.

1.D. Each closed and each open set in a semi-compact can be written as the sum of a denumerable number of compact subsets.

Proof of 1.A. Let $\tilde{\mathcal{C}} \subseteq \mathcal{C}$ be a denumerable base of the semi-compact $(E, \mathcal{C})$. We write $\tilde{\mathcal{C}}'$, for the subsystem of system $\tilde{\mathcal{C}}$ consisting of all the elements of $\tilde{\mathcal{C}}$ with compact closures. Let $x \in E$. In view of the local compactness of $(E, \mathcal{C})$, there exists a neighbourhood U of the point x with a compact closure. Since $\tilde{\mathcal{C}}$ is a base, there exists $G \in \tilde{\mathcal{C}}$ such that

*)A subsystem $\tilde{\mathcal{C}}$ of a system $\mathcal{C}$ is said to be a base of the topological space $(E, \mathcal{C})$ if every set $\Gamma \in \mathcal{C}$ can be written as the sum of elements of $\tilde{\mathcal{C}}$.

$x \in G \subseteq U$. Clearly, $G \in \tilde{\mathcal{C}}'$. Thus every point $x \in E$ belongs to some set $G \in \tilde{\mathcal{C}}'$, and $\tilde{\mathcal{C}}'$ is a covering of space E. The closures of the elements of $\tilde{\mathcal{C}}'$ form a denumerable system of compacts adding up to the sum E.

Proof of 1.B. Discarding a point from a compact evidently leads to a semi-compact. We show that a compact can be got from any semi-compact of $(E, \mathcal{C})$ by adding a single point a. We put $E_1 = E \cup \{a\}$ and write $\mathcal{C}_1$ for the system of all subsets appearing in $\mathcal{C}$ and of all sets of the form $\{a\} \cup \{E \setminus \Gamma\}$, where Γ is any compact subset of space $(E, \mathcal{C})$. It may easily be seen that $(E_1, \mathcal{C}_1)$ is a compact.

Proof of 1.C. In view of 1.B we can assume that $E = E_1 \setminus \{a\}$, where $(E_1, \mathcal{C}_1)$ is a compact, into which some metric $\rho_1(x, y)$ is introduced*). This metric may easily be seen to be complete. The expression

$$\rho(x, y) = \rho_1(x, y) + |\rho_1(x, a)^{-1} - \rho_1(y, a)^{-1}| \quad (x, y \in E)$$

is readily seen to define a complete metric in E.

Proof of 1.D. In accordance with 1.A, $E = \bigcup_{m=1}^{\infty} E_m$, where the E_m are compact sets. If Γ is closed, we have

$$\Gamma = \bigcup_{m=1}^{\infty} \Gamma E_m$$

and the ΓE_m are clearly compact. Now let G be open, and let $\rho(x, y)$ be any metric in $(E, \mathcal{C})$ (existing by virtue of 1.C). We put

$$\Gamma_n = \left\{ y : \rho(x, E \setminus G) \geqslant \frac{1}{n} \right\}.$$

Obviously, Γ_n is closed and

$$G = \bigcup_{n=1}^{\infty} \Gamma_n = \bigcup_{n=1}^{\infty} \bigcup_{m=1}^{\infty} \Gamma_n E_m.$$

The sets $\Gamma_n E_m$ are compact.

2. We shall write $\mathcal{K}(E, \mathcal{C})$ for the class of all compact subsets of the topological space $(E, \mathcal{C})$, $\mathcal{K}_\sigma(E, \mathcal{C})$ for the class

*)The proof of the metrizability of any compact can be found e.g. in Ref. 25.

of all subsets which are the sums of a denumerable number of compact subsets, and $\mathscr{K}_{\sigma\delta}(E, \mathcal{C})$ for the class of all subsets expressible as the intersections of a denumerable number of sets of $\mathscr{K}_{\sigma}(E, \mathcal{C})$.

We shall describe a subset Γ of the space $(E, \mathcal{C})$ as <u>analytic</u> if, in some compact $(E', \mathcal{C}')$ a set $\mathrm{B} \in \mathscr{K}_{\sigma\delta}(E', \mathcal{C}')$ can be constructed which permits a continuous mapping on to Γ.

<u>Lemma 1</u>. Every Borel set in the semi-compact $(E, \mathcal{C})$ is an analytic set.

Proof. Let $\mathscr{S}$ denote the class of all analytic sets in the space $(E, \mathcal{C})$.

1°. We show that, if $\Gamma_n \in \mathscr{S}$ $(n = 1, 2, \ldots)$ and

$$\Gamma = \bigcup_{n=1}^{\infty} \Gamma_n,$$

then $\Gamma \in \mathscr{S}$.

By hypothesis, there exists for any n a compact $(E_n, \mathcal{C}_n)$ and a set $\mathrm{B}_n \in \mathscr{K}_{\sigma\delta}(E_n, \mathcal{C}_n)$ admitting a continuous mapping f_n in Γ_n.

Let

$$\widetilde{E} = \bigcup_{n=1}^{\infty} E_n$$

and let $\widetilde{\mathcal{C}}$ be the class of all subsets of the set $\widetilde{E}$ expressible in the form $\bigcup_{n=1}^{\infty} U_n$, where $U_n \in \mathcal{C}_n$. The topological space $(E, \mathcal{C})$ is a semi-compact, so that (see 1.B) it can be got by discarding a point from some compact $(E', \mathcal{C}')$. We put

$$\mathrm{B} = \bigcup_{n=1}^{\infty} \mathrm{B}_n$$

and define a mapping $f: \mathrm{B} \to E$ by the expression $f(x) = f_n(x)$, if $x \in \mathrm{B}_n$. It is easily verified that $\mathrm{B} \in \mathscr{K}_{\sigma\delta}(E', \mathcal{C}')$ and f is a continuous mapping of B on to Γ.

2°. We now show that, if

$$\Gamma_n \in \mathscr{S} \qquad (n = 1, 2, \ldots)$$

and

$$\Gamma = \bigcap_{n=1}^{\infty} \Gamma_n,$$

then $\Gamma \in \mathscr{S}$.

Let $(E_n, \mathcal{C}_n)$, B_n and f_n have the same meanings as in sec. 1°. The space

$$(E', \mathcal{C}') = \\ = (E_1 \times E_2 \times \dots \times E_n \times \dots, \mathcal{C}_1 \times \mathcal{C}_2 \times \dots \times \mathcal{C}_n \times \dots)$$

is a compact. The set

$$\widetilde{B} = B_1 \times B_2 \times \dots \times B_n \times \dots$$

is the intersection of sets $E_1 \times \dots \times E_{n-1} \times B_n \times E_{n+1} \times \dots \in \mathscr{K}_{\sigma\delta}(E', \mathcal{C}')$. Consequently $\widetilde{B} \in \mathscr{K}_{\sigma\delta}(E', \mathcal{C}')$.

We take the mappings $f_n : \widetilde{B} \to E$ defined by

$$f_n(x_1, \dots, x_n, \dots) = f_n(x_n).$$

Each of these mappings is continuous, and the set

$$B = \{x : f_1(x) = f_2(x) = \dots = f_n(x) = \dots\}$$

is therefore closed with respect to $\widetilde{B}$, i.e. $B = \widetilde{B}\hat{B}$, where $\hat{B}$ denotes the closure of B in E'. The set $\hat{B}$ is compact. Therefore $B = \widetilde{B}\hat{B} \in \mathscr{K}_{\sigma\delta}(E', \mathcal{C}')$. The mappings f_n all induce the same mapping f of set B in E. Obviously $f(B) \subseteq \Gamma_n$ for any n, so that $f(B) \subseteq \Gamma$. We show that f maps B on to Γ. For let $c \in \Gamma$. There exists $x_n \in B_n$ such that $f_n(x_n) = c$ for any n. The point $x = (x_1, x_2, \dots, x_n, \dots)$ of E' belongs to B and $f(x) = c$.

3°. All the open and all the closed subsets of $(E, \mathcal{C})$ belong to $\mathscr{S}$.

For $\mathscr{S}$ contains any compact set Γ (since we can put $E' = B = \Gamma$ and take the identity mapping for f). By 1.D, every closed and every open set can be expressed as the sum of a sequence of compact sets. Our assertion therefore follows from sec. 1°.

4°. We put $\Gamma \in \mathscr{S}'$ if $\Gamma \in \mathscr{S}$ and $\overline{\Gamma} \in \mathscr{S}$. It follows from sec. 1° and 2° that $\mathscr{S}'$ is closed with respect to the operations of denumerable summation and denumerable intersection. Since it follows obviously from $\Gamma \in \mathscr{S}'$ that $\overline{\Gamma} \in \mathscr{S}'$, $\mathscr{S}'$ is a σ-algebra. In accordance with 3°, $\mathscr{S}' \supseteq \mathcal{C}$. Consequently $\mathscr{S}' \supseteq \sigma(\mathcal{C})$, i.e. it contains all the Borel sets of the space $(E, \mathcal{C})$.

3. Let $\mathscr{F}$ be any system of subsets of the semi-compact

$(E, \mathcal{C})$ such that it contains all open and all compact sets. We shall call the function φ, defined on $\mathcal{F}$ and taking values from the segment $[0, 1]$, a capacity if the following conditions are fulfilled:

3.A. If $\Gamma_1 \subseteq \Gamma_2$ and $\Gamma_1, \Gamma_2 \in \mathcal{F}$, then $\varphi(\Gamma_1) \leqslant \varphi(\Gamma_2)$.

3.B. If $\Gamma_n \uparrow \Gamma$ and $\Gamma_n \in \mathcal{F}$, then $\Gamma \in \mathcal{F}$ and $\varphi(\Gamma_n) \uparrow \varphi(\Gamma)$.

3.C. Given any compact set Γ and any $\varepsilon > 0$, a $G \in \mathcal{C}$ can be found such that $G \supseteq \Gamma$ and

$$\varphi(G) - \varphi(\Gamma) < \varepsilon.$$

3.D. If $\Gamma, \tilde{\Gamma}, B \in \mathcal{F}$ and $\tilde{\Gamma} \subseteq \Gamma$, then

$$\varphi(\Gamma \cup B) - \varphi(\tilde{\Gamma} \cup B) \leqslant \varphi(\Gamma) - \varphi(\tilde{\Gamma}).$$

The following property is a consequence of 3.D:

3.E. For any $\tilde{\Gamma}_i \subseteq \Gamma_i (i = 1, 2, \ldots, n)$ of $\mathcal{F}$:

$$\varphi\left(\bigcup_1^n \Gamma_i\right) - \varphi\left(\bigcup_1^n \tilde{\Gamma}_i\right) \leqslant \sum_1^n [\varphi(\Gamma_i) - \varphi(\tilde{\Gamma}_i)].$$

For,

$$\varphi\left(\bigcup_1^n \Gamma_i\right) - \varphi\left(\bigcup_1^n \tilde{\Gamma}_i\right) = \sum_1^n [\varphi(\Gamma_i \cup B_i) - \varphi(\tilde{\Gamma}_i \cup B_i)],$$

where

$$B_i = \Gamma_1 \cup \ldots \cup \Gamma_{i-1} \cup \tilde{\Gamma}_{i+1} \cup \ldots \cup \tilde{\Gamma}_n \qquad (i = 1, 2, \ldots, n).$$

For each $\Gamma \subseteq E$ we shall write $\varphi^*(\Gamma)$ for the lower bound of $\varphi(G)$ with respect to all open sets G containing Γ, and $\varphi_*(\Gamma)$ for the upper bound of all $\varphi(\tilde{\Gamma})$ over all the closed sets $\tilde{\Gamma}$ contained in Γ.

Our purpose is to prove the following theorem regarding the extension of capacities.

Theorem 1. Whatever the capacity φ in the semi-compact $(E, \mathcal{C})$, we have for any analytic (and in particular, any Borel) set Γ:

$$\varphi_*(\Gamma) = \varphi^*(\Gamma).$$

4. We shall need some lemmas before proving theorem 1.

Lemma 2. For any sets $\widetilde{\Gamma}_i \subseteq \Gamma_i \subseteq E$ $(i=1, 2, \ldots, n)$

$$\varphi^*\left(\bigcup_1^n \Gamma_i\right) - \varphi^*\left(\bigcup_1^n \widetilde{\Gamma}_i\right) \leqslant \sum_1^n [\varphi^*(\Gamma_i) - \varphi^*(\widetilde{\Gamma}_i)]. \tag{1}$$

If $\Gamma_n \uparrow \Gamma$, we have

$$\varphi^*(\Gamma_n) \uparrow \varphi^*(\Gamma). \tag{2}$$

Proof. Let $\varepsilon > 0$. We choose open sets G_i $(i=1, 2, \ldots, n)$ and $\widetilde{G}$ such that $\Gamma_i \subseteq G_i$, $\widetilde{G} \supseteq \bigcup_1^n \widetilde{\Gamma}_i$ and

$$\left.\begin{aligned} &\varphi(G_i) \leqslant \varphi^*(\Gamma_i) + \varepsilon \qquad (i=1, 2, \ldots, n), \\ &\varphi(\widetilde{G}) \leqslant \varphi^*\left(\bigcup_1^n \widetilde{\Gamma}_i\right) + \varepsilon. \end{aligned}\right\} \tag{3}$$

We put $\widetilde{G}_i = \widetilde{G} G_i$. Obviously $\widetilde{G} \supseteq \widetilde{G}_i \supseteq \widetilde{\Gamma}_i$ and

$$\varphi\left(\bigcup_1^n \widetilde{G}_i\right) \leqslant \varphi^*\left(\bigcup_1^n \widetilde{\Gamma}_i\right) + \varepsilon. \tag{4}$$

We have on the basis of (3), (4) and 3.E:

$$\begin{aligned} &\varphi^*\left(\bigcup_1^n \Gamma_i\right) - \varphi^*\left(\bigcup_1^n \widetilde{\Gamma}_i\right) \leqslant \varphi\left(\bigcup_1^n G_i\right) - \varphi\left(\bigcup_1^n \widetilde{G}_i\right) + \varepsilon \leqslant \\ &\leqslant \sum_1^n [\varphi(G_i) - \varphi(\widetilde{G}_i)] + \varepsilon \leqslant \sum_1^n [\varphi^*(\Gamma_i) - \varphi^*(\widetilde{\Gamma}_i)] + (n+1)\varepsilon. \end{aligned} \tag{5}$$

Since ε is arbitrary, (1) follows from (5).

Now let $\Gamma_n \uparrow \Gamma$. For any $\varepsilon > 0$ we can choose open sets G_n such that $G_n \supseteq \Gamma_n$ and

$$\varphi(G_n) < \frac{\varepsilon}{2^n} + \varphi^*(\Gamma_n).$$

We put

$$G^{(n)} = \bigcup_1^n G_i.$$

In view of (1):

$$\begin{aligned} \varphi(G^{(n)}) - \varphi^*(\Gamma_n) = \varphi\left(\bigcup_1^n G_i\right) - \varphi^*\left(\bigcup_1^n \Gamma_i\right) &\leqslant \\ \leqslant \frac{\varepsilon}{2} + \ldots + \frac{\varepsilon}{2^n} &< \varepsilon. \end{aligned} \tag{6}$$

We put

$$G=\bigcup_{1}^{\infty} G_i=\bigcup_{1}^{\infty} G^{(n)}.$$

By 3.B:

$$\varphi\left(G^{(n)}\right) \uparrow \varphi(G). \tag{7}$$

From (6) and (7):

$$\varphi(G)-\lim_{n\to\infty} \varphi^*(\Gamma_n) \leqslant \varepsilon. \tag{8}$$

Since $\varphi(G) \geqslant \varphi^*(\Gamma_n)$, (2) follows from (8).

Lemma 3. If $\Gamma \in \mathscr{K}_{\sigma\delta}(E, \mathcal{C})$, we have

$$\varphi_*(\Gamma)=\varphi^*(\Gamma).$$

Proof. Let $\Gamma \in \mathscr{K}_{\sigma\delta}(E, \mathcal{C})$. Then Γ can be expressed as

$$\Gamma=\bigcap_{n=1}^{\infty} \Gamma_n \qquad (\Gamma_n \in \mathscr{K}_\sigma(E, \mathcal{C})).$$

We can choose the sets $\Gamma_n^k \in \mathscr{K}(E, \mathcal{C})$ such that $\Gamma_n^k \uparrow \Gamma_n$. We assign any positive ε and put

$$B_1^k=\Gamma_1^k\Gamma.$$

Obviously, $B_1^k \uparrow \Gamma$ and by (2), $\varphi^*\left(B_1^k\right) \uparrow \varphi^*(\Gamma)$. We select k_1 so that

$$\varphi^*(\Gamma)-\varphi^*\left(B_1^{k_1}\right)<\frac{\varepsilon}{2}.$$

We put

$$B_2^k=B_1^{k_1}\Gamma_2^k.$$

We have $B_2^k \uparrow B_1^{k_1}$. By (2), $\varphi^*\left(B_2^k\right) \uparrow \varphi^*\left(B_1^{k_1}\right)$. We choose k_2 so that

$$\varphi^*\left(B_1^{k_1}\right)-\varphi^*\left(B_2^{k_2}\right)<\frac{\varepsilon}{4}.$$

On continuing these constructions, we get a sequence of sets

$$B_3^{k_3}=B_2^{k_2}\Gamma_3^{k_3},$$

$$\cdots\cdots$$

$$B_n^{k_n}=B_{n-1}^{k_{n-1}}\Gamma_n^{k_n},$$

$$\cdots\cdots$$

such that

$$\varphi^*\left(B_{n-1}^{k_{n-1}}\right) - \varphi^*\left(B_n^{k_n}\right) < \frac{\varepsilon}{2^n}.$$

Thus for any n:

$$\varphi^*(\Gamma) - \varphi^*\left(B_n^{k_n}\right) < \frac{\varepsilon}{2} + \ldots + \frac{\varepsilon}{2^n} < \varepsilon. \tag{9}$$

We put

$$B_\varepsilon = \bigcap_{n=1}^{\infty} B_n^{k_n} = \Gamma\Gamma_1^{k_1} \ldots \Gamma_n^{k_n} \ldots,$$

$$A_n = \Gamma_1^{k_1}\Gamma_2^{k_2} \ldots \Gamma_n^{k_n}.$$

Since $\Gamma_n^{k_n} \subseteq \Gamma_n$ and $\bigcap_1^\infty \Gamma_n = \Gamma$, we have

$$\bigcap_1^\infty \Gamma_n^{k_n} \subseteq \Gamma$$

and

$$B_\varepsilon = \bigcap_1^\infty \Gamma_n^{k_n}$$

is a compact set. By 3.C, we can choose an open set $G \supseteq B_\varepsilon$ such that

$$\varphi(G) - \varphi(B_\varepsilon) < \varepsilon. \tag{10}$$

We observe that

$$B_n^{k_n} = A_n\Gamma \text{ and } A_n \downarrow B_\varepsilon.$$

Hence (in view of the compactness of A_n), as from a certain n, $B_n^{k_n} \subseteq A_n \subseteq G$ and by (9) and (10):

$$\varphi^*(\Gamma) < \varphi^*\left(B_n^{k_n}\right) + \varepsilon \leqslant \varphi(G) + \varepsilon < \varphi(B_\varepsilon) + 2\varepsilon.$$

Since B_ε is compact and contained in Γ, we have

$$\varphi(B_\varepsilon) \leqslant \varphi_*(\Gamma) \text{ and } \varphi^*(\Gamma) < \varphi_*(\Gamma) + 2\varepsilon.$$

It follows from this, in view of the fact that ε is arbitrary, that $\varphi^*(\Gamma) = \varphi_*(\Gamma)$.

5. Proof of theorem 1. Let Γ_0 be an arbitrary analytic set of the space $(E, \mathcal{C})$. We can construct in some compact

$(E', \mathcal{C}')$ a set $B \in \mathscr{K}_{\sigma\delta}(E', \mathcal{C}')$ admitting a continuous mapping f on the set Γ_0. We take the space $(\widetilde{E}, \widetilde{\mathcal{C}}) = (E \times E', \mathcal{C} \times \mathcal{C}')$ (it is clearly a semi-compact) and write p for the projection of $\widetilde{E}$ to E, i.e. the mapping given by

$$p(x, x') = x \qquad (x \in E, \ x' \in E').$$

The set of all points $(f(x'), x')$ $(x' \in B)$ will be denoted by $\widetilde{\Gamma}_0$. If $p(\widetilde{\Gamma}) \in \mathscr{F}$, we put $\widetilde{\Gamma} \in \widetilde{\mathscr{F}}$ and

$$\widetilde{\varphi}(\widetilde{\Gamma}) = \varphi(\Gamma). \tag{11}$$

1°. We show that the function $\widetilde{\varphi}(\widetilde{\Gamma})$ $(\widetilde{\Gamma} \in \widetilde{\mathscr{F}})$ is a capacity in the space $(\widetilde{E}, \widetilde{\mathcal{C}})$. Firstly, $\widetilde{\mathscr{F}}$ contains all the compact and all the open sets of the space $(\widetilde{E}, \widetilde{\mathcal{C}})$. For $p(\widetilde{\Gamma})$ is open if $\widetilde{\Gamma}$ is open, and compact if $\widetilde{\Gamma}$ is compact. Moreover, the mapping p preserves the operation of summation and the inclusion relationship. Hence, since conditions 3.A-3.B and 3.D hold for the function φ, it follows that they also hold for the function $\widetilde{\varphi}$. We prove 3.C by observing that, if $\widetilde{\Gamma}$ is a compact subset in $(\widetilde{E}, \widetilde{\mathcal{C}})$ and if $G \in \mathcal{C}$ is such that

$$\varphi(G) - \varphi[p(\widetilde{\Gamma})] < \varepsilon,$$

the set $\widetilde{G} = G \times E'$ belongs to $\widetilde{\mathcal{C}}$, and at the same time we have

$$\widetilde{\varphi}(\widetilde{G}) - \widetilde{\varphi}(\widetilde{\Gamma}) < \varepsilon.$$

2°. We show that $\widetilde{\Gamma}_0 \in \mathscr{K}_{\sigma\delta}(\widetilde{E}, \widetilde{\mathcal{C}})$. To start with, it may easily be deduced from the continuity of f that

$$\widetilde{\Gamma}_0 = (E \times B)\widetilde{\Gamma}_0', \tag{12}$$

where $\widetilde{\Gamma}_0'$ is the closure of $\widetilde{\Gamma}_0$ in $(\widetilde{E}, \widetilde{\mathcal{C}})$. In accordance with 1.D, the closed set $\widetilde{\Gamma}_0'$ in the semi-compact $(\widetilde{E}, \widetilde{\mathcal{C}})$ can be written as

$$\widetilde{\Gamma}_0' = \bigcup_1^\infty K_n,$$

where $K_n \in \mathscr{K}(\widetilde{E}, \widetilde{\mathcal{C}})$. On the other hand,

$$E = \bigcup_1^\infty E_m, \quad B = \bigcap_{k=1}^\infty \bigcup_{i=1}^\infty B_k^i,$$

where sets E_m and B_k^i are compact. We have from (12):

$$\widetilde{\Gamma}_0 = \bigcap_{k=1}^\infty \bigcup_{i, m, n=1}^\infty (E_m \times B_k^i) K_n.$$

The sets $(E_m \times B_k^i) K_n$ are evidently compact, so that $\widetilde{\Gamma}_0 \in \mathscr{K}_{\sigma\delta}(\widetilde{E}, \widetilde{\mathcal{C}})$.

3°. It follows from 2° and lemma 3 that

$$\widetilde{\varphi}_*(\widetilde{\Gamma}_0) = \widetilde{\varphi}^*(\widetilde{\Gamma}_0). \tag{13}$$

We observe that

$$\varphi_*(\Gamma_0) = \sup_{\substack{\Gamma \in \mathscr{K}(E, \mathcal{C}) \\ \Gamma \subseteq \Gamma_0}} \varphi(\Gamma) \geqslant \sup_{\substack{\widetilde{\Gamma} \in \mathscr{K}(\widetilde{E}, \widetilde{\mathcal{C}}) \\ \widetilde{\Gamma} \subseteq \widetilde{\Gamma}_0}} \varphi[p(\widetilde{\Gamma})] = \widetilde{\varphi}_*(\widetilde{\Gamma}_0) \tag{14}$$

$$\varphi^*(\Gamma_0) = \inf_{\substack{G \in \mathcal{C} \\ G \supseteq \Gamma_0}} \varphi(G) \leqslant \inf_{\substack{\widetilde{G} \in \widetilde{\mathcal{C}} \\ \widetilde{G} \supseteq \widetilde{\Gamma}_0}} \varphi[p(\widetilde{G})] = \widetilde{\varphi}^*(\widetilde{\Gamma}_0). \tag{15}$$

It follows from (13), (14) and (15) that $\varphi_*(\Gamma_0) \geqslant \varphi^*(\Gamma_0)$. But since $\varphi_*(\Gamma_0) \leqslant \varphi^*(\Gamma_0)$ in view of 3.A, we have $\varphi_*(\Gamma_0) = \varphi^*(\Gamma_0)$.

2. Measurability Theorems for the Instants of First Departure

6. Let $X = (x_t, \zeta, \mathscr{M}_t^s, \mathbf{P}_{s,x})$ be a Markov process in the measurable space $(E, \mathscr{B})$. For every $\omega \in \Omega_\tau$ we write $F_t^s = F_t^s(\omega)$ for the segment of the trajectory during the time $[s, t]$, i.e. the set of points $x_u(\omega)$, where $u \in [s, t]$.

If the process X is given in a topological measurable space, we shall write $\dot{F}_t^s$ for the closure of the set F_t^s.

Lemma 4. Let X be a Markov process continuous from the right in the topological measurable space $(E, \mathcal{C}, \mathscr{B})$. Then for any closed set $\Gamma \in \mathscr{B}$ and any $0 \leqslant s \leqslant t$:

$$\{\dot{F}_t^s \subseteq \Gamma\} = \{F_t^s \subseteq \Gamma\} \in \mathscr{N}_t^s. \tag{16}$$

Let $U \in \mathcal{C}\mathscr{B}$. We assume that one of the following conditions is fulfilled:

6.A. $(E, \mathcal{C}, \mathscr{B})$ satisfies condition 1.9.B and the closure of U is compact.

6.B. $(E, \mathcal{C}, \mathscr{B})$ is metrizable, $\mathscr{B} \supseteq \mathcal{C}$ and $E \setminus U$ is compact.

Then we can construct a sequence of measurable closed sets $\Gamma_n \uparrow U$ such that, for any $0 \leqslant s \leqslant t$:

$$\{\hat{F}_t^s \subseteq \Gamma_n\} \uparrow \{\hat{F}_t^s \subseteq U\} \tag{17}$$

and

$$\{\hat{F}_t^s \subseteq U\} \in \mathcal{N}_t^s. \tag{18}$$

Proof. Let Γ be a measurable closed set and let Λ be any denumerable everywhere dense subset of the segment $[s, t]$, containing the point t. Obviously,

$$\{\hat{F}_t^s \subseteq \Gamma\} = \{F_t^s \subseteq \Gamma\} = \bigcap_{r \in \Lambda} \{x_r \in \Gamma\},$$

so that (16) holds.

Furthermore, let U be an open measurable set. In case 6.A we take the function $f(x)$ defined by condition 1.9.B. In case 6.B we put $f(x) = \rho(x, \overline{U})$. The sets

$$\Gamma_n = \left\{x : f(x) \geqslant \frac{1}{n}\right\}$$

are closed and measurable and $\Gamma_n \uparrow U$. Evidently,

$$\{\hat{F}_t^s \subseteq U\} \supseteq \bigcup_{n=1}^{\infty} \{\hat{F}_t^s \subseteq \Gamma_n\}.$$

We can prove (17) simply by proving that the converse inclusion also holds. All we have to do for this is to show that

$$\{\hat{F}_t^s \subseteq U\} \subseteq \{\inf_{x \in \hat{F}_t^s} f(x) > 0\}. \tag{19}$$

In case 6.A, this inclusion follows from the fact that the continuous function $f(x)$ attains a minimum on the compact set $\hat{F}_t^s$. In case 6.B, the continuous function $\rho(y, \hat{F}_t^s)$ attains a minimum on the compact set $\overline{U}$. If

$$\hat{F}_t^s \overline{U} = \emptyset,$$

this minimum is positive and we have

$$\inf_{x \in \hat{F}_t^s} f(x) = \rho(\hat{F}_t^s, \overline{U}) > 0.$$

As already mentioned, (17) is a consequence of inclusion (19) just proved. Expression (18) is a fairly obvious consequence of (16) and (17).

7. We put $A \in \bar{\mathcal{N}}_t^s$ if, for every measure μ on the σ-algebra $\mathscr{B}$ there exist sets A_1 and A_2 of $\mathcal{N}_t^s$ such that $A_1 \subseteq A \subseteq A_2$ and $\mathbf{P}_{s,\mu}(A_1) = \mathbf{P}_{s,\mu}(A_2)$*).

Theorem 2. Let $(E, \mathcal{C})$ be a semi-compact, let $\mathscr{B}$ be the σ-algebra in E containing $\mathcal{C}$, and let X be a Markov process continuous from the right in the topological measurable space $(E, \mathcal{C}, \mathscr{B})$.

Then for any Borel set Γ and any $0 \leqslant s \leqslant t$:

$$\{\hat{F}_t^s \subseteq \Gamma\} \in \bar{\mathcal{N}}_t^s. \tag{20}$$

Given any Borel set Γ, any measure μ on the σ-algebra $\mathscr{B}$ and any $0 \leqslant s \leqslant t$, we can construct a sequence of closed sets

$$\Gamma_1 \subseteq \Gamma_2 \subseteq \ldots \subseteq \Gamma_n \subseteq \ldots \subseteq \Gamma$$

and a sequence of open sets $U_1 \supseteq U_2 \supseteq \ldots \supseteq U_n \supseteq \ldots \supseteq \Gamma$ with compact complements such that

$$\begin{aligned} &\mathbf{P}_{s,\mu}\{\hat{F}_t^s \subseteq \Gamma_n\} \uparrow \mathbf{P}_{s,\mu}\{\hat{F}_t^s \subseteq \Gamma\}, \\ &\mathbf{P}_{s,\mu}\{\hat{F}_t^s \subseteq U_n\} \downarrow \mathbf{P}_{s,\mu}\{\hat{F}_t^s \subseteq \Gamma\}. \end{aligned} \tag{21}$$

Proof. We fix the $0 \leqslant s \leqslant t$ and put $\Gamma \in \mathscr{F}$ if

$$\{\hat{F}_t^s \subseteq E \setminus \Gamma\} \in \bar{\mathcal{N}}_t^s.$$

In view of lemma 4, the system $\mathscr{F}$ contains all compact and all open sets. Having fixed a probability measure μ on the σ-algebra $\mathscr{B}$, we put for each $\Gamma \in \mathscr{F}$:

$$\varphi(\Gamma) = \mathbf{P}_{s,\mu}\{\hat{F}_t^s \Gamma \neq \emptyset\} = \mathbf{P}_{s,\mu}\{\Omega_t \setminus [\hat{F}_t^s \subseteq E \setminus \Gamma]\}^{**)} \tag{22}$$

We show that the function φ is a capacity, i.e. satisfies conditions 3.A-3.D. It is obvious that 3.A-3.B are fulfilled.

---

*)Cf. foot-note on p.55.

**)This expression is meaningful because the set in brackets belongs to $\bar{\mathcal{N}}_t^s \subseteq \bar{\mathcal{N}}^s$ and, in accordance with sec. 2.3, the measures $\mathbf{P}_{s,\mu}$ can be extended to $\bar{\mathcal{N}}^s$.

Conditions 3.C follows from relationship (17) which we proved in lemma 4. It remains to consider condition 3.D.

We notice that, if $\Gamma, \widetilde{\Gamma}, \mathrm{B} \in \mathscr{F}$ and $\widetilde{\Gamma} \subseteq \Gamma$, then

$$\begin{gathered}\varphi(\Gamma \cup \mathrm{B})= \\ =\mathbf{P}_{s,\mu}\{\hat{F}_t^s(\Gamma \cup \mathrm{B}) \neq 0\}=\mathbf{P}_{s,\mu}\{(\hat{F}_t^s\Gamma \neq 0) \cup (\hat{F}_t^s\mathrm{B} \neq 0)\}= \\ =\mathbf{P}_{s,\mu}\{\hat{F}_t^s\Gamma \neq 0\}+\mathbf{P}_{s,\mu}\{\hat{F}_t^s\mathrm{B} \neq 0\}-\mathbf{P}_{s,\mu}\{\hat{F}_t^s\Gamma \neq 0,\ \hat{F}_t^s\mathrm{B} \neq 0\}= \\ =\varphi(\Gamma)+\varphi(\mathrm{B})-\mathbf{P}_{s,\mu}\{\hat{F}_t^s\Gamma \neq 0,\ \hat{F}_t^s\mathrm{B} \neq 0\}.\end{gathered} \tag{23}$$

Similarly,

$$\varphi(\widetilde{\Gamma} \cup \mathrm{B})=\varphi(\widetilde{\Gamma})+\varphi(\mathrm{B})-\mathbf{P}_{s,\mu}\{\hat{F}_t^s\widetilde{\Gamma} \neq 0,\ \hat{F}_t^s\mathrm{B} \neq 0\}. \tag{24}$$

We get from (23) and (24):

$$\begin{aligned}-\varphi(\Gamma \cup \mathrm{B})+\varphi(\widetilde{\Gamma} \cup \mathrm{B})+\varphi(\Gamma)-\varphi(\widetilde{\Gamma})= \\ =\mathbf{P}_{s,\mu}\{\hat{F}_t^s\widetilde{\Gamma}=0,\ \hat{F}_t^s\Gamma \neq 0,\ \hat{F}_t^s\mathrm{B} \neq 0\} \geqslant 0,\end{aligned}$$

whence 3.D follows.

Let Γ be any Borel set. Then $\overline{\Gamma}$ is also a Borel set and, by theorem 1, we can find for each n a compact set Γ^n and an open set U^n such that

$$\Gamma^n \subseteq \overline{\Gamma} \subseteq U^n$$

and

$$0 \leqslant \varphi(U^n)-\varphi(\Gamma^n) \leqslant \frac{1}{n}.$$

It follows from this last expression and (22) that $\overline{\Gamma}^n \supseteq \Gamma \supseteq \overline{U}^n$ and

$$0 \leqslant \mathbf{P}_{s,\mu}\{\hat{F}_t^s \subseteq \overline{\Gamma}^n\}-\mathbf{P}_{s,\mu}\{\hat{F}_t^s \subseteq \overline{U}^n\} \leqslant \frac{1}{n}.$$

The sets

$$\Gamma_n=\bigcup_{k=1}^n \overline{U}^k,\quad U_n=\bigcap_{k=1}^n \overline{\Gamma}^k$$

satisfy the inclusions

$$\Gamma_1 \subseteq \ldots \subseteq \Gamma_n \subseteq \ldots \subseteq \Gamma \subseteq \ldots \subseteq U_n \subseteq \ldots \subseteq U_1,$$

whilst

$$0 \leqslant \mathbf{P}_{s,\mu}\{\hat{F}_t^s \subseteq U_n\} - \mathbf{P}_{s,\mu}\{\hat{F}_t^s \subseteq \Gamma_n\} \leqslant \frac{1}{n}. \qquad (25)$$

We put

$$A_1 = \bigcup_{n=1}^{\infty}\{\hat{F}_t^s \subseteq \Gamma_n\}, \quad A_2 = \bigcap_{n=1}^{\infty}\{\hat{F}_t^s \subseteq U_n\}.$$

Obviously,

$$A_1 \subseteq \{\hat{F}_t^s \subseteq \Gamma\} \subseteq A_2. \qquad (26)$$

In view of lemma 4, A_1 and A_2 belong to $\mathcal{N}_t^s$. Furthermore,

$$\begin{aligned} \mathbf{P}_{s,\mu}(A_1) &= \lim_{n\to\infty} \mathbf{P}_{s,\mu}\{\hat{F}_t^s \subseteq \Gamma_n\}, \\ \mathbf{P}_{s,\mu}(A_2) &= \lim_{n\to\infty} \mathbf{P}_{s,\mu}\{\hat{F}_t^s \subseteq U_n\} \end{aligned} \qquad (27)$$

and by (25):

$$\mathbf{P}_{s,\mu}(A_1) = \mathbf{P}_{s,\mu}(A_2).$$

Relationship (20) therefore holds.

We conclude from (26) and (27) that relationship (21) also holds.

Remark. The reader will observe on going through the proof that the theorem still holds in the case when Γ is the complement of any analytic set.

8. Let $X = (x_t, \zeta, \mathcal{M}_t^s, \mathbf{P}_{s,\mu})$ be a Markov process in the measurable space $(E, \mathcal{B})$. The instant of first departure after s from the set Γ *) is given by

$$\xi_s(\Gamma) = \begin{cases} \sup\{t : F_t^s \subseteq \Gamma\}, & \text{if } \zeta(\omega) > s, \\ s, & \text{if } \zeta(\omega) \leqslant s \end{cases} \qquad (28)$$

(this may easily be seen to be equivalent to the definition given in sec. 3.8).

*)This magnitude can also be called the instant of first reaching the set $E - \Gamma$.

If process X is given in a topological measurable space, the function

$$\hat{\xi}_s(\Gamma) = \begin{cases} \sup\{t : \hat{F}_t^s \subseteq \Gamma\}, & \text{if } \zeta(\omega) > s, \\ s, & \text{if } \zeta(\omega) \leqslant s \end{cases} \tag{29}$$

will be described as <u>the instant of first departure after</u> s from inside the set Γ *).

<u>Theorem 3</u>. Let X be a Markov process continuous from the right in the topological measurable space $(E, \mathcal{C}, \mathcal{B})$.

If Γ is a closed measurable set, we have for any $0 \leqslant s \leqslant t$:

$$\{\hat{\xi}_s(\Gamma) > t\} = \{\xi_s(\Gamma) > t\} \in \mathcal{N}_{t+0}^s. \tag{30}$$

If $\Gamma \in \mathcal{C}\mathcal{B}$ and if one of conditions 6.A-6.B is fulfilled, we have for any $0 \leqslant s \leqslant t$:

$$\{\hat{\xi}_s(\Gamma) > t\} \in \mathcal{N}_t^s. \tag{31}$$

Finally, if $(E, \mathcal{C})$ is a semi-compact and $\mathcal{B} \supseteq \mathcal{C}$, then for any Borel**) set Γ and any $0 \leqslant s \leqslant t$

---

*)Alternatively, we can call $\hat{\xi}_s(\Gamma)$ <u>the instant of first contact with set</u> $E-\Gamma$.

We defined in sec. 3.13 the instant of first departure after s from inside the open set Γ as the instant of first departure after s from the normal system $\mathcal{F}$ for which

$$\bigcup_{\Gamma \in \mathcal{F}} \Gamma = G.$$

If G has a compact closure, the earlier and the new definition are easily shown to lead to the same function (cf. the proof of lemma 3.8).

**)And in fact for any set Γ whose complement is an analytic set.

$$\{\hat{\xi}_s(\Gamma) > t\} \in \bar{\mathcal{N}}^s_{t+0}\ ^{*)}. \tag{32}$$

In this case, we can construct for any $s \geqslant 0$ and any measure μ on $\mathscr{B}$ a sequence of closed sets $\Gamma_1 \subseteq \ldots \subseteq \Gamma_n \subseteq \ldots$ contained in Γ and a sequence of open sets $U_1 \supseteq \cdots \supseteq U_n \supseteq \ldots$ contained in Γ with compact complements such that

$$\mathbf{P}_{s,\mu}\{\hat{\xi}_s(\Gamma_n) \uparrow \hat{\xi}_s(\Gamma)\} = \mathbf{P}_{s,\mu}\{\hat{\xi}_s(U_n) \downarrow \hat{\xi}_s(\Gamma)\} = 1. \tag{33}$$

Proof. Let $\xi_s = \xi_s(\Gamma)$, $\hat{\xi}_s = \hat{\xi}_s(\Gamma)$. We have for any $v > t$ and any integer m:

$$\{\hat{\xi}_s > t,\ \Omega_v\} = \bigcup_{n=m}^{\infty} \left\{\hat{F}^s_{t+\frac{1}{n}} \subseteq \Gamma,\ \Omega_v\right\}. \tag{34}$$

Suppose that Γ is closed. Then by lemma 4:

$$\left\{\hat{F}^s_{t+\frac{1}{n}} \subseteq \Gamma\right\} \in \mathcal{N}^s_{t+\frac{1}{n}}.$$

Consequently,

$$\{\hat{\xi}_s > t,\ \Omega_v\} \in \mathcal{N}^s_v$$

for any $v > t$, so that $\{\hat{\xi}_s > t\} \in \mathcal{N}^s_{t+0}$. Since $\xi_s = \hat{\xi}_s$ for a closed set, relationship (30) holds.

Now let Γ be open and one of conditions 6.A-6.B be satisfied. It follows easily from relationship (19) that we deduced when proving lemma 4 that

$$\{\hat{\xi}_s > t\} = \{\hat{F}^s_t \subseteq \Gamma\}.$$

Since by lemma 4:

$$\{\hat{F}^s_t \subseteq \Gamma\} \in \mathcal{N}^s_t,$$

---

*)We put $A \in \mathcal{N}^s_{t+0}$ if $A \subseteq \Omega_t$ and $A\Omega_v \in \mathcal{N}^s_v$ for any $v > t$. Obviously, $\mathcal{N}^s_{t+0}$ is a σ-algebra in the space Ω_t. The σ-algebra $\mathcal{N}^s_{t+0}$ is similarly defined. It will be noticed that $A \in \bar{\mathcal{N}}^s_{t+0}$ when and only when there exist for every measure μ in the σ-algebra $\mathscr{B}$ sets $A', A'' \in \mathcal{N}^s_{t+0}$ such that $A' \subseteq A \subseteq A''$ and $\mathbf{P}_{s,\mu}(A') = \mathbf{P}_{s,\mu}(A'')$ (cf. foot-note on p.55).

relationship (31) holds.

Finally, let $(E, \mathcal{C})$ be a semi-compact, let $\mathcal{B} \supseteq \mathcal{C}$ and let Γ be an arbitrary Borel set. By theorem 2:

$$\left\{\hat{F}^s_{t+\frac{1}{n}} \subseteq \Gamma\right\} \in \bar{\mathcal{N}}^s_{t+\frac{1}{n}}.$$

We can therefore conclude from (34) that

$$\{\hat{\xi}_s > t\} \in \bar{\mathcal{N}}^s_{t+0}.$$

We now number all the rational numbers $r_1, r_2, \ldots, r_n, \ldots$. By theorem 2, for each k we can choose sequences

$$\Gamma_1^k \subseteq \ldots \subseteq \Gamma_n^k \subseteq \ldots \subseteq \Gamma \subseteq \ldots \subseteq U_n^k \subseteq \ldots \subseteq U_1^k$$

(the Γ_n^k being closed, and the U_n^k open with compact complements) such that, as $n \to \infty$,

$$\mathbf{P}_{s,\mu}\{\hat{F}^s_{r_k} \subseteq \Gamma_n^k\} \uparrow \mathbf{P}_{s,\mu}\{\hat{F}^s_{r_k} \subseteq \Gamma\},$$
$$\mathbf{P}_{s,\mu}\{\hat{F}^s_{r_k} \subseteq U_n^k\} \downarrow \mathbf{P}_{s,\mu}\{\hat{F}^s_{r_k} \subseteq \Gamma\}.$$

We put

$$\Gamma_n = \bigcup_{k=1}^n \Gamma_n^k, \quad U_n = \bigcap_{k=1}^n U_n^k.$$

Since

$$\Gamma_1 \subseteq \ldots \subseteq \Gamma_n \subseteq \ldots, \quad U_1 \supseteq \ldots \supseteq U_n \supseteq \ldots$$

and

$$\Gamma_n^k \subseteq \Gamma_n \subseteq \Gamma \subseteq U_n \subseteq U_n^k,$$

for $n \geqslant k$, we have for each k as $n \to \infty$:

$$\mathbf{P}_{s,\mu}\{\hat{F}^s_{r_k} \subseteq \Gamma_n\} \uparrow \mathbf{P}_{s,\mu}\{\hat{F}^s_{r_k} \subseteq \Gamma\}, \tag{35}$$

$$\mathbf{P}_{s,\mu}\{\hat{F}^s_{r_k} \subseteq U_n\} \downarrow \mathbf{P}_{s,\mu}\{\hat{F}^s_{r_k} \subseteq \Gamma\}. \tag{36}$$

Clearly,

$$\hat{\xi}_s(\Gamma_1) \leqslant \ldots \leqslant \hat{\xi}_s(\Gamma_n) \leqslant \ldots \leqslant \hat{\xi}_s(\Gamma) \leqslant \ldots$$
$$\ldots \leqslant \hat{\xi}_s(U_n) \leqslant \ldots \leqslant \hat{\xi}_s(U_1).$$

so that

$$\{\hat{\xi}_s(\Gamma_n) \not\uparrow \hat{\xi}_s(\Gamma)\} = \bigcup_{k=1}^{\infty} \bigcap_{n=1}^{\infty} \{\hat{\xi}_s(\Gamma_n) < r_k < \hat{\xi}_s(\Gamma)\} \subseteq \subseteq \bigcup_{k=1}^{\infty} \bigcap_{n=1}^{\infty} \{[\hat{F}^s_{r_k} \subseteq \Gamma] \setminus [\hat{F}^s_{r_k} \subseteq \Gamma_n]\}. \quad (37)$$

It follows from (35) and (37) that

$$\mathbf{P}_{s,\mu}\{\hat{\xi}_s(\Gamma_n) \uparrow \hat{\xi}_s(\Gamma)\} = 1.$$

Similarly, it can be seen on the basis of (36) that

$$\mathbf{P}_{s,\mu}\{\hat{\xi}_s(U_n) \downarrow \hat{\xi}_s(\Gamma)\} = 1.$$

9. The functions $\xi_s(\Gamma)$ and $\hat{\xi}_s(\Gamma)$ do not increase as s decreases, with the result that there exist the limits:

$$\xi_{s+0}(\Gamma) = \lim_{t \downarrow s} \xi_t(\Gamma),$$
$$\hat{\xi}_{s+0}(\Gamma) = \lim_{t \downarrow s} \hat{\xi}_t(\Gamma).$$

Theorem 3′. Let X be a process continuous from the right in the topological measurable space $(E, \mathcal{C}, \mathcal{B})$.

If Γ is a closed measurable set, we have for any $0 \leqslant s \leqslant t$:

$$\{\hat{\xi}_{s+0}(\Gamma) > t\} = \{\xi_{s+0}(\Gamma) > t\} \in \mathcal{N}^s_{t+0}. \quad (38)$$

If $\Gamma \in \mathcal{C}\mathcal{B}$ and if condition 6.A or 6.B is fulfilled, we have for any $0 \leqslant s < t$:

$$\{\hat{\xi}_{s+0}(\Gamma) > t\} \in \mathcal{N}^s_t. \quad (39)$$

Finally, if $(E, \mathcal{C})$ is a semi-compact and $\mathcal{B} \supseteq \mathcal{C}$, then

$$\{\hat{\xi}_{s+0}(\Gamma) > t\} \in \mathcal{N}^s_{t+0}, \quad (40)$$

for any Borel*) set Γ and any $0 \leqslant s \leqslant t$.

In this case, given any $s \geqslant 0$ and any measure μ in $\mathcal{B}$, we

*) And for any set Γ which is the complement of an analytic set.

can construct a sequence of open sets $U_1 \supseteq \ldots \supseteq U_n \supseteq \ldots \supseteq \Gamma$ such that their complements $\bar{U}_1, \ldots, \bar{U}_n, \ldots$ are compact and

$$\mathbf{P}_{s,\mu}\{\hat{\xi}_{s+0}(U_n) \downarrow \hat{\xi}_{s+0}(\Gamma)\} = 1. \tag{41}$$

If $\mu(\bar{\Gamma}) = 0$*), we can construct a sequence of closed sets $\Gamma_1 \subseteq \ldots \subseteq \Gamma_n \subseteq \ldots \subseteq \Gamma$ such that

$$\mathbf{P}_{s,\mu}\{\hat{\xi}_{s+0}(\Gamma_n) \uparrow \hat{\xi}_{s+0}(\Gamma)\} = 1. \tag{42}$$

Proof. Let Γ be a closed measurable set. If $s < u < t$, we have by (30):

$$\{\hat{\xi}_u(\Gamma) > t\} = \{\xi_u(\Gamma) > t\} \in \mathcal{N}^u_{t+0} \subseteq \mathcal{N}^s_{t+0}.$$

We conclude on letting $u \downarrow s$ that (38) is satisfied for $s < t$. If we now let t tend to s, it will be seen that (38) also holds for $t = s$. Expressions (39) and (40) may be verified similarly.

Relationship (42) follows from (33) on taking into account the fact that $\hat{\xi}_{s+0}(\Gamma) \geqslant \hat{\xi}_s(\Gamma)$ for any set Γ and $\mathbf{P}_{s,\mu}\{\hat{\xi}_{s+0}(\Gamma) = \hat{\xi}_s(\Gamma)\} = 1$ if $\mu(\Gamma) = 0$.

We still have to prove (41). We choose a sequence $s_n \downarrow s$ and put

$$\mu_n(\Gamma) = \mathbf{P}_{s,\mu}\{x_{s_n} \in \Gamma\} \qquad (\Gamma \in \mathscr{B}).$$

Using theorem 3, we construct for each n a sequence of open sets $U_n^1 \supseteq U_n^2 \supseteq \ldots \supseteq U_n^k \supseteq \ldots \supseteq \Gamma$, having compact complements and such that

$$\mathbf{P}_{s_n,\mu_n}\{\xi_{s_n}(U_n^k) \downarrow \xi_{s_n}(\Gamma)\} = 1.$$

By (32):

$$A = \{\xi_{s_n}(U_n^k) \downarrow \xi_{s_n}(\Gamma)\} \in \mathcal{N}^{s_n}.$$

*) The following example shows that this condition is essential. Let X be a determinate motion on a straight line with velocity 1 and let $\Gamma = (0, \infty)$. Then for any closed set $\tilde{\Gamma} \subseteq \Gamma$:

$$\mathbf{P}_{s,0}\{\xi_{0+0}(\tilde{\Gamma}) = 0,\ \hat{\xi}_{0+0}(\Gamma) = \infty\} = 1.$$

By theorem 2.1′:

$$\mathbf{P}_{s,x}(A) = \mathbf{M}_{s,x}\mathbf{P}_{s_n, x_{s_n}}(A)$$

so that

$$\mathbf{P}_{s,\mu}(A) = \mathbf{M}_{s,\mu}\mathbf{P}_{s_n, x_{s_n}}(A) = \mathbf{P}_{s_n, \mu_n}(A) = 1.$$

Thus we have

$$\xi_{s_n}(U_n^k) \downarrow \xi_{s_n}(\Gamma) \qquad (\text{a.c. } \Omega,\ \mathbf{P}_{s,\mu}).$$

for each n as $k \to \infty$. We put $U_k = U_1^k \cap \ldots \cap U_k^k$. Clearly, $U_1 \supseteq \ldots \supseteq U_k \supseteq \ldots \supseteq \Gamma$ and $\xi_{s_n}(U_k) \leqslant \xi_{s_n}(U_n^k)$ for $k \geqslant n$. Hence

$$\xi_{s_n}(U_k) \downarrow \xi_{s_n}(\Gamma) \qquad (\text{a.c. } \Omega,\ \mathbf{P}_{s,\mu}), \tag{43}$$

for any n as $k \to \infty$. We have, moreover, for any n and k,

$$\xi_{s_n}(U_k) \geqslant \xi_{s+0}(U_k) \geqslant \xi_{s+0}(\Gamma)$$

and by virtue of (43):

$$\xi_{s_n}(\Gamma) \geqslant \lim_{k \to \infty} \xi_{s+0}(U_k) \geqslant \xi_{s+0}(\Gamma) \qquad (\text{a.c. } \Omega,\ \mathbf{P}_{s,\mu}).$$

Since

$$\lim_{n \to \infty} \xi_{s_n}(\Gamma) = \xi_{s+0}(\Gamma),$$

we get

$$\lim_{k \to \infty} \xi_{s+0}(U_k) = \xi_{s+0}(\Gamma) \qquad (\text{a.c. } \Omega,\ \mathbf{P}_{s,\mu}).$$

10. Theorem 4. Let $(E, \mathscr{C})$ be a semi-compact, $\mathscr{B}$ a σ-algebra in E, containing $\mathscr{C}$, and X a Markov process continuous from the right and quasi-continuous from the left*) in the space $(E, \mathscr{C}, \mathscr{B})$ such that

$$\mathscr{N}_{t+0}^s \subseteq \mathscr{M}_t^s$$

for all $0 \leqslant s \leqslant t$. Then

$$\mathbf{P}_{s,x}\{\hat{\xi}_s(\Gamma) \neq \xi_s(\Gamma)\} = 0. \tag{44}$$

---

*) see sec. 6.17.

for any Borel*) set Γ and any $s \geqslant 0$, $x \in E$.

Proof. Let U be any open set. By theorem 3, a sequence of closed sets $\Gamma_1 \subseteq \ldots \subseteq \Gamma_n \subseteq \ldots \subseteq U$ can be constructed for any $s \geqslant 0$, $x \in E$, such that

$$\mathbf{P}_{s,x}\{\hat{\xi}_s(\Gamma_n) \uparrow \hat{\xi}_s(U)\} = 1. \tag{45}$$

In accordance with 1.C we can introduce a metric $\rho(x, y)$ into the space $(E, \mathcal{C})$. We put

$$\widetilde{\Gamma}_n = \Gamma_n \cup \left\{x : \rho(x, \overline{U}) \geqslant \frac{1}{n}\right\}.$$

Obviously, $\widetilde{\Gamma}_1 \subseteq \ldots \subseteq \widetilde{\Gamma}_n \subseteq \ldots \subseteq U$ and $\Gamma_n \subseteq \widetilde{\Gamma}_n$. Hence

$$\{\hat{\xi}_s(\Gamma_n) \uparrow \hat{\xi}_s(U)\} \subseteq \{\hat{\xi}_s(\widetilde{\Gamma}_n) \uparrow \hat{\xi}_s(U)\}$$

and

$$\mathbf{P}_{s,x}\{\hat{\xi}_s(\widetilde{\Gamma}_n) \uparrow \hat{\xi}_s(U)\} = 1. \tag{45}$$

It is clear from theorem 3 that the $\xi_s(\widetilde{\Gamma}_n)$ are random variables independent of the future and s-past, and it follows from (45), since X is quasi-continuous from the left, that

$$x_{\hat{\xi}_s(\widetilde{\Gamma}_n)} \to x_{\hat{\xi}_s(U)} \qquad (\text{a.c. } \Omega_{\hat{\xi}_s(U)}, \mathbf{P}_{s,x}). \tag{46}$$

But $\xi_s(\widetilde{\Gamma}_n) = \hat{\xi}_s(\widetilde{\Gamma}_n)$ for the closed set $\widetilde{\Gamma}_n$, and $\rho(x_{\xi_s(\widetilde{\Gamma}_n)}, \overline{U}) \leqslant \frac{1}{n}$ since X is continuous from the right. It follows from this, in view of (46), that

$$\rho(x_{\hat{\xi}_s(U)}, \overline{U}) = 0 \qquad (\text{a.c. } \Omega_{\hat{\xi}_s(U)}, \mathbf{P}_{s,x}). \tag{47}$$

Since

$$\{\xi_s(U) \neq \hat{\xi}_s(U)\} \subseteq \{x_{\hat{\xi}_s(U)} \in U\} = \{\rho(x_{\hat{\xi}_s(U)}, \overline{U}) > 0\}.$$

it follows from (47) that

$$\mathbf{P}_{s,x}\{\hat{\xi}_s(U) \neq \xi_s(U)\} = 0.$$

This proves the theorem for open sets.

---

*)See footnote on p.191.

Now let Γ be any Borel set. By theorem 3, for each $s \geqslant 0$, $x \in E$, a sequence of open sets $U_1 \supseteq U_2 \supseteq \ldots \supseteq U_n \supseteq \ldots \supseteq$ can be constructed such that

$$\mathbf{P}_{s,x}\{\hat{\xi}_s(U_n) \downarrow \hat{\xi}_s(\Gamma)\} = 1.$$

By what has been proved

$$\mathbf{P}_{s,x}\{\hat{\xi}_s(U_n) = \xi_s(U_n) \text{ for } n = 1, 2, \ldots\} = 1.$$

Hence

$$\mathbf{P}_{s,x}\{\xi_s(U_n) \downarrow \hat{\xi}_s(\Gamma)\} = 1. \tag{48}$$

But

$$\xi_s(U_n) \geqslant \xi_s(\Gamma) \geqslant \hat{\xi}_s(\Gamma),$$

and (44) therefore follows from (48).

Remark 1. Let $(E, \mathcal{C})$ be a semi-compact and $P(s, x; t, \Gamma)$ any transition function in the measurable space $(E, \mathfrak{z}(\mathcal{C}))$ that satisfies the conditions of theorem 6.8 (sec. 6.17). Then it follows from theorems 6.8 and 5.11 (sec. 5.21) that a Markov process X exists with the transition function $P(s, x; t, \Gamma)$, for which all the conditions of theorem 4 are fulfilled, so that (43) holds.

Remark 2. Let X be a process satisfying the conditions of theorem 4. It follows from theorems 3 and 4 that, if we take the σ-algebras $\mathfrak{R}_t^s$ in the sense indicated in the footnote to p. 55, all Borel sets are admissible (see sec. 3.8) for process X (and indeed all sets which are the complements of analytic sets).

The same statement holds true without the requirement of quasi-continuity of the process from the left if the functions $\hat{\xi}_s(\Gamma)$ are considered instead of functions $\xi_s(\Gamma)$.

SUPPLEMENTARY NOTES

Chapter 1

The reduction of the basic ideas of probability theory to measure theory is due to A.N. Kolmogorov (Ref. 19).

Chapter 1 gives a brief résumé of the results of measure theory which are used in the present book. A more detailed treatment can be found in the monographs by Halmos (Ref. 23) and Loeve (Ref. 20).

Article 1. The concepts of a π-system and λ-system of sets and of an $\mathscr{L}$-system of functions are introduced for the first time. Lemma 1.5 is due to Doob (Ref. 7, supplement, theorem 1.6).

Article 2. The proofs of propositions 1.4.A-1.4.C can be found in the works of Halmos (Ref. 23) and Loeve (Ref. 20).

Article 3. The general definitions of conditional probability and conditional mathematical expectation were given by Kolmogorov (Ref. 19). We follow Doob (Ref. 7) and Loeve (Ref. 20) in the formulation of these problems. The only new feature here is that we consider functions and σ-algebras defined in some subset of, instead of throughout, the space Ω. (Doob mentioned the possibility of carrying over the normal definitions to this case in Ref. 8).

Article 4. The definitions relating to topological and metric spaces can be found, for instance, in works by Hausdorff (Ref. 25), Loeve (Ref. 20) and Halmos (Ref. 23). The concept of topological measurable space appears to be investigated for the first time in the general form.

Article 5. Theorem 1.1 is often called the theorem on the extension of measure. It is generally proved in a somewhat different form (see, e.g. Loeve, Ref. 20, 4.1 or Halmos, Ref. 23, sec. 13), for the case when the system $\mathcal{C}$ is an algebra, i.e. contains the complement of each set as well as the set itself and the intersection of every pair of contained sets. This case is readily obtained from the more general case considered in theorem 1.1 (see Halmos, Ref. 23, sec. 8, problem 5).

Theorem 1.2 is due to Daniell (Refs. 3, 4) and Kolmogorov (Ref. 19, chapter III, sec. 4). (See also Halmos, Ref. 23, chapter 9, sec. 49.) Kolmogorov stated this theorem only for the case when $(E, \mathcal{C})$ is a straight line with its usual topology and $\mathscr{B} = \sigma(\mathcal{C})$; but his proof stands unchanged in the more general case considered here.

Chapter 2

Article 1. The principle of the independence of the "future" from the "past" for a known present was first stated (as applied to sequences of random variables) by Markov (Ref. 2). This and subsequent work by Markov reveal the actual history of the theory of Markov random processes. Processes with discrete time (Markov chains) were considered almost exclusively in the first period of this history.

The foundations of the general theory of Markov processes were laid by Kolmogorov (Ref. 18). The transition probabilities $P(s, x; t, \Gamma)$ formed the main subject of study in Ref. 18 and in subsequent works. The systematic investigation of Markov processes in the sense of random functions began somewhat later (Levy, Doeblin, and others). The creation of a satisfactory, general logical concept of the Markov process as a random function subject to definite requirements is primarily due to Doob. His work on the subject is brought together in the monograph of Ref. 8.

Doob started out from a general concept of probability process. This is defined as a function $x_t(\omega)$ with values in the measurable space $(E, \mathscr{B})$, where the argument t runs over some numerical interval I and the argument ω over some probability space $(\Omega, \mathscr{M}, \mathbf{P})$. (It is assumed that $\{\omega : x_t(\omega) \in \Gamma\} \in \mathscr{M}$ for any $t \in I, \Gamma \in \mathscr{B}$). The condition for a process to be Markov is stated as: for any $\Gamma \in \mathscr{B}, t \leqslant u \in I$,

$$\mathbf{P}\{x_u \in \Gamma \| \mathscr{N}_t\} = \mathbf{P}\{x_u \in \Gamma \| x_t\} \qquad (\text{a.c. } \Omega, \mathbf{P}) \tag{1}$$

($\mathscr{N}_t$ denotes the σ-algebra in Ω generated by sets $\{\omega : x_s(\omega) \in \Gamma\}$ $(\Gamma \in \mathscr{B}, s \in I, s \leqslant t))$.

Development of the theory of Markov processes in recent years has shown that:

a) it is useful to consider events not appearing in the

σ-algebra $\mathcal{N}_t$, and to take as basis the strengthened variant of relationship (1):

$$\mathbf{P}\{x_u \in \Gamma \mid \mathcal{M}_t\} = \mathbf{P}\{x_u \in \Gamma \mid x_t\} \qquad (\text{a.c. } \Omega, \mathbf{P}),$$

where $\mathcal{M}_t$ are σ-algebras satisfying the inclusions $\mathcal{M} \supseteq \mathcal{M}_t \supseteq \mathcal{N}_t$, $\mathcal{M}_t \supseteq \mathcal{M}_s$ for $t \geqslant s \in I$;

b) it is advantageous to allow that the process may cut off at a random instant $\zeta(\omega)$.

If we take this into account, we arrive at the general concept of Markov random function given in sec. 2.1. (This concept was first considered by Doob in Ref. 8 (and see Ref. 27).

In the theory of Markov processes it is usually a question of dealing, not with a single random function, but with a family of such functions, corresponding to all the possible initial instants of time and all the possible initial states. It is therefore natural to assume that the theory is primarily concerned with what we have called Markov families of random functions. Various special classes of Markov family have been discussed in a number of works but this is the first time that the general case has been mentioned*). We apply the term "Markov process" to a somewhat simpler formation than the Markov family. There is no loss of generality in taking the process as our main subject of discussion (see the end of sec. 2.1) and we gain at the same time in compactness and simplicity as regards the propositions and expressions.

Articles 2-3. Almost all the results of these articles are new. The basic idea of the proof of theorem 2.8 can be traced to Doob. In the investigation of the trajectory properties theorem 2.8 replaces Doob's separability theorem (Ref. 7, chapter 2, theorem 2.4).

Chapter 3

The basic ideas and results of chapter 3 are due to the author. The proofs of these results are published for the first time. Integral equation (3.76) was first deduced by

---

*) The Markov random function corresponding to the transition function $P(s, x; t, \Gamma)$ is quite often taken as the starting-point. This concept occupies an intermediate position between the concepts of Markov random function and Markov family.

another method and with different assumptions in the work by Blanc-Lapierre and Fortet (Ref. 1, chapter 6, sec. 14). We reproduce the method of deducing the equation published in Ref. 9.

Chapter 4

Theorem 4.1 can be regarded as familiar (see e.g. Ref. 7 or 20). The basic idea of theorem 4.2 was employed, for instance, in Ref. 8.

Chapter 5

Up to 1955-1956 the strictly Markov property had undergone virtually no logical analysis. Many authors have used this property without any basis, apparently on the assumption that it is a general property of all Markov processes.

Doob (Ref. 6) was the first to give a clear formulation and proof of the strictly Markov property of certain processes. He showed in the work in question that all stationary Markov processes continuous from the right with a denumerable set of states are strictly Markov*). Doob's result was later extended to wider classes of stationary Markov processes with denumerable sets of states (Yushkevich, Ref. 27, and Ref. 28; K.L. Chung, Ref. 26).

The study of strictly Markov processes as an independent class was begun in 1955-1956 by Dynkin (Refs. 11, 12**), 13), Dynkin and Yushkevich (Ref. 16) and Ray (Ref. 22). Dynkin showed that, by starting from the strictly Markov property and attaching definite requirements to the nature of the trajectories, infinitesimal operators can be evaluated for the processes and a complete classification thus obtained of certain important classes of process. The work of Dynkin and Yushkevich (Ref. 16) gives the first general definition of strictly Markov processes (for the stationary case), shows that the class of strictly Markov processes is considerably narrower than the class of all Markov processes, and deduces the sufficient conditions for a Markov process to be strictly Markov. Ray's work (Ref. 22) is devoted specially to continuous one-dimensional stationary Markov processes. The

---

*)The strictly Markov property is understood in a slightly different sense to ours in Ref. 6, and the class of processes discussed there is in fact a little wider than the class of processes continuous from the right.

**)Detailed proofs of the results stated in Ref. 12 are published in Ref. 15.

condition for such processes to be strictly Markov is stated (more weakly than in Ref. 16)*) and the necessary and sufficient conditions for the process to be strictly Markov are deduced in terms of the transition function**).

Hunt's work (Ref. 24) is independent of those mentioned above. The strictly Markov property is stated here in a form suitable for stationary Markov processes with independent increments, and the Wiener process is shown to possess this property.

The concept of strictly Markov process and the criteria for such a process was extended in 1957 to stationary cut-off processes (Blumenthal, Ref. 2) and non-stationary processes (Dynkin, Ref. 14; Yushkevich, Ref. 28).

The general theory which is developed in chapter 5 includes the basic results of Refs. 16, 14, 28, and 2 in a modified form. In particular, the connexion between theorems 5.9-5.10 and the fundamental theorem of Ref. 16 is readily seen (theorem 5 of Ref. 14 and theorem 1 of Ref. 28 occupy an intermediate position between these results). The "law of zero or unity" (sec. 5.21) was discovered by Blumenthal (Ref. 2), who also first discussed the example of sec. 5.22.

Chapter 6

The main sources of the theorems of this chapter are the results of Doeblin (Ref. 5), Dynkin (Ref. 9), Kinney (Ref. 17) and Blumenthal (Ref. 2). In order to adapt these results to the definition of Markov process given in article 1 of chapter 2, the proofs had to be modified considerably.

Theorem 6.2 can be looked on as a generalization of theorem 2.1 of Ref. 2 (Blumenthal only considered the case when the process is given in a locally compact separable Hausdorff space and $\mathscr{F} = \{E_n\}$ is a sequence of compact sets of this space). Ref. 17 contains somewhat different conditions for boundedness.

---

*)Instead of all random variables independent of the future, only the instants $\xi(a, b)$ of first departure of the trajectory from the interval (a, b) appear in Ray's statement.

**)The problem of discovering the necessary and sufficient conditions remains open to date if the description "strictly Markov" is taken in the more rigid sense of Ref. 16 and the present book.

Theorem 6.3 is a "localization" of theorem V of Kinney's work (Ref. 17) (Kinney takes the case $\Gamma = E$)*).

Theorem 6.4 is due to Doeblin (Ref. 5).

Theorem 6.5 is due to Seregin. It is a "localization" of the theorem proved by Dynkin (Ref. 9) and Kinney (Ref. 17).

Finally, theorem 6.7 is a generalization of a theorem of Blumenthal (Ref. 2).

The example of a Markov, but not strictly Markov, process described in sec. 6.18.5 was first constructed by Yushkevich and published in Ref. 16.

Addendum

Article 1. The results described in this article are due to Choquet (Ref. 29).

Article 2. The measurability properties of the instants of first reaching the set Γ (or, what amounts to the same thing, the instants of first departure from $E\setminus\Gamma$)) were studied in Hunt's work (Ref. 30) for the case of non-cut-off stationary strictly Markov processes that have no discontinuities of the second kind, are continuous from the right and quasi-continuous from the left, and satisfy the condition $\overline{\mathcal{N}}_{t+0} \subseteq \mathcal{M}_t$. The general theorems for wider classes of Markov process proved in article 2 are published for the first time.

---

*)A result analogous to Kinney's theorem was obtained also in Ref. 9, but with a tighter condition :

$$\alpha^{\varepsilon}(\delta) = o(\sqrt{\delta}).$$

REFERENCES

1. A. BLANC-LAPIERRE, R. FORTET, Theorie des fonctions aléatoires, Paris (1953).

2. R. BLUMENTHAL, Trans. Am. Math. Soc., 85, 52-72 (1957).

3. P.J. DANIELL, Ann. Math. (2), 20, 281-288 (1918-1919).

4. P.J. DANIELL, Ann. Math. (2), 21, 30-38 (1919-1920).

5. W. DOEBLIN, Scand. Aktuarietidskr., 22, 211-222 (1939).

6. J.L. DOOB, Trans. Am. Math. Soc., 58, 455-473 (1945).

7. J.L. DOOB, Stochastic processes, John Wiley, New York - London (1953).

8. J.L. DOOB, Teor. ver. i ee prim., 2, 3-33 (1957).

9. E.B. DYNKIN, Izv. Akad. Nauk SSSR (ser. Matem), 16, 563-572 (1952).

10. E.B. DYNKIN, Dokl. Akad. Nauk. SSSR, 104, 691-694 (1955).

11. E.B. DYNKIN, Dokl. Akad. Nauk. SSSR, 105, 206-209 (1955).

12. E.B. DYNKIN, Dokl. Akad. Nauk. SSSR, 105, 405-408 (1955).

13. E.B. DYNKIN, Teor. ver. i ee prim., 1, 38-60 (1956).

14. E.B. DYNKIN, Dokl. Akad. Nauk. SSSR, 113, 261-263 (1957).

15. E.B. DYNKIN, Teor. ver. i ee prim. 4, 3-54 (1959).

16. E.B. DYNKIN and A.A. YUSHKEVICH, Teor. ver. i ee prim., 1, 149-155 (1956).

17. J.R. KINNEY, Trans. Am. Math. Soc., 74, 280-302 (1953).

18. A.N. KOLMOGOROV, Usp. matem. nauk, 5, 5-41 (1938); Math. Ann., 104, 415-458 (1931).

19. A.N. KOLMOGOROV, Grundbegriffe der Wahrscheinlichkeitsrechnung, Erg. Math., 2, no. 3, Berlin (1933).

20. M. LOEVE, Probability theory, New York - London - Toronto (1955).

21. A.A. MARKOV, *Izv. fiz.-matem. obshch. pri Kazansk. un-te* (2), 15, 135-156 (1906).

22. D. RAY, *Trans. Am. Math. Soc.* 82, 452-493 (1956).

23. P. HALMOS, Measure theory, New York (1950).

24. G.A.HUNT, *Trans. Am. Math. Soc.*, 81, 294-319 (1956).

25. F. HAUSDORFF, Mengenlehre, Berlin-Leipzig (1927).

26. K.L. CHUNG, Proc. Third Berkeley Symposium Math. Stat. and Prob., 30-40 (1956).

27. A.A. YUSHKEVICH, On the differentiability of the transition probabilities of a stationary Markov process with a denumerable number of states (O differentsiryemosti perekhodnykh veroyatnostei odnorodnogo markovskogo protsessa so schetnym chislom sostoyanii), Thesis, Moscow Univ. (1953).

28. A.A. YUSHKEVICH, *Teor. ver. i ee prim.*, 2, 187-213 (1957).

29. G. CHOQUET, *Ann. Inst. Fourier*, Grenoble, 5, 131-295 (1953-1954).

30. G.A. HUNT, *Illinois J. Math.* 1, 44-93 (1957).

INDEX

INDEX OF LEMMAS AND THEOREMS

INDEX OF LEMMAS AND THEOREMS

INDEX OF NOTATION

A CATALOG OF SELECTED

DOVER BOOKS

IN SCIENCE AND MATHEMATICS

Astronomy

BURNHAM'S CELESTIAL HANDBOOK, Robert Burnham, Jr. Thorough guide to the stars beyond our solar system. Exhaustive treatment. Alphabetical by constellation: Andromeda to Cetus in Vol. 1; Chamaeleon to Orion in Vol. 2; and Pavo to Vulpecula in Vol. 3. Hundreds of illustrations. Index in Vol. 3. 2,000pp. 6⅛ x 9¼.
Vol. I: 0-486-23567-X
Vol. II: 0-486-23568-8
Vol. III: 0-486-23673-0

EXPLORING THE MOON THROUGH BINOCULARS AND SMALL TELESCOPES, Ernest H. Cherrington, Jr. Informative, profusely illustrated guide to locating and identifying craters, rills, seas, mountains, other lunar features. Newly revised and updated with special section of new photos. Over 100 photos and diagrams. 240pp. 8¼ x 11. 0-486-24491-1

THE EXTRATERRESTRIAL LIFE DEBATE, 1750–1900, Michael J. Crowe. First detailed, scholarly study in English of the many ideas that developed from 1750 to 1900 regarding the existence of intelligent extraterrestrial life. Examines ideas of Kant, Herschel, Voltaire, Percival Lowell, many other scientists and thinkers. 16 illustrations. 704pp. 5⅜ x 8½. 0-486-40675-X

THEORIES OF THE WORLD FROM ANTIQUITY TO THE COPERNICAN REVOLUTION, Michael J. Crowe. Newly revised edition of an accessible, enlightening book recreates the change from an earth-centered to a sun-centered conception of the solar system. 242pp. 5⅜ x 8½. 0-486-41444-2

A HISTORY OF ASTRONOMY, A. Pannekoek. Well-balanced, carefully reasoned study covers such topics as Ptolemaic theory, work of Copernicus, Kepler, Newton, Eddington's work on stars, much more. Illustrated. References. 521pp. 5⅜ x 8½.
0-486-65994-1

A COMPLETE MANUAL OF AMATEUR ASTRONOMY: TOOLS AND TECHNIQUES FOR ASTRONOMICAL OBSERVATIONS, P. Clay Sherrod with Thomas L. Koed. Concise, highly readable book discusses: selecting, setting up and maintaining a telescope; amateur studies of the sun; lunar topography and occultations; observations of Mars, Jupiter, Saturn, the minor planets and the stars; an introduction to photoelectric photometry; more. 1981 ed. 124 figures. 25 halftones. 37 tables. 335pp. 6½ x 9¼. 0-486-40675-X

AMATEUR ASTRONOMER'S HANDBOOK, J. B. Sidgwick. Timeless, comprehensive coverage of telescopes, mirrors, lenses, mountings, telescope drives, micrometers, spectroscopes, more. 189 illustrations. 576pp. 5⅝ x 8¼. (Available in U.S. only.)
0-486-24034-7

STARS AND RELATIVITY, Ya. B. Zel'dovich and I. D. Novikov. Vol. 1 of *Relativistic Astrophysics* by famed Russian scientists. General relativity, properties of matter under astrophysical conditions, stars, and stellar systems. Deep physical insights, clear presentation. 1971 edition. References. 544pp. 5⅝ x 8¼. 0-486-69424-0

Chemistry

THE SCEPTICAL CHYMIST: THE CLASSIC 1661 TEXT, Robert Boyle. Boyle defines the term "element," asserting that all natural phenomena can be explained by the motion and organization of primary particles. 1911 ed. viii+232pp. 5⅜ x 8½. 0-486-42825-7

RADIOACTIVE SUBSTANCES, Marie Curie. Here is the celebrated scientist's doctoral thesis, the prelude to her receipt of the 1903 Nobel Prize. Curie discusses establishing atomic character of radioactivity found in compounds of uranium and thorium; extraction from pitchblende of polonium and radium; isolation of pure radium chloride; determination of atomic weight of radium; plus electric, photographic, luminous, heat, color effects of radioactivity. ii+94pp. 5⅜ x 8½. 0-486-42550-9

CHEMICAL MAGIC, Leonard A. Ford. Second Edition. Revised by E. Winston Grundmeier. Over 100 unusual stunts demonstrating cold fire, dust explosions, much more. Text explains scientific principles and stresses safety precautions. 128pp. 5⅜ x 8½. 0-486-67628-5

THE DEVELOPMENT OF MODERN CHEMISTRY, Aaron J. Ihde. Authoritative history of chemistry from ancient Greek theory to 20th-century innovation. Covers major chemists and their discoveries. 209 illustrations. 14 tables. Bibliographies. Indices. Appendices. 851pp. 5⅜ x 8½. 0-486-64235-6

CATALYSIS IN CHEMISTRY AND ENZYMOLOGY, William P. Jencks. Exceptionally clear coverage of mechanisms for catalysis, forces in aqueous solution, carbonyl- and acyl-group reactions, practical kinetics, more. 864pp. 5⅜ x 8½. 0-486-65460-5

ELEMENTS OF CHEMISTRY, Antoine Lavoisier. Monumental classic by founder of modern chemistry in remarkable reprint of rare 1790 Kerr translation. A must for every student of chemistry or the history of science. 539pp. 5⅜ x 8½. 0-486-64624-6

THE HISTORICAL BACKGROUND OF CHEMISTRY, Henry M. Leicester. Evolution of ideas, not individual biography. Concentrates on formulation of a coherent set of chemical laws. 260pp. 5⅜ x 8½. 0-486-61053-5

A SHORT HISTORY OF CHEMISTRY, J. R. Partington. Classic exposition explores origins of chemistry, alchemy, early medical chemistry, nature of atmosphere, theory of valency, laws and structure of atomic theory, much more. 428pp. 5⅜ x 8½. (Available in U.S. only.) 0-486-65977-1

GENERAL CHEMISTRY, Linus Pauling. Revised 3rd edition of classic first-year text by Nobel laureate. Atomic and molecular structure, quantum mechanics, statistical mechanics, thermodynamics correlated with descriptive chemistry. Problems. 992pp. 5⅜ x 8½. 0-486-65622-5

FROM ALCHEMY TO CHEMISTRY, John Read. Broad, humanistic treatment focuses on great figures of chemistry and ideas that revolutionized the science. 50 illustrations. 240pp. 5⅜ x 8½. 0-486-28690-8

Engineering

DE RE METALLICA, Georgius Agricola. The famous Hoover translation of greatest treatise on technological chemistry, engineering, geology, mining of early modern times (1556). All 289 original woodcuts. 638pp. 6¾ x 11. 0-486-60006-8

FUNDAMENTALS OF ASTRODYNAMICS, Roger Bate et al. Modern approach developed by U.S. Air Force Academy. Designed as a first course. Problems, exercises. Numerous illustrations. 455pp. 5⅜ x 8½. 0-486-60061-0

DYNAMICS OF FLUIDS IN POROUS MEDIA, Jacob Bear. For advanced students of ground water hydrology, soil mechanics and physics, drainage and irrigation engineering and more. 335 illustrations. Exercises, with answers. 784pp. 6⅛ x 9¼. 0-486-65675-6

THEORY OF VISCOELASTICITY (Second Edition), Richard M. Christensen. Complete consistent description of the linear theory of the viscoelastic behavior of materials. Problem-solving techniques discussed. 1982 edition. 29 figures. xiv+364pp. 6⅛ x 9¼. 0-486-42880-X

MECHANICS, J. P. Den Hartog. A classic introductory text or refresher. Hundreds of applications and design problems illuminate fundamentals of trusses, loaded beams and cables, etc. 334 answered problems. 462pp. 5⅜ x 8½. 0-486-60754-2

MECHANICAL VIBRATIONS, J. P. Den Hartog. Classic textbook offers lucid explanations and illustrative models, applying theories of vibrations to a variety of practical industrial engineering problems. Numerous figures. 233 problems, solutions. Appendix. Index. Preface. 436pp. 5⅜ x 8½. 0-486-64785-4

STRENGTH OF MATERIALS, J. P. Den Hartog. Full, clear treatment of basic material (tension, torsion, bending, etc.) plus advanced material on engineering methods, applications. 350 answered problems. 323pp. 5⅜ x 8½. 0-486-60755-0

A HISTORY OF MECHANICS, René Dugas. Monumental study of mechanical principles from antiquity to quantum mechanics. Contributions of ancient Greeks, Galileo, Leonardo, Kepler, Lagrange, many others. 671pp. 5⅜ x 8½. 0-486-65632-2

STABILITY THEORY AND ITS APPLICATIONS TO STRUCTURAL MECHANICS, Clive L. Dym. Self-contained text focuses on Koiter postbuckling analyses, with mathematical notions of stability of motion. Basing minimum energy principles for static stability upon dynamic concepts of stability of motion, it develops asymptotic buckling and postbuckling analyses from potential energy considerations, with applications to columns, plates, and arches. 1974 ed. 208pp. 5⅜ x 8½. 0-486-42541-X

METAL FATIGUE, N. E. Frost, K. J. Marsh, and L. P. Pook. Definitive, clearly written, and well-illustrated volume addresses all aspects of the subject, from the historical development of understanding metal fatigue to vital concepts of the cyclic stress that causes a crack to grow. Includes 7 appendixes. 544pp. 5⅜ x 8½. 0-486-40927-9

ROCKETS, Robert Goddard. Two of the most significant publications in the history of rocketry and jet propulsion: "A Method of Reaching Extreme Altitudes" (1919) and "Liquid Propellant Rocket Development" (1936). 128pp. 5⅜ x 8½. 0-486-42537-1

STATISTICAL MECHANICS: PRINCIPLES AND APPLICATIONS, Terrell L. Hill. Standard text covers fundamentals of statistical mechanics, applications to fluctuation theory, imperfect gases, distribution functions, more. 448pp. 5⅜ x 8½. 0-486-65390-0

ENGINEERING AND TECHNOLOGY 1650–1750: ILLUSTRATIONS AND TEXTS FROM ORIGINAL SOURCES, Martin Jensen. Highly readable text with more than 200 contemporary drawings and detailed engravings of engineering projects dealing with surveying, leveling, materials, hand tools, lifting equipment, transport and erection, piling, bailing, water supply, hydraulic engineering, and more. Among the specific projects outlined-transporting a 50-ton stone to the Louvre, erecting an obelisk, building timber locks, and dredging canals. 207pp. 8⅜ x 11¼. 0-486-42232-1

THE VARIATIONAL PRINCIPLES OF MECHANICS, Cornelius Lanczos. Graduate level coverage of calculus of variations, equations of motion, relativistic mechanics, more. First inexpensive paperbound edition of classic treatise. Index. Bibliography. 418pp. 5⅜ x 8½. 0-486-65067-7

PROTECTION OF ELECTRONIC CIRCUITS FROM OVERVOLTAGES, Ronald B. Standler. Five-part treatment presents practical rules and strategies for circuits designed to protect electronic systems from damage by transient overvoltages. 1989 ed. xxiv+434pp. 6⅛ x 9¼. 0-486-42552-5

ROTARY WING AERODYNAMICS, W. Z. Stepniewski. Clear, concise text covers aerodynamic phenomena of the rotor and offers guidelines for helicopter performance evaluation. Originally prepared for NASA. 537 figures. 640pp. 6⅛ x 9¼. 0-486-64647-5

INTRODUCTION TO SPACE DYNAMICS, William Tyrrell Thomson. Comprehensive, classic introduction to space-flight engineering for advanced undergraduate and graduate students. Includes vector algebra, kinematics, transformation of coordinates. Bibliography. Index. 352pp. 5⅜ x 8½. 0-486-65113-4

HISTORY OF STRENGTH OF MATERIALS, Stephen P. Timoshenko. Excellent historical survey of the strength of materials with many references to the theories of elasticity and structure. 245 figures. 452pp. 5⅜ x 8½. 0-486-61187-6

ANALYTICAL FRACTURE MECHANICS, David J. Unger. Self-contained text supplements standard fracture mechanics texts by focusing on analytical methods for determining crack-tip stress and strain fields. 336pp. 6⅛ x 9¼. 0-486-41737-9

STATISTICAL MECHANICS OF ELASTICITY, J. H. Weiner. Advanced, self-contained treatment illustrates general principles and elastic behavior of solids. Part 1, based on classical mechanics, studies thermoelastic behavior of crystalline and polymeric solids. Part 2, based on quantum mechanics, focuses on interatomic force laws, behavior of solids, and thermally activated processes. For students of physics and chemistry and for polymer physicists. 1983 ed. 96 figures. 496pp. 5⅜ x 8½. 0-486-42260-7

Mathematics

FUNCTIONAL ANALYSIS (Second Corrected Edition), George Bachman and Lawrence Narici. Excellent treatment of subject geared toward students with background in linear algebra, advanced calculus, physics and engineering. Text covers introduction to inner-product spaces, normed, metric spaces, and topological spaces; complete orthonormal sets, the Hahn-Banach Theorem and its consequences, and many other related subjects. 1966 ed. 544pp. 6⅛ x 9¼. 0-486-40251-7

ASYMPTOTIC EXPANSIONS OF INTEGRALS, Norman Bleistein & Richard A. Handelsman. Best introduction to important field with applications in a variety of scientific disciplines. New preface. Problems. Diagrams. Tables. Bibliography. Index. 448pp. 5⅜ x 8½. 0-486-65082-0

VECTOR AND TENSOR ANALYSIS WITH APPLICATIONS, A. I. Borisenko and I. E. Tarapov. Concise introduction. Worked-out problems, solutions, exercises. 257pp. 5⅝ x 8¼. 0-486-63833-2

AN INTRODUCTION TO ORDINARY DIFFERENTIAL EQUATIONS, Earl A. Coddington. A thorough and systematic first course in elementary differential equations for undergraduates in mathematics and science, with many exercises and problems (with answers). Index. 304pp. 5⅜ x 8½. 0-486-65942-9

FOURIER SERIES AND ORTHOGONAL FUNCTIONS, Harry F. Davis. An incisive text combining theory and practical example to introduce Fourier series, orthogonal functions and applications of the Fourier method to boundary-value problems. 570 exercises. Answers and notes. 416pp. 5⅜ x 8½. 0-486-65973-9

COMPUTABILITY AND UNSOLVABILITY, Martin Davis. Classic graduate-level introduction to theory of computability, usually referred to as theory of recurrent functions. New preface and appendix. 288pp. 5⅜ x 8½. 0-486-61471-9

ASYMPTOTIC METHODS IN ANALYSIS, N. G. de Bruijn. An inexpensive, comprehensive guide to asymptotic methods–the pioneering work that teaches by explaining worked examples in detail. Index. 224pp. 5⅜ x 8½ 0-486-64221-6

APPLIED COMPLEX VARIABLES, John W. Dettman. Step-by-step coverage of fundamentals of analytic function theory–plus lucid exposition of five important applications: Potential Theory; Ordinary Differential Equations; Fourier Transforms; Laplace Transforms; Asymptotic Expansions. 66 figures. Exercises at chapter ends. 512pp. 5⅜ x 8½. 0-486-64670-X

INTRODUCTION TO LINEAR ALGEBRA AND DIFFERENTIAL EQUATIONS, John W. Dettman. Excellent text covers complex numbers, determinants, orthonormal bases, Laplace transforms, much more. Exercises with solutions. Undergraduate level. 416pp. 5⅜ x 8½. 0-486-65191-6

RIEMANN'S ZETA FUNCTION, H. M. Edwards. Superb, high-level study of landmark 1859 publication entitled "On the Number of Primes Less Than a Given Magnitude" traces developments in mathematical theory that it inspired. xiv+315pp. 5⅜ x 8½. 0-486-41740-9

CALCULUS OF VARIATIONS WITH APPLICATIONS, George M. Ewing. Applications-oriented introduction to variational theory develops insight and promotes understanding of specialized books, research papers. Suitable for advanced undergraduate/graduate students as primary, supplementary text. 352pp. 5⅜ x 8½. 0-486-64856-7

COMPLEX VARIABLES, Francis J. Flanigan. Unusual approach, delaying complex algebra till harmonic functions have been analyzed from real variable viewpoint. Includes problems with answers. 364pp. 5⅜ x 8½. 0-486-61388-7

AN INTRODUCTION TO THE CALCULUS OF VARIATIONS, Charles Fox. Graduate-level text covers variations of an integral, isoperimetrical problems, least action, special relativity, approximations, more. References. 279pp. 5⅜ x 8½. 0-486-65499-0

COUNTEREXAMPLES IN ANALYSIS, Bernard R. Gelbaum and John M. H. Olmsted. These counterexamples deal mostly with the part of analysis known as "real variables." The first half covers the real number system, and the second half encompasses higher dimensions. 1962 edition. xxiv+198pp. 5⅜ x 8½. 0-486-42875-3

CATASTROPHE THEORY FOR SCIENTISTS AND ENGINEERS, Robert Gilmore. Advanced-level treatment describes mathematics of theory grounded in the work of Poincaré, R. Thom, other mathematicians. Also important applications to problems in mathematics, physics, chemistry and engineering. 1981 edition. References. 28 tables. 397 black-and-white illustrations. xvii + 666pp. 6⅛ x 9¼. 0-486-67539-4

INTRODUCTION TO DIFFERENCE EQUATIONS, Samuel Goldberg. Exceptionally clear exposition of important discipline with applications to sociology, psychology, economics. Many illustrative examples; over 250 problems. 260pp. 5⅜ x 8½. 0-486-65084-7

NUMERICAL METHODS FOR SCIENTISTS AND ENGINEERS, Richard Hamming. Classic text stresses frequency approach in coverage of algorithms, polynomial approximation, Fourier approximation, exponential approximation, other topics. Revised and enlarged 2nd edition. 721pp. 5⅜ x 8½. 0-486-65241-6

INTRODUCTION TO NUMERICAL ANALYSIS (2nd Edition), F. B. Hildebrand. Classic, fundamental treatment covers computation, approximation, interpolation, numerical differentiation and integration, other topics. 150 new problems. 669pp. 5⅜ x 8½. 0-486-65363-3

THREE PEARLS OF NUMBER THEORY, A. Y. Khinchin. Three compelling puzzles require proof of a basic law governing the world of numbers. Challenges concern van der Waerden's theorem, the Landau-Schnirelmann hypothesis and Mann's theorem, and a solution to Waring's problem. Solutions included. 64pp. 5⅜ x 8½. 0-486-40026-3

THE PHILOSOPHY OF MATHEMATICS: AN INTRODUCTORY ESSAY, Stephan Körner. Surveys the views of Plato, Aristotle, Leibniz & Kant concerning propositions and theories of applied and pure mathematics. Introduction. Two appendices. Index. 198pp. 5⅜ x 8½. 0-486-25048-2

INTRODUCTORY REAL ANALYSIS, A.N. Kolmogorov, S. V. Fomin. Translated by Richard A. Silverman. Self-contained, evenly paced introduction to real and functional analysis. Some 350 problems. 403pp. 5⅜ x 8½. 0-486-61226-0

APPLIED ANALYSIS, Cornelius Lanczos. Classic work on analysis and design of finite processes for approximating solution of analytical problems. Algebraic equations, matrices, harmonic analysis, quadrature methods, much more. 559pp. 5⅜ x 8½. 0-486-65656-X

AN INTRODUCTION TO ALGEBRAIC STRUCTURES, Joseph Landin. Superb self-contained text covers "abstract algebra": sets and numbers, theory of groups, theory of rings, much more. Numerous well-chosen examples, exercises. 247pp. 5⅜ x 8½. 0-486-65940-2

QUALITATIVE THEORY OF DIFFERENTIAL EQUATIONS, V. V. Nemytskii and V.V. Stepanov. Classic graduate-level text by two prominent Soviet mathematicians covers classical differential equations as well as topological dynamics and ergodic theory. Bibliographies. 523pp. 5⅜ x 8½. 0-486-65954-2

THEORY OF MATRICES, Sam Perlis. Outstanding text covering rank, nonsingularity and inverses in connection with the development of canonical matrices under the relation of equivalence, and without the intervention of determinants. Includes exercises. 237pp. 5⅜ x 8½. 0-486-66810-X

INTRODUCTION TO ANALYSIS, Maxwell Rosenlicht. Unusually clear, accessible coverage of set theory, real number system, metric spaces, continuous functions, Riemann integration, multiple integrals, more. Wide range of problems. Undergraduate level. Bibliography. 254pp. 5⅜ x 8½. 0-486-65038-3

MODERN NONLINEAR EQUATIONS, Thomas L. Saaty. Emphasizes practical solution of problems; covers seven types of equations. ". . . a welcome contribution to the existing literature...."–*Math Reviews*. 490pp. 5⅜ x 8½. 0-486-64232-1

MATRICES AND LINEAR ALGEBRA, Hans Schneider and George Phillip Barker. Basic textbook covers theory of matrices and its applications to systems of linear equations and related topics such as determinants, eigenvalues and differential equations. Numerous exercises. 432pp. 5⅜ x 8½. 0-486-66014-1

LINEAR ALGEBRA, Georgi E. Shilov. Determinants, linear spaces, matrix algebras, similar topics. For advanced undergraduates, graduates. Silverman translation. 387pp. 5⅜ x 8½. 0-486-63518-X

ELEMENTS OF REAL ANALYSIS, David A. Sprecher. Classic text covers fundamental concepts, real number system, point sets, functions of a real variable, Fourier series, much more. Over 500 exercises. 352pp. 5⅜ x 8½. 0-486-65385-4

SET THEORY AND LOGIC, Robert R. Stoll. Lucid introduction to unified theory of mathematical concepts. Set theory and logic seen as tools for conceptual understanding of real number system. 496pp. 5⅜ x 8¼. 0-486-63829-4

TENSOR CALCULUS, J.L. Synge and A. Schild. Widely used introductory text covers spaces and tensors, basic operations in Riemannian space, non-Riemannian spaces, etc. 324pp. 5⅜ x 8¼. 0-486-63612-7

ORDINARY DIFFERENTIAL EQUATIONS, Morris Tenenbaum and Harry Pollard. Exhaustive survey of ordinary differential equations for undergraduates in mathematics, engineering, science. Thorough analysis of theorems. Diagrams. Bibliography. Index. 818pp. 5⅜ x 8½. 0-486-64940-7

INTEGRAL EQUATIONS, F. G. Tricomi. Authoritative, well-written treatment of extremely useful mathematical tool with wide applications. Volterra Equations, Fredholm Equations, much more. Advanced undergraduate to graduate level. Exercises. Bibliography. 238pp. 5⅜ x 8½. 0-486-64828-1

FOURIER SERIES, Georgi P. Tolstov. Translated by Richard A. Silverman. A valuable addition to the literature on the subject, moving clearly from subject to subject and theorem to theorem. 107 problems, answers. 336pp. 5⅜ x 8½. 0-486-63317-9

INTRODUCTION TO MATHEMATICAL THINKING, Friedrich Waismann. Examinations of arithmetic, geometry, and theory of integers; rational and natural numbers; complete induction; limit and point of accumulation; remarkable curves; complex and hypercomplex numbers, more. 1959 ed. 27 figures. xii+260pp. 5⅜ x 8½. 0-486-63317-9

POPULAR LECTURES ON MATHEMATICAL LOGIC, Hao Wang. Noted logician's lucid treatment of historical developments, set theory, model theory, recursion theory and constructivism, proof theory, more. 3 appendixes. Bibliography. 1981 edition. ix + 283pp. 5⅜ x 8½. 0-486-67632-3

CALCULUS OF VARIATIONS, Robert Weinstock. Basic introduction covering isoperimetric problems, theory of elasticity, quantum mechanics, electrostatics, etc. Exercises throughout. 326pp. 5⅜ x 8½. 0-486-63069-2

THE CONTINUUM: A CRITICAL EXAMINATION OF THE FOUNDATION OF ANALYSIS, Hermann Weyl. Classic of 20th-century foundational research deals with the conceptual problem posed by the continuum. 156pp. 5⅜ x 8½. 0-486-67982-9

CHALLENGING MATHEMATICAL PROBLEMS WITH ELEMENTARY SOLUTIONS, A. M. Yaglom and I. M. Yaglom. Over 170 challenging problems on probability theory, combinatorial analysis, points and lines, topology, convex polygons, many other topics. Solutions. Total of 445pp. 5⅜ x 8½. Two-vol. set. Vol. I: 0-486-65536-9 Vol. II: 0-486-65537-7

INTRODUCTION TO PARTIAL DIFFERENTIAL EQUATIONS WITH APPLICATIONS, E. C. Zachmanoglou and Dale W. Thoe. Essentials of partial differential equations applied to common problems in engineering and the physical sciences. Problems and answers. 416pp. 5⅜ x 8½. 0-486-65251-3

THE THEORY OF GROUPS, Hans J. Zassenhaus. Well-written graduate-level text acquaints reader with group-theoretic methods and demonstrates their usefulness in mathematics. Axioms, the calculus of complexes, homomorphic mapping, *p*-group theory, more. 276pp. 5⅜ x 8½. 0-486-40922-8

Math–Decision Theory, Statistics, Probability

ELEMENTARY DECISION THEORY, Herman Chernoff and Lincoln E. Moses. Clear introduction to statistics and statistical theory covers data processing, probability and random variables, testing hypotheses, much more. Exercises. 364pp. 5⅜ x 8½. 0-486-65218-1

STATISTICS MANUAL, Edwin L. Crow et al. Comprehensive, practical collection of classical and modern methods prepared by U.S. Naval Ordnance Test Station. Stress on use. Basics of statistics assumed. 288pp. 5⅜ x 8½. 0-486-60599-X

SOME THEORY OF SAMPLING, William Edwards Deming. Analysis of the problems, theory and design of sampling techniques for social scientists, industrial managers and others who find statistics important at work. 61 tables. 90 figures. xvii +602pp. 5⅜ x 8½. 0-486-64684-X

LINEAR PROGRAMMING AND ECONOMIC ANALYSIS, Robert Dorfman, Paul A. Samuelson and Robert M. Solow. First comprehensive treatment of linear programming in standard economic analysis. Game theory, modern welfare economics, Leontief input-output, more. 525pp. 5⅜ x 8½. 0-486-65491-5

PROBABILITY: AN INTRODUCTION, Samuel Goldberg. Excellent basic text covers set theory, probability theory for finite sample spaces, binomial theorem, much more. 360 problems. Bibliographies. 322pp. 5⅜ x 8½. 0-486-65252-1

GAMES AND DECISIONS: INTRODUCTION AND CRITICAL SURVEY, R. Duncan Luce and Howard Raiffa. Superb nontechnical introduction to game theory, primarily applied to social sciences. Utility theory, zero-sum games, n-person games, decision-making, much more. Bibliography. 509pp. 5⅜ x 8½. 0-486-65943-7

INTRODUCTION TO THE THEORY OF GAMES, J. C. C. McKinsey. This comprehensive overview of the mathematical theory of games illustrates applications to situations involving conflicts of interest, including economic, social, political, and military contexts. Appropriate for advanced undergraduate and graduate courses; advanced calculus a prerequisite. 1952 ed. x+372pp. 5⅜ x 8½. 0-486-42811-7

FIFTY CHALLENGING PROBLEMS IN PROBABILITY WITH SOLUTIONS, Frederick Mosteller. Remarkable puzzlers, graded in difficulty, illustrate elementary and advanced aspects of probability. Detailed solutions. 88pp. 5⅜ x 8½. 65355-2

PROBABILITY THEORY: A CONCISE COURSE, Y. A. Rozanov. Highly readable, self-contained introduction covers combination of events, dependent events, Bernoulli trials, etc. 148pp. 5⅜ x 8¼. 0-486-63544-9

STATISTICAL METHOD FROM THE VIEWPOINT OF QUALITY CONTROL, Walter A. Shewhart. Important text explains regulation of variables, uses of statistical control to achieve quality control in industry, agriculture, other areas. 192pp. 5⅜ x 8½. 0-486-65232-7

Math–Geometry and Topology

ELEMENTARY CONCEPTS OF TOPOLOGY, Paul Alexandroff. Elegant, intuitive approach to topology from set-theoretic topology to Betti groups; how concepts of topology are useful in math and physics. 25 figures. 57pp. 5⅜ x 8½. 0-486-60747-X

COMBINATORIAL TOPOLOGY, P. S. Alexandrov. Clearly written, well-organized, three-part text begins by dealing with certain classic problems without using the formal techniques of homology theory and advances to the central concept, the Betti groups. Numerous detailed examples. 654pp. 5⅜ x 8½. 0-486-40179-0

EXPERIMENTS IN TOPOLOGY, Stephen Barr. Classic, lively explanation of one of the byways of mathematics. Klein bottles, Moebius strips, projective planes, map coloring, problem of the Koenigsberg bridges, much more, described with clarity and wit. 43 figures. 210pp. 5⅜ x 8½. 0-486-25933-1

THE GEOMETRY OF RENÉ DESCARTES, René Descartes. The great work founded analytical geometry. Original French text, Descartes's own diagrams, together with definitive Smith-Latham translation. 244pp. 5⅜ x 8½. 0-486-60068-8

EUCLIDEAN GEOMETRY AND TRANSFORMATIONS, Clayton W. Dodge. This introduction to Euclidean geometry emphasizes transformations, particularly isometries and similarities. Suitable for undergraduate courses, it includes numerous examples, many with detailed answers. 1972 ed. viii+296pp. 6⅛ x 9¼. 0-486-43476-1

PRACTICAL CONIC SECTIONS: THE GEOMETRIC PROPERTIES OF ELLIPSES, PARABOLAS AND HYPERBOLAS, J. W. Downs. This text shows how to create ellipses, parabolas, and hyperbolas. It also presents historical background on their ancient origins and describes the reflective properties and roles of curves in design applications. 1993 ed. 98 figures. xii+100pp. 6½ x 9¼. 0-486-42876-1

THE THIRTEEN BOOKS OF EUCLID'S ELEMENTS, translated with introduction and commentary by Sir Thomas L. Heath. Definitive edition. Textual and linguistic notes, mathematical analysis. 2,500 years of critical commentary. Unabridged. 1,414pp. 5⅜ x 8½. Three-vol. set.
Vol. I: 0-486-60088-2 Vol. II: 0-486-60089-0 Vol. III: 0-486-60090-4

SPACE AND GEOMETRY: IN THE LIGHT OF PHYSIOLOGICAL, PSYCHOLOGICAL AND PHYSICAL INQUIRY, Ernst Mach. Three essays by an eminent philosopher and scientist explore the nature, origin, and development of our concepts of space, with a distinctness and precision suitable for undergraduate students and other readers. 1906 ed. vi+148pp. 5⅜ x 8½. 0-486-43909-7

GEOMETRY OF COMPLEX NUMBERS, Hans Schwerdtfeger. Illuminating, widely praised book on analytic geometry of circles, the Moebius transformation, and two-dimensional non-Euclidean geometries. 200pp. 5⅝ x 8¼. 0-486-63830-8

DIFFERENTIAL GEOMETRY, Heinrich W. Guggenheimer. Local differential geometry as an application of advanced calculus and linear algebra. Curvature, transformation groups, surfaces, more. Exercises. 62 figures. 378pp. 5⅜ x 8½. 0-486-63433-7

History of Math

THE WORKS OF ARCHIMEDES, Archimedes (T. L. Heath, ed.). Topics include the famous problems of the ratio of the areas of a cylinder and an inscribed sphere; the measurement of a circle; the properties of conoids, spheroids, and spirals; and the quadrature of the parabola. Informative introduction. clxxxvi+326pp. 5⅜ x 8½. 0-486-42084-1

A SHORT ACCOUNT OF THE HISTORY OF MATHEMATICS, W. W. Rouse Ball. One of clearest, most authoritative surveys from the Egyptians and Phoenicians through 19th-century figures such as Grassman, Galois, Riemann. Fourth edition. 522pp. 5⅜ x 8½. 0-486-20630-0

THE HISTORY OF THE CALCULUS AND ITS CONCEPTUAL DEVELOPMENT, Carl B. Boyer. Origins in antiquity, medieval contributions, work of Newton, Leibniz, rigorous formulation. Treatment is verbal. 346pp. 5⅜ x 8½. 0-486-60509-4

THE HISTORICAL ROOTS OF ELEMENTARY MATHEMATICS, Lucas N. H. Bunt, Phillip S. Jones, and Jack D. Bedient. Fundamental underpinnings of modern arithmetic, algebra, geometry and number systems derived from ancient civilizations. 320pp. 5⅜ x 8½. 0-486-25563-8

A HISTORY OF MATHEMATICAL NOTATIONS, Florian Cajori. This classic study notes the first appearance of a mathematical symbol and its origin, the competition it encountered, its spread among writers in different countries, its rise to popularity, its eventual decline or ultimate survival. Original 1929 two-volume edition presented here in one volume. xxviii+820pp. 5⅜ x 8½. 0-486-67766-4

GAMES, GODS & GAMBLING: A HISTORY OF PROBABILITY AND STATISTICAL IDEAS, F. N. David. Episodes from the lives of Galileo, Fermat, Pascal, and others illustrate this fascinating account of the roots of mathematics. Features thought-provoking references to classics, archaeology, biography, poetry. 1962 edition. 304pp. 5⅜ x 8½. (Available in U.S. only.) 0-486-40023-9

OF MEN AND NUMBERS: THE STORY OF THE GREAT MATHEMATICIANS, Jane Muir. Fascinating accounts of the lives and accomplishments of history's greatest mathematical minds–Pythagoras, Descartes, Euler, Pascal, Cantor, many more. Anecdotal, illuminating. 30 diagrams. Bibliography. 256pp. 5⅜ x 8½. 0-486-28973-7

HISTORY OF MATHEMATICS, David E. Smith. Nontechnical survey from ancient Greece and Orient to late 19th century; evolution of arithmetic, geometry, trigonometry, calculating devices, algebra, the calculus. 362 illustrations. 1,355pp. 5⅜ x 8½. Two-vol. set. Vol. I: 0-486-20429-4 Vol. II: 0-486-20430-8

A CONCISE HISTORY OF MATHEMATICS, Dirk J. Struik. The best brief history of mathematics. Stresses origins and covers every major figure from ancient Near East to 19th century. 41 illustrations. 195pp. 5⅜ x 8½. 0-486-60255-9

Physics

OPTICAL RESONANCE AND TWO-LEVEL ATOMS, L. Allen and J. H. Eberly. Clear, comprehensive introduction to basic principles behind all quantum optical resonance phenomena. 53 illustrations. Preface. Index. 256pp. 5⅜ x 8½. 0-486-65533-4

QUANTUM THEORY, David Bohm. This advanced undergraduate-level text presents the quantum theory in terms of qualitative and imaginative concepts, followed by specific applications worked out in mathematical detail. Preface. Index. 655pp. 5⅜ x 8½. 0-486-65969-0

ATOMIC PHYSICS (8th EDITION), Max Born. Nobel laureate's lucid treatment of kinetic theory of gases, elementary particles, nuclear atom, wave-corpuscles, atomic structure and spectral lines, much more. Over 40 appendices, bibliography. 495pp. 5⅜ x 8½. 0-486-65984-4

A SOPHISTICATE'S PRIMER OF RELATIVITY, P. W. Bridgman. Geared toward readers already acquainted with special relativity, this book transcends the view of theory as a working tool to answer natural questions: What is a frame of reference? What is a "law of nature"? What is the role of the "observer"? Extensive treatment, written in terms accessible to those without a scientific background. 1983 ed. xlviii+172pp. 5⅜ x 8½. 0-486-42549-5

AN INTRODUCTION TO HAMILTONIAN OPTICS, H. A. Buchdahl. Detailed account of the Hamiltonian treatment of aberration theory in geometrical optics. Many classes of optical systems defined in terms of the symmetries they possess. Problems with detailed solutions. 1970 edition. xv + 360pp. 5⅜ x 8½. 0-486-67597-1

PRIMER OF QUANTUM MECHANICS, Marvin Chester. Introductory text examines the classical quantum bead on a track: its state and representations; operator eigenvalues; harmonic oscillator and bound bead in a symmetric force field; and bead in a spherical shell. Other topics include spin, matrices, and the structure of quantum mechanics; the simplest atom; indistinguishable particles; and stationary-state perturbation theory. 1992 ed. xiv+314pp. 6⅛ x 9¼. 0-486-42878-8

LECTURES ON QUANTUM MECHANICS, Paul A. M. Dirac. Four concise, brilliant lectures on mathematical methods in quantum mechanics from Nobel Prize-winning quantum pioneer build on idea of visualizing quantum theory through the use of classical mechanics. 96pp. 5⅜ x 8½. 0-486-41713-1

THIRTY YEARS THAT SHOOK PHYSICS: THE STORY OF QUANTUM THEORY, George Gamow. Lucid, accessible introduction to influential theory of energy and matter. Careful explanations of Dirac's anti-particles, Bohr's model of the atom, much more. 12 plates. Numerous drawings. 240pp. 5⅜ x 8½. 0-486-24895-X

ELECTRONIC STRUCTURE AND THE PROPERTIES OF SOLIDS: THE PHYSICS OF THE CHEMICAL BOND, Walter A. Harrison. Innovative text offers basic understanding of the electronic structure of covalent and ionic solids, simple metals, transition metals and their compounds. Problems. 1980 edition. 582pp. 6⅛ x 9¼. 0-486-66021-4

A TREATISE ON ELECTRICITY AND MAGNETISM, James Clerk Maxwell. Important foundation work of modern physics. Brings to final form Maxwell's theory of electromagnetism and rigorously derives his general equations of field theory. 1,084pp. 5⅜ x 8½. Two-vol. set. Vol. I: 0-486-60636-8 Vol. II: 0-486-60637-6

QUANTUM MECHANICS: PRINCIPLES AND FORMALISM, Roy McWeeny. Graduate student-oriented volume develops subject as fundamental discipline, opening with review of origins of Schrödinger's equations and vector spaces. Focusing on main principles of quantum mechanics and their immediate consequences, it concludes with final generalizations covering alternative "languages" or representations. 1972 ed. 15 figures. xi+155pp. 5⅜ x 8½. 0-486-42829-X

INTRODUCTION TO QUANTUM MECHANICS With Applications to Chemistry, Linus Pauling & E. Bright Wilson, Jr. Classic undergraduate text by Nobel Prize winner applies quantum mechanics to chemical and physical problems. Numerous tables and figures enhance the text. Chapter bibliographies. Appendices. Index. 468pp. 5⅜ x 8½. 0-486-64871-0

METHODS OF THERMODYNAMICS, Howard Reiss. Outstanding text focuses on physical technique of thermodynamics, typical problem areas of understanding, and significance and use of thermodynamic potential. 1965 edition. 238pp. 5⅜ x 8½. 0-486-69445-3

THE ELECTROMAGNETIC FIELD, Albert Shadowitz. Comprehensive undergraduate text covers basics of electric and magnetic fields, builds up to electromagnetic theory. Also related topics, including relativity. Over 900 problems. 768pp. 5⅝ x 8¼. 0-486-65660-8

GREAT EXPERIMENTS IN PHYSICS: FIRSTHAND ACCOUNTS FROM GALILEO TO EINSTEIN, Morris H. Shamos (ed.). 25 crucial discoveries: Newton's laws of motion, Chadwick's study of the neutron, Hertz on electromagnetic waves, more. Original accounts clearly annotated. 370pp. 5⅜ x 8½. 0-486-25346-5

EINSTEIN'S LEGACY, Julian Schwinger. A Nobel Laureate relates fascinating story of Einstein and development of relativity theory in well-illustrated, nontechnical volume. Subjects include meaning of time, paradoxes of space travel, gravity and its effect on light, non-Euclidean geometry and curving of space-time, impact of radio astronomy and space-age discoveries, and more. 189 b/w illustrations. xiv+250pp. 8⅜ x 9¼. 0-486-41974-6

STATISTICAL PHYSICS, Gregory H. Wannier. Classic text combines thermodynamics, statistical mechanics and kinetic theory in one unified presentation of thermal physics. Problems with solutions. Bibliography. 532pp. 5⅜ x 8½. 0-486-65401-X